The C. S. Lewis Phenomenon

Christianity and the Public Sphere

MERCER
UNIVERSITY PRESS

*Endowed by*
TOM WATSON BROWN
*and*
THE WATSON-BROWN FOUNDATION, INC.

# The C. S. Lewis Phenomenon

# Christianity and the Public Sphere

*Samuel Joeckel*

MERCER UNIVERSITY PRESS
MACON, GEORGIA

MUP/ P463

© 2013 Mercer University Press
1400 Coleman Avenue
Macon, Georgia 31207

First Edition

Books published by Mercer University Press are printed on acid-free paper that meets the requirements of the American National Standard for Information Sciences—Permanence of Paper for Printed Library Materials.

A version of Chapter 1 appeared previously as "C.S. Lewis, Public Intellectual" in *Sehnsucht: The C.S. Lewis Journal* 4 (2010): 43-66. Copyright (c) 2010 by *Sehnsucht: The C.S. Lewis Journal*.

A version of Chapter 5 appeared previously as "C.S. Lewis and the Art of the Allegory" in *SEVEN: An Anglo-American Review* 27 (2010): 69-84. Copyright (c) 2010 by *SEVEN: An Anglo-American Review*.

Mercer University Press is a member of Green Press Initiative (greenpressinitiative.org), a nonprofit organization working to help publishers and printers increase their use of recycled paper and decrease their use of fiber derived from endangered forests. This book is printed on recycled paper.
ISBN      978-0-88146-437-5
Cataloging-in-Publication Data is available from the Library of Congress

# Contents

*To Mira and Reed*

# Acknowledgments

I am grateful to all who have helped make this book possible. Palm Beach Atlantic University awarded me a sabbatical leave in 2009 and a Quality Initiative grant in 2010. I enlisted the help of Chris Jensen when he was a freshman at PBAU. For three years, he served as my unfailing research and editorial assistant. I look forward to returning the favor someday. James Carter III also provided me with editorial assistance. My colleague Jenifer Elmore gave me invaluable advice that strengthened the focus of my project; I am thankful for her warm collegiality and critical acumen. I greatly benefited from the wisdom of Roger Chapman, Dave Athey, and Brenton Dickieson, all of whom offered guidance and encouragement. Nerolie Ceus of the PBAU library processed over a thousand inter-library loans for me. Anthony Verdesca, also on staff at the PBAU library, provided me with some last-minute assistance with bibliographical material. The staff at the Wade Center on the campus of Wheaton College welcomed me with generous hospitality during a research visit in 2010, ensuring that my week spent there was productive. My mother-in-law, Lenore Dingle, offered me a quiet place to read and write during the summer months and during my sabbatical. Finally, I am grateful for the support from my private sphere: my wife Tory, daughter Mira, and son Reed. To these, I need not say more, for "I am sure my love's more ponderous than my tongue."

# General Introduction

The history of C. S. Lewis scholarship presents meta-critical challenges to any new book on Lewis. Various commentators over the years have noted the poor quality of many Lewis studies, highlighting their tendencies toward unimaginative paraphrase and uncritical praise. In 1988, for instance, Peter Kreeft proclaimed, "Books on Lewis have multiplied like rabbits, or like flies around honey." Kreeft added that "most [of these books] are not worth reading because they do little more than rehash what Lewis already said much, much more effectively than any of his summarizers and commentators can."[1] As recently as 2010, Robert MacSwain coined the term "Jacksploitation"; drawn from Lewis's nickname, Jack, the neologism describes "a work related to Lewis that has no scholarly substance or originality whatsoever, produced by someone whose only credential is that the work is related to Lewis. The world is awash in Jacksploitation."[2] Any new book on Lewis must thus negotiate this foreboding scholarly context, carving out a critical space under the historical weight of meta-critical baggage. In short, the author of a new book on Lewis apparently has some explaining to do.

Venturing unique and occasionally provocative arguments, this study seeks to overcome what MacSwain also calls the current "impasse" in Lewis scholarship.[3] It offers an interpretive framework for understanding not only Lewis's accomplishment but also the critical preoccupations of Lewis studies, preoccupations that have helped generate uncreative, hagiographical, and thus mediocre books. It offers a new way to understand Lewis's ambitious project, explores some complications along the way, and explains the often underwhelming scholarship that follows in his wake.

The C. S. Lewis phenomenon names the way in which Lewis's presentations of Christianity in both his fiction and non-fiction depend upon the conventions of the public sphere. This study explores three facets of that phenomenon. The first concerns Lewis's accomplishment as a public

---

[1] Peter Kreeft, *C. S. Lewis: A Critical Essay* (Front Royal VA: Christendom College Press, 1988) 5.

[2] Robert MacSwain, introduction to *The Cambridge Companion to C. S. Lewis*, ed. Robert MacSwain and Michael Ward (Cambridge: Cambridge University Press, 2010) 11.

[3] Ibid., 9.

intellectual, a term coined by Russell Jacoby in 1987 and occasionally ascribed to Lewis, but never fully developed.[4] A public intellectual couples the expertise of a scholar with the communicative skills of a journalist. Lewis adopts this role by making the truth claims of Christianity understandable to the layperson, in short performing the work of a religious public intellectual. I connect the necessary conditions for this accomplishment to the public sphere, which arose at the turn of the eighteenth century. The public sphere seminally established the conventions of public discourse and thus also the rules and guidelines by which the public intellectual operates.

Lewis's mastery of these conventions, along with various cultural crises and technological innovations of the twentieth century, occasioned his success as a public intellectual. Standing on a larger stage than the professional scholar, the public intellectual performs in a polemical register attuned to a differentiated audience, calculated to unite people around commonalities, to find homogeneity amidst heterogeneity. The public intellectual is thus often compelled to offer grandiose claims that appeal to universal human experience. Posing as hyperbolically objective and

---

[4] Every now and then, at a conference or on a website, in a book or journal article, C. S. Lewis is referred to as a "public intellectual." Volume four of Bruce Edwards's four-volume Lewis reference set, for instance, is subtitled *Scholar, Teacher, and Public Intellectual*. In the opening essay of the volume, Edwards hints at the true role of the public intellectual when he identifies Lewis as "a learned pundit whose opinions provoked the self-satisfied and resisted the zeitgeist...." He further discloses Lewis's public-intellectual identity by emphasizing Lewis's appeal to the "earnest and respectfully skeptical 'man (or woman) in the street....'" (See Bruce L. Edwards, "The Christian Intellectual in the Public Square: C. S. Lewis's Enduring American Reception," in *C. S. Lewis: Life, Works, Legacy*, ed. Bruce L. Edwards [London: Praeger Perspectives, 2007] 4:2, 13.) Likewise, in an article titled "C. S. Lewis in the Public Square," the late Richard John Neuhaus evokes the concept of the public intellectual when he notes that Lewis engaged in "public discourse" and remarks that "one might even risk calling him a populist." (See Richard John Neuhaus, "C. S. Lewis in the Public Square," in *First Things* vol. 88 [December 1, 1988]: 30.) Despite such hints and evocations, it appears that no one has attempted a systematic analysis of Lewis as a public intellectual. That is, no one has methodically employed extant theories on the concept of the public intellectual to assess how he fits the bill. No one has used these theories as an interpretive lens for analyzing Lewis's writings. No one has analyzed the historical conditions during Lewis's lifetime that pushed him into the role of public intellectual. No one has explored how Lewis adheres to the conventions of public discourse, the language of the public intellectual. And finally no one has considered how Lewis's identity as public intellectual might shift our understanding of his accomplishment as a Christian writer, offering new critical vantage points from which to interpret his individual works.

repeatedly drawing from what Lewis calls the Law of Human Nature and what I term "high tradition," the collective wisdom of Western civilization, Lewis stresses throughout most of his works a uniformity of human experience, an essentialism minimizing difference that resonates within the public sphere.

In his fiction, Lewis makes use of what I call the "transcendent character." Adopting a perspective that transcends the epistemological limitations endemic to the human condition (an Olympian perspective), the transcendent character possesses knowledge that approximates absolute truth. The transcendent character inhabits the fictional geography of nearly all of Lewis's imaginative works and endows them with a sense of authority from which spiritual truths and moral precepts proceed with such rhetorical power. I highlight the importance of these truths and precepts by recasting much of Lewis's fiction as examples of a literary genre known as the "apologue," which, as Sheldon Sacks explains, "is a work organized as a fictional example of the truth of a formulable statement or a series of such statements."[5] Re-classifying Lewis's imaginative writings in this way underscores the literary formula that Lewis fleshes out in his scholarship and follows in his own fiction: to convey and cultivate stock reader responses under the assumption of essentialist ethics and experiential uniformity. Lewis thus adroitly harnessed and conveyed forms of authority that proved formidable upon the universal stage of the public sphere. I analyze this first facet of the C. S. Lewis phenomenon in Part 1 of the book.

Not long after Lewis's death, the public sphere fragmented and crumbled; the public space of critical-rational debate ceased to exist in the form it maintained for centuries. That is, the public sphere lost its universal reach and splintered into pockets of particular interests and ideological commitments. Gone were the principles designed to unite diverse people around commonalities, the principles that operated in such traditional public spaces as print journalism, popular books on politics, philosophy, and religion, and (in older incantations) coffee houses and pubs. These developments contributed to the disintegration of the public sphere by replacing impartial, universalized, unifying discourse with partisan, esoteric, polarizing discourse. A number of developments led to this demise: postmodernism, communitarian epistemology, the specialization of the academy, the culture wars, and the World Wide Web. Consequently, Lewis's accomplishment was both unprecedented and inimitable: He made use of the public sphere like

---

[5] Sheldon Sacks, *Fiction and the Shape of Belief* (Berkeley: University of California Press, 1967) 26.

no other Christian in history, and since the public sphere no longer exists, his accomplishment will never be repeated.

Lewis remains popular today because he transmitted his ideas in the public sphere before its devolution; although the metaphorical launching pad imploded, the ideas reached their destination and irreversibly made their mark. Nevertheless, a few of Lewis's books employ a rhetorical orientation and an artistry that stretch the outline of his public-intellectual identity; that is, some of Lewis's books do not abide by the conventions of the public sphere. These books are the subject of Part 2. The Lewis who surfaces in their pages abandons the fundamental conventions of the public sphere: the adoption of hyperbolic neutrality and the use of universalizing forms of authority. Operating beyond the public sphere, this Lewis emphasizes particularity rather than universality. He is more interested in exploring the precognitive factors that contextualize beliefs than in painstakingly marshaling evidence to defend beliefs.

Forged in the crucible of pain and loss, for instance, the Lewis of *A Grief Observed* divests himself of his typical rhetorical stance, calculated to appeal to the uniform experience of the hypothetical, differentiated audience of the public sphere; instead, *A Grief Observed* particularizes Lewis's experiences and localizes the problem of evil. The novel *Till We Have Faces* privileges the role that perspective plays in finding truth, setting forth a pre-analytical orientation called preconditionalism: the notion that the heart (or non-rational faculties) needs to meet certain conditions—such as exercising empathy and altruism—in order to perceive truth. Like *A Grief Observed*, *Till We Have Faces* troubles the conventions operative in the public sphere, conventions that Lewis, as public intellectual, incorporates with such dexterity in his other popular works. For these reasons, *A Grief Observed* and *Till We Have Faces* constitute anomalies in the Lewis *oeuvre*, nudging him beyond the public sphere. Part 2 addresses this second facet of the Lewis phenomenon, what I term a "counter-narrative" to the first.

Conceiving Lewis as a public intellectual provides a useful meta-critical lens for exploring Lewis's symbiotic relationship to the public sphere. An historical survey of secondary sources on Lewis—from the 1940s to 2010— reveals how Lewis's place within the public sphere mirrors the public sphere's rupture. Through the 1960s, Lewis mostly maintained his position on the universal stage, elevated above sectarian and political difference. Once ideological contestation parceled the public sphere into warring camps (especially with the rise of the culture wars in the 1980s), however, Lewis increasingly became appropriated by evangelical Christian fans, thereby linking him to politically conservative evangelicalism within the public imagination. This link increasingly positioned Lewis as the animus for religious and political diatribes within the post-public-sphere culture wars.

A meta-critical analysis also sheds light on the Lewis industry, helping to explain the jeremiads of Kreeft, MacSwain, and other commentators. As previously noted, many books on Lewis begin in a defensive tone, acknowledging the glut of other books on the subject. Some Lewis scholars even verge on apologizing for contributing to this glut. Like any public intellectual, Lewis generates a fan base that unifies itself around his message, what Richard A. Posner calls "solidarity goods"[6]; that fundamental message is that Christianity is both rationally defensible and experientially compelling. Most writers of Lewis books thus carry on the project of Lewis himself, transmitting that message to as large an audience as possible. Lewis identified himself as a "translator," rendering Christian doctrine into the vernacular to be easily understood by the layperson. Sustaining Lewis's project, many books on Lewis thus tautologically function as translations of Lewis's translations.

In addition, Lewis advocated certain methodological principles as he translated Christian doctrine. For instance, he downplayed the role that originality plays in the transmission of the message; in fact, he denied ever trying to be original. Commitment to Lewis's message spills over into adherence to his methodological principles: Originality is thus suspect, and interpretive risks are discouraged. Perhaps no methodological principle looms larger in Lewis criticism than what Lewis referred to as the "personal heresy," committed when a critic attempts to show ways in which an author's work reflects that author's personality, beliefs, or experiences. Wary of falling victim to this heresy, many books on Lewis are restrained by a tight interpretive leash, tiptoeing around analyses that make correlations between Lewis's ideas and his life.

In short, positioning Lewis as a public intellectual discloses the heartbeat of the Lewis industry: the commitment to Lewis's message, mobilization around Lewis's solidarity goods, and veneration of the man himself. Just as Lewis has become associated with evangelicals, so has Lewis become associated with the Lewis industry. Engaging Lewis's ideas in critical studies often means first negotiating the Lewis industry, a negotiation that inflects and shapes interpretation, structuring the approach to Lewis. A formidable weight of meta-critical baggage has accumulated around him; this baggage

---

[6] Richard A. Posner, *Public Intellectuals: A Study of Decline* (Cambridge MA: Harvard UP, 2002) 42.

has influenced the way he is understood and analyzed. This third facet of the Lewis phenomenon is the subject of Part 3, which, drawing from the title of one of Lewis's own works, I call "An Experiment in Meta-criticism."

Analyzing Lewis within the context of the public sphere occasionally requires me to historicize and thus de-mythologize Lewis, divesting him of his status as—in the words of A. N. Wilson—a "plaster saint."[7] The context of my analysis also compels me in Part 3 to critique the Lewis industry. For these reasons, I anticipate spirited responses from those who disfavor my critical perspective. While such risks are probably unavoidable within the field of Lewis studies, I hope the merits of my book will convince the impartial reader that I at least need not apologize for writing it.

---

[7] A. N. Wilson, *C. S. Lewis: A Biography* (New York: Norton, 1990) xvii.

# 1

# C. S. Lewis, Public Intellectual

## I. The Public Intellectual: A Basic Overview

At the heart of what I identify as the first aspect of the C. S. Lewis phenomenon lies the creation of a distinct persona, made visible in the public sphere, acutely sensitive to audience, strategically and passionately positioned on a host of issues of key concern to a culture. This persona, that of the public intellectual, fulfills this role through a combination of historical opportunity and talent in the art of rhetoric and polemical persuasion. Coined by Russell Jacoby in his 1987 book, *The Last Intellectuals: American Culture in the Age of Academe,* the term "public intellectual" specifically refers to a figure who defends religious, political, or ideological beliefs in a manner that requires the expertise of a scholar, possessing the learning and critical acumen to engage with proficiency complex issues, and the communicative skills of a journalist, capable of making those complex beliefs under-standable to the layperson.

To become visible in the public sphere, however, the public intellectual first requires a medium to transmit ideas to a broad swath of the population that cuts across socio-economic and class distinctions. Whether the salons and coffee houses of eighteenth-century Europe or the editorial page of a major newspaper, the medium must be accessible to a diverse audience. Not only must the public intellectual live during an opportune historical moment when such mediums are available, but the most influential public intellectuals engage issues of profound historical weight due to their watershed significance. Such issues often emerge from moments of radical cultural change and social transformation, moments contingent upon the unpredictable flux of history.

Because of the wide accessibility of the medium, available to both patrician and plebian, bourgeoisie and proletariat, rich and poor, educated and semi-educated, specialist and non-specialist, the public intellectual must be acutely sensitive to audience, speaking in a language intelligible to this diverse audience; this language is the vernacular. Jacoby shows, for instance, that Galileo's "crime...was less what he discovered or said but how and where he said it."[1] As a prototypical public intellectual, Galileo wrote in Italian—not in Latin, the language of the learned—avoiding the universities as his channel of communication and instead addressing himself to the educated general public. Following Morris Dickstein, Richard A. Posner holds that the term "public intellectual" became prominent in the late twentieth century because influential intellectuals like Barthes, Lyotard, Lacan, and Derrida did not write for the educated general public. These intellectuals employed a jargon-heavy language and a labyrinthine style, unintelligible to most outside the setting of the university.[2]

The public intellectual also positions himself or herself in a strategic role, often as outsider or nonconformist. Arthur M. Melzer argues that the public intellectual is "committed" and "engaged."[3] However, although the public intellectual "has a vital concern for the practical application of ideas and the welfare of society," he or she "regards direct political involvement as something that would compromise his [*sic*] very being as an intellectual. He [*sic*] is not part of the establishment."[4] The outsider identity provides the strategic vantage point from which to critique popular trends entering or dominating the cultural mainstream. Indeed, Posner names one type of intellectual discourse the "jeremiad," a discourse that "must be nostalgic, pessimistic, predictive, and judgmental,"[5] a discursive mode both powerful and necessary for an outsider looking in and denouncing what he or she finds there.

Strategically positioned in this way, the pessimistic outsider generates the publicity necessary to brand his or her name (what Posner calls "brand identification"[6]); that is, the public intellectual's name becomes associated with his or her religious or political position(s). As an outsider, the public intellectual elicits predictable responses. To the insider, the public intellectual becomes the object of hatred and verbal vituperation, a response that serves merely to multiply the publicity and further brand the name; to the fellow outsider, the public intellectual becomes a flag bearer, a

---

[1] Russell Jacoby, *The Last Intellectuals: American Culture in the Age of Academe* (New York: Basic Books, 1987) 8.

[2] Richard A. Posner, *Public Intellectuals: A Study of Decline* (Cambridge MA: Harvard UP, 2002) 26.

[3] Arthur M. Melzer, "What Is an Intellectual?" in *The Public Intellectual: Between Philosophy and Politics*, ed. Arthur M. Melzer et al. (New York: Rowman & Littlefield Publishers, Inc., 2003) 4.

[4] Ibid., 7.

[5] Posner, *Public Intellectuals*, 9.

[6] Ibid., 72.

passionate and polemically formidable representative of the position(s) he or she defends. Posner states that the public intellectual deals in "'solidarity goods', symbolic goods that provide a rallying point for like-minded people."[7]

The public intellectual must summon the rhetorical authority to appeal to a diverse audience. While professional scholars assume a clearly delineated readership that shares basic, often esoteric discursive practices, the public intellectual writes for, and speaks to, a wider audience, thus conveying authority through more universal, less arcane discursive practices. Standing on a larger stage than the professional scholar, the public intellectual performs in a polemical register attuned to a differentiated audience. The public intellectual is thus often compelled to offer grandiose claims that appeal to universal human experience.

## II. C. S. Lewis, Public Intellectual

### a. Name-branding, Controversy, and Cultural Change

In most of his published writings and radio broadcasts, C. S. Lewis follows the model of the public intellectual sketched above. His conversion to Christianity and commitment to apologetics fortuitously coincided with the rise of the radio celebrity, which Lewis undeniably became as a result of his broadcast talks over the British Broadcasting Company (BBC)[8], enabling his voice to be heard by hundreds of thousands of people. His name thus established or branded, he became associated with the religious positions he defended—traditional, conservative positions that, because of the forces of secularization as well as the forces of progress, became increasingly controversial. The combination of name-branding and controversy ensured healthy sales of his other popular books, each of which solidified the name-branding and stoked the controversies, nudging Lewis further into the public sphere.

Lewis wrote and spoke during a period of staggering cultural and social change in England and beyond. As alluded to above, the forces of secularization became increasingly aggressive during Lewis's lifetime. Lewis's career as a Christian writer is tellingly sandwiched between the publications of Bertrand Russell's influential 1927 pamphlet *Why I Am Not a Christian* and John A.T. Robinson's 1963 *Honest to God*, both unabashed in

---

[7] Ibid., 42.

[8] These talks were subsequently edited and published as *Mere Christianity*.

their direct challenge to traditional Christianity. The forces of secularization also surrounded Lewis at Oxford University, where he was a fellow of Magdalen College for nearly thirty years and which continued to distance itself from its Christian identity during Lewis's lifetime, a fact more striking when one considers that John Wycliffe, the fourteenth-century English reformer, once referred to the university as a "Vineyard of the Lord."[9] V. H. H. Green affirms, "The half-century which has elapsed since the start of the First World War witnessed as great a revolution in the history of Oxford and Cambridge as any that had taken place in their long history. Although the process was not elucidated clearly until after the end of the Second World War, the secularisation of the Universities proceeded steadily."[10] Green also notes that most of the Oxford colleges dropped compulsory attendance at chapel between 1918 and 1939, the period during which Lewis converted to Christianity and began his public defense of the faith.[11] Although Christian revivals occurred during Lewis's time at Oxford, particularly after World War II, the overall trend was toward unbelief. Alan Jacobs tellingly refers to the Inklings as "a kind of tiny counterculture."[12]

The rise of what Lewis calls "subjectivism" also brought society into the crucible of cultural change. Increasingly, beliefs once held to be objectively true were not simply rejected; the very analytical framework from which objectivity proceeds was dismissed. The dismissal of this framework, which Lewis identifies as the *Tao* in *The Abolition of Man*, robbed reason of its arbitrative power, leaving matters of truth and falsity, right and wrong, good and bad as mere subjective preferences. As Lewis repeatedly warned, with appeals to reason now discredited or rendered useless, subjectivism undermines traditional morality and meaningful aesthetic judgments, leaving humankind in epistemological chaos and civilization in peril; truth then becomes whatever anyone can make it. The following warning in *The Abolition of Man* is representative of Lewis's position:

> Values are now mere natural phenomena. Judgements of value are to be produced in the pupil as part of the conditioning. Whatever *Tao* there is will be the product, not the motive, of education. The Conditioners have been emancipated from all that.... The Conditioners, then, are to choose

---

[9] Jan Morris, *Oxford* (Oxford: Oxford UP, 1965) 164.

[10] V. H. H. Green, *Religion at Oxford and Cambridge* (London: SCM Press, 1964) 338.

[11] Ibid., 338.

[12] Alan Jacobs, *The Narnian: The Life and Imagination of C. S. Lewis* (San Francisco: HarperSanFrancisco, 2005) 203.

what kind of artificial *Tao* they will, for their own good reasons, produce in the Human race.[13]

The elimination of the stabilizing role that reason, allied with objectivity, historically played creates for Lewis a vacuum filled by nefarious alternatives. Guided by a Nietzschean will to power or a diabolical attempt to redefine human nature, this subjectivism is illustrated in the machinations of the National Institute for Co-ordinated Experiments (N.I.C.E.) in Lewis's *That Hideous Strength.*

What bolsters Lewis's identity as public intellectual is the fact that what Lewis calls "subjectivism" overlaps with moral relativism; moral relativism, in turn, would later become associated with postmodernism, which rose to prominence after Lewis's death. A sweeping intellectual movement with strong cultural repercussions, postmodernism is often vilified by evangelical Christians, who make up a large segment of Lewis's fan base. Thus we see once again how Lewis was born at the right time in order to emerge and flourish as a public intellectual. Addressing the rise of postmodernism, Nancey Murphy writes, "Changes as sweeping as those now occurring in the intellectual world happen only rarely—perhaps the most recent such change was 300 years ago, although we need more historical perspective to make sound judgments here."[14] For the C. S. Lewis industry, postmodernism constitutes a paradox: while, from the perspective of the average evangelical Christian, it produces a toxic effect on society, it also keeps the Lewis industry churning, for fans can turn for guidance to Lewis, who presciently offers cogent critiques of some principles of postmodernism, even though he lived before its birth. Transcending his own time, Lewis engages postmodernism, thereby further branding his name.

### b. Science and Literary Criticism

Subjectivism is fueled to a large extent by a twentieth-century philosophic offshoot of science, founded on materialism, and often referred to as scientism; the ascendency of science in the twentieth century, as well as the materialist philosophies that it generates, constitutes another historical moment that enabled Lewis's accomplishment as a public intellectual. According to one scientific account (a scientific account that obviously caught Lewis's attention), if the human body evolves by chance, unguided by the providential guidance of a creator, then reason amounts to little more

---

[13] C. S. Lewis, *The Abolition of Man* (New York: Collier Books, 1955) 74.

[14] Nancey Murphy, "Philosophical Resources for Postmodern Evangelical Theology," *Christian Scholar's Review* 26/2 (1996): 205.

than neuron firings. The deliverances of reason thus robbed of ontological meaning and value, subjectivism becomes the final court of arbitration in matters central to humankind, from ethics to aesthetics.[15]

The ascendancy of science in the twentieth century transformed other disciplines as well; the influence of science was inescapable. Philosophers, for instance, appropriated scientific methodologies in the creation of what became known as logical positivism, a philosophy widely popular in the early to mid twentieth century. Rejecting metaphysics and upholding scientific method, logical positivism insisted that only empirically verifiable propositions—what A. J. Ayer refers to as "factual propositions"—could count as true.[16] Rendering theological claims meaningless, logical positivism and its variations created an intellectual climate unfriendly to Christianity: a climate paradoxically favorable to Lewis's project because of its oppositional stance. Resisting philosophies of near hegemonic status among the scholarly elite, Lewis created the sensation and controversy that propelled him onto the public stage.

The ascendancy of science creates another intellectual animus—this one in Lewis's own field of literary criticism—that sharpened Lewis's oppositional stance, the rhetorical posture that well-served him as a public intellectual. The preeminence of science in the early twentieth century set the field of literary criticism back on its heels. In a world in which only science supposedly held the promise of bettering society and improving the lot of humankind, what role was left for literature? What was the value of literature? Science sent the field of literary study into an identity crisis, forcing it to carve out and justify its place in the life of the mind.

A major literary scholar of Lewis's era, along with the influential movement he created, confronted this crisis with ambitious plans and tactics. With the publication of numerous books and with the founding in 1932 of the quarterly periodical *Scrutiny*, F. R. Leavis embarked on a project amounting to nothing less than an effort of cultural renewal. Dismayed by (among other innovations) the pervasiveness of radio and the proliferation of popular books—the artifacts of low-brow culture—Leavis sought to rehabilitate society through the cultivation of a more refined sensibility; as Ian Wright notes, "mass civilization" became Leavis's sarcastic shorthand for

---

[15] This issue is at the heart of Lewis's famous, well-rehearsed debate with G. E. M. Anscombe during a meeting of the Oxford Socratic Club.

[16] A. J. Ayer, introduction to *Logical Positivism*, ed. A. J. Ayer (New York: The Free Press, 1959) 8.

"pulp fiction, commercialized journalism and manipulative advertising."[17] Appropriating the legacy of Matthew Arnold, Leavis endowed literature with the talismanic power to perform this overhaul of civilization. Combating the spreading ignorance of "mass civilization," Leavis launched a social campaign or, in Terry Eagleton's words, " a moral and cultural crusade" in which the "Scrutineers" would "go out to the schools and universities to do battle there, nurturing through the study of literature the kind of rich, complex, mature, discriminating, morally serious responses (all key *Scrutiny* terms) which would equip individuals to survive in a mechanized society of trashy romances, alienated labour, banal advertisements and vulgarizing mass media."[18] Along with I. A. Richards, Leavis found salvific value in literature, the social function of which was to improve civilization. Indeed, because—at least in part—Lewis did not share this view, Leavis once remarked that Lewis "hated literature."[19]

Leavis's crusade further helped create the cultural milieu that made Lewis's stance so oppositional and thus, once again, so favorable for Lewis's becoming a public intellectual. Lewis consistently denied such restorative power of literature for a society and instead assigned literature a much more limited role: the Horatian formula of delighting and teaching. His ingrained conservatism and very intellectual temperament placed him at odds with the theorizing of Leavis as well as the quixotic calls for progress from science and scientism. In his 1954 inaugural address at Cambridge University, Lewis identified himself as a "dinosaur," a rare specimen embalmed in the past, immune to the fluctuations of intellectual fads and fashions: an identity formulation consonant with the counter-cultural posture of the public intellectual.

*c. Christianity and the Oppositional Stance*

Of course, Lewis adopts his most prominent counter-cultural stance with respect to his faith, as mentioned earlier.[20] Adrian Hastings describes the ebbing plausibility of Christianity beginning in the 1920s in England:

---

[17] F. R. Leavis, *For Continuity* (Freeport NY: Books for Libraries Press, 1933) 38.

[18] Terry Eagleton, *Literary Theory: An Introduction*, 2nd ed. (Minneapolis: University of Minnesota Press, 1996) 29.

[19] Quoted in John Wain, "C. S. Lewis," *American Scholar* 50/issue no. 1 (Winter 1980–1981): 73–80.

[20] Lewis thus upends the pattern typical to most public intellectuals. That is, the public intellectual is most commonly associated with progress and liberal causes (from Voltaire to Norman Mailer). But because of the intellectual milieu in which he

Orthodox Christianity appeared for very solid reasons increasingly implausible to the intelligent man. To believe meant standing out against every single one of the giants of modernity, the prophets who had established the framework of understanding wherein which intellectual discourse, the whole modern civilization of the mind, seemed newly established.[21]

As a Christian, Lewis flourished within such an intellectual milieu. The son of a forceful solicitor and educated under a tutor sometimes referred to as a "purely logical entity," Lewis thrived on debate, whether on the printed page or in ordinary conversation during meetings of the Oxford Socratic Club, of which he served as president for many years. In addition, from an early age, Lewis centered his identity on opposition, on what he refers to in *Surprised by Joy* as a "vision of the world which comes most naturally to me": "'we two' or 'we few' (and in a sense 'we happy few') stand[ing] together against something stronger and larger."[22] Thomas Molner describes Lewis's tone as "that of the last lonely man, engaged in a losing battle with the all-engulfing Collectivity, Party, Bureaucracy, or simply, the Modern World."[23] This defiant attitude sustains Lewis's popularity and extends his service to the twenty-first-century Christian, who faces similar adversity as a citizen in the now well-established post-Christian world. Antagonists now abound—witness the rise of the so-called New Atheists—and Lewis's model of the public intellectual remains relevant: vigorous and cogent debate against a stronger and numerically larger opponent.

### III. The Language of the Public Intellectual: Lewis as Translator

The oppositional stance creates problems of communication. How do the "we few" talk to the "something stronger and larger"? How can the Christian intelligibly transmit ideas to the post-Christian world? Here, Lewis fulfills another criterion of the public intellectual: his ability to communicate clearly to a wide and diverse audience.

Lewis's public exchange with W. Norman Pittenger, a controversy played out in the pages of the *Christian Century* wherein Pittenger critiqued

---

worked, one in which traditionalism comes under attack, the conservative Lewis finds himself an outsider, holding positions that once would have made him an insider.

[21] Adrian Hastings, *A History of English Christianity* (London: SCM Press, 1991) 221.

[22] C. S. Lewis, *Surprised by Joy* (San Diego: Harcourt Brace & Company, 1956) 32.

[23] Thomas Molner, *The Decline of the Intellectual* (New York: Meridian Books, 1961) 181.

Lewis's apologetics, illustrates this communicative ability. Multipronged in its points of attack, including accusations that Lewis's portrayal of the naturalist falls into the fallacy of the straw man, the critique concludes with Pittenger's damning estimation that Lewis "substitute[s] smart superficiality for careful thought, reasonable statement and credible theology."[24] Clearly, discourse aimed at the educated layperson can easily be mistaken for "smart superficiality," and such is the main thrust of Lewis's self-defense: "He judges my books *in vacuo*, with no consideration of the audience to whom they were addressed or the prevalent errors they were trying to combat. The Naturalist becomes a straw man because he is not found among 'first-rate scientists' and readers of Einstein. But I was writing *ad populum*, not *ad clerum*."[25] Lewis continues, "Most of my books are evangelistic, addressed to *tous exo* [those without; with a view toward outsiders]. It would have been inept to preach forgiveness and a Saviour to those who did not know they were in need of either."[26]

In the same essay, Lewis deploys a trope that threads its way through some of his other essays. Identifying himself as "translator," Lewis emphasizes the importance of this position while also admitting that it risks a polemical strategy given to simplification at the possible expense of nuance. Eschewing the "highly emotional form offered by revivalists" as well as the "unintelligible language of highly cultured clergyman," Lewis engages the trope:

> My task was therefore simply that of a *translator*—one turning Christian doctrine, or what he believed to be such, into the vernacular, into language that unscholarly people would attend to and could understand. For this purpose a style more guarded, more *nuanced*, finelier shaded, more rich in fruitful ambiguities—in fact, a style more like Dr Pittenger's own—would have been worse than useless.[27]

In an address titled "Christian Apologetics," delivered in 1945 to an assembly of Anglican priests and youth leaders, an address, in fact, that could be read as a how-to manual for performing the task of "translation," Lewis positions England as a missionary field: "Now if you were sent to the

---

[24] W. Norman Pittenger, "Apologist Versus Apologist: A Critique of C. S. Lewis as 'Defender of the Faith,'" *Christian Century* vol. 75 (1 October 1958): 1107.

[25] C. S. Lewis, "Rejoinder to Dr Pittenger," in *God in the Dock: Essays on Theology and Ethics*, ed. Walter Hooper (Grand Rapids: Eerdmans, 1970) 182. Originally published in *Christian Century* vol. 75 (26 November 1958): 1359–61.

[26] Ibid., 181.

[27] Ibid., 183.

Bantus you would be taught their language and traditions. You need similar teaching about the language and mental habits of your own uneducated and unbelieving fellow countrymen."[28] Lewis then provides in this address a virtual lexicon for facilitating the act of translation, offering definitions of certain key words according to their popular usage, words like "atonement," "Christian," "morality," and "spirituality."[29]

Lewis filled a vacuum left by scholars becoming increasingly esoteric in their work and specialized in their focus, speaking more and more to each other and less and less to the populace. In the 1950s, intellectuals like Maritain and Bergson converted to Christianity, a seeming boon for the cause of the faith. Lewis, however, was not so optimistic. He writes,

> But this phenomenon would be more hopeful if it had not occurred at a moment when the Intelligentsia (scientists apart) are losing all touch with, and all influence over, nearly the whole human race. Our most esteemed poets and critics are read by our most esteemed critics and poets (who don't usually like them much) and nobody else takes any notice. An increasing number of highly literate people simply ignore what the 'Highbrows' are doing. It says nothing to them. The Highbrows in return ignore or insult them. Conversions from the Intelligentsia are not therefore likely to be very widely influential.[30]

As the "Highbrows" isolated themselves within their arcane cultural niche, Lewis embraced the opportunity of communicating to a much larger readership.

Lewis acutely felt the demands of writing for and speaking to a range of popular audiences. One need only browse the contents of Lewis's collection of essays and articles published in *God in the Dock* to appreciate his sensitivity to a non-specialized audience, which includes the following diverse array of laypeople: auditors of his many sermons and readers of a pamphlet by the Electrical and Musical Industries Christian Fellowship, of the *Coventry Evening Telegraph*, of a pamphlet by the Student Christian Movement in Schools, of *St James' Magazine* (published by St James' Church in England), of a pamphlet by the New England Anti-Vivisection Society, and of the *Saturday Evening Post*. The segmentation of readers into two types, specialist and non-specialist, necessitating two different forms of discourse, scholarly and popular, creates problems and challenges relatively recent in history. So explains Lewis in *Miracles*: "All over the world, until quite

---

[28] C. S. Lewis, "Christian Apologetics," in *God in the Dock*, 94.

[29] Ibid., 96–98.

[30] Lewis, "Revival or Decay?" in *God in the Dock*, 251.

modern times, the direct insight of the mystics and the reasonings of the philosophers percolated to the mass of the people by authority and tradition; they could be received by those who were no great reasoners themselves in the concrete form of myth and ritual and the whole pattern of life."[31] Robbed of this process of percolation, the modern world teeters on cataclysm, the populace left to fend for itself absent the guidance and direction from the learned: "A society where the simple many obey the few seers can live: a society where all were seers could live even more fully. But a society where the mass is still simple and the seers are no longer attended to can achieve only superficiality, baseness, ugliness, and in the end extinction."[32] And when the process of percolation does occur, it misleads the populace through distortions of what the seers truly believe. Thus, when it comes to the discipline of science, it is significant that Lewis does not chiefly object to the beliefs of scientists but rather to the transmogrified beliefs that have filtered down from the scientists to the populace in the form of the "Scientific Outlook" or, to use Lewis's favored term, "Wellsianity," named after H. G. Wells.[33]

It is therefore no coincidence that Lewis's representations of near apocalypse in *That Hideous Strength* (the final book in Lewis's space trilogy) and total apocalypse in *The Last Battle* (the seventh and final Narnian story) involve duplicitous communications between (diabolical) seers and the general population, ill-willed percolations descending from the cognoscenti to the populace. Indeed, *That Hideous Strength* is a book about communication; the protagonist Mark Studdock, though a sociologist by academic training, is recruited by the nefarious N.I.C.E. for his persuasive writing ability and his potential to shape public opinion. In the book, the press, what Jürgen Habermas refers to as the "public sphere's preeminent institution,"[34] is the medium used by the N.I.C.E. speciously to justify their horrific experimentations under the guise of remedial punishment: "As regards crime in general, they had already popularised in the press the idea that the Institute should be allowed to experiment pretty largely in the hope of discovering how far humane, remedial treatment could be substituted for

---

[31] C. S. Lewis, *Miracles: A Preliminary Study* (New York: Collier Books, 1947) 42.

[32] Ibid., 43.

[33] C. S. Lewis, "Is Theology Poetry?" in *The Weight of Glory and Other Addresses*, ed. Walter Hooper (New York: Simon & Schuster, 1980) 98.

[34] Jürgen Habermas, *The Structural Transformation of the Public Sphere: An Inquiry into a Category of Bourgeois Society*, trans. Thomas Burger (Cambridge: MIT Press, 1989) 180.

the old notion of 'retributive' or 'vindictive' punishment."[35] Through manipulation of public opinion, the N.I.C.E. cloaks its malevolent intentions, ingratiating itself to the world powers. Thus Mark Studdock, who because of various character flaws falls victim (and, again, through his writing skills, contributes) to the N.I.C.E.'s propaganda, finds out too late that there is no sanctuary from its public influence:

> Even the vague idea of escaping to America which, in a simpler age, comforted so many a fugitive, was denied him. He had already read in the papers the warm approval of the N.I.C.E. and all its works which came from the United States and from Russia. Some poor tool just like himself had written them. Its claws were embedded in every country: on the liner, if he should ever succeed in sailing; on the tender, if he should ever make some foreign port; its ministers would be waiting for him.[36]

The N.I.C.E.'s grip on the mass populace thus precludes open attack from the forces of good, as explained by Ransom to Merlin the magician: "'It could not be done now. They have an engine called the Press whereby the people are deceived. We should die without even being heard of.'"[37]

Likewise, in *The Last Battle*, Shift the ape deceives Narnians into believing that Aslan has returned. The Aslan that Shift proclaims, however, bears little resemblance to the real Aslan. Thus Shift distorts the meaning of the refrain that has echoed through Narnian history, passed on from generation to generation: "Aslan is not a tame lion." In its original rendering, the phrase connotes the holiness of the lion as divine; through manipulation in the public square—the open space outside the hut where Aslan supposedly resides and where Narnians gather to hear Shift's speeches— Shift manipulates the phrase through linguistic sleights of hand, convincing the public that the phrase gives license for Aslan to commit whatever heinous act he desires. The people are fooled, and the new (and false) revelations about Aslan spread.

In fact, the manipulation of public opinion becomes more sophisticated and devastating. When Narnian King Tirian, along with Eustace Scrubb and Jill Pole, discover that the newly revealed "Aslan" is just Puzzle the donkey poorly fitted with a lion costume, they launch a rescue operation, liberating the dim-witted Puzzle from the hut as well as from the machinations of Shift. Shift, however, with the help of Ginger the cat and the Calormene Captain Rishda Tarkaan, then deploys a strategy that preemptively negates the force

---

[35] C. S. Lewis, *That Hideous Strength* (New York: Simon & Schuster, 1996) 69.
[36] Ibid., 213.
[37] Ibid., 292.

of this discovery to sway public opinion. Summoning the Narnians, Shift proclaims that a donkey has been spotted that pretends to be Aslan and that this donkey should be executed upon sight. As the narrator comments, "By mixing a little truth with [their plan, the enemies] had made their lie far stronger."[38] This plan, deployed in the public sphere and effective primarily insofar as it fools Narnian commoners, ushers in the Narnian eschaton.[39]

Lewis's sensitivity to a popular audience inflects his literary and cultural criticism as well. In *The Allegory of Love*, for instance, Lewis bestows upon Boethius the glowing epithet, "the divine popularizer."[40] In an essay titled "Christianity and Culture," Lewis censures Milton for betraying in the *Areopagitica* an elitist, spiritually toxic attitude, "based on an aristocratic preoccupation with great souls and a contemptuous indifference to the mass of mankind which, I suppose, no Christian can tolerate."[41]

Of even more import to my argument is Lewis's critical attitude toward Edmund Spenser, who exerted tremendous influence on Lewis. In a key passage in *The Allegory of Love*, Lewis considers the allegory in *The Faerie Queene*, noting the diverse interpretive speculations concerning the allegorical significance of Una and the lamb, who figure prominently in Book I of Spenser's poem. For Lewis, these speculations amount to scholarly much ado about what is obvious. What is required to understand and appreciate Spenser's allegories is not critical erudition, but a vicarious reading of the text from the position of Spenser's original appreciators: those familiar with popular images and motifs. (Note once again Lewis's sensitivity to audience.) Thus, remarks Lewis, "the two figures which meet us at the beginning of *The Faerie Queene* were instantly recognized by

---

[38] C. S. Lewis, *The Last Battle* (New York: Harper Trophy, 1994) 127.

[39] Lewis was thus clearly wary of propaganda: of powerful institutions and people trying to manipulate the populace. It is for this reason, I believe, that of all the ghosts who reject heaven in *The Great Divorce*, it is the ghost of a "hard-bitten man" who comes closest to persuading the narrator that heaven is a sham. When asked by the narrator if he plans to accept the invitation to proceed to heaven, the ghost of the hard-bitten man responds, "'That's all propaganda.… Of course there never was any question of our staying. You can't eat the fruit and you can't drink the water and it takes you all your time to walk on the grass. A human being couldn't live here. All that idea of staying is only an advertisement stunt.…'" The narrator later confesses, "This account of the matter struck me as uncomfortably plausible. I said nothing" (*The Great Divorce* [San Francisco: HarperSanFrancisco, 2001] 52, 54).

[40] C. S. Lewis, *The Allegory of Love: A Study in Medieval Tradition* (Oxford: Oxford University Press, 1936) 46.

[41] C. S. Lewis, "Christianity and Culture" in *Christian Reflections*, ed. Walter Hooper (Grand Rapids: Eerdmans, 1967) 18.

Spenser's first readers, and were clothed for them not in literary or courtly associations, but in popular, homely, patriotic associations."[42] The two figures of Una and the lamb were inscribed in early legends of St. George, legends with which the common folk were conversant. "We have long looked for the origins of *The Faerie Queene* in Renaissance palaces and Platonic academies, and forgotten that it has humbler origins of at least equal importance in the Lord Mayor's show, the chap-book, the bedtime story, the family Bible, and the village church. What lies next beneath the surface in Spenser's poem is the world of popular imagination: almost, a popular mythology."[43]

The scholar/lay-reader dichotomy also figures in Lewis's analysis of Spenser in *Studies in Medieval and Renaissance Literature*. The "sophisticated, self-conscious frame of mind" endemic to the project of scholarly analysis has caused us to misread Spenser's poem, which, instead, "demands of us a child's love of marvels and dread of bogies, a boy's thirst for adventures, a young man's passion for physical beauty.... The poem is a great palace, but the door into it is so low that you must stoop to go in."[44] Because of his sensitivity to audience, Lewis could not dismiss or look down his nose at the importance of popular imagination, tradition, myth, and experience. "No prig," Lewis insists, "can be a Spenserian."[45]

Translative discourse—the language of the public intellectual—shapes Lewis's apologetics, fiction, and (as we now see) literary analyses. But these sensitivities are more deeply seeded. In *Surprised by Joy*, Lewis describes his experiences as an infantryman in World War I. Lewis's battalion consisted of a diverse group of men: "a minority of good regulars ruling a pleasantly mixed population of promoted rankers (west country farmers, these), barristers, and university men. You could get as good talk there as anywhere."[46] As a result of these experiences, Lewis "came to know and pity and reverence the ordinary man...."[47] To reach his intended audience in a text such as *Mere Christianity*, Lewis need only imaginatively invoke some of these conversations with "regulars" and "rankers," for I maintain that the image of the "ordinary man" was never far from mind when Lewis sat down with pen and paper.

---

[42] Lewis, *Allegory of Love*, 310.

[43] Ibid., 312.

[44] C. S. Lewis, *Studies in Medieval and Renaissance Literature* (Cambridge: Cambridge University Press, 1998) 132.

[45] Ibid., 133.

[46] Lewis, *Surprised by Joy*, 193.

[47] Ibid.

Lewis's discursive identity as translator once again places him at odds with yet another major literary scholar of the twentieth century: I. A. Richards. In *Principles of Literary Criticism,* Richards observes that the growth of the population widens the gulf between learned and unlearned, thereby burdening the cognoscenti with a cultural mandate: to inform the unenlightened what is good and bad. Doing so, of course, puts the sage in an uncomfortable position: "The expert in matters of taste is in an awkward position when he differs from the majority. He is forced to say in effect, 'I am better than you. My taste is more refined, my nature more cultured, you will do well to become more like me than you are.' It is not his fault that he has to be so arrogant." Risking accusations of arrogance is necessary, however, for what is at stake is "a transvaluation by which popular taste replaces trained discrimination."[48] In *For Continuity,* Leavis echoes Richards:

> In any period it is upon a very small minority that the discerning appreciation of art and literature depends: it is...only a few who are capable of unprompted, first-hand judgment.... Upon this minority depends our power of profiting by the finest human experience of the past; they keep alive the subtlest and most perishable parts of the tradition. Upon them depend the implicit standards that order the finer living of an age, the sense that this is worth more than that, this rather than that is the direction in which to go, that the centre is here rather than there.[49]

The elitism here contrasts starkly with Lewis's populism. Lewis's ability and willingness to reach a wide audience equips him with the requisite skills to succeed as a public intellectual; his opposition to two major literary scholars of his day further places him in the countercultural posture characteristic of the public intellectual.

## IV. A Brief Overview of Lewis's Rhetorical Strategies as Public Intellectual

Lewis also summoned the rhetorical authority necessary to appeal to a diverse popular audience. Operating on the large stage of the public intellectual, Lewis creates arguments fashioned to rise above particularities and contingencies. Avoiding claims that are culturally and theologically specific (hence Lewis's appeal to mere Christianity), Lewis constructs

---

[48] I. A. Richards, *Principles of Literary Criticism* (New York: Harcourt Brace & World, 1925) 36–37.
[49] Leavis, *For Continuity*, 15.

arguments that presuppose a basic uniformity of experience, arguments that unite a diverse audience around what it holds in common.

These rhetorical strategies will be discussed in detail in chapters 3, 4, and 5; for now, I will briefly describe some of them. First, Lewis engages in what I will refer to as *de-conversion*. Although an odd term to apply to a thinker whom Walter Hooper calls the "most thoroughly *converted* man I ever met," de-conversion refers not to a religious position but an analytical orientation.[50] Similar to Cartesian methodology, de-conversion means the stripping away of biases before engaging in analysis; it is an analytical posture of neutrality. Second, Lewis mobilizes in both his fiction and non-fiction what he calls *high tradition*: the cumulative wisdom of Western civilization as recorded in its literature, history, philosophy, and theology. Lewis, in fact, acts as a cipher of this wisdom, channeling the sages of the centuries, allowing them to support, enrich, contextualize, and, in the end, universalize the claims proffered either in his own voice (for instance, *The Problem of Pain* and *Miracles*) or in the voice of his characters (such as Screwtape or George MacDonald in *The Great Divorce*). Lewis's translations of high tradition, in fact, reconnect him to an important function of the public intellectual: to "elaborate, apply, and popularize the thought of the great, epoch-making thinkers."[51] Finally, Lewis employs in his fiction what I will call *transcendent characters*. Adopting an Olympian perspective, transcending the intellectual limitations endemic to the human condition, the transcendent character possesses knowledge that approximates absolute truth. Inhabiting the fictional geography of nearly all of Lewis's imaginative works—Mother Kirk (among others) in *The Pilgrim's Regress*, the *Oyarasu* in the space trilogy, Aslan in the Narnian books—the transcendent character endows Lewis's texts with Olympian perspectives from which spiritual truths and moral precepts proceed with such rhetorical power. Lewis as narrator serves as the intermediary between the immortal (and apothegmatic) truths of transcendent characters and the limited understanding of ordinary, mortal readers.

All of these strategies give Lewis's texts considerable rhetorical power on the public stage. They unite the public intellectual's diverse audience around universal truths and experiences: de-conversion strips the mind to its essence, setting subjectivity aside; high tradition coalesces the collective wisdom of the western world, privileging only the ideas that have stood the

---

[50] Walter Hooper, preface to *God in the Dock*, 12.

[51] Melzer, "What is an Intellectual?," 5.

test of time; and the transcendent character magisterially transmits absolute truths, mediated only by the Lewisian narrator.

## V. The Commitment of the Public Intellectual: Division, Polarization, and Sacrifice

Finally, like most public intellectuals, Lewis creates a divisive body of work. As explained above, the public intellectual becomes identified with his or her position on an issue—the more controversial the position, the more divisive the public intellectual. Throughout history, nothing has proven more polarizing than uncompromising positions on religion. For devoted believers, Lewis stands for Christianity, a religion at the core of their being, a religion for which they would sacrifice their lives. For devoted unbelievers, Lewis represents intolerant, superannuated dogma and/or philosophical sophistry at the service of a desperate faith that fills a psychological need. Thus, on the one hand, Lewis admirers write books and articles identified as hagiography, consisting of summaries of Lewis's ideas and testimonies of their cogency. On the other hand, skeptics write books and articles that mercilessly critique Lewis's arguments[52] and call into question Lewis's saintly image.[53] And never the polarized twain shall meet. Lewis devotees, who run the Lewis industry, marginalize Lewis's critics, dismissing them in annotated bibliographies and reviews. Lewis's critics, in turn, impugn the work of the Lewis devotees as shoddy scholarship, their analyses blinded by their own devotion to the man.[54]

---

[52] John Beversluis, *C. S. Lewis and the Search for Rational Religion*, rev. ed. (Grand Rapids: Eerdmans, 1985; repr. Amherst NY: Prometheus, 2007).

[53] A. N. Wilson, *C. S. Lewis: A Biography* (New York: Norton, 1990).

[54] Lewis scholars Diana Glyer and David Bratman, for instance, assess A. N. Wilson's controversial biography thusly: "Wilson writes engagingly, but commits serious gaffes in fact, interpretation, and tone that overshadow any value in the book." See "C. S. Lewis Scholarship: A Bibliographical Overview," in *C. S. Lewis: Life, Works, and Legacy*, vol. 4, *Scholar, Teacher, and Public Intellectual*, ed. Bruce Edwards (London: Praeger Perspectives, 2007) 285. Lewis scholar and former curator of the Wade Center at Wheaton College Lyle Dorsett comments that Wilson's biography is "...so filled with factual errors and inaccurate interpretations that it is useless to the serious student of C. S. Lewis's life and writings." See *Seeking the Secret Place: The Spiritual Formation of C. S. Lewis* (Grand Rapids: Brazos Press, 2004) 24. Reviewing Wilson's biography for *Modern Fiction Studies*, Brian Murray conversely offers praise of the biography while also commenting on Lewis's devotees: "The lively but judicious tone he sustains throughout this thoroughly researched work suggests that Wilson's interest in such matters is sparked not by prurient curiosity, but derives in

To make his religious position even more charged, Lewis presents Christianity in various books and essays with strongly conservative inflections. His traditional position on the role of women, for instance, constitutes a lightning rod, with devotees rushing to his defense, supporting or qualifying his position, and skeptics eager to pounce, quick with

---

part from his desire to correct the image—kept especially vivid in evangelical circles—that Lewis was quite free of the more fleshly drives and desires that can dog and distract lesser mortals." See *Modern Fiction Studies* 36/4 (1990): 618. Wilson, meanwhile, maintains that for "the cult" of Lewis, "Evidence is only of peripheral interest when the idolatrous imagination gets to work." See *C. S. Lewis: A Biography* (New York: Norton, 1990) 309, 305. Polarization also characterizes responses to John Beversluis's *C. S. Lewis and the Search for Rational Religion*, rev. ed. (Grand Rapids: Eerdmans, 1985; repr. Amherst NY: Prometheus, 2007). Long-time Lewis scholar Peter Kreeft calls the book the "abomination of desolation." See *C. S. Lewis: A Critical Essay* (Front Royal VA, 1998) 5. James Como, a founding member of the New York C. S. Lewis Society, states that Beversluis is "generically tone deaf," betraying his "profound ignorance of the demands of rhetoric." See *Branches to Heaven: The Geniuses of C. S. Lewis* (Dallas: Spence, 1998) 174. Others who do not identify themselves as Lewis scholars offer different assessments. Basil Mitchell, Oxford professor and Lewis's successor as president of the Socratic Club, refers to Beversluis's "really rather devastating critique of Lewis' work...." See "Reflections on C. S. Lewis, Apologetics, and the Moral Tradition: Basil Mitchell in Conversation with Andrew Walker," in *A Christian for All Christians: Essays in Honor of C. S. Lewis*, ed. by Andrew Walker and James Patrick (Washington DC: Regnery, 1992) 15. Christopher Derrick, one of Lewis's students at Oxford, favorably reviewed Beversluis's critique and here recalls the vitriol he received in the form of letters from Lewis fans: "More recently, I reviewed a book which cast doubt upon what some consider the flawless rationality of—once again—Lewis's religious thinking. It seemed to me that the writer, Beversluis by name, had done his chosen task rather well, and I said so. Once again, the angry letters came, and their dominant tone was 'Hey, Derrick—which side are you on?'" See "Some Personal Angles on Chesterton and Lewis," in *G. K. Chesterton and C. S. Lewis: The Riddle of Joy*, ed. Michael H. MacDonald and Andrew A. Tadie (Grand Rapids: Eerdmans, 1989) 10. For his part, like Wilson, Beversluis minces no words in condemning the scholarly rigor and integrity of much of what makes up Lewis studies, or what he calls "the increasing crop of almost wholly uncritical studies of Lewis the thinker": "Their discussions are seldom suggestive or illuminating. They have next to nothing to offer by way of analysis or elucidation. They never probe. Their rare attempts at criticism are timid, addressed to tiny points, and dropped almost the instant they are raised. Wishing (but invariably failing) to do more than repeat what Lewis has already said, they write books that lack direction, thesis, and, in the end, substance. Though brimming over with good intentions, they seldom transcend a sort of doting worshipfulness." See *C. S. Lewis and the Search for Rational Religion*, xiv 1st edition. I explore these meta-critical phenomena in chapters 12 and 13.

accusations of misogyny.[55] Similar polarizations characterize responses to Lewis's position on, and fictional representations of, war and violence. War and violence conducted in the name of Aslan in the Narnian stories, for instance, evoke for some formulations of a militant, belligerent, and dangerous Christianity.[56] The baggage that accompanies Lewis's presentation of Christianity thus intensifies the polarized responses to his work.

---

[55] Walter Hooper provides an example of this pattern in his essay "C. S. Lewis and C. S. Lewises." He notes that some unfriendly critics have created false Lewises, one of which is the misogynist Lewis, a judgment that Hooper reduces to a knee-jerk response, similar in intellectual depth to a children's card game called Snap, in which participants smack a card when they find a match and yell, "Snap!" Hooper thus calls those who accuse Lewis of misogyny "snappers." See "C. S. Lewis and C. S. Lewises," in *G. K. Chesterton and C. S. Lewis*, ed. MacDonald and Tadie, 39. Mary Stewart Van Leeuwen is a scholar who has attempted to qualify accusations of misogyny directed toward Lewis, maintaining that Lewis's putative sexism was blunted primarily after his relationship with Joy Davidman. See "A Sword between the Sexes: C. S. Lewis's Long Journey to Gender Equality," in *Christian Scholar's Review* 36/4 (Summer 2007): 391–414; see also Stewart Van Leeuwen's *A Sword Between the Sexes: C. S. Lewis and the Gender Debates* (Grand Rapids:Brazos Press, 2010). Philip Pullman and Phillip Hensher have both accused Lewis of misogyny. See Pullman's "The Dark Side of Narnia," in *Guardian*, 1 October 1998; and Hensher's "Don't Let Your Children Go to Narnia," in *Independent*, 4 December 1998.

[56] Polly Toynbee, for instance, writes, "Christ would surely be no lion…. He was the lamb, representing the meek of the earth, weak, poor, and refusing to fight." She claims that "Narnia is the perfect Republican, muscular Christianity for America— that warped, distorted neo-fascist strain that thinks might is proof of right." See "Narnia represents everything that is most hateful about religion," *Guardian*, 5 December 2005, 8. Hensher likewise uses the phrase "muscular Christianity" in his broadside against the Narniad ("Don't Let Your Children," 4). Such accusations can be traced at least as far back as 1973 when David Holbrook published an essay in *Children's Literature in Education* ([March 1973]) titled "The Problem of C. S. Lewis," an article that culminated in his 1991 monograph, *The Skeleton in the Wardrobe: C. S. Lewis's Fantasies* (London: Associated University Press, 1991). Holbrook's major claim is that Lewis's God is belligerent: "his Christ is too severe an authoritarian power to whom one needs masochistically to submit" (*Skeleton in the Wardrobe*, 11). Consistent with the polarized-response pattern, Walter Hooper identified Holbrook's article as "the most hostile piece of criticism I have ever seen," though Hooper does not identify Holbrook by name, for he "cannot bear that it should appear on the same page with that of C. S. Lewis." Hooper goes so far as to challenge Holbrook to a lie-detector test, insisting that not even Holbrook believes what he has written. See *Past Watchful Dragons: The Narnian Chronicles of C. S. Lewis* (New York: Collier Books, 1970) 26–27.

These polarized responses proceed, again, from Lewis's uncompromising commitment to Christianity. It is important to emphasize that, with the exception of his literary scholarship, *all* of Lewis's books convey this commitment in one way or another, thus assuring his brand identification as a public intellectual. This truism leads me to the conclusion that Lewis's works of fiction are, to varying extents, ideologically driven. That is, Lewis never created art for art's sake; he was no artist simpliciter; didactic elements are never subtle. This is not to affirm what Lewis plainly denied: that when he sat down to write, he first devised ways in which he could incorporate Christian messages in his work. Rather, it is to argue that Christianity was paramount in his life and unavoidably manifested itself in his books, often with masterful artistry. But the faith comes first, not the art.

Such a claim runs the risk of perpetrating a false distinction, since compelling presentations of Christianity require artistry, but as future chapters will show, Lewis lived during a time when Christianity was particularly embattled, demanding of him an aggressively didactic voice in his fiction that lacks the nuance and artistic fine touches of, say, Spenser in his *Faerie Queene*. This is why Owen Barfield identifies in Lewis's fiction something he called "the expository demon," or what Lewis himself defines as his "native tendency to be too argumentative and make people talk like a Platonic dialogue."[57] Lewis's argumentativeness—his fiery passion for defending the faith—elicited concern from Dorothy Sayers: "One trouble about C. S. Lewis, I think, is his fervent missionary zeal. I welcome his able dialectic, and he is a tremendous hammer for heretics. But he is apt to think that one should rush into every fray and strike a blow for Christendom, whether or not one is equipped by training and temperament for that particular conflict."[58]

More evidence of Lewis's commitment to art in the service of faith (rather than art for art's sake) abounds. Lewis categorically rejected Matthew Arnold's high view of literature as a substitute for a declining faith.[59] This rejection shapes nearly all of Lewis's iterations on the relationship between Christianity and literature. "But the Christian knows from the outset," writes

---

[57] C. S. Lewis to Katharine Farrer, 9 July 1955, in *The Collected Letters of C. S. Lewis*, vol. 3, *Narnia, Cambridge, and Joy, 1950–1963*, ed. Walter Hooper (San Francisco: HarperSanFrancisco, 2007) 630.

[58] Dorothy Sayers, "Letter to Brother George Every," 10 July 1947, in *The Letters of Dorothy L. Sayers*, vol. 3, ed. Barbara Reynolds (Cambridge: The Dorothy L. Sayers Society, 1998) 314.

[59] See "Learning in War-Time" in *The Weight of Glory and Other Addresses*, ed. Walter Hooper (New York: Simon & Schuster, 1980) 41–52.

Lewis, "that the salvation of a single soul is more important than the production or preservation of all the epics and tragedies of the world...."[60] Lewis approaches the subject systematically in his essay, "Christianity and Culture." Lewis wonders what place culture, which he defines as "intellectual and aesthetic activity," has for the Christian, for whom the "salvation of souls...is the real business of life."[61] As he considers this question, Lewis proceeds inductively, first identifying culture as a "weapon" for conversion: "If we are to convert our heathen neighbours, we must understand their culture."[62] Later, Lewis finds in culture "sub-Christian" values and experiences, such as honor and *"Sehnsucht* awakened by the past, the remote, or the imagined."[63] Representations of these values and experiences in literature may pave the way to a conversion to Christianity: "On these grounds I conclude that culture has a distinct part to play in bringing certain souls to Christ. Not all souls—there is a shorter, and safer, way which has always been followed by thousands of simple affectional natures who begin, where we hope to end, with devotion to the person of Christ."[64] In a 1940 letter to Dom Bede Griffiths, Lewis explains,

---

[60] C. S. Lewis, "Christianity and Culture" in *Christian Reflections*, ed. Walter Hooper (Grand Rapids: Eerdmans, 1967) 10.

[61] Lewis, "Christianity and Culture," 12, 14.

[62] Ibid., 17.

[63] Ibid., 22.

[64] Ibid., 24. Donald T. Williams suggests that Lewis's argument in "Christianity and Culture" reflects his earlier thought, which would develop as he matured: "...but in later essays Lewis would go on to develop much more fully not just the innocence but also the positive values of literary culture." While Lewis's ideas may have developed (following the trajectory established in "Christianity and Culture"), I do not believe this development marks any significant change. Williams identifies four specific developments in Lewis's subsequent writings: (1) literature "enlarges our world of experience...." (2) "...this expansion of horizons makes it possible for literature to strip Christian doctrines of their 'stained glass and Sunday School associations' and allow them to appear in their 'real potency,' a possibility Lewis himself magnificently realized in the Narnia books and the Space Trilogy." (3) "In the third place, literature can have some of the significance Lewis seemed to deny it in 'Christianity and Culture' through the creation of positive role models and the reinforcement of healthy 'stock responses.'" And (4) "Finally, literature can cure our chronological snobbery and provincialism and fortify us in the "mere Christianity' that has remained constant through the ages" (Donald T. Williams, *Mere Humanity* [Nashville, Tennessee: Broadman & Holman Publishers, 2006] 141, 143, 145, 148]. These developments solidify the points that Lewis made in "Christianity and Culture": that the salvation of souls is paramount and that, as we shall see, literature should serve as the handmaiden of religion and morality. Chapter 5 will show how

I do most thoroughly agree with what you say about Art and Literature. To my mind they are only healthy when they are either (a) Definitely the handmaids of religious, or at least moral, truth—or (b) Admittedly aiming at nothing but innocent recreation or entertainment. Dante's alright, and *Pickwick* is alright. But the great *serious irreligious* art—art for art's sake—is all balderdash; and, incidentally, never exists when art is really flourishing.[65]

Lewis's position on Christianity and art further solidifies his status as public intellectual. His commitment to the message within the art—not the art that packages the message—harmonizes with the function of the public intellectual. By transmitting that message in the vernacular to a diverse audience that spans many decades, Lewis assured himself a prominent place on the public stage.

It is also important to note the sacrifices Lewis made in carving out that public role. Becoming a well-known advocate of Christianity made Lewis unpopular with some. In a 1946 essay titled "The Decline of Religion," Lewis states that the claims of Christianity create in many "dislike, terror, and finally hatred..." and that "to be on the Christian side would be costing a man (at the least) his career."[66] Biographically, it is not difficult to notice the self-reflexive nature of Lewis's admonition: the career being sacrificed may well have been his own. On more than one occasion during Lewis's thirty-five-year term of office, for example, Oxford University failed to elect him to a professorial chair. Walter Hooper, who served as Lewis's secretary for a brief time at the end of Lewis's life, reports that J. R. R. Tolkien told him that "No Oxford don was forgiven for writing books outside his field of study—except for detective stories which dons, like everyone else, read when they are down with the 'flu. But it was considered unforgiveable that Lewis wrote international best-sellers, and worse still that many were of a religious

---

Lewis parlays "stock responses" into a method of conveying authority as a distinctly public intellectual, a move that ultimately advances the claims of Christianity.

[65] C. S. Lewis to Dom Bede Griffiths, 16 April 1940, in *The Collected Letters of C. S. Lewis*, vol. 2, *Books, Broadcasts, and the War, 1931–1949*, ed. Walter Hooper (San Francisco: HarperSanFrancisco, 2004) 391.

[66] C. S. Lewis, "The Decline of Religion," in *God in the Dock*, 223.

nature."[67] Harry Blamires reports that Lewis once told him, "'You don't know how I'm hated.'"[68]

It is ironic that the public role that may have cost Lewis a professorship at Oxford is precisely the role that contributed to the longevity of his reputation as a writer. During his own life, brand identification already attached itself to Lewis's name, following him wherever he went, predisposing many of his colleagues (at Oxford and Cambridge) and students toward predictably polarized responses. For instance, in 1955, Graham Hough explained that auditors of Lewis's inaugural address at Cambridge responded less to the contents of his speech than to his popular Christian works with which he was inextricably associated. That is, Lewis's address was ostensibly focused on the subject of intellectual history and the nature of historical change, with Lewis clearly staking out his conservative position as "Old Western Man." But the address contained a subtext: whether Christianity is true. Because of Lewis's popularity as a Christian writer, that subtext transformed itself into the main text in the days that followed as the Cambridge community wrestled with Lewis's ideas. I quote at length from Hough's eye-witness account because of the importance of this transformation:

> Let us change the scene from the crowded and expectant lecture room to a crowded and argumentative sherry party a little later. The guests were divided into several groups. Some didn't need any sherry as they were already quite drunk with rhetoric; the lecture had proved a heady beverage. Some had decided that they were Old Western Men, and very nice too. Some violently denied the validity of the distinction, some merely denied Professor Lewis's claim to be a genuine Old Western Man, while others maintained that the whole thing was an Anglo-Catholic plot and that the lecture was Christian propaganda in disguise. The last three points of view are the ones that interest me, and the odd thing about them is that a number of people tried to maintain all three simultaneously. Let us take the last first. Professor Lewis is well known to believe—to have come to believe—in a supernatural order. He has written a number of books to that effect—books that might be labeled popular theology. It is true that neither theologians nor skeptics were greatly satisfied by them. The logic of the essay on *Miracles* was not compelling; the moral theology

---

[67] Walter Hooper, *Through Joy and Beyond: A Pictorial Biography of C. S. Lewis* (New York: Macmillan Publishers Company, Inc., 1982) 125.

[68] Harry Blamires, "Teaching the Universal Truth: C. S. Lewis among the Intellectuals," in *The Pilgrim's Guide: C. S. Lewis and the Art of Witness*, ed. David Mills (Grand Rapids: Eerdmans, 1998) 16.

of *The Screwtape Letters* was less than profound. But these were not the subjects under discussion at our lecture. It was tolerably clear, even before the final passage, that when professor Lewis distinguished between an antique-Christian civilization on the one hand, and a modern one on the other, that he preferred the former; but his point was the objective difference, not the subjective preference. However, it seems to have been immediately clear to a large part of his audience that, because he had written *The Screwtape Letters* and the little book on *Miracles*, which were both overtly Christian propaganda, his inaugural lecture must be propaganda too—a covert attempt to put the clock back on the pretence of telling the time. How this could be when the burden of his discourse was that a great historical change, involving among other things the unchristening of Europe, was already far advanced, I do not know. But so it seemed to many.... Hardly anyone, for example, had time to listen to Professor Lewis's argument, which was about the Renaissance and whether it really marked a crisis in our civilization; they were far too busy lining up for or against his essay on miracles. The fact that he obviously approved of a culture based on supernatural presuppositions aroused such intense partisanship, or intense disgust, that the really important matter that lay behind his lecture, and behind the whole discussion, went quite unnoticed.[69]

Hough's analysis of this single speech event helps to explain the sociological forces, spanning decades, that transformed Lewis into a public intellectual: the outsider status (the Old Western Man, a dying breed), the brand identification, and the polarized responses. As long as Christianity remains embattled in the public sphere; as long as those passionately committed to various religious, intellectual, and cultural issues self-organize into irreconcilable camps designated as conservative and liberal; and as long as his books remain in print, Lewis will continue to generate controversy, for his place has already been secured on the public stage.

Posner confirms Lewis's place on this stage. In his book on the public intellectual, Posner constructs a table of what he considers to be 546 of the most influential public intellectuals of recent times. He ranks the public influence of these intellectuals with respect to three categories: "scholarly citations," "media mentions," and "Web hits" from 1995 to 2000. Out of these 546 public intellectuals, Lewis is unimpressively tied for 132nd (with Elaine Scarry) in scholarly citations; however, he ranks 31st in media

---

[69] Graham Hough, "Old Western Man," in *Critical Thought Series: C. S. Lewis*, ed. George Watson (Cambridge: Cambridge UP, 1992) 241–43.

mentions; and he comes in at second place in Web hits.[70] Lewis is thus not merely a public intellectual, but, according to Posner's data, one of the most influential public intellectuals of the turn of the century. Having explored the characteristics that qualify Lewis as a public intellectual, the rest of this chapter will chart his meteoric rise to this position.

## VI. The Radio Celebrity and the Birth of the Public Intellectual

Sometime in 1940 or 1941, J. W. Welch read Lewis's *The Problem of Pain*. Like many, Welch benefitted from the book and accordingly wrote Lewis a letter of appreciation. What distinguished Welch from Lewis's other grateful readers was that he was director of the Religious Broadcasting Department of the British Broadcasting Center (BBC), and what made his letter unique was that it included an invitation to give a talk over the airwaves of the BBC on some aspect of Christianity. Despite Lewis's dislike of modern technology, he accepted Welch's invitation and gave his first of a series of radio talks in 1941, talks that elevated him onto a wider stage and transformed him into the public intellectual.

Fortuitous historical circumstances created the conditions that made this transformation possible. The timing was uncanny: Lewis's unlikely conversion to Christianity and the beginning of his career as a public defender of the faith coincided with what Asa Briggs and Peter Burke call a "communication revolution" in the form of radio.[71] During World War II, the power of radio was unleashed in the form of political propaganda. At the first Nazi radio exhibition in 1933, Goebbels, the "manager of the Nazi propaganda machine," maintained that radio would eclipse the press as the most powerful purveyor of political ideology.[72]

In 1941, Rogers Majestic Limited, a company that produced radio tubes, released an advertisement confirming Goebbels's prognosis. A menacing picture of Hitler and a Nazi soldier covers the center of the ad. Above the picture are printed the words, "Always the first order of the Nazi invader." Below the picture the text reads, "Seize the Radio Station!" And below that: "Make no Mistake, Hitler knows the power of radio. But in his hands, it is a power for evil—a force to smash men's liberty.... And so that these fighting

---

[70] Posner, *Public Intellectuals*, 194.
[71] Asa Briggs and Peter Burke, *A Social History of the Media: From Gutenberg to the Internet* (Cambridge: Polity Press, 2002) 1.
[72] Ibid., 217.

men may have ample resources of vital equipment, Rogers Majestic has converted its factories and its research laboratories 100% to war purposes."[73]

The BBC began broadcasting in 1922; by 1924, over one million British citizens possessed licenses to access these broadcasts. But the radio phenomenon of the twentieth century concerns more than its popularity; it created a cultural shift along socioeconomic lines, empowering the ordinary citizen with easy access to inexpensive news, information, and entertainment. In Hastings's words, radio created a "mini-revolution," resulting in the "formation of popular culture" and the "tilting of the scales away from aristocracy and towards the satisfaction of more ordinary mortals of the lower classes, male and female...."[74] Radio thus created an audience of socioeconomic and educational diversity, an audience that placed specific communicative demands upon the broadcaster: an audience, in short, tailor-made for the public intellectual.

Lewis possessed the skills, motivation, and right timing to engage this audience with virtuosity. George Watson calls Lewis a "media-don," which was "an extreme rarity before the 1960s."[75] In a 1945 review of *Beyond Personality*, one of the published versions of Lewis's broadcast talks, Anne Fremantle calls Lewis an "English radio star."[76] In a 1943 article, Robert Speaight writes, "Mr. Lewis is that rare being—a born broadcaster; born to the manner as well as the matter."[77] George C. Anderson affirms in a 1946 article that "unquestionably not a clergyman in all Britain has the influence exercised by this ordinary lay lecturer on English literature."[78] Indeed, *Time* magazine, in its 1947 cover story on Lewis, estimates that Lewis's broadcast talks reached 600,000 people. In fact, some evidence suggests that the impact of his Christian books would have been minimal were it not for the medium of radio. In his 1944 review of *Christian Behavior*, another published version of one of Lewis's broadcast talks, Alistair Cooke contends that, without the radio broadcasts, Lewis's books might have fallen quietly, if not stillborn, from the press:

---

[73] Neil Strauss, ed. *Radiotext(e)* (New York: Semiotext(e), 1993) 228.

[74] Hastings, *A History of English Christianity*, 23.

[75] George Watson, introduction to *Critical Thought Series: C. S. Lewis*, 1.

[76] Anne Fremantle, "Beyond Personality," *Commonweal* vol. 42 (14 September 1945): 528.

[77] Robert Speaight, "To Mixed Congregations," *Tablet* vol. 81 (26 June 1943): 308.

[78] George C. Anderson, "C. S. Lewis: Foe of Humanism," *Christian Century* (25 December 1946): 1563.

In the days before radio, Mr. Lewis' little volume would have been reviewed politely in the well bred magazines and no harm would have been done... Mr. Lewis has a real radio talent. He is not, like most publicists and professional men called to the radio, a statesman or editorial writer merely wiring his normal writing style for sound. He knows that radio should find an idiom, and images, that will mean the same thing to people of very different background, an ambition that only our radio gag-writers seem to sweat over. He knows it is the first task of radio to make difficult ideas honestly clear. Since his subject is morality, or as he calls it "directions for running the human machine," and since this is the topic above all others that has exercised the finest agonies of the saints, and the best skill of poets, philosophers and psychiatrists since the beginning of time, he is tackling about the toughest assignment ever known to radio. He has to explain the Beatitudes in words of one syllable.[79]

The rise of radio and Lewis's aptitude for communicating Christian principles clearly and compellingly converge to produce Lewis the public intellectual.

This chapter has outlined some cultural crises of the twentieth century (and other watershed historical moments) that, coupled with Lewis's strategies for addressing them, create the necessary conditions for Lewis's accomplishment. However, the roots of the public-intellectual identity grow even deeper, reaching beyond the twentieth century. The stage of the public intellectual descends from the public sphere, born in the eighteenth century, and the subject of the next chapter.

---

[79] Alastair Cooke, "Mr. Anthony at Oxford," *New Republic* (24 April 1944): 579.

# 2

# The Rise of the Public Sphere, the Challenge of Atheism, and the Transformation of Christian Apologetics

The twentieth-century public intellectual is a product of the Enlightenment, a massively influential historical phenomenon whose origins I trace to the late seventeenth century. Thomas L. Pangle likewise finds the roots of the public intellectual in the soil of the Enlightenment: "Indeed, I am under the impression that there is no place for the idea of the public intellectual in any text written prior to the modern era. The idea of the public intellectual is, I would contend, a distinctly modern idea. It is an idea born in, and inseparable from, the Enlightenment."[1] Bold in its challenges to the religious and political status quo, the Enlightenment endorsed independent inquiry, creating a climate of intellectual exploration in which audacious, charismatic, and innovative figures like Voltaire and Jean-Jacque Rousseau could generate publicity in both France and England. Encouraging open debate, the Enlightenment likewise created the conditions for Samuel Johnson—an equally audacious and charismatic, yet reactionary and traditional-leaning personality—to achieve cultic status. The competition of ideas animates the spirit of the Enlightenment.

The competition of ideas requires a public space—literal or figurative—for debate. This space is the public sphere, an invention of the late seventeenth century that has seminally shaped the conventions of public discourse. Thus, the public sphere creates both the space for debate as well as the procedural guidelines governing the discourse of the very debate it enables. This chapter begins by exploring the genesis of the public sphere and the discursive conventions that arise from its development. Such an exploration will situate Lewis's accomplishment as a public intellectual within the sweep of intellectual history, setting up my analysis in subsequent chapters of Part 1, where I will illustrate how dexterously Lewis mobilized the conventions of the public sphere.

---

[1] Thomas L. Pangle, "A Platonic Perspective on the Idea of the Public Intellectual," in *The Public Intellectual: Between Philosophy and Politics*, ed. Arthur M. Melzer, et al. (New York: Rowman & Littlefield Publishers, Inc., 2003) 15.

## I. The Rise of the Public Sphere

According to Jürgen Habermas, the public sphere develops at the turn of the eighteenth century. Habermas traces this development to (among other historical events) the shifting oppositional dynamic between "court and town."[2] During the first half of the seventeenth century in England, the court served as the epicenter for learned discourse; as Habermas puts it, "literature and art served the representation of the king."[3] The age of courtly patronage kept artists and intellectuals beholden to the monarch. Toward the end of the seventeenth century, however, the town began to eclipse the court in influence, becoming the new cradle of learned culture. Habermas specifically dates the cultural decline of the court to the Glorious Revolution (1688), after which the prestige of the court waned. Meanwhile, the cultural influence of the town gained more and more strength with the advent of novel institutions: the coffee house and the salon. Acting as social spaces for public dialogue, literary discourse, intellectual debate, and information exchange, the coffee houses and salons assumed the "social functions" once held by the court.[4] Unlike the court, however, the coffee houses and salons "preserved a kind of social intercourse that, far from presupposing the equality of status, disregarded status altogether. The tendency replaced the celebration of rank with a tact befitting equals. The parity on whose basis alone the authority of the better argument could assert itself against that of social hierarchy and in the end can carry the day meant, in the thought of the day, that parity of 'common humanity....'"[5] John Bender reiterates the primacy of parity, calling this public sphere "an arena of conversational and written exchange, epitomized by early English coffee houses and newspapers," whereby "discourse was reordered to allow easy flow of ideas from one field of interest to another and from one social stratum to another...."[6] A byproduct of the rise of the public sphere is the birth of public opinion, forged by the debates among these various social strata. "The medium of this public confrontation," writes Habermas, "was peculiar and

---

[2] Jürgen Habermas, *The Structural Transformation of the Public Sphere: An Inquiry into a Category of Bourgeois Society*, trans. Thomas Burger (Cambridge: MIT Press, 1989) 32.

[3] Ibid., 32.

[4] Ibid.

[5] Ibid., 36.

[6] John Bender, *Imagining the Penitentiary* (Cambridge: Cambridge University Press, 1977) 6.

without historical precedent: people's use of their reason."[7] The rise of the public sphere, in fact, helped secure the legacy of the Enlightenment as expressed in the following procedural guideline: reason is the preeminent faculty of humankind; it is the chief source of authority—not faith, not tradition, not religious or political powers.

Reason within the public sphere differs qualitatively from earlier forms of reason. It lacks the sweeping metaphysical implications with which thinkers of the classical period endowed it; that is, reason of the public-sphere variety is not enlisted in, say, a process of platonic dialectic whereby a philosopher achieves metaphysical clarity on the nature of reality as well as heightened self-awareness. In addition, the medieval synthesis had been dismantled: Reason no longer operates at the Thomistic service of faith, deployed to unite all branches of learning under the auspices of God's providential design.[8] Instead, Enlightenment reason operates much more pragmatically: its purpose is merely to find truth on a particular issue in a forum neutral with respect to religion and politics. The public sphere provides the fair and impartial space for the deliverances of reason to be aired. Moreover, the public sphere places unique demands upon reason as it carries out this function.

Fulfilling the pragmatic purpose of finding truth, reason within the public sphere must prove rationally compelling (as suggested above) to an increasingly pluralistic audience with divergent beliefs: religious, irreligious, high church, low church, Anglicans, dissenters, Tories, Whigs, etc. As Habermas notes, "The issues discussed became 'general' not merely in their significance, but also in their accessibility: everyone had to *be able* to participate."[9] Performing this task necessitates a unification of the diversity, a method of appealing to commonalities lying beyond the differences. The public sphere vouchsafes a critical unifying principle by assuming the existence of uniform experience across the religious, philosophical, political, and socio-economic spectrum. While particularities divide those of conflicting convictions, at the root of all experience exists a foundational sameness. Thus, despite the increasing heterogeneity of the period, the principle of homogeneity paradoxically becomes the operative principle of the public sphere as well as an assumed pillar in the framework of

---

[7] Habermas, *Structural Transformation*, 27.

[8] Gone also was the assumption of the Cambridge Platonists: that "…reason had a place for an intuition of the divine." Charles Taylor, *A Secular Age* (Cambridge, Mass: The Belknap Press of Harvard University Press, 2007) p.226.

[9] Ibid., 37.

Enlightenment discourse. Predisposed to favor homogeneity, public discourse acts as a unifying agent, uniting people around what they have in common rather than how they differ. As Alasdair MacIntyre explains, during the Enlightenment, "Rational justification was to appeal to principles undeniable by any rational person and therefore independent of all those social and cultural particularities which the Enlightenment thinkers took to be the mere accidental clothing of reason in particular times and places."[10]

*a. The Public Sphere in Action: Illustrations From the Eighteenth Century*

Evidence of a basic commonality across humanity—this notion of uniform experience—abounds in various eighteenth-century texts. In *An Enquiry Concerning Human Understanding* (1748), David Hume speaks of the universality of human nature, whose similarities cut across particularizing lines of culture and context:

> It is universally acknowledged that there is a great uniformity among the actions of men, in all nations and ages, and that human nature remains the same, in its principles and operations. The same motives always produce the same actions: The same events follow from the same causes. Ambition, avarice, self-love, vanity, friendship, generosity, public spirit: these passions, mixed in various degrees, and distributed through society, have been, from the beginning of the world, and still are, the source of all the actions and enterprises, which have ever been observed among mankind. Would you know the sentiments, inclinations, and course of life of the Greeks and Romans? Study well the temper and actions of the French and English: You cannot be much mistaken in transferring to the former most of the observations which you have made with regard to the latter. Mankind are so much the same, in all times and places, that history informs us of nothing new or strange in this particular. Its chief use is only to discover the constant and universal principles of human nature, by showing men in all varieties of circumstances and situations, and furnishing us with materials from which we may form our observations and become acquainted with the regular springs of human action and behaviour.[11]

Hume thus rules out—or at least minimizes—the possibility that cultural contexts frame experiences and conceptions of reality. Such conception-

---

[10] Alasdair MacIntyre, *Whose Justice? Which Rationality?* (Notre Dame: University of Notre Dame Press, 1988) 6.

[11] David Hume, *An Enquiry Concerning Human Understanding*, in *Modern Philosophy*, ed. Forrest E. Baird and Walter Kaufmann (Upper Saddle River NJ: Prentice Hall, 1996) 370.

al contexts bend to the foundational nature of human experience. Leo Damrosch points in this direction when he asserts that the "goal of eighteenth-century thought" is "to dispel illusions and identify a bedrock of experience that underlies psychology."[12]

Perhaps no one appealed to this "bedrock of experience" more vehemently than did Samuel Johnson. In *Idler* no. 51 (1759), he remarks how difficult it is to be original, to be remarkable, when humankind is essentially uniform in its experiences: "Whatever any man may have written or done, his precepts or his valor will scarcely overbalance the unimportant uniformity which runs through his time."[13] And in *Rambler* no. 60 (1750), Johnson praises the didactic value of biography: because of the uniformity of humankind, when one reads about another's life, one in fact learns about oneself:

> I have often thought that there has rarely passed a Life of which a judicious and faithful Narrative would not be useful. For, not only every Man has in the mighty Mass of the World great Number in the same Condition with himself, to whom his Mistakes and Miscarriages, Escapes and Expedients would be of immediate and apparent Use; but there is such an Uniformity in the state of Man, considered apart from adventitious and separable Decorations and Disguises, that there is scarce any Possibility of Good or Ill, but is common to Humankind.[14]

Then, in a similar vein to Hume, he continues, "We are all prompted by the same Motives, all deceived by the same fallacies, all animated by Hope, obstructed by Danger, entangled by Desire, and seduced by Pleasure."[15]

We achieve an idea of how this presupposition of uniformity in experience influenced aesthetic sensibilities in Joshua Reynolds's *Discourse VII* (1776). Reynolds maintains that the productions of the artistic imagination remain qualitatively the same across the aesthetic board. Consequently, this similarity creates a unanimity of affections within the public sphere:

---

[12] Leo Damrosch, *Fictions of Reality in the Age of Hume and Johnson* (Madison: University of Wisconsin Press, 1989) 23.

[13] Samuel Johnson, *Idler* no. 51, in *The Yale Edition of the Complete Works of Samuel Johnson*, vol. 2, ed. Jean H. Hagstrum and James Gray, (New Haven: Yale University Press, 1978) 160.

[14] Samuel Johnson, *Rambler* no. 60, in *The Yale Edition of the Complete Works of Samuel Johnson*, vol. 3, ed. Jean H. Hagstrum and James Gray (New Haven: Yale University Press, 1978) 320.

[15] Ibid., 320.

The internal fabrick of our minds, as well as the external form of our bodies, being nearly uniform; it seems then to follow of course, that as the imagination is incapable of producing any thing originally of itself, and can only vary and combine those ideas with which it is furnished by means of the senses, there will be necessarily an agreement in the imaginations as in the senses of men. There being this agreement, it follows, that in all cases, in our lightest amusements, as well as in our most serious actions and engagements of life, we must regulate our affections of every kind by that of others. The well-disciplined mind acknowledges this authority, and submits its own opinion to the public voice.[16]

Affections, in other words, must be regulated by and conform to the authoritative opinion of public discourse. Prescribing uniformity and homogeneity, eighteenth-century experience is laid upon a Procrustean bed. Patricia Spacks significantly notes that many characters in novels of the period are fundamentally static, "absolutely fixed" in their identity.[17] The Tom Jones on page one is the same Tom Jones on page 762. Clearly, then, the idealization of a mythic uniform experience within the public sphere served to standardize particular, individual types of experience that usually vary from person to person. Adam Potkay affirms that the "eighteenth-century man of letters generalized his experience into a rule: all seek the particular pleasure of social love and approval, and all do so within the broader pursuit of happiness."[18]

The myth of uniform experience thus acts as the unifying principle within the public sphere, creating the semblance of homogeneity within the reality of heterogeneity. Bonamy Dobree, for instance, identifies a "general process," completed in the 1730s, which witnessed the "convergence from above and below of distinct reading classes, which came together to form one large homogenous group."[19] Appropriating a metaphor crafted by the French *philosophes*, Peter Gay identifies the Enlightenment as a "philosophic family," with "common loyalties and a common world view."[20] The metaphor also appears in A. R. Humphreys's assessment of the eighteenth

---

[16] Joshua Reynolds, *Discourses* (New York: E.P. Dutton & Company, 1906) 1217.

[17] Patricia Spacks, *Imagining a Self: Autobiography and the Self in Eighteen-Century England* (Cambridge: Harvard University Press, 1976) 8.

[18] Adam Potkay, *The Passion for Happiness: Samuel Johnson and David Hume* (Ithaca: Cornell University Press, 2000) 64.

[19] Bonamy Dobree, *English Literature in the Early Eighteenth Century* (Oxford: Oxford University Press, 1959) 4.

[20] Peter Gay, *The Enlightenment: An Interpretation* (New York: Knopf, 1966) 6.

century. In the Augustan world, "Perpetually one seems to be part of a large but very real family. London provided an audience coherent enough to give writers an understood body of communal experience, expressed in the sharing of scandal, gossip, and allusion in a freely-comprehending way.... [O]ne feels the social world of literate London bound together in a close linkage of experience."[21]

Entrance into this family (or community) necessitates that the private emerge from the enclosed spaces of idiosyncratic, inner experience in order to participate in that "close linkage of experience" forged in the public sphere. In *Spectator* no. 10 (1711), in fact, Joseph Addison proclaims, "I shall be ambitious to have it said of me, that I have brought Philosophy out of closets and libraries, schools and colleges, to dwell in clubs and Assemblies, at tea tables, and in coffee houses."[22] In *Tatler* no. 1 (1704), Joseph Steele illustrates the preeminence of public discourse: he assigns various conversations to various public locations in London. "All accounts of gallantry, pleasure, and entertainment," Steele declares, will be discussed at White's Chocolate House; poetry will be analyzed at Will's Coffee House; the Graecian will be the site for inquiries into learning; foreign and domestic news will be the subject at the St. James Coffee House; any other subject, Steele concludes, will be entertained "at my own apartment."[23] The expanding public sphere even encompasses novelistic discourse. In *Tom Jones* (1749), Fielding analogizes his narrative to a conversation he might conduct with his readers, "fellow-travellers in a stage coach, who have passed several days in the company of each other...."[24]

### b. The Role of Puritanism in the Formation of Public Discourse

The experiential homogeneity assumed in public discourse has as its animus a concomitant distaste for the local and private. Issues of warrant hinge on the question of public acceptability: does any given argument uphold the criterion of uniform experience, which forces private judgments to shed the idiosyncrasies of personal difference, so out of place on the universal stage of the Enlightenment? The distrust of the local and private finds a historical source in an event of the late seventeenth century that helps shape the distinguishing features of public discourse. This event is the

---

[21] A. R. Humphreys, *The Augustan World* (New York: Harper & Row, 1963) 44.
[22] Joseph Addison, *The Spectator* (London: J. M. Dent & Sons, 1950) 32.
[23] Joseph Steele, *The Tatler* (New York: Clarendon, 1977) 296.
[24] Henry Fielding, *Tom Jones* (Oxford: Oxford University Press, 1991) 808.

Puritan-led revolt in England, eventuating in the failed political experiment known as the Interregnum (1649–1660), during which time England had no monarch and the parliamentarians or, to use their Puritan-inflected moniker, the Roundheads, ruled the country.

With the chaotic, destructive rise and fall of the Puritan-led Interregnum indelibly ingrained in their collective minds, Augustans developed a contempt for all things Puritan. The foremost object of contempt was Puritan enthusiasm, the private and passionate convictions which Puritans claimed to have received from the Holy Spirit. To counter these supposed supernatural, idiosyncratic, private deliverances, Augustans privileged the faculties maintained to be more uniform, more publicly acceptable. As George Sherburn points out, "The spectrum of religious opinion would range from this belief in a universal, uniform perception of truth through the light of reason to a belief in private revelations of an inner light, which was purely individual."[25] And as Sherburn later explains, British Anglicans and Catholics united in their protest against this inner light as it appeared in sects with Puritan leanings: "Strong in their concept of the light of reason, which the orthodox insisted was uniform and universal, both Protestants and Catholics were bitterly scornful of the inner or private light so valued by the Quakers and by some other sects—and called by their enemies "enthusiasm."[26] In the preface to the *Religio Laici*, Dryden labels the Puritan "Fanaticks" as "Enemies," because "they have assum'd what amounts to an Infallibility, in the private Spirit: and have detorted those Texts of Scripture, which are not necessary to Salvation, to the damnable uses of Sedition, disturbance and destruction of the Civil Government."[27] Consistent with his Latitudinarianism, which upholds external, demonstrable works of faith rather than the internal, private movements of faith, Henry Fielding robustly registers his disapproval of enthusiasm. In *Joseph Andrews* (1742), Parson Adams is initially drawn by George Whitefield's sermons. However, "when [Whitefield] began to call Nonsense and Enthusiasm to his Aid, and to set up the detestable Doctrine of Faith against Works, I was [Whitefield's] friend no longer...."[28] In *Tom Jones*,

---

[25] George Sherburn, "The Restoration and Eighteenth Century," in *A Literary History of England*, ed. Albert C. Baugh (New York: Appleton-Century Crofts, 1948) 705.

[26] Ibid., 705.

[27] John Dryden, "Religio Laici," in *Eighteenth-Century English Literature*, ed. Geoffrey Tillotson, et al. (New York: Harcourt Brace Jovanovich, 1969) 153.

[28] Henry Fielding, *Joseph Andrews* (Oxford: Oxford University Press, 1991) 72.

Whitefield's sister-in-law is also initially intrigued by Methodism; but her interest is short-lived:

> ...for she freely confesses that her brother's documents made at first some impression upon her, and that she had put herself to the expense of a long hood in order to attend the extraordinary emotions of the spirit; but having found, during an experiment of three weeks, no emotions, she says, worth a farthing, she very wisely laid by her hood, and abandoned the sect.[29]

Indeed, Fielding's repulsion to enthusiasm partially explains his scathing reaction to Samuel Richardson's *Pamela* (1740–1741), a novel that preserves the integrity of a young maid's private, inner experience as a faithful transcription of truth. The narrative ideology of *Pamela* suggests a sympathy for enthusiasm; it is this narrative ideology, among other things, that Fielding attacks. The reaction against enthusiasm was so charged that, in Smollett's *Humphrey Clinker*, Matthew Bramble refuses to answer to his own first name because it is associated with Puritanism.[30]

The hostile, often visceral reaction to Puritan enthusiasm spills over into eighteenth-century experience as a whole, thereby creating a suspicion of private emotion in general. Out of place on the universal stage of the Enlightenment, such emotion is deemed disruptive. In Alexander Pope's *The Rape of the Lock* (1714), for example, the Cave of Spleen represents the region farthest from the universal stage, farthest from reason and rationality. It is a region where imagination and emotion unite to create a bizarre, surreal, topsy-turvy world—a world that threatens the orderly world of public acceptability:

> A constant Vapour o'er the Palace flies;
> Strange Phantoms rising as the Mists arise;
> Dreadful, as Hermit's Dreams in haunted Shades,
> Or bright as Visions of expiring Maids.
> Now glaring Fiends, and Snakes on rolling Spires,
> Pale Spectres, gaping Tombs, and Purple Fires:
> Now Lakes of liquid Gold. Elysian Scenes,

---

[29] Fielding, *Tom Jones*, 373–74.

[30] Tobias Smollett, *The Expedition of Humphrey Clinker* (Oxford: Oxford University Press, 1984) 191.

And Crystal Domes, and Angels in Machines.[31]

And in his lectures, Hugh Blair (1718–1800) warns of the ode as a poetic genre, a genre which permits the poet to indulge in his emotional extravagance and unrestrained flights of passion and imagination. Such a poet, Blair explains, "is out of sight in a moment. He gets up in the clouds; becomes so abrupt in his transitions; so eccentric and irregular in his notions, and of course so obscure, that we essay in vain to follow him, or to partake in his raptures."[32] The eccentricities and irregularities of such a poet diverge from the collective sensibilities of an era committed to public discourse and uniform experience.

### c. Illustrating the Foundations of the Public Sphere: The Theme of Sympathy

The standardizing influence of public discourse universalizes a popular eighteenth-century emotion: sympathy and its inevitable appearance in the sympathetic or sentimental scene. The universalizing tendency evident in the sympathy motif illustrates the conventions of the burgeoning public sphere.

Formulated and shaped by public discourse, sympathy achieves the sort of uniformity that we would expect. The fact alone that sympathy is thematized in the sentimental scene makes this point; to become a conventional rhetorical or narrative device, sympathy must obviously possess standard features that are readily identifiable by the reader. We might note a few of these standard features. For one, the sentimental scene involves witnessing the suffering of a virtuous person, which, in turn, stimulates similar feelings in the beholder. The beholder thus vicariously experiences the sufferings of the sufferer. The experience is intensely emotional, whereby the beholder is typically "cut to the heart" or, if the beholder is a female, "faints away." The entire spectacle is thus labeled an "affecting scene." Also, the sufferer and beholder engage in non-verbal communication, arriving at a profound understanding of each other through a languishing glance or a wilting gesture. The scene is then typically pronounced to be ineffable.

---

[31] Alexander Pope, "The Rape of the Lock," *in Eighteenth-Century English Literature,* ed. Geoffrey Tillotson et al. (New York: Harcourt Brace Jovanovich, 1969) 4:39–46.

[32] Hugh Blair, *Lectures of Rhetoric and Belles Lettres* (Carbondale: Southern Illinois University Press, 1965) 356.

Adam Smith codified many of the conventional attributes of sympathy. In the opening sections of *The Theory of Moral Sentiments* (1759), he underscores the vicarious emotive power of suffering—the ease with which it is transmitted from sufferer to beholder, producing an encompassing and penetrating sense of sympathy:

> Tho our brother is upon the rack, as long as we ourselves are at our ease, our senses will never carry us beyond our own person, and it is by the imagination only that we can form any conception of what are his sensations.... By the imagination we place ourselves in the situation, we conceive ourselves enduring all the same torments, we enter as it were into his body, and become in some measure the same person with him, and thence form some idea of his sensations, and even feel something, which, tho weaker in degree, is not altogether unlike them.[33]

It is also important to notice how this whole process necessitates the exposure of the private, the relocation of the personal into the public. Private emotion is brought onto the Enlightenment stage, where it is assessed according to the guidelines of public discourse and approved if it conforms to the general consensus. The public, in other words, places itself in the place of an individual and asks, "Does this emotion that we vicariously experience agree with our own understanding of emotional experiences?" As Smith claims, "To approve or disapprove of the opinions of others is acknowledged to mean no more than to observe their agreement or disagreement with our own."[34] Privately experienced and privately held emotions and opinions are removed from their particular contexts and evaluated within the context of the public sphere.

### d. The Public Sphere: Conclusions

The public sphere created the conventions to which the public intellectual of the twentieth century adhered. No doubt this claim sounds tenuous considering the fact that a public intellectual like C. S. Lewis was separated by some two hundred years from the rise of the public sphere. But one must never underestimate the weighty influence of the Enlightenment and its discursive manifestations. After all, it was not until the late twentieth century that the fundamental procedural mechanisms of the Enlightenment were significantly called into question with the advent of postmodernism.

---

[33] Adam Smith, *The Theory of Moral Sentiments* (Amherst NY: Prometheus Books, 2000) 9.
[34] Ibid., 17.

As we have seen, the threat of heterogeneity within the public sphere necessitates presumptions of uniform experience that serve to unite disparate groups; the myth of homogeneity subsumes the reality of heterogeneity. This myth, in turn, exerts a gate-keeping influence on the public sphere, requiring all entrants to shed the particularities deemed threatening to public discourse. The transformation of the private individual into public individual thus yields a persona: an idealized, de-contextualized figure, an embodiment of uniform experience. Michael Warner writes,

> As the subjects of publicity—its hearers, speakers, viewers, and doers—we have a different relation to ourselves, a different affect, from that which we have in other contexts. No matter what particularities of culture, race, and gender, or class we bring to bear on public discourse, the moment of apprehending something as public is one in which we imagine, if imperfectly, indifference to those particularities, to ourselves. We adopt the attitude to the public subject, marking to ourselves its nonidentity with ourselves. There are any number of ways to describe this moment of public subjectivity: as a universalizing transcendence, as ideological repression, as utopian wish, as schizocapitalist vertigo, or simply as a routine difference of register.[35]

What Warner refers to as a "moment of subjectivity" I refer to throughout this book as de-conversion: a pose, assumed in the public sphere, of analytical neutrality, of a denuded self participating in "ideological repression" and a "utopian wish." It is also my contention that Lewis played this role with virtuosity, as will be described in the next chapter.

The presumption of homogeneity and uniform experience also champions the role of reason. Unlike imagination, which privileges originality and individual creativity, and unlike faith, which allows for the private deliverances of the Holy Spirit (vis-à-vis Puritan enthusiasm), reason positions itself as the universalizing faculty, heeding laws of logic that transcend the particular and local. Commenting on Habermas's theory of communicative action, Christian Delacampagne explains, "Participants in any discussion must jointly agree upon certain logical norms if the course of the argument is to lead to conclusions that they can all accept. Thus reason can be unambiguously defined as that set of norms guaranteeing the democratic and rigorous character of all debate."[36] Here too, Lewis, as public

---

[35] Michael Warner, "The Mass Public and the Mass Subject," in *Habermas and the Public Sphere*, ed. Craig Calhoun (Cambridge: MIT Press, 1992) 376.

[36] Christian Delacampagne, *A History of Philosophy in the Twentieth Century*, trans. M. B. DeBevoise (Baltimore: Johns Hopkins University Press, 1999) 271.

intellectual, proves himself beholden to the conventions of the public sphere. Lewis not only wields reason like a sword, but he also repeatedly reveals his reliance upon it as well as his confidence that it will lead his readers into accepting the claims of Christianity. In *Mere Christianity*, for instance, Lewis insists that his readers should not accept the case for faith if their reason leads them in another direction. In *The Screwtape Letters*, Screwtape warns Wormwood about appealing to his "patient's" reason; doing so too easily leads the patient to God.

Enlightenment reason thus serves as a fundamental source of authority in the public sphere. As was alluded in the previous chapter and will be fleshed out in the next, Lewis also employs rhetorical devices that further summon the authority to marshal his arguments with cogency (in nonfiction) and to thematize Christian principles with compelling representations (in fiction). These rhetorical devices are consonant with the conventions of the public sphere. By invoking high tradition, Lewis not only grounds his claims in the collective wisdom of Western civilization; he also divests his perspective of subjectivism. High tradition, in fact, becomes synonymous with uniform experience and universal truth, thus suitable for presentation in the public sphere. Lewis's transcendent characters in fiction perform the same function: rising above the particularities of time and place, transcendent characters offer an Olympian point of reference anchored in the absolute. This preference for the absolute in contradistinction to the particular stems from what Lewis writes in a 1940 letter as his "partly pathological hostility to what is fashionable...."[37]

While Lewis upholds most of the conventions of the public sphere, he nevertheless finds himself in obvious opposition to one of its fundamental assumptions: the irrationality of revealed religion. Although the claims of Christianity may have been tolerated during the early phase of the public sphere—thanks to James Boswell, Samuel Johnson gave Christianity strong footing in the public arena—with the passage of time the public sphere repeatedly pushes religion into the private realm. Birgit Meyer and Annelies Moors show that the marginalization of religion is central to Habermas's analysis of the public sphere: "Habermas saw the emergence of the public sphere and the public decline of religion as dependent on each other. He regarded religion as privatized, stating that religious convictions emerge in public debate only as opinions and thus have to engage with other (non-

---

[37] C. S. Lewis to to Mary Neylan, 26 March 1940, in *The Collected Letters of C. S. Lewis*, vol. 2, *Books, Broadcasts, and the War, 1931–1949*, ed. Walter Hooper (San Francisco: HarperSanFrancisco, 2007) 372.

religiously informed) opinions in line with agreed-upon, rational discursive rules."[38] Lewis thus finds himself in the same position as many Christian thinkers after the Enlightenment: defending the faith using a procedural framework that assumes the irrelevance, at best, and irrationality, at worst, of Christianity.

## II. The Challenge of Atheism and the Transformation of Christian Apologetics

Increasingly embattled during the Enlightenment, Christianity drew defenders to its side. The strategy of many of these defenders was often reactionary, developing arguments in response to the mounting attacks on revealed religion. Consequently, defenders of the faith often adopted the very interpretive framework and assumptions of the other side.

For instance, Stanley Hauerwas contends that the philosophical problem of evil (which asks, "Why does God allow bad things to happen?") is a development of the seventeenth century. The rising interest during the eighteenth century in the problem of evil, in turn, generates a discourse known as the "theodicy," a word coined by Gottfried Wilhelm Leibniz in 1710, which denotes an attempt to defend God's existence and nature in the face of suffering. Thus, the rise of atheism issued a specific challenge to the faith in the form of the problem of evil, which subsequently generated the Christian, reactionary discourse known as the theodicy. Hauerwas notes that "the assumptions that there is something called the problem of evil which creates a discourse called 'theodicy' occurred at the same time that modern atheism came into being."[39] According to Hauerwas's account, evil counts as a strike against God's existence only when evil is viewed through an interpretive lens that holds God's existence in skeptical abeyance to begin with. Enlightenment thought—with its posture of tradition-free, autonomous inquiry—creates this conceptual scheme which in turn transforms evil into a problem that undermines God's supposed existence or nature.

Claims about God and evil are thus wrenched from the interpretive community (the community of faith) which had traditionally framed those claims, supplying them with contextual meaning. Alasdair MacIntyre likewise points out that only after the seventeenth century did the existence

---

[38] Birgit Meyer and Annelies Moors, introduction to *Religion, Media, and the Public Sphere*, ed. Birgit Meyer and Annelies Moors (Bloomington: Indiana University Press) 4.

[39] Stanley Hauerwas, *Naming the Silences* (Grand Rapids: Eerdmans, 1990) 41.

of evil become a problem that challenged the "coherence and intelligibility of Christian belief per se."[40] Prior to this time, truth claims about God and evil achieved coherence within a narrative that held certain presuppositions about those very truth claims. According to an Enlightenment model, on the other hand, as Hauerwas contends, the assumption is that "we are most fully ourselves when we are free of all traditions and communities other than those we have chosen from the position of complete autonomy." "In such a context," Hauerwas concludes, "suffering cannot help but appear absurd, since it always stands as a threat to that autonomy."[41]

In this way, the challenge of atheism during the Enlightenment transformed Christian apologetics. Prior to the eighteenth century, defenses of Christian truth claims often operated at the service of much larger theological projects. For instance, while Thomas Aquinas offered arguments for God's existence in *Summa Contra Gentiles*, the text's primary purpose was to offer what Kenneth Boa and Robert Bowman call a "sweeping, comprehensive Christian philosophy in Aristotelian terms."[42] Likewise, while the *Summa Theologiciae* contains apologetic dimensions, its main function was to provide a systematic theology. Arguments for God's existence thus addressed the whole person, mind and soul. Boa and Bowman also note that, while a few passages in Scripture emphasize the importance of defending the faith, "no science or formal academic discipline of apologetics is contemplated."[43]

Beginning in the eighteenth century, all of this changes. Apologetics becomes its own field within theology in direct response to increasingly unabashed challenges to the faith. As Boa and Bowman affirm, "Until the post-Reformation period most Europeans took Christianity for granted, and the major religious debates were primarily intra-Christian disputes about the *meaning* of specific key doctrines of the faith. But the seventeenth century saw the rise of religious skepticism that challenged the very *truth* of the Christian faith. This skepticism led to new developments in apologetics."[44] Among these developments is the apologists' willingness to confront the new challenges on the opponents' own ground: to "accept the rationalistic

---

[40] Alasdair MacIntyre, quoted in Kenneth Surin, *Theology and the Problem of Evil* (Oxford: Basil Blackwell, 1986) 97.

[41] Hauerwas, *Naming the Silences*, 53–54.

[42] Kenneth D. Boa and Robert M. Bowman, *Faith Has Its Reasons: Integrative Approaches to Defending the Christian Faith*, 2nd ed. (Waynesboro GA: Paternoster, 2005) 20.

[43] Ibid., 3.

[44] Ibid., 21.

challenge and [seek] to answer it by proving that Christianity was just as rational as the conclusions of modern science."[45] Avery Dulles also points to the reactionary nature of apologetics beginning in the sixteenth century and culminating in the Enlightenment: The "initiative," he writes, "in this period no longer lies with the protagonists of the cause but rather with the adversaries. The apologists, rushing to answer one objection after another, are vexed and harassed, anxious and defensive."[46]

The challenge of atheism and the transformation of Christian apologetics are significant to this study for two reasons. First, they solidify Lewis's standing as a public intellectual. As chapter 1 showed, the public intellectual by nature adopts a reactionary stance; he or she is a counterpuncher—confronting and opposing the spirit of the times. To emphasize the contentious intellectual milieu at Oxford during Lewis's career—a milieu that demands the counterpunching skills of a Christian public intellectual like Lewis—one might appeal to James Patrick's characterization of Oxford: "...the university was more and more an intellectual battlefield—lively, fragmented, dangerous to careers."[47] A public intellectual thrives in such an environment.

Second, the transformation of Christian apologetics into a specialized discipline creates a bifurcated approach to faith. As previously explained, early Christian philosophers and theologians incorporated apologetics into a much larger project, one that engaged the mind and the soul in a holistic approach to faith. The evolution of apologetics in the seventeenth and eighteenth centuries transforms the discipline into a purely rational or empirical discourse, a discourse restricted to propositional claims that must meet rational standards of justification. The narrowing of apologetic discourse is encouraged by the prominence of reason and what I have called de-conversion, both of which originate from the rise of the public sphere.

In his essay "Is Theism Important?" Lewis evidences the bifurcated approach to faith occasioned by the specialized discipline of Christian apologetics. Lewis makes a distinction between two species of faith—one he calls "Faith-A" and another he calls "Faith-B." He defines Faith-A as "a settled intellectual assent" and Faith-B as "a trust, or confidence, in the God

---

[45] Ibid., 22.

[46] Avery Dulles, *A History of Apologetics* (London: Hutchinson, 1971) 156.

[47] James Patrick, *The Magdalen Metaphysicals: Idealism and Orthodoxy at Oxford, 1901–1945* (Macon GA: Mercer University Press, 1985) 135.

whose existence is thus assented to."[48] His point is that Christian apologetics can produce Faith-A but not Faith-B. As "a settled intellectual assent," Faith-A operates primarily on rational and empirical grounds; it is a propositionally construed faith that engages the mind alone. As "a trust, or confidence, in the God whose existence is thus assented to," Faith-B is holistic and existential, summoning the faculties of the mind, soul, and heart. I suggest that the transformation of Christian apologetics during the Enlightenment constitutes the subtext of Lewis's distinction and subsequent argument. Lewis thus appropriates a tradition of modern apologetic discourse that implicitly partitions human faculties, marks out the intellect as its battleground, and employs the conventions of the public sphere as the weapons most suitable for the field of engagement. Equally importantly, this process occurs to the neglect of the human faculties that cultivate trust and confidence.

## III. Conclusion

The rise of the public sphere, the challenge of atheism, and the subsequent transformation of Christian apologetics create a discourse unique to modernity. This chapter has shown how this discourse involves intricately linked assumptions: assumptions about rhetorical efficacy (the primacy of pragmatic reason and de-conversion), audience (uniformity of experience), and attitudes toward religion (the presumption of atheism or, at the least, antagonism toward theism). As a public intellectual, Lewis necessarily adopts all three assumptions. His appropriation of the first two assumptions will be discussed in the next chapter. For now, I want to linger on Lewis's adoption of the last assumption.

As explained above, Christian apologists after the Enlightenment and the rise of the public sphere confront the challenges of unbelief on their adversary's own turf. As a public intellectual, Lewis is no exception. To combat the atheist challenge, Lewis presupposes the polemical perspective from which that very challenge emerges, namely because the perspective and the challenge developed in an almost symbiotic relationship during the advent of the Enlightenment and the rise of the public sphere. Once again, the public sphere creates both the space for discourse as well as the conventions that determine the rules of that very discourse. Lewis himself recognizes the unique character of the debate involving religious claims in

---

[48] C. S. Lewis, "Is Theism Important?" in *God in the Dock: Essays on Theology and Ethics*, ed. Walter Hooper (Grand Rapids: Eerdmans, 1970) 172–73.

his essay "God in the Dock": "The ancient man approached God (or even the gods) as the accused person approaches his judge. For the modern man the roles are reversed. He is the judge: God is in the dock. He is quite a kindly judge: if God should have a reasonable defence for being the god who permits war, poverty and disease, he is ready to listen to it. The trial may even end in God's acquittal. But the important thing is that Man is on the Bench and God in the Dock."[49]

More than simply acknowledging the unique and modern character of this debate, Lewis participates in the very phenomenon that he observes. That is, it is clear that nearly all of Lewis's post-conversion works themselves place God in the dock. The starting point of inquiry presupposes the non-existence of God, implicitly recognizing the legitimacy of the atheist challenge. Thus in *Mere Christianity*, Lewis's incremental argument proceeds from the initial assumption that God does not exist—the assumption of the public sphere. As the argument builds momentum, Lewis departs from that assumption with qualifications and polemical delicacy. At the conclusion of chapter 4 of Book 1, for instance, he assures his readers that he has not yet parted complete company with the skeptical starting point: "Do not think I am going faster than I really am. I am not yet within a hundred miles of the God of Christian theology." In the next chapter, he repeats that assurance: "Then, secondly, this has not yet turned exactly into a 'religious jaw'. We have not yet got as far as the God of any actual religion, still less the God of that particular religion called Christianity."[50] In *The Problem of Pain*, Lewis begins his introductory chapter by momentarily re-adopting his pre-Christian perspective as an atheist: "Not many years ago when I was an atheist, if anyone had asked me, 'Why do you not believe in God?' my reply would have run something like this...."[51] Lewis thus adopts once again the assumptions of the public sphere. In fact, before Lewis even addresses the problem of evil, he first must establish that God exists, a proof he endeavors in the introductory chapter.

The situation in Lewis's fiction is more complex. Lewis's fictional works do not project worlds that assume the legitimacy of atheism; because of their supernatural subjects, texts like *The Screwtape Letters*, *The Great Divorce*, and the space trilogy cannot make that assumption. Nevertheless, much of Lewis's fiction is quick to argue, to debate, to withdraw from the artistry of narrative and follow dialectic excursions. Lewis admits as much in a 1955

---

[49] C. S. Lewis, "God in the Dock," in *God in the Dock*, 244.

[50] C. S. Lewis, *Mere Christianity* (San Francisco: HarperSanFrancisco, 2001) 25, 29.

[51] C. S. Lewis, *The Problem of Pain* (San Francisco: HarperSanFrancisco, 2001) 1.

letter to Katharine Farrer in which he explains what he tried to avoid in writing *Till We Have Faces*: "…what Owen Barfield calls 'the expository demon', my native tendency to be too argumentative and make people talk like a Platonic dialogue."[52] Lewis strikes a similar chord when he describes his attraction to the form of the fairy story: "…its brevity, its severe restraints on description, its flexible traditionalism, its inflexible hostility to all analysis, digression, reflections and 'gas'."[53] Lewis was drawn to the fairy story because the genre preempted his natural proclivity for argument. As John Wain states,

> Lewis's father was a lawyer, and the first thing that strikes one on opening any of his books is that he is always persuading, always arguing a case…. To him, every important issue lay in the domain of public debate. Whether it was the choice of a book to read or the choice of a God to believe in, Lewis argued the matter like a counsel. His personal motives were kept well back from the reach of curious eyes. All was forensic; the jury were to be won over and that was all.[54]

Dorothy Sayers describes Lewis thusly in a 1947 letter to George Every:

> One trouble about C. S. Lewis, I think, is his fervent missionary zeal. I welcome his able dialectic, and he is a tremendous hammer for heretics. But he is apt to think that one should rush into every fray and strike a blow for Christendom, whether or not one is equipped by training and temperament for that particular conflict. If one objects that God has put nothing into one's mind on the subject, he darkly hints that one has probably mistaken one's own artistic preferences for the voice of the Holy Ghost. I am not strong on pneumatology, but I know when I am merely talking hot air without conviction, and I refuse to believe that that is the operation of the Holy Ghost. But Lewis seems to feel it wrong to refuse any challenge: if the Bishop of Bootle says that the Christian doctrine of

---

[52] C. S. Lewis to Katharine Farrer, 7 September 1955, in *The Collected Letters of C. S. Lewis*, vol. 3, *Narnia, Cambridge, and Joy, 1950–1963*, ed. Walter Hooper (San Francisco: HarperSanFrancisco, 2007).

[53] C. S. Lewis, "Sometimes Fairy Stories May Say Best What's to Be Said," in *On Stories and Other Essays on Literature*, ed. Walter Hooper (San Diego: Harcourt Brace & Company, 1982) 47.

[54] John Wain, "C. S. Lewis," in *Critical Thought Series: C. S. Lewis*, ed. George Watson (Cambridge: Cambridge UP, 1992) 26.

marriage must be upheld, Lewis makes haste to uphold it, although, very obviously, he has no practical experience in the matter.[55]

The polemical thrust in most of Lewis's works of fiction further enacts what was referred to in the last chapter as name-branding: the ready association between Lewis and his vigorously defended Christian message. Inexhaustibly argumentative, Lewis effectively confronts the challenge of atheism employing a Christian discourse that has appropriated the transformation of apologetics. While doing so, he generates the controversy that ensures his place in the public sphere.

The context into which I have placed Lewis—the rise of the public sphere, the challenge of atheism, and the transformation of apologetics—also provides the lens to view tensions in Lewis's project as a Christian writer. As explained in the previous chapter, the public intellectual plays a role, engages in a performance. Adopting such a role widens the gulf between the public self and the private self, between writerly voice and personal voice, between the expositor of ideas and the real human being behind the exposition.

Lewis occasionally speaks of this tension in ways that suggest his identity as public intellectual. In "Sometimes Fairy Stories May Say Best What's to Be Said," for instance, Lewis affirms that engaging in imaginative writing creates a split persona: the "Author" versus the "Man." The Author is the persona under the throes of inspiration seeking to embody his imaginative ideas into narrative form. The Man, on the other hand, has more practical concerns: "He will ask how the gratification of this [imaginative] impulse will fit in with all the other things he wants, and ought to do or be. Perhaps the whole thing is too frivolous and trivial (from the Man's point of view, not the Author's) to justify the time and pains it would involve."[56] While all writers may experience this two-voiced inner-dialogue, Lewis's version of this internal negotiation suggests the pressing influence of his time and place as public intellectual, for the "other things he wants, and ought to do," the demands placed upon him as Man, not Author, are the personal convictions that compel him to defend his faith. Lewis writes,

> Then of course the man in me began to have his turn. I thought I saw how stories of this kind could steal past a certain inhibition which had paralysed much of my own religion in childhood. Why did one find it so

---

[55] Dorothy L. Sayers to George Every, 10 July 1947, in *The Letters of Dorothy L. Sayers*, vol. 3, ed. Barbara Reynolds (Cambridge: The Dorothy L. Sayers Society, 1998) 314.

[56] Ibid., 46.

hard to feel as one was told one ought to feel about God or about he sufferings of Christ? I thought the chief reason was that one was told one ought to. An obligation to feel can freeze feelings. And reverence itself did harm. The whole subject was associated with lowered voices; almost as if it were something medical. But supposing that by casting all these things into an imaginary world, stripping them of their stained-glass and Sunday school association, one could make them for the first time appear in their real potency? Could one not thus steal past those watchful dragons? I thought one could. That was the Man's motive.[57]

The Man, set in an intellectual and cultural milieu hostile to Christianity, demands that the Author direct the imagination toward an exposition and defense of Christianity.

Lewis likewise alludes to this split persona in an essay titled "The Language of Religion." He explains that "Poetic language" cannot communicate with scientific precision:

I think Poetic language does convey information, but it suffers from two disabilities in comparison with Scientific. (1) It is verifiable or falsifiable only to a limited degree and with a certain fringe of vagueness. Not all men, only men of some discrimination, would agree, on seeing Burn's mistress that the image of "a red, red rose" was good, or (as might be) bad. In that sense, Scientific statements are, as people say now, far more easily "cashed".... Such information as Poetic language has to give can be received only if you are ready to meet it half-way. It is no good holding a dialectical pistol to the poet's head and demanding how the deuce a river could have hair, or thought be green, or a woman a rose. You may win, in the sense of putting him to a *non-plus*. But if he had anything to tell you, you will never get it by behaving in that way. You must begin by trusting him.[58]

Poetic language thus has a unique relationship to its reader: it demands that the reader adhere to the presuppositions implicit in its images, conceits, and themes. The reader must momentarily assume the particularities of the poetic persona. Poetic language, as Lewis defines it here, is thus at odds with the conventions of the public sphere, which insists upon what I have called de-conversion, the posture of impartiality and neutrality. Within the public sphere, no textual representation can be afforded trust until it proves its merit by adhering to the public sphere's conventions; on the other hand, the

---

[57] Ibid., 47.

[58] C. S. Lewis, "The Language of Religion," in *Christian Reflections*, ed. Walter Hooper (Grand Rapids: Eerdmans, 1967) 135.

poetic text, as Lewis states, begins with trust, assuming what cannot be assumed in the public sphere.

Poetic language places readers into an elaborate context—created, again, by its images, conceits, and themes—that makes that very language meaningful. Thus, while poetic language begins with a rich context, locutions within the public sphere begin from a de-contextualized starting point.

The difficulty for a writer like Lewis is occasioned by the nature of apologetics. Unlike poetical language, apologetics must employ "terms as definable and univocal as possible," terms that are "always abstract."[59] While apologetics communicate in abstract language, poetic language is preeminently concrete. Thus, when Lewis melds the poetic and the apologetic (which many of his works of fiction attempt to do) the result is a tension manifested in alternating and contrasting modes of discourse. The second book in Lewis's space trilogy, *Perelandra*, illustrates these contrasting modes of discourse. The narrator's depiction of Venus and its geographical features is rich in poetic imagery: the golden sky, the flora and fauna of the floating islands, and the lofty heights of the Fixed Land. However, the lengthy conversations between Ransom, Weston, and Tinidril interrupt the poetic language, replacing it with a philosophical/theological/apologetic discourse. In short, Lewis's fiction almost always gravitates toward the expository mode, eager to flesh out arguments and defend claims that lead readers to what is of paramount concern to Lewis: the truth of Christianity.

This gravitation toward the expository mode proceeds from the fundamental impulse of a public intellectual: to fight for a belief in an arena of intense contestation. This is thus one of many ways in which Lewis is a product of his time: To put it more strongly, this is one of many ways in which Lewis's historical/intellectual context *shapes* the form and purpose of his work. As a result of historical chance and personal talent, Lewis found himself in the public sphere, conventionalized with its own rules of engagement, where the one belief he held most dearly was embattled, and where he took up the fight on the enemy's own territory.

Without succumbing to melancholy reverie or quixotic re-creations of the past, and without downplaying Lewis's prodigious accomplishment, one can imagine how it might have been different. What if Lewis had been born in another era, an era that did not compel him to adhere to the conventions of the public sphere and adopt the persona of the public intellectual? The reincarnation of Lewis in a bygone epoch might be glimpsed in the

---

[59] Ibid., 136.

sixteenth-century poet Edmund Spenser. Both Lewis and Spenser possessed a mythopoeic imagination, and both used mythopoeic images to embody or convey religious beliefs and to transmit moral axioms; both, that is, wrote strongly didactic literature. In addition, both filtered their created myths through the collective wisdom of classical philosophers: Platonism operates in Lewis's books as strongly as Aristotelianism operates in Book II of *The Faerie Queene*. Spenser's influence on Lewis was significant; many of Lewis's works of fiction bear the fingerprints of *The Faerie Queene*.

Lewis, however, points to one way in which Spenser differs from moderns like himself:

> When a modern writer is didactic he endeavours, like Shaw or M. Sartre, to throw his own "ideas" into sharp relief, distinguishing them from the orthodoxy which he wants to attack. Spenser is not at all like that. Political circumstances lead him at times to stress his opposition to Roman Christianity; and if pressed, he would no doubt admit that where the pagan doctors differed from the Christian, the pagan doctors were wrong. But in general he is concerned with agreements, not differences. He is, like nearly all his contemporaries, a syncretist.[60]

Lewis too poses as a syncretist: he claims to avoid all attempts at originality, instead relaying what all Christians through the centuries held in common as true. The difference is that the ideas of Lewis, entering the public sphere after the challenge of atheism and the transformation of Christian apologetics, cannot avoid being placed into "sharp relief." Lewis enters the public sphere as a controversialist; his ideas are embattled at the outset. Moreover, the public sphere was designed to adjudicate between differences in a setting of contestation. As a result of entering the public sphere, Lewis could never become the Spenser of the twentieth century. While Spenser creates a world of pure mythopoeic imagination, Lewis's fiction evidences the tension described above, the forestalling of the mythopoeic for the sake of the argument—an argument Lewis felt had to be made in response to the aggressive hostility toward his Christian beliefs. The public intellectual is, by nature, reactionary.

---

[60] C. S. Lewis, *English Literature in the Sixteenth Century Excluding Drama* (Oxford: Clarendon Press, 1944) 386.

# 3

## The Basic Stance: The Vantage Point of the Outsider and Other Advantageous Perspectives

### I. Preliminary Considerations on Writerly Personas

All writing scenarios entail a space between the person wielding the pen and the persona that person assumes in print: To employ Lewis's own nomenclature, there exists an ontological gap between the "Man" and the "Author."[1] Poets of the Romantic period in England attempted to collapse that space, adopting personas of authenticity that minimized the visibility of self-conscious artistry by employing what Wordsworth called the "very language of men."[2] Modernist poets of the twentieth century, on the other hand, enlarged that space, creating texts with shifting voices and with networks of references, texts that thus scream, "I am artifice!"

As mentioned in chapter 1, the public intellectual is a persona, one made even more artificial by the fact that the very term "public intellectual" implies a divide between the public and private. The transformation of the private person into the public intellectual necessitates an argumentative, defensive stance that downplays doubt and rests upon certainty, a certainty that, in the public sphere, is easily read as rightness of position. Thus, of all species of writers, public intellectuals experience most acutely the cognitive dissonance and the schizophrenic sensations endemic to any writing scenario. Lewis speaks to this phenomenon when he confides to Dorothy Sayers in a 1946 letter, "A doctrine never seems dimmer to me than when I have just successfully defended it."[3] The fact that this confession occurs in a

---

[1] C. S. Lewis, "Sometimes Fairy Stories May Say Best What's to Be Said," in *On Stories and Other Essays on Literature*, ed. Walter Hooper (San Diego: Harcourt Brace & Company, 1982) 47.
[2] William Wordsworth, "Preface to Lyrical Ballads" (1800 edition), ed. R. L. Brett and A. R. Jones, 2nd ed. (London: Routledge, 1991) 250.
[3] C. S. Lewis to Dorothy Sayers, 2 August 1946, in *The Collected Letters of C. S. Lewis*, vol. 2, *Books, Broadcasts, and the War, 1931–1949*, ed. Walter Hooper (San Francisco: HarperSanFrancisco, 2004) 730.

private letter underscores the paradox of the public-intellectual persona: the public Lewis alleviates doubt while the private Lewis remains doubtful.[4]

The adoption of writerly personas in Lewis's case becomes more complex when one attends to some of his various biographical peculiarities. Owen Barfield, one of Lewis's closest lifelong friends, traces an abstruse change in Lewis's behavior to his Christian conversion (though Barfield places the date "from about 1935 onwards"). At that time, Barfield explains, "I had the impression of living with, not one, but two Lewises; and this was so as well when I was enjoying his company as when I was absent from him."[5] Barfield subsequently struggles to explain the precise nature of the doubled Lewis, ultimately availing himself of a few sentences from Robert Southey's *Life of Wesley*, an "acute analysis of John Wesley's mental temper," which, explains Barfield, "seems to me to have some bearing on Lewis's." Here is Southey's analysis:

> I am persuaded that Wesley never rose above the region of logic and strong volition. The moment an idea presents itself to him, his understanding intervenes to eclipse it, and he substitutes a conception by some process of deduction. Nothing is *immediate* to him. Nor could it be otherwise with a mind so ambitious, so constitutionally—if not a commanding—yet a *ruling* genius; i.e. no genius at all, but a height of talent with unusual strength and activity of individual will.[6]

Although difficult to interpret, Southey's analysis suggests that ideas never seemed to reach the heart, the core of Wesley's consciousness. Driven by intense theological commitments (the "region" of "strong volition" as well as the "strength and activity of individual will"), Wesley forges a mental buffer in the form of a conceptual framework that intercepts ideas before they penetrate too deeply, then processes them through that framework within "the region of logic." Nothing is cognitively immediate when the understanding intervenes to eclipse an idea.

One also clearly notices the use of spatial terms in Southey's analysis: "region of logic and strong volition"; the intervention of reason to eclipse an idea; "nothing is immediate to him." This language of spatiality hearkens back to Lewis's situation: the intervening space between the private self and the public intellectual. Both cases involve a disconnect: doubled selves that

---

[4] Of course, even private correspondence involves the creation of a persona—thus the fascinating complexity of personas within personas.

[5] Owen Barfield, introduction to *Light on C. S. Lewis*, ed. Jocelyn Gibb (New York: Harcourt Brace & World, 1965) xiv.

[6] Ibid., xvii, emphasis in original.

process and transmit ideas differently, an understanding that prevents an idea from becoming too immediate. Both cases also involve a cognitive dissonance: a divided self or divided psyche, each side of which operates on different impulses. Applied to Lewis specifically after his conversion (as Barfield has done), Southey's analysis of Wesley indicates that Lewis's newfound faith shaped the understanding whereby it intercepted ideas, holding them at a distance until they could be analyzed within a faith-informed framework, thereby readied for public argument.

Lewis occasionally acknowledges not only the constructedness of identity but also a hiddenness or privacy in his own identity that lends itself to shifting personas. In *Letters to Malcolm: Chiefly on Prayer*, for instance, he writes,

> For what I call "myself" (for all practical, everyday purposes) is also a dramatic construction; memories, glimpses in the shaving glass, and snatches of the very fallible activity called "introspection" are the principal ingredients. Normally I call this construction "me," and the stage set "the real world." Now the moment of prayer is for me—or involves for me as its condition—the awareness, the re-awakened awareness, that this "real world" and "real self" are very far from being rock-bottom realities.[7]

Lacking an ontological essence, identity is thus subject to fluctuations; all subjectivities are constructs, not to be mistaken for real selves.

In *The Four Loves*, Lewis states that some subjectivities should remain hidden; his explanation of *philia* discloses an impersonality that Lewis believes should obtain between friends:

> For of course we do not want to know our Friend's affairs at all. Friendship, unlike Eros, is uninquisitive. You become a man's Friend without knowing or caring whether he is married or single or how he earns his living. What have all these "unconcerning things, matters of fact" to do with the real question, *Do you see the same truth*? In a circle of true Friends each man is simply what he is: stands for nothing but himself. No one cares two-pence about anyone else's family, profession, class, income, race, or previous history.[8]

Certainly Lewis's description here is at least somewhat idiosyncratic. To claim that friends do not care in the least about each others' personal lives is

---

[7] C. S. Lewis, *Letters to Malcolm: Chiefly on Prayer* (San Diego: Harcourt Brace, 1964) 81.

[8] C. S. Lewis, *The Four Loves* (New York: Harcourt Brace & Company, 1988) 70.

indeed overstated; while the focus of friendship might be on perceiving and discussing the same truths—to use Lewis's image, standing side-by-side versus the face-to-face stance characteristic of *eros*—certainly such a focus does not imply that friends need remain so personally aloof.

Lewis's oddly conceived definition of friendship points to the hiddenness of his own identity, as confirmed by many of his friends. Robert Havard, Lewis's longtime friend and doctor, felt that Lewis's autobiography, *Surprised by Joy*, should be renamed "Suppressed by Jack" because it is so thin on self-disclosing autobiographical details.[9] Commenting on his review of *Surprised by Joy*, Malcolm Muggeridge strikes a similar chord: "I felt something inscrutable did not come out in the book. There is something strange in him that I don't fully understand. I mean, I feel in his life there is an element of mystery."[10] Leo Baker, a close friend during Lewis's early years at Oxford, asks, "Why was Lewis so remote from normal university life, so secretive, one who literally shied away from friendship?"[11] Echoing Barfield, John Wain proposes the existence of two Lewises: "Everyone knew Lewis was aware of this strange dichotomy. The outer self—brisk, challenging, argumentative, full of an overwhelming physical energy and confidence—covered an inner self as tender and as well-hidden as a crab's. One simply never got near him."[12] (Wain's formulation of the doubled Lewis re-invokes the dual nature of the public intellectual.) Wain also notes that "every [Oxford] don is equipped with a persona, a set of public characteristics that he finds hard to lay aside even in private."[13] Alan Bede Griffiths comments on the enigmatic personality of Lewis: "I was thus quite unaware that there was anything exceptional in this friendship, and it was only years afterward that I began to discover other aspects of his mind and character, which were then completely hidden from me."[14] John Lawlor notes "Lewis's determined impersonality towards all except his very closest

---

[9] C. S. Lewis to Arthur Greeves, 13 May 1956, in *The Collected Letters of C. S. Lewis*, vol. 3, *Narnia, Cambridge, and Joy, 1950–1963*, ed. Walter Hooper (San Francisco: HarperSanFrancisco, 2007) 750.

[10] Malcolm Muggeridge, "The Mystery," in *In Search of C. S. Lewis*, ed. Stephen Schofield (South Plainfield NJ: Bridge Logos, 1983) 127.

[11] Leo Baker, "Near the Beginning," in *Remembering C. S. Lewis: Recollections of Those Who Knew Him*, ed. James T. Como (San Francisco: Ignatius Press, 2005) 67.

[12] John Wain, "C. S. Lewis," in *Critical Thought Series: C. S. Lewis*, ed. George Watson (Cambridge: Cambridge UP, 1992) 28.

[13] Ibid., 24.

[14] Alan Bede Griffiths, "The Adventure of Faith," in *Remembering C. S. Lewis*, ed. James T. Como, 77.

friends."[15] A student of Lewis beginning in 1947, Peter Bayley likewise affirms the hiddenness of Lewis:

> Lewis was forty-two. He seemed older. He was already a well-known figure and beginning to be famous. He gave us a heartily friendly welcome, and my dominating recollection of him is of forced geniality, which I think he adopted partly because he wanted to seem friendly and partly to preserve impersonality. It was not false or insincere, and I think it had become an inseparable part of his public persona. It gave one an impression of a more toughly masculine and aggressive character than perhaps he was.[16]

Richard W. Ladborough, Lewis's friend at Cambridge, writes, "I am convinced that his fundamental shyness (part of his modesty) caused him, during the first years of his Cambridge career, to appear more aggressive than he really was. It was not that he outshone us all in conversation but that he felt that brilliance was expected. There was, perhaps, something of the poseur about him when he first arrived at his new college."[17]

Even Lewis's fiction inscribes the slipperiness of identity, the self as construct. The distance between personas is embodied in Lewis's symbol of the mask, which appears in both *The Pilgrim's Regress* and *Till We Have Faces*.[18] In *The Pilgrim's Regress*, the Steward of Puritania dons a mask while giving John religious instruction; the Steward's religiosity is thus figured as a pose. Before Psyche in *Till We Have Faces* undergoes her sacrificial ritual, her face is painted, obscuring her identity. Her older sister Orual subjects herself to veilings and unveilings, maskings and unmaskings. In fact, Orual exhibits alternating identities, evident after her father dies and she perhaps foolhardily proposes individual combat with a rival from another kingdom: "Ever since Arnom [the priest] had said hours ago that the King was dying, there seemed to be another woman acting and speaking in my place. Call her the Queen; but Orual was someone different and now I was Orual again."[19]

---

[15] John Lawlor, *C. S. Lewis: Memories and Reflections* (Dallas: Spence Publishing, 1998) 6.

[16] Peter Bayley, "From Master to Colleague," in *Remembering C. S. Lewis*, ed. James T. Como, 166.

[17] Richard W. Ladborough, "In Cambridge," in *Remembering C. S. Lewis*, ed. James T. Como, 192.

[18] See Peter Schakel, *Reason and the Imagination in C. S. Lewis: A Study of* Till We Have Faces (Grand Rapids: Eerdmans, 1984) for a close reading of masks in the two books.

[19] C. S. Lewis, *Till We Have Faces: A Myth Retold* (San Diego: Harcourt Brace & Company, 1984) 201.

These two texts, the metaphorical bookends of Lewis's career as a fiction writer, thematize the very issues that so puzzled Lewis's friends about Lewis himself.

These issues have not escaped the attention of Lewis scholars. Stephen Medcalf, for instance, traces the various personas of Lewis and how they influenced his writing style. The "midlife persona" is evident in *Surprised by Joy* and the Narniad: "the classic English prose style we have described that relies on stock response in choice of words, easily and unironically employed allusion and quotation, architectonic syntax with a tendency to long sentences harmonious in stress and sound, and narrative and description implying one universal observer—adding up in Barfield's phrase to 'the sort of thing a man might say.'" Medcalf notices a change in persona and thus in style in 1955: "It became and remained much more personal—he shed a skin. Some attribute the various changes which came upon him at this period to his acquaintance with, and double marriage to, Joy Gresham." Medcalf argues that, throughout much of his life, Lewis attempted to create a self made fit for God, an endeavor captured in *Mere Christianity* wherein Lewis "compares the self to a telescope in that 'the instrument through which you see God is your whole self.'" Medcalf continues, "That is why, as he says, horrible nations have horrible gods. He thought in consequence that it was his duty to build up a good self as a telescope through which to see God, to build it up in this manner was a persona, not the 'he' that was choosing the materials and doing the building up. There was built up an artificiality in his relation to himself which lasted twenty years."[20]

These biographical and critical commentaries as well as the symbols of the mask all show that Lewis was attentive to the dynamic of adopting personas. However it is figured—impersonality, hiddenness, mystery, secretiveness, privacy, dichotomy, poseur, or artificiality—the art of playing a role well-served Lewis throughout his career, enabling him to adopt the stances and perspectives from which the public intellectual approaches issues and marshals arguments.

---

[20] Stephen Medcalf, "Language and Self-Consciousness: The Making and Breaking of C. S. Lewis's Personae," in *Word and Story in C. S. Lewis*, ed. Peter J. Schakel and Charles A. Huttar (Columbia: University of Missouri Press, 1991) 129, 135.

## II. The Vantage Point of the Outsider

Chapter 1 showed how the public intellectual often poses as an outsider, set apart from the political or cultural mainstream, issuing critiques from the ideological periphery. Arthur Melzer explains that this position is necessary in order to avoid the taint of mere partisanship: "It is only this extreme detachment and withdrawal—founded on the love of ideas and a certain contempt for society—that can render a man relatively immune to the seductions of interest and partisanship and thus make him a worthy guide for society. Thus the public intellectual is *necessarily* defined by a posture of detachment, alienation, and nonconformity: he is the outsider, the misfit, the bohemian."[21]

While Lewis assumes the vantage point of an outsider, his case is unique. As explained in previous chapters, Lewis lived during the rise of modernism, scientism, and intense secularization. As a medievalist, intellectual conservative, supernaturalist, and Christian, Lewis was clearly out of sync with the twentieth-century *Zeitgeist*, thus forcing him into the position of outsider, adopting a persona of "detachment and withdrawal." In fact, Lewis embodied a set of values and beliefs of which many of his contemporaries were simply ignorant. (This is why, as described earlier, Lewis fulfills the significant role of public intellectual as translator of ideas.) Simply put, the language of Christianity had become for many in the twentieth century a foreign tongue, thus prompting Lewis to serve as translator. As outsider, Lewis thus presents ideas and arguments that come across as strange and new to the insiders of the secularized mainstream. One of Nevill Coghill's remembrances of Lewis illustrates this phenomenon. Coghill once asked Lewis how he came to write so regularly for American audiences:

> How did he know what to write about or what to say? "Oh," he said, "they have somehow got the idea that I am an unaccountably paradoxical dog, and they name the subject on which they want me to write; and they pay generously." "And so you set to work and invent a few paradoxes?" "Not a bit of it. What I do is to recall, as well as I can, what my mother used to say on the subject, eke it out with a few similar thoughts of my

---

[21] Arthur M. Melzer, "What Is an Intellectual?" in *The Public Intellectual: Between Philosophy and Politics*, ed. Arthur M. Melzer et al. (New York: Rowman & Littlefield Publishers, Inc., 2003) 11, emphasis in original.

own, and so produce what would have been strict orthodoxy in about 1900."[22]

The outsider persona gives Lewis's arguments their unique rhetorical spin: the presentation of orthodoxy to an audience that has lost all memory of orthodoxy.

This rhetorical situation recapitulates a phenomenon of reception theory that Lewis himself explores in Edmund Spenser's *Faerie Queene*. Analyzing Book III of that text, Lewis shows that the character of Britomart symbolizes not only chastity but, more specifically, "married love," a species a love in stark contrast to the adulterous love of earlier romances. In fact, Lewis argues that *The Faerie Queene* instantiates the substitution of "romance of marriage" for "romance of adultery"; "in the history of sentiment he is the greatest among the founders of that romantic conception of marriage which is the basis of all our love literature from Shakespeare to Meredith." Lewis goes on to explain that the symbolism of Britomart, which was obvious to previous generations, is "platitude no longer": "The whole conception is now being attacked. Feminism in politics, reviving ascetism in religion, animalism in imaginative literature, and, above all, the discoveries of the psycho-analysts, have undermined that monogamic idealism about sex which served us for three centuries. Whether society will gain or lose by the revolution, I need not try to predict; but Spenser ought to gain."[23]

Lewis's analysis of *The Faerie Queene* spells out the very role he plays as public intellectual: just as the poem represents "monogamic idealism about sex" for a twentieth-century audience hostile to that idealism—an audience of feminists, ascetics, and animalists—so too Lewis the public intellectual defends arguments within an oppositional, increasingly secularized *milieu*; and just as the poem's depiction of monogamy as an ideal is foreign to twentieth-century readers, so too is the orthodoxy Lewis defends foreign to a post-Christian world. Like Spenser, Lewis stands to gain from this dynamic, for the pseudo-novelty and controversy of his arguments brand his name, securing his place in the public sphere.

Another example illustrates Lewis's unique stance as outsider. In 1940, Lewis's friend Charles Williams gave a lecture at Oxford. As Lewis writes in a letter to his brother, the subject of the lecture was "nominally on [John Milton's] *Comus* but really on Chastity." While Lewis was impressed with

---

[22] Nevill Coghill, "The Approach to English," in *Light on C. S. Lewis*, ed. Jocelyn Gibb (New York: Harcourt Brace & World, 1965) 65.

[23] C. S. Lewis, *The Allegory of Love: A Study in Medieval Tradition* (Oxford: Oxford University Press, 1936) 360.

Williams's lecture, he was equally intrigued by the reaction of the students: "It was a beautiful sight to see a whole room full of modern young men and women sitting in that absolute silence which can *not* be faked, very puzzled, but spell-bound: perhaps with something of the same feeling which a lecture on *un*chastity might have evoked in their grandparents—the forbidden subject broached at last."[24] Lewis believed that his books could evoke a similar reaction, thus the perception of paradox for what is actually orthodoxy.

Lewis plays the role of outsider for holding beliefs that push him outside the cultural mainstream. These are the same beliefs—enshrined as they are in the past—that would once have made him an insider, safely ensconced *within* the cultural mainstream. This paradox is what George Watson has in mind when he applies the following oxymoronic epithet to Lewis: "conservative iconoclast."[25] Lewis conserves and defends the values of the past while challenging and tearing down the icons of the present. He is simultaneously marginalized (because of his rejection of twentieth-century dogmas) and centralized, firmly allied to the once hegemonic authority of Christendom, espousing the values and traditions of Western civilization, both of which were fading from the collective memory of twentieth-century England. As conservative iconoclast, Lewis is simultaneously a heretic, by the standards of his present, and a believer, by the standards of the past.

## III. The Strategy of Re-conceptualization

This unique perspective as outsider strengthens a key rhetorical strategy that threads its way through Lewis's *oeuvre*. This strategy, in turn, can be traced to Lewis's war experiences and his early career as a poet, as demonstrated by K. J. Gilchrist. Traumatized by the realities of war, Lewis, like other war poets, "attempts to rebuild shattered assumptions" in a process Gilchrist calls "paradigmatic rupture." That is, the experience of war unsettles one's mental bearings, necessitating a reorganized paradigm to orient one's worldview. Gilchrist notes how this same process operates when Lewis converts to Christianity, forcing him to reassess his assumptions about God and, when Lewis's wife dies, forcing him—yet again—to reexamine his

---

[24] C. S. Lewis to Warren Lewis, 11 February 1940, in *Collected Letters*, 2:344–45.

[25] George Watson, introduction to *Critical Thought Series: C. S. Lewis*, ed. George Watson, 1.

beliefs about Christianity vis-à-vis the problem of evil.[26] These experiences of questioning, reassessment, and reevaluation become the basis for a rhetorical strategy that resembles what Stanley Fish refers to as a "dialectical presentation," which "is disturbing, for it requires of its readers a searching and rigorous scrutiny of everything they believe in and live by. It is didactic in a special sense; it does not preach the truth, but asks that its readers discover the truth for themselves, and this discovery is often made at the expense not only of a reader's opinions and values, but of his self-esteem." The dialectical presentation, Fish continues, is often "humiliating."[27]

While Lewis's dialectical presentations are intended to produce discomforting effects on readers, they do—unlike Fish's formula—"preach the truth." That is, Lewis does challenge the assumptions implicit in secular, anti-traditional beliefs (a rigorous scrutiny of everything the modern world lives by), not so that readers can discover truth for themselves, but so that he can direct them to truth. Lewis's version of the dialectical presentation is a carefully *guided* process, with the reader being led from a position of dislocation and uncertainty to faith and conviction. Nevertheless, the experiences Gilchrist identifies and the rhetorical strategy Fish explains point to a fundamental dynamic in Lewis's writings, a dynamic I will refer to simply as *re-conceptualizations*.

Lewis's stance as outsider makes the strategy of re-conceptualization particularly effective. Because the modern world possesses an incomplete or deficient understanding of the basic concepts of Christianity and traditional values, Lewis can challenge assumptions in obvious ways: by re-framing the ideas that have been misunderstood by the secular world. And since Lewis was once an atheist (an *insider*), he is particularly adept at this form of re-conceptualization because he is conversant in the languages of both the Christian and post-Christian worlds.

Thus, in his first book published after his conversion, *The Pilgrim's Regress*, Lewis re-conceptualizes a fundamental human experience: what German Romantics referred to as *Sehnsucht* and what Lewis calls Joy in his autobiography. Through the thinly veiled autobiographical character of John, Lewis shows how this experience of strong desire is most often misunderstood, leading one down false paths that lead to frustration, sin, and personal harm. For instance, having first experienced this intense

---

[26] K. J. Gilchrist, *A Morning after War: C. S. Lewis and WWI* (New York: Peter Lang, 2005) 191, 217–18.

[27] Stanley Fish, *Self-Consuming Artifacts: The Experience of Seventeenth-Century Literature* (Berkeley: University of California Press, 1972) 2.

longing during a romantic reverie, embodied in his vision of an Island, John attempts to fulfill the desire through sexual escapades; this course of action leads to disappointment and self-disgust. Nearly the rest of the book charts John's failed attempts to trace the experience of *Sehnsucht* to its source, all of which lead to dead-ends: nineteenth-century rationalism, various aesthetic experiences, the philosophy of Absolute Idealism, etc. Not until the end of the book does John come to understand that the desire inherent in *Sehnsucht* can only be fulfilled in heaven, that God has implanted it within his creatures, pointing them toward their true home. In the afterword to the third edition of the book, Lewis refers to John's circuitous journey to God and a proper understanding of *Sehnsucht* as a type of "dialectic": "The dialectic of Desire, faithfully followed, would retrieve all mistakes, head you off from all false paths, and force you not to propound, but to live through, a sort of ontological proof."[28] Thus, *The Pilgrim's Regress* implicitly offers an argument for the Judeo-Christian God as it also re-conceptualizes the concept of *Sehnsucht*.

Because of the significant disconnect between the Christian and post-Christian worlds—between the outsiders and insiders—Lewis occasionally endeavors re-conceptualizations that can come across as shocking, wrenching the secular reader out of his or her definitional obtuseness. One such re-conceptualization concerns the very definition of God. In *Mere Christianity*, for instance, Lewis describes the Law of Human Nature as a standard of right and wrong that we fail to keep; he also identifies God as the "Power behind the law" and, now shifting to a direct second-person address, informs his reader that "you have broken that law and put yourself wrong with that Power...." Lewis thus concludes, "God is the only comfort, He is also the supreme terror: the thing we most need and the thing we most want to hide from. He is our only possible ally, and we have made ourselves His enemies. Some people talk as if meeting the gaze of absolute goodness would be fun. They need to think again."[29] In *The Problem of Pain*, Lewis replaces the notion of God as a gentle, grandfatherly deity with a similarly startling reality:

> You asked for a loving god: you have one. The great spirit you so lightly invoked, the "lord of terrible aspect", is present: not a senile benevolence that drowsily wishes you to be happy in your own way, not the cold philanthropy of a conscientious magistrate, nor the care of a host who

---

[28] C. S. Lewis, afterword to *The Pilgrim's Progress, The Pilgrim's Regress*, 3rd ed. (Grand Rapids: Eerdmans, 1981) 205.

[29] C. S. Lewis, *Mere Christianity* (San Francisco, HarperSanFrancisco, 2001) 31.

feels responsible for the comfort of his guests, but the consuming fire Himself, the Love that made the world, persistent as the artist's love for his work and despotic as a man's love for a dog, provident and venerable as a father's love for a child, jealous, inexorable, exacting as love between the sexes.[30]

These re-conceptualizations of God are inscribed in the refrain repeated throughout Narnia, famously uttered by Mr. Beaver in *The Lion, the Witch and the Wardrobe*: "'Course [Aslan] isn't safe. But he's good. He's the king, I tell you."[31] Colin Manlove explains how the Pevensie children "continually have their assumptions displaced," assumptions not merely relating to Aslan: "Mr. Tumnus is not just the jolly domestic host he appears to be; the wardrobe is more than a wardrobe; Narnia is not an illusion; Edmund is not rewarded by the witch; Edmund's rescue from the witch is not final; Aslan is not dead, but even more alive than before; they who were kings and queens of Narnia are in an instant returned to being modern children. Reality is not to be appropriated; its richness and depth elude ready absorption by mind."[32] This pattern of displaced assumptions proceeds from Lewis's writerly position: the outsider making old concepts new to the insider.

Lewis's stance enables re-conceptualizations on a host of issues. For instance, through the voice of the devil Screwtape, Lewis counters the notion that Christianity is an ascetic religion, suitable only for dour-faced killjoys. Screwtape avers, "He [God, the "Enemy"] made the pleasures: all our research so far has not enabled us to produce one. All we can do is to encourage the humans to take the pleasures which our Enemy has produced, at times, or in ways, or in degrees, which He has forbidden."[33] Taking a theological principle about the nature of good and evil that has roots in the centuries-old writings of Augustine, Lewis makes the idea new for the secularized reader, challenging stereotypes of a prim Christianity. Later, in fact, Screwtape admits that God is "a hedonist at heart. All those fasts and vigils and stakes and crosses are only a façade."[34] Lewis thus fully exploits the opportunity to re-conceptualize this aspect of Christianity. He makes a similar ambitious move in his sermon, "The Weight of Glory": "Our Lord finds our desires not too strong, but too weak. We are half-hearted creatures,

---

[30] C. S. Lewis, *The Problem of Pain* (San Francisco: HarperSanFrancisco, 2001) 39.

[31] C. S. Lewis, *The Lion, the Witch and the Wardrobe* (New York: Harper Trophy, 1994) 86.

[32] Colin Manlove, *The Chronicles of Narnia: The Patterning of a Fantastic World* (New York: Twayne Publishers, 1993) 38.

[33] C. S. Lewis, *The Screwtape Letters* (San Francisco: HarperSanFrancisco, 2001) 40.

[34] Ibid., 118.

fooling about with drink and sex and ambition when infinite joy is offered us, like an ignorant child who wants to go on making mud pies in a slum because he cannot imagine what is meant by the offer of a holiday at the sea. We are far too easily pleased."[35] As with other instances of re-conceptualization, this veritable affront to common assumptions disorients the reader, instigating an uncomfortable process of reassessment.

Lewis mastered the art of re-conceptualization—so much so that it became a *leitmotif* in his works—because it proved effective in offering a compelling picture of Christianity from his position as outsider. It is true, however, that Lewis appropriates the rhetorical strategy of re-conceptualization from G. K. Chesterton, whose influence on Lewis was seminal. Chesterton was likewise the master of challenging assumptions and disorienting readers, often through apothegmatic gems like the following: "Pessimism is not in being tired of evil but in being tired of good. Despair does not lie in being weary of suffering, but in being weary of joy."[36] It is also true that Lewis's re-conceptualizations can prove as disorienting to those inside the faith as they are to those outside; indeed, Lewis's theological and moral formulations often liberate God from the proverbial box into which believers confine him.

But it is also true that nearly every book he wrote constituted a response in one way or another to the modern movements that embattled his religious and moral beliefs. Even in a scholarly work like *The Discarded Image*, Lewis fleshes out his picture of the medieval world by challenging modern assumptions. "I have read a novel," Lewis explains, "which represents all the Pagans of the day as carefree sensualists, and all the Christians as savage ascetics. It is a grave error. They were in some ways far more like each other than either was like a modern man."[37] By thrusting upon his modern readers a historical consciousness that acknowledges the historical contingency of modern beliefs, making the modern man the anomaly—not the Christian or pagan—Lewis distances himself from modernism, carving out his identity as outsider. This position lends his art of re-conceptualization its distinct argumentative edge, overturning the false assumptions, making room for

---

[35] C. S. Lewis, "The Weight of Glory," in *The Weight of Glory and Other Addresses*, ed. Walter Hooper (New York: Simon & Schuster, 1980) 26.

[36] G. K. Chesterton, *The Everlasting Man* (Radford VA: Wilder Publications, 2008) 96.

[37] C. S. Lewis, *The Discarded Image: An Introduction to Medieval and Renaissance Literature* (Cambridge: Cambridge University Press, 1964) 46.

what alone stands after the dialectical presentations have cleared the field: the truth of Christianity and traditional values.

## IV. Science Fiction, Myth, and Otherness

What I have identified as a *leitmotif* in Lewis's work naturally appears in his science fiction. Both *Out of the Silent Planet* and *Perelandra* re-conceptualize the angelic and the supernatural in ways reminiscent of Lewis's re-conceptualization of God analyzed earlier: an unbearable presence replacing a comfortable, undemanding companionship. Elwin Ransom's encounter with the Oyarsa of Malacandra (the tutelary spirit of the planet Mars) in *Out of the Silent Planet* is eerie and disconcerting: "Ransom felt a tingling of his blood and a pricking on his fingers as if lightning were near him; and his heart and body seemed to him to be made of water [....] 'What are you so afraid of, Ransom of Thulcandra?' it said."[38] Lewis, who plays a role as character in both *Out of the Silent Planet* and *Perelandra*, is unnerved by the presence of the Oyarsa even after he learns of its identity as angelic servant of Maleldil (God). Lewis as narrator describes his experience upon entering Ransom's domicile and finding himself in the company of the Oyarsa: "Here at last was a bit of that world from beyond the world, which I had always supposed that I loved and desired, breaking through and appearing to my senses: and I didn't like it, I wanted it to go away."[39] Similar to his analysis of the Narniad, Manlove observes that, in *Perelandra*, "Ransom is continually being thrown out of his previous assumptions [...] and that is how the whole book works, shifting us out of assumptions to deeper knowledge, and revealing even that deeper knowledge to be of only provisional reality...."[40] In a similar vein, David Downing observes, "Lewis's portrayal of the eldila clearly illustrates his strategy of inviting readers to look at old doctrines with new eyes. He well knew that angels in the Bible are never portrayed with harps and halos."[41]

I wish to draw attention, however, to the way in which re-conceptualizations in the science fiction trilogy emerge organically from the very genre of science fiction itself and therefore why Lewis gravitated

---

[38] C. S. Lewis, *Out of the Silent Planet* (New York: Macmillan Publishing Company, 1965) 119.

[39] C. S. Lewis, *Perelandra* (New York: Macmillan Publishing Company, 1965) 19.

[40] Colin Manlove, *Christian Fantasy: From 1200 to the Present* (Notre Dame: University of Notre Dame Press, 1992) 249–50.

[41] David Downing, *Planets in Peril: A Critical Study of C. S. Lewis's Ransom Trilogy* (Amherst: University of Massachusetts Press, 1992) 42.

toward the genre because of his perspective as outsider. It is important to note that when *Out of the Silent Planet* was published in 1943, science fiction was still in its preadolescent phase as a genre. Neil Barron notes that, while the term "science fiction" was first used in 1851, it was not employed again until 1929.[42] Lewis himself was not even sure how to identify the new genre, referring in a 1943 letter to I. O. Evans as "a brother 'scientifictionist' or 'scientifictor.'"[43]

Lewis was much surer, however, about why the genre appealed to him. He first came under the spell of science fiction after reading David Lindsay's *Voyage to Arcturus*. In a 1947 letter to Ruth Pitter, Lewis writes, "From Lyndsay [*sic*] I first learned what other planets are really good for: for *spiritual* adventures."[44] Lewis records this same sort of appreciation in his essay, "On Stories." He there asserts,

> In each chapter [of Lindsay's book] we think we have found [Lindsay's] final position; each time we are utterly mistaken…. There is no recipe for writing of this kind. But part of the secret is that the author (like Kafka) is recording a lived dialectic. His Tormance [the planet in outer space where much of the novel is set] is a region of the spirit. He is the first writer to discover what "other planets" are really good for in fiction. No merely physical strangeness or merely spatial distance will realise that idea of otherness which is what we are always trying to grasp in a story about voyaging through space: you must go into another dimension. To construct plausible and moving "other worlds" you must draw on the only real "other world" we know, that of the spirit.[45]

These qualities of Lindsay's novel are foundational to the genre of science fiction, especially when Lewis enumerates the qualities of dialectic and otherness. Darko Suvin, for instance, defines science fiction as "a literary genre whose necessary and sufficient conditions are the presence and interaction of estrangement and cognition, and whose main formal device is an imaginative framework alternative to the author's empirical environment."[46] Adam Roberts observes that numerous definitions of science fiction share a common component: "the encounter with difference…articulated through a

---

[42] Neil Barron, *Anatomy of Wonder: A Critical Guide to Science Fiction*, 5th ed. (London: Libraries Unlimited, 2004) 3.

[43] C. S. Lewis to I. O. Evans, 7 July 1943, *Collected Letters*, 2:584.

[44] C. S. Lewis to Ruth Pitter, 4 January 1947, *Collected Letters*, 2:753.

[45] C. S. Lewis, "On Stories," in *On Stories and Other Essays on Literature*, ed. Walter Hooper (San Diego: Harcourt Brace & Company, 1982) 12.

[46] Darko Suvin, *Metamorphoses of Science Fiction: On the Poetics and History of a Literary Genre* (New Haven: Yale University Press, 1979) 8–9.

'novum', a conceptual, or more usually material embodiment of alterity...."
Roberts continues,

> This serves as the basis of many critics' affection for the genre, the fact
> that SF provides a means, in a popular and accessible fictional form, for
> exploring alterity. Specific SF nova are more than just gimmicks, and
> much more than clichés: they provide a symbolic grammar for
> articulating the perspectives of normally marginalized discourses of race,
> of gender, of non-conformism and alternative ideologies.[47]

These definitions and elaborations return us to Lewis's stance as
outsider. Lewis turned to science fiction because embedded in its generic
identity is the representation of otherness and the exploration of "perspectives of normally marginalized discourses." For Lewis, otherness revolves
around the spiritual world (what other planets are really good for), a world
adopting a discourse increasingly marginalized and misunderstood—
especially Lewis's Judeo-Christian version of the discourse—during the
twentieth century. Lewis thus depicts the realities and truths of this spiritual
world within a genre that not only encourages but necessitates re-
conceptualizations through, in Lewis's case, the narrative device of space
travel. Lewis's readers experience not only the alien worlds of otherness
found on Mars and Venus but a likewise alien spiritual world, an
"alternative ideology" rendered other by the hegemonic ideologies of the
twentieth century. Thus the character of Maleldil, the sovereign power of the
universe in all three books of the trilogy, is actually God; the eldila,
Maleldil's servants, are angels; and the Bent One, Maleldil's enemy, is Satan.
From this set of characters alone, Lewis can project worlds that recast
Christian principles in a new light, re-conceptualizing them according to the
narrative demands of the science-fiction genre itself.[48]

Dialectical representations of otherness are not unique to the genre of
science fiction; they are also central to the genre of myth. In an essay titled
"Tolkien's *The Lord of the Rings*," Lewis explains,

---

[47] Adam Roberts, *Science Fiction* (London: Routledge, 2000) 28.

[48] After reading reviews of *Out of the Silent Planet,* Lewis was unsure about how
well he accomplished this task, though he was aware of the task's value for the cause
of Christianity. In 1939 letter to Sister Penelope, he writes, "You will be both grieved
and amused to learn that out of about 60 reviews, only 2 showed any knowledge that
my idea of a fall of the Bent One was anything but a private invention of my own. But
if only there were someone with a richer talent and more leisure, I believe this great
ignorance might be a help to the evangelisation of England: any amount of theology
can now be smuggled into people's minds under cover of romance without their
knowing it" (C. S. Lewis to Sister Penelope, 9 July 1939, *Collected Letters,* 2:262).

The value of the myth is that it takes all the things we know and restores to them the rich significance which has been hidden by "the veil of familiarity". The child enjoys his cold meat (otherwise dull to him) by pretending it is buffalo, just killed with his own bow and arrow. And the child is wise. The real meat comes back to him more savoury for having been dipped in a story; you might say that only then is it the real meat. If you are tired of the real landscape, look at it in a mirror. By putting bread, gold, horse, apple, or the very roads into a myth, we do not retreat from reality: we rediscover it.[49]

Likewise, Christian principles are rediscovered and re-understood when they are placed into a myth. Elsewhere, Lewis writes that myth "gets under our skin, hits us at a level deeper than our thoughts or even our passions, troubles oldest certainties till all questions are reopened, and in general shocks us more fully awake than we are for most of our lives."[50]

We see here that myth deploys the strategy of re-conceptualization: challenging assumptions, disorienting readers, and revealing truth. Thus, texts with mythic qualities—like *The Great Divorce* and the Narniad—imitate the rhetorical patterns of the science-fiction trilogy. Lewis makes use of genres that by their very nature engage in the art of re-conceptualization: an art particularly compelling when one poses as an outsider within the public sphere.

## V. Other Advantageous Stances: The Perspective of De-conversion

From its beginnings, the public sphere compelled its participants to adopt a stance of neutrality—to marshal arguments from an oxymoronic impartial perspective. The neutral stance is consistent with the procedural guidelines of the Enlightenment, especially as those guidelines descend from the ideas of Rene Descartes, whose process of methodological doubt influenced the philosophical strategies of centuries of thinkers. Doubting everything that he had been taught and had assumed, Descartes proceeds with (hyperbolic) impartiality to arrive at truth.[51] In an earlier chapter, I have identified this procedure as de-conversion and have argued that it is a characteristic stance of the public intellectual. Within the context of this chapter on perspectives and stances, I can now fully exploit the way in

---

[49] Lewis, "Tolkien's The Lord of the Rings," in *On Stories and Other Essays on Literature*, ed. Walter Hooper, 90.

[50] C. S. Lewis, introduction to *George MacDonald: 365 Readings*, ed. C. S. Lewis (New York: Collier Books, 1974) xxviii.

[51] See the first meditation in *Meditations on First Philosophy*

which the term, applied to the Christian Lewis, underscores the dissembling role that personas play, forcing Lewis momentarily to divest himself of his religious beliefs within the public sphere—becoming hyperbolically neutral—for the precise and paradoxical purpose of defending those very beliefs.

A convention of the public sphere and a procedural guideline of the Enlightenment, de-conversion enables the public intellectual to shore up authority and credibility by posing as a commentator not sullied by the distortions of bias. The stance of de-conversion is also consistent with a conventional assumption of the public sphere described in the last chapter: the myth of the uniformity of experience. By emphasizing objectivity, the de-converted stance downplays experiential particularities and historical fads, placing humankind on a Procrustean bed for purposes of analysis.

(Of course, postmodern public intellectuals are exceptions to the rule. A public intellectual like Stanley Fish argues that such objectivity can never be attained. As chapter 6 will show, however, postmodernism contributes to the demise of the public sphere, thereby creating a different sort of intellectual. Fish, after all, enters the public sphere by attacking the very conventions of the public sphere.)

Lewis adopts the stance of de-conversion in multiple ways. His intellectual conservatism—like many forms of conservatism—encourages de-conversion because of its opposition to modern ideas not only on the basis of their inaccuracies and dangers, but on their transience as well. To dismiss nontraditional, new ideas as ephemeral, fleeting, and merely subjective—proverbial flashes in the pan—one must appeal to a context that immunizes ideas from the vicissitudes of time: The next chapter will show how Lewis's appeal to high tradition performs that function. For now, it is sufficient to recognize that Lewis's basic conservative orientation inclines him toward de-conversion because both conservatism and de-conversion insulate ideas from the fluctuations wrought by subjectivity and innovation; both stances stabilize arguments by elevating them above the happenstances of personal preference and historical contingency.

A few examples will illustrate the conservative orientation that inclines Lewis toward de-conversion. Consider Lewis's warning against "chronological snobbery." He defines the phrase as "the uncritical acceptance of the intellectual climate common to our own age and the assumption that whatever has gone out of date is on that account discredited."[52] To what

---

[52] C. S. Lewis, *Surprised by Joy: The Shape of My Early Life* (San Diego: Harcourt Brace & Company, 1984) 207.

extent Lewis believes that those who adopt the beliefs of his own age do so on the basis of "uncritical acceptance" is unclear, but his definition does seem to be loaded, suggesting that new ideas are accepted and old ideas are rejected irrationally. (Indeed, Lewis affirms that he himself was guilty of chronological snobbery, but it is hard to believe that Lewis, especially after his education under Kirkpatrick, would accept any proposition uncritically.) Lewis's opposition to popular ideas (read: *ephemeral* ideas) is crystallized in a passage from *The Four Loves*: "All that is not eternal is eternally out of date."[53] Indeed, Lewis admitted to a "partly pathological hostility to what is fashionable."[54] In a 1940 letter to his brother, Lewis emphatically expresses his distrust of, and confusion with, the modern world: "I am afraid the truth is in this, as in nearly everything else I think about at present, that the world, as it is now becoming and has partly become, is simply *too much for* people of the old square-rigged type like you and me. I don't understand its economics, or its politics, or any dam' thing about it."[55]

While Lewis's conservatism inclines him toward de-conversion, some of his analyses exhibit how he practices it. An obvious starting point is his essay titled "The Poison of Subjectivism." Demonstrating his conservative bent, Lewis states that, for centuries, values were held to be objective. "The modern view," explains Lewis, "is very different." He continues, "It does not believe that value judgements are really judgements at all. They are sentiments, or complexes, or attitudes, produced in a community by the pressure of its environment and its traditions, and differing from one community to another. To say that a thing is good is merely to express our feeling about it; and our feeling about it is the feeling we have been socially conditioned to have."[56] Moral judgments are objective, a conclusion that inflects his own analysis: an argument *for* objectivity, discounting the role that feeling plays in informing judgments, is naturally and logically an argument that *proceeds* objectively, likewise minimizing subjective influences.

Lewis defines one species of reasoning (in Lewis's mind, pseudo-reasoning) that attends to pre-theoretical considerations as "Bulverism." Bulverism refers to pre-analytical factors that shape one's beliefs, and, in the essay, Lewis chiefly has in mind Freudians and Marxists. "In the old days,"

---

[53] Lewis, *The Four Loves*, 137.

[54] C. S. Lewis to Mary Neylan, 26 March 1940, *Collected Letters*, 2:372.

[55] C. S. Lewis to Warren Lewis, 18 February 1940, *Collected Letters*, 2:350.

[56] C. S. Lewis, "The Poison of Subjectivism," in *Christian Reflections*, ed. Walter Hooper (Grand Rapids: Eerdmans, 1967) 73.

writes Lewis, "it was supposed that if a thing seemed obviously true to a hundred men, then it was probably true in fact." Freudians and Marxists, on the other hand, attribute the espousal of some truth claims to unconscious desires and socioeconomic identities; we believe what we believe because of who we are—"psychological causes," as Lewis later puts it. Here is Lewis's conclusion on the matter:

> Now this is obviously great fun; but it has not always been noticed that there is a bill to pay for it. There are two questions that people who say this kind of things ought to be asked. The first is, Are *all* thoughts thus tainted at the source, or only some? The second is, Does the taint invalidate the tainted thought—in the sense of making it untrue—or not? If they say that *all thoughts* are thus tainted, then, of course, we must remind them that Freudianism and Marxism are as much systems of thought as Christian theology or philosophical idealism. The Freudian and the Marxian are in the same boat with all the rest of us, and cannot criticize us from outside. They have sawn off the branch they were sitting on. If, on the other hand, they say that the taint need not invalidate their thinking, then neither need it invalidate ours. In which case they have saved their own branch, but also saved ours with it. The only line they can really take is to say that some thoughts are tainted and others are not—which has the advantage (if Freudians and Marxians regard it as an advantage) of being what every sane man has always believed. But if that is so, we must then ask how you find out which are tainted and which are not.[57]

While Lewis later explains that truth claims must be analyzed on their own merits before one can assess how psychological factors influence one to adopt them, his conclusion here reveals the practice of de-conversion and his strong commitment to objectivity. First, Lewis casts the pre-analytical factors that shape theorizing as a "taint": "tainted at the source," "tainted thought." Theorizing is *tainted* by subjective influences. Second, Lewis employs a preemptive move—a polemical strategy threading its way through much of Lewis's non-fiction—that disables the subjectively derived arguments of his opponents while commending his own objectively grounded reasoning: Bulverism is self-refuting. That is, if the Freudian argues that the Christian believes a certain claim merely because he or she is Christian, the Christian can retort that the Freudian says *that* only because he or she is a Freudian.

---

[57] C. S. Lewis, "'Bulverism,' or, the Foundation of 20th Century Thought," in *God in the Dock: Essays on Theology and Ethics*, ed. Walter Hooper (Grand Rapids: Eerdmans, 1970) 272.

This move is preemptive because it never allows his opponent out of the gate: the very terms of his opponent's argument are self-contradictory.

More importantly, the move necessarily privileges objectivity and implicitly encourages de-conversion. Given the taint of subjectivity, the prudent inquirer is the de-converted inquirer, advancing claims that cannot be read as idiosyncratic. Thus, Lewis explains in the preface to *Mere Christianity*: "For I am not writing to expound something I could call 'my religion,' but to expound 'mere' Christianity, which is what it is and what it was long before I was born and whether I like it or not."[58] And in *The Problem of Pain*, Lewis likewise writes, "I write, of course, as a layman of the Church of England: but I have tried to assume nothing that is not professed by all baptized and communicating Christians."[59] These pre-analytical attestations endow Lewis's perspective with credibility and authority, stripped as it is of subjective influences.

Lewis practices de-conversion as a critic. And while his books on literary theory are written primarily for the specialist, the basic orientation that Lewis adopts obviously informs his work as a public intellectual. In *An Experiment in Criticism*, for instance, Lewis explains that true appreciation of art necessitates a process that amounts to what I call de-conversion:

> We must not let loose our own subjectivity upon the pictures and make them its vehicles. We must begin by laying aside as completely as we can all our own preconceptions, interests, and associations. We must make room for Botticelli's Mars and Venus, or Cimabue's Crucifixion, by emptying our own. After the negative effort, the positive. We must use our eyes. We must look, and go on looking till we have certainly seen exactly what is there. We sit down before the picture in order to have something done to us, not that we may do things with it. The first demand any work of any art makes upon us is surrender. Look. Listen. Receive. Get yourself out of the way.[60]

Divested of our particularities, stripped of our subjective lenses, we see the work of art as it truly presents itself. Subjectivism is further doomed when Lewis equates its presence with aesthetic narcissism. Those who do not lay aside their subjectivity "*use* art," seeing only what they want to see; they "never get beyond [themselves]." On the other hand, those who do lay aside their subjectivity—those who properly de-convert—"*receive*" the work

---

[58] Lewis, *Mere Christianity*, ix.

[59] Lewis, *The Problem of Pain*, xii.

[60] C. S. Lewis, *An Experiment in Criticism* (Cambridge: Cambridge University Press, 1961) 18–19.

of art, seeing "the pictures as they are."[61] Aesthetic de-conversion, like all forms of de-conversion, affords a context-less perspective, thus guaranteeing objective judgments, which are therefore accurate judgments.

This orientation, this perspective of de-conversion, as previous chapters have shown, provides a compelling stance from which to articulate and defend positions within the public sphere. Composed of a diverse, differentiated audience, the public sphere requires a discourse that finds common ground. Lewis finds this common ground by marshaling arguments that purport to be presupposition-less—or, at the very least, arguments that minimize presuppositions. As he testily writes to Dom Bede Griffiths, with whom he carried on an occasionally heated debate on Roman Catholicism, "If I object at all to what you said, I object not as a friend or as a guest, but as a logician. If you are going to argue with me on the points at issue between our churches, it is obvious that you must argue *to* the truth of your position, not *from* it."[62]

In addition, the presupposition-less, de-converted stance operates powerfully in the public sphere because it underscores the efficacy of reason, obviously the public intellectual's most potent weapon. Once presuppositions are swept aside, the objective, universal faculty of reason can lead to the truths that transcend subjectivity. Thus Lewis, as *Christian* public intellectual, presents arguments for the existence of God that should appear valid—perhaps obviously so—to anyone with an open mind and the capacity to follow the dictates of reason: "I do not maintain that God's creation of Nature can be proved as rigorously as God's existence, but it seems to me overwhelmingly probable, so probable that no one who approached the question with an open mind would very seriously entertain any other hypothesis."[63] Likewise, in *The Screwtape Letters*, Screwtape suggests that reason is God's natural ally, inevitably leading, if faithfully followed, to the truth of Christianity: The devil, on the other hand, can only make use of propaganda, which merely manipulates emotions: "The trouble about argument is that it moves the whole struggle on to the Enemy's [God's] own ground. He can argue too; whereas in really practical propaganda of the kind I am suggesting He has shown for centuries to be

---

[61] Ibid., 19, 21. Lewis allows for little shades on nuance in his analysis. He sets up an either/or scenario: either people use art, or they receive it. No careful consideration is given to the ways in which "preconceptions, interests, and associations" can enhance the apprehension of art without devolving into narcissism.

[62] C. S. Lewis to Dom Bede Griffiths, 26 December 1934, *Collected Letters*, 2:150, emphasis in original.

[63] C. S. Lewis, *Miracles: A Preliminary Study* (New York: Collier Books, 1947) 33.

greatly inferior of Our Father Below. By the very act of arguing, you awake the patient's reason; and once it is awake, who can foresee the result?"[64] And in *Mere Christianity*, Lewis endows reason with enormous power in converting to Christianity. God, after all, "is the source from which all your reasoning power comes: you could not be right and He wrong any more than a stream can rise higher than its own source."[65]

In fact, the process of reasoning constitutes Lewis's litmus test: if the claims of Christianity cannot meet the demands of reason, then Christianity should be abandoned. He writes, "I am not asking anyone to accept Christianity if his best reasoning tells him that the weight of the evidence is against it. That is not the point at which Faith comes in. But supposing a man's reason once decides that the weight of the evidence is for it."[66] Once reason verifies the claims of Christianity, then faith becomes engaged, nourishing beliefs after they have passed reason's criterion. Lewis first presented this process in a 1941 essay, wherein he explains, "Now I define Faith as the power of continuing to believe what we once honestly thought to be true until cogent reasons for honestly changing our minds are brought before us."[67]

Thus, reason operates not only as the gatekeeper to the entrance of faith but to the exit leading away from faith as well. At least, that is how the process should operate. Too often, Lewis believes, people lose their faith not because their reason has rejected it, but simply because they lose interest. As Lewis explains in *Mere Christianity*, "And as a matter of fact, if you examined a hundred people who had lost their faith in Christianity, I wonder how many of them would turn out to have been reasoned out of it by honest argument? Do not most people simply drift away?"[68] Lewis's tone here suggests that such a form of apostasy is an intellectual cop out, unsanctioned by the dictates of reason; to lose faith by simply drifting away is unreasonable. Lewis's emphasis on reason becomes even more pronounced when one considers the assumption buried in the process Lewis describes. If most people simply drift away from faith, what prevents one from concluding that many people likewise simply drift *into* faith? Why assume that the process of religious-belief acquisition is such a *rational* process?

---

[64] Lewis, *The Screwtape Letters*, 2.
[65] Lewis, *Mere Christianity*, 48.
[66] Ibid., 140.
[67] C. S. Lewis, "Religion: Reality or Substitute?" in *Christian Reflections*, 42.
[68] Lewis, *Mere Christianity*, 141.

Lewis's assumption privileges reason, the preeminent faculty of the public sphere.

Lewis's adherence to the conventions of the public sphere overlaps with certain components of his commitment to Christianity. In *Perelandra*, for instance, the character of Weston becomes possessed by Satan (the "Bent One"). For a brief moment near the end of Weston's life, Satan momentarily relaxes his stranglehold on Weston's body and mind long enough for the real Weston to emerge and express his nihilistic fear and terror over the doom of humankind:

> "Haven't you seen the real meaning of all this modern stuff about the dangers of extrapolation and bent space and the indeterminacy of the atom? They don't say in so many words, of course, but what they're getting to, even before they die nowadays, is what men get to when they're dead—the knowledge that reality is neither rational nor consistent nor anything else. In a sense you might say it isn't there. 'Real' and 'Unreal,' 'true' and 'false'—they're all only on the surface. They give way the moment you press them."[69]

In this scene, Satanic dread is linked to subjectivism: The psychology of possession has affinities to the rejection of objectivity and thus the rejection of reason and rationality.

In *That Hideous Strength*, the poison of subjectivism spreads throughout all the branches of the N.I.C.E. as it calls upon diabolical forces to reconstitute humankind and overtake the world:

> Despair of objective truth had been increasingly insinuated into the scientists; indifference to it, and a concentration upon mere power, had been the result.... What should they find incredible, since they believed no longer in a rational universe? What should they regard as too obscene, since they held that all morality was a mere subjective by-product of the physical and economic situations of men? The time was ripe. From the point of view which is accepted in Hell, the whole history of our Earth had led up to this moment.

A science and epistemology built upon subjectivity occasion near apocalypse in the novel. The rejection of reason and rationality carries eschatological ramifications, signifying Lewis's belief that an attack on reason and objectivity constitutes an assault on Christianity itself.

The perspective of de-conversion thus enables Lewis's success in the public sphere. Along with the position of outsider, the de-converted stance

---

[69] Lewis, *Perelandra*, 169.

provides Lewis with the authority and credibility necessary to play the role of public intellectual. The de-converted, outsider stance also well-serves Lewis's defense of Christianity. Christianity, after all, began as a religion for outsiders, marginalized in the first century by both Jews and pagans. And the faith has most flourished from marginalized positions, vitalized when it is embattled and immunized from the sort of corruption that inevitably ensues when it is institutionalized within the mainstream. In addition, the de-converted stance aligns Christianity with rationality, thereby situating it as a reasonable faith. In short, the perspectives sketched in this chapter create personas seemingly antithetical: Lewis the public intellectual, champion of Enlightenment procedures, and Lewis the Christian, for whom, as Paul writes, "the wisdom of this world is foolishness in God's sight" (1 Cor 3:19).

# 4

## Forms and Sources of Authority

All polemical writing must anchor itself to some form or source of authority. Indeed, Phyllis Tickle asserts that human existence without authority, which grounds and guides beliefs, is unlivable: "The question of 'Where now is our authority?' is the fundamental or foundational question of all human existence and/or endeavor, be it individual or that of a larger, social unit. Without an answer to it, the individual personality or the personality of the group at large alike falls into disarray and ultimate chaos. It is Hell where there is no answer to that question."[1] Within the putatively neutral space of the public sphere, consolidating beliefs around authority presents unique challenges, for the forms and sources of authority must appeal to a diverse, differentiated audience: Like the presentation of the beliefs themselves, the forms and sources of authority must aspire toward universality, adhering to that convention of the public sphere which I have termed de-conversion, the achievement of hyperbolic objectivity. The last chapter sketched some writerly stances and personas that facilitate this process. This chapter analyzes concepts and techniques that enable Lewis to garner even more authority within the public sphere, further filling out his identity as public intellectual.

Lewis's affiliation with the Anglican church created both the challenges and opportunities that yielded forms of authority with strong resonance in the public sphere. Aidan Nichols notes the elasticity of Anglican theology: its flexibility of belief proceeding from the lack of a strong centralized, standardized authority. He explains,

> The Anglican Church is one of the most pluralistic churches in the world, certainly the most pluralistic of the historic churches. It has never had a single theological orthodoxy. Although it has promulgated confessional statements, and above all the Thirty Nine Articles of Religion of 1571, it has never committed itself to a single theological elucidation of those statements. There is no one theologian, in other words, who plays

---

[1] Phyllis Tickle, *The Great Emergence: How Christianity Is Changing and Why* (Grand Rapids: Baker Books, 2008) 72.

anything like the role of Calvin in the Reformed churches, or even that of Luther in Lutheranism.[2]

Without a strong authority to consolidate beliefs, Anglicanism incorporates a wide variety of believers, spanning the theological spectrum from liberal to conservative. As a 1963 *Time* magazine article on the declining membership within English parishes explains, "The Anglican faith encompasses Evangelical missionaries as fundamentalist as any Southern Baptist and such subtle, sophisticated minds as San Francisco's Bishop James A. Pike, who questions the virgin birth and speaks of 'demythologizing' the Resurrection." In the article, Einar Molland describes Anglicanism as "the most elastic church in Christendom."[3]

Given this malleability, Lewis must find authority within relatively wide theological parameters. He cannot avail himself of, say, the narrow and focused *ex cathedra* teachings of Roman Catholicism or the exacting doctrine of biblical inerrancy among American fundamentalists and evangelicals; authority must come elsewhere. In addition, authority must have widespread appeal, consolidating diverse believers around unifying forms of authority. Consequently, Anglicanism constitutes a microcosm of the public sphere—albeit a more homogenous microcosm since the Anglican church *does* unite most communicants around shared beliefs that normally do not require justification (whereas nearly all beliefs require justification within the public sphere). While Anglicanism recognizes Scripture, reason, and tradition as authoritative guides for belief, these forms of authority are, again, elastic. The plasticity of Lewis's own faith tradition not only explains the ecumenical spirit of a book like *Mere Christianity*, with its appeal to beliefs that unite Christians throughout time and throughout the world. It also explains Lewis's pressing need to shore up his various arguments by aligning them with the universalizing forms and sources of authority analyzed in this chapter.

## I. The Law of Human Nature

The Law of Human Nature constitutes a source of authority most prominently in *Mere Christianity* and *The Abolition of Man*. However, since the Law refers to innate, divinely originating standards of right and wrong, and

---

[2] Aidan Nichols, preface to *The Panther and the Hind: A Theological History of Anglicanism* (Edinburgh: T & T Clark, 1993) xvi–xvii.

[3] "Anglicans: Empty Pews, Full Spirit," *Time* (16 August 1963) Accessed 25 August 2009. http://www.time.com/time/magazine/article/0,9171,894600,00.html.

since nearly all of Lewis's popular books concern virtue and religion, the Law appears, either explicitly or implicitly, throughout the Lewis corpus.

It is illuminating for the purposes of my analysis that Richard Hooker's *Of the Laws of Ecclesiastical Polity* (1593) informs and influences Lewis's development of the Law, for Hooker's stance and strategy overlap with those of Lewis as public intellectual. Of course, Hooker wrote *Laws* before the rise of the public sphere, but Hooker confronted an historical event— continuing well beyond Hooker's lifetime—that developed alongside the birth of the public sphere, helping to shape its conventions. This historical event was the political rise and fall of Puritanism (as explained in chapter 2), the opposition to which generated a mythical notion of uniform human experience.

Hooker wrote *Laws* in order to defend the Anglican establishment from the charges of Puritan dissenters who denounced the Anglican prelatical organization as a diabolical, humanly constructed scheme: The Puritans instead upheld the primacy of Scripture to the complete exclusion of human reason, which, they claimed, as a quality of post-lapsarian humanity, is corrupt. As Peter Munz writes, the Puritans "did not believe that human or natural law, promulgated or discovered by reason, could have any validity whatever."[4] Thus, the Puritans questioned the orthodoxy of the Anglican belief system and considered it suspect within the pale of true Christianity. Hooker explains, "…we are accused as men that will not have Christ Jesus to rule over them, but have wilfully cast his statutes behind their backs, hating to be reformed and made subject unto the scepter of discipline."[5]

Hooker defends Anglicanism by appealing to a concept whose stabilizing and universalizing tendencies contrast with another form of Puritan authority, this one even more polarizing and subjectively interpreted than the Bible: "enthusiasm," the private, emotionally charged, and potentially volatile deliverances of the Holy Spirit. The first two definitions of the term in Samuel Johnson's 1755 dictionary underscore these qualities of enthusiasm: "1. A vain belief of private revelation; a vain confidence of divine favour or communication. 2. Heat of imagination; violence of passion; confidence of opinion."[6] The oppositional nature of Hooker's text includes a

---

[4] Peter Munz, *The Place of Hooker in the History of Thought* (London: Routledge & Kegan, 1952) 33.

[5] Richard Hooker, *Of the Laws of Ecclesiastical Polity*, ed. A. S. McGrade (New York: St. Martin's Press, 1975) 109.

[6] Samuel Johnson, "enthusiasm," in *Samuel Johnson's Dictionary: Selections from the 1755 Work that Defined the English Language*, ed. Jack Lynch (New York: Walker Publishing Company, Inc., 2003) 166.

rejection of Puritan enthusiasm and its potential for divisiveness, a potential later actualized during the English civil war.[7] Hooker writes of the dissenters, "When they and their Bibles were alone together, what strange and fantastical opinion soever at any time entered into their heads, their use was to think the Spirit taught it them."[8]

In defending the Law of Nature from the attacks of the Puritans, Hooker is thus likewise fending off the volatility and subjectivism of enthusiasm, appealing to a stabilizing concept that is universally binding on all humankind, regardless of creed or religious practice. Hooker defines the Law as "an infallible knowledge imprinted in the minds of all the children of men."[9] Here then is a solid and authoritative guide for theologizing, a guide that presupposes uniformity of experience because it directs through infallible knowledge the moral behavior of all humankind: Unlike Puritan enthusiasm, the Law is a form of knowledge that is undeniable to any who employ reason. Hooker's moves will become the process by which arguments, adhering to Enlightenment conventions, succeed in the public sphere.

They are the moves that Lewis follows, step by step, in *Mere Christianity*. The Law provides the basis authoritative enough for Lewis to marshal his most extensive argument for the existence of God. We might begin, however, by noting Lewis's respect for Hooker and his work. In *English Literature in the Sixteenth Century Excluding Drama*, he writes that *Laws* is the first work "on the Anglican side that was a resounding success." He praises its style: "The style is, for its purpose, perhaps the most perfect in English." But Lewis reserves his highest respect for Hooker's explanation of the forms of authority man is "created to live by." The first is Scripture. Lewis articulates the second: "There is another part, no less God-given, which Hooker calls 'nature' (Pref. vi. I), 'law rational, which men commonly use to call the Law of Nature' (I. viii. 9), 'the light of reason' (I. viii. 3). The most permanent value of Hooker's work lies in his defence of that light."[10]

Thus Lewis models his argument in *Mere Christianity* after Hooker's defense. Like Hooker, Lewis endows the Law of Nature with authority by emphasizing its universality. He writes,

---

[7] See part 1, ch. 2 for a more thorough assessment of these events.

[8] Hooker, *Of the Laws of Ecclesiastical Polity*, 97.

[9] Ibid., 183.

[10] C. S. Lewis, *English Literature in the Sixteenth Century Excluding Drama* (Oxford: Clarendon Press, 1944) 451–62.

This law was called the Law of Nature because people thought that every one knew it by nature and did not need to be taught it. They did not mean, of course, that you might not find an odd individual here and there who did not know it, just as you find a few people who are colour-blind or have no ear for a tune. But taking the race as a whole, they thought that the human idea of decent behaviour was obvious to every one.[11]

Those unaware of the Law of Nature are aberrations, possessing defects or deficiencies that exclude them from what Lewis calls in *The Problem of Pain* "the common ground of humanity."[12] Like Hooker, Lewis shows that no one can abide by the Law of Nature; that is, no one can follow the dictates of right and wrong that exist naturally in the individual. Like Hooker, Lewis affirms that humankind's innate awareness of general morality, which exists universally in the minds of men and women, and which, nevertheless, cannot be upheld, finds its source in the wellsprings of God's being.

The comparison between Hooker and Lewis illustrates the process by which the Law of Nature amasses authority in the public sphere. The sort of opposition Hooker registers to Puritan accusations will become the animus that helps give birth to the public sphere. Distrust of enthusiasm (a subjective, unpredictable, and unverifiable experience) motivates the formation of an objective, neutral space of rational/critical debate: a space where the Law of Nature, with its universalizing sweep, achieves authority and compels assent. After all, how can one disagree with an argument that is built upon a uniform moral experience? With the exception of those with defective faculties, *all* humankind is experientially aware of these moral precepts. Hooker thus participates in a polemical phenomenon that will become definitive of public discourse and the procedural guidelines of the Enlightenment, conventionalized into what I have termed de-conversion and uniform experience. (Phrased differently, justifying truth claims in the public sphere will recapitulate some of the moves of Hooker's argument.) Like Hooker, Lewis operates within a faith tradition that operates as a microcosm of the public sphere—in Hooker's case, of course, a proleptic microcosm of the public sphere. Unlike Hooker, Lewis, as public intellectual, marshals arguments after the public sphere has fundamentally structured public discourse, after its conventions—so amenable to the Law of Nature—have been hardened. For Lewis, then, the Law of Nature is an especially powerful source and form of authority.

---

[11] C. S. Lewis, *Mere Christianity* (San Francisco: HarperSanFrancisco, 2001) 5.

[12] C. S. Lewis, *The Problem of Pain* (San Francisco: HarperSanFrancisco, 2001) 14–15.

The Law of Nature as Lewis develops it does not merely refer to moral precepts. It also refers to basic emotional responses, especially emotional responses to aesthetic experiences. Lewis registers this aspect of the Law in *The Abolition of Man*, though he there employs the term *Tao*. He defines it thusly: "It is the reality beyond all predicates, the abyss that was before the Creator Himself. It is Nature, the Way, the Road."[13] The *Tao* resembles the Law of Nature in its universality; it is not localized in a specific society or culture, but transcends them all. Neither is it of human origin; it is built into the cosmos. It also resembles the Law of Nature because it is a "recognition of objective value," value that is measured not only in terms of right and wrong, but good and bad as well. Thus, the *Tao* encompasses both ethics and aesthetics. It builds and expands upon the authority that the Law of Nature commands by endowing both morality and aesthetic value judgments with objectivity.

Like the Law of Nature, the *Tao* presupposes a type of uniform experience. In *The Abolition of Man*, Lewis critiques an English textbook that renders as purely subjective all emotional responses to nature and art. The authors of the textbook claim, for instance, that when we describe a waterfall as being "sublime," "we '*appear* to be saying something very important' when in reality we are '*only* saying something about our own feelings.'" Such teaching, Lewis warns, reduces "all values" to something "subjective and trivial." [14]

Lewis refutes this teaching, of course, by appealing to the *Tao*, which provides "an objective order" whereby "emotional states can be in harmony with reason (when we feel liking for what ought to be approved) or out of harmony with reason (when we perceive that liking is due but cannot feel it). No emotion is, in itself, a judgement: in that sense all emotions and sentiments are alogical. But they can be reasonable or unreasonable as they conform to Reason or fail to conform."[15] Lewis's objection to the subjective ("and trivial") compels him to underscore the objective. In Lewis's formulation, to experience the waterfall or a work of art under the guiding principles of the *Tao* is to experience it as all properly reasonable people would experience it; it is to enter the common ground of humanity. Like the Law of Nature, the *Tao* universalizes: with the exception of those with defective faculties—those who do not conform to reason—all people recognize the principle of objective value. Both the Law of Nature and the

---

[13] C. S. Lewis, *The Abolition of Man* (New York: Collier Books, 1955) 28.
[14] Ibid., 17.
[15] Ibid., 30.

*Tao* presuppose a uniformity of experience that resonates in the public sphere, making them powerful sources and forms of authority.

Lewis's adherence to the universalizing guidelines of the public sphere should not be taken to mean that he was not attentive to difference. He obviously was. However, his position on difference varies depending upon the two perspectives he most commonly adopted during his career: Christian writer (public intellectual) or literary scholar. I begin with the position that proceeds from his identity as Christian writer/public intellectual.

## II. Difference from the Perspective of the Public Intellectual

Lewis as public intellectual is ever the polemicist, defending either the existence or Judeo-Christian nature of God or general principles (like the Law of Nature and the *Tao*) that are consistent with Christianity. Consequently, qualifications with respect to difference that allow for too much flexibility within these claims and principles concede too much. The positions most associated with Lewis's name as public intellectual—all of which arise from his fundamental commitment to "mere Christianity"—minimize difference and emphasize continuity.

I take as representative the argument Lewis fleshes out in his essay titled "Dogma and the Universe," an essay that aims, in fact, to adjudicate between the rival demands of progress, on the one hand, and the immutability of Christian dogma, on the other. As Lewis puts it, "How can an unchanging system survive the continual increase of knowledge?" Lewis answers this question by first clarifying terms, making a distinction between "change" and "progress." By virtue of his commitment to essentialism and conservatism, Lewis assumes progress can only build upon a core or essence that has already been established. Change occurs when that core or essence is altered, resulting in "chaos." Lewis illustrates his position by proposing a hypothetical "great statesman" who must consider a law that carries moral repercussions for a society. He states that "…only in so far as that first knowledge of the great moral platitudes survives unimpaired in the statesman will his deliberation be moral at all. If that goes, then there has been no progress, but only mere change."[16] In this instance, then, progress can only occur when what Lewis considers to be the foundations of

---

[16] C. S. Lewis, "Dogma and the Universe," in *God in the Dock: Essays on Theology and Ethics*, ed. Walter Hooper, ed. Walter Hooper (Grand Rapids: Eerdmans, 1970) 44–45.

morality—the Law of Nature, the *Tao*—remain intact. Difference is thus minimized when progress is given a short leash; progress follows the trajectory established by the core or essence.

The minimization of difference applies to the doctrines of Christianity as well. In the same essay, Lewis addresses the problem of conflicting interpretations of the creation account in the book of Genesis:

> When the author of Genesis says that God made man in His own image, he may have pictured a vaguely corporeal God making man as a child makes a figure out of plasticine. A modern Christian philosopher may think of a process lasting from the first creation of matter to the final appearance on this planet of an organism fit to receive spiritual as well as biological life. But both mean essentially the same thing. Both are denying the same thing—the doctrine that matter by some blind power inherent in itself has produced spirituality. Does this mean that Christians on different levels of general education conceal radically different beliefs under an identical form of words? Certainly not. For what they agree on is the substance, and what they differ about is the shadow.[17]

The first of these disparate interpretations of Genesis follows what Lewis would probably have recognized as a fundamentalist position: that God *directly* created humankind. The second is the position Lewis himself proposes in *The Problem of Pain*, a position that admits certain aspects of the evolutionary account: that man evolved from single-cell organisms, becoming *Homo sapiens*, at approximately which time he was fitted to receive the breath of God and become a biological *and* spiritual creature. That these disparate interpretations amount to a nominal difference is possible. But the testament of history—from the formation of fundamentalism in the early twentieth century to the culture wars of the late twentieth century—suggests that the conflicting opinions on this issue have been acrimoniously disputed among many Christians and that they do produce, in the minds of the disputants, "radically different beliefs" about the nature of God and the inspiration of Scripture. Of course, as an Englishman and practicing Anglican, Lewis was positioned to steer clear of the heated controversies that embroiled American Christianity. My purpose, however, is not to show why or how he minimized differences of opinion, but *that* he minimized differences of opinion specifically when they pertain to Christian doctrine and its underlying philosophical principles.

In an essay entitled "On Ethics," Lewis minimizes some of these underlying philosophical principles as they concern ethical differences

---

[17] Ibid., 46.

across cultures. He asks, "…may we not recognize in modern thought a very serious exaggeration of the ethical differences between different cultures?" Lewis traces this exaggeration to the modern fixation on "ideologies," a "word that suggests that the whole moral and philosophical outlook of a people can be explained without remainder in terms of their method of production, their economic organization, and their geographical position."[18] A focus on ideology connects a culture's moral and philosophical outlook to that culture's particularities: its means of subsistence and location on a map. It reduces fundamental beliefs to anthropological contingency.

Such a focus unmoors the moral and philosophical outlook from the core or essence described earlier. In short, such a focus overemphasizes difference. "But is [such difference]," asks Lewis, "what we actually find? Much anthropology seems at first to encourage us to answer Yes. But if I may venture an opinion in a field where I am by no means an expert, I would suggest that the appearance is somewhat illusory."[19] Lewis's opposition to ideology (as a hermeneutical grid) thus resembles his opposition to Bulverism. Both forms of opposition privilege objectivity, mobilize what I have called de-conversion, and minimize differences across societies and cultures.

## III. Difference from the Perspective of the Literary Scholar

As a scholar of literary history, Lewis was aware of the ways in which historical time and place shape literary representations. In fact, in *A Preface to Paradise Lost*, Lewis explores how students can fully enter the fictional worlds projected by poets of a bygone era whose society, customs, and ideas differ radically from those of the modern world; his exploration is informed by an acknowledgment of historical particularity. In addition, Lewis rejects one method of bridging the gaps between historical epochs—a method built upon a principle he calls "The Unchanging Human Heart"—because it minimizes difference. "According to this method," writes Lewis, "the things which separate one age from another are superficial. Just as, if we stripped the armour off a medieval knight or the lace off a Caroline courtier, we should find beneath them an anatomy identical with our own, so, it is held, if we strip off from Virgil his Roman imperialism…we shall find the

---

[18] C. S. Lewis, "Christianity and Culture," in *Christian Reflections*, ed. Walter Hooper (Grand Rapids: Eerdmans, 1967) 54.
[19] Ibid.

Unchanging Human Heart, and on this we should concentrate."[20] Stripping humankind to its essence is not conducive to a meaningful reading of poetry. Instead, Lewis counters, students of poetry must momentarily *become* a part of the world the text projects, acknowledging and experiencing historical difference. Lewis explains,

> To enjoy our full humanity we ought, so far as is possible, to contain within us potentially at all times, and on occasion to actualize, all the modes of feeling and thinking through which man has passed. You must, so far as in you lies, become an Achaean chief while reading Homer, a medieval knight while reading Malory, and an eighteenth century Londoner while reading Johnson. Only thus will you be able to judge the work "in the same spirit that its author writ" and to avoid chimerical criticism.[21]

Lewis's opposition to the doctrine of the Unchanging Human Heart may seem to contravene his essentialism—his belief, for instance, in moral absolutes that fundamentally structure all experience, constituting the essence of what it means to be human. However, the passage above shows that Lewis simply reconstitutes essentialism in a different form. He universalizes not by reduction (the doctrine of the Unchanging Human Heart) but by accumulation. He locates the foundations of human experience not by stripping man to his essence but by harmonizing the differences that proceed from the assumed essence. Containing within us "all modes of feeling and thinking through which man has passed" engages our "full humanity." Employing Lewis's reading strategy, difference, in short, will amount to unity.

Universalizing by accumulation is what Lewis has in mind in his volume of the *Oxford History of English Literature* when he identifies Edmund Spenser, Philip Sidney, and Shakespeare (in fact, any "sincere and serious poet") as syncretists. Such poets meld diverse expressions of human experience—"all the modes of feeling and thinking through which man has passed"—to create representations of "full humanity." They find the bedrock of human experience by uniting the particularized forms of thought and feeling into a unified whole. "The agreements," writes Lewis, "are the important thing, the useful and interesting thing." United into a whole, what

---

[20] C. S. Lewis, *A Preface to Paradise Lost* (Oxford: Oxford University Press, 1961) 64–65.
[21] Ibid., 64.

Shakespeare creates cannot be identified as "his philosophy"; "he would have called it," concludes Lewis, "common knowledge."[22]

Awareness of "common knowledge" and of the agreements that overarch differences becomes most acute when historical consciousness is broadened—when wide swaths of time are mobilized for the actualization of modes of thought and experience. For this reason, Lewis cannot restrict a literary text's meaning to its author's intentions. In his essay "On Criticism," Lewis defines literary meaning as "the series or system of emotions, reflections, and attitudes produced by reading [a literary text]."[23] While an author can intend to produce certain emotions, reflections, and attitudes in the readers, only readings and re-readings of the text across the centuries can identify which of those emotions, reflections, and attitudes are most consonant with the common experience of humankind. Lewis explains,

> The ideally true or right "meaning" would be that shared (in some measure) by the largest number of the best readers after repeated and careful readings over several generations, different periods, nationalities, moods, degrees of alertness, private pre-occupations, states of health, spirits, and the like cancelling one another out when (this is an important reservation) they cannot be fused so as to enrich one another.[24]

Subjected to centuries of interpretation, the literary text passes through a hermeneutical crucible that forges its true meaning, which accumulates over time through a process of interpretive syncretism. Idiosyncratic interpretations—that is, readings characterized by difference—are rejected when they cannot be harmonized with the syncretized interpretive core: the unified interpretation. In a 1952 letter, Lewis identifies this process as interpretation "by a composite mind."[25] Achieving an Olympian interpretive perspective, the composite mind minimizes difference, winnowing out interpretive aberrations that do not accord with "common knowledge," and finds literary meaning in the deliverances of a critical voice that speaks for generations. This critical voice is a powerful source and form of authority, one that overlaps with the next form of authority I wish to analyze in Lewis's writings.

---

[22] Lewis, *English Literature in the Sixteenth Century*, 387.

[23] C. S. Lewis, "On Criticism," in *On Stories and Other Essays on Literature*, ed. Walter Hooper (San Diego: Harcourt Brace & Company, 1982) 139.

[24] Ibid., 139–40.

[25] C. S. Lewis to Wayland Hilton Young, 24 February 1952, *The Collected Letters of C. S. Lewis*, vol. 1, *Family Letters, 1905–1931*, ed. Walter Hooper (San Francisco: HarperSanFrancisco, 2007) 168.

## IV. High Tradition

From a young age, Lewis filtered life experiences through the books he read. He tended to orient his perspective of the world around descriptions in books. For instance, here is Lewis's description of Great Bookham in 1914, when he was just fifteen years old: "One was strongly reminded of 'As you like it [sic]'. The village is one such as I have often read of, but never before seen. The little row of red roofed cottages, the old inn, and the church dating from the Conquest might all have stepped out of the Vicar of Wakefield."[26] A letter written one year later shows how he lived vicariously through the experiences of poets and literary characters: "But though I have no personal experience of the thing they call love, I have what is better—the experience of Sapho [sic], of Euripides of Catullus of Shakespeare of Spenser of Austen of Bronte of, of—anyone else I have read. We see through their eyes."[27] Indeed, the recipient of this letter—Lewis's longtime friend Arthur Greeves—became frustrated and hurt by Lewis's literary tunnel vision, annoyed that their conversations always fell back upon the subject of books and *belles lettres*. This frustration and annoyance are evident in a 1916 letter that Lewis wrote to Greeves:

> So you feel hurt that I should think you worth talking to only about books, music, etc.: in other words that I keep my friendship with you only for the highest plane of life: that I leave to others all the sordid and uninteresting worries about so-called practical life, and share with you those joys and experiences which make that life desirable: that—but now I am getting rhetorical. It must be the influence of dear Sidney and his euphuism I suppose. But seriously, what can you have been thinking about when you said "only" books, music, etc., just as if these weren't the real things![28]

For Lewis, literature was more than a mere simulacrum of reality; literature was constitutive of reality. K. J. Gilchrist crystallizes this claim when he observes "Lewis's persistence in viewing a fictional world and its characters as Real, viewing literary experience, despite its vicarious nature, as existing on the same plane as one's own actual experience."[29]

---

[26] C. S. Lewis to Albert Lewis, 21 September 1914, *Collected Letters*, 1:69.

[27] C. S. Lewis to Arthur Greeves, 12 October 1915, *Collected Letters*, 1:146.

[28] C. S. Lewis to Arthur Greeves, 4 July 1916, *Collected Letters*, 1:205.

[29] K. J. Gilchrist, *A Morning after War: C. S. Lewis and WWI* (New York: Peter Lang, 2005) 22.

Lewis's literary-infused perspective explains his ubiquitous appeal to what I call *high tradition*, a form of authority in the public sphere that refers to the cumulative wisdom of Western civilization.[30] High tradition crystallizes into one principle what Lewis considers the syncretist function of great poets, as explained earlier: shoring up consensus from a sea of particularity, finding unity that supersedes diversity. The appeal to high tradition, of course, is not unique to Lewis. It is woven into the fabric of the Great Books curriculum at Oxford; it is therefore part of the intellectual spirit that Lewis imbibed for approximately thirty years. High tradition lies at the heart of what T. S. Eliot calls in a 1919 essay the "historical sense," which, he insists,

> we may call nearly indispensable to any one who would continue to be a poet beyond his twenty-fifth year; and the historical sense involves a perception, not only of the pastness of the past, but of its presence; the historical sense compels a man to write not merely with his own generation in his bones, but with a feeling that the whole of the literature of Europe from Homer and within it the whole of the literature of his own country has a simultaneous existence and composes a simultaneous order.[31]

The historical sense is an expanding literary consciousness that absorbs the past and the present.

While the historical sense and high tradition clearly share commonalities, high tradition takes on near divine qualities. For instance, it possesses—in a God-like manner—both transcendence and imminence: transcendence in that it rises above the volatility of the discrete present moment and arranges itself into an ordered, continuous whole; imminence in that the transcendent order engages the present moment, appropriating it into something larger than itself. One of Lewis's own felicitous phrasings to describe God aptly characterizes the nature of high tradition: "unbounded Now"—a phrase Lewis derives (in the very spirit of high tradition) from

---

[30] I am indebted here to Michael D. Aeschliman, who writes, "What Lewis trusted was the fund of 'common sense' of men throughout history, the *communis sensus* of Vincent of Lerins, what Alexander Pope was referring to when he wrote that 'whatever is very good sense must have common sense in all times': the vast common sense of humanity, of which he felt he was a trustee and which he articulated and defended in all of his writing, speaking, and living." See *The Restitution of Man: C. S. Lewis and the Case Against Scientism* (Grand Rapids: Eerdmans, 1983) 3.

[31] T. S. Eliot, "Tradition and the Individual Talent," in *Selected Essays* (New York: Harcourt, Brace & World, 1964) 4.

Boethius.[32] These divine qualities link high tradition to the Law of Nature as well as the *Tao*. They all transcend time and place, essentialize human experience, and offer universal and immutable truth. These qualities make all three formidable sources of authority within the public sphere. The difference between these forms of authority concerns their origin: while the Law of Nature and the *Tao* flow from the wellspring of God's being, high tradition is of human origin; but the vast accumulation of human thought and feeling achieves, over time, a divine status.

While high tradition finds individual expression in the theories of Eliot and institutional expression in the Great Books curriculum at Oxford, Lewis's unique appropriation of the concept relates back to his function as public intellectual. Lewis presents high tradition (as a form of authority) to the diverse audience of the public sphere. As James Patrick explains, "There had been many notable advocates of the unity of the European mind, among them Hulme, Collingwood, and Eliot. But it was in Lewis's works that the quest for unity in its inescapable combination with Christianity passed out of the academy and into the lives of ordinary folk."[33] Lewis stands alone as translator to the lay audience of high tradition, assembling arguments upon this authoritative foundation.

## V. High Tradition and Literary Studies

It is helpful, however, to examine Lewis's development of high tradition in his literary scholarship. Doing so will help us understand the theoretical principles that undergird the practical task of bringing high tradition to the layperson. *The Discarded Image* reveals that employing high tradition involves much more than simply quoting from authors of the past. The medieval writer, as Lewis characterizes him in that text, serves as an exponent of high tradition. First, medieval writers make little attempt at originality; they *depend* upon earlier writers, borrowing and recapitulating their ideas. Second, medieval writers used books as a fundamental source of authority. While pagan civilization developed a culture, "in part unconsciously, from participation in the immemorial pattern of behaviour, and in part by word of mouth, from the old men of the tribe"; and while knowledge in the twentieth century is derived from observation, the

---

[32] C. S. Lewis, *The Screwtape Letters* (San Francisco: HarperSanFrancisco, 2001) 150.

[33] James Patrick, *The Magdalen Metaphysicals: Idealism and Orthodoxy at Oxford 1901–1945* (Macon GA: Mercer University Press, 1985) 131.

formation of culture and the acquisition of knowledge in "the Middle Ages depended predominately on books." Medieval people, Lewis succinctly states, "are bookish." Finally, medieval writers, like the "serious and sincere" poets discussed earlier, were syncretists. They "were, perhaps half-consciously, gathering together and harmonising views of very different origin: building a syncretistic Model not only out of Platonic, Aristotelian, and Stoical, but out of Pagan and Christian elements. This Model the Middle Ages adopted and perfected."[34] Lewis's fondness for the Middle Ages spills over into his own practice: these three qualities of the medieval writer characterize Lewis as well. In following earlier writers (making no attempt at originality), using them as his authorities, and harmonizing their ideas, Lewis follows what he calls the "Model of the Middle Ages," summoning high tradition as a form of authority.

In *An Experiment in Criticism*, Lewis shows how high tradition avoids the myopia of individual perspectives, which, at best, particularize and thus distort views of reality and, at worst, taint vision with a toxic narcissism. "In coming to understand anything," contends Lewis as he clarifies the nature of true knowledge, "we are rejecting the facts as they are for us in favour of the facts as they are." This contention seems motivated in part by Lewis's antipathy toward subjectivism and consequently his reliance upon objectivity, which in turn evokes what I have called the process of de-conversion. De-conversion momentarily empties the self, a process that seems implicit when Lewis avers that the biased and self-serving perspective of the individual compels us to "want to be more than ourselves."[35] Reading good literature written over the centuries—i.e., participating in high tradition—enables this expansion of being. As Lewis states in his essay titled "On the Reading of Old Books," the "only palliative" for the provincialism and narrow mindedness of the modern view "is to keep the clean sea breeze of the centuries blowing through our minds...."[36]

Employing a paradox found throughout his writings, however, Lewis maintains that high tradition—"literary experience" is the term he uses in this context—"heals the wound, without undermining the privilege, of individuality."[37] That is, high tradition creates true individuality by

---

[34] C. S. Lewis, *The Discarded Image: An Introduction to Medieval and Renaissance Literature* (Cambridge: Cambridge University Press, 1964) 11.

[35] C. S. Lewis, *An Experiment in Criticism* (Cambridge: Cambridge University Press, 1961) 137.

[36] C. S. Lewis, "On the Reading of Old Books," in *God in the Dock*, 202.

[37] Lewis, *An Experiment in Criticism*, 140.

expanding individual consciousness—a process identical to Eliot's notion of the "historical sense"—and thus enlarges the self while avoiding the biased obfuscations and poisonous narcissism of subjectivism. Lewis explains, "But in reading great literature I become a thousand men and yet remain myself. Like the night sky in the Greek poem, I see with myriad eyes, but it is still I who see. Here, as in worship, in love, in moral action, and in knowing, I transcend myself; and am never more myself than when I do."[38] The modes of feeling and thought that have endured through the centuries thus permeate the individual consciousness, correcting its particularities and thus forging an oxymoronic collective individuality.

Lewis invokes this paradox in *Mere Christianity* when he explains how believers submit themselves to God—dying to self—and become part of the body of Christ, a collective affiliation that generates true individuality: "It is only Christians who have any idea of how human souls can be taken into the life of God and yet remain themselves—in fact, be very much more themselves than they were before."[39] High tradition thus has its equivalent in the spiritual realm, the two types mirroring each other by enlarging identity and universalizing consciousness into a transcendent, invisible collective body: high tradition in the worldly realm and the Church in the spiritual realm.

Unlike its mirrored counterpart in the spiritual realm, however, high tradition is beholden to Enlightenment principles and thus the conventions of the public sphere. This is evident in high tradition's functional reliance upon objectivity, de-conversion, and universalizing tendencies. The indebtedness appears in more subtle ways when Lewis analogizes the expansion of the self through literary experience to the expansion of the self in the moral sphere. Within that sphere, Lewis writes, "every act of justice or charity involves putting ourselves in the other person's place and thus transcending our own competitive particularity."[40] Lewis here draws from the ideas of Adam Smith in his 1759 text, *The Theory of Moral Sentiments* (1759), a work squarely ensconced within the tradition and assumptions of the Enlightenment.

Smith codified many of the conventional attributes of sympathy, a popular eighteenth-century emotion that is often thematized in sentimental scenes of novels of the period, like Oliver Goldsmith's *The Vicar of Wakefield* (1766) and Laurence Sterne's *A Sentimental Journey* (1768). In the opening

---

[38] Ibid., 141.

[39] Lewis, *Mere Christianity*, 161.

[40] Lewis, *An Experiment in Criticism*, 141.

sections of *The Theory of Moral Sentiments,* Smith underscores the vicarious emotive power of suffering—the ease with which it is transmitted from sufferer to beholder, producing an encompassing and penetrating sense of sympathy: This quotation from the opening section also informs Lewis's statement above on the moral sphere:

> Tho our brother is upon the rack, as long as we ourselves are at our ease, our senses will never carry us beyond our own person, and it is by the imagination only that we can form any conception of what are his sensations.... By the imagination we place ourselves in the situation, we conceive ourselves enduring all the same torments, we enter as it were into his body, and become in some measure the same person with him, and thence form some idea of his sensations, and even feel something, which, tho weaker in degree, is not altogether unlike them.[41]

This whole process necessitates the exposure of the private, the relocation of the personal into the public. Private emotion is brought onto the Enlightenment stage, where it is assessed according to the guidelines of public discourse and approved if it conforms to the general consensus. The public, in other words, places itself in the place of an individual and asks, "Does this emotion that we vicariously experience agree with our own understanding of emotional experiences?" As Smith claims, "To approve or disapprove of the opinions of others is acknowledged to mean no more than to observe their agreement or disagreement with our own."[42] Privately experienced and privately held emotions and opinions are removed from their particular contexts and evaluated within the context of the public sphere. Lewis's allusion to Smith thus highlights high tradition's affinity for the universalizing tendencies of Enlightenment discourse.

Lewis's assumptions about the nature of literature and learning endow his appeal to high tradition with the potential ability not only to convey authoritative knowledge but to shape behavior and transform worldview. Literature, as Lewis sees it, has power to shape emotions and change lives. In *The Screwtape Letters,* for instance, the eponymous character endorses for his demonic purposes something he calls the "Historical Point of View," a perspective adopted primarily by the learned. According to the Historical Point of View, in studying writers of the past, the learned person restricts inquiry to esoteric scholarly questions—for instance, "who influenced the ancient writer, and how far the statement is consistent with what he said in

---

[41] Adam Smith, *The Theory of Moral Sentiments* (Amherst NY: Prometheus Books, 2000) 9.

[42] Ibid., 17.

other books, and what phase in the writer's development, or in the general history of thought, it illustrates, and how it affected later writers, and how often it has been misunderstood (specially by the learned man's own colleagues) and what the general course of criticism on it has been for the last ten years, and what is the 'present state of the question'."[43] The Historical Point of View, Screwtape implies, de-capacitates literature, confining its use to mere pedantry.

Consistent with the very principles of high tradition, Lewis instead follows the literary models of the Western civilization—Horace, Philip Sidney, Johnson—in maintaining that the purpose of literature, as well as the Great Books tradition in general, is to delight and instruct. Concluding his thoughts on the Historical Point of View, Screwtape remarks, "To regard the ancient writer as a possible source of knowledge—to anticipate that what he said could possibly modify your thoughts or your behaviour—this would be rejected as unutterably simple-minded."[44] This didacticism—the performativity of high tradition—well serves Lewis as public intellectual, for, by virtue of this identity, Lewis's arguments appeal to the layperson, not getting bogged down in scholarly minutiae, and (when most successful) engage the whole person, mind and soul, and thereby transforming lives.

## VI. High Tradition and Transcendence

Arguments from high tradition—like arguments from the Law of Nature—proceed from a transcendent authority, one that overarches the vicissitudes of time and unites humankind around the notion of uniform experience. In the letter quoted above, Screwtape asserts that the Historical Point of View helps "to cut every generation off from all others; for where learning makes a free commerce between the ages there is always the danger that the characteristic errors of one may be corrected by the characteristic truths of another."[45] High tradition, the antithesis of the Historical Point of View, places all ages into dialogue (the Great Conversation of the Oxford curriculum), enabling universal truth and uniform experience to emerge from the dialectic of the generations. One sees this process in action in Lewis's essay, "Why I Am Not a Pacifist." He holds this position on war because to do otherwise would be to defy high tradition: "To be a Pacifist, I must part company with Homer and Virgil, with Plato and Aristotle, with

---

[43] Lewis, *The Screwtape Letters*, 150–51.
[44] Ibid., 151.
[45] Ibid.

Zarathustra and the *Bhagavad-Gita*, with Cicero and Montaigne, with Iceland and with Egypt." The voices of the past unite in chorus, proclaiming the occasional necessity of war. "From this point of view," Lewis concludes, "I am almost tempted to reply to the Pacifist as Johnson replied to Goldsmith, 'Nay, Sir, if you will not take the universal opinion of mankind, I have no more to say.' I am aware that, though Hooker thought 'the general and perpetual voice of men is as the sentence of God Himself,' yet many who hear will give it little or no weight."[46]

The accumulation of assent through the ages on any given issue approximates the very pronouncement of the Almighty. Although it has human origins, high tradition, in fact, constitutes a simulacrum of God. In this way, Lewis smuggles transcendence into the secular public sphere, resting his arguments on a quasi-divine form and source of authority.

As a simulacrum of God, high tradition naturally evidences the existence of the deity. Like the Law of Nature, high tradition flows from the wellsprings of God's being. Affirmation of Christianity in the canonical writers of Western civilization constitutes an authoritative testament to the truth of the faith. Such is Lewis's claim in his essay titled "On the Reading of Old Books":

> In the days when I still hated Christianity, I learned to recognize, like some familiar smell, that almost unvarying *something* which met me, now in Puritan Bunyan, now in Anglican Hooker, now in Thomist Dante. It was there (honeyed and floral) in Francois de Sales; it was there (grave and homely) in Spenser and Walton; it was there (grim but manful) in Pascal and Johnson; there again, with a mild, frightening, Paradisial flavour, in Vaughan and Boehme and Traherne. In the urban sobriety of the eighteenth century one was not safe—Law and Butler were two lions in the path. The supposed "Paganism" of the Elizabethans could not keep it out; it lay in wait where a man might have supposed himself safest, in the very centre of *The Faerie Queene* and the *Arcadia*. It was, of course, varied; and yet—after all—so unmistakably the same; recognizable, not to be evaded, the odour which is death to us until we allow it to become life....[47]

---

[46] C. S. Lewis, "Why I Am Not a Pacifist," in *The Weight of Glory and Other Addresses*, ed. Walter Hooper (New York: Simon & Schuster, 1980) 65.

[47] C. S. Lewis, "On the Reading of Old Books," in *God in the Dock*, 203–204. Lewis also describes the inescapably Christian identity of writers within the sweep of Western Civilization in chapter fourteen of *Surprised by Joy* (1984).

We see here again the self-correcting function of high tradition: through the erosion of time, the diverse expressions of Christianity are reduced to an essence; permutations of doctrine are either abandoned or are harmonized with the core. From the temporal tumults of sectarian strife and denominational difference emerges a trans-temporal, mere Christianity. In a 1939 letter to his brother, Lewis suggests that the historical testament to Christianity in the great writers of the past must unnerve the atheist: "...how on earth did we manage to enjoy all these books so much as we did in the days when we had really no conception of what was at the centre of them [when they were atheists]? Sir, he who embraces the Christian revelation rejoins the main tide of human existence!"[48] Like the pacifist, the atheist ignores or denies "common knowledge"; both the pacifist and the atheist are aberrations in history, denying the truths that have withstood and thus transcended the passage of time. Lewis's claims about the existence and Judeo-Christian nature of God proceed with borrowed momentum, for the source of authority from which he draws presumes from the outset the truth of the very arguments he constructs.

## VII. High Tradition and the Lay Reader

As public intellectual, Lewis must marshal these arguments from high tradition with widespread appeal. Indeed, the role of the public intellectual highlights the demanding requirement placed upon this discursive identity: a scholar, with a solid command of intellectual history, translating with journalistic accessibility complex ideas and arguments to the layperson. The very presence of high tradition within the public sphere emblematizes the tension between the erudite, elite scholar and the populist nature of his or her audience.

As a previous chapter has shown, however, Lewis was far from elitist: his concern for the salvation of one person—scholar or not—far outweighed his allegiance to his guild. High tradition is thus not merely academic territory, the domain of the scholar. It is a source of authority universally relevant, binding on everyone from the Oxford don to the chimney sweep. This is a lesson that Lewis learned, at least in part, from Owen Barfield. When Lewis once referred to philosophy as "'a subject," Barfield retorted, "'It wasn't a *subject* to Plato...it was a way.'"[49] Lewis's popular books operate on this same principle: high tradition is a way.

---

[48] C. S. Lewis to Warren Lewis, 18 December 1939, *Collected Letters*, 2:305.
[49] Lewis, *Surprised by Joy*, 225.

An overview of some of Lewis's popular books reveals the crucial presence of high tradition. In *Mere Christianity*, Lewis employs an analogy to convey its principles. Responding to a military officer who rejects theology, having no use for it since he claims to have had firsthand experiences of God in the desert, Lewis contrasts the authority of experience and the authority of tradition. Writes Lewis of the military officer, "I think he had probably had a real experience of God in the desert. And when he turned from that experience to the Christian creeds, I think he really was turning from something real to something less real." Lewis then deploys an analogy:

> In the same way, if a man has once looked at the Atlantic form the beach, and then goes and looks at a map of the Atlantic, he also will be turning from something real to something less real: turning from real waves to a bit of coloured paper. But here comes the point. The map is admittedly only coloured paper, but there are two things you have to remember about it. In the first place, it is based on what hundreds and thousands of people have found out by sailing the real Atlantic. In that way it has behind it masses of experience just as real as the one you could have from the beach; only, while yours would be a single glimpse, the map fits all those different experiences together.[50]

The shortsightedness of the single glimpse—the individual's experience of God—contrasts with the bird's-eye view afforded by the study of theology, the metaphorical map that is sketched by hundreds of Christians through the centuries who also have had experiences of God. High tradition enters *Mere Christianity* through Lewis's winsomely drawn analogy.

High tradition in *The Screwtape Letters* is more straightforward. Screwtape seems aware of the authority that high tradition possesses, fearful that humans might use it for guidance. For instance, Screwtape writes to Wormwood that humans' misunderstanding of God's relation to time leads to subsequent confusion about petitionary prayer. How can God answer prayers if he knows in advance the outcome? Screwtape, of course, knows that God exists above time and therefore knows nothing in advance but in an eternal present; God can thus hear the prayer and answer the prayer simultaneously in some ineffable, temporality-defying fashion. Then comes Screwtape's warning: "It may be replied that some meddlesome human writers, notably Boethius, have let this secret out."[51] Screwtape even seems to be aware of Hooker's and Aquinas's theories of communion, for he uses them to orient his advice to Wormwood on the subject: "The real fun is

---

[50] Lewis, *Mere Christianity*, 154.
[51] Lewis, *The Screwtape Letters*, 150.

working up hatred between those who *say* 'mass' and those who *say* 'holy communion' when neither party could possibly state the difference between, say, Hooker's doctrine and Thomas Aquinas', in any form which would hold water for five minutes."[52]

The following list of authors and thinkers quoted or referenced in *The Screwtape Letters* attests that high tradition plays an important role in the text (even if it is for Screwtape's diabolical purposes): Homer, Maritain, Byron, Goethe, Coleridge, Hooker, Aquinas, Milton, Shaw, Boethius, Shakespeare, Swift, Socrates, Marx, and Kant. Even in the brief *Screwtape Proposes a Toast*, Screwtape grounds and hinges his address on the authors of high tradition: Rousseau, Hegel, Aristotle, Aeschylus, and Dante. Lewis's works of nonfiction make use of an even more extensive network of references, all of which engage high tradition.

Here are the quoted or referenced authors in *The Problem of Pain*: Ptolemy, Rudolph Otto, Shakespeare, Kenneth Grahame, Malory, Ovid, Virgil, a fragment attributed to Aeschylus, Dante, Plato, Aristotle, Milton, George MacDonald, Zarathustra, Gautama Buddha, Marcus Aurelius, William Law, Augustine, Newman, Hobbes, Hardy, Housman, Aldous Huxley, Kant, Johnson, William Paley, Hooker, William Cowper, Marlowe, Aquinas, von Hugel, and the anonymous author of *Theologica Germanica*.

In *The Four Loves*, the references include Plato, MacDonald, Lewis Carroll, Thomas á Kempis, M. Denis de Rougemont, Browning, Coventry Patmore, Shakespeare, Sidney, Wordsworth, Coleridge, Kipling, Chesterton, the author of the *Song of Roland*, the author of the French romance *Amis et Amiles*, Aristotle, Cicero, Dante, the *Beowulf* author, Boswell, Melville, Emerson, Jean Froissart, Bunyan William Dunbar, George Orwell, Lucretius, Milton, Freud, Richard Wagner, Mozart, Thomas Browne, St. Francis, Shaw, Tolstoy, William Morris, Augustine, Richard Lovelace, Lady Julian of Norwich, Housman, and Hardy.

One would be hard pressed to identify any other popular books—that is, books written for the non-specialist—with such extensive references as *The Screwtape Letters*, *The Problem of Pain*, and *The Four Loves*. Throughout all of these works and more, Lewis operates as mediator of high tradition, a source and form of authority that, like the Law of Nature, acquires divine status by transcending the particularities of time and place. These two forms of authority can make the logic of Lewis's arguments irresistible. Since these arguments are based upon a notion of uniform experience, skeptical readers who demur cast themselves as the aberrations referred to earlier. The

---

[52] Ibid., 84.

formidability of these arguments—their polemical strong-arming—intensifies when one considers Lewis's occasional method for conveying this authority, which is the subject of the next chapter.

# 5

# Conveying Authority

## I. Preliminary Considerations: Stock Responses

As public intellectual, C. S. Lewis conveys to the layperson the forms of authority described in the last chapter; these forms of authority serve as the foundation for his arguments about God and ethics. The form of authority I call high tradition requires Lewis's mediation. That is, to become accessible to a general audience, high tradition requires the learning and communication skills of a scholar, who by training has absorbed high tradition and by rhetorical mastery disseminates it within the public sphere. Simply put, the truths that descend from high tradition are not self-evident. Lewis siphons the modes of thought and feeling of western civilization into time-tested principles that fundamentally inform, shape, and authoritatively support his arguments. This is Lewis's scholarly service to his lay audience: crystallizing over two millennia of wisdom into accessible truths, most of which, of course, align with those he defends.

Unlike high tradition, however, the Law of Nature and the *Tao*—the other two forms of authority analyzed in the last chapter—are self-evident to all (with the exception of those whom Lewis casts as aberrations of history, misfits whose defective faculties or willful ignorance corrupt their understanding). Like high tradition, the Law and the *Tao* constitute universal moral and aesthetic realities, inclining us toward transcendent truths rooted in a cosmic order. Unlike high tradition, the Law and the *Tao* are knowable through direct experience; standards of right and wrong, good and bad are written on the hearts of all people. Nevertheless, the Law and the *Tao* do require Lewis's mediation: the mediation not of a scholar but a moralist. This distinction leads me to the notion of "stock responses."

The phrase "stock responses" signifies moral and aesthetic attitudes proceeding ontologically from experiential correlatives—thus constancy proceeds from the experience of love, acknowledgment of sublimity proceeds from the experience of a towering waterfall. For a scholar such as I. A. Richards, who was Lewis's contemporary, "stock response" is a pejorative term.[1] In *Practical Criticism*, Richards writes that stock responses "have their opportunity whenever a poem seems to, or does, involve views and emotions already fully prepared in the reader's mind, so that what happens appears to be more of the reader's doing than the poet's."[2] Richards's objection to stock responses reveals his critical orientation: Richards is no aesthetic essentialist. That is, Richards does not believe that beauty is a quality that inheres in an object; instead, beauty is a subjective experience caused by external stimuli. Richards writes in *Principles of Literary Criticism*,

> Even to-day, such is the insidious power of grammatical forms, the belief that there is such a quality or attribute, namely Beauty, which attaches to the things which we rightly call beautiful, is probably inevitable for all reflective persons at a certain stage of their mental development. Even among those who have escaped from this delusion and are well aware that we continually talk as though things possess qualities, when what we ought to say is that they cause effects in us of one kind or another, the fallacy of "projecting" the effect and making it a quality of its cause tends to recur.[3]

Not objectively attaching itself to a work of art, aesthetic value comes under the sole purview of the trained critic. Possessing a refined sensibility, the critic serves as arbiter of value, insuring that popular taste does not replace trained discrimination.

As the last chapter showed, Lewis's critical orientation is at the opposite pole. Lewis's profound disagreement with moral and aesthetic theories like those of Richards constitutes the polemical heart of *The Abolition of Man*. The anonymous antagonists of this book, Gaius and Titius, whose English textbook for children serves as the springboard for Lewis's exhortations against subjective values, evidence the influence exerted by Richards's ideas on pedagogy in English schools. Marshaling as evidence universal moral axioms that cross cultures, Lewis identifies the *Tao* as the "doctrine of objective value, the belief that certain attitudes are really true, and others really false, to the kind of thing the universe is and the kind of things we are."[4] Lewis's essentialist orientation attests that value does not merely

---

[1] For a sustained contrast between the views of Lewis and Richards, see part 1, ch. 1.

[2] I. A. Richards, *Practical Criticism* (London: Transaction Publishers, 2004) 14.

[3] I. A. Richards, *Principles of Literary Criticism* (New York: Harcourt Brace & World, 1925) 20–21.

[4] C. S. Lewis, *The Abolition of Man* (New York: Collier Books, 1955) 29.

descend from the trained judgments of discriminating cognoscenti; rather, as stated above, value is, under the right conditions, self-evident. Consistent through time and civilizations, moral value and principles present themselves to all but the morally corrupt, those who try to live outside the *Tao*. Thus, it is not a lack of training, discrimination, or sensibility that disqualifies one from apprehending value; instead, it is a lack of virtue, a quality available to specialist and non-specialist, scholar and layperson. All but those who willfully reject conventional morality can know the principles of the *Tao*.

Nevertheless, as mentioned previously, the Law and the *Tao* require some mediation on Lewis's part. That is, some training is necessary to perceive what Lewis calls "first principles in Ethics."[5] This training eventuates not in a refined sensibility but in a basic moral orientation. Lewis describes the process:

> St. Augustine defines virtue as *ordo amoris*, the ordinate condition of the affections in which every object is accorded that kind and degree of love which is appropriate to it. Aristotle says that the aim of education is to make the pupil like and dislike what he ought. When the age for reflective thought comes, the pupil who has been thus trained in "ordinate affections" or "just sentiments" will easily find the first principles in Ethics: but to the corrupt man they will never be visible at all and he can make no progress in that science. Plato before him had said the same. The little human animal will not at first have the right responses. It must be trained to feel pleasure, liking, disgust, and hatred at those things which really are pleasant, likeable, disgusting, and hateful.[6]

Cultivating right responses leads us to the distinctly literary component of Lewis's dispute with Richards. In *A Preface to Paradise Lost*, Lewis directly addresses Richards's objections to stock responses. Lewis notes how this "elementary rectitude of human response" is denigrated with classist and priggish inflections, the "unkind epithets of 'stock', 'crude', 'bourgeois', and 'conventional.'"[7] In fact, Lewis accepts Richards's loaded definition of the phrase—a "deliberately organized attitude which is substituted for 'the direct free play of experience'"—and upholds the process it describes as central to the purpose of literature: "In my opinion such deliberate

---

[5] Ibid., 27.

[6] Ibid., 26–27.

[7] C. S. Lewis, *A Preface to Paradise Lost* (Oxford: Oxford University Press, 1961) 55–56.

organization is one of the first necessities of human life, and one of the main functions of art is to assist it."[8]

The question then is this: how can art best fulfill this function? What genre of literature most effectively assists the cultivation of stock responses? How can Lewis best convey the authority of the Law of Nature and the *Tao*?

## II. The Genre of the Apologue

Out of Lewis's disagreement with Leavis and Richards emerges the following principle: a main function of literature is to cultivate the stock responses presupposed by an essentialist theory of ethics: Although associated with "bourgeois" and "conventional" culture, these responses are of dire importance to civilization, for they foster "trained habits... on the maintenance of which depend both our virtues and our pleasures and even, perhaps, the survival of our species."[9] Most of Lewis's works instantiate this principle. They train readers in the habits of what Lewis considers to be universal virtues, all of which fall under the auspices of the *Tao*. Clearly didactic in nature, these texts attempt to teach truths that Lewis holds to be universal, objective and thus, again under the right conditions, available to all. Moreover, in addition to being already associated with bourgeois culture, the stock responses that these texts cultivate contain widespread appeal—so important within the public sphere—because they also assume a uniformity of experience. Despite their fantastical settings, most of Lewis's texts engage the quotidian, the everyday realities of common culture which, as Lewis would have it, is *all* culture in the eschatological sweep of history.

Given this literary formula—to convey and cultivate stock responses under the assumption of essentialist ethics and experiential uniformity— many of Lewis's books are best conceived as examples of what Sheldon Sacks calls apologues in his classic analysis of narrative structure, *Fiction and the Shape of Belief.* Although numerous texts within the Lewis corpus possess qualities of the apologue, I restrict my analysis to two books that can be read as pure apologue: *The Screwtape Letters* and *The Great Divorce.*[10] "An

---

[8] Ibid., 54–55.

[9] Ibid., 57.

[10] Empirical evidence suggests that these two works have had an enormous influence in the public sphere, second only to *Mere Christianity.* I base this claim on personal correspondence with a representative from HarperOne Publishing, who provided me with the following sales numbers of Lewis's best-selling books from 2001–2009: *Mere Christianity*: 1.5 million; *The Screwtape Letters*: 1.3 million; *The Great Divorce*: 600,000.

apologue," explains Sacks, "is a work organized as a fictional example of the truth of a formulable statement or a series of such statements."[11] Among Sacks's examples of this genre are Spenser's *Faerie Queene* and Bunyan's *Pilgrim's Progress*. However, an apologue need not be allegorical or even possess allegorical elements, evident in Sacks's inclusion of Johnson's *Rasselas* on his list of apologues. Conceived as such, *The Screwtape Letters* and *The Great Divorce* evince their appeal to the differentiated audience of the public sphere and its populist character. Consider their literary predecessors: chapter 1 explored, via Lewis's own literary analyses, the reliance of Spenser's poem on popular myth and imagination. Bunyan's allegory was one of the first national bestsellers, finding a place in numerous British homes. And Samuel Johnson wrote *Rasselas* during the rise of the public sphere, a time—as chapter 2 explained—that witnessed an explosion of

---

[11] Sheldon Sacks, *Fiction and the Shape of Belief* (Berkeley: University of California Press, 1967) 26. As mentioned, other Lewis texts besides *The Screwtape Letters* and *The Great Divorce* possess characteristics of the apologue. Witness Richard Purtill's comment on the space trilogy: "Note that what Lewis is doing is not like most illustrative fantasy, where the real interest is in certain aspects of human nature or the human condition, which are merely isolated and exaggerated by the supposal. Rather, Lewis is interested in these supposals partly for their own sake and partly because they provide a restatement in new terms of ideas which Lewis held to be true on other grounds" (Richard Purtill, *Lord of the Elves and Eldils: Fantasy and Philosophy in C. S. Lewis and J. R. R. Tolkien* [Grand Rapids: Eerdmans, 1974] 137). Or consider Jared C. Lobdell's estimation that the Ransom stories are "in part novels of intellect or ideas," influenced by novels of the eighteenth century and participating in what Nikolaus Pevsner calls "Englishness": "the belief that art exists to preach and that the best preaching comes from the detailed observation of daily life." Thus, Lobdell links *Out of the Silent Planet* and Johnson's *Rasselas*, "both being travels intermixed with philosophy, the story being more in the philosophy than in the travels" (Jared C. Lobdell, "C. S. Lewis's Ransom Stories and Their Eighteenth-Century Ancestry," in *Word and Story in C. S. Lewis*, ed. Peter J. Schakel and Charles A. Huttar [Columbia: University of Missouri Press, 1991] 214, 216). Also witness Peter Schakel's reflections on *Out of the Silent Planet*: "The narrative, however, is not left to convey these themes on its own. The conceptual truths which underlie the story are spelled out in statement form, in the account of the war in heaven at the time of Satan's rebellion and in the extended conversation between the Oyarsa and Weston, with Ransom as interpreter" (Peter Schakel, *Reason and the Imagination in C. S. Lewis: A Study of* Till We Have Faces [Grand Rapids: Eerdmans, 1984] 126). Purtill's, Lobdell's, and Schakel's observations are in close proximity to my contention that the Ransom stories, as well as other Lewis texts, contain elements of the apologue.

social spaces for public dialogue and information exchange, what Jürgen Habermas calls a "public sphere of a rational-critical debate."[12]

Descending from this literary lineage, *The Screwtape Letters* and *The Great Divorce* wrap narratives around "formulable statements" that proceed from the Law and the *Tao,* thereby conveying their authority.[13] While a number of formulable statements emerge from *The Screwtape Letters* and *The Great Divorce,* one that unites them both may be summarized as follows: The apparently small, quotidian decisions one makes and actions one commits on a daily basis cumulatively carry eternal consequences. Or, as Walter Hooper describes the chief theme of *Screwtape*: "the main interest is meant to be the immortal consequences of seemingly small and insignificant choices in the every-day life of Everyman."[14] Because these decisions and actions are of immense importance, both books carry out what Lewis felt was the first function of art: cultivating in his readers stock responses, a task clearly consonant with the characteristics of the apologue.

This generic identity not only helps clarify the fundamental mission of Lewis's *oeuvre,* but it also situates his texts for proper analysis, precluding misinterpretations caused by misunderstandings of their literary function. Such misunderstandings have attended Lewis scholarship from the 1940s to the present. Chad Walsh's early study of Lewis, for instance, observes the following critique directed toward Lewis's fiction: "The other charges

---

[12] Jürgen Habermas, *The Structural Transformation of the Public Sphere: An Inquiry into a Category of Bourgeois Society,* trans. Thomas Burger (Cambridge: MIT Press, 1989) 51.

[13] To identify these texts as apologues is not to suggest that they are works of philosophy disguised as literature, though apologues often include strong philosophical dimensions. Lewis writes, "And we may also—which is less important—expect to find in [poetry] many psychological truths and profound, at least profoundly felt, reflections. But all this comes to us, and was very possibly called out of the poet, as the 'spirit' (using that word in a quasi-chemical sense) of a work of art, a play. To formulate it as a philosophy, even if it were a rational philosophy, and regard the actual play as primarily a vehicle for that philosophy, is an outrage to the thing the poet has made for us" (*An Experiment in Criticism* [Cambridge: Cambridge University Press, 1961] 104). I draw a strong distinction between a work of literature as a vehicle for a philosophy and a work of literature as an exemplification of a formulable statement. As Lewis writes elsewhere, "Being a skill of utterance, [poetry] can be used to utter almost anything; to draw attention (though not, of course, to demonstrate) a fact, to tell lies, to tell admitted fictions, to describe your own real or feigned emotions, to make jokes" (*The Personal Heresy: A Controversy* [London: Oxford University Press, 1939] 112).

[14] Walter Hooper, *C. S. Lewis: A Companion and Guide* (San Francisco: HarperSanFrancisco, 1996) 270.

commonly leveled against Lewis are patness, glibness, oversimplification. He is accused of making black too black, white too white."[15] As we have seen, what Walsh identifies as oversimplification are the epistemological conditions and narrative framework that solidify the function of the apologue. In her 1958 caustic indictment of Lewis and Dorothy Sayers, Kathleen Nott discredits Lewis and Sayers for "an incapacity or a dislike for analyzing and comprehending concrete individual human character, which was always characteristic of them."[16] Nott's accusation could just as well apply to Johnson's *Rasselas*, the characters of which are in many respects indistinguishable, lacking individualized qualities; they serve as the mouthpiece for Johnson's formulable statements. But such, of course, is the function of the apologue. Nott is not issuing a critique; she is stating a truism or even a tautology. She also betrays her misunderstanding when she complains that Lewis (and Sayers) substitutes in his characters "theological generalisations for a sound psychology...."[17] In the case of Lewis, the theological generalizations are the point, not the sound psychology. Attention to genre reveals the unfairness of Nott's charge.

More modern scholarship reveals the same misunderstanding. Consider, for instance, the judgment rendered by Corbin Scott Carnell: "Occasionally his imaginative works are overloaded with meanings and subliminal echoes of meaning. His earnestness sometimes leads him to caricature in his fictional characters (character being the most difficult aspect of fiction for Lewis)."[18] Once Lewis's imaginative works are recast as apologues, however, these criticisms evaporate. The expatiation of a formulable statement accounts for the overload of meaning. Character development does not amount to caricature; rather, character development operates at the service of the formulable statement, as Sacks explains: "What is revealed about any major character is, almost of necessity and almost ruthlessly, limited to qualities directly required for their role in the apologue."[19] Margaret Patterson Hannay comments that the "total effect" of character development in *The Great Divorce* "...is that of a sermon rather than a

---

[15] Chad Walsh, *C. S. Lewis: Apostle to the Skeptics* (New York: Macmillan, 1949) 164.

[16] Kathleen Nott, *The Emperor's Clothes* (Bloomington: Indiana University Press, 1958) 256.

[17] Ibid.

[18] Corbin Scott Carnell, *Bright Shadow of Reality: C. S. Lewis and the Feeling Intellect* (Grand Rapids: Eerdmans, 1974) 161.

[19] Sacks, *Fiction and the Shape of Belief*, 60.

vision."[20] Likewise, Peter Schakel surmises that Lewis "held back, in his own stories, from the commitment to the imagination required for pure fantasy."[21] He faults *The Great Divorce* for not engaging in pure myth: "its effect is to convey a message, not to give an imaginative experience,"[22] an effect which, as my argument contends, is not a weakness of the text but rather its primary purpose. In addition, Peter Kreeft writes, "Because Lewis's writing is so very rational, one gets the impression that his characters are all very rational…[and that Lewis] often seems to *use* his characters as bearers of philosophical points, often by means of rational, expository conversation, rather than as objects of the author's interest for their own sake."[23] Of course, that is precisely the point of Lewis's characters, at least in *The Screwtape Letters* and *The Great Divorce*, once we conceive them as apologues.

Some critics thus seem to want to read these works as they would read novels, finding faults on that basis. Unlike the apologue, the novel, as Sacks explains, is a "represented action" involving "characters about whose fates we are made to care [and who] are introduced in unstable relationships which are then further complicated until the complications are finally resolved by the complete removal of the represented instability."[24] Using this literary grid as criterion for assessment, *The Screwtape Letters* and *The Great Divorce* will certainly be found wanting, but that is only because that criterion is alien to the generic form that the texts assume. Placed amid the complicated, messy world that a novel projects, formulable statements come across as glib—and are as equally unpleasant as preeminently reasonable characters. Such statements and characters in an apologue, on the other hand, when successfully marshaled and depicted, contribute to the artistry of the form. Consider the musings of David Downing: "The question remains why Lewis was drawn to genres that did not require characters with 'insides.' One answer would be that he tended to view things in black-and-white terms—'we few' against the world."[25] Another answer could be the one offered in this chapter: that simplistically drawn characters further the

---

[20] Margaret Patterson Hannay, *C. S. Lewis* (New York: Frederick Ungar, 1981) 112–13.

[21] Peter Schakel, *Reason and the Imagination in C. S. Lewis: A Study of* Till We Have Faces (Grand Rapids: Eerdmans, 1984) 126.

[22] Ibid., 147.

[23] Peter Kreeft, *C. S. Lewis: A Critical Essay* (Front Royal VA: Christendom College Press, 1988) 56–57.

[24] Sacks, *Fiction and the Shape of Belief*, 15.

[25] David Downing, *Planets in Peril: A Critical Study of C. S. Lewis's Ransom Trilogy* (Amherst: University of Massachusetts Press, 1992) 143.

aim of the apologue. Kath Filmer's praise for *Till We Have Faces* comes at the expense of Lewis's other works of fiction: "This is the novel which portrays flawed humanity more eloquently, more sensitively, than many contemporaneous novels; and because of its honesty, it does much to redeem the image of Lewis as novelist from that of the rather banal and superficial defender of the supernatural he adopts in his earlier works."[26] But *Till We Have Faces* is the only true novel Lewis ever wrote; the purpose of the "earlier works" to which Filmer refers is to defend the supernatural, not to offer the sensitive representations characteristic of the novel. Finally, here is Adam Gopnick's critique in a 2005 issue of the *New Yorker*:

> For, throughout his own imaginative writing, Lewis is always trying to stuff the marvelous back into the allegorical—his conscience as a writer lets him see that the marvelous should be there for its own marvelous sake, just as imaginative myth, but his Christian duty insists that the marvelous must (to use his own giveway language) be reinfected with belief. He is always trying to inoculate metaphor with allegory, or, at least, drug it, so that it walks around hollow-eyed, saying just what it's supposed to say.[27]

If Gopnick has *The Screwtape Letters* and *The Great Divorce* in mind here, then his issue is not with Lewis but with the genre within which the two imaginative works can be classified. The apologue, above all else, says "just what it's supposed to say."

I conclude this section with brief close readings of *The Screwtape Letters* and *The Great Divorce*, analyzing how they fulfill the purpose of the apologue. Organized as a series of letters from one devil of hell (Screwtape) to a subordinate devil (Wormwood), *The Screwtape Letters* assumes the instability inherent in the epistolary form. An unreliable narrator seemingly unsettles meanings upon which formulable statements rely. However, because of the way Lewis draws his eponymous character, the narrative paradoxically registers a network of stable meanings that suits the form of the apologue. Since Screwtape is superlatively evil, he (unlike Milton's Satan, not to mention any character in a novel) is never conflicted; because he is never conflicted, his evil is utterly transparent. Consequently, the formulable statement and stock responses that the text registers are neatly

---

[26] Kath Filmer, *The Fiction of C. S. Lewis: Mask and Mirror* (New York: St. Martin's Press, 1993) 4.

[27] Adam Gopnik, "Prisoner of Narnia: How C. S. Lewis Escaped," *New Yorker*, 21 November 2005. Accessed 8 September 2010 <http://www.newyorker.com/archive/2005/11/21/051121crat_atlarge>.

assembled as the antithesis of whatever Screwtape advocates. Lewis refers to this dynamic as a "photographic negative," wherein Screwtape's whites should be our blacks, and his blacks should be our whites.[28] In short, Screwtape's uncomplicated psychology well serves the expository aim of Lewis's text as apologue.

In fact, rather simple binary oppositions (like black and white) form the organizing principle of the book. In Screwtape's first letter, he sets forth the dualism out of which formulable statements can felicitously emerge: "He [the patient, the human Wormwood tempts] doesn't think of doctrines as primarily 'true' or 'false', but as 'academic' or 'practical', 'outworn' or 'contemporary', 'conventional' or 'ruthless.'"[29] Consistent with the nature of the apologue, this binary opposition—true or false—deemphasizes character motivations, downplays the contexts that shape approaches to "doctrines." The text minimizes the innumerable factors that predispose us to belief or unbelief (whatever the doctrine), thereby clearing the way for formulable statements that rise above the pre-analytical nature of decision-making. A similar dualism occurs when Screwtape explains to Wormwood the "Historical Point of View," which "means that when a learned man is presented with any statement in an ancient author, the one question he never asks is whether it is true. He asks who influenced the ancient writer, and how far the statement is consistent with what he said in other books, and what phase in the writer's development, or in the general history of thought, it illustrates, and how it affected later writers...."[30] Screwtape thus distills the study of the ancients into a direct question: is it true or false? Again, this dichotomy—simple, direct, devoid of the nuance that other considerations bear, yet of eternal importance in the projected world of the text—establishes the conditions that enable the apologue. These conditions favor the truths of Christianity, for direct questions about truth and falsity lead to arguments, and as Screwtape admits, "The trouble about argument is that it moves the whole struggle on to the Enemy's ground."[31] These considerations provide the epistemological framework for an apologue: only when arguments lead to clear truths can a text advocate formulable statements.

Wandering around the foothills of heaven that constitute the fictional geography of *The Great Divorce*, Lewis as narrator is accosted by his spiritual mentor, George MacDonald, the nineteenth-century Scottish minister and

---

[28] C. S. Lewis, Screwtape Proposes a Toast (New York: Macmillan, 1982) 151.
[29] C. S. Lewis, *The Screwtape Letters* (San Francisco: HarperSanFrancisco, 2001) 1.
[30] Ibid., 150.
[31] Ibid., 2.

fantasist. Commenting on the interactions between Ghosts (souls of the deceased on holiday from hell) and Solid People (inhabitants of heaven who entreat and beckon the Ghosts to join them in eternal bliss), MacDonald utters the truth that *The Great Divorce* exemplifies: "'There is always something they [the Ghosts] prefer to joy—that is, to reality.'"[32] That alternative to joy is essentially pride, and it is the function of *The Great Divorce* as apologue to cultivate in readers stock responses that protect against these sins. Indeed, in his preface, Lewis articulates a formulable statement along these lines, the truth of which the text exemplifies: "If we insist on keeping Hell (or even Earth) we shall not see Heaven: if we accept Heaven we shall not be able to retain even the smallest and most intimate souvenirs of Hell."[33]

Like the *Screwtape Letters*, *The Great Divorce* establishes the narrative framework that makes this and other formulable statements compelling. For instance, the ghost of an apostate bishop of the Anglican church cannot relinquish the scholarly pedantry that characterized his mortal life; he has interest not in finding truth but in complicating scholarly questions and achieving academic fame. Before advancing to heaven, the bishop wants assurance that his scholarly talents will find a home, an assurance that his attendant Solid Person cannot grant: "'No,' said the other. 'I can promise you none of these things. No sphere of usefulness: you are not needed there at all. No scope for your talents: only forgiveness for having perverted them. No atmosphere of inquiry, for I will bring you to the land not of questions but of answers, and you shall see the face of God."[34] The bishop does not realize that, in the epistemological geography of the foothills of heaven, the apprehension of truth overshadows intellectual pursuits. "We know nothing of speculation," the Solid Person continues, "Come and see. I will bring you to Eternal Fact, the Father of all other facthood."[35] Within the projected world of the text, reality unmasks itself, truth becomes knowable, and issues of ultimate concern thus shed their ambiguities. Such a world stabilizes and secures formulable statements.

The uncomplicated psychology of the Ghost characters also secures this function. The Ghosts who reject the invitation to enter heaven are simplistically developed, transparently motivated by variations of pride:

---

[32] C. S. Lewis, *The Great Divorce* (San Francisco: HarperSanFrancisco, 2001) 71.

[33] Ibid., vii–ix.

[34] Ibid., 40.

[35] Ibid., 42.

self-absorption or a sense of self-importance.[36] This assessment does not constitute a critique for reasons previously explained on the nature of the apologue. While robbing the novel of the psychological depth and richness expected of a genre characterized by realism, simplistic characters in an apologue provide the platform for the promulgation of direct and clear truths. Perhaps this is why A. C. Deane, in a 1946 review of *The Great Divorce*, writes, "The narrator seems, as it were, to place each Ghost in turn on the lecture-table, to exhibit with deliberate skill his special follies and impenitence, and then to drop him back whence he came."[37] The Ghost of the apostate bishop, for instance, rejects the idea of an objectively existing God by concluding, "'God, for me, is something purely spiritual. The spirit of sweetness and light and tolerance—and, er, service, Dick [the Solid Person], service. We mustn't forget that, you know.'"[38] The solecistic "er," the fragmented and incomplete thoughts, the desperate and asinine reminder of the importance of "service"—all of these rhetorical devices serve to reduce the apostate bishop's position to absurdity.

Lewis's apologue systematically sets up such characters only to knock them down, a process that solidifies the truth that the text ultimately sets up as an alternative to the folly of the Ghost characters. As in Lewis's non-fiction apologetics, *The Great Divorce* makes use of the *reductio ad absurdum*: the viewpoints represented by the Ghost characters are reduced to absurdity, rendering the various objections to entering Heaven nonsense.[39] Consider also the Ghost character who in her mortal life was a domineering wife driving her husband to exhaustion and death. She demands that the Solid Person attending her (called Hilda) return her husband to her. Otherwise, she refuses to enter heaven: "'There's lots, lots, lots of things I still want to do with him. No, listen, Hilda. Please, please! I'm so miserable. I must have someone to—to do things to.'"[40]

Character after character, the narrator overhears such conversations—framed by MacDonald's authoritative commentary—that cumulatively

---

[36] Of course, before they were Ghosts, when they were alive on earth, they might have been more complicated, demonstrating a psychology characterized by mixed motives; they may have been less one dimensional. Such identities would have made Lewis's task much more difficult.

[37] A. C. Deane, "A Nightmare," *Spectator* 176 (1946): 96.

[38] Lewis, *The Great Divorce*, 42.

[39] In this respect, *The Great Divorce* resembles another apologue: Samuel Johnson's *Rasselas*, which, character after character, shows that happiness in this life is unattainable; exponents of happiness are repeatedly reduced to absurdity.

[40] *Great Divorce*, 95.

establish the truth that lies at the heart of the apologue: pride, which assumes many forms and poisons many souls through gradual means, must be expurgated in order eventually to see God. The closing lines of the text attach a sense of urgency to this purgation process. The reader realizes that the narrative was a dream, from which Lewis awakens: "I awoke in a cold room, hunched on the floor beside a black and empty grate, the clock striking three, and the siren howling overhead."[41] Awakening from a nightmare into another nightmare—the "siren" is possibly an air-raid warning during a German attack—the narrator can sense the proximity of death and the concomitant need for reform, which is implicitly called for in those readers who heed the formulable statement(s) that *The Great Divorce* exemplifies. A 1946 review of the book in the *Times Literary Supplement* accords, I believe, with Lewis's theory of good art as well as the function of the apologue: "The book succeeds because its readers will forget that it is a work of art, and remember not so much what happened in it as what it made them think."[42]

### III. Transcendent Characters

Lewis employs in his fiction a sort of character that solidifies the purpose of the apologue. I coin a phrase to describe this character type: the *transcendent character*. Transcending the epistemological limitations endemic to the human condition, the transcendent character possesses knowledge that approximates absolute truth. Inhabiting the fictional geography of nearly all of Lewis's imaginative works, the transcendent character endows Lewis's texts with a sense of authority—Olympian perspectives—from which spiritual truths and moral precepts proceed with such rhetorical power. In this capacity, Lewis once again performs acts of mediation: Lewis as narrator serves as the intermediary between the immortal (and apothegmatic) truths of transcendent characters (that is, truths properly translated) and the limited understanding of ordinary, mortal readers.

Screwtape draws attention to this chasm separating ordinary mortals and transcendent truths by pointing to what has been called through history the Great Chain of Being. Represented in widely diverging texts like Giovanni Pico della Mirandola's *Oration on the Dignity of Man* and Shakespeare's *Antony and Cleopatra*, the Great Chain of Being maps the relational position of all created and uncreated entities. Half spirit and half

---

[41] Ibid., 146.

[42] "Dream of the After-World." *Times Literary Supplement*, 2 February 1946, 58.

animal, thus occupying a middle position on the Great Chain, humankind possesses faculties that are simultaneously divine and corrupt, with a capacity to seek eternal knowledge but a fallen, time-bound nature that thwarts that capacity. As Screwtape explains, "As spirits they belong to the eternal world, but as animals they inhabit time. This means that while their spirit can be directed to an eternal object, their bodies, passions, and imaginations are in continual change, for to be in time means to change."[43] As spirit, Screwtape transcends these limitations; although, of course, as a devil his eternal object is himself, a locus of hatred and anger. As collector and editor of Screwtape's "letters," Lewis distills from Screwtape's transcendent perspective (through the process of the photographic negative) the prescriptive beliefs and ethical norms that undergird the apologue. Screwtape, for instance, observes that the existence of hypocritical Christians cannot be logically used to disprove Christianity: He then remarks, "You may ask whether it is possible to keep such an obvious thought from occurring even to a human mind. It is, Wormwood, it is! Handle him properly and it simply won't come into his head."[44] Manipulating his transcendent character, Lewis ensures that the obvious truths do not escape his mortal readers and their limited perspective.

The dichotomy between transcendent/spiritual and mortal/animal becomes literalized in an early letter in which Screwtape reminisces to Wormwood about a "patient" he once had. One day, the patient sat reading in the British Museum when Screwtape "saw a train of thought in his mind beginning to go the wrong way."[45] Screwtape also saw that the "Enemy" (God) was present during this act of introspection, leading the patient toward thoughts of eternity and transcendence. In his moment of victory, Screwtape manages to convince the patient to leave the museum; once outside, the patient finds himself reabsorbed into the busy-ness of life, with a "newsboy shouting the midday paper, and a No. 73 bus going past...."[46] Screwtape thus convinces the patient that "whatever odd ideas might come into a man's head when he was shut up alone with his books, a healthy dose of 'real life' [by which he meant the bus and the newsboy] was enough to show him that all 'that sort of thing' just couldn't be true."[47] Thanks to Screwtape's mental manipulations and suggestions, the patient, in short,

---

[43] Lewis, *The Screwtape Letters*, 37.
[44] Ibid., 8.
[45] Ibid., 2.
[46] Ibid., 3.
[47] Ibid.

dismisses the transcendent ("that sort of thing,"), momentarily literalized by the act of reading, as shadowy and vague; the patient instead accepts as truth "real life," embodied in the figures of the bus and newsboy. As a result of the photographic-negative technique operating on Screwtape as a transcendent character, the text is organized to ensure that the formulable statements align with transcendence in the immortal/mortal dichotomy. In the conclusion of the text, Wormwood's patient dies in God's graces and "is caught up into that world where pain and pleasure take on transfinite values...."[48] *The Screwtape Letters* serves as a simulacrum of that world, where readers can more easily glimpse the stock responses that, Lewis believed, art should assist.

Indeed, certain moments in *The Screwtape Letters* suggest that Lewis had to apply the brakes on the religious instruction implicit in the book; textual cues suggest that Lewis saw his didacticism becoming too heavy-handed. This is what Graham Hough has in mind when he writes, "[Screwtape] so far forgets himself as to give at times much straightforward exposition of Christian morals."[49] Consider this passage:

> What he wants of the layman in church is an attitude which may, indeed, be critical in the sense of rejecting what is false or unhelpful, but which is wholly uncritical in the sense that it does not appraise—does not waste time in thinking about what it rejects, but lays itself open in uncommenting, humble receptivity to any nourishment that is going. (You see how groveling, how unspiritual, how irredeemably vulgar He is!) This attitude, especially during sermons, creates the conditions (most hostile to our whole policy) in which platitudes can become really audible to a human soul.[50]

Here, again by manipulating the transcendent perspective of Screwtape, Lewis communicates the optimal attitude for religious instruction during a church service. But the instruction becomes so transparent that readers might forget the diabolical perspective of the speaker: Thus, the parenthetical remarks cue the readers, re-directing their attention to the photographic-negative technique, reminding them of Screwtape's infernal perspective. These parenthetical cues emphasize the strongly didactic function of the text. And this function, typically foreign to the genre of fantasy and pure mythopoeia, is central to the apologue—in the case of *The*

---

[48] Ibid., 175.

[49] Graham Hough, "The Screwtape Letters," *London Times*, 10 February 1966, 15.

[50] Lewis, *The Screwtape Letters*, 82.

*Screwtape Letters,* an apologue with strong fantastical and mythopoeic elements.

In *The Great Divorce,* the Solid People serve as transcendent characters. As such, they possess the authority and knowledge to which the formulable truths of an apologue can be anchored. Lewis describes the formidable approach of the Solid People: "Long after that I saw people coming to meet us. Because they were bright I saw them while they were still very distant, and at first I did not know that they were people at all. Mile after mile they drew nearer. The earth shook under their tread as their strong feet sank into the wet turf."[51] The Solid People also possess trans-mortal knowledge. Consider the Solid Person who attends the ghost of the apostate bishop analyzed earlier. This Solid Person dismisses the bishop's life work, the theological speculations upon which the bishop built his career. "You see," the Solid Person proclaims, "I *know* now";[52] emphasis in original). The Solid Person possesses knowledge that approximates omniscience, knowledge which, again, anchors the statements of the apologue.

Of course, George MacDonald operates as the most important transcendent character in the text, serving as Lewis's guide through the foothills of heaven, a role not unlike the one Virgil plays to Dante in the *Divine Comedy*. Relieved to receive guidance from his master, the narrator pays him warm homage, confessing how MacDonald's *Phantastes* initiated in him a Dantean New Life: "I started to confess how long that Life had delayed in the region of imagination merely: how slowly and reluctantly I had come to admit that his Christendom had more than an accidental connexion with it, how hard I had tried not to see that the true name of the quality which first met me in his books is Holiness. He laid his hand on mine and stopped me."[53]

With this guide, the narrator describes events as framed by the commentaries of MacDonald from his Olympian perspective. Consequently, the moral, theological, and philosophical significance of the exchanges between Solid People and Ghosts never goes unexplained: MacDonald aids the narrator by fleshing out of these exchanges moral axioms and theological/philosophical truths, thus unfailingly securing the didactic function of the apologue. Lewis's respect and admiration for his guide transforms MacDonald into the transcendent translator, evident in this utterance that returns us to Lewis's preface and the fundamental formulable

---

[51] Lewis, *The Great Divorce,* 23.

[52] Ibid., 37.

[53] Ibid., 67.

statement of the book: "'Milton was right,' said my Teacher. 'The choice of every lost soul can be expressed in the words "Better to reign in Hell than serve in Heaven." There is always something they insist on keeping even at the price of misery. There is always something they prefer to joy—that is, to reality.'"[54] With its narrative framework, epistemological geography, and transcendent characters, *The Great Divorce* falls within the same genre as *The Screwtape Letters*: an apologue with strong fantastical and mythopoeic elements.[55]

Transcendent characters operate in Lewis's other works of fiction, all of which possess, in varying degrees, characteristics of the apologue. I briefly analyze three of them now.

### a. Father History in The Pilgrim's Regress

In *The Pilgrim's Regress*, both Mother Kirk and Father History adopt a transcendent perspective, assessing the allegorical geography of the land, revealing to the text's protagonist, John, the pitfalls particular to various regions, and pointing him in the right direction. I wish to focus my analysis on Father History, for his unique identity illustrates Lewis's strategy of distilling transcendence from contingency. "'I know all parts of this country,'"[56] Father History declares to John, who earlier embarked on a search for an Island, a vision allegorizing what Lewis refers to in the afterword to the third edition as *Sehnsucht* (German for "longing") and elsewhere as Joy. John's circuitous journey brings him hardship and disappointment.

As transcendent character, elevated in his lofty cliff-side cave, Father History orients both John and the reader, explaining the false ideas of the country's inhabitants below, from the fuzzy-minded romantics to the tough-minded stoics. Earlier, the reader shared John's confusion as these characters offered various accounts of the Island, some claiming that it can be

---

[54] Ibid., 72.

[55] Again, my contention is that, while *The Screwtape Letters* and *The Great Divorce* are pure apologues, other Lewis's texts contain characteristics of the apologue. Consider Charles Moorman's pronouncement on the science-fiction trilogy, a pronouncement that points to the qualities of the apologue: "Lewis's main aim in the creation of the silent-planet myth is to create and maintain a metaphor that will serve to carry in fictional form the basic tenets of Christianity and present them from a non-Christian point of view, but without reference to normal Christian symbols" (quoted in David Downing, *Planets in Peril: A Critical Study of C.S. Lewis's Ransom Trilogy.* Amherst, MA: University of Massachusetts Press, 1992. 109).

[56] C. S. Lewis, *The Pilgrims Regress* (Grand Rapids: Eerdmans, 1992) 143.

recaptured (through illicit means), others insisting it does not even exist. Father History's perspective, however, immediately distinguishes his position: "You may be sure," he tells John of one particular group, "that they make the same mistake about the Island that they make about everything else. But what is the current lie at present?"[57] Father History's question implicitly communicates important points about his authoritative position: first, that his Olympian perspective is nearly infallible because it transcends the vicissitudes of time. He need not even know the current explanation of the Island to dismiss it as a lie. Concomitantly, he can dismiss it as a lie because it *is* rooted in time. Temporality produces fashion; transcendence yields truth.

As transcendent character, Father History is able to explain the Island to John. Consistent with his character, he draws conclusions from an overarching view of the past. He informs John that the vision comes in different forms, not always that of an Island: "What is universal is not the particular picture, but the arrival of some message...."[58] History traces the vision from the pagans, who, like John, perceived an Island, to people of the Middle Ages, who thanks to the courtly-love tradition, experienced the vision in the form of a lady. In each case, as Father History explains, the vision "sets men longing for something East or West of the world...to lead him at last where true joys are to be found."[59] Like the Law of Nature and the *Tao*, the vision finds its source in God himself. Father History enlightens John on a subject of which other characters, mired in temporality, remain ignorant: The vision of the Island, if interpreted correctly, will lead John to the Christian faith. Father History thus not only sets John on the right path but also helps secure the apologetic function of *The Pilgrim's Regress*.

Father History is an unlikely transcendent character by virtue of his very name and identity. History, after all, is a discipline committed to the temporal: the discrete day, week, year, or century. History is the study of that which is time-bound. Even assuming a historiography that permits the valid discernment of larger patterns through time, history cannot easily be pressed into the service of Lewis's character. History is limited to the descriptive mode; it cannot advocate moral truths.

This is what Philip Sidney, the Elizabethan poet and diplomat, has in mind when he evaluates the merits of history, philosophy, and literature with respect to their potential for encouraging virtue. Philosophy, Sidney

---

[57] Ibid., 145–46.
[58] Ibid., 151.
[59] Ibid.

contends, is too "abstract and general," possessing the "precept" but lacking the "example" to motivate; it lacks a concrete narrative to make the pursuit of virtue salient. Sidney then notes the limitations of history: "On the other side, the historian, wanting the precept, is so tied, not to what should be but to what is, to the particular truth of things and not to the general reason of things, that his example draweth no necessary consequence, and therefore a less fruitful doctrine."[60] In addition to temporal restrictions—the "particular truth of things"—history is limited because it cannot avail itself of prescriptive discourse; it can only state what is, not what should be. Father History's explanation of John's vision abounds with moral judgments—evident in phrases like "vile satisfaction," "true joys," and "spurious satisfactions."[61] These moral judgments, a component of prescriptive discourse, lie outside the purview of the discipline of history. Father History performs what, according to Sidney, is only possible for the poet: to couple "the general notion with the particular example."[62]

Lewis's view of history, however, is shaped by his Christian conviction, which makes the character of Father History possible. In a 1950 article, Lewis defines historicism as "the belief that men can, by the use of their natural powers, discover an inner meaning in the historical process." Lewis states that such a belief is unwarranted, but is at least theoretically possible *only* from a Christian perspective:

> What appears, on Christian premises, to be true in the Historicist's position is this. Since all things happen either by the divine will or at least by the divine permission, it follows that the total content of time must in its own nature be a revelation of God's wisdom, justice, and mercy. In this direction we can go as far as Carlyle or Novalis or anyone else. History is, in that sense, a perpetual Evangel, a story written by the finger of God. If, by one miracle, the total content of time were spread out before me, and if, by another, I were able to hold all that infinity of events in my mind and if, by a third, God were pleased to comment on it so that I could understand it, then, to be sure, I could do what the Historicist says he is doing. I could read the meaning, discern the pattern.[63]

---

60 Philip Sidney, *A Defence of Poetry*, ed. Jan Van Dorsten (Oxford: Oxford University Press, 1996) 32.

61 Lewis, *The Pilgrims Regress*, 151–52.

62 Sidney, *A Defence of Poetry*, ed. Jan Van Dorsten, 32.

63 C. S. Lewis, "Historicism," in *Christian Reflections*, ed. Walter Hooper (Grand Rapids: Eerdmans, 1967) 104.

This is the miracle that Father History enacts. He uncovers the inner meaning of history with respect to John's vision. And since it is a "revelation of God's wisdom, justice, and mercy," history assumes God's moral calculus. Moral judgments are not alien to history when all events "happen either by the divine will or at least by divine permission," especially when we assume that God has morally sufficient reasons for causing or permitting those events. From Lewis's Christian perspective, history is thus not a record of random events, but instead bears the marks of providential design. Father History employs prescriptive discourse because God's fingerprints on the past endow history with meaning and purpose, revealing the standards by which Father History issues moral judgments.

Father History is, in fact, an embodiment of high tradition, one of the forms of authority analyzed in the last chapter. Culling the cumulative wisdom of western civilization is tantamount to reading the meaning of history. In both cases, transcendent truths emerge from a past superintended by God. Despite the temporal limitations implicit in his very name, Father History paradoxically conveys authority that is trans-historical.

### b. *Augray and the Sorns in* Out of the Silent Planet

The Oyarsa of Mars—that is, the archangel of Mars—perhaps serves as the best example of a transcendent character in *Out of the Silent Planet*. As the highest ranking angel in the cosmic order, the Oyarsa possesses transcendent knowledge. At the end of the narrative, the Oyarsa performs the role typical of transcendent characters: orienting both the protagonist and the reader, tying up narrative loose ends, and assisting the didactic function of the text. I focus, however, on a character whose knowledge does not so closely approximate omniscience and who thus illustrates the fact that transcendent characters need not be polymathic—as long as they orient the reader and stabilize the narrative's meaning.

Augray is a type of creature known as a *sorn*, inhabiting the planet Mars. Like all *seroni*, he is of immense height and, like Father History, dwells in a mountainside cave. And like his physiological features and geographical location, Augray holds a perspective that towers above that of most other creatures. Consequently, as transcendent character, he orients both Ransom (the protagonist of the book) and the reader, explaining the flora and fauna of Mars as well as the divine order of the cosmos, from *Maleldil* (God) to the beaver-like *hrossa* (other inhabitants of Mars).

Various moments in the text illustrate and symbolize Augray's Olympian perspective. It is from Augray that Ransom learns about the *eldila*.

Throughout his adventures on Mars, Ransom has been made aware of their fleeting and ethereal presence, but unable to understand their nature and purpose. Augray instructs Ransom, who learns that they are angels:

"But the body of an *eldil* is a movement swift as light; you may say its body is made of light, but not of that which is light for the *eldil*. His 'light' is a swifter movement which for us is nothing at all; and what we call light is for him a thing like water, a visible thing, a thing he can touch and bathe in—even a dark thing when not illumined by the swifter. And what we call firm things—flesh and earth—seem to him thinner, and harder to see, than our light, and more like clouds, and nearly nothing. To us the *eldil* is a thin, half-real body that can go through walls and rocks: to himself he goes through them because he is solid and firm and they are like cloud. And what is true light to him and fills the heaven, so that he will plunge into the rays of the sun to refresh himself from it, is to us the black nothing in the sky at night. These things are not strange, Small One, though they are beyond our senses. But it is strange that the *eldila* never visit Thulcandra."[64]

Augray organizes his explanation around dueling perspectives, that of the *eldila* themselves and that of mortal creatures: "you may say..."; "...for the *eldil*"; "...for us..."; "and what we call..."; "...seem to him..."; "To us..."; and "to himself...." The perspectivism of this account underlines the limitations of all *hnau*, Augray included. (In the Old Solar language, *hnau* signifies sapient, mortal creatures above beasts and below angels in the chain of being.) The *eldila* apprehend the divine reality, which the faculties of the *hnau* are too weak to comprehend.

However, despite his limited faculties, Augray possesses sufficient knowledge to contrast the rival perspectives. That is, his knowledge is sufficient to explain—as accurately as his vantage point will allow—the *eldila*'s perspective to Ransom: His knowledge is also sufficient momentarily to stand outside his own perspective to notice its limitations. In this act, Augray achieves a meta-perspective, a point of reference characteristic of the transcendent character, albeit one whose knowledge is not exhaustive.

Transcendence in this case comes not from Augray's inerrant knowledge, but from his possession of universal, though incomplete, truth. That is, what authorizes Augray's utterances is their claim to universality: Augray does not possess the entire truth, but the sliver of it that he holds and shares with Ransom (and the reader) is sufficient to elide perspectival limitations and the taint of subjectivism. It is significant that Ransom

---

[64] C. S. Lewis, *Out of the Silent Planet* (New York: Collier Books, 1944) 94–95.

contrasts Augray's account of the *eldila* with theories postulated by anthropologists on his home planet: theories to explain the "recurrent human tradition of bright, elusive people sometimes appearing on the Earth...."[65] As we saw in the last chapter, Lewis connects anthropology with difference; anthropology privileges particularity in its study of individual cultures. (And, of course, Lewis rejects this particularity, maintaining that cultural difference is not as great as anthropologists contend.[66]) By pitting Augray's account against that of the anthropologists, the narrator aligns Augray's explanation with universality, with trans-cultural application. Given this conceptual alignment, the truth of Ransom's speculation, grounded in Augray's teaching, is irresistible: The evanescent appearance of irradiated people on earth "...might after all have another explanation than the anthropologists had yet given."[67]

Ransom later learns the cosmic place of the *eldila* during a conversation that occurs in the cave of a venerable and esteemed acquaintance of Augray. Augray and this acquaintance, referred to simply as the "old *Sorn*," along with his students, question Ransom about earth—its civilizations, languages, methods of production, etc. When they learn about "war, slavery and prostitution," they are "astonished." The following dialogue among the *sorns* ensues:

"It is because they have no Oyarsa," said one of the pupils.

"It is because every one of them wants to be a little Oyarsa himself," said Augray.

"They cannot help it," said the old *sorn*. "There must be rule, yet how can creatures rule themselves? Beasts must be ruled by *hnau* and *hnau* by *eldila* and *eldila* by *Maleldil*. These creatures have no *eldila*. They are like one trying to lift himself by his own hair—or one trying to see over a whole country when he is on a level with it—like a female trying to beget young on herself."[68]

This conversation among the *sorns* exemplifies their roles as transcendent characters, for within this dialogue are embedded theological and moral principles that undergird the narrative and that orient Ransom and the reader. The fundamental principle evident in the dialogue is that the universe is divinely arranged into a hierarchy that structures authority.

---

[65] Ibid., 95.

[66] C. S. Lewis, "Christianity and Culture" in *Christian Reflections*, 54.

[67] Lewis, *Silent Planet*, 95.

[68] Ibid., 102.

Created beings obey in love those above them on the hierarchy and lead, again in love, those below. (It is fitting that these points about hierarchy should be offered within a pseudo-classroom setting, as the old *Sorn*'s pupils heed his authority and learn alongside Ransom and the reader.) The principle of hierarchy catalyzes the narrative, for the villains of the book, Dick Devine and Edward Weston, overstep their bounds, playing God through their attempt at colonizing Mars and other planets. Ransom overcomes his initial horror of the *sorns* and repulsion from the *hrossa* by interacting with them personally—as opposed to casting them as Other from a distance—eventually learning of their valued place in the cosmic hierarchy as beloved creatures of *Maleldil*.

Indeed, in the history of the genre of science fiction, Lewis, at least according to his own estimation, was a pioneer in crafting the benevolent Martian. This is what he writes in his 1963 essay originally titled "Onward, Christian Spacemen": "In [the early days of science fiction] writers in that genre almost automatically represented the inhabitants of other worlds as monsters and the terrestrial invaders as good. Since then the opposite set-up has become fairly common. If I could believe that I had in any degree contributed to this change, I should be a proud man."[69] If we assume he is correct about changing the common conception of the alien, Lewis redirects the genre of science fiction on the basis of his Christian conviction, for it is his faith that compels him to believe that aliens from outer space might find a place on God's chain of being and thus be an object of his love. More importantly, their comparatively lofty place on the hierarchy might also warrant our respect and submission. In the same essay, Lewis contemplates the prospect of space travel: "Must we go on to infect new realms? Of course we might find a species stronger than ourselves. In that case we shall have met, if not God, at least God's judgement in space."[70] Lewis's supposition about extraterrestrial life here overlaps with the function of transcendent characters in *Out of the Silent Planet*.

Like Father History in *The Pilgrim's Regress*, the *sorns* embody high tradition, though, of course, their version of high tradition collects the cumulative wisdom of Martian—not terrestrial—learning. During his time with the *sorns*, Ransom notices they possess few books. "'It is better to remember,' said the *sorns*."[71] Lacking books, the *sorns* become the literal

---

[69] C. S. Lewis, "The Seeing Eye," in *Christian Reflections*, 175.

[70] Ibid., 173.

[71] Ibid., 101.

repositories of Martian wisdom, endowing them with the authority to serve as transcendent characters.

### *Ransom in* That Hideous Strength

After his space flights to Mars (in *Out of the Silent Planet*) and Venus (in *Perelandra*), Ransom appears in *That Hideous Strength* as a transformed character. Imbibing the fecundity and unblemished beauty of the unfallen planet Perelandra, Ransom, now an older man, maintains a youthful—in fact, a divine—appearance. Adopting the title "Mr. Fisher-King," Ransom nurses a perpetual wound, like his Arthurian namesake. Having defeated Satan in the possessed body of Weston, Ransom—like another transcendent character—reenacts or re-fulfills the prophecy of Genesis 3:15: that Adam and Eve's offspring will crush the serpent's head, and the serpent will strike his heel. In *Perelandra*, Ransom literally smashes Weston/Satan's head. During their fight, Ransom—completing the prophecy—receives a wound to his heel. In *That Hideous Strength*, his leadership of a small coterie in England united against the nefarious plot of a diabolical organization called the National Institute of Co-ordinated Experiments (N.I.C.E.) proves pivotal in a cosmic battle between good and evil. Ransom thus once again plays a central role in a confrontation whose outcome determines the fate of an entire world and its inhabitants. His preternatural appearance, interplanetary experiences, and allusive likenesses to the Fisher King and to Christ position him as a transcendent character.

One representation of Ransom's character in *That Hideous Strength* engages a rhetorical dynamic analyzed in chapter 3: the re-conceptualization, a dialectical presentation consonant with Lewis's stance as outsider, not conforming to the twentieth-century *Zeitgeist*. This dynamic occurs when Jane Studdock first glimpses and then meets Ransom:

> Pain came and went in his face: sudden jabs of sickening and burning pain. But as lightning goes through the darkness and the darkness loses up again and shows no trace, so the tranquility of his countenance swallowed up each shock of torture. How could she have thought him young? Or old either? It came over her, with a sensation of quick fear, that this face was of no age at all…. Shortly after this she found herself seated before the Director. She was shaken: she was even shaking. She hoped intensely that she was not going to cry, or be unable to speak, or do

anything silly. For her world was unmade: anything might happen now.[72]

As chapter 3 explained, God and angelic beings are often subjected to Lewis's art of re-conceptualization; their power, knowledge, and goodness overwhelm human faculties. Lewis reframes the apprehension of such beings, a process that elicits in the reader reverential fear. Figured in a similar fashion, Ransom assumes the transcendent—and thus unnerving—qualities of the divine.

Like all transcendent characters, Ransom orients and instructs other characters as well as the reader. Ransom, for instance, helps clarify one of Jane's important visions, highlighting its religious and moral significance, thus safeguarding the apologic qualities of the text.[73] In this vision, Jane is visited by the terrestrial Venus, earth's representative of the celestial Venus. The terrestrial Venus appears to Jane in her bedroom as a giantess, resembling (but only through distortion) Mother Dimble, a matronly, Christian woman of Ransom's coterie. The terrestrial Venus is unruly and terrifying, adorned in "flame-robed" attire and brandishing a torch, threatening to set Jane's bedroom on fire. Lewis's position on myth as it relates to transcendence will be explored in the next section. For now, it will be sufficient to show how Ransom's knowledge of myth elevates him to his position as transcendent character.

Relating this vision to Ransom, Jane learns that Venus appeared to her in such a frightening manner because Jane is not a Christian. Venus came to her in pagan form: wide-eyed and violent. While she resembles Mother Dimble, Jane's vision of the terrestrial Venus lacks the sanctifying influence of Mother Dimble's Christianity, taming the wildness of Venus's pagan incarnation. As Ransom explains, "[Mother Dimble] is a Christian wife. And you, you know, are not. Neither are you a virgin. You have put yourself where you must meet that Old Woman [the terrestrial Venus] and you have rejected all that has happened to her since *Maleldil* came to Earth. So you get her raw—not stronger than Mother Dimble would find her, but untransformed, demoniac. And you don't like it."[74] The nature of Venus's

---

[72] C. S. Lewis, *That Hideous Strength* (New York: Simon & Schuster, 1996) 142–43.

[73] Again, I do not consider *That Hideous Strength*, or any of the texts analyzed in this section, as examples of pure apologue. Nevertheless, they contain features of the apologue given the strong didactic function of the text: "to assist" the "deliberate organization of attitudes." *A Preface to Paradise Lost* (Oxford: OUP, 1901), 56.

[74] *That Hideous Strength*, 314.

appearance thus hinges on the beliefs of those who behold her theophany: terrifying to the non-Christian, awe-inspiring to the Christian.

With Ransom's guidance, Jane gains a new understanding of spiritual realities. His explanation of the terrestrial Venus/celestial Venus dichotomy narrows the viable options with respect to ultimate concerns. As Ransom informs her, "'I'm afraid there's no niche in the world for people that won't be either Pagan or Christian."[75] Ransom's position here resembles Lewis's own: that the pagan imagination, as expressed in myth, record archetypal realities that, descending through time, can be baptized by Christianity (like the terrestrial Venus). Ransom, in short, helps Jane (and the reader) understand, from a Christian perspective, the fundamental realities of myth as networks of meaning that make the concrete apprehension of truth possible; he possesses and disseminates the archetypal knowledge that serves as the phenomenological foundation of the text, a foundation wherein Christianity appropriates pagan myths, which Lewis believed narrativized the quintessence of human experience.

Ransom and Jane's conversation about her vision concludes with the topic of archetypes. Although an agnostic, Jane acknowledges that her vision revealed to her a spiritual world, but she conceived "this world as 'spiritual' in the negative sense—as some neutral, or democratic, vacuum where differences disappeared, where sex and sense were not transcended but simply taken away."[76] This conception of the spiritual world appealed to Jane because, her own marriage in jeopardy, she guarded her individuality against the distinctly male presence of her spouse and the patriarchy that he symbolized. A spiritual world that effaced that masculine quality attracted Jane.

However, as a result of her visions and Ransom's guidance, Jane realizes that gender differences are not culturally constructed, but are rooted in a transcendent order. This realization gives Jane a jolt: "How if this invasion of her own being in marriage from which she had recoiled, often in the very teeth of instinct, were not, as she had supposed, merely a relic of animal life or patriarchal barbarism, but rather the lowest, the first, and the easiest form of some shocking contact with reality which would have to be repeated—but in ever larger and more disturbing modes—on the highest levels of all?"[77] Ransom teaches Jane (and, again, the reader) that, while the concept of male and female exist "only on the biological level," masculine and feminine

---

[75] Ibid., 315.
[76] Ibid.
[77] Ibid.

record fundamental realities built into the universe, emanating from God himself. "'The male you could have escaped,'" Ransom explains, "'for it exists only on the biological level. But the masculine none of us can escape. What is above and beyond all things is so masculine that we are all feminine in relation to it.'" Jane must acknowledge the archetypal realities of gender, a reality descending from God, who is the very quintessence of masculinity. "'You had better agree with your adversary [God] quickly,'" Ransom advises.

"'You mean I shall have to become a Christian?' said Jane.

"'It looks like it,' said [Ransom]."[78]

Ransom's knowledge of pagan myth as well as the archetypes and the spiritual, quintessential realities that they produce occasion Jane's conversion to Christianity. As transcendent character, Ransom adopts an Olympian perspective from which the reader discerns with clarity the spiritual and moral *desiderata* of the text.

## IV. Conveying Authority through Myth

The analysis of Jane's vision of the terrestrial Venus in *That Hideous Strength* leads me to a more thorough analysis of Lewis's understanding of myth. Like the apologue, mythopoeia is an effective genre for conveying authority. The two operate in different modes, however. The apologue cultivates stock responses by exemplifying formulable statements: for Lewis, statements that concern Christian ethics and doctrine. Mythopoeia, on the other hand, represents transcendent, pre-Christian realities, for myth, as we saw within the context of *That Hideous Strength*, inscribes the archetypes foundational to human experience. As we also saw, *That Hideous Strength*, like most of Lewis's works with mythopoeic elements, baptizes myth, sublimating it so that the realities of myth and of Christianity form one continuous whole. This function of myth now requires elaboration.

It is in his essay titled "Myth Became Fact" that Lewis identifies myth as a touchstone for reality: its capacity to bear the phenomenological weight of experiences that unite all humankind. Lewis writes, "What flows into you from the myth is not truth but reality (truth is always *about* something, but reality is that *about which* truth is), and, therefore, every myth becomes the father of innumerable truths on the abstract level. Myth is the mountain whence all the different streams arise which become truths down here in the

---

[78] Ibid., 316.

valley; *in hac valle abstractionis.*"[79] Reality proceeds from myth. Consequently, myth provides the conditions for truth to exist. Lewis's mountain metaphor illustrates this principle: Truth is contingent upon the reality that myth provides. Elsewhere, Lewis refers to myth as a "master key; use it on what door you like."[80] That is, since myth figures reality, it can unlock the truths that lie behind the doors of various branches of learning, from theology to psychology.

Because of its ontological status, myth obviously avoids the taint of subjectivism. It transcends the particular and the contingent: the individual perspective. Lewis notes, for instance, that tragic myths evoke in us sympathy not for the individual character within the myth, but for humankind in general: "The story of Orpheum makes us sad; but we are sorry for all men rather than vividly sympathetic with him, as we are, say, with Chaucer's Troilus."[81] In fact, because it registers a universal reality, myth is not indebted to the individual mythmaker. In the introduction to his edited volume on George MacDonald, Lewis asserts, "When I think of the story of the Argonauts and praise it, I am not praising Apollonium Rhodius (whom I never finished) nor Kingsley (whom I have forgotten) nor even [William] Morris, though I consider his version a very pleasant poem." What Lewis does praise is "a particular pattern of events" that is not beholden to the creative faculties of the writer or even dependent on artifice at all. As Lewis contends, "The critical problem which we are confronted is whether this art—the art of myth-making—is a species of the literary art. The objection to so classifying it is that the Myth does not essentially exist in *words* at all."[82] Myth records a non- or trans-verbal phenomenon, a reality that precedes not only truth but language as well.

For purposes of elucidation, we might contrast Lewis's position on myth as a pre-linguistic reality with Richard Rorty's conception of truth as a linguistic construct and thus—necessarily—a human construct: "Since truth is a property of sentences, since sentences are dependent for their existence on vocabularies, and since vocabularies are made by human beings, so are

---

[79] C. S. Lewis, "Myth Became Fact," in *God in the Dock: Essays on Theology and Ethics,* ed. Walter Hooper (Grand Rapids: Eerdmans, 1970) 66.

[80] C. S. Lewis, "Tolkien's *The Lord of the Rings*," in *On Stories and Other Essays on Literature,* ed. Walter Hooper (San Diego: Harcourt Brace & Company, 1982) 85.

[81] Lewis, *An Experiment in Criticism,* 6.

[82] C. S. Lewis, introduction to *George MacDonald: 365 Readings,* ed. C. S. Lewis (New York: Collier Books, 1974) xxvii.

truths."[83] Rorty's utterance, setting humans at the center of reality and truth making, underscores by contrast Lewis's essentialism. For Lewis, it is doubtful that vocabularies—let alone truth—are made by human beings. (This is evident when Ransom speaks Old Solar, which is described in *That Hideous Strength* as "Language herself, as she first sprang at *Maleldil's* bidding out of the molten quicksilver of the star called Mercury on Earth, but Viritrilbia in Deep Heaven."[84]) Since truth proceeds from myth, since myth records into archetypal patterns a fundamental reality, and since that reality was created by God, so is truth.

The archetypal patterns that eventuate in truth inform Lewis's reading of Milton's *Paradise Lost*, which represents "...certain very basic images in the human mind...of Heaven, Hell, Paradise, God, Devil, the Winged Horse, the Naked Bride, the Outer Void." According to Lewis, Milton—like all good mythopoeic writers—captures these images by distancing them from local and individual associations; the images are too grand, too universal for a particularized perspective. Lewis explains, "His own private image of the happy garden, like yours and mine, is full of irrelevant particularities—notably, of memories from the first garden he ever played in as a child. And the more thoroughly he describes those particularities the further we are getting away from the Paradisal idea as it exists in our minds, or even in his own." Mythopoeia captures the idea of the image from which all particularized ideas are the shadow. The universal image is planted within the uniform experience of humankind. Here Lewis explains how Milton connects readers to this uniform experience, evoking in them an image not of his own creation, but one already printed in their own hearts: "While seeming to describe his own imagination he must actually arouse ours, and arouse it not to make definite pictures, but to find again in our own depth the Paradisal light of which all explicit images are only the momentary reflection. We are his organ: when he appears to be describing Paradise he is in fact drawing out the Paradisal Stop in us."[85] Inscribing these archetypal images in *Paradise Lost*, Milton mitigates his own subjectivity, a process we must imitate if we read his poem correctly, for the world Milton projects in his poem contains the realities he already shares with his readers.

Archetypes descending from pagan myth figure in Lewis's account of sex in *The Four Loves*. During sex, explains Lewis, lovers enact a "Pagan

---

[83] Richard Rorty, *Contingency, Irony and Solidarity* (Cambridge: Cambridge University Press, 1989) 21.

[84] Lewis, *That Hideous Strength*, 229.

[85] Lewis, *Preface to Paradise Lost*, 48–49.

sacrament" during which the male becomes "Sky-Father," representing the quintessence of masculinity, and the female becomes "Earth-Mother," embodying pure femininity. Sex is a "mystery-play or ritual" during which lovers assume archetypal roles. Indeed, in shedding their clothes, lovers also shed their individuality: "By nudity the lovers cease to be solely John and Mary; the universal He and She are emphasised."[86] Once again, we see the authority commanded by myth: its phenomenological access to reality, transcending the particular, rooted in the uniform experience of humankind, establishing the conditions for universal truth.

In fact, myth resembles the Law of Nature and the *Tao* in its authoritative reach. All three convey or imply a transcendent reality. All three stress objectivity, epistemologically privileged by remaining immune to the subjectivism of Conditioners, Innovators, and others who adhere to ephemeral cultural movements and intellectual fads. Concomitantly, all three depend upon the presumption of uniform experience; human experience over the course of millennia verifies their universality, making the truths they offer undeniable. Unlike the Law of Nature and the *Tao*, however, myth contains malleable content. While the Law of Nature and the *Tao* unwaveringly prescribe moral and aesthetic absolutes, myth encompasses varying subject matter. For Lewis, as we saw, myth is a "master key." This is what makes myth so instrumental for Lewis in conveying authority in his works of fiction, nearly all of which contains elements of mythopoeia. By virtue of its generic identity, mythopoeia sustains essentialism through archetypal images, committing itself to the phenomenological and epistemological assumptions upon which Lewis's Christian worldview is built. It is no wonder that myth appealed to Lewis, given his philosophical orientation and given his polemical task as public intellectual: mythopoeia is a ready-made genre for authoritatively conveying a reality consonant with Lewis's Christian conviction.

In this respect, then, myth *does* resemble the Law of Nature and the *Tao*; faithfully traced and followed, all three will lead to the throne of God. Like moral absolutes, mythic archetypes find their source in the wellspring of God's being. This is why Lewis cannot dismiss religions other than Christianity as simply false; they all are anchored—in varying degrees—to a fundamental reality. In *Mere Christianity*, Lewis writes, "If you are a Christian you do not have to believe that all the other religions are simply wrong all through.... If you are a Christian, you are free to think that all those religions, even the queerest ones, contain at least some hint of the

---

[86] C. S. Lewis, *The Four Loves* (New York: Harcourt Brace & Company, 1988) 103.

truth."[87] Lewis draws a similar conclusion in his essay, "Is Theology Poetry?": "Supposing, for purposes of argument, that Christianity is true; then it could avoid all coincidence with other religions only on the supposition that all other religions are one hundred percent erroneous.... We should, therefore, expect to find in the imagination of great Pagan teachers and myth makers some glimpse of that theme which we believe to be the very plot of the whole cosmic story—the theme of incarnation, death, and rebirth."[88] This plot and these themes constitute the fundamental archetypes, the "pattern of events" that transforms myth into the touchstone of God's reality. Pagan myths of dying and resurrecting gods that predate Christianity do not rattle Lewis's faith; on the contrary, they attest to the reality that lies beyond them. Lewis, in fact, refers to Christianity as a myth that became fact:

> The heart of Christianity is a myth which is also a fact. The old myth of the Dying God, *without ceasing to be myth*, comes down from the heaven of legend and imagination to the earth of history. It *happens*—at a particular date, in a particular place, followed by definable historical consequences. We pass from a Balder or an Osiris, dying nobody knows when or where, to a historical Person crucified (it is all in order) *under Pontius Pilate*. By becoming fact it does not cease to be myth: that is the miracle. I suspect that men have sometimes derived more spiritual sustenance from myths they did not believe than from the religion they professed. To be truly Christian we must both assent to the historical fact and also receive the myth (fact though it has become) with the same imaginative embrace which we accord to all myths. The one is hardly more necessary than the other.[89]

Lewis's high view of myth helps explain the prevalence of mythopoeia in his fiction. My analysis contravenes the common view that Lewis's imaginative side exists in disharmony with his apologetic side. Instead, I contend that all of Lewis's writerly personas, forms of authority, and methods for conveying authority operate at the service of his function as public intellectual. Mythopoeia summons principles that resonate in the public sphere: the presumption of uniform experience and an objective order binding on all humankind. In this respect, the loftiest flights of mythopoeic fancy in, say, *The Great Divorce*, are not operationally different than the most

---

[87] C. S. Lewis, *Mere Christianity* (San Francisco: HarperSanFrancisco, 2001) 35.

[88] C. S. Lewis, "Is Theology Poetry?" in *The Weight of Glory and Other Addresses*, ed. Walter Hooper (New York: Simon & Schuster, 1980) 98.

[89] Lewis, "Myth Became Fact," 66–67.

rigorously argued sections of polemical prose in *The Problem of Pain*. Both engage the procedural guidelines of public discourse, thereby summoning the authority to make the case for Christianity compelling within the public sphere.

# Introduction to Part 2

## C. S. Lewis beyond the Public Sphere

In his provocative essay, "Why We Can't All Just Get Along," Stanley Fish offers counsel to Christians who wish to bring their faith to bear on discussions and debates within the public sphere: "To put the matter baldly, a person of religious conviction should not want to enter the marketplace of ideas but to shut it down, at least insofar as it presumes to determine matters that he believes have been determined by God and faith. The religious person should not seek an accommodation with liberalism; he should seek to rout it from the field, to extirpate it, root and branch."[1] Fish contends that the "modern liberal-enlightenment picture of cognitive activity,"[2] which by and large overlaps with the Enlightenment procedural guidelines and conventions of the public sphere as outlined in the previous chapters, will never give religion a fair hearing. While it proclaims to champion tolerance, the public sphere marginalizes faith perspectives by virtue of evidential criteria: ideas achieve credence when verified by hyperbolically objective reasoning. Faith is a category of belief ill-fitted to this Enlightenment process of verification. Fish's point, however, is that *all* beliefs—religious or not—proceed upon faith: "That is to say, evidence is never independent in the sense of being immediately perspicuous; evidence comes into view (or doesn't) in the light of some first premise or 'essential axiom' that cannot itself be put to the test because of the protocols of testing are established by its pre-assumed authority."[3] The result is a stalemate within the public sphere, a war unwinnable due to "deep conflict over basic and *nonnegotiable* issues." This stalemate exposes liberalism's attenuated definition of tolerance as well as its bias: the very conditions of the public sphere favor anti-religious perspectives. Warfare that results from the stalemate, as Fish explains, "…was precisely what liberalism was invented to deny; and it manages that denial by excluding from the tolerance it preaches anyone who will not pledge allegiance to the mimicry of tolerance."[4] For this reason,

---

[1] Stanley Fish, "Why We Can't All Just Get Along?," *First Things* vol. 60 (February 1996): 21.

[2] Ibid., 19.

[3] Ibid., 23.

[4] Ibid., 25.

Christians should not seek accommodation with the liberal-Enlightenment paradigm; we simply can't all get along.

Fish's thought-provoking essay provides a vantage point to consider the transition this book makes in Part 2. The stalemate and subsequent warfare alluded to by Fish signal the demise of the public sphere, its failure to provide the rational-critical space of exchange where dispassionate reasoners could arrive at truth by consensus. Chapter 6 explores this demise, showing how this consensus, for a variety of reasons, never materialized.

Despite this demise, and Fish's cogent argument notwithstanding, Part 1 of this book shows that Lewis entered the public sphere, employed its conventions, played by the rules of the liberal-Enlightenment paradigm, and did so with great success. Many converted Christians would agree, from Joy Davidman Gresham to Chuck Colson, both of whom were reasoned into faith because of the writings of C. S. Lewis. Scores of Christian philosophers and apologists have not abandoned evidentialism and thus have not given up on the basic Enlightenment paradigm. For these holdouts, the Lewis analyzed in Part 1—Lewis the public intellectual—still speaks to current generations.

It remains to be seen how long the holdouts can cling to the crumbling stage of the Enlightenment. Again, my contention is that Lewis died near the beginning stages of the demise of the public sphere; he employed its conventions before they were seriously challenged and found wanting. His accomplishment as public intellectual is thus inimitable, constituting the first phenomenon of my analysis. Writing in the mid 1990s, thirty years after the death of C. S. Lewis, Fish is in a position to declare, "'We already had the Enlightenment' and religion lost."[5] Fish shows little optimism for the holdouts who follow the model of Lewis as public intellectual. Fish identifies one of these as George Marsden, a scholar of higher education and its intersections with religion. Fish's critique of Marsden provides a springboard for Part 2, Lewis beyond the public sphere.

In many ways, Marsden's orientation as a distinctly Christian scholar overlaps with the theoretical assumptions of Lewis. As Lewis heeds the conventions of the public sphere, Marsden insists that religious scholars must accommodate the pluralistic setting of the modern academy. That is, "If [religious scholars] wish to participate in such a setting (and some may not), they need to respect some conventions that make it possible for people to communicate and to get along when they differ as to first principles." Marsden identifies these conventions as "basic standards of evidence and

---

[5] Ibid., 26. Fish here is borrowing some words from the work of Stephen Carter.

argument. These standards work in separating good arguments from bad, and on many topics they can establish a sort of 'public knowledge' that persons from many ideological sub-communities can agree on and which are not simply matters of opinion." And so Marsden concludes, "Religious beliefs must be defended with arguments and evidence that are publicly accessible."[6] Marsden's repeated appeal to the gate-keeping function of the public links his advice to the accomplishment of Lewis as public intellectual: knowledge must be public to be meaningful, accessible to a wide swath of disparate individuals—i.e., the differentiated audience of the public sphere.

Fish finds Marsden's project self-defeating and thus futile. Fish's specific point of attack is relevant to my analysis. By virtue of his insistence on public knowledge, Marsden claims that Christians can approach the study of faith and faith-inflected issues with objectivity and dispassionate detachment: "It is perfectly possible to have strong evaluative interests in a subject, and yet treat it fairly and with a degree of detachment."[7] Marsden here endorses a mitigated version of what I referred to as *de-conversion* in chapter 3: an analytical pose in which pre-analytical convictions—i.e., biases—are held in momentary abeyance.

Fish's refutation of Marsden's claim is powerful and, I think, ultimately devastating:

> But it is possible to detach yourself from a "strong evaluative interest" only if you believe in a stage of perception that exists *before* interest kicks in; and not only is that a prime tenet of liberal thought, it is what makes possible the exclusionary move of which Marsden...complain[s]. If such a base-level stage of perception does in fact exist, it can be identified as the common ground in relation to which *uncommon*—that is, not universally shared—convictions (like, for example, Christ is risen) can be marginalized and privatized. By claiming to have set aside his strongly held values in deference to the virtue of fairness—a virtue only if you are committed to the priority of procedure over substance—Marsden agrees to play by the rules of the very ideology of which his book is in large part a critique.[8]

Fish thus contends that Marsden's advocacy of detachment—his very belief in a "base-level stage of perception"—concedes too much; it sanctions the

---

[6] George Marsden, *The Outrageous Idea of Christian Scholarship* (Oxford: Oxford University Press, 1997) 11, 47, 48.

[7] George Marsden, *The Soul of the American University: From Protestant Establishment to Established Nonbelief* (Oxford: Oxford University Press, 1994) 8.

[8] Fish, "Why We Can't All Just Get Along?," 25–26.

liberal commitments that marginalize religion in the first place. It should be clear by now that the grounds upon which Fish critiques Marsden could very well serve for a critique of Lewis. The analytical strategy of detachment and the assumption of a base-level stage of perception constitute in part the conventions of the public sphere that Lewis, as public intellectual, had mastered. Fish's reference to a "common ground," which is "universally shared," evokes my notion of the myth of uniform experience, an assumption of the Enlightenment that remained operative in the twentieth-century public sphere. Again, as public intellectual, Lewis espoused this myth. So, from our post-Enlightenment perspective, we might ask whether Lewis concedes too much.

Part 2 analyzes how Lewis operates beyond the public sphere. This is not to claim that Lewis abandons the public sphere and engages merely in private, personal writing, though my analysis of *A Grief Observed* reveals that this is partly the case. This is also not to claim that, at some point later in life, Lewis changed his *basic* orientation with respect to reason and belief-acquisition. (Indeed, sections of Part 2 will show how Lewis retained his commitment to Enlightenment principles to the end.) Rather, it is to claim that Lewis in his later work does occasionally jettison those conventions that Fish describes as too accommodating. In the case of texts like the Narniad and *Till We Have Faces*, Lewis's abandonment of these conventions is deliberate, though, of course, he would not describe it as such; his self-professed motivation was to exorcise his "expository demon"—mixing metaphors, to purge his writing of rhetorical "gas." In the case of *A Grief Observed*, the departure from the public sphere was an experiential necessity; the throes of despair drove him to a radically different discursive strategy.

In the case of all these texts, which span Lewis's later career from the 1950s till his death in 1963, a process of interested perception intermittently replaces the objective, universalizing conventions of the public sphere. The sense of detachment becomes less prominent. Pre-theoretical convictions are shown to shape belief; particularized perspectives localize abstract issues. Lewis operates beyond the public sphere, a move I identify as the second C. S. Lewis phenomenon.

# 6

## The Demise of the Public Sphere

Previous chapters have shown how Lewis, conceived as a public intellectual, offers representations and defenses of faith and virtue that are rooted in the procedural guidelines of the public sphere. Lewis's articulations of ultimate concerns conform to the conventions of public discourse. My critical narrative cast these articulations as rhetorical strategies proceeding from Lewis's adoption of various writerly stances from which he conveys powerful forms of authority. The writerly stances combine into what I call the de-converted outsider, a countercultural thinker who assumes a hyperbolically objective vantage point for critique. The forms of authority include the Law of Human Nature, the *Tao*, and what I call high tradition, the cumulative wisdom of western civilization. The genre of the apologue, the use of what I call transcendent characters, and mythopoeia (with its archetypal truths) constitute Lewis's method of conveying those forms of authority. Throughout this process, Lewis abides by what Alasdair MacIntyre calls "a central aspiration of the Enlightenment": "Rational justification was to appeal to principles undeniable by any rational person and therefore independent of all those social and cultural particularities which the Enlightenment thinkers took to be the mere accidental clothing of reason in particular times and places."[1] I have linked this process to Lewis by noting that the cumulative effect of his forms of authority and methods of conveying them is the presumption of an Olympian perspective, rising above the welter of localized viewpoints. This effect lies at the heart of Lewis's accomplishment as a public intellectual.

This chapter examines the demise of the public sphere: specifically, the historical events, particularly those of the twentieth century, that precipitated its degeneration. The public sphere underwent a transition that undermined the conventions and guidelines by which it was characterized for centuries. These conventions and guidelines are precisely those that Lewis mastered as public intellectual. In short, the transformation of the public sphere marked the deterioration of the conventions and guidelines

---

[1] Alasdair MacIntyre, *Whose Justice? Which Rationality?* (Notre Dame: University of Notre Dame Press, 1988) 6.

upon which Lewis garnered fame as Christian apologist, both in nonfiction and fiction. This chapter will thus bring into focus the first C. S. Lewis phenomenon: With the demise of the public sphere, Lewis's accomplishment is inimitable.[2] The conditions that helped enable Lewis's accomplishment have evaporated. This chapter also serves as a transition to part 2: Lewis beyond the public sphere.

## I. Jürgen Habermas and the "Decomposition" of the Public Sphere

Published in 1989, Habermas's *The Structural Transformation of the Public Sphere* traces the gradual demise of the public sphere.[3] This decomposition stems in large part from the expansion of the public sphere and, consequently, its increasing inclusiveness. Homogeneity within the public sphere began to unravel as class and education disparities often made differences of opinion irreconcilable: "The public was expanded, informally at first, by the proliferation of the press and propaganda; along with its social exclusiveness it also lost the coherence afforded by the institutions of sociability and a relatively high level of education."[4] The result was that the public sphere occasionally "...became an arena of competing interests fought out in the coarser forms of violent conflict."[5] Admitting diverse and divisive voices, the public sphere lost its unity, transforming public opinion from a

---

[2] This inimitable quality lies behind, I think, Alan Jacobs's concerns about the fascination with Lewis from so many Christians: "...there is the danger that Lewis will so dominate our picture of what a Christian apologist should be that we will be looking for someone to address the challenges of fifty years ago, not today—someone who has a response to Freud or Marx but not to Richard Rorty or Andrea Dworkin.... His apologetic works presuppose, and rarely make any argument for, the criteria for rationality themselves. Today those criteria simply cannot be assumed, and yet many Christians still persist in assuming them.... For these and other reasons it is an open question whether orthodox Christians' continued fascination with Lewis is a good or a bad thing. There is much to be gained from reading him; I say this as one who has over the last fifteen years drawn considerable spiritual nourishment from his cornucopia of works, and who expects to draw more in the future. But more attention must be given to following his example rather than imitating his productions—that is, to making the case for Christianity to our world rather than to his. Lewis wrote most of his major apologetic works more than fifty years ago, and in this century fifty years is a long, long time." See Jacobs, "The Second Coming of C. S. Lewis," *First Things* 47 (1994): 29–30.

[3] Jurgen Habermas, *The Structural Transformation of the Public Sphere: An Inquiry into a Category of Bourgeois Society*, trans. Thomas Burger (Cambridge: MIT, 1989) 4.

[4] Ibid., 131–32.

[5] Ibid., 132.

site of contestation and adjudication into a mechanism for political leverage. Habermas cites the sentiments of John Stuart Mill as evidence: "Thus Mill even deplored the 'yoke of public opinion' or 'moral means of coercion in the form of public opinion.'"[6] Where it once served to ameliorate conflict through the use of reason, the public sphere increasingly became the *source* of conflict.

However, it was not until the late twentieth century that the public sphere underwent the changes most profound for the purposes of my analysis: changes that undermined the guidelines and conventions of the public sphere. Today, writes Habermas, "...the mass media have transmogrified [the public sphere] into a sphere of culture consumption."[7] Consumerism now defines the public sphere; "it assumes the form of a consumer item."[8] Of course, from its early formation, the public sphere depended on consumers, who purchased books and theater, concert, and museum tickets, cultural artifacts that generated the discussions constitutive of public discourse. In the late twentieth century, however, the discussions themselves have become absorbed into the consumer culture. Explains Habermas,

> Today the conversation itself is administered. Professional dialogues from the podium, panel discussion, and round table shows—the rational debate of private people becomes one of the production numbers of the stars in radio and television, a salable package ready for the box office; it assumes commodity form even at "conferences" where anyone can "participate." Discussion, now a "business," becomes formalized; the presentation of positions and counterpositions is bound to certain prearranged rules of the game; consensus about the subject matter is made largely superfluous by that concerning form.[9]

The consumerization of discussion restructures public discourse, reconstituting it as a cultural product and often limiting it to the modes of presentation characteristic of new media.

Indeed, Habermas notes the way that radio, film, and television transform the way we process ideas. The new media render its audience passive by virtue of its immediacy, their totalizing effect on the listener or viewer. In short, the new media reduce the space for rational-critical debate. As Habermas explains, "Under the pressure of the 'Don't talk back!' the conduct of the public assumes a different form. In comparison with printed

---

[6] Ibid., 133.
[7] Ibid., 162.
[8] Ibid., 164.
[9] Ibid.

communications the programs sent by the new media curtail the reactions of their recipients in a peculiar way. They draw the eyes and ears of the public under their spell but at the same time, by taking away its distance, place it under 'tutelage,' which is to say they deprive it of the opportunity to say something and to disagree."[10]

Habermas notes another way in which the public sphere has been compromised. The rise of intellectual specialization has polarized two groups of people: "the productive and critical minorities of specialists and specializing amateurs," on the one hand, and, on the other, "the great public of mass media."[11] While the specialists become more insular, reasoning critically to each other while marginalizing their public relevance, the consumers of mass media monopolize the public space, but do so with a "receptiveness" that is "uncritical."[12] Consequently, the public sphere has been fractured along this schism, with the groups on either side engaging different forms of culture and grappling with different ideas. Reflecting on the early phase of the public sphere, Habermas observes, "Of Richardson's *Pamela* it could be said that it was read by the entire public, that is, by 'everyone' who read at all."[13] In modern times, no cultural production enjoys the ubiquity of Richardson's novel, a ubiquity that indicates not only the cohesion of the public sphere but the myth of uniform experience. The lack of cohesion dispels the myth, undermining the traditional conventions of public discourse.

## II. The Decline of the Public Intellectual

Expectedly, the factors that engendered the demise of the public sphere contribute to the decline of the public intellectual. Richard A. Posner lays the blame at the feet of the late twentieth-century university: "I believe that it is fair to say that the position, the contribution, most precisely the social *significance* of the public intellectual is deteriorating in the United States and that the principal reasons are the growth and character of the modern university."[14] At the heart of that character is, as in Habermas's critical narrative, specialization, the splintering of scholarship into focused niches, an enterprise that dominates the academy. "The chief culprit in the quality

---

[10] Ibid., 170–171.

[11] Ibid., 175.

[12] Ibid.

[13] Ibid., 174.

[14] Richard A. Posner, *Public Intellectuals: A Study of Decline* (Cambridge MA: Harvard UP, 2001) 6.

problems of the public-intellectual market," writers Posner, "is the modern university."[15]

Occasioning the "professionalization of knowledge,"[16] the university creates at least two unfavorable conditions for the livelihood of the public intellectual. First, the professionalization of knowledge remaps the intellectual terrain, dividing it into smaller and smaller segments, thereby leaving the public intellectual, as generalist, with no ground to stand on. Second, the university lures the would-be public intellectual into its environs, offering a safe and comfortable life. Both of these unfavorable conditions require some exploration.

Prior to the specialization endemic to the modern university, the various fields of knowledge admitted entrée to non-university critics. From G. K. Chesterton to George Orwell, such critics could at least theoretically speak and write with as much authority as academicians. Specialization, however, subdivided and shrank the fields of inquiry, requiring expertise in narrowly focused subjects. By definition, public intellectuals do not deal in such scholarly minutiae, leaving them disinclined and/or unable to engage in debates fostered by the leading scholars of rapidly growing (and esoteric) fields. As John Patrick Diggins writes, "Given the exponential expansion of academia and hence the competitive quest for differentiation and specialization, more and more is asked about less and less in ever more arcane ways."[17] The restructuring of the intellectual map marginalizes the sort of perspectives that offer generalizations across disciplines and fields, attempts at which rankle the scholarly experts and lead to charges of amateurism. As the university expands and knowledge becomes more professionalized, the public intellectual is increasingly squeezed out of the debates: "When self-contained (or worse, self-referential) expert communities define the supply side of the market, there will be a dearth of those either polyglot or capable of transcendence. In a world of such archipelagoes, the public intellectual literally has no ground to stand on. Either he remains on his little island or he drowns."[18] As Posner aptly puts it, "The professionalization of knowledge has made it much more difficult for intellectual freebooters to range across different fields...."[19]

---

[15] Ibid., 188.

[16] Ibid., 54.

[17] John Patrick Diggins, "The Changing Role of the Public Intellectual in American History," in *The Public Intellectual: Between Philosophy and Politics*, ed. Arthur M. Melzer et al. (New York: Rowman & Littlefield Publishers, Inc., 2003) 114.

[18] Ibid., 115.

[19] Posner, *Public Intellectuals*, 54.

For these reasons, would-be public intellectuals enter the university to pursue their career; the university, Posner states, "...has shrunk the ranks of the 'independent' intellectual."[20] Becoming academic scholars, these intellectuals do not play the role of translators, disseminating in vernacular language their ideas to laypeople. As Russell Jacoby puts it, "As intellectuals became academics, they had no need to write in a public prose; they did not, and finally they could not." Trained in specialized graduate programs, playing by the rules of the academy, would-be public intellectuals did not cease to exist: "They became radical sociologists, Marxist historians, feminist theorists, but not quite public intellectuals."[21]

The decline of the public intellectual reflects large shifts in culture. Specialization in the academy finds its parallel in an increasingly diverse culture that offers specialized forms of entertainment and information to a niche market. Jacoby explains,

> There is no doubt that the demise of public intellectuals reflects the recomposition of the public itself; it coincides with the wild success of television, the expansion of the suburbs, the corrosion of the cities, the fattening of the universities. The eclipse of the big general magazines, such as *Look* and *Life*, itself registers a parcellation of a once more homogeneous public; they have been replaced by "special interest" magazines—tennis, computer, travel, sports. In view of these developments, the disappearance of general intellectuals into professions seems completely understandable, inevitable, and perhaps desirable.[22]

Diggins echoes Jacoby:

> What about the public, the demand side, so to speak? By definition, a public intellectual requires an intellectual public. What are we to make of the demise of *Encounter, Preuves*, and *Monat*, the waning of once powerful reviews with names such as *Partisan, Edinburgh, Westminister*, the nonbirth of a "Berlin Review of Books," and the failure to establish *Transatlantik*, a German version of the *New Yorker*, which folded after a few years? All this suggests two possible explanations: Either the "intellectual public" has also contracted, or it, too, has "specialized."[23]

---

[20] Ibid., 188.

[21] Russell Jacoby, *The Last Intellectuals: American Culture in the Age of Academe* (New York: Basic Books, 1987) 7 and 8.

[22] Ibid., 236–37.

[23] Diggins, "The Changing Role of the Public Intellectual in American History," 115.

Both Jacoby and Diggins describe the effects of an increasingly heterogeneous public, which, by virtue of its diversity, strains the social cohesion upon which public discourse is predicated. A fragmented public pursues different intellectual and cultural interests that often never overlap. Consequently, the public sphere has no foundation, no essence; the common intellectual denominator that unites the public becomes smaller and smaller. Indeed, a fragmented public reflects the dissolution of social spaces that once served as the locus for intellectual and cultural activity. Coffee houses, tea houses, and editorial pages of widely read periodicals once provided the space for rational-critical debate on issues that concerned the informed public as a whole. Writing just two years after the death of C. S. Lewis, Lewis A. Coser observes,

> At the present time, political life is centered in Washington, the world of publishing and editing is in New York, Los Angeles remains the movie capital, the musical and art world is located in New York, and the world of scholarship is dispersed throughout such major university centers as Cambridge, Berkeley, and New Haven. The geographical fragmentation of cultural life is not conducive to the emergence of a sense of cohesion among the intellectuals, nor does it encourage the rise of a cohesive public for them. The professors, scholars, and scientists gathered in a vast university center like Cambridge may have only minimal contact or even acquaintance with the New York intellectual *milieu*....[24]

As chapter 2 showed, the conventions of the traditional public sphere depend to a large extent on a homogenous public as well as the myth of uniform experience. Arguments that once held sway in the public sphere— arguments that appealed to universal truths and essential human experiences—lose cogency in a world that privileges difference and diversity. When Lewis died in 1963, the stage upon which the public intellectual stood, a stage that commanded the attention of a unified public, was crumbling to the ground.

### III. Post-Enlightenment Epistemology
### (and the Rise of Postmodernism)

Postmodernism is a massive event of the mid to late twentieth century, though, as this section will show, its precursors stretch back to at least the early part of the century. Because of its multifarious nature, postmodernism

---

[24] Lewis A. Coser, *Men of Ideas: A Sociologist's View* (New York: The Free Press, 1965) 350.

defies definition. Consequently, I narrow its scope in this section to issues of epistemology, drawing a distinction between Enlightenment epistemology and post-Enlightenment epistemology. It should be understood that post-Enlightenment epistemology is indebted—or at least affined—to postmodernism or some of its tenets. This section will explore the contours of post-Enlightenment epistemology first by way of contrast: by showing how Enlightenment epistemology helps to structure the conventions of the public sphere, thereby creating opportune conditions for the public intellectual. I will then explore how post-Enlightenment epistemology challenges the conventions of the public sphere; its success in doing so contributes to the demise of the public sphere.

### a. Enlightenment Epistemology.

With the 1690 publication of John Locke's *An Essay Concerning Human Understanding*, empiricism became the dominant philosophy of England, constituting a radical break from seventeenth-century rationalism. My contention, however, is that there exists some continuity between the rival philosophical traditions—a continuity obtained by a shared commitment to the Enlightenment project. Although empiricism depends upon the senses for knowledge-acquisition and rationalism expressly avoids sense data, basic procedural guidelines remain—to some extent—constant. I begin my analysis of these procedural guidelines by turning first to one of the founding fathers of the Enlightenment project, Rene Descartes.

In 1637, Descartes helped to codify the Enlightenment project with the publication of his *Discourse on Method*. Employing mathematical methods and universal doubt, he sought to break down knowledge and experience to indubitable certainties. This rationalist approach was highly optimistic because it held that truth was "out there" and merely needed to be "discovered." Descartes wrote, "...there is only one truth to each thing, whoever finds it knows as much about the thing as there is to be known."[25] The one truth that Descartes claimed he knew for certain is expressed in the celebrated phrase, "*cogito ergo sum*," "I think, therefore I am."[26] The search for truth, Descartes maintained, could be built upon this certain and unshakable foundation; the search for truth was furthermore undergirded by the belief that truth was stable and knowable.

---

[25] Rene Descartes, *Discourse on Method and the Meditations*, trans. F. E. Sutcliffe (New York: Penguin Books, 1968) 43.

[26] Ibid., 103.

Pursuing his project, Descartes implemented three procedural guidelines that I wish to identify as hallmarks of the Enlightenment; these guidelines are then appropriated by eighteenth-century empiricists and seminally influence public discourse and thus the playing field for the twentieth-century public intellectual. First, Descartes established foundationalism as the normative blueprint for epistemological structures. Such structures must rise upwardly upon a foundation of propositions that need no justification, that are self-evident. Propositions higher up on the structure attain their truth status by virtue of their logical and coherent relationship to propositions lower on the structure, all of which are anchored by the foundational beliefs. Nancey Murphy and James Wm. McClendon define foundationalism this way:

> The foundationalist doctrine, a legacy from Descartes, assumes that it is the philosopher's job to justify the knowledge claims of other disciplines by finding indubitable or incorrigible beliefs upon which they depend. The reasoning behind the search for foundations is this: In the attempt to justify a given belief, the chain of supporting beliefs must not be circular or form an infinite regress. Therefore one must at some point reach a belief that needs no further justification—it must be something that cannot fail to be believed.[27]

For Descartes, that something was not only the existence of self but the existences of God and the external world. These beliefs constituted the foundation of Descartes's epistemological structure.

It must be noted that in the history of modern philosophy (from, say, the early seventeenth century to the late nineteenth century) all epistemologies were by and large foundational in nature.[28] However, within this history, there do exist various forms of foundationalism. The Enlightenment project, I suggest, espouses *strong* foundationalism—a variation that sets up stringent criteria for justifying truth claims. These stringent criteria become apparent when we look at the other two procedural guidelines—both of which are components of strong foundationalism—adopted by Descartes.

---

[27] Nancey Murphy and James Wm. McClendon, "Distinguishing Modern and Postmodern Theologies," *Modern Theology* 5/3 (1989): 192.

[28] In the mid-twentieth century, Willard V. O. Quine eschewed foundationalism when he developed his web theory of belief—a holistic approach to epistemology in which beliefs assume an interdependence within a non-foundational architecture. Beliefs are not built upon indubitable certainties but are rather interlocked in an elaborate pattern of mutual dependence. See Quine's "Two Dogmas of Empiricism," *Philosophical Review* 40 (1951); reprinted in T. Olshewsky, ed., *Problems in the Philosophy of Language* (New York: Holt, 1969).

The second procedural guideline concerns Descartes's method for building his epistemological foundation. As stated above, Descartes resolved to doubt everything that he had been taught in order to arrive at certainty, in order to find his foundations. He thus assumes a hyperbolically objective, impartial, and assumedly neutral stance that involves what I called in chapter 2 *de-conversion*. If conversion refers to the acceptance of particular beliefs and views, Descartes reverses that process and assumes that he can strip away particular beliefs and views in order to achieve that objective stance. De-conversion involves a self-imposed manipulation of one's own identity whereby the self is supposedly cleansed of all presuppositions in order to apprehend truth impartially. The self thus sheds the incrustations of historical, political, social, religious, and communal contingencies and particularities. Having done so, the self assumes a new identity—one of a neutral inquisitor.

Assuming that anyone can undergo this de-conversion experience, Descartes maintained that this neutral inquisitor will render philosophical conclusions that any reasonable or rational person must agree with. (The subtext here is the homogenous public of the public sphere.) Claims built upwardly on the foundation thus achieve the status of universal truth. This need for unanimity—guaranteed by the "de-converted" neutral inquisitor—constitutes the third procedural guideline I wish to note.

Admittedly, one finds that applying these three procedural guidelines to late seventeenth- and eighteenth-century empiricists is problematic. Reasoning *a priori*—as rationalists are wont to do—more readily yields the certainty and unanimity upon which foundationalism depends. For rationalists, truth exists independently of sense experience, thereby immune to the idiosyncratic fashion in which individuals might acquire and process sense data empirically. Thus, empirical foundationalism seems to be an oxymoron; this is not the case, however. Other critics have noted the empiricists' commitment to foundationalism. In his study on eighteenth-century hermeneutics, Joel C. Weinsheimer observes that much of the empirical thought of the period resists interpretation because its foundational claims are held to be indubitable—as foundational claims necessarily are:

> Most of the nonhermeneutic aspects of Hume's thought, as of Locke's, can be grouped under the rubric...of what we would now call "foundationalism." In the sense employed here, foundationalism is logically antithetical to hermeneutics, in that a foundation is defined as something that grounds interpretation but is not itself an interpretation. On this definition, foundational visions posit some ultimate given, some

bedrock of solidity where muddiness comes to an end, some hard knowledge that marks the limit—hence the secondariness—of interpretation.[29]

Nancey Murphy and James Wm. McClendon asseverate that "David Hume, following earlier British empiricists, continued Descartes's foundationalism,"[30] and, elsewhere, Murphy explains that, though they differed in their understanding of the nature of foundations and methods of attaining them, Descartes and Hume shared the overarching commitment to foundationalism:

> In Descartes's day deductive reasoning could be assumed to be the means of constructing the chain, once given the foundation. But when the foundations came to be thought of as sense experience, as already in Hume's day, the means of construction became problematic. In fact, one way of looking at Hume's famous problem of induction is to see it as simply drawing attention to the fact that because deduction only spells out consequences already implicit in the premises, there can be no deductive argument from a limited number of observations to a general conclusion. Hume's solution was finally to accept the necessity of proportioning one's belief to the strength of evidence. Thus, in empiricist epistemology, both the nature of the foundations and the method of construction differ from the corresponding Cartesian elements, but the underlying assumption is the same—namely, that it is the business of philosophy to examine the justification of the putative knowledge claims of other disciplines by attempting to derive them from immediately given foundations.[31]

Empiricists often located these foundations and simultaneously avoided the idiosyncratic, individualistic tendencies that empiricism would seemingly promote by appealing to Nature and/or Human Nature, a move similar to the one Lewis makes when he appeals to the Law of Human Nature and the *Tao* (see chapter 4). In such a way, many empiricists found order and stability in a world cut off from external truths and instead constituted by sense perception and associated ideas.

Appeals to Nature often provided empirical foundationalism with the universality and essentialism that characterize such epistemological

---

[29] Joel C. Weinsheimer, *Eighteenth-Century Hermeneutics: Philosophy of Interpretation in England from Locke to Burke* (New Haven: Yale University Press, 1993) 107.
[30] Murphy and McClendon, "Distinguishing Modern and Postmodern Theologies," 193.
[31] Nancey Murphy, *Theology in the Age of Scientific Reasoning* (Ithaca: Cornell University Press, 1990) 6–7.

structures. Basil Willey claims that "...no conception played a more significant part [in the eighteenth century] than that of 'Nature'....."; he continues, "Nature was the grand alternative to all that man had made of man; upon her solid ground therefore—upon the *tabula rasa* prepared by the true philosophy—must all the religion, the ethics, the politics, the law, and the art of the future be constructed."[32] S. N. Hampshire highlights the importance of Nature in Hume's philosophy: "For Hume the ultimate appeal in any argument, whether it is a moral or a philosophical argument, whether it is a matter of politics or aesthetics or of economics, is always an appeal to nature, to the regular order of our experience, to the normal course of things, as we actually observe them."[33] The Third Earl of Shaftesbury's portrayal of nature has affinities to my notion of the de-conversion experience in that they both rest upon a de-particularized, de-contextualized vantage point. In *An Essay Concerning Virtue and Merit*, he writes that we must regulate our behavior by Nature, "beyond which there is no measure or rule of things. Now Nature may be known from what we see of the natural state of creatures, and of man himself, when unprejudiced by vicious education."[34]

Appeals to Nature thus implicitly make a distinction between unnatural behavior and natural behavior. Unnatural behavior may stem, as in Shaftesbury's case, from "vicious education"; or, more generally, it may proceed from a deleterious overbalance of particularities—emotional, religious, etc.—within an individual's psyche. Natural behavior, on the other hand, is publicly acceptable behavior; it encompasses an ideal common denominator that unites individuals under that famous eighteenth-century collective noun, "Man." Natural behavior, in fact, is embodied in the de-contextualized, de-converted Cartesian inquirer.

We can see then that appeals to Nature reflect the eighteenth-century ideal of uniform experience (sketched in chapter 2). When a writer of the period appeals to Nature, the myth of uniform experience is presupposed. Thus, Joseph Addison, in *Spectator* no. 70, can blithely proclaim, "Human Nature is the same in all reasonable creatures; and whatever falls in with it, will meet with Admirers amongst Readers of all Qualities and Conditions."[35] Appeals to Nature and the ideal of uniform experience go hand in hand to

---

[32] Basil Willey, *The Eighteenth Century Background* (London: Chatto & Windus, 1946) 1–2.

[33] S. N. Hampshire, "Hume's Place in Philosophy," in *David Hume: A Symposium*, ed. D. F. Pears (New York: St. Martin's Press, 1966) 6–7.

[34] Anthony Earl of Shaftesbury, *Characteristics of Men, Manners, Opinions, Times, Etc.*, ed. John M. Robertson (Gloucester MA: Peter Smith, 1963) 325.

[35] Joseph Addison, *The Spectator*, vol. 1 (London: J. M. Dent & Sons, 1950) 263.

underwrite epistemological universality—an empirical foundation that is universally binding.

As should be evident by now, all three procedural guidelines outlined above inform Lewis's writing in one way or another. In addition, the eighteenth-century appeal to Nature and to uniform experience finds expression in the Lewis corpus. These Enlightenment guidelines and eighteenth-century concepts converged within the formation of the public sphere, which, as chapter 2 showed, provided the conditions for the twentieth-century public intellectual. Post-Enlightenment epistemology challenges these guidelines and concepts; in so doing, it also undermines the conditions that help produce the public intellectual.

### b. Post-Enlightenment Epistemology.

Late twentieth-century thinkers turned the Enlightenment on its head when they questioned the de-converted starting point of the Enlightenment project, particularly as it was codified by Descartes. To recapitulate the Cartesian epistemological narrative, Descartes claimed to assume nothing when he began his inquiry. Careful to avoid any *a priori* deductions, inductions, or assumptions, Descartes attempted to divest himself of all interpreted data to reach an unquestionable epistemological foundation. But as William Placher shows, uninterpreted data, whether rational or empirical, are never truly uninterpreted; inquiries are never conducted without assumptions; and foundationalism is never truly foundational: "Only in the context of assuming *some* things can he question *other* things.... We cannot build knowledge on a foundation of uninterpreted sense-data, because we cannot know particular sense-data in isolation from the conceptual schemes we use to organize them."[36] Those "conceptual schemes" may include the language with which knowledge itself is made communicable, the society or culture of which the inquirer is a member, or the historical time period in which the inquirer lives. Epistemological starting points, in other words, cannot be purely objective. All observations, as Placher writes, are "theory-laden."[37] The result, then, of post-Enlightenment thinking is the belief that there exists no universal standard by which we may judge rationality and truth—no Olympian point of reference. Any understanding of the world is necessarily a *contextualized* understanding.

---

[36] William Placher, *Unapologetic Theology: A Christian Voice in a Pluralistic Conversation* (Louisville: Westminster/John Knox Press, 1989) 26 and 29, emphasis in original.

[37] Ibid., 27.

It would be difficult to pinpoint one twentieth-century philosopher who was most influential in derailing the Enlightenment project and proposing an epistemological alternative. One could do worse, however, than to consider the work of William James, who serves as a precursor to postmodernism and whose *Pragmatism* (1907) seminally directed the post-Enlightenment turn. James steps outside the Enlightenment tradition when he underscores the contextual nature of knowledge and shies away from claims to privileged, objective points of reference from which to judge truth claims. James hints at the inevitability of contextualized understandings of the world. At the beginning of *Pragmatism*, for example, James indicates that a philosopher's temperament necessarily influences and colors his or her judgment. James, therefore, casts off any pretension to neutrality: "...of whatever temperament a professional philosopher is, he tries, when philosophizing, to sink the fact of his temperament. Temperament is no conventionally recognized reason, so he urges impersonal reasons only for his conclusions. Yet his temperament really gives him a stronger bias than any of his more strictly objective premises."[38] The denial of what I have called de-conversion thus complicates questions of truth. "The whole notion of truth," asserts James, "which naturally and without reflection we assume to mean the simple duplication by the mind of a ready-made and given reality, proves hard to understand clearly."[39]

James also develops one facet of post-Enlightenment thinking known as perspectivalism. Harold Heie defines perspectivalism as "the view that our claims to knowledge unavoidably reflect our particular perspectives as members of different interpretive communities."[40] Thus, not only can the temperament of a philosopher affect his or her judgments, but so can the perspective from which he or she judges as well. James provides perhaps his most explicit assent to perspectivalism (even though it had not yet at the time been developed into a specifically philosophic construct) when he writes: "What we say about reality thus depends on the perspective into which we throw it. The *that* of it is its own, but the *what* depends on the *which*; and the which depends on us."[41]

A student of James, Richard Rorty has wielded an enormous influence on post-Enlightenment thought, fully developing pragmatism into a political

---

[38] William James, *Pragmatism* (Indianapolis: Hackett, 1981) 8.

[39] Ibid., 87.

[40] Harold Heie, "The Postmodern Opportunity: Christians in the Academy." *Christian Scholar's Review* 26/2 (1996): 138.

[41] James, *Pragmatism*, 111, emphasis in original.

program. Like James (but with added vitriol), Rorty denounces the intellectual tradition of the seventeenth and eighteenth centuries, and announces the death of the Enlightenment project. This death involves the failure of those Enlightenment procedural guidelines described earlier as well as the various appeals to nature in order to shore up an epistemological consensus. In "Solidarity or Objectivity," he writes,

> To most thinkers of the eighteenth century, it seemed clear that the access to Nature which physical science had provided should now be followed by the establishment of social, political, and economic institutions which were in accordance with Nature. Ever since, liberal social thought has centered around social reform as made possible by objective knowledge of what human beings are like—not knowledge of what Greeks or Frenchman or Chinese are like, but of humanity as such. We are the heirs of this objectivist tradition, which centers around the assumption that we must step outside our community long enough to examine it in the light of something which transcends it, namely, that which it has in common with every other actual and possible human community. This tradition dreams of an ultimate community which will have transcended the distinction between the natural and the social, which will exhibit a solidarity which is not parochial because it is the expression of an ahistorical human nature.[42]

Rejecting the "objectivist tradition" and the notion of an "ahistorical human nature," Rorty likewise rejects epistemological foundationalism and its quest for de-converted starting points. In *The Consequences of Pragmatism*, he denounces philosophy that tries to "find natural starting points which are distinct from cultural traditions...."[43] He vehemently rejects setting up "criteria to which all sides must appeal"[44] and attempts to cultivate in his readers the "...sense that there is nothing deep down inside us except what we have put there ourselves, no criterion that we have not created in the course of creating a practice, no standard of rationality that is not an appeal to such a criterion, no rigorous argumentation that is not obedient to our own conventions."[45]

Another prominent exponent of post-Enlightenment thought, Alexander Nehamas, arguing in the tradition of Nietzsche and expanding on James,

---

[42] Richard Rorty, "Solidarity or Objectivity?," in *Post-Analytic Philosophy*, ed. John Rajchman and Cornel West (New York: Columbia University Press, 1985) 4.
[43] Richard Rorty, *Consequences of Pragmatism* (Minneapolis: University of Minnesota Press, 1982) xxxvii.
[44] Ibid., xli.
[45] Ibid., xlii.

details the nature of perspectivalism, which "implies that our many points of view cannot be smoothly combined into a unified synoptic picture of their common object."[46] In opposition to Weinsheimer's notion of Hume's uninterpretive foundationalism, Nehamas, summarizing Nietzsche, identifies our views of life itself as "interpretations," "in order to call to our attention the fact that they are never detached or disinterested, that they are not objective in a traditional sense."[47] According to the post-Enlightenment model, all propositions are not only interpretations but *interested* interpretations. This claim alone contravenes those three procedural guidelines of the Enlightenment project: foundationalism, de-conversion, and epistemological consensus among reasonable people (embodied in the public sphere).

Though less influential than Rorty and Nehamas, Alasdair MacIntyre has developed a communal system of ethics that proceeds from post-Enlightenment presuppositions. Though his is just one of the many tents in the post-Enlightenment camp, his position—as articulated in *Whose Justice? Which Rationality?*—builds upon the rubble of the public sphere.

MacIntyre recognizes the hegemony of the Enlightenment project, noting that it has dictated the norms of rational inquiry:

> Rationality requires, so it has been argued by a number of academic philosophers, that we first divest ourselves of allegiance to any one of the contending theories and also abstract ourselves from all those particularities of social relationship in terms of which we have been accustomed to understand our responsibilities and our interests. Only by so doing, it has been suggested, shall we arrive at a genuinely neutral, impartial, and, in this way, universal point of view, freed from the partisanship and the partiality and onesidedness that otherwise affect us.[48]

MacIntyre, however, like other post-Enlightenment thinkers, realizes that we would be best served to abandon such a definition of rationality and its repercussions for justification. He contends that "the legacy of the Enlightenment has been the provision of an ideal of rational justification which it has proved impossible to attain."[49] The universal stage of the Enlightenment simply cannot encompass humankind. Contextual conside-

---

[46] Alexander Nehamas, *Nietzsche: Life as Literature* (Cambridge: Harvard University Press, 1985) 49.

[47] Ibid., 72.

[48] MacIntyre, *Whose Justice? Which Rationality?*, 3.

[49] Ibid., 6.

rations determine the way we think, enclosing us within cultural, religious, or intellectual traditions. MacIntyre thus explodes the myth of a universal stage as well as the illusion of a universal rationality.

He explains that "what many of us are educated into is, not a coherent way of thinking and judging, but one constructed out of an amalgam of social and cultural fragments inherited from different traditions...."[50] And this fact about rationality—its situatedness—is the one fact that prominent empiricists like John Locke and David Hume, ensconced within the Enlightenment tradition, could not perceive. MacIntyre's narrative of the Enlightenment's blindness to its own shortcomings is particularly poignant; I thus quote it at length:

> In not perceiving that what he took to be universal was to a significant degree local and particular, Hume was at one with most of his contemporaries, perhaps indeed at one with most human beings of the time. The interest lies not so much in the type of error which Hume made as in the consequences for his own specific doctrines. What then were the highly specific social and cultural forms and attitudes which the Hume of the *Treatise* falsely identified with human nature as such? To what type of social and cultural order did they belong?... A system in which pride in houses and other such possessions, and in one's place within a hierarchy, is the keystone of a structure of reciprocity and mutuality, in which property determines rank, and in which law and justice have as their distinctive function the protection of the propertied, so that principles of justice provide no recognizable ground for appeals against the social order: this is the type of social and cultural order portrayed by Hume in the *Treatise* as exhibiting the characteristics of universal human nature, but it is also of course the type of social and cultural order described...as constituting the highly specific way of life of the eighteenth-century English landowning class and its clients and dependents. What Hume presents as human nature as such turns out to be eighteenth-century English human nature, and indeed only one variant of that, even if the dominant one.[51]

Once removed from the universal stage of the Enlightenment, issues of justification attend to principles of rationality that had previously gone unrecognized. Justification no longer appeals to non-existent universal standards of rationality but instead proceeds from the forthright assumptions and perspectives of a tradition-informed inquirer. From the rubble of the demolished universal stage emerges enclosed areas of tradition

---

[50] Ibid., 2.
[51] Ibid., 293, 295.

and community, each of which goes about justifying beliefs, experiences, ideas, or (in the largest sense of the term) interpretations based upon the contextualized geography of that enclosed area. Justificatory methods differ from tradition to tradition, and from community to community. The rise of post-Enlightenment epistemology thus builds upon the fragmentation of the public sphere. Its focus on localized interpretations stands in stark contrast to the Olympian perspective of the Enlightenment project. The new attentiveness to particularity and context creates a whole new set of procedural guidelines: a set of guidelines completely alien to public discourse, and thus to the project of the public intellectual, as they both had been traditionally conceived.

## IV. Post-Enlightenment Philosophy of Religion

The radical challenge of postmodernism reverberated throughout the disciplines, prompting scholars in various fields to rethink theoretical assumptions and transform modes of practice. One discipline reshaped by the postmodern turn is the philosophy of religion. Scholars of faith began to reevaluate the basic categories of their discipline, from natural theology to spiritual discipleship; these scholars began to talk about God and religious faith in much different ways than their Enlightenment predecessors. Like post-Enlightenment epistemology, post-Enlightenment philosophy of religion challenges the basic principles of the public sphere and thus shifts the ground upon which the traditional public intellectual stands. Post-Enlightenment philosophy of religion also calls into question traditional methods of conceptualizing Christianity, dislodging the faith from the interpretive framework established by Enlightenment principles. Since Lewis lived before the postmodern turn, the project of post-Enlightenment philosophy of religion challenges the model Lewis created as a distinctly *Christian* public intellectual.

Let us turn, then, to post-Enlightenment philosophy of religion. George Lindbeck develops what he calls "postliberal theology" by first abandoning foundationalism. His apologetics, which "must be *ad hoc* and nonfoundational,"[52] do not seek universal standards of rationality as a preliminary move for establishing common grounds for theological discussion. Neither do his apologetics assume a objective, disinterested stance; they do not claim to render universally binding conclusions with

---

[52] George Lindbeck, *The Nature of Doctrine: Religion and Theology in a Postliberal Age* (Philadelphia: Westminster, 1984) 129.

which any reasonable person must agree. Instead, Lindbeck contextualizes theological discourse within communities of faith, enclosing narratives of God within traditions, which provide the hermeneutical guidelines whereby members of religious communities and traditions develop interpretations. To use Lindbeck's term, these interpretations are "intratextual."[53] In defiance of the Enlightenment project, starting points are, so to speak, *re*-converted. Lindbeck, for example, maintains that the "proper way to determine what 'God' signifies…is by examining how the word operates within a religion and thereby shapes reality and experience…."[54] Sustaining the hermeneutical metaphor, Lindbeck suggests that a "scriptural world…supplies the interpretive framework within which believers seek to live their lives and understand reality."[55] "Intratextual theology," he continues, "redescribes reality within the scriptural framework rather than translating Scripture into extrascriptural categories. It is the text, so to speak, which absorbs the world, rather than the world the text."[56] Following post-Enlightenment theories of perspectivalism, religious communities thus admit that their perspectives are "prejudiced" by their interpretive framework, but they also realize that all perspectives, religious or not, are prejudiced in one way or another. What such communities refuse to do is allow their perspectives to be prejudiced by the hegemony of the Enlightenment interpretive framework, which is alien and often hostile to the structure of their own faith.

Like Lindbeck, William Placher is made uneasy by Christian apologetics. He senses that they place theologians in an unfair position of rationally defending Christian truth claims using the Enlightenment methods of justification. In the past, Placher explains, such justificatory methods have pushed Christians off the Enlightenment stage:

> Contemporary Christian theology often seems to adopt such an "apologetic" tone. Perhaps one reason is that ever since the Enlightenment in the seventeenth century, many forces in our culture have taught that "being rational" meant questioning all inherited assumptions and then accepting only those beliefs which could be proven according to universally acceptable criteria. "Tradition" and "authority" were bad words. If Christians wanted to join the general conversation, it seemed that these were the rules which they would have to play. If that

---

[53] Ibid., 114.
[54] Ibid., 114.
[55] Ibid., 117.
[56] Ibid., 118.

meant that there were some things they could not say, or some ways they could not say them, then they would have to adjust accordingly—or else find themselves in increasing intellectual isolation.[57]

Like other post-Enlightenment thinkers, Placher perceives the fatal flaws of those Enlightenment rules. Contrary to Enlightenment assumptions, he explains that "...there is no absolute standpoint, no place to stand outside any tradition, no universal criterion for judging truth and rationality...."[58]; in addition, he asserts that "...we cannot evaluate the reasonableness of assertions, or even understand their meaning, in isolation from the values and practices of the culture in which they are made."[59] Perspectivalism necessitates the particularity of our interpretative strategies.

Placher thus develops what he calls an "unapologetic theology," a pun that registers a refusal to allow Christian theology to be compromised by the Enlightenment project. Like Lindbeck, Placher "insist[s] that Christian theology should focus primarily on describing the internal logic of Christian faith—how Christian beliefs relate to each other and function within the life of a Christian community."[60] Christian theology must speak the language of that community, careful to avoid the universal vocabulary of the Enlightenment project.[61] This method of communication provides definite challenges to conversation. For Placher, theology should rise to this challenge by seeking common ground that participants in the conversation may share, without assuming that that common ground constitutes an area of *universal* commonality—a de-converted starting point. Placher admits that he "do[es] not know how to defend Christian faith—or any other belief system—in terms that all rational human beings would have to accept. We

---

[57] Placher, *Unapologetic Theology*, 11.

[58] Ibid., 158.

[59] Ibid., 74.

[60] Ibid., 18.

[61] This is not to say that Placher and thinkers like him believe that Christianity is not universally true. He is simply making a distinction between the justification of truth claims and truth claims themselves. As he explains, "The way we can go about justifying a belief is always context dependent, but the truth claimed for that belief is not" (*Unapologetic Theology*, 120). Here, Placher borrows from Jeffrey Stout's *Ethics After Babel*. "As Stout says," writes Placher, "a big part of the solution to the puzzle lies in distinguishing between claims about truth and claims about justification. To use his example: he believes that slavery is wrong—not just wrong in some times and places but everywhere and always. Maybe he is wrong to make that claim across all cultures, but that really is what he believes. On the other hand, he does not know of any way to argue for that belief except in the context of some particular tradition" (*Unapologetic Theology*, 120).

argue within the context of some tradition, and we begin with the rules and assumptions a particular conversation partner happens to share."[62] This is what Lindbeck refers to as "*ad hoc* and nonfoundational" apologetics. Methods of justification proceed hand in hand with context, contingency, and particularity.

Perhaps no Christian thinker has argued more cogently against Enlightenment methods of justification than has Alvin Plantinga. This may seem odd considering that Plantinga identifies himself as a foundationalist.[63] However, as stated at the outset, various forms of foundationalism exist, and Plantinga identifies his as *weak* foundationalism, qualitatively distinct from the Enlightenment variety of strong foundationalism.[64] Strong or Enlightenment foundationalism is "a thesis about rational noetic structures. A noetic structure is rational if it could be the noetic structure of a person who was completely rational."[65] As we have seen, Enlightenment rationality erects stringent criteria that demand conformity to universal standards. "From this point of view," explains Plantinga, "a rational person is one whose believings meet the appropriate standards; to criticize a person as irrational is to criticize her for failing to fulfill these duties or responsibilities, for failing to conform to the relevant norms or standards."[66] Of course, certain standards are unacceptable for establishing epistemological foundations: "From the foundationalist point of view, not just any kind of belief can be found in the foundations of a rational noetic structure; a belief, to be properly basic (i.e., basic in a rational noetic structure) must meet certain conditions."[67] What are these conditions for basicality? Plantinga considers some of them here: "Many philosophers have endorsed the idea that the strength of one's belief ought always to be proportional to the strength of the evidence for that belief. Thus, according to John Locke a mark of the rational person is 'the not entertaining any proposition with greater

---

[62] Ibid., 123.

[63] It should also be noted that Plantinga expresses strong objections to postmodernism—at least postmodernism of the Richard Rorty variety. See Stephen Louthan, "On Religion—A Discussion with Richard Rorty, Alvin Plantinga and Nicholas Wolterstorff," *Christian Scholar's Review* 26/2 (1996): 177–83.

[64] See, for example, Plantinga's "The Reformed Objection to Natural Theology" *Christian Scholar's Review* 11/3 (1982): 193.

[65] Alvin Plantinga, "Reason and Belief in God," in *Faith and Rationality: Reason and Belief in God*, ed. Alvin Plantinga and Nicholas Wolterstorff (Notre Dame: Notre Dame University Press, 1983) 52.

[66] Ibid.

[67] Alvin Plantinga, "The Reformed Objection to Natural Theology," *Christian Scholar's Review* 11/3 (1982): 194.

assurance than the proofs it is built upon will warrant.' According to David Hume, 'A wise man...proportions his belief to the evidence."[68]

Resonating with Placher's distaste for apologetics, Plantinga explains that Christians have unfortunately appropriated this Enlightenment paradigm of evidentialism, aligning their theology with the Enlightenment procedural guidelines. Such Christians frantically search for evidence for God's existence—evidence that is built upon the basic beliefs of the foundational structure—in order rationally to meet the objections of the evidentialist. But as Plantinga points out, such conformity to evidentialism validates the rigorous criteria that make justification difficult. According to such criteria, "...a good theistic argument must have premises accepted by nearly everyone, or nearly everyone who thinks about the topic, or nearly everyone who thinks about it and has a view on the topic. But this requirement is much too strong."[69]

Plantinga thus contends that such apologetic work is unnecessary, mainly because the evidentialist program—informed by foundationalism—is in error. He explains that some beliefs are accepted without evidence and are not, consequently, excoriated as irrational:

> Presumably the [evidentialist] objector does not mean to suggest that *no* proposition can be believed or accepted without evidence, for if you have evidence for *every* proposition you believe, then (granted certain plausible assumptions about the formal properties of the evidence relation) you will believe infinitely many propositions; and no one has time, these busy days, for that. So presumably *some* propositions can properly be believed and accepted without evidence.[70]

Plantinga then contends that God's existence is just such a proposition; belief in God itself is properly basic. "Why is it not entirely acceptable, desirable, right, proper, and rational to accept belief in God without any argument or evidence whatever?" he asks.[71] "[T]he believer," Plantinga maintains, "is entirely within his epistemic rights in believing that God has created the world, even if he has no argument at all for that conclusion."[72]

Like Lindbeck and Placher, Plantinga appeals to community and the epistemological assumptions that structure its beliefs. The Christian community employs a conceptual framework that organizes its perspective,

---

[68] Plantinga, "Reason and Belief in God," 24.
[69] Alvin Plantinga, "Augustinian Christian Philosophy," *Monist* 75/3 (1992): 294.
[70] Plantinga, "Reason and Belief in God," 39, emphasis in original.
[71] Ibid., 39.
[72] Plantinga, "Reformed Objection to Natural Theology," 188.

just as other communities employ other conceptual frameworks. Objective, neutral, de-converted epistemological posturing is a hollow philosophical gesture: "But we come to philosophy with pre-philosophical opinions; we can do no other. And the point is: the Christian has as much right to his pre-philosophical opinions as others have to theirs."[73] The Christian community is enclosed within the context of its own opinions—pre-philosophical or otherwise—and need not conform to other contexts:

> The Christian will of course suppose that belief in God is entirely proper and rational; if he doesn't accept this belief on the basis of other propositions, he will conclude that it is basic for him and quite properly so. Followers of Bertrand Russell and Madalyn Murray O'Hair may disagree; but how is that relevant? Must my criteria, or those of the Christian community, conform to their examples? Surely not. The Christian community is responsible to *its* set of examples, not to theirs.[74]

Situated within the contextual space of the Christian community, belief in God achieves basicality, thereby re-formulating noetic structures and justificatory methods that were summarily dismissed from the universal stage of the Enlightenment. Post-enlightenment thinking thus makes room for various interpretive communities, which, though engaged in dialogue with other communities, retain their intellectual integrity and validity within the enclosed area provided for by their own conceptual framework.

We can see, then, that some influential Christian thinkers have fleshed out philosophies of religion that reject the presuppositions of the Enlightenment project and thus the conventions of the public sphere. Like various postmodernists, these thinkers emphasize context, localizing issues of epistemology within traditions and interpretive communities; they do so by dismantling the universal stage of the Enlightenment. Once again, the public intellectual—in this case, the *Christian* public intellectual—has little ground upon which to stand.

### V. Two Final Contributing Factors to the Demise of the Public Intellectual: Modern Technology and the Culture Wars

I conclude this chapter by making brief forays into two other factors that contribute to the transformation of public discourse. Like the other subjects

---

[73] Alvin Plantinga, "Advice to Christian Philosophers," *Faith and Philosophy* 1/3 (1984): 268.
[74] Plantinga, "Reformed Objection to Natural Theology," 197, emphasis in original.

of the chapter, these factors are massive in scope. My modest, focused goal is to extract from them plausible answers to the operative question of this chapter: How do they assist in undermining the conditions that enabled the rise of the public intellectual?

### a. Modern Technology

An earlier analysis in this chapter revealed ways in which Jürgen Habermas believed modern technology contributed to the dissolution of the public sphere. Habermas contends that radio and television render the listener/viewer passive, discouraging the sort of critical engagement necessary for public discourse. This section supplements that analysis by attending to the work of Neil Postman, who has explored the ramifications of these relatively new media with acute insight.

In *Amusing Ourselves to Death: Public Discourse in the Age of Show Business*, Postman argues that new media—television in particular—has transformed public discourse into mere entertainment: "Our politics, religion, news, athletics, education and commerce have been transformed into congenial adjuncts of show business, largely without protest or even much popular notice. The result is that we are people on the verge of amusing ourselves to death."[75] Postman maintains that the mid twentieth century witnessed "the decline of the Age of Typography," during which print media structured public discourse, and "the ascendency of the Age of Television."[76] "This change-over," continues Postman, "has dramatically and irreversibly shifted the content and meaning of public discourse, since two media so vastly different cannot accommodate the same ideas. As the influence of print wanes, the content of politics, religion, education, and anything else that comprises public business must change and be recast in terms that are most suitable to television."[77] Public discourse during the "Age of Typography" had real content: what Postman calls "a semantic, paraphrasable, propositional content."[78] The "Age of Television" empties public discourse of content by reducing information and idea exchange to entertainment: "Entertainment is the supra-ideology of all discourse on television. No matter what is depicted or from what point of view, the overarching presumption is that it is there for our amusement and

---

[75] Neil Postman, *Amusing Ourselves to Death: Public Discourse in the Age of Show Business* (New York: Penguin Books, 1985) 3–4.

[76] Ibid., 8.

[77] Ibid.

[78] Ibid., 49.

pleasure."[79] Postman's argument overlaps with Habermas's claim about the consumerism of the new media: Discussion has become a "business," and, assuming Postman is correct, in order to sell it must entertain.

Of course, Habermas's and Postman's books predate the monolithic presence of the Internet, a form of media whose influence has certainly rivaled that of the radio and television. Nevertheless, the World Wide Web has affected public discourse in ways analyzed by Habermas as well as scholars of the public intellectual: Like older media of the twentieth century, the Internet has fostered the exponential growth of specialized niches of interest, intellectual and cultural ghettos closed off from each other by diverse consumer demands. As Melissa Rogers, director of the Center for Religion and Public Affairs at Wake Forest School of Divinity, comments (with tongue-in-cheek), "It's much better to be a news junky today. A fix is always a click away. This has allowed me to do something I couldn't have imagined ten years ago: construct a daily newsfeed tailored to my particular interests."[80]

Once again, then, we see how the public sphere has been chopped and diced, broken into fragments that cater to individual consumers. The public sphere obviously lacks the cohesion it possessed before the advent of the World Wide Web. Stewart M. Hoover notes that "...a variety of audience practices and technological arrangements today present themselves as being 'interactive' or 'bottom up.'"[81] That is, the Internet and "...the general self-oriented social consciousness of today's consumers has [the consumer], rather than the advertiser or the marketer, in the 'driver's seat....'"[82] From this position, consumers create their own customized sphere of ideas. (One cannot really identify this sphere as public.) Without a unified public, the public intellectual addresses a dwindled audience, one perhaps with specialized interests. Consequently, the public intellectual is hurled into the intellectual ghetto, marginalized by his or her very admirers.[83]

### b. The Culture Wars

Talk radio and cable-news channels have infused public rhetoric with rancor and animosity. Commentators demonize opponents in twenty-second

---

[79] Ibid., 87.

[80] Melissa Rogers, "Navigating the New Media News Filter," *Christian Century* 126/20 (September 2009): 24.

[81] Stewart M. Hoover, *Religion in the Media Age* (London: Routledge, 2006) 46.

[82] Ibid., 47.

[83] This is a component of the third C. S. Lewis phenomenon, analyzed in part 3.

sound bites as incivility becomes normalized within the public square. Much of this incivility proceeds from divisions that separate Americans in the so-called culture wars. From entrenched positions on religious and moral issues, combatants in these wars launch verbal assaults that tear down not only their opponents but the conventions of the public sphere as well. In this final section, I draw from James Davison Hunter's magisterial *Culture Wars: The Struggle to Define America* as I pinpoint one final factor that contributes to the demise of the public intellectual.

At the root of the culture wars are not mere differences of opinion; rather, the culture wars stem from rival bases of authority that form the opinions that generate the differences. These questions constitute the heart of the culture wars: What are the criteria for moral judgment? Where does moral authority reside? How does one authorize moral decisions? Hunter identifies two possible answers to these questions: two different answers that irreparably divide Americans of the late twentieth and early twenty-first centuries. Hunter writes, "To come right to the point, the cleavages at the heart of the contemporary culture war are created by what I would like to call *the impulse toward orthodoxy* and *the impulse toward progressivism*." Hunter defines orthodoxy as "...the commitment on the part of adherents to an external, definable, and transcendental authority." Hunter defines the latter thusly, "Within cultural progressivism, by contrast, moral authority tends to be defined by the spirit of the modern age, a spirit of rationalism and subjectivism.... In other words, what all *progressivist* world views share in common is *the tendency to resymbolize historic faiths according to the prevailing assumptions of contemporary life.*"[84] Thus, the schism at the heart of the culture wars is deep-seated: "What ultimately explains the realignment in America's public culture are *allegiances to different formulations and sources of moral authority.*"[85]

Like other factors contributing to the demise of the public intellectual, the culture wars splinter the public sphere; specialization becomes the *modus operandi.* To advance their agendas, warring sides require narrowly focused, highly specialized scholars and public figures, what Hunter calls "'knowledge workers'": "public policy specialists located in think tanks, special interest lobbyists, public interest lawyers, independent writers and

---

[84] James Davison Hunter, *Culture Wars: The Struggle to Define America* (New York: Basic Books, 1990) 43, 44, and 45, italics in original. One can see how Lewis's forms of authority clearly align with the orthodox view. Part 3 analyzes how Lewis has been enlisted in the culture wars.

[85] Ibid., 118, italics in original.

ideologues, journalists and editors, community organizers, and movement activists—the national and regional leadership of grass-roots social and political organizations."[86] Para-church organizations have also been influential in waging culture wars. And while Hunter notes that such organizations "have long played a conspicuous role in the course of American religious life," what is unprecedented is "growth in number, their increasing variety, and their rising political impact."[87] Para-church groups increasingly serve the focused needs of political agendas.

Most significantly, the culture wars mark the deterioration of the rational-critical debate that once characterized the public sphere. Because the impulses toward orthodoxy and progressivism are foundational, uncompromising, and non-negotiable, debates reach predictable stalemates. As Hunter explains,

> But in the end, whether concerned with abortion, homosexuality, women's rights, day care, or any other major moral or political issue of the day, the tools of logic and the evidence from science, history, and theology can do nothing to alter the opinions of their opposition. Because each side interprets them differently, logic, science, history, and theology can only serve to enhance and legitimate particular ideological interests. The willingness or unwillingness of opposing groups to have a "dialogue" about their differences is largely irrelevant. Even a spirit of compromise maintained by either side would be irrelevant. *In the final analysis, each side of the cultural divide can only talk past the other.*[88]

Hunter later adds,

> Given the incompatible nature of the polarizing cultural impulses, positive moral argument is simply insufficient as a way of achieving any real advantage over the opposition. In other words, because each side operates out of a fundamentally different conception of moral authority, because each side uses a radically different measure of moral sensibility, because each side employs a markedly different kind of moral logic, neither side will ever be able to persuade the other of the superiority of its own claims.[89]

The culture wars have rendered the public sphere ineffective. The inflexibility of combatants, anchoring their positions to uncompromising

---

[86] Ibid., 60.
[87] Ibid., 90.
[88] Ibid., 130–31, italics in original.
[89] Ibid., 136.

impulses, replaces the traditional public sphere with a battleground, a belligerent social space where angry voices drown each other out.

Of course, not all voices are angry. Many Americans advocate a multitude of middle-ground positions, adjudicated by reason and discussion. Hunter emphasizes, "Voices of moderation and restraint do exist. Public opinion research reveals a rich complexity of ideas, beliefs, and commitments among the leadership of the nation's public institutions as well as ordinary citizens.... Without doubt, public discourse is more polarized than the American public itself."[90] Why is this the case? What accounts for the "eclipse of the middle"?[91]

While Hunter offers several reasons, I focus on one here because it converges with the theorizing of Postman: entertainment and sensationalism. Extreme, polarizing figures are simply more interesting than those who speak with moderation; middle-ground positions, though often accurate and more representative of the American public, are also unexciting—even boring. Hunter connects this to our need "to be stirred and titillated." "Thus," he concludes, "public debate that is sensational is more likely to arouse and capture the attention of ordinary people than are methodical and reflective arguments. For this reason, the shrill pitch of harsh moral criticism and blunt commentary is much more likely to sell newspapers, build audience ratings, or raise money."[92] As David von Drehle puts it, "The mutual contempt of the American extremes draws crowds and fattens wallets at bookstores, cable-news departments, AM radio stations and documentary film fests."[93] The extremes depend upon the new media and the way it structures public discourse. Rodney Clapp pinpoints a pivotal year in the development of this phenomenon: 1980, "when CNN, the first 24/7 new network, premiered on cable television." As a result, news became reported continuously, with little reflection and nuance:

> Previously, news organizations operated on a news cycle that pivoted around a morning and an evening newscast. That cycle allowed journalists and producers a few moments to catch their breath. They had some time to think twice and to stay mindful of their civic and professional responsibilities before rushing a piece of gossip or glamorous gore onto the air. The need for programming 24 hours a day intensified

---

[90] Ibid., 159.

[91] Ibid., 160.

[92] Ibid.

[93] David von Drehle, "Mad Man: Is Glenn Beck Bad for America?," *Time* (17 September 2009): 34.

the pressure to lead with the gut, to run immediately with the sensational—even if it is unverified and only rumored. What little inhibition remained evaporated with the rise of the Internet in the mid-1990s.[94]

Cable news and the Internet display the visceral responses—often angry and ill-conceived responses—that ensue when modern media removes the filter of time and reflection.

Of course, as my précis of Hunter's book shows, the incivility of public discourse is not particular to the new media; rather, it is a deeply seated contempt proceeding from basic, rival impulses that manifest themselves in various skirmishes of the cultural wars. This contempt is writ large in the writings of the so-called New Atheists. The latest combatants in the culture wars, the New Atheists are of interest to my analysis because they are, for the most part, public intellectuals. For instance, writing for a general audience, translating complex ideas to the layperson, Richard Dawkins certainly comes across as a public intellectual, but of a different sort: one characterized by the sensationalism of contemporary discourse, lacking nuance and generating rancor. (Perhaps the New Atheists exemplify the methods—post public sphere—of the new public intellectual.)

Consider, for instance, the first sentence of chapter 2 in Dawkins's *The God Delusion*: "The God of the Old Testament is arguably the most unpleasant character in all fiction: jealous and proud of it; a petty, unjust, unforgiving control-freak; a vindictive, bloodthirsty ethnic cleanser; a misogynistic, homophobic, racist, infanticidal, genocidal, filicidal, pestilential, megalomaniacal, sadomasochistic, capriciously malevolent bully."[95] Clearly adopting sarcastic and inflammatory language, Dawkins defies the conventions of the public sphere: the attempt to find common ground with his audience. Dawkins's hyperbole rallies those who already agree with him and alienates those who do not. Dawkins's sensational remark may generate sales, but it does so by invoking the spirit of the culture wars. Consider also Dawkins's opening salvo in his refutation of the ontological argument for the existence of God:

Let me translate this infantile argument into the appropriate language, which is the language of the playground:

---

[94] Rodney Clapp, "Our Stalker Culture," *Christian Century* 126/23 (17 November 2009): 45.

[95] Richard Dawkins, *The God Delusion* (Boston: Houghton Mifflin Company, 2006) 31.

"Bet you I can prove God exists."

"Bet you can't."

"Right then, imagine the most perfect perfect *perfect* thing possible."

"Okay, now what?"

"Now, is that perfect perfect *perfect* thing real? Does it exist?"

"No, it's only in my mind."

"But if it was real it would be even more perfect, because a really really perfect thing would have to be better than a silly old imaginary thing. So I've proved that God exists. Nur Nurny Nur Nur. All atheists are fools."[96]

The ontological argument can perhaps be refuted. But considering that it has stood the test of time for approximately 1,000 years, one can hardly reduce it to Dawkins's petty and unfair synopsis.

The degeneration of discourse is obviously not restricted to the progressive side of the cultural-war divide, however. If we are to believe New Atheist Sam Harris, Christians likewise convey the sort of hostility that undermines public discourse:

> Since the publication of my first book, *The End of Faith*, thousands of people have written to tell me that I am wrong not to believe in god. The most hostile of these communications have come from Christians. This is ironic, as Christians generally imagine that no faith imparts the virtues of love and forgiveness more effectively than their own. The truth is that many who claim to be transformed by Christ's love are deeply, even murderously, intolerant of criticism. While we may want to ascribe this to human nature, it is clear that such hatred draws considerable support from the Bible. How do I know this? The most disturbed of my correspondents always cite chapter and verse.[97]

Vitriolic language undermines the process by which public arguments nudge readers and listeners toward truth; caustic discourse enervates the adjudicating powers of reason and clouds the critical faculties. Indeed, in one of his last books published during his lifetime (*Studies in Words*, 1960), Lewis reflects upon the effects of bellicose book reviews. While he notes the social indecorum of such reviews, he pays particular attention to what he calls "their inutility." They may please if we already agree with the reviewer, but they do little "to inform our judgment," a phrase that captures an

---

[96] Ibid., 80.

[97] Sam Harris, *Letter to a Christian Nation* (New York: Knopf, 2006) vii.

important function of the public sphere.[98] Pugnacious rhetoric distracts the reader away from this function. Lewis describes the impact of reading "...some unusually violent reviews lately which were all by the same man. Automatically, without thinking about it, willy-nilly, one's mind discounts everything he says; as it does when we are listening to a drunk or delirious man. Indeed we cannot even think about the book under discussion. The critic rivets our attention on himself."[99] For the reader, bewildered fascination replaces reflective analysis in such a scenario. The unintended results of adverse criticism that Lewis observes in 1960 become absorbed into public discourse on the frontlines of the late-twentieth-century culture wars. Hostility disarms critical faculties as combatants talk past each other.

This chapter has described a number of factors that transformed the public sphere, altering its conventions and restructuring public discourse. As a result of this re-landscaped intellectual terrain, the accomplishment of C. S. Lewis cannot be imitated. Seizing an historical moment, Lewis became a public intellectual, availing himself of a public sphere and conventions of public discourse that no longer exist. Nevertheless, a few Lewis texts operate beyond the public sphere, a process I explore in the next three chapters.

---

[98] C. S. Lewis, *Studies in Words*, 2nd ed. (Cambridge: Cambridge University Press, 1967) 329.
[99] Ibid., 330.

# 7

# Hesitant Steps beyond the Public Sphere:
# Tensions and Dilemmas

## I. Re-Mapping the Critical Geography

The writings of C. S. Lewis underwent a change in the 1950s, for this was the decade that witnessed the publication of the Narnia chronicles and Lewis's only true novel, *Till We Have Faces*, two texts in genre and substance that depart from earlier works. Scholars have attempted to understand what exactly defines this change as well as what motivated it.[1] Peter Schakel argues that Lewis texts composed during the 1930s and most of the 1940s relied predominately upon reason; beginning in the late 1940s, Schakel maintains, Lewis gave fuller expression to his imagination, which subsequently brought balance to his writings, correcting the tilt toward reason.[2] Adam Barkman disagrees, insisting that reason remained for Lewis till the end the preeminent faculty, residing in "the citadel of the soul": From this position, reason evaluates the workings of the imagination, identifying

---

[1] The most commonly invoked theory to explain this change concerns Lewis's 1948 debate with Elizabeth Anscombe on the subject of miracles; Anscombe critiqued elements of Lewis's argument concerning this subject during a meeting of the Socratic Club. As a result of this confrontation, so the theory goes, Lewis realized the weaknesses of his philosophical approach to Christianity and thus abandoned straightforward apologetic writing. Defenders of Lewis often reject this theory and associate it with A. N. Wilson, who develops it in his provocative 1990 work, *C. S. Lewis: A Biography*. The theory, however, predates Wilson's book. As far back as 1979, Humphrey Carpenter wrote, "Lewis had learnt his lesson [from the debate]: for after this he wrote no further books of Christian apologetics for ten years, apart from a collection of sermons; and when he did publish another apologetic work, *Reflections on the Psalms*, it was notably quieter in tone and did not attempt any further intellectual proofs of theism or Christianity" (*The Inklings: C. S. Lewis, J. R. R. Tolkien, Charles Williams, and Their Friends* [Boston: Houghton Mifflin Company, 1979] 217). In 1981, Margaret Patterson Hannay claimed, "His argument having been, at least by some accounts, defeated by the Catholic philosopher Elizabeth Anscombe, he produced no more combative apologetics" (*C. S. Lewis* [New York: Frederick Ungar Publishing Company, 1981] 262).

[2] Peter J. Schakel, *Reason and the Imagination in C. S. Lewis: A Study of* Till We Have Faces (Grand Rapids: Eerdmans, 1984) x.

what is true and what is false. This process "demanded the kingship of reason."[3]

It seems to me that Barkman misrepresents Schakel's position. According to Barkman, under Schakel's influence, numerous Lewis scholars have appointed imagination "as the most exalted faculty in Lewis's mature thought." This is because Schakel "declares that during the 1940s, Lewis thought that reason was more important than imagination, but then later, in the 1950s, 'reversed' this order."[4] This declaration is overstated. Schakel does affirm that "imagination becomes the more striking feature of his work from 1950 on—in the chronicles of Narnia, for example." But Schakel also emphasizes that this is "a shift, not in basic positions or theory but certainly in emphasis and practice...."[5] Barkman's sketch of the place of reason and imagination within Lewis's epistemology is not inconsistent with Schakel's argument. Indeed, Schakel's thesis, the very purpose of his book, is not to show that Lewis reversed the order of importance between reason and imagination but that "reason and imagination are, at last, reconciled and unified."[6]

Nevertheless, one senses some definitional imprecision in Schakel's analysis or—to phrase it more accurately and charitably—some conceptual overlap. Schakel occasionally associates (and other times nearly equates) reason with objectivity and imagination with subjectivity. For instance, Schakel writes, "It appears to me, however, that for the final decade and a half of his life Lewis gradually shifted his emphasis to give fuller consideration to the self and the subjective, simultaneous with and related to an altered emphasis on reason and imagination, all of which leads to a noticeably different approach and tone in his later works."[7] Later, Schakel attributes one cause of Lewis's fuller investment in imagination as "an acknowledgment that an element of subjectivity is inherent in perception, and that a degree of self-consciousness is necessary to sound under-

---

[3] Adam Barkman, *C. S. Lewis & Philosophy as a Way of Life: A Comprehensive Historical Examination of His Philosophical Thoughts* (Wayne PA: Zossima Press, 2008) 314.

[4] Ibid., 314. Barkman also faults Schakel for not defining his terms. Barkman subdivides imagination into various types, including primary imagination and deliberative imagination, which Barkman defines as the faculty used in creating art. I think it is pretty clear that Schakel's analysis of imagination refers to the deliberative variety.

[5] Schakel, *Reason and the Imagination in C. S. Lewis*, x.

[6] Ibid., x.

[7] Ibid., 89–90.

standing." This acknowledgement corresponds with "[h]is movement away from an almost mechanical approach to the objective...."[8] Of course, reason need not be associated with objectivity, nor imagination with subjectivity (as my analysis of myth and archetypes in chapter 5 illustrates, as will my fuller exploration of myth in this chapter). Objectivity and subjectivity are categories of experience and knowledge in the writings of Lewis that merit their own critical investigation; that is, objectivity and subjectivity must be regarded independently of their associations with the categories of reason and imagination. Conflating the former category with the latter too easily produces misunderstandings.

On the other hand, the category of objectivity and subjectivity is central to the division separating Lewis the public intellectual and Lewis beyond the public sphere. Part 1 employed critical terms—de-conversion, universality, the myth of uniform experience—that underscore the public intellectual's dependence upon objectivity, or at least an appearance of objectivity: an objective pose. Lewis outside the public sphere is more attentive to the subjective, or as Schakel puts it, how "an element of subjectivity is inherent in perception." This chapter explores this subjective element and how it defines Lewis beyond the public sphere. I begin by taking two detours: the first an exploration of theories, both secular and Christian, that will help me flesh out how exactly this subjective element operates; the second a brief examination of some writers who most likely influenced Lewis to consider how perception shapes belief. These detours provide the context for my analysis of Lewis in this chapter.

## II. The First Detour: Post-Enlightenment Subjectivity

I begin with the theorizing of Stanley Fish. Obviously, Fish's philosophy is a long way from that of Lewis. Nevertheless, an analysis of Fish's critique of liberal thought—continued from the introduction to part 2—will provide us with a conceptual framework for seeing more clearly how Lewis's later works move beyond the conventions of the public sphere. (It is interesting to note that Lewis exerted a profound influence on Fish, who writes, "I would have loved to have saluted C. S. Lewis, not only for his enormous contribution to medieval and Renaissance studies, but for the extraordinary

---

[8] Ibid., 150–51.

fact of his prose style, on which I have modeled my own with results that fall far short of his example."[9])

As described in the introduction to part 2, Fish sees through the supposed neutrality of the liberal marketplace of ideas. While it promises to give all its participants a fair hearing, the public sphere marginalizes certain beliefs by virtue of the very procedures it has established. Paramount among these procedures is the operation of reason, which, as it descends from the Enlightenment, privileges objectivity. Unbiased and freely available to all, reason authorizes the public sphere as the final court of arbitration for all intellectual disputes.

However, Fish points out that unreasonable or, perhaps better put, pre-reasonable factors influence the operations of reason. Disputants within the public sphere engage reason from a particular perspective that shapes the way they use it. Perspectives, along with their many assumptions, cannot be divorced from the operations of reason as they materialize during the course of the argument. "This is so," writes Fish,

> because the reasons you think to give will always be a function of the personal and institutional history that has brought you to a moment of dispute. If, for example, you ask me to give reasons for my reading of a poem, I would surely be able to do so; but the reasons I then proceeded to give would rest on assumptions—about the nature of poetry, the practice of literary interpretation, the difference between poetry and other forms of discourse or the absence of any such difference, and a thousand other things—that gave to those reasons the intelligibility and force they would have for *me* and for those whose intellectual and institutional history was commensurate with mine. Others would not hear them as reasons at all, at least not as *good* ones, but would hear them as mistakes and perhaps, were the dispute heated enough, as instances of *ir*rationality. At that moment the appeal to reason will have run its course and produced the kind of partisan impasse from which reason supposedly offers us an escape.[10]

Disputants are thus left with warring assumptions. But might not those assumptions be evaluated in an attempt to discover which can reasonably support the respective arguments? Fish responds, "To this suggestion I would pose a simple question: if you propose to examine and assess

---

[9] Stanley Fish, "Milton, Thou Shouldst Be Living in this Hour," in *There's No Such Thing as Free Speech and It's a Good Thing, Too* (Oxford: Oxford University Press, 1994) 269.

[10] Fish, introduction to *There's No Such Thing as Free Speech*, 16–17.

assumptions, what will you examine and assess them *with*? And the answer is that you will examine and assess them with forms of thought that themselves rest on underlying assumptions. At any level, the tools of rational analysis will be vulnerable to the very deconstruction they claim to perform."[11] In short, one can never get *behind* the assumptions; there exists no Olympian reference point by which they may be assessed by the adjudicating process of reason.

As a convention of the public sphere, reason—that is, Enlightenment reason—is not the only fatality of Fish's argument, which likewise calls into question the myth of uniform experience. As a neutral, de-contextualized arbiter, reason collectivizes humankind; a good reason within the public sphere is a universal reason, binding on all rational people. But as Fish shows, in the course of actual arguments, reasons are always particularized, embedded within the interpretive framework from which the argument proceeds. As he states, "In short, what is and is not a reason will always be a matter of faith, that is, of the assumptions that are bedrock within a discursive system which because it rests upon them cannot (without self-destructing) call them into question."[12] Assumptions—matters of faith—seminally shape the way in which we process truth claims as well as the way in which we defend them.[13]

Often associated with relativism (an accusation he denies and refutes), Fish may seem an unlikely exponent of any theory that can contextualize an analysis of Lewis. In a sense, however, Fish's theory is not as radically postmodern or, in the minds of some, inimical to a Christian worldview as it appears. For instance, Charles Taylor (certainly no "radical" thinker) coins the phrase "social imaginary," which refers to the way people "imagine their social existence" by using, in part, pre-theoretical background beliefs, beliefs

---

[11] Ibid., 18.

[12] Fish, "Liberalism Doesn't Exist," in *There's No Such Thing as Free Speech*, 136.

[13] My foray into the philosophy of Fish compels me to address an apparent contradiction in my analysis. Fish is occasionally referred to as a public intellectual, yet it is clear that at the heart of his thought is a critique of the public sphere as well as its conventions. Fish is thus a public intellectual after the demise of the public sphere. I frankly consider Fish to be an exception to the rule, to be, in fact, an anomaly. His contrarian, often feisty, attitude toward mainstream ideas provides him with the countercultural pose typical of the public intellectual, but his critique of Enlightenment thought positions him in opposition to the conventions upon which the traditional public intellectual depends. My analysis does not hold, however, that the public intellectual ceases to exist: just the traditional public intellectual. Fish's identity as a non-traditional public intellectual, a post-public-sphere public intellectual, is the subject of another book.

not always articulated or even capable of being articulated in propositional terms. Here is Taylor's definition of the term:

> It is in fact that largely unstructured and inarticulate understanding of our whole situation, within which particular features of our world show up for us in the sense they have. It can never be adequately expressed in the form of explicit doctrines, because of its very unlimited and indefinite nature. That is another reason for speaking here of an "imaginary", and not a theory.[14]

Taylor's concept calls attention to the numerous factors—presumably including assumptions and matters of faith—that shape our perception of the world, a perception that amounts to the "unstructured and inarticulate understanding of our whole situation." Our place within this situation—the context we inhabit—determines not only which "particular features of our world" we perceive but how we process and make sense of them. The apprehension of truth claims involves much more than the mere deliberations of reason.

Fish's theory, in fact, even has a conceptual kinship with certain strands of Christian thought. The Reformed tradition has long valued the place of presuppositional thinking: the idea that the most important philosophical action takes place not in the actual processing of truth claims but in the presuppositions that one brings to those truth claims, before the processing even starts. Cornelius Van Til, like other important figures in the Reformed tradition, holds that belief in God is the key presupposition for clear and right thinking: "...man's consciousness of self and of objects presuppose for their intelligibility the self-consciousness of God. In asserting this we are not thinking of psychological and temporal priority. We are thinking only of the question as to what is the final reference point in interpretation."[15] Interpretation is thus not a task that requires that the object of interpretation be submitted to the public sphere and scrutinized according to the Enlightenment guidelines of objective reason. Instead, accurate interpretation depends upon religious and, by the standards of the public sphere, highly subjective and thus corrupt presuppositions. Van Til's hermeneutic stands in stark and almost defiant contrast to the conventions of the public sphere: knowledge of God "is the final reference point in interpretation."

---

[14] Charles Taylor, *A Secular Age* (Cambridge: Belknap Press of Harvard University, 2007) 172–73.

[15] Cornelius Van Til, *The Defense of the Faith*, 3rd ed. (Phillipsburg NJ: Presbyterian and Reformed Publishing Company, 1967) 77.

Van Til's Reformed hermeneutic finds epistemological formulation in a process called preconditionalism: the idea that one cannot arrive at truth until one's cognitive faculties have been properly prepared; one's noetic faculties operate properly on the condition that one's faith is intact. As Nicholas Wolterstorff explains, "Faith is seen as a condition for arriving at a fully comprehensive, coherent, consistent, and true body of theories in the sciences."[16] The concept of preconditionalism finds its source in Scripture, though it finds significant development in other writers of the Christian tradition. For example, in the eleventh century, Anselm's notion of "faith seeking understanding" implies that it is faith that makes knowledge possible; faith serves as the epistemological illumination for understanding. (See chapter 1 of Anselm's *Proslogion*.) Similarly, Augustine explained in the fourth century that antecedent belief guides the acquisition of knowledge. (See *De Libero Arbitrio*, Book I, paragraph 4.) In the Protestant era, John Calvin also inscribed preconditionalism in his theology. In his *Institutes of the Christian Religion*, Calvin suggests that the Holy Spirit can recuperate to some extent an individual's fallen faculties on the condition that one's faith remains vigorous. (See II.ii.12.) Calvin, I believe, finds precedence for this position in (among other places) Jesus' proclamation in John 8:31-32: "If you hold to my teaching, then you are truly my disciples; then you will know the truth, and the truth will set you free." Here again, faith is epistemologically antecedent to knowledge-acquisition. To use the language of epistemology, faith is the control belief, the central concept in the web of beliefs. Reason is thus not a universalized, one-size-fits-all tool, transcending the subjective, belief-shaping factors that it is intended to objectify and then adjudicate; rather, reason is inflected by those very subjective factors, which, in the formation of belief, are not only antecedent to reason but determinative of reason's application and use.

James K. A. Smith provides an example that nicely illustrates reason's subordinate role in the formation of belief. He contends that "liturgies," which can be either sacred or secular, shape our identities more definitively than reason. Our liturgies include what we do, how we behave, and, most importantly, what we love. By thus shaping our identities, liturgies largely determine what we believe. This identity-formation occurs before reason even kicks in; or, to be more precise, reason is involved in a process much larger and more important than itself, a process involving the whole body (not just the brain). For this reason, Smith makes use of key words to

---

[16] Nicholas Wolterstorff, *Reason within the Bounds of Religion* (Grand Rapids: Eerdmans, 1984) 31.

describe this process: words like "precognitive," "pretheoretical," and "prereflective." Here, for instance, is James's explanation of how liturgies produce knowledge:

> In short, every liturgy constitutes a pedagogy that teaches us, in all sorts of precognitive ways, to be a certain kind of person. Hence every liturgy is an education, and embedded in every liturgy is an implicit worldview or "understanding" of the world. And by this I don't mean that implanted in the liturgies are all kind of ideas to be culled from them; rather, implicit in them is an understanding of the world that is pretheoretical, that is on a different register than ideas.[17]

Smith applies his notion of liturgy to a theory of education. Because "we are shaped by material bodily practices,"[18] he replaces the traditional understanding of education with an alternative: Education is "not primarily a heady project concerned with providing *information*; rather, education is most fundamentally a matter of *formation*, a task of shaping and creating a certain kind of people."[19] Smith's project rests upon a traditional Christian belief that what we believe is in large part determined by what we do and by what we love. My analysis of Fish within this section reveals one way in which this belief gains significant momentum after the demise of the public sphere, when reason becomes implicated in the subjective factors—which is to say embodied and localized factors—that it was long held to transcend.

This is precisely the momentum that launches Lewis beyond the public sphere. His later works closely attend to pre-analytical factors that shape knowledge-acquisition and belief. (One also catches glimpses of these factors in his earlier work: thus my characterization of Part 2 as a counter-narrative.) *Till We Have Faces*, as we will see, even exemplifies the process of preconditionalism. Before turning to Lewis, however, I wish briefly to examine some of those who influenced him, for as we will see, these influences occasionally engage the concerns of this section.

### III. The Second Detour: Lewis's Influences

Lewis would of course have had ample opportunity to perceive ways in which reason and belief-acquisition operate beyond what has become called the Enlightenment paradigm. These opportunities are certainly not limited

---

[17] James K. A. Smith, *Desiring the Kingdom: Worship, Worldview, and Cultural Formation* (Grand Rapids: Baker Academic, 2009) 25.

[18] Ibid., 131.

[19] Ibid., 26.

to the few notable influences surveyed in this section. As we have seen, alternatives to the Enlightenment paradigm can be found in the writings of important thinkers who precede the Enlightenment: Anselm, Augustine, and Calvin. (Indeed, one explanation for the three-hundred-year staying power of the Enlightenment is that its principles of reasoning were accepted as normative; *all* forms of valid reasoning are Enlightenment forms of reasoning, even for those who precede the Enlightenment.) Nevertheless, it is clear that a few writers made a profound impact on Lewis.

George MacDonald, for instance, famously "baptized" Lewis's imagination. Although his reading of *Phantastes* constituted a life-changing moment, Lewis obviously read MacDonald's sermons. In one such sermon, "The Truth in Jesus," MacDonald provides the basis for an epistemology that has affinities to preconditionalism: "'Do I believe or feel this thing right?'— the true question is forgotten: 'Have I left all to follow him?' To the man who gives himself to the living Lord, every belief will necessarily come right; the Lord himself will see that his disciple believe aright concerning him."[20] MacDonald here attends to the pre-rational concerns that fashion beliefs; one can only acquire right knowledge about God after one has first committed wholeheartedly to God, a proposition that contrasts with Lewis's position in his essay, "Is Theism Important?" There, Lewis distinguishes between two types of faith: Faith-A and Faith-B, the former defined as "a settled intellectual assent" and the latter as "a trust, or confidence, in the God whose existence is thus assented to." Lewis maintains that Faith-A "is a necessary pre-condition of Faith-B."[21] Lewis thus suggests that intellectual matters must first be settled before the heart and will can follow. That this essay was published in 1962 reminds us that Lewis's basic epistemological orientation never changed, that what I call his movement beyond the public sphere is not systematic and complete. Nevertheless, within that same essay, Lewis does admit that there exists something "quasi-religious" within Faith-A, something that operates beyond the purely rational.[22]

Lewis was also influenced by Edwyn Bevan's *Symbolism and Belief* (1938).[23] Bevan's conception of belief at times diverges greatly from the

---

[20] George MacDonald, *Unspoken Sermons* (Whitethorn CA: Johannesen, 1997) 392.

[21] C. S. Lewis, "Is Theism Important?," in *God in the Dock: Essays on Theology and Ethics*, ed. Walter Hooper (Grand Rapids: Eerdmans, 1970) 172–73.

[22] Ibid., 174.

[23] In a 1959 letter to Mary van Deusen, Lewis writes, "Have I recommended to you Edwyn Bevan's *Symbolism and Belief*? I think it helps more than any book I know to keep one right on all 'modernism'" (*The Collected Letters of C. S. Lewis*, vol. 3, *Narnia*,

evidentialism characterizing most of Lewis's work: instances of divergence that signal departures from Enlightenment assumptions about belief-acquisition. Bevan, for instance, maintains that those who are not compelled by the Christian worldview can overcome those doubts by inhabiting it more intensively—not merely by overcoming intellectual objections. He writes, "Thus the best answer which Christians can give to those who say they cannot see value in the Christian life, is to live the life more truly and thoroughly. In the end every man must see or not see its value for himself." Like Blaise Pascal, Bevan reposes little hope in arguments for the existence of God; they occasion few conversions: "It is highly improbable that anyone who had no belief in God was ever led to believe in God by any of the standard 'proofs' for God's existence—the ontological, cosmological, teleological proof. They were thought of by men who already believed in God as considerations for harmonizing their belief, for themselves, and for others, with a general view of the universe."[24] In fact, Bevan seems to reverse the order into which Lewis places Faith-A and Faith-B: For Bevan, belief— the movement of the heart and the effort of the will—precedes rational assent, for as Bevan states, "It is only, I think, in the sense of giving rational comfort to people who already believe in God that the standard arguments can be regarded as demonstrating the existence of God."[25]

The conceptual framework undergirding these standard arguments is the object of severe critique in a book that greatly influenced Lewis: Rudolf Otto's *The Idea of the Holy*.[26] Otto laments the intellectualizing of faith within Christianity, a process that robs religion of its non-rational elements and its numinous richness:

> It is rather that orthodoxy found in the construction of dogma and doctrine [has] no way to do justice to the non-rational aspect of its subject. So far from keeping the non-rational element in religion alive in the heart of the religious experience, orthodox Christianity manifestly failed to recognize its value, and by this failure gave to the idea of God a one-sidedly intellectualistic and rationalistic interpretation. This bias to

---

*Cambridge, and Joy, 1950–1963*, ed. Walter Hooper [San Francisco: HarperSanFrancisco, 2007] 1012). Lewis offers similar reading advice to Margaret Gray in 1961 (ibid., 1264).

[24] Edwyn Bevan, *Symbolism and Belief* (Port Washington NY: Kennikat Press, Inc., 1938) 256, 386.

[25] Ibid., 386.

[26] In its June 6, 1962, issue, *Christian Century* interviewed Lewis, asking him, "What books did most to shape your vocational attitude and your philosophy of life?" Lewis placed The Idea of the Holy at number six in his top-ten list. List is reprinted in *The Canadian C.S. Lewis Journal* No.58 (Spring 1987), p.27.

rationalization still prevails, not only in theology but in the science of comparative religion in general, and from top to bottom of it.[27]

While various events and movements have contributed to the overly intellectualized character of Christianity, there is little doubt the "bias to rationalization" is heavily indebted to the Enlightenment. And as we will see, it is partly from the influence of Otto that Lewis occasionally operates beyond the public sphere, imaging the numinous in his works of non-fiction to produce visceral responses—independent of reason—that frame an alternative perception of Christianity.

Lewis grappled with the notion of a reality-shaping role of perception during the course of his longstanding friendship with Owen Barfield, whose influence of all the thinkers surveyed in this section was most profound. Lewis's early relationship with Barfield was of course marked by the so-called "Great War," an extended debate between the two men, carried out in letters and conversations from about 1927 to 1931; these conversations concerned such topics as the imagination and anthroposophy, a religious view developed by Rudolf Steiner in the early twentieth century. As the title of their exchange suggests, their debate was characterized by significant disagreements. Lewis Barfield's anthroposophical beliefs as well as Barfield's notion that imagination can convey truth; that function, Lewis insisted, was reason's domain. Lewis never faltered from these basic positions; these fundamental points of disagreement remained. Nevertheless, Lewis does admit that, as a result of their friendship, Barfield "changed me a good deal more than I him."[28] And as Phyllis Tickle sagely reminds, "An old axiom of folk wisdom holds that one always picks up a bit of whatever it is that one opposes simply by virtue of wrestling with it."[29]

I maintain that Lewis specifically assimilated many of Barfield's beliefs about the role of perception: that perception is not simply a direct apprehension of the external world solely afforded by the deliverances of the senses. I therefore agree with Peter Schakel's estimation: "[Lewis] came to accept Barfield's ideas about the importance of the perceiver and a subjective element in perception."[30] And I am sympathetic with Doris T. Myers's claim: "As can be seen in his mature writings, Lewis ultimately adopted most of

---

[27] Rudolf Otto, *The Idea of the Holy*, trans. John W. Harvey (Oxford: Oxford University Press, 1969) 3.

[28] C. S. Lewis, *Surprised by Joy* (San Diego: Harcourt Brace & Company, 1984) 200.

[29] Phyllis Tickle, *The Great Emergence: How Christianity Is Changing and Why* (Grand Rapids: Baker Books, 2008) 90.

[30] Schakel, *Reason and the Imagination in C. S. Lewis*, 42.

Barfield's theory of language while rejecting its basis in anthroposophy."[31] Barfield explains his theory of language in *Poetic Diction*, of which Lewis wrote, "Much of the thought which he afterward put into *Poetic Diction* had already become mine before that important little book appeared."[32]

This "important little book" engages large issues of perception. Barfield holds that during the early stages of language—a "pre-logical age"— meaning was unified and whole, abiding by what he calls the "poetic principle" whereby the "connections between discrete phenomena...[were] perceived as immediate realities"[33]; myths exemplified this poetic principle, conveying a unified meaning through the use of "concrete vocabulary": the "world's first 'poetic diction.'"[34] Later stages in the evolution of language witnessed the rise of the "rational principle," which fractured the original unity of meaning, dividing meaning into "contrasted pairs—the abstract and the concrete, particular and general, objective and subjective."[35] The shift in language likewise engendered a change in human consciousness: The rational principle privileges analysis and conceptual understanding; by contrast, during the early stages of language, the meanings built in to the universe and conveyed through poetic diction "could not be *known*, but only experienced, or lived."[36]

This admittedly oversimplified précis (which does not do justice to Barfield's complex argument) reveals the ways in which language shapes our perception of the world; two different linguistic principles generate two radically different modes of consciousness. Indeed, the divergent modes of consciousness are mutually exclusive, as Barfield explains, "The absolute rational principle is that which makes conscious of poetry but cannot create it; the absolute poetic principle is that which creates poetry but cannot make conscious of it."[37] In addition, the opening pages of Barfield's book explore the nature of aesthetic experience, an exploration that serves as a prolegomenon to his analysis of poetic consciousness. His contention is that aesthetic experiences enhance our consciousness. They do so by changing

---

[31] Doris T. Myers, *C. S. Lewis in Context* (Kent: Kent State University Press, 1994) 6–7.

[32] Lewis, *Surprised by Joy*, 200.

[33] Owen Barfield, *Poetic Diction: A Study in Meaning* (New York: McGraw-Hill Company, 1964) 93.

[34] Ibid., 92.

[35] Ibid., 85.

[36] Ibid., 102.

[37] Ibid., 104.

(for the better) the way we see the world through, for instance, our encounter with a metaphor in poetry:

> Now my normal everyday experience, as human being, of the world around me depends entirely on what *I* bring to the sense-datum from within; and the absorption of this metaphor into my imagination has enabled me to bring more than I could before. It has created something in me, a faculty or a part of a faculty, enabling me to observe what I could not hitherto observe.[38]

Barfield describes in strong terms here the reality-shaping power of perception, a power that forms the very analytic foundation of *Poetic Diction*.[39]

These influences help explain the two different modes of discourse found in Lewis's writings, thus necessitating the critical narrative/counter-narrative approach of my study. As public intellectual, Lewis adhered to the conventions of the public sphere, rendering reason immune to the reality-shaping power of individual perception and thus overly committing Lewis to a notion of universalized human experience. Eventually, Lewis's influences helped nudge him toward a different mode of discourse, one more attentive to perception and particularity. (Lewis's account of how Barfield identified an "expository demon" in his earlier writings offers some palpable proof of this influence.[40]) The following two chapters examine this mode of discourse in *Till We Have Faces* and *A Grief Observed*; the remainder of this one begins my counter-narrative by exploring this mode in other works.

## IV. Launching the Counter-Narrative

### a. Hesitant Steps beyond the Public Sphere

Mere Christianity, The Great Divorce, *and a Re-Consideration of Stock Responses.* It bears repeating that Lewis's movement beyond the public sphere

---

[38] Ibid., 55.

[39] Issues of perception also figure strongly in Barfield's later book, *Saving the Appearances: A Study in Idolatry*: "On almost any received theory of perception the familiar world—that is, the world which is apprehended, not through instruments and inference, but simply—is for the most part dependent upon the percipient" ([London: Faber and Faber, 1959] 21). In 1957, Lewis wrote to Barfield, "The book is a stunner. It rapt me out of myself at a time when I needed nothing more & expected nothing less" (*Collected Letters*, 3:853).

[40] C. S. Lewis to Katharine Farrer, 9 July 1955, *Collected Letters*, 3:630.

is not a radical shift in philosophical orientation; it is rather a shift in emphasis and, in his fiction, method of representation. Thus, one finds in Lewis's midlife writings *some* attentiveness to pre-rational, pre-analytic concerns, although those moments are relatively rare. For instance, one finds in *Mere Christianity* that coming to faith does not amount merely to accepting a proposition (that Jesus Christ is one's Lord and Savior). Rather, becoming a Christian means becoming a different person, purging certain qualities of character and refining others. As Lewis explains, "The point is not that God will refuse you admission into His eternal world if you have not got certain qualities of character: the point is that if people have not got at least the beginning of those qualities inside them, then no possible external conditions could make a 'Heaven' for them—that is, could make them happy with the deep, strong, un-shakable kind of happiness God intends for us."[41] Without these qualities of character—qualities that obviously include more than just the intellect—people cannot perceive the reality of God and the goodness he offers them.

This version of preconditionalism clearly operates in *The Great Divorce*. As argued in chapter 5, this text can be conceived as an apologue, a generic identity that highlights Lewis's role as public intellectual. But the formulable statements that *The Great Divorce* exemplifies concern the very issues of preconditionalism. In chapter 5, these formulable statements were articulated thusly: (1) The seemingly small, quotidian decisions one makes and actions one commits on a daily basis cumulatively carry eternal consequences; (2) Pride, which assumes many forms and poisons many souls through gradual means, must be expurgated in order eventually to see God. Thus, on the one hand, according to my critical narrative in part 1, *The Great Divorce* is a strongly philosophical text, functioning almost like an argumentative essay, rationally defending a thesis (the formulable statements of the apologue).

On the other hand, according to the counter-narrative offered here, *The Great Divorce* ultimately commits itself to pre-analytical concepts, for the formulable statements it exemplifies affirm that truth can only be perceived when one's loves and affections are rightly prioritized to direct the will: a process clearly indebted to Augustine, who, as we saw earlier, helps give shape to concepts of preconditionalism. The narrative/counter-narrative dichotomy can be expressed in oxymoronic formulations: *The Great Divorce*, leans heavily upon reason and polemics as it exemplifies the proposition that the process of coming to faith involves more than simply accepting a

---

[41] C. S. Lewis, *Mere Christianity* (San Francisco, HarperSanFrancisco, 2001) 81.

reasonable proposition; the text offers representations that rationally show how coming to faith involves pre-rational behavioral adjustments.

At this point, some textual evidence is in order. The objections of nearly every character in *The Great Divorce* to traveling to the Mountains (Heaven) reveal flaws within those characters that prevent them from thinking and seeing clearly. The "Big Man" who appears primarily in chapter 4, for instance, exemplifies a stubborn insistence upon his rights, clouding his ability to understand grace and forgiveness. The apostate Bishop of chapter 5 cannot relinquish his liberal views of Christianity because he is afraid of ridicule and "(above all) of real spiritual fears and hopes."[42] Pride for reputation blinds the Painter of chapter 9. Shame blinds the well-dressed woman of chapters 8 and 9. To release her from her blindness (resulting from her inability to swallow her shame), the Spirit attending her summons a herd of unicorns, whose purpose is to frighten the shame out of her. The narrator's guide, George MacDonald, comments, "Ye will have divined that he [the well-dressed woman's attendant spirit] meant to frighten her, not that fear itself could make her less a Ghost, but if it took her mind a moment off herself, there might, in that moment, be a chance."[43] MacDonald's assessment is relevant to nearly every ghost character, returning us to one of the formulable statements of the book: pride, self-centeredness, or any form of over-attentiveness to self results in an inability to see what is apparent to those who have submitted to God and relinquished self. Pam, the selfishly possessive mother of chapter 11, has wrongly prioritized her loves, valuing her son over God, turning God into, at best, a means for reuniting with her son, and, at worst, a tyrant for taking him away from her in the first place. The vision of Frank, the short ghost on a chain in chapters 12 and 13, is blinded by his selfish use of pity, which he cruelly employs to emotionally blackmail his wife, Sarah Smith of Golders Green.

Ironically, then, the very function of the apologue both situates Lewis as a public intellectual and nudges him beyond the public sphere. Exemplifying formulable statements, the apologue is conducive to Lewis's role as public intellectual, staking out a position and defending it to the last. However, the formulable statements that *The Great Divorce* exemplifies concern principles of preconditionalism, which radically depart from the conventions of the public sphere and are thus not conducive to Lewis's role as public intellectual. This tension in *The Great Divorce*—evident in my oxymoronic figurations of their appearance—suggests that they emerge inorganically.

---

[42] Ibid., 37.
[43] Ibid., 79.

This is because, at this stage in his career (the 1940s), Lewis was wholly committed to his role as public intellectual, defending the faith in print and on the airwaves.

This is why the tension also appears in *Mere Christianity* (and earlier, of course, in the broadcast talks). As part 1 showed, *Mere Christianity* evidences Lewis's prowess as a public intellectual and his adherence to the conventions of the public sphere. However, in Book Four of the text (the fourth series of broadcast talks), Lewis addresses concepts central to the phenomenon of preconditionalism. The relevant passage is found in the chapter on the Trinity but actually describes the process by which one comes to be a Christian—to be more specific, the process by which you—to adopt Lewis's second-person address—may be "drawn into that three-personal life—tonight, if you like."[44] This is not the first altar-call moment in *Mere Christianity*. At the conclusion of Book Two, Lewis presented readers (and, in the broadcast talks, listeners) with a moment of decision: "Now, to-day, this moment, is our chance to choose the right side. God is holding back to give us that chance. It will not last for ever. We must take it or leave it."[45] The altar-call moment in Book Four, however, comes after Lewis has begun explaining the specific doctrines of the faith, contextualizing the act of conversion within a larger and richer (and more particularized) framework. I quote it at length:

> When you come to knowing God, the initiative lies on His side. If He does not show Himself, nothing you can do will enable you to find Him. And, in fact, He shows much more of Himself to some people than to others—not because He has favourites, but because it is impossible for Him to show Himself to a man whose whole mind and character are in the wrong condition. Just as sunlight, though it has no favourites, cannot be reflected in a dusty mirror as clearly as in a clean one.
>
> You can put this another way by saying that while in other sciences the instruments you use are things external to yourself (things like microscopes and telescopes), the instrument through which you see God is your whole self. And if a man's self is not kept clean and bright, his glimpse of God will be blurred—like the Moon seen through a dirty telescope. That is why horrible nations have horrible religions: they have been looking at God through a dirty lens.[46]

---

[44] Ibid., 163.
[45] Ibid., 65.
[46] Ibid., 164–65.

This is one of Lewis's fullest expressions of a species of preconditionalism in his entire corpus: one can only see God rightly on the condition that one's "mind and character" are operating according to their God-ordained function—that is, the *whole* person (not just intellect) must be in proper working condition.

Thus, on the one hand, Lewis affirms a principle that moves beyond the conventions of the public sphere, a principle that testifies to the noetic power of pre-analytical factors. On the other hand, the affirmation of this principle occurs within the latter pages of a book committed to the conventions of the public sphere. That is, Lewis begins the text from a deconverted starting point, never assuming that God exists and accepting the burden of proof—in effect, placing God in the dock. He then builds his argument upon a universal principle—the Law of Human Nature—upon which any rational person should agree, a principle that moreover presupposes the myth of uniform experience. How does one then explain the unlikely appearance of preconditionalism given the procedural guidelines to which the text adheres, procedural guidelines beholden to the public sphere?

Comparing the two altar-call moments referenced earlier may provide an answer. As mentioned, the first moment occurs at the end of Book Two, which, like Book One, is heavily philosophical and polemical. Having built his argument upon the universal Law, Lewis adopts a voice in these two Books that speaks in a register attuned to generalities. (The finer points of Christian doctrine will come in Books Three and Four.) The polemical tone and generalized thrust of the first two books require keeping the particularities of the faith at a distance, lest those particularities alienate the differentiated audience of the public sphere. Lewis of course removes that distance in Books Three and Four, but not before the cogency of his fundamental argument—the argument for the existence of God from the Law of Nature—compels assent. In short, Lewis employs in Books One and Two a distinctly public discourse. Thus, the invitation to faith in Book Two is generic and vague, de-contextualized from the partisan articles of faith that both particularize Christianity and make its presentation within the public sphere awkward at best and—given its secularized environment—transgressive at worst.

Assuming the success of his argument at the conclusion of Book Two, Lewis liberates God from the dock; that is, he provides the audience within the public sphere with good reasons for believing in the Judeo-Christian God. It is only after the liberation of God that Lewis can begin outlining the unique details of Christian dogma; he can proceed from the general to the specific. He has satisfied the demands of public discourse, fulfilled the conventions of the public sphere, and met the necessary prerequisites for traversing the divide that separates the secular (universal) from the religious (particular). Consequently, the altar-call moment in Book Four is *re-contextualized*, reconnected to the framework—the distinctly religious framework—that particularizes its process, providing it with contextual coherence and meaning. This is why the affirmation of preconditionalism falls hard upon the heels of the invitation to faith. Preconditionalism signals the primacy of articles of faith, not the conventions of the public sphere. In fact, it upends those conventions; the discernment of truth comes not from a de-converted starting point but from its opposite: a fully converted mind and will that reveal the very beliefs to which the conversion was directed. Again, Lewis attends to issues of preconditionalism after successfully conforming to the mode of public discourse. This, then, is the source of tension within *Mere Christianity*: Lewis arrives at his affirmation of preconditionalism by first adhering to the conventions of the public sphere, conventions that are fundamentally at odds with preconditionalism.[47]

The tensions within *Mere Christianity* and *The Great Divorce* lead me to a brief reconsideration of the stock response, first analyzed within the context of Lewis's identity as a public intellectual in chapter 5. The principles of the Law of Human Nature in *Mere Christianity* (as well as the *Tao* in *The Abolition of Man*) lend themselves to stock responses. The Law (and *Tao*) reveals objective moral precepts of which humankind is universally cognizant (with varying levels of awareness). Stock responses sharpen the awareness of these precepts by objectively correlating responses and ethical and aesthetic data. Thus, certain actions should objectively warrant our moral approbation and others our moral disapprobation; certain natural landscapes should elicit our appreciation as being objectively sublime (to use Lewis's famous illustration in *Abolition*). Moreover, we have seen how, for Lewis, "one of the main functions of art is to assist it [the stock response]."[48] Certainly Lewis includes his own works of art within this declaration.

Stock responses, as they develop from Lewis's arguments in *Mere Christianity* and *The Abolition of Man*, are implicated in the tensions analyzed

---

[47] It is also interesting to note that Lewis affirms preconditionalism within a paragraph that emphasizes God's "initiative" in the act of conversion, an emphasis that obviously invokes the tenets of the Reformed tradition. As explained earlier, the phenomenon of preconditionalism develops within the Calvinist community. Lewis treads heavily here upon Reformed territory.

[48] C. S. Lewis, *A Preface to Paradise Lost* (Oxford: Oxford University Press, 1961) 55–56.

above. Indeed, the specific tensions in *The Great Divorce* descend from Lewis's critical appraisal of stock responses, for stock responses are built upon the generalized concepts of the Law and the *Tao*, which are utterly objective in nature and universal in application. As we have seen, these qualities of the concepts make them powerful forms of authority in the public sphere, for their claims to objectivity and universality harmonize them with the conventions of the public sphere.

However, those who successfully cultivate the stock response adopt at that moment a perspective that particularizes their vision of the world. They see reality differently than the idealized inhabitant of the public sphere. First, their perspective is hardly neutral: They are predisposed to see the world in stark moral terms that dictate from the outset what constitutes right and wrong. The possession of a preexisting moral framework belies any claim to neutrality. Second, the moral framework they possess is partial to Christianity because it facilitates the apprehension of God and the acknowledgment of Christian truth. Thus, Lewis grounds his advocacy of stock responses in a procedure—seen most clearly in the first two Books of *Mere Christianity* and in *The Abolition of Man*—that de-perspectivizes critical inquiry, yielding the objective, deconverted analysis, universal to all, but specific to none. However, once acquired, stock responses perform the opposite function, supplying an interpretive lens that suggests the important role that perspective plays in seeing reality properly. Lewis's development of the stock response thus serves his purpose within the public sphere while simultaneously nudging him beyond the public sphere.

### b. Further Hesitant Steps Beyond the Public Sphere

Out of the Silent Planet, *the Narniad, and a Re-Consideration of Myth.* Published in 1938, *Out of the Silent Planet* is situated in what I consider Lewis's early public-intellectual phase. However, consistent with my counter-narrative approach, the text shows some evidence of the reality-shaping power of perception. For instance, when Ransom first finds himself on Malacandra, he struggles to take in his surroundings. In a passage probably indebted to the influence of Barfield, Lewis writes, "He [Ransom] saw nothing but colours—colours that refused to form themselves into things. Moreover, he knew nothing yet well enough to see it: you cannot see things till you know roughly what they are."[49] Understanding reality depends upon the conceptual categories that organize them. A variation of

---

[49] C. S. Lewis, *Out of the Silent Planet* (New York: Macmillan Publishing Company, 1965) 42.

preconditionalism also comes into play when Ransom joins the community of *hrossa* (one of the three main species of Malacandra). Occasionally, Ransom notices that *hrossa* hold seemingly imaginary conversations with invisible creatures. He later learns that they are actually talking to *eldila* (angels), largely invisible to his eye and inaudible to his ears. Ransom lacks the perception to detect these angelic beings because he inhabits earth, the "silent planet," subjected to Satan's dominion after the Fall. His senses are dulled presumably by the sin that he inherits from his species.

A more explicit representation of preconditionalism occurs later in the novel when Ransom, along with the villains Weston and Devine, is brought before the *Oyarsa* of Malacandra, the archangel of Mars. The *Oyarsa* explains that Weston's fear clouded his judgment: "'When first you came here, I sent for you, meaning you nothing but honour. The darkness in your own mind filled you with fear. Because you thought I meant evil to you, you went as a beast goes against a beast of some other kind, and snared this Ransom.'"[50] Despite the *Oyarsa's* charity and grace, Weston remains fearful, not to mention covetous and murderous. Weston consequently misjudges the inhabitants of Malacandra. Indeed, the comical dialogue that follows between Weston and the *Oyarsa*—with Ransom serving as translator—reveals how "fear and death and desire" are deeply entrenched in Weston's perspective, rendering it defective, obtuse to the benevolence and richness of Martian civilization.

As we have seen, by the time Lewis created the world of Narnia in the late 1940s, his methods and emphases underwent a shift that signals further movement beyond the public sphere. Instances of preconditionalism thus abound in the Narniad. In *The Lion, the Witch and the Wardrobe*, Lucy and Edmund hold diametrically opposed views of the White Witch. Lucy rightly observes that she is evil; Edmund is not convinced. But given his spiteful attitude toward his siblings and greed for Turkish Delight, Edmund betrays a flawed perspective that unfolds a false picture of reality; Edmund is self-deceived. In *Prince Caspian*, Lucy, whose faith exceeds that of the other Pevensie children, is the first to see the great Lion. More, she continues to trust in—and thus see—Aslan even when the other children do not believe her. Eventually, all the children do see Aslan, Susan being the last, who offers this explanation: "'But I've been far worse than you know. I really believed it was him—he, I mean—yesterday. When he warned us not to go down to the fir wood and I really believed it was him tonight, when you woke us up. I mean, deep down inside. Or I could have, if I'd let myself. But

---

[50] Ibid., 134.

I just wanted to get out of the woods and—and—oh, I don't know.'"[51] In a moment that resembles Orual's willful blindness to Psyche's palace in *Till We Have Faces*, Susan demonstrates how a distorted perspective occasions the inability or refusal—in the epistemology of preconditionalism, the two are indistinguishable—to see and know truth. Aslan later lovingly chastises Susan: "'You have listened to fears, child,' said Aslan. 'Come, let me breathe on you. Forget them. Are you brave again?'"[52] Forgiven and emboldened by Aslan, Susan achieves a restored perspective, affording her with clear knowledge and a firm commitment that replace the elliptical indecisiveness with which she concluded her apology to Lucy (as quoted above).

For the most part in the Narniad, the process of preconditionalism is inscribed in self-centered and stubborn characters: characters who are thus morally and epistemologically blind. In *The Voyage of the* Dawn Treader, the creatures known as Dufflepuds are convinced that their ruler, the magician Coriakin, has made them ugly through a spell he cast upon them. They therefore later sneak into Coriakin's house, consult his magic book, and incant a spell that makes them invisible. When she later reverses the invisibility spell, Lucy asks Coriakin if he will de-uglify them: "'Well, that's rather a delicate question,' said the Magician. 'You see, it's only *they* who think they were so nice to look at before. They say they've been uglified, but that isn't what I called it. Many people might say the change was for the better.'"[53] The Dufflepuds's faulty self-perception stems from their own outrageous self-conceit; they are unable to see themselves as they truly appear. In *The Magician's Nephew*, Uncle Andrew and Jadis dislike the beautiful song of creation with which Aslan brings Narnia to life: an aesthetic defect resulting from moral turpitude and close-mindedness. Uncle Andrew, in fact, cannot hear the song for what it truly is:

"Of course it can't really have been singing," he thought, "I must have imagined it. I've been letting my nerves get out of order. Who ever heard of a lion singing?" And the longer and more beautiful the Lion sang, the harder Uncle Andrew tried to make himself believe that he could hear nothing but roaring. Now the trouble about trying to make yourself stupider than you really are is that you very often succeed. Uncle Andrew did. He soon did hear nothing but roaring in Aslan's song.[54]

---

[51] C. S. Lewis, *Prince Caspian* (New York: HarperTrophy, 1979) 161.

[52] Ibid., 162.

[53] C. S. Lewis, *The Voyage of the Dawn Treader* (New York: HarperTrophy, 1980) 176.

[54] C. S. Lewis, *The Magician's Nephew* (New York: HarperTrophy, 1980) 149–50.

Later, Uncle Andrew cannot understand the Talking Animals. The narrator describes the nature of Uncle Andrew's failure of perception, a description that resonates with the principles of preconditionalism: "For what you see and hear depends a good deal on where you are standing: it also depends on what sort of person you are."[55]

Numerous representations of preconditionalism exist in the seventh and final book of the series, *The Last Battle*. Perhaps it is fitting that defective perception—and thus faulty thinking and rash actions—should precipitate the end of Narnia. When they observe that Narnians are denuding the forests of the land, selling the trees to the Calormenes, Tirian, King of Narnia, and Jewel the Unicorn become enraged: "They were too angry to think clearly. But much evil came of their rashness in the end."[56] Their judgment clouded by anger, Tirian and Jewel, though well intentioned, inadvertently help set into place the conditions and events that will lead to the Narnian apocalypse. And when that apocalypse does descend upon Narnia, the recalcitrant dwarfs are unwilling/unable—again, no real distinction here—to perceive the reality of the real Narnia: the heavenly realm that lies inside the stable door. As Aslan explains, "'They will not let us help them. They have chosen cunning instead of belief. Their prison is only in their own minds, yet they are in that prison; and so afraid of being taken in that they cannot be taken out.'"[57] Because of their hard hearts, the dwarfs' perspective is skewed; they cannot see the truth, the reality of what lies in the stable.

Not all representations of preconditionalism in *The Last Battle*, however, involve darkened perspectives. The Calormene soldier Emeth is admitted into Aslan's realm despite the fact that he was a lifelong follower of the false god Tash. As Aslan tells him, "'Child, all the service thou hast done to Tash, I account as service done to me.'"[58] Although serving a false god, Emeth possesses the qualities of character—noble, entirely good qualities—that predispose him to find the truth, for as Aslan explains, "'For all find what they truly seek.'"[59] Unlike the dwarfs, Emeth has a trusting and openminded perspective, a clear lens to behold reality; despite being born a Calormene, he is able to see through the falseness of Tash to the reality of Aslan.[60]

---

[55] Ibid., 148.

[56] C. S. Lewis, *The Last Battle* (New York: Harper Trophy, 1994) 25.

[57] Ibid., 185–86.

[58] Ibid., 205.

[59] Ibid., 206.

[60] Barkman identifies some of these instances of preconditionalism in the Narniad as exemplifications of virtue epistemology, an epistemology indebted to

(Perhaps representations of preconditionalism explain why some have connected Lewis with universalism: Anyone, even followers of other gods, who possess the right qualities of character will eventually find God. Lewis's belief in purgatory and the post-mortal opportunities for Emeth and the characters of *The Great Divorce* complicate the matter.[61])

The genre of the Narniad lends itself well to representations of preconditionalism. In his essay "Sometimes Fairy Stories May Say Best What's to Be Said," Lewis explains why he was drawn to fairy tale: "...its brevity, its severe restraints on description, its flexible traditionalism, its inflexible hostility to all analysis, digression, reflections and 'gas.'"[62] As we saw in part 1, Lewis's analyses, digressions, reflections, and gas conform to the conventions of the public sphere. Thus, a departure from the former entails a departure from the latter, both of which might lead to closer attentiveness to the phenomenon of preconditionalism. But the genre of the Narniad overlaps with the genre of *The Great Divorce*: Both are specimens of mythopoeia. As apologue, *The Great Divorce* exemplifies formulable statements, performing expository functions—i.e., indulging in analysis and "gas"—alien to mythopoeia. Thus, the genre of mythopoeia as Lewis employs it seems to operate both inside and outside the public sphere: It generates the sort of exposition that necessitates the use of objective reason (inside the public sphere), but also engages pre-reflective factors that operate beyond reason (outside the public sphere), factors equally—if not more so—determinative of belief than reason itself. How does one explain this?

As Lewis develops it, mythopoeia unites two contradictory elements, two divergent modes of experience that Lewis struggled throughout his life to harmonize. On the one hand, myth, as we saw in part 1, is abstract and universal; it figures archetypes foundational to all human experience, archetypes that can be analytically positioned to generate large conclusions about the nature of humankind. On the other hand, myth is concrete and particular; it embodies the archetypes in a narrative that defies analysis by becoming absorbed into the stream of experience. These two antithetical modes of apprehension create a daunting polarity within human consciousness. As Lewis explains,

---

post-Enlightenment thinking and thus further illustrative of Lewis's movement beyond the public sphere. See Barkman, *C. S. Lewis & Philosophy as a Way of Life*, 116.

[61] See, for instance, Elissa McCormack, "Inclusivism in the Fiction of C. S. Lewis: The Case of Emeth," *Logos* 11/4 (Fall 2008).

[62] C. S. Lewis, "Sometimes Fairy Stories May Say Best What's to Be Said," in *On Stories and Other Essays on Literature*, ed. Walter Hooper (San Diego: Harcourt Brace & Company, 1982) 46.

Human intellect is incurably abstract. Pure mathematics is the type of successful thought. Yet the only realities we experience are concrete—this pain, this pleasure, this dog, this man. While we are loving the man, bearing the pain, enjoying the pleasure, we are not intellectually apprehending Pleasure or Personality. When we begin to do so, on the other hand, the concrete realities sink to the level of mere instances or examples: we are no longer dealing with them, but with that which they exemplify. This is our dilemma—either to taste and not to know or to know and not to taste—or, more strictly, to lack one kind of knowledge because we are in an experience or to lack another kind because we are outside it.[63]

For Lewis, myth unifies the opposites: "Of this tragic dilemma myth is the partial solution. In the enjoyment of a great myth we come nearest to experiencing as a concrete what can otherwise be understood only as an abstraction."[64] Myth affords the opportunity both to know and taste; it is a "concrete universal."[65]

But with the possible exception of *Till We Have Faces*, the unification of these opposites never appears fully complete in Lewis's fiction: The universal is never fully reconciled to the particular; the abstract is never fully harmonized with the concrete. Lewis's public-intellectual persona—what Barfield called his "expository demon"—intrudes upon the narrative. Thus *The Great Divorce* functions as both myth and apologue. No doubt by the time Lewis wrote the Narnian stories the harmonization between the opposites was much more fully actualized (though the impulse of the public intellectual was still present, evident in Lewis's stated intention of "casting all these things [religious beliefs] into an imaginary world, stripping them of their stained-glass and Sunday school association..." thereby making "them for the first time appear in their real potency"[66]).

The presence of stark polarities within myth—the unification of opposites that demarcate a fundamental division of human consciousness—explains Lewis's use of both the analytical and pre-analytical mode in his fiction. As public intellectual, Lewis is drawn to the universal, the abstract, and thus ultimately the polemical element of myth; as fantasist, he engages

---

[63] C. S. Lewis, "Myth Became Fact," in *God in the Dock: Essays on Theology and Ethics*, ed. Walter Hooper (Grand Rapids: Eerdmans, 1970) 65.

[64] Ibid., 66.

[65] Barkman, *C. S. Lewis & Philosophy as a Way of Life*, 111. Northrop Frye's use of the phrase "concrete universal" as applied to myth predates Barkman's. See *Anatomy of Criticism: Four Essays*. Princeton: Princeton University Press, 1975. p. 192.

[66] Lewis, "Sometimes Fairy Stories," 47.

the particular, the concrete, and thus the pre-reflective element of myth. Like the stock response, myth is fraught with tension in Lewis's writings; both hold the potential to serve him within the public sphere or to carry him beyond it.

### C. Enlarging the Context: Lewis's Joy, Burke's Sublime, and the Inadequacy of Theory

The bifurcation between the abstract and the concrete, ostensibly harmonized within myth, constitutes a challenge for both the study of aesthetics and the study of humankind, for, as described above, the abstract and the concrete modes of apprehension divide human consciousness. Lewis analyzes a variation of this bifurcation in *Surprised by Joy* when he explores the nature of Joy or *Sehnsucht*, the immortal longing, the infinite desire. He maintains that the experience of Joy is incompatible with the analysis of Joy; drawing from Samuel Alexander's *Space Time and Deity*, he classifies the two modes of apprehension as Enjoyment and Contemplation, respectively. Overwhelmed by the throes of the immortal longing, one becomes immersed in the experience of Joy. Seeking to understand this longing, one necessarily exits that experience to analyze it. By doing so, the experience is lost, and the analysis fails: analysis necessitates the momentary abandonment of the experience it seeks to understand. In Lewis's words, "...the enjoyment and the contemplation of our inner activities are incompatible. You cannot hope and also think about hoping at the same moment; for in hope we look to hope's object and we interrupt this by (so to speak) turning round to look at the hope itself."[67] The enjoyment of Joy and the contemplation of Joy are distinct experiences and do not even wholly concern the same phenomenon. This section in *Surprised by Joy* reveals some ways in which Lewis was attentive to the reality-shaping power of conceptual lenses: the lens of analysis discloses a different reality than the lens of immediate experience.

As we saw, Barfield was closely attentive to conceptual lenses and perceptual influences. For the moment, I want to focus on his dichotomy that we explored earlier: the dichotomy between the poetic principle and the rational principle. Lewis's observation of the problems of analysis in *Surprised by Joy* recapitulates a fundamental incompatibility within Barfield's dichotomy in *Poetic Diction*. Barfield explains this incompatibility: "The absolute rational principle is that which makes conscious of poetry but cannot create it; the absolute poetic principle is that which creates poetry but

---

[67] Lewis, *Surprised by Joy*, 218.

cannot make conscious of it."[68] Like Enjoyment and Contemplation, the rational principle and the poetic principle occupy two separate spaces of experience, employing different modes of apprehension, and affording two separate perceptions of reality. What is important for my purposes is that Barfield's polarity suggests the terms with which I have defined Lewis's *modus operandi* both inside and outside the public sphere. The rational principle demonstrates clear affinities to the conventions of the public sphere, while the poetic principle abides by a different set of conventions altogether.

I mention Barfield's elucidation of these two principles here not only because it helps flesh out the tension within Lewis's body of work, but because it turns our attention to the large sweep of intellectual history— Barfield, after all, offers a grand narrative about how people think and write. I want to connect the tension found in some of Lewis's writings and described in this chapter to one specific moment in intellectual history that loosely overlaps with Barfield's analysis. This was a crucial moment in the history of aesthetics that takes place in the century that witnessed the rise of the public sphere. This moment is the publication of Edmund Burke's *A Philosophical Enquiry into the Origins of Our Ideas of the Sublime and Beautiful* (1757), a text that, like many of Lewis's own, attempts to analyze a concept that defies analysis. Like Joy, the sublime constitutes a totalizing experience that becomes a mere shadow of itself when laid upon the dissecting table. My brief analysis of Burke's *Enquiry* will provide a larger context for considering Lewis's dilemma, returning us to the very century from which the conventions of the public sphere originate.

The eighteenth-century discourse of the sublime poses challenges to its own discursiveness. How is one to give expression to the inexpressible and to reason about what often transcends reason? The procedural guidelines of the Enlightenment structure Burke's approach to the problem, not to mention that of most eighteenth-century thinkers. Burke appeals to fittingness in order to stabilize, tame, and gain control over his unpliable, messy subject matter. He defines the sublime as "whatever is fitted in any sort to excite the ideas of pain and danger."[69] Consistent with empiricism, Burke launches a taxonomic analysis of the sublime, cataloging qualities that are foundational to sublimity, for example, infinity, obscurity, darkness, etc. These qualities and properties of both natural and artificial phenomena are naturally fitted to produce the experience of the sublime. Enabling Burke to

---

[68] Barfield, *Poetic Diction*, 104.
[69] Edmund Burke, *An Enquiry* (Oxford: Oxford University Press, 1998) 35.

harness his difficult subject, taxonomy informed by empiricism constitutes the analytic mechanism whereby he systematizes the sublime and attempts to overcome its discursive challenges.

Inserting itself into Burke's analytic mechanism is the procedural framework of de-contextualized spatiality—procedural in the sense that notions of spatiality dictate a metaphorical analytic space, removed from the context of the sublime experience, that Burke marks off for himself in order to examine the sublime itself. This is, of course, the exact procedure that Lewis critiques in *Surprised by Joy*. Burke's analytic space, I suggest, is further informed by the myth of uniform experience, which, as we saw in Part 1, de-contextualizes experience, divesting it of its particularities in order to make it suitable for the universal stage of the Enlightenment. And as we saw, Lewis's work as a public intellectual upholds the myth of uniform experience.

Burke's best-known usage of spatiality in the *Enquiry* occurs in his discussion of the aesthetic distance necessary for sublime experiences. After isolating pain and danger as the sources of the sublime, Burke asserts that, if the danger threatens the spectator, if it comes too near to the spectator, the sublime experience is impossible: the spectator will simply fear for his or her life. Later, however, spatiality becomes transferred from the subject of analysis to the procedure of the analysis itself.

This phenomenon of spatiality turning itself upon Burke as critic manifests itself when Burke asks who is most qualified to describe the sublime. He eliminates the artists themselves because they, as Burke writes, "have been too much occupied in the practice." Burke continues, "As for the critics they have generally sought the rule of the arts in the wrong place; they sought it among poems, pictures, engravings, statues and buildings. But art can never give the rules that make an art.... I can judge but poorly of any thing whilst I measure it by no other standard than itself."[70]

Artists and critics are unfit judges of the sublime because they are too immersed in it to speak truly of it. They cannot get outside of their own production of, and engagement with, the sublime. For Burke, the standard of the sublime must locate itself outside the metaphorical arena of the sublime. Burke suggests that the judicious analyst of the sublime must be distanced from that arena in order to arrive at that standard. Indeed, as the spectator of the sublime must allow a certain distance between him- or herself and the danger that causes sublimity, so the critic of the sublime must allow a certain distance between him- or herself and the intense experiences of the sublime.

---

[70] Ibid., 49.

Why Burke imposes a space between sublime experiences and analyses of the sublime—why he seeks a standard for the sublime *outside* the sublime—finds expression, I believe, in his introduction. Written twelve years after the original text, the introduction enters a discourse popular in the eighteenth century that revolves around the standard of taste.[71] Neoclassical in intellectual temperament, this discourse seeks rational principles upon which to ground ideas of taste and beauty. It generally maintains that there exist certain principles in true art that will always evoke the sentiment of beauty in the beholder, a principle that, as we saw in chapters 4 and 5, Lewis himself follows. This discourse forges a universal basis for the standard of taste, privileging objective aesthetic judgments that make rational inquiry possible. "The whole ground-work of taste," Burke asserts, "is common to all, and therefore there is a sufficient foundation for a conclusive reasoning on these matters."[72]

In this groundwork that Burke lays in his introduction, spatiality and discursiveness converge on the sublime. By emphasizing aesthetic universality and the faculty of reason, Burke is cordoning off the critical space that he feels is necessary for evaluating sublimity. He is, in fact, reaching toward a standard for measuring the sublime that is external to the sublime arena. Once the universality of taste is posited, a methodical reasoning process combs the human passions in order to find the principles upon which the sublime operates. Unlike the artist or typical critic, Burke steps outside the sublime experience and into a critical space that analyzes it. But in doing so, Burke reprises the fundamental questions of the discourse of the sublime. If Burke creates a critical space outside the sublime, and if his critical space—informed by the discourse of the standard of taste—employs reason to analyze the sublime, we now ask: can one reason about something that often transcends reason? How much can the space of critical reason, in other words, say about the sublime space of intense passion?

This brief overview underscores the explicit and implicit dilemmas inherent in the subject of this chapter: Lewis's tentative movement away from the public sphere. Like this very movement, Burke's text is located in a moment marked by the transition from an insistence upon the conventions

---

[71] Evidence of this discourse, all of which makes similar pronouncements on the nature of taste, can be found in the following eighteenth-century texts: the Third Earl of Shaftesbury's *Characteristics* (1711); Joseph Addison's *Spectator no. 409* (1712); Francis Hutcheson's *An Inquiry into the Original of Our Ideas of Beauty and Virtue* (1725); David Hume's essay, "Of the Standard of Taste," in *Essays Moral, Political, and Literary: Part I* (1742); and Hugh Blair's *Lectures on Rhetoric and Belles Lettres* (1784).

[72] Ibid., 22.

of the Enlightenment to an irrepressible interest in that which defies those conventions, like the sublime, the Gothic, and the subject-matter of the so-called graveyard poets. The tension in Lewis's writings is thus a microcosm of this moment in history, a moment when two discourses converge, the newer discourse giving representation to trans-rational, pre-analytical experiences, the older discourse subjecting those experiences to the (inadequate) procedure of rational analysis. What Burke's analysis of the sublime and Lewis's analysis of Joy show are that some experiences are too large for the public sphere; they may be subjected to analysis, to Contemplation, to the rational principle, but in so doing they become something else, something attenuated and thin.

But the commitment to the public sphere dies hard. Lewis, unlike Burke, can see that analysis diminishes his subject. Nevertheless, as public intellectual, Lewis remains largely committed to the conventions of the public sphere exemplified in Burke's *Enquiry*. Lewis's explanation of the *Tao* in *The Abolition of Man*, especially the aesthetic considerations at the beginning of the book, overlap with Burke's deployment of the concept of taste: both appeal to objective qualities in natural phenomena and art that are fitted to produce certain aesthetic feelings. Burke and Lewis protect against the dangers of subjectivism by privileging the universal, which in turn commits them to a myth of uniform experience.

In short, when Lewis attends to pre-analytical phenomena, when he acknowledges the reality-shaping power of perception, he generally has one foot remaining in the public sphere. And yet those movements beyond the public sphere—however partial—are compelling. One thinks, for instance, of the epilogue to *The Discarded Image*. Lewis there explains that the explanatory models that humans create to understand their world do not gain traction simply because they objectively correlate to all available empirical data. (We must bear in mind that this was published just two years after Thomas Kuhn's *The Structure of Scientific Revolutions*, 1962.) Rather, people are drawn to explanatory models simply because they find themselves drawn to them for a variety of non-rational reasons, oftentimes independently of facts; certain models simply strike an age as appealing, powerful, or interesting. As Lewis explains, each model "reflects the prevalent psychology of an age almost as much as it reflects the state of that age's knowledge."[73] In yet another instance of preconditionalism, Lewis states that a change in perspective occasions a change in model. And neither

---

[73] C. S. Lewis, *The Discarded Image: An Introduction to Medieval and Renaissance Literature* (Cambridge: Cambridge University Press, 1964) 222.

change comes necessarily from scientific discovery; indeed, the scientific discovery may come as a result of the change in perspective or model: "But I think it [our own model] is more likely to change when, and because, far-reaching changes in the mental temper of our descendants demand that it should."[74]

By comparing Lewis and Burke, I have returned us to the century that produced the conventions so central to my analysis. The comparison illustrates how the public sphere, from its beginnings through the twentieth century, commits itself to a discourse ill-equipped for the apprehension of certain powerful experiences—powerful aesthetic and religious experiences. The public sphere, in other words, is inadequate to the task of doing justice to experiences that defy reason. This inadequacy manifests itself when analysis falters, producing the sort of tensions and dilemmas we have noted in the writings of both Burke and Lewis.

## V. Conclusion

This chapter has explored ways in which mental tempers of a wide variety in Lewis's fictional characters shape understandings of reality. But one wonders how willing Lewis would be to apply his theory of model-change in *The Discarded Image* to his own thinking: that is, how willing he would be to admit that his changing mental temper demands a new model, a model to replace the one that adheres to the conventions of the public sphere, propped up by universalizing principles like the Law of Nature and the *Tao*. To admit as much necessitates the concomitant admission that our knowledge is provisional, that the models of our creation are tentative and temporary, that the subjectively refracted lenses through which we see the world give us an incomplete picture. As we saw in chapter 1, the public sphere is a space of certainty, of uncompromising commitment; provisionality betrays an epistemological weakness that the public intellectual cannot reveal. And thus we are brought back again to the tension in Lewis's writings; movement beyond the public sphere unmasks Lewis's uncertainty, his provisional understanding.

Lewis's last book—*Letters to Malcolm: Chiefly on Prayer*—positions him outside the public sphere by virtue of its form. Written as a series of letters to a fictitious friend, the book begins with a context already in place. Lewis as narrator is not writing to the differentiated audience of the public sphere; he is writing to a particular (imaginary) friend, who even has a wife and son of

---

[74] Ibid.

whom Lewis must take account. Such a writing scenario necessarily particularizes the issues that are universalized in most of Lewis's works of theology and apologetics. *Letters to Malcolm* presents itself as a private, not public, text. Consequently, the text lends itself to admissions of tentativeness in thought. Consider, for instance, this passage in which Lewis proposes a solution to the problem of coming before God in prayer without pretenses or facades: "The two facades—the 'I' as I perceive myself and the room as I perceive it—were obstacles as long as I mistook them for ultimate realities. But the moment I recognized them as facades, as mere surfaces, they became conductors. Do you see? A lie is a delusion only so long as we believe it; but a recognised lie is a reality—a real lie—and as such may be highly instructive."[75] Here Lewis recognizes a provisionality not only in his own identity but in the external world as he perceives it. And prayer, which can be a private act, is the actual recognition of that provisionality: "Now the moment of prayer is for me—or involves for me as its condition—the awareness, the re-awakened awareness, that this 'real world' and 'real self' are very far from being rock-bottom realities."[76]

This is Lewis with his back turned to the public sphere: a rare moment, usually fraught, as we have seen, with tension, but brought to bloom in this passage from *Letters to Malcolm* and, as we shall see in the next two chapters, most fully in *Till We Have Faces* and *A Grief Observed*.

---

[75] C. S. Lewis, *Letters to Malcolm: Chiefly on Prayer* (San Diego: Harcourt Brace, 1964) 80.
[76] Ibid., 81.

# 8

# "Water-Spouts of Truth from the Very Depth of Truth": Perspective, Preconditionalism, and the Actualization of Myth in *Till We Have Faces*

## I. Introduction: The Place of *Till We Have Faces* in the Lewis Corpus

In some respects, the novel *Till We Have Faces* is a typical C. S. Lewis text. Like other works in his post-Christian-conversion *oeuvre*, *Till We Have Faces* engages huge religious questions: Does God (or do the gods) exist? What is his (or their) nature? How does he (or how do they) reveal himself (or themselves) to humankind? What does he (or they) require of us? In addition, the novel harmonizes with earlier Lewis works by putting God (or the gods) in the dock. That is, *Till We Have Faces*—through the protagonist Orual—adopts a skeptical stance toward religious claims, subjecting them to rigorous interrogation. The religious position assumes the burden of proof, not the skeptical (or secular) position, a polemical scenario inherent in nearly all works of Christian apologetics since the Enlightenment, evident, for instance, in the very assumptions with which Lewis begins *The Problem of Pain* and *Mere Christianity*: The starting points of inquiry presuppose the non-existence of God or, at the very least, hold God's existence in abeyance. Finally, *Till We Have Faces* assumes an audience similar to that for which Lewis writes his more straightforward apologetic works, from *The Screwtape Letters* to *Miracles*. The protagonist of *Till We Have Faces*, Orual, affirms that she writes her autobiographical narrative for the Greeks, for whom "there is great freedom of speech even about the gods themselves."[1] This freedom of speech, a central characteristic of the public sphere, wherein Lewis, as public intellectual, makes his case for theistic supernaturalism in earlier works, generates a putative neutral space for argumentation where no claim is privileged by authority or tradition. Only the most reasonable claims survive, which is to say that only the claims that adhere to the conventions of the public sphere deserve assent. Orual realizes that the open-minded Greeks, by virtue of their exposure to wide-ranging beliefs, are more likely to

---

[1] C. S. Lewis, *Till We Have Faces: A Myth Retold* (San Diego: Harcourt Brace & Company, 1984) 3–4.

resonate with her religious skepticism than the superstitious inhabitants of her own kingdom of Glome, where the cult of Ungit holds the religious monopoly, restricting free speech by limiting what can publicly and safely be said about the gods. Orual's intended audience proleptically imitates the audience for which Lewis wrote his apologetic fiction and non-fiction.

Despite these similarities, it is obvious that *Till We Have Faces* holds an anomalous place in the Lewis corpus. It is arguably the only true novel Lewis ever wrote.[2] Indeed, this generic identity accounts for much of its uniqueness, primarily its non-polemical nature. As Doris T. Myers writes, the novel "is a radical departure from the beautiful fantasies and religious teaching that loyal readers are accustomed to associate with Lewis."[3] This chapter analyzes this radical departure as a movement away from the public sphere and its conventions. Even allowing for its unique identity as a novel, the work develops themes and deploys images that require Lewis to shed his identity as public intellectual. Consequently, Lewis engages those huge religious questions enumerated above from a different vantage point, one that lies beyond the public sphere. This vantage point specifically accounts for the following qualities that differentiate *Till We Have Faces* from earlier works: the uncertainty that abounds throughout the narrative, what we might call epistemological provisionality; the privileging of context, perspectivism, and thick narrativity that proceed precisely from this

---

[2] David Downing echoes this opinion, claiming that *Till We Have Faces* is "...probably [Lewis's] only book that he would consider a novel in the strict sense of the term" (*Planets in Peril: A Critical Study of C. S. Lewis's Ransom Trilogy* [Amherst: University of Massachusetts Press, 1992] 84). This generic identification holds true if we espouse Ian Watt's foundational formulation that "formal realism" lies at the heart of the novel (*The Rise of the Novel* [New York: Kessinger Publishing, 2009] 32). One would be hard-pressed to identify any Lewis text other than *Till We Have Faces* that offers such realistic representations as the following: "I was leaning my head on my window-sill to dry my hair after the bath, and they were walking in the garden" ([San Diego: Harcourt Brace & Company, 1984] 13). This generic identification also holds true if we consider Watt's association of the novel with individualism. Indeed, Watt traces the emergence of the individual alongside the rise of the novel in the eighteenth century. He writes that "both philosophers and novelists paid greater attention to the particular individual than had been common before" (*The Rise of the Novel*, 18); Watt attends to the eighteenth-century emphasis of the particular rather than the universal; he argues that novels like Moll Flanders propagate an "individualist ideology" (*The Rise of the Novel*, 59). Emphasis on the particularities of the narrative endows *Till We Have Faces* with the artistic fine touches mentioned above.

[3] Doris T. Myers, *Bareface: A Guide to C. S. Lewis's Last Novel* (Columbia: University of Missouri Press, 2004) 1.

uncertainty[4]; character development informed by preconditionalism, the idea that one cannot arrive at truth until one's cognitive and moral faculties have been properly prepared; and an actualization of myth unparalleled in Lewis's other works, evident in the novel's representation of fertility and sacrifice, archetypal images of primitive mythology. Thus, the radical departure of *Till We Have Faces* entails more than a turning away from straightforward Christian apologetics, a species of writing that served Lewis well as a public intellectual. Rather, the novel crystallizes Lewis's departure from the public sphere and its conventions, the abandonment of which generates a text unlike anything Lewis had previously written.

## II. Uncertainty and Epistemological Provisionality

We have seen how the public intellectual necessarily adopts an argumentative, defensive stance that downplays doubt and rests upon certainty, a certainty that, in the public sphere, is easily read as rightness of position. For the public intellectual, uncertainty betrays a chink in the armor. In apologetic works like *The Problem of Pain*, *Mere Christianity*, and *Miracles*, Lewis exudes confidence; he manages his argument like a master chess player, always in control, never exposing vulnerabilities, striking the polemical nail directly on the head. Even works of fiction like *The Screwtape Letters* and *The Great Divorce* downplay doubt, precluding uncertainty by virtue of their form and function. As apologues (see chapter 5), these texts project worlds that clearly and unambiguously demarcate the boundaries between religious truth and error as well as between moral right and wrong. In addition, characters in these texts are simplistically drawn, at times verging on caricatures, thereby insuring that they transparently illustrate the vices and virtues from which the texts perform what Sheldon Sacks identifies as the purpose of the apologue: to serve as "a fictional example of the truth of a formulable statement or a series of such statements."[5] Consequently, *The Screwtape Letters* and *The Great Divorce* provide the reader with stable epistemological ground: Truth and goodness are never hard to discern.

---

[4] Again, I admit that this quality in particular stems from the work's identity as a novel. But even for a novel, the text exhibits an especially thick narrativity, a Faulknerian emphasis on perspective and context.

[5] Sheldon Sacks, *Fiction and the Shape of Belief* (Berkeley: University of California Press, 1967) 26.

*Till We Have Faces*, on the other hand, can occasionally leave the reader with epistemological vertigo. As the only true novel that Lewis wrote, the text employs the characteristic that Ian Watt seminally identifies as the core ingredient of the novel: formal realism.[6] And reality in *Till We Have Faces* proves to be complex, generating the uncertainty and provisionality that remove Lewis from the public sphere.

Much of the uncertainty in the novel surrounds issues of identity. As we have seen, the public sphere requires its participants to undergo a process of de-conversion, a divestment of subjectivity and particularity, resulting in a de-contextualized, hyperbolically neutral inquirer who can dispassionately and objectively adjudicate between rival claims. *Till We Have Faces*, on the other hand, spotlights the complexity of identity, its function as a lens for the perception of reality. While composing the addendum to her autobiography (Part II of the novel), Orual realizes just how difficult it is to understand herself. She describes the attempt as "a labour of sifting and sorting, separating motive from motive and both from pretext...." This labor invades her dreams, assuming the form of an impossible task: separating an enormous pile of assorted seeds into individual piles, each of one kind of seed. Orual estimates, "There was one chance in ten thousand of finishing the labour in time, and one in a hundred thousand of making no mistake."[7] Unlike characters in texts written during Lewis's public-intellectual phase— Screwtape; George MacDonald, the ghosts, and Solid People (in *The Great Divorce*); and Ransom as well as the various villains in the Ransom trilogy— Orual is a nuanced, complex, and conflicted character.

In fact, struggling to cope with the pain and shame she experiences after the ordeal with her sister Psyche, Orual adopts a persona, further complicating her identity. She becomes Queen of Glome, a metamorphosis that transforms not only her personality but her appearance, signaled by the donning of a veil. A richly symbolic image, the veil suggests (among other things) the inscrutability of identity and, more specifically, its pretenses that mask a reality often beyond discernment. As analyzed in chapter 3, some evidence indicates that Lewis himself adopted a persona after his conversion to Christianity. As Owen Barfield explains, "I had the impression of living with, not one, but two Lewises; and this was so as well when I was enjoying

---

[6] Ian Watt, *The Rise of the Novel: Studies in Defoe, Richardson and Fielding* (Berkeley: University of California Press, 2001) 9-34.

[7] Lewis, *Till We Have Faces*, 256–57.

his company as when I was absent from him."[8] Lewis admits that "what I call 'myself' (for all practical, everyday purposes) is also a dramatic construction...."[9] Lewis seems to have understood firsthand the layers of pretense that can insulate the elusive raw self. *Till We Have Faces* explores with unflinching honesty the damage that these layers of pretense can wreak, laying bare what we might call the self-deception of the self, the enigma of subjectivity. Written from Orual's first-person perspective, the novel projects a world that is likewise enigmatic, shrouded by layers of false appearances.

Orual struggles not only to understand herself but to understand other people as well. Uncertainty surrounds the identity of other characters. As previously stated, Part II of the novel consists of Orual's addendum to her first accusation against the gods. What inspires this addendum, at least in part, is Orual's realization that she misunderstood individuals from her past. As she writes, "The past which I wrote down was not the past that I thought I had (all these years) been remembering."[10] In fact, her misunderstanding was so profound that she is tempted to rewrite her entire history; she is prevented from doing so only because she does not have sufficient time in her old age.

Orual's misjudgment primarily concerns her sister Redival and Ansit, the wife of Bardia, captain of the Glomian guards with whom Orual is secretly in love. For most of her life, Orual considered Redival to be petty, lascivious, and vindictive. It is Redival, after all, who in her youth arranges a tryst with Tarin, which results in his castration by the King her father. It is also Redival who out of jealousy reports to the Priest of Ungit that the people revere Psyche as a god, a communiqué that rankles the Priest and ultimately occasions the sacrifice of Psyche to the god of the mountain.

However, in her addendum, Orual receives a revelation during a chance encounter with Tarin, who now serves as eunuch in the court of a different king. Tarin recounts that Redival was terribly lonely as a girl, a loneliness that began after Psyche was born, when Orual spent every waking hour in devotion to Psyche to the complete neglect of Redival. Orual thus realizes how she herself wounded Redival and that Redival's spiteful actions stem not from mere ill-will but from the pain of abandonment. Orual's new understanding of a complex relationship explodes her previously facile

---

[8] Owen Barfield, introduction to *Light on C. S. Lewis*, ed. Jocelyn Gibb (New York: Harcourt Brace & World, 1965) xiv.

[9] Lewis, *Letters to Malcolm*, 81.

[10] Lewis, *Till We Have Faces*, 253.

conception of a good sister/bad sister dichotomy. Similarly, facile conceptions crumble to pieces when Orual comes face-to-face for the first time with Ansit. Previously, Orual looked upon Ansit as a domineering wife, an attitude sharpened by Orual's jealousy. However, a short conversation with Ansit brings another revelation, further dismantling the perception of matters that Orual long took for granted. Ansit explains that she was in fact jealous of Orual, that Orual, once she became queen, kept Bardia on duty for interminable lengths of time, and that only a piece of Bardia—an exhausted, spent piece—remained after he finally returned home. With emotionally raw audacity, Ansit implicitly places the cause of Bardia's death at the feet of Orual, likening her to the very gods that Orual despises: a devourer of men and women. Orual's long-settled beliefs about Redival and Ansit become unsettled: She realizes that the identity of others, just like her own identity, is more complex than she imagined. The novel inscribes this complexity in more subtle ways as well. Orual's servant girl Poobi, an apparent simpleton, plays a game with beads. Orual comments, significantly in a parenthetical locution, "(she once tried to teach it to me, but I could never learn)."[11]

The nature of the gods constitutes the most significant source of confusion and provisionality in the novel. The rationalizing tendencies of Lewis's apologetic works, marshaling logically strong-armed arguments for the existence of God that resonate in the public sphere, give way in this novel to the presence of a shadowy deity perceived as through a dark glass. This perceptual darkness and divine hiddenness frustrate and madden Orual. Contemplating the gods' ambiguous presence, she agonizes,

> But to hint and hover, to draw near us in dreams and oracles, or in a waking vision that vanishes as soon as seen, to be dead silent when we question them and then glide back and whisper (words we cannot understand) in our ears when we most wish to be free of them, and to show to one what they hide from another; what is all this but cat-and-mouse play, blindman's buff, and mere jugglery? Why must holy places be dark places?[12]

Orual aptly refers to her attitude toward the gods as one of "infinite misgiving," which she contrasts with its apparent opposite, "plain belief."[13] It would seem that Orual craves the sort of lucidity that characterizes Lewis's apologetic works. One could imagine her receptivity to the following sentence in the conclusion of Book One of *Mere Christianity*: "All I am doing

---

[11] Ibid., 147.

[12] Ibid., 249.

[13] Ibid., 118.

is to ask people to face the facts...."[14] For Orual, there are no facts—only fleeting visions, mystical dreams, and unbelievable testimonies. Orual's accusation against the gods (Part I of the novel) ends with the words, "no answer."[15]

The pre-Christian setting of *Till We Have Faces* accounts in part for the spiritual tenuousness of the novel. Lewis simply could not avail himself of Christian revelation in a text chronicling events that predate the advent of Christianity. It is possible that Lewis simply could not have portrayed such ambiguity any other way. The explanatory power and comprehensiveness of Christianity problematize—at least for a writer like Lewis—the writing of a novel characterized by uncertainty and provisionality. For Lewis, Christianity answers all of the important questions, taking on the doubts and uncertainties that, on the one hand, must be mitigated to achieve the salvation of souls but, on the other, help establish the conditions that make a novel like *Till We Have Faces* so rich and profound. In other words, doubts and uncertainties constitute obstacles to be overcome for the apologist; for the novelist, they afford opportunities for authentic artistic representation.

---

[14] C. S. Lewis, *Mere Christianity* (New York: Collier Books, 1952) 32.

[15] Lewis, *Till We Have Faces*, 250. Such a capitulatory response, "no answer," would of course be impossible for Lewis the public intellectual, the unflappable defender of the faith. A few trivial exceptions may exist: For instance, Lewis has no answer for those deliberating over which Christian denomination to join. But this is a tangential issue, outside the periphery of mere Christianity, wherein Lewis offers an abundance of answers. One finds a more significant exception in a paper he read on 8 December 1953. The paper was addressed to the Oxford Clerical Society and grapples with two different models of prayer, both of which Jesus exemplifies. In the first model, Jesus instructs his followers to pray without doubt, expecting to receive what they ask for: "… if you have faith and do not doubt, you will not only do what has been done to the fig tree, but even if you say to this mountain, 'Be taken up and thrown in to the sea,' it will happen" (Matt 21:21; ESV). Jesus demonstrates the second model in the Garden of Gethsemane, where he prays, "…not my will, but yours be done" (Luke 22:42). Lewis struggles to reconcile these two models: Do we pray with full expectation of a granted prayer or not? The parting words of his talk—a plea to his audience of priests—resembles the no-answer conclusion to Part One of *Till We Have Faces*: "I have no answer to my problem, though, I have taken it to about every Christian I know, learned or simple, lay or clerical, within my own Communion or without…. But at present I have got no further. I come to you, reverend Fathers, for guidance. How am I to pray this very night?" ("Petitionary Prayer: A Problem without an Answer," in *Christian Reflections*, ed. Walter Hooper [Grand Rapids: Eerdmans, 1967] 150–51). It is significant for my purposes that this address was delivered outside the public sphere to a group of fellow Christians.

This diametrical role of doubt and uncertainty reinvokes my reflections on Lewis as public intellectual. Judging by the anomalous place of this novel within the Lewis corpus, we may conclude that the existential probing of *Till We Have Faces* does not come naturally to Lewis, that it does not emerge organically from the structure of his thought and from his project as a Christian writer. Instead, as uncompromising public defender of the faith, as what Dorothy Sayers calls "God's terrier,"[16] as, in short, Christian public intellectual, Lewis aims to make everything clear, downplaying ambiguity, so that articles of faith are opportunely positioned for acceptance by the public. In doing so, Lewis abides by the conventions of the public sphere. So committed is Lewis to these conventions (whether knowingly or not) that his only recourse to abandon them is to place characters of a novel within a setting before Christianity solved life's spiritual mysteries. By doing so, Lewis adopts a different writerly orientation and voice, one clearly distinct from his persona as public intellectual—in his own words, a movement away from the "expository demon" within him who makes characters sound like they are participating in a "Platonic dialogue."[17]

I have identified what I consider to be a conflict in Lewis's project as Christian writer. Lewis realized that his Christian commitment as public intellectual inclined him toward what he called in a 1945 paper "clear" religion, by which he meant a religion which was "philosophical, ethical, and universalizing...." Christianity, Lewis avers, must also be "thick," involving "...ecstasies and mysteries and local attachments...." Thus, Lewis adds, the thick part of Christianity "takes a twentieth-century academic prig like me and tells me to go fasting to a Mystery, to drink the blood of the Lord."[18] Lewis was sufficiently influenced by Rudolph Otto's *Idea of the Holy* to acknowledge the numinous and ineffable in many of his apologetic works. The opening chapter of *The Problem of Pain*, in fact, explains the mystical concept of the uncanny. But it seems to me that the overarching message of Otto's book is occasionally lost on Lewis: that the intellectualizing impulse of Western Christianity robs the faith of its reason-defying qualities, its unspeakable otherness. Thus, while Lewis may recognize these qualities, he

---

[16] Dorothy Sayers to George Every, 10 July 1947, *The Letters of Dorothy Sayers*, vol. 3, 1944–1950, ed. Barbara Reynolds (Cambridge: The Dorothy L. Sayers Collection, 1998) 315.

[17] C. S. Lewis to Katharine Farrer, 9 July 1955, in *The Collected Letters of C. S. Lewis*, vol. 3, *Narnia, Cambridge, and Joy, 1950–1963*, ed. Walter Hooper (San Francisco: HarperSanFrancisco, 2007) 630.

[18] C. S. Lewis, "Christian Apologetics," in *God in the Dock: Essays on Theology and Ethics*, ed. Walter Hooper (Grand Rapids: Eerdmans, 1970) 102–103.

implicitly downplays their importance by writing apologetic books (like *The Problem of Pain*) that erect a preeminently rationalizing framework upon which to hang truth claims for intellectual assent. The discourse of apologetics by its very nature domesticates the idea of the holy. Because of its discursive commitments, the conventions of the public sphere attempt to make understandable that which defies understanding. The pre-Christian setting of *Till We Have Faces* releases Lewis from this self-defeating crux. It enables Lewis, moving beyond the public sphere, to put the following words into the mouth of one of his characters: "I...have dealt with the gods for three generations of men, and I know that they dazzle our eyes and flow in and out of one another like eddies on a river, and nothing that is said clearly can be said truly about them."[19]

### III. Context, Perspective, and Deep Narrativity

The tone of uncertainty and provisionality throughout *Till We Have Faces* has a corollary: the contextualizing of events that perspectivize abstract issues. Unlike Lewis's earlier works of fiction, *Till We Have Faces* lacks a figure who consistently serves as what I identified in chapter 5 as a transcendent character—a character who serves as an authoritative guide through the theological geography of the projected world of the text and thereby offers inerrant, universal truths. Admittedly, in the conclusion of *Till We Have Faces*, the Fox does come close to serving that role; for Lewis, old habits die hard.

Nevertheless, the reality-shaping power of perspective augments the tone of uncertainty and provisionality throughout most of the novel. We have already seen this power at work in Orual's reformulated understanding of her own identity as well as the identities of others. The seed of this perspectivizing is planted in Orual early on, evident when Bardia offers an opinion of the King that challenges Orual's settled notions. Orual long considered her father a tyrant, abusive to all his subjects and intimidated by none. Bardia, however, offers a different perspective: "'For all his hard words he's no bad master to soldiers, shepherds, huntsmen, and the like. He understands them and they him. You see him at his worst with women and priests and politic men. The truth is, he's half afraid of them.'" Orual's comment on this assertion is telling: "This was very strange to me."[20] The presence of dueling perspectives tends to breed uncertainty and

---

[19] Lewis, *Till We Have Faces*, 50.
[20] Ibid., 93.

provisionality. What kind of character is the King really? A violent monster? Or a conflicted leader sympathetic to some of his male subjects and careful to mask the anxiety within him? Orual cannot understand why the Fox spent so much time at the foot of the King's bed as the King lay dying; after all, the Fox was the King's slave, occasionally mistreated and threatened. The Fox sees something in the King that escaped the notice of Orual.

Contexts shape truth claims in *Till We Have Faces*. Orual informs both Bardia and the Fox of her strange and unexpected experience on the Gray Mountain, where she finds the sacrificed Psyche alive and well. Bardia offers a religious explanation of the experience, and the Fox offers a skeptical/materialist explanation. Orual comments, "I now saw that I had, strangely, taken both Bardia's explanation and the Fox's (each while it lasted) for certain truth. Yet one must be false. And I could not find out which, for each was well-rooted in its own soil."[21] Given Bardia's and the Fox's rival philosophical orientations—one pagan and the other Stoic—the respective explanations they offer are entirely consistent, logical, and warranted. They are also utterly mutually exclusive. Without a transcendent character elevated above the noetic limitations of the individual perspective, rival truth claims cannot be infallibly adjudicated.

This perspectival characteristic, perhaps more than any other, distinguishes *Till We Have Faces* from Lewis's other fiction and most definitively distances him from the public sphere: Lewis's earlier fictional works universalize and de-contextualize truth, an abstracted, undeniable truth *simplicitir*; *Till We Have Faces* localizes and particularizes a hard-won, humanly inhabited truth. As she struggles to comprehend her mountain-top experience, reflecting upon the explanations of her friends, Orual finds that she cannot escape the prior commitments and beliefs that ineluctably structure perspectives of reality and thus accounts of truth. And since she herself has no real prior commitments, since her beliefs are unsettled, held in agnostic abeyance, Orual simply cannot produce her own account of the truth.

In *Till We Have Faces*, truth operates on a concrete rather than abstract level and, unlike in Lewis's earlier fiction, is rarely obvious. It achieves coherence in precisely the opposite fashion as Lewis's earlier works: through human mediation, localized within a specific context, rather than through the divine authority of a transcendent character, detached from all the contingencies of perspective. On the night before her sacrifice, Psyche contemplates her imminent death in terms that exemplify these disparate

---

[21] Ibid., 151.

orientations. These are her words to Orual: "Are these things so evil as they seemed? The gods will have mortal blood. But they say whose. If they had chosen any other in the land, that would have been only terror and cruel misery. But they chose me. And I am the one who has been made ready for it ever since I was a little child in your arms, Maia [Psyche's pet name for Orual]."[22] Abstractly considered, mortal sacrifice strikes fear and repulsion in the heart of any disinterested observer. From a distance, it simply seems horrific. In Psyche's case, however, once that distance is removed, once the prospect of sacrifice is localized within the life of a specific individual, the situation metamorphoses, assuming different significance and contours. For it is context that gives not only individual lives but truth claims meaning and coherence. The abstract contemplation of sacrifice creates a vastly different affective response and intellectual apprehension than the narrative depiction of the specific sacrifice of Psyche, daughter of King Trom, Princess of Glome. Psyche, like all realistically drawn characters, has a story that localizes and thus reconstitutes abstract concepts.

Narrative operates on a different level of cognition than abstraction. Its immersion in particular experience contrasts with abstraction's attempt to transcend it. Without such transcendence, narrative is deeply perspectivized and thus fallible. In the case of *Till We Have Faces*, a first-person narrator and, even more significantly, the presence of narratives within narratives augment that fallibility, solidifying the tone of uncertainty and provisionality in the novel. Orual is an obviously unreliable narrator, evident in the repeated misjudgments of herself and others that we noted earlier.

In addition, the novel contains a network of stories whose accounts of events do not always jibe. *Till We Have Faces* is Orual's first-person account of events that compel her to indict the gods. But at one point in her story, Orual encounters the Priest of Essur, who himself relays the central event in Orual's life from a different, mythically transmogrified vantage point: The Priest's narrative undermines the main narrative of the novel. In fact, it is the Priest's story that generates Orual's narrative to begin with; incensed by what she believes are false depictions, she is determined to respond and offer a counter-narrative. We encounter another narrative (within a narrative) at the end of the novel, when Orual is brought before the mystical court of the gods and the dead. There, she finds herself reading from a book, which mysteriously materialized in her hands, that consists of what she really meant to say in her own narrative. Even though this book contains

---

[22] Ibid., 75.

damning contents, once again undermining her own narrative, she finds herself compulsively and involuntarily reading and re-reading the book aloud. The narratives within narratives presuppose a divergent array of audiences: Orual writes for the refined Greeks; the Priest of Essur spins his tale to travelers and Essurians; and Orual reads her book to an assembly of gods and dead. We might also recount that Lewis's novel itself is a borrowing from Apuleius's *The Golden Ass*; Lewis's own story is an adaptation of another story.

The result of these multilayered perspectives and diverse audiences is what we might call a *thick narrative*: a highly perspectival narrative that consequently leaves the reader off-balance, establishing a tone of uncertainty and provisionality. In such a narrative, character motives and perceptions conflict, rendering the discernment of truth problematic. As readers, for instance, we are caught off-balance when the transparent selfishness of Redival, which so obviously catches our attention, distracts our attention from the far more egregious (and far subtler) form of selfishness betrayed by the character of Orual—this despite her uncompromising love and nobility of character. Such unstable fictional ground and such ambiguity remove Lewis from the public sphere.

## IV. Preconditionalism

The previous chapter explained how Lewis, in part influenced by Owen Barfield, increasingly sanctioned—in fiction and non-fiction—a version of preconditionalism, an implicit assumption of which is that non- or supra-rational factors influence the acquisition of beliefs. To put it more strongly, truth cannot be found until the moral and affective components of identity have been properly prepared. I claim in this section that preconditionalism in *Till We Have Faces* replaces the cerebral-oriented epistemologies that predominate in his earlier works, epistemologies that rest primarily on rational foundations, implicitly downplaying the role that emotions, loves, and moral orientations play in coming to knowledge and finding truth. To say that preconditionalism operates in *Till We Have Faces* means that, to an extent unrivalled in any other Lewis text, the focus is not on truth claims— their expatiation and defense—but on the perspective with which truth claims are processed. I showed in the last chapter how Peter Schakel finds in the later Lewis "an acknowledgment that an element of subjectivity is inherent in perception, and that a degree of self-consciousness is necessary to sound understanding."[23] Addressing this element more specifically in *Till We Have Faces*, Schakel argues "…that belief, or even the will to believe, can be one of the factors that affect perception. Thus, as Orual sits on the steps of the god's house, her perceptual mechanism is not in a state which will enable her to experience it."[24] Schakel thus shows how Lewis in general and *Till We Have Faces* in particular engage one component of preconditionalism, although Schakel never uses the term. This section will more fully develop how preconditionalism operates in the novel and thus further distances it from the public sphere.

We might note the pervasiveness of preconditionalism in *Till We Have Faces* by observing that, although its principles most visibly operate in the character of Orual (the protagonist of the novel), it functions less apparently—but no less importantly—in other characters. For instance, when the Priest of Ungit identifies Psyche as the agreed-upon sacrificial victim, Orual desperately and tearfully pleads with the King to spare her sister's life, pressuring him to overrule the Priest's decree. The King is nonplussed by Orual's insistence, proclaiming, "It's I who have a right to rage and blubber if anyone has. What did I beget her for if I can't do what I think best with my own? What is it to you? There's some cursed cunning that I haven't yet smelled out behind all your sobbing and scolding. You're asking me to believe that any woman, let alone such a fright as you, has much love for a pretty half-sister? It's not in nature. But I'll sift you yet."[25] Accustomed to viewing people as possessions, the King cannot understand the true nature of love. The King's defective moral faculties preclude him from discerning the truth that love is blind and unconditional.[26]

---

[23] Peter J. Schakel, *Reason and the Imagination in C. S. Lewis: A Study of* Till We Have Faces (Grand Rapids: Eerdmans, 1984) 150–51.

[24] Ibid., 43.

[25] Lewis, *Till We Have Faces*, 60–61.

[26] This scene has a parallel in the last letter of *The Screwtape Letters*. Screwtape explains what happens to Wormwood's patient upon death: everlasting life with God. Just as the King cannot understand why Orual responds to the Priest's decree as she does, so Screwtape cannot understand the love that motivates God: "If only we could find out what He [God] is really up to!" (*The Screwtape Letters* [San Francisco: HarperSanFrancisco, 2001] 175). Like the King, Screwtape cannot understand unconditional love because the motives that lie at the heart of his identity cloud his vision. This parallel underscores the qualifications I have placed upon my argument: I do not contend that preconditionalism does not operate in other Lewis texts—only that in *Till We Have Faces* does it operate so thoroughly, playing a central role in the characters and thus the plot of the novel.

Preconditionalism operates in the character of the Fox as well. When Orual returns from her salvage mission on the Gray Mountain (to retrieve Psyche's remains), she does not even bother telling the Fox that she caught a fleeting vision of Psyche's god-husband. She knows that he would never believe her. His unbelief ostensibly proceeds from his adherence to Stoicism, the naturalism of which rules out the existence of the sort of deity Orual glimpsed. However, the Fox's adherence to Stoicism is hardly the result of a strictly intellectual assent to the most rational worldview. As a Greek slave in a barbaric, primitive land, the Fox harbors a prejudicial attitude toward Glome and its people, quickly and summarily dismissing their supposed backwards beliefs. Thus, stubborn pride and arrogance sharpen the Fox's attitude. The Fox is simply not in a cognitive position to discern the reality of the gods because of his experiences as a slave, his pride in Greek learning, and the animosity that develops from their convergence. Non-rational factors intensify his apparent rational rejection of the gods of Glome. Like the King, then, defective moral faculties, stemming from wounded pride and intellectual arrogance, prevent the Fox from perceiving reality.

Of course, the character of Orual, as protagonist, best demonstrates the phenomenon of preconditionalism. As we have seen, Schakel notes how Orual's "perceptual mechanism" prevents her from seeing Psyche's palace, the house she shares with the god. But analyzing the defects of this mechanism as an elucidation of the process of preconditionalism pushes the point in a different direction: Orual simply will not see truth until she acquires the right perspective. She cannot perceive, know, or understand the gods in her present condition. It is not that her intellectual faculties are malfunctioning—that she is not thinking clearly or logically. Rather, it is that she is not behaving virtuously; her moral faculties are in disarray. Removing the possessive quality of her love for Psyche as well as rightly ordering her loves in general will help enable Orual to meet the conditions for discerning divine truth—to the extent, of course, that mere mortals can discern such things. Orual embodies the principle that Lewis borrowed from M. Denis de Rougemont: "love ceases to be a demon only when he ceases to be a god."[27] Once she understands this concept, Orual will have wiped clean the lens of her perceptual mechanism.

Employing preconditionalism as a hermeneutical prism in analyzing *Till We Have Faces* affords an interpretive approach that contrasts with approaches to Lewis's other works: a focus on character rather than argument, psychology rather than philosophy/theology, individual motive

---

[27] C. S. Lewis, *The Four Loves* (New York: Harcourt Brace & Company, 1988) 6.

rather than universal truth. Such an approach applied to the character of Orual uncovers the extent to which her possessive love for Psyche clouds her judgment. Once the King submits to the Priest's decree that Psyche must die by sacrifice, Orual desires to comfort Psyche, but her possessiveness hampers the attempt. Orual longs to mother a grief-stricken Psyche, but Psyche does not meet Orual's expectations. A hopeful rather than lachrymose Psyche, for instance, informs Orual that she always felt an immortal longing directed toward the Grey Mountain; she further believes that she might, in fact, truly become the bride of a god and that there are more things in heaven and on earth that are dreamt of in the Fox's naturalistic philosophy. Orual's response to this courage and optimism betrays her selfishness: "'O cruel, cruel!' I wailed. 'Is it nothing to you that you leave me here alone? Psyche, did you ever love me at all?'"[28] Orual becomes jealous of the gods; she wants Psyche's love all to herself.

After Psyche's sacrifice, Orual refuses to let joy and laughter enter her life. She nurses her grief while her animosity toward the House of Ungit and, more importantly, the god who supposedly inhabits it, grows more encompassing, poisoning her outlook and obscuring her judgment. Even when Orual later finds Psyche alive and well on the mountain, she still cannot entertain happiness, for Psyche declares that she is now married to the god, even though she cannot see him, and that she dwells in a palace, even though Psyche claims not to see it. Orual's jealously and possessiveness prompt her reflection, "Gods, and again gods, always gods...they had stolen her. They would leave us nothing."[29] Later, when Psyche enthusiastically informs Orual that her husband the god can help Orual see the palace, Orual responds with close-minded, spiteful finality: "'I don't want it!' I cried, putting my face close to hers, threatening her almost, till she drew back before my fierceness. 'I don't want it. I hate it. Hate it, hate it, hate it. Do you understand?'"[30] Orual's desire for Psyche to return to her is so intense and consuming that she threatens to kill Psyche if she does not cooperate. This prompts the Fox to respond to Orual, "'There's one part love in your heart, and five parts anger, and seven parts pride.'"[31]

In earlier works, Lewis had represented characters similar in psychology to Orual. Numerous ghost characters in *The Great Divorce*, for instance, cannot see truth simply because they prefer not to; like Orual, they struggle

---

[28] Lewis, *Till We Have Faces*, 73.
[29] Ibid., 120–21.
[30] Ibid., 124.
[31] Ibid., 148.

to relinquish the strong-willed pessimism, the fierce sense of self-sufficiency, or the consuming possessiveness that structure a particularly jaded view of the world and the transcendent. Pam, the over-possessive mother in *The Great Divorce*, demands to be reunited with her son on her own terms: "'I want my boy, and I mean to have him. He is mine, do you understand? Mine, mine, mine, for ever and ever.'"[32] Similarly, Orual says of Psyche, "'She was mine. *Mine*. Do you not know what that word means? Mine!'"[33] As I have been arguing, the difference between the two representations is that Lewis wraps Orual in a thick narrative, one characterized by the perspectivism explored in the last section. The result is a more realistic—and less philosophical and apologetic—account of how subjectivity shapes the apprehension of reality. The result is also the depiction of complex images, couched within a rich narrative context, operating at various registers of meaning, and developing the principles of preconditionalism with a complexity lacking in Lewis's earlier works.

The veil constitutes one such image in *Till We Have Faces*. Orual first dons a veil permanently after her two journeys to the Gray Mountain. She resolves never to remove it, a rule she identifies as "a sort of treaty made with my ugliness."[34] As an evocation of that ugliness, the veil complicates the character of Orual: Her damaging, possessive love for Psyche is not merely an inherent, de-contextualized vice. Rather, it is an overcorrected response to pain, the desperate and insecure attempt to cling to sisterly intimacy by a character for whom romantic intimacy is unlikely because she is not attractive. The novel shows that Orual was made aware of her ugliness as a child: Her father ridiculed her appearance, and other girls in the court laughed at her. The novel thus inscribes a pathetic truth: People are often cruel because they have been hurt. The veil thus both evokes Orual's ugliness and emblematizes the cruelty that results: her tendency to cause harm in response to her own insecurity, neediness, and pain.

The veil also symbolizes secrecy. As Orual writes, "Hitherto, like all my country-women, I had gone bareface; on those two journeys up the Mountain I had worn a veil because I wished to be secret. I now determined that I would go always veiled."[35] From whom or what, exactly, does Orual wish to be hidden? Why this attempt at permanent secrecy? One answer is that Orual is hiding from her own pain. The veil shields her own wounds,

---

[32] C. S. Lewis, *The Great Divorce* (San Francisco: HarperSanFrancisco, 2001) 103.
[33] Lewis, *Till We Have Faces*, 292.
[34] Ibid., 180–81.
[35] Ibid., 180.

removing her vulnerability from exposure. After her ordeal on the mountaintop, Orual finds her imagination playing tricks on her, believing she hears the sound of a weeping Psyche outside her bedchamber. Upon investigation, Orual learns that the wind produces the sound as it blows the chains of a well. Demonstrating her obsessive attempt to protect herself, she commands her mason to build a thick wall around the well so that she need never hear the sound again. Orual then comments, "For a while after that an ugly fancy used to come to me in my dreams, or between sleeping and waking, that I had walled up, gagged with stone, not a well but Psyche (or Orual) herself."[36] This dreamlike conceit reveals that Orual's counterproductive defense mechanism operates at the expense of her own identity, enslaving herself within the very attempt at self-protection. The veil thus symbolizes a false sense of security, the futile attempt to hide from the past and achieve invulnerability as a re-created person.

Indeed, the image of the veil divides Orual's identity, segmenting her life into two parts, before and after her experience on the mountaintop. During the former, Orual is simply Orual; during the latter, she becomes the veiled Queen, an identity construct ostensibly beyond the reach of pain. These bifurcated identities undergo an uneasy, though progressively seamless, division. For instance, prior to her duel with Argan, Prince of Phars, the Queen experiences a fear that momentarily summons Orual: "I was mostly the Queen now, but Orual would whisper a cold word in the Queen's ear at times."[37] After her father dies, the Queen liberates the Fox from slavery; later, the old Priest of Ungit dies, deaths and liberation that signal just how much the Queen's life has changed, dismantling the world of her youth. To the Queen's surprise, this change engenders a general sense of sorrow, which, in her new role as Queen, she struggles to feel acutely: "This astonished me. One part of me made to snatch that sorrow back; it said, 'Orual dies if she ceases to love Psyche.' But the other said, 'Let Orual die. She would never have made a queen.'"[38] Later, the Queen speaks of killing Orual,[39] culminating in this reflection: "I must now pass quickly over many years (though they made up the longest part of my life) during which the Queen of Glome had more and more part in me and Orual had less and less. I locked Orual up or laid her asleep as best I could somewhere deep down inside me; she lay curled there. It was like being with child, but reversed; the

---

[36] Ibid., 235.
[37] Ibid., 205.
[38] Ibid., 211.
[39] Ibid., 225.

thing I carried in me grew slowly smaller and less alive."[40] The veil emblematizes this process, in which the birth of a barricaded persona comes at the expense of the death of an authentic, though tragically flawed identity.

Another important, though under-analyzed, image in *Till We Have Faces* is the mirror. Like the veil, the mirror richly symbolizes the bifurcation of Orual's identity and thus narrativizes the principles of preconditionalism, illustrating the shortcomings in Orual's character that preclude the discernment of truth. The image of the mirror first appears in the palace's Pillar Room, where the King's great mirror hangs. Orual describes it thusly: "Our common mirrors were false and dull; in this you could see your perfect image."[41] Within this Pillar Room, Orual pleads with her father to accept her as the sacrifice rather than Psyche. The King then violently drags Orual before the mirror: "'Ungit asked for the best in the land as her son's bride,' he said. 'And you'd give her *that*.'"[42] The mirror thus ascertains her ugliness, crushing the young and impressionable girl, mercilessly replacing her naïve self-conception–reflected self mercilessly pronounced hideous by her own father. Again like the veil, the mirror thematizes a key movement of the text: the division of Orual's identity.

Orual's comment that the mirror reflects a "perfect image" may be ironic on a couple of levels: First, her image in the mirror is hardly perfect, due to her ugliness; also, she is much more than an image reflected by a mirror—a mirror calculates perfection by a superficial calculus. However, evidence later in the novel suggests that the mirror does perform a revelatory function with respect to questions of identity. During one of her visions toward the end of the novel, her dead father, the King, drags her underground into a subterranean Pillar Room. There Orual espies the great mirror. As he did once before his death, the King drags Orual before the mirror, where she gazes upon her reflection to find that her face had become the face of Ungit, the god she despised throughout her life. Like the goddess, she was a devourer of men and women, ruining lives through her outrageous demands for sacrifice. Thus, the image of the mirror introduces another identity within Orual's complex character. She is Orual, she is the Queen, and now, in this vision, she is Ungit.

On the one hand, the mirrored reflection of Ungit further complicates the character of Orual, exacerbating the problems of her unintegrated identity. On the other hand, her appearance as Ungit generates the

---

[40] Ibid., 226.

[41] Ibid., 61.

[42] Ibid., 62.

denouement of the novel, eventually silencing her false selves and mitigating the deficiencies of character that cloud her vision of truth. For In seeing her reflection as Ungit, in realizing the burdens she has placed upon those she loved, and in recognizing herself as a devourer of men and women, Orual experiences the remorse that leads to regeneration.

This process involves Orual's final loss of her multiplied identities, a metamorphosis into nothing, in which she literally becomes a void. Orual describes Ungit as possessing no face, an undecipherable blankness. Like her mirrored image, Orual too is a cipher. Busied with her duties as Queen, Orual laments the inevitable conclusion of the day: a return "to my own chamber to be alone with myself—that is, with a nothingness."[43] Later, when Bardia dies, Orual's "craving" for him—a craving she identifies as love—dies along with him. Orual writes, "But when the craving went, nearly all that I called myself went with it. It was as if my whole soul had been one tooth and now that tooth was drawn. I was a gap."[44] Figured as a "nothing-ness" and a "gap," Orual assumes the characteristics of the Ungit idle in the temple: cold, implacable, powerful, and faceless, inhumanly demanding blood sacrifices. Nothingness at this point suggests Orual's attempt to disguise herself with a veil, an attempt that simply masks the possessive love that destroys, a craving love so intense that it becomes hatred, a de-humanizing, monomaniacal need. Thus, the mirror in Orual's envisioned Pillar Room provides an accurate representation of what she has become: a tyrannical nothingness. Acknowledging the truth of this representation, however, occasions her regeneration, initiating what a god tells her in another vision: "'Die before you die.'"[45]

Once Orual begins this process of regeneration, the trope of nothingness itself undergoes a transformation. In Orual's vision of herself in the court of the gods, invisible hands forcibly remove her veil, stripping her of the nothingness that denoted her possessive love. In fact, the hands in the land of the dead divest Orual of all her clothing, fully exposing the vulnerabilities she tried desperately to protect during her lifetime. Reunited with Psyche during this vision, Orual confesses to her selfishness: "'I never wished you well, never had one selfless thought of you. I was a craver.'"[46] Stripped of her veil, clothes, and possessive love, Orual is then greeted by the god of the mountain.

---

[43] Ibid., 236.
[44] Ibid., 267.
[45] Ibid., 280.
[46] Ibid., 305.

It is at this point that the trope of nothingness changes; Orual describes her experience as the god approaches: "Each breath I drew let into me new terror, joy, overpowering sweetness. I was pierced through and through with the arrows of it. I was being unmade. I was no one."[47] Becoming no one—achieving another sort of nothingness—here signals the death of the needy love that controlled Orual, a selfishness purged by the divine presence of selfless love. Nothingness no longer conveys the attempt to hide—to disguise craving as love and to protect vulnerabilities; rather, nothingness now inscribes a humility that mortifies selfishness, a fulfillment of the god's injunction to die before death. Most importantly, this new form of nothingness enables Orual to love Psyche truly: "I loved her as I would once have thought it impossible to love, would have died any death for her."[48]

The images of the veil, the mirror, and nothingness focus the narrative lens of the novel upon the flaws and eventual redemption of the character of Orual. Like Lewis's apologetic works, the novel engages religious questions, but it does so at a different level of analysis: a psychological, pre-philosophical level. The novel interrogates not truth claims but the interpretive framework by which truth claims are processed. This level of analysis I have identified as preconditionalism. Spotlighting the prominent role subjectivity plays in belief-formation and consequently presupposing an epistemological uncertainty and provisionality, the preconditionalism in *Till We Have Faces* positions Lewis outside the public sphere.

## V. The Actualization of Myth

### a. Nonverbal, Trans-rational Reality

Myth obviously plays a prominent role in nearly all of Lewis's writings, both fiction and non-fiction. However, myth in earlier works often operates at the service of Lewis's larger polemical design. An earlier chapter developed *The Screwtape Letters* and *The Great Divorce* as apologues; thus mythic elements in these texts contribute to the exemplification of formulable statements. Similarly, *The Pilgrim's Regress* subordinates myth to the purpose of allegorical argument. Even the Ransom trilogy often includes mythic patterns and images that primarily serve the expository function of the texts. Explanations of myth in Lewis's non-fiction usually operate as a move in Lewis's larger apologetic argument—for instance, the argument that

---

[47] Ibid., 307.
[48] Ibid.

Christianity fulfills pagan myths about a dying and resurrecting god. Although it may recapitulate some of these subordinating tendencies, *Till We Have Faces* constitutes Lewis's purest actualization of myth. In this section, I explore how this actualization further removes Lewis from the public sphere by equating myth with a trans-rational reality.

Myth records a non-verbal reality. Such was Lewis's contention in the introduction to his volume on George MacDonald: "The critical problem with which we are confronted is whether this art—the art of myth-making—is a species of the literary art. The objection to so classifying it is that the Myth does not essentially exist in *words* at all."[49] Myth precedes language, operating in a register often inaudible to the intellect and even consciousness itself. During one of her visions, Orual finds her story recorded as one such myth. Removed from the menacing environment of the god's courtroom, Orual suddenly inhabits a pleasant room with sunshine reflecting off of pillars and leaves. She is attended by the Fox, who, unlike her Father in an earlier vision, leads her not to a mirror, that symbol of her divided self, but to a series of pictures on walls. These pictures come to life and record stories that weave Orual's past with mystical visions and parallel, mythically inflected realities in which Psyche's fate converges with Orual's. The pictures on the walls reveal how the prophecy of the god was fulfilled, the prophecy that Orual would become Psyche. Conveying a belief most likely indebted to Charles Williams's notion of the way of exchange, these pictures specifically uncover how Orual shared the torment visited upon Psyche upon her banishment from her mountain-top palace.[50] As the Fox explains, "'We're all limbs and parts of one Whole. Hence, of each other. Men, and gods, flow in and out and mingle.'"[51]

The pictures on the wall thus illustrate Lewis's notion of the nonverbal quality of myth, its resistance to lucid exposition. Of course, the Fox serves for Orual as interpreter of these pictures; as such, he approximates the status of what I called in chapter five a transcendent character, achieving an Olympian point of reference by offering unimpeachable commentary. But the Fox confesses to his limitations as now a spirit in the land of the dead: "'They [the gods] say...but even I, who am dead, do not yet understand

---

[49] C. S. Lewis, introduction to *George MacDonald: 365 Readings*, ed. C. S. Lewis (New York: Collier Books, 1974), xxvii.

[50] Charles Williams, "The Way of Exchange," in *The Image of the City and Other Essays*, ed. Anne Ridler (London: Oxford University Press, 1958) 147–54. The idea here is that pain and suffering can be exchanged from one person to another.

[51] Ibid., 300–301.

more than a few broken words of their language.'"[52] Even the Fox, Orual's guide in the underworld, cannot bring complete lucidity to the ineffable meanings conveyed by the pictures and communicated by the gods. Thus, while shedding light on these conveyances and communications, the Fox's exposition is ultimately eclipsed by the enigmatic, mythic qualities of his world.

Indeed, throughout the novel, representations of the gods and the myths that surround them falter in the very attempt at representation, testifying to the inadequacy of exposition in the face of such mysteries—and testifying to the inadequacy of the conventions of the public sphere in engaging ultimate concerns. For instance, Psyche explains to Orual that the only consideration that gave her consolation on the morning of her sacrifice concerned the gods and the profundity of divine rituals, but she struggles to articulate these thoughts:

> "The only thing that did me good," she continued, "was quite different. It was hardly a thought, and very hard to put into words. There was a lot of the Fox's philosophy in it—things he says about gods or 'the divine nature'—but mixed up with things the Priest said, too, about the blood and the earth and how sacrifice makes the crops grow. I'm not explaining it well. It seemed to come from somewhere deep inside me, deeper than the part that sees pictures of gold and amber palaces, deeper than fears and tears. It was shapeless, but you could just hold onto it; or just let it hold onto you.[53]

Psyche's inability fully to explain herself, as well as her faltering syntax, evokes the nonverbal quality of myth; words are inadequate to the task of conveying the importance of mythic archetypes that involve blood, earth, and sacrifice. This is because these archetypes transcend mere cognitive faculties; they are existential realities dwelling in the nearly inaccessible regions of an individual's spirit—as Psyche puts it, "...somewhere deep inside me...deeper than fears and tears." Whatever the source of her consolation, Psyche says, it cannot be considered a thought.

A metaphorical reading of Psyche's mountaintop experience crystallizes the trans-rational status of myth in the novel. Coerced by Orual, Psyche beholds the physical form of her husband the god after he has fallen asleep in their bed, even though he forbade her from doing so. Incensed by her betrayal of his trust, the god subsequently banishes Psyche from the palace and from the mountain. This scene constitutes a fictional emblem. Psyche's

---

[52] Ibid., 305.
[53] Ibid., 109–110.

lamp represents the light of analysis, the attempt to verify either empirically or rationally the realities of deep myth. When she applies the light of analysis, Psyche finds that the god has flown, that empirical or rational analysis not only betrays a lack of trust, but is inherently incompatible with. the shadowy experience of the gods and their ways (the stuff of myth). Lewis describes in *Surprised by Joy* a similar problem with respect to the phenomenon he calls Joy. He explains that the experience of Joy is destroyed by the attempt to analyze it. Appropriating Samuel Alexander's terminology, Lewis maintains that "...the enjoyment and the contemplation of our inner activities are incompatible."[54] Analysis is likewise incompatible with the existential apprehension of deep myth.

Thus, the novel fittingly ends with Orual's attestation of the inadequacy of analysis and even of words themselves. Addressing the very god who was once her enemy, she writes, "I ended my first book with the words *no answer*. I know now, Lord, why you utter no answer. You are yourself the answer. Before your face questions die away. What other answer would suffice? Only words, words; to be led out to battle against other words."[55] The methods of exposition and of rational/empirical interrogation disintegrate in the presence of deep myth.[56] The novel ends by underscoring the futility of words in coming to terms with a nonverbal, trans-rational reality. Consequently, the novel likewise rejects the very methods upon which Lewis depended as a public intellectual.

### b. The Mythic Archetype of Fertility

Ancient myths generally revolve around issues of fertility. In the Greek world, Dionysian rituals were often fertility rituals that involved various activities to promote healthy crops and an abundant harvest: activities that included sexual unions (to tell the land symbolically to be fertile), human sacrifice (of those who represent sterility), and phallic processions. According to one theory, dramatic comedy finds its origins in these very

---

[54] Lewis, *Surprised by Joy*, 218. All citations from *Surprised by Joy* come from the 1989 version.

[55] Lewis, *Till We Have Faces*, 308.

[56] Orual's formulation, "Before your face questions die away," finds a structural parallel in Lewis's *A Grief Observed*, in which he writes, "Can a mortal ask questions which God finds unanswerable? Quite easily, I should think. All nonsense questions are unanswerable. How many hours are there in a mile? Is yellow square or round?" (*A Grief Observed* [San Francisco: HarperSanFrancisco, 1994] 87). This sort of parallel explains in part why I identify *Till We Have Faces* and *A Grief Observed* in particular as illustrations of Lewis's movement beyond the public sphere.

rituals. (See, for example, F. M. Cornford's *The Origins of Attic Comedy* Cambridge University Press, 1939, 2nd edition.) Most of the elements of these Dionysian rituals thus find their way into dramatic comedy, from Aristophanes to Shakespeare. The human to be sacrificed as representative of sterility and thus hostile to fertility is depicted in dramatic comedy as the figure of the killjoy, who is often a repressed, dour-faced, prudish villain who blocks young lovers from marriage. In addition, dramatic comedy often concludes with a feast, a wedding, and the promise of children, all of which symbolize the triumph of fertility.

Historically, then, literary expression and fertility rites as practiced in ancient myth have developed symbiotically. The purpose of this section is to attend to the representations of fertility in *Till We Have Faces*, explaining how they solidify the actualization of myth in the novel and subsequently further remove Lewis from the public sphere. I begin, however, by showing how one book in the Narniad—*Prince Caspian*—recapitulates the patterns of Dionysian fertility rites as they were practiced in ancient rituals and incorporated into dramatic comedy. Doing so will provide a fuller context for exploring fertility images in *Till We Have Faces*.[57]

### c. Enlarging the Context: Dionysus and Dionysian Ritual in Prince Caspian

Dionysus/Bacchus makes a few cameos in the Narniad. In *The Lion, the Witch and the Wardrobe*, Mr. Tumnus the faun tells Lucy that, during summer in Narnia before the White Witch cast a spell causing a never-ending winter, revelries took place in the woods; "and sometimes," says Tumnus, "Bacchus himself...would come to visit them...and then the streams would run with wine instead of water and the whole forest would give itself to jollification for weeks on end."[58] In *Prince Caspian*, in moment of epiphany during which Aslan reveals himself to the Pevensie children, Bacchus and a riotous train of revelers dance across Aslan's How. The narrator gives us this description of Bacchus: "One [of the revelers] was a youth, dressed only in a fawn-skin, with vine-leaves wreathed in his curly hair. His face would have been almost too pretty for a boy's, if it had not looked so extremely wild. You felt, as

---

[57] As explained in the introduction, the Narnian stories evidence a Lewis both inside and outside the public sphere; within my hermeneutical framework, they are liminal texts, adhering to a fundamental assumption of the public sphere—to bolster a position—but, on the other hand, animated by a mythic spirit. In this chapter, I emphasize the latter, momentarily aligning the Narniad with *Till We Have Faces*.

[58] C. S. Lewis, *The Lion, the Witch and the Wardrobe* (New York: Harper Trophy, 1994) 17.

Edmund said when he saw him a few days later, 'There's a chap who might do anything—absolutely anything.'" Attending Bacchus is a group of girls, "as wild as he"[59]; these girls are undoubtedly the Maenads, Bacchus's female devotees. It is not until Bacchus's raucous procession is out of sight that the children realize who the vine-wearing, wine-drinking god is; the following conversation between Susan and Lucy ensues:

> "I say, Su, I know who they are."
> "Who?"
> "The boy with the wild face is Bacchus.... Don't you remember
>     Mr. Tumnus telling us about them long ago?"
> "Yes, course. But I say, Lu—"
> "What?"
> "I wouldn't have felt safe with Bacchus and all his wild girls if
>     we'd met them without Aslan."
> "I should think not," said Lucy.[60]

Susan and Lucy have reason not to feel safe. A brief overview of the figure of Dionysus reveals how Aslan's shoulder-rubbing with Dionysus might give one pause. Walter Otto writes, "All of antiquity extolled Dionysus as the god who gave men wine. However, he was known also as the raving god whose presence makes man mad and incites him to savagery and even to lust for blood."[61] Marcel Detienne describes Dionysus as the god who "snatches his victim by surprise, who trips his prey and drags it down into madness, murder, and defilement...."[62] To begin at the beginning, Dionysus was the offspring of Zeus and the mortal Semele. When Dionysus was in utero, Semele died when Zeus appeared to her. However, Hermes saved Dionysus by sewing him up in Zeus's thigh, where he gestated for another three months and then was successfully delivered. When she heard of Dionysus's existence, a jealous Hera commanded the Titans to tear Dionysus into pieces, boiling his body parts in a cauldron. However, Dionysus's grandmother Rhea resurrected the boy, who was raised by nymphs on Mount Nysa, thus accounting for his effeminacy. From this time

---

[59] C. S. Lewis, *Prince Caspian* (New York: Harper Trophy, 1994) 167.

[60] Ibid., 169.

[61] Walter Otto, *Dionysus: Myth and Cult*, trans. Brian B. Palmer (Bloomington: University of Indiana Press, 1965) 49.

[62] Marcel Detienne, *Dionysos at Large*, trans. Arthur Goldhammer (Cambridge: Harvard University Press, 1989) 2.

on, much of Dionysus's existence was spent overseeing orgiastic rituals and waging war on those who deny his godhood. In Euripedes' *The Bacchae*, women start rumors that Dionysus was not the son of Zeus. "Therefore," proclaims Dionysus,

> ...I've stung them
> with madness, and goaded them raving from their houses.
> They're living on the mountain now, delirious,
> dressed, as I've compelled them to be dressed,
> in the garments of my rituals.

The women thus become Maenads.

Dionysus then directs his wrath toward Pentheus, King of Thebes, who, as Dionysus rages, "is warring with divinity / by excluding me from rituals / and not invoking my name in prayers."[63] Dionysus brings madness upon not only Pentheus, who subsequently dons women's clothing, but the entire city of Thebes, resulting in Pentheus's brutal death: He is torn to pieces—at the hands of his own mother as well as the Maenads. On another occasion, Dionysus's vindictiveness is directed toward Athens. Because the Athenians would not recognize his statue, he afflicted the entire male population with a "painful state of erection that nothing seemed to alleviate."[64]

The presence of Dionysus/Bacchus as well as the fingerprints of Dionysian rituals and fertility rites is most apparent in *Prince Caspian*. As the Narnian forces defeat the evil King Miraz and his army, Bacchus is summoned to free a river god from the Fords of Beruna, a god who had been enchained by a river bridge. Bacchus and his Maenads splash into the water and wreak havoc on the bridge: "Great, strong trunks of ivy came curling up all the piers of the bridge, growing as quickly as a fire grows, wrapping the stones round, splitting, breaking, separating them."[65] As in Greek myth, Bacchus here is capable of great destruction; his vines operate like tentacles, ripping the bridge from its foundations. In addition, Bacchus is also figured in this passage as a liberator. In dramatic comedy, Bacchus-as-liberator translates into a liberation from repressive social conventions, resulting in the creation of a topsy-turvy world that often defies reason, order, propriety, common sense, and predictability. (One thinks, for example, of

---

[63] Euripedes, *The Bacchae*, trans. C. K. Williams (New York: Farrar Straus Giroux, 1990) 4.

[64] Detienne, *Dionysos at Large*, 32.

[65] Lewis, *Prince Caspian*, 221.

Aristophanes' *Lysistrata* or Shakespeare's *A Midsummer Night's Dream*.) By destroying the bridge, Lewis's Bacchus operates more at the service of the plot; after all, Aslan needs a force powerful enough to take down the bridge. In addition, Bacchus lacks the moral ambiguity he possesses in Greek myth: Bacchus destroys the bridge so that good can triumph over evil.

However, as Bacchus proceeds through Narnia, his wild disregard for constraint and order become more apparent, suggestive of his originally dubious moral character (at least as suggestive as one can expect in a book for children). As Bacchus and his train dance in celebration of Narnia's victory over King Miraz, they come across a school instituted under Miraz's rule: a school, explains the narrator, "where a lot of Narnian girls, with their hair done very tight and ugly tight collars round their necks and thick tickly stocking on their legs, were having a history lesson."[66] Lewis's language here evokes the repressive morality and confining social milieu against which the spirit of comedy militates: "hair done very tight," "tight collars round their necks," and "thick tickly stockings" constitute constrictions upon the body that discourage fertility. With the help of Aslan's roar, Bacchus once again employs his ivy, this time to take down the school. Once it is destroyed, most of the students ("prim little girls") flee in terror—an effect that Bacchus's presence has on many in the original myths. However, one student asks to join the procession: "Instantly [the girl] joined hands with two of the Maenads, who whirled her round in a merry dance and helped her take off some of the unnecessary and uncomfortable clothes that she was wearing."[67] One hears in the echoes of this narration the original phallic processions, orgiastic celebrations, and wine- and lust-induced insanity that were hallmarks of the rites of Dionysus.

Among those who flee in terror at the sight of Bacchus is Miss Prizzle, who, as the strict, sour-faced, joyless teacher of the school, resembles the killjoy figure of dramatic comedy. Her name itself, Prizzle, sounds like "prissy." Also, when one of the students exclaims that there is a lion outside the school, Miss Prizzle chastises the student for "talking nonsense."[68] Resistant to nonsense, Miss Prizzle is also inimical to the spirit of comedy.

The Telmarine soldiers—who opposed the Narnian forces—also possess attributes of the killjoy. Like Miss Prizzle, the Telmarines are humorless and morose. They are described as "sulky" and "hat[ing] and fear[ing] running

---

[66] Ibid., 213.
[67] Ibid., 214.
[68] Ibid., 213.

water just as much as they hated and feared woods and animals."[69] Their disposition is at odds with the feast and celebration with which the narrative concludes; thus, consistent with killjoy figures in dramatic comedy, the Telmarines are expelled from the metaphorical stage. Aslan creates a magic door that leads them to the world from where they came.

The feast and celebration from which the Telmarines are expelled are, of course, key structural elements to any dramatic comedy. Lewis describes in great detail the food and drink that Bacchus and the Maenads create through a "magic dance of plenty": "sides of roasted meat that filled the grove with delicious smell, and wheaten and oaken cakes, honey and many-colored sugars and cream as think as porridge and as smooth as still water.... Then, in great wooden cups and bowls and mazers, wreathed with ivy, came the wines; dark, thick ones like syrups of mulberry juice, and clear red ones like red jellies liquefied, and yellow wines and green wines and yellow-green and greenish-yellow."[70] How can such a bacchanalia not lead to intoxication?

And though *Prince Caspian* does not conclude with a wedding and the consequent promise of children, the denouement does include the sustaining and prolonging of life. During the procession, Bacchus encounters a dying woman. Dipping a pitcher into the cottage well, the vessel emerges filled not with water but the "richest wine, red as red-currant jelly, smooth as oil, strong as beef, warming as tea, cool as dew."[71] Quaffing Bacchus's wine, the woman is healed. The structural elements of *Prince Caspian* thus recapitulate the basic patterns of dramatic comedy as it descends from Dionysian fertility rituals: the elimination of killjoys, as well as the prudery and behavioral constraints they represent; the eventual indulgence in festivity; and the promise and restoration of life.

### d. Fertility Archetypes in Till We Have Faces

Some of these basic patterns operate in *Till We Have Faces*. However, because the novel accomplishes Lewis's fullest actualization of myth, representations of fertility emerge more organically from the text; they are structurally and thematically more consonant with the world that *Till We Have Faces* projects.[72] Of course, the religion of Glome accounts for some of

---

[69] Ibid., 229, 224.
[70] Ibid., 225–26.
[71] Ibid., 217.
[72] It is well known that Joy Davidman Gresham helped Lewis write *Till We Have Faces*. She writes in a 1955 letter, "Though I can't write one-tenth as well as Jack, I can

this more natural representation of mythic fertility. The Fox informs Orual that Ungit is Glome's barbaric version of the Greek goddess Aphrodite. When he relays the story of Aphrodite to Orual, the Fox includes the goddess's affair with Anchises, a dalliance that results in the birth of Aeneas. Aeneas would later flee a burning Troy and found the civilization of Rome. Thus, through the character of the Fox, the novel associates the religion of Ungit/Aphrodite with fertility and the renewal/birth of a society.

Moreover, the Temple of Ungit in Glome assumes a "holy shape": that of an egg "from which the whole world was hatched or the womb in which the whole world once lay."[73] As part of a fertility rite taking place every spring, the Priest of Ungit engages in a ritualistic struggle to exit the temple, thereby hatched from the egg, signifying the birth of a new year. This ritual is a ceremonial reenactment of the birth of Ungit herself, who, according to the ancient stories, "...had pushed her way up out of the earth...." As Arnom the Priest informs Orual, Ungit "'signifies the earth, which is the womb and mother of all living things.'"[74]

Traveling beyond the borders of Glome, Orual finds that Psyche herself has been deified into a fertility goddess of sorts. At a temple in Essur, a priest tells Orual the sacred story of Istra (Psyche), who is a goddess during the fertile seasons of spring and summer. In winter, however, the lighting of a lamp signifies the departure of her god-husband, at which point "'...all winter she is wandering and suffering; weeping, always weeping....'"[75] The sacred story of Istra resembles the myth of Demeter and her daughter, Persephone, goddesses who superintend the fertility of the earth. In light of these religions and rituals, it is not insignificant that Orual's attention (and thus the narrative focus of the text) is drawn to issues of fertility: the procurement of a new wife for the king (for the purpose of producing a son)

---

tell him how to write more like himself! He is now about three-quarters of the way through his new book (what I'd give for that energy!) and says he finds my advice indispensable" (letter to William Lindsay Gresham, 29 April 1955, in *Out of My Bone: The Letters of Joy Davidman*, ed. Don W. King [Grand Rapids: Eerdmans, 2009] 246). In *A Grief Observed*, Lewis uses two images to describe Davidman Gresham: a sword and a garden. The latter image is evocative of fertility: "I see I've described H. as being like a sword. That's true as far as it goes. But utterly inadequate by itself, and misleading. I ought to have balanced it. I ought to have said, 'But also like a garden. Like of nest of gardens, wall within wall, hedge within hedge, more secret, more full of fragrant and fertile life, the further you entered'" (80). Thus, the fertility imagery in the novel is associated with the very person who inspired it: Lewis's wife.

[73] Ibid., 94.
[74] Ibid., 270.
[75] Ibid., 246.

in the very first chapter; the repeated fact that Ansit, wife of Bardia, has eight children; that Redival bore many children and that Orual could love at least one of them; and that Orual's ugliness is connected to her sterility.

This connection structures the mythic elements of the novel as they pertain to the archetype of fertility. Indeed, the first chapter begins and ends with contrasting images of female bodies. In the first paragraph, Orual describes her body as "lean carrion"; she is old, possessing "no husband nor child...."[76] By contrast, the last paragraph of the chapter focuses on the ritually prepared royal bedchamber and the naked body of the new queen, made ready for the arrival of the king shortly after their marriage. These vivid set pieces establish the thematic importance of fertility/sterility. Central to the latter set piece is the royal bed, "...made of an eastern wood which was said to have such virtue that four of every five children begotten in such a bed would be male."[77] Later, when the queen becomes pregnant and goes into labor, ritual observances once again underscore the importance of fertility. For instance, the door between the Pillar Room and the Bedchamber must remain open, for as Orual explains, "...the shutting of a door might shut up the mother's womb."[78] Again, in juxtaposition to these images and rites of fertility, sterility characterizes representations of the character of Orual. She inauspiciously begins her narrative with the day her mother died; the death of this central fertility image inflects her story with a tone of sterility. As we have seen, repeated depictions of Orual's ugliness sustain this tone, amplified by the consideration that in Apuleius's original, all three daughters of the king were beautiful. Lewis's novel thus isolates the character of Orual, setting her apart from the spirit of fertility that animates her world.

The birth of Psyche, whose superlative beauty contrasts with Orual's ugliness, draws further attention to the importance of fertility in the novel. As Erich Neumann observes, commenting on Apuleius's original story, Psyche is "'a second Aphrodite,' newly begotten and newly born."[79] Like Aphrodite herself, Psyche is the apotheosis of love and beauty as well as the fecundity that those two qualities tend to produce. Evoking the seasonal rituals that would come to be associated with Psyche after her deification,

---

[76] Ibid., 3.
[77] Ibid., 10.
[78] Ibid., 14.
[79] Erich Neumann, *Amor and Psyche: The Psychic Development of the Feminine: A Commentary on the Tale by Apuleius*, trans. Ralph Manheim (New York: Pantheon Books, 1956) 58.

Orual comments that, after Psyche's birth, "...in my memory it seems to have been all springs and summers."[80] Espying the new princess, the inhabitants of Glome equate Psyche's beauty with divinity. Thus, when the plague strikes Glome, the people initially identify Psyche as their savior, calling upon her to touch and heal them, thereby bringing new life and restoration to society. Psyche emblematizes fertility operating on a societal level. Of course, the people quickly turn on Psyche, identifying her not as the healer of the plague but its cause. The Priest of Ungit concurs: the casting of holy lots identifies Psyche as the Accursed, a verdict requiring the sentence of death by sacrifice.

Here we arrive at the heart of the actualization of myth in *Till We Have Faces*: the convergence of fertility and sacrifice, the latter producing the former, death providing life. Such sacrifice lies at the heart of all myths, both pagan and Christian. Rene Girard calls the set of circumstances that occasion this sacrifice the "initial mythic situation": a communal crisis that necessitates violence. As Girard writes, "All mythical and biblical dramas, including the Passion, represent the same type of collective violence against a single victim."[81] In depicting such a sacrifice within the fictional world of *Till We Have Faces*—a world, as we have seen, characterized by uncertainty and ambiguity—Lewis moves beyond the public sphere, employing a discourse at odds with its conventions. The convergence of fertility and sacrifice underscores the trans-rational quality of myth; the "initial mythic situation" engages a dimly lit area of human consciousness, removed from the intellectual lucidity that typifies public discourse. Moreover, representations of these mythic archetypes of fertility and sacrifice starkly contrast with the polemical thrust of the public intellectual. And although *Till We Have Faces* concludes with a Christian appropriation of pagan myths, the *denouement* is less a staked-out position than a possibility, a vision seen as through a dark glass—in short, a conclusion faithful not to the conventions of the public sphere, where myth operates at the service of argument, but to the shadowy, logic-defying spirit of deep myth itself.

The confusion that befalls the Fox, the exemplar of reason, when questioning the Priest of Ungit on the nature of sacrifice reveals the extent to which *Till We Have Faces* subverts the preeminent faculty of the public sphere—that is, reason. The Fox rejects the Priest's mythic notion that Psyche can be both the Accursed, "the wickedest person in the whole land," and a

---

[80] Lewis, *Till We Have Faces*, 22.

[81] Rene Girard, *I See Satan Fall like Lightning*, trans. James G. Williams (Maryknoll: Orbis Books, 2001) 63, 1.

spotless sacrifice, "the perfect victim—married to the god as a reward." The Fox cannot understand how Psyche can assume such mutually exclusive roles. "Ask him which he means," the Fox concludes, "It can't be both." Orual registers her disappointment in the Fox's seemingly devastating critique; her response is telling: "If any hope had put up its head within me when the Fox began, it was killed. This sort of talk could do no good." It is not that the Fox's critique does not succeed on its own terms—that is, given its own analytic framework and subsequent high estimation of logic; rather, it is that the Priest as well as the deep myth that he embodies does not operate by that very framework. The Fox adopts a mode of discourse—"this sort of talk"—foundationally different than that of the Priest. Within the former discourse, myths are suspect because they break the laws of contradiction; within the latter discourse, myths suspend the laws of contradiction and, in fact, are holy and revered precisely *because* they break the laws of contradiction. Indeed, the Priest later distinguishes between two mutually opposed types of wisdom, one—"holy wisdom"—identified with myth and its opposite associated with the rational framework of the Fox: "Holy wisdom is not clear and thin like water, but thick and dark like blood. Why should the Accursed not be both the best and the worst?"[82]

Within this mythic paradigm, how might one understand the double identity of Psyche as perfect sacrifice and Accursed? The theorizing of Girard proves helpful here. Girard contends that sacrificial victims in myth undergo a "double transformation." During the first transformation, the sacrificial victim is made into a pariah (whether deserved or not), an evil-doer who threatens the community and thus must be put to death. During the second transformation, taking place after his or her death, the sacrificial victim is made into a god who restores harmony to society. Of course, Psyche undergoes both transformations before her sacrifice, thus departing from Girard's model. On the other hand, the worship of Istra in the kingdom of Essur does exemplify the second transformation of Girard's theory: Psyche becomes a god after her death. We might say, then, that Psyche undergoes a triple transformation: She is hailed as a goddess while alive, called upon to heal the plague-stricken Glomians; she is then reviled as the Accursed, identified as the very cause of the plague by virtue of posing as a god, thus drawing Ungit's anger and jealously; and then after death, she is once again deified as Istra.

The character of Psyche thus participates in paradoxical mythic patterns. It is important to note that Orual undergoes similar transformations—

---

[82] Lewis, *Till We Have Faces*, 49–50.

transformations that link her mythic role to the destiny of her sister Psyche. After all, the god of the west wind informs Orual, "'You also shall be Psyche.'"[83] This character overlap first becomes evident when Orual is escorted through the city to face Argan in individual combat: just as Psyche, thinks Orual, was led from the city to be sacrificed to the god of the mountain. As Orual reflects, "I also might be an offering."[84] My contention is that Orual assumes throughout her life the accursed part of Psyche's mythic role, the first of Girard's double transformation: being made into an outcast and pariah. Indeed, Girard maintains that even after the sacrificial victim is posthumously deified, a "vestige of the original demon"[85] remains; characteristics of the first transformation carry over into the second transformation. Orual becomes this vestige of the original demon; she embodies the accursed side of the mythicized Psyche figure. A picture that appears on the wall during one of Orual's visions reveals that Psyche collects golden wool from the pasture of the gods only after Orual redirects the charging rams toward herself. The Fox comments, "Another bore nearly all the anguish."[86] Shouldering the burden of Psyche's accursed role, embodying Girard's vestigial demon, Orual, like Psyche, becomes a sacrifice.

This sacrificial role represented on the storied pictures of the wall emblematizes Orual's sacrifices during life. Here the themes of fertility and sacrifice converge. Just as Psyche was sundered from her husband, evicted from the warm, fertile valley of her husband / god, so Orual is consigned to a sterile existence: the sacrifice she must endure. Her veil not only hides her ugliness, which itself evokes infertility, but also symbolizes "nothingness," a sexless, sterile identity that results when Orual assumes the mannish role of Queen. Orual explains, "I locked Orual up or laid her asleep as best I could somewhere deep down inside me; she lay curled there. It was like being with child, but reversed; the thing I carried in me grew slowly smaller and less alive."[87] Orual's simile figures a process of reverse gestation, highlighting the infertility of her new identity; her womb is the locus of decay and death. Her ugliness de-sexes her: She writes of the Fox and Bardia, "they did not think of me as a woman."[88] In her old age, Orual longs to talk to Bardia on his deathbed, for she has long been secretly in love with him. Her self-

---

[83] Ibid., 174.

[84] Ibid., 216.

[85] Girard, *I See Satan Fall like Lightning*, 74.

[86] Lewis, *Till We Have Faces*, 300.

[87] Ibid., 226.

[88] Ibid., 228.

description while she waits to see him underscores the infertility of their relationship: "Three days [I waited] (I, the old fool, with hanging dugs and shriveled flanks)."[89] The abundance of infertility imagery surrounding Orual suggests that part of her sacrifice—the "burden" that she bore—includes the pain of an isolated, sterile existence, the weight of isolation and loneliness that Psyche also experienced but that Orual must shoulder on her behalf.

As we have seen, Orual experiences regeneration as a result of her visions: She acknowledges the tyrannical possessiveness she exercised over those closest to her and subsequently reorders—rightly prioritizes—her loves. She experiences a spiritual rebirth; consequently, toward the end of the novel, fertility imagery associated with her rejuvenation replaces the sterility proceeding from her former, neutered identity. In one vision, Orual's father leads her farther and farther underground, to Pillar Room beneath Pillar Room, where she receives revelations that engender her rebirth. As we have seen, Ungit herself "'signifies the earth, which is the womb and mother of all living things.'" [90] Thus, in descending into the earth, Orual literally returns to the womb to be reborn; she travels to the foundational site of fertility, the archetypal image of birth. Moreover, Orual's father comments on their surroundings, "'There's no Fox to help you here.... We're far below any dens that foxes can dig.'"[91] A world beyond the reaches of the Fox, who embodies reason, intimates a world beyond the reaches of reason itself. Thus, Orual's rebirth, rooted in mystical experience and mythic archetypes, begins in a region removed from the lucidity of rationality and the explanatory power of analysis. No fox can dig this deep; no light can illuminate these mysteries. Or, to reiterate my larger point, the discursive mode of the public sphere cannot apprehend the mythic properties of this novel.

Later visions also include rich fertility imagery, underscoring Orual's rebirth. The room with the painted walls, described earlier, teems with fecundity: "[The Fox] was leading me somewhere and the light was strengthening as we went. It was a greenish, summery light. In the end it was sunshine falling through vine leaves. We were in a cool chamber, walls on three sides of us, but on the fourth side only pillars and arches with a vine growing over them on the outside."[92] Later, the Fox leads Orual into a court where she is reunited with Psyche: "...a fair, grassy court, with blue, fresh

---

[89] Ibid., 258.

[90] Ibid., 270.

[91] Ibid., 275.

[92] Ibid., 297.

sky above us; mountain sky. In the center of the court was a bath of clear water in which many could have swum and sported together."[93] The room and the court resemble in their fecundity not only the islands of Cytherea and Cyprus, both attributed as the birthplace of Aphrodite,[94] but also the mountain valley that Psyche, along with her husband/god, once called home. Orual describes this valley thusly: "It was like looking down into a new world. At our feet, cradled amid a vast confusion of mountains, lay a small valley bright as a gem, but opening southward to our right.... I never saw greener turf. There was gorse in bloom, and wild vines, and many groves of flourishing trees, and great plenty of bright water—pools, streams, and little cataracts."[95] The painted-wall room and the court of Orual's visions thus serve as mythic recreations or fulfillments of the mountain valley of the god, signaling the newfound presence of life and growth, once terminated by Orual's earlier possessiveness but now restored through her rebirth. For the first time in the novel, Orual begins to dwell in harmony with fertile landscapes.

As Orual shares Psyche's burden, so she also participates in her restoration. The god's prophecy that Orual will become Psyche is fulfilled. Orual's final vision reveals an image of herself standing beside her sister: "Two Psyches, the one clothed, the other naked? Yes, both Psyches, both beautiful (if that mattered now) beyond all imagining, yet not exactly the same."[96] Having retrieved the casket of beauty from the land of the dead, Psyche heralds the return of the god, at which point Orual becomes like Psyche, shedding her ugliness, the symbol of infertility. The mythic patterning of double—or triple—transformation (goddess, Accursed, goddess) is itself transformed. No longer accursed, Psyche and Orual become a twinned goddess, the apotheosis of life and beauty.

## VI. Conclusion

The *denouement* of *Till We Have Faces* ultimately gestures toward the metaphysical ultimacy of Christianity. That is, the pagan, mythic archetypes of sacrifice, beauty, and fertility flow from the wellsprings of Christian reality. Thus, the sacrifices of Glome—the collective violence of a community

---

[93] Ibid., 305.

[94] Artistic representations of Aphrodite's birthplace vividly depict this fecundity. See, for instance, Botticelli's *Birth of Venus*, and Jean-Antoine Watteau's *The Embarkation for Cythera*.

[95] Ibid., 100–101.

[96] Ibid., 307–308.

directed toward a scapegoat figure—dimly reflect the truer sacrifice that Orual undergoes: bearing the burden of another person. Orual's sacrifice, in turn, anticipates the truest of all sacrifices: "Greater love hath no man than this, that a man lay down his life for his friends," a love and sacrifice of which Jesus Christ serves as the preeminent model (John 15:13). Thus, with the help of the Fox, Orual stumbles upon the larger truth behind the meaning of sacrifice. The Fox informs her,

> "Only that the way to the true gods is more like the house of Ungit...oh, it's unlike too, more unlike than we yet dream, but that's the easy knowledge, the first lesson; only a fool would stay there, posturing and repeating it. The Priest knew at least there must be sacrifices. They will have sacrifice—will have man. Yes, and the very heart, center, ground, roots of a man; dark and strong and costly as blood."[97]

For Lewis, love and sacrifice in pagan myth—the world of Orual and Psyche—are perfected with the coming of true myth—the myth that became fact when God became man. The Fox attempts to communicate above his incomplete knowledge of this fact: that the religion of Ungit merely approximates some larger, obscured truth. In this sense, *Till We Have Faces* recapitulates the more polemical use of myth in Lewis's earlier work as a public intellectual. Or, to be more precise, *Till We Have Faces* is faithful to the position that Lewis staked out in his apologetic work.

As in the apologetic work, *Till We Have Faces* demonstrates how Christianity's fulfillment of pagan myths lends those myths moments of reflected metaphysical profundity and insight. Here the novel reengages the tropes of beauty and fertility. Psyche's completion of her third task—retrieving the casket of beauty from the land of the dead—not only contributes to the regeneration of Orual, transforming her into something beautiful, but it also beautifies and sanctifies—at least partially—Ungit herself. Upon Psyche's completion of this third task, the Fox speaks of a "...distant day when the gods become wholly beautiful, or we at least are shown how beautiful they always were...."[98] That distant day occurs with Jesus's death and resurrection, the ultimate fertility ritual, when sacrifice creates an abundance of life and a new form of (spiritual) re-birth. In short, *Till We Have Faces* resembles Lewis's earlier work in that it supports the proposition that pagan myth prefigures Christianity.

---

[97] Ibid., 295.
[98] Ibid., 304.

This chapter has argued, however, that the novel absorbs this proposition into a unique narrative context, one removed from the public sphere. With its representation of uncertainty and provisionality and its emphasis on perspective and preconditionalism, *Till We Have Faces* engages key Lewisian concepts of myth from a radically different perspective. In fact, the term "proposition" ill-defines the depiction of myth found in the novel, for the term connotes a universalized, disembodied belief and presupposes a polemically driven writing scenario. Discursive contexts shape the signification of any concept. Inhabiting the context of the public sphere, the concept of myth provides Lewis with a polemical weapon in his apologetic arsenal; the discursive tone of exposition and argumentation, whether in Lewis's fiction or non-fiction, modulates myth to the key of certainty and clarity, necessarily subordinating myth's mysteries. Located outside the public sphere, localized within a particular narrative, and perspectivized by a limited narrator, the concept of myth remains mysterious; it also loses the universalized polemical reach it acquired within the public sphere. Orual herself provides an alternative to the term "proposition" as she describes one of her visions, a term that more accurately describes the apprehension of myth in the novel:

> Of the things that followed I cannot at all say whether they were what men call real or what men call dream. And for all I can tell, the only difference is that what many see we call a real thing, and what only one sees we call a dream. But things that many see may have no taste or moment in them at all, and things that are shown only to one may be spears and water-spouts of truth from the very depth of truth.[99]

Outside the public sphere, myth occupies a shadowy world where, like the kingdom of Glome, "nothing that is said clearly can be said truly about [the gods]."

In *Till We Have Faces*, the representation of propositions does not yield truth. Rather, consistent with the principles of preconditionalism, truth describes the hint of awareness that Orual receives only after her labors of sacrifice and suffering sharpen her moral vision. And while the subject of her visions ultimately prefigures Christianity, the knowledge she obtains remains vague and ineffable, contrasting with the illuminated God made lucid by the intellectualizing methods of the public sphere. The "Lord" whom Orual addresses in her visions is too large for the projected world of the novel, ultimately unknowable within its epistemological geography.

---

[99] Ibid., 277.

Readers of the novel do not ascend a series of propositions to reach Truth with a capital T; rather, like Orual, occupying her richly interpretive world, they linger in uncertainty and consider in wonderment how visions and myths reveal "water-spouts of truth from the very depth of truth."

# 9

# "The Best Is Perhaps What We Understand Least":
# Localizing the Problem of Evil in *A Grief Observed*

## I. Introduction

If God is omnipotent, then he possesses the power to prevent evil from occurring. If God is perfectly good, then he likewise possesses the desire to prevent evil from occurring. Evil occurs. Why? These propositions and this question reveal points of attack for skeptics and demand answers from Christian apologists. The arguments that ensue and the structure of discourse that such arguments necessitate are distinctly Enlightenment phenomena. Terrence W. Tilley observes, "The practice of constructing theodicies only became possible in the context of the Enlightenment."[1] Tilley's observation is supported by the fact that the very word "theodicy," the attempt to defend God's existence and nature given the reality of evil in the world, was invented in the eighteenth century by Wilhelm Leibnitz. Kenneth Surin notes, "Pre-seventeenth century Christian thinkers were certainly not unaware of the conceptual difficulties that these antinomies [between divine omnipotence and worldly evils] generated; but, unlike their post-seventeenth century counterparts, they did not regard these problems as constituting *any* sort of ground for jettisoning their faith."[2] Alasdair MacIntyre echoes Surin, noting that only after the seventeenth century did the existence of evil become a problem that challenged the "coherence and intelligibility of Christian belief per se."[3] The evolution of evil into a distinct problem occurred during the Enlightenment because the seventeenth and eighteenth centuries witnessed the birth of modern atheism.[4] Evil counts as a strike against God's existence only when evil is viewed through an interpretive lens that holds God's existence in skeptical abeyance to begin with. Enlightenment thought—with its posture of tradition-free, autono-

---

[1] Terrence W. Tilley, *The Evils of Theodicy* (Washington D.C.: Georgetown University Press, 1991) 221.

[2] Kenneth Surin, *Theology and the Problem of Evil* (Oxford: Basil Blackwell, 1986) 9.

[3] Alasdair MacIntyre, quoted in Surin, *Theology and the Problem of Evil*, 97.

[4] Stanley Hauerwas, *Naming the Silences* (Grand Rapids: Eerdmans, 1990) 41.

mous inquiry—creates this conceptual scheme that in turn transforms evil into a problem that undermines God's supposed existence or nature. The issue of God and evil thus hinges upon methodological assumptions, contexts, and perspectives.[5]

The birth of the Enlightenment coincides with the creation of the public sphere. Thus, the Enlightenment methodological assumptions about God

---

[5] For these and other reasons, many Christian scholars have abandoned the project of theodicy-making. Although well intentioned, and though important for a well-conceived Christian theology, the theodicy has often proved to be inadequate and even hurtful. Nancy Eiesland recalls the "folk theodicies" directed toward her when she was a child: "'You are special in God's eyes. That's why you were given this disability'; 'Don't worry about your pain and suffering now, in heaven you will be made whole'; and 'Thank God it isn't worse.' I was told that God gave me a disability to develop my character. But at age 6 or 7, I was convinced that I had enough character to last a lifetime" ("Barriers and Bridges: Relating the Disability Rights Movement and Religious Organizations," in *Human Disability and the Service of God: Reassessing Religious Practice*, ed. Nancy Eiesland and Don Saliers [Nashville: Abingdon, 1998] 218). Likewise, in an almost hostile tone, Reynolds Price affirms how he avoided the theodicy questions: "But with all the morbidity of such parlor games, some vital impulse spared my needing to reiterate the world's most frequent and pointless question in the face of disaster—*Why? Why me?* I never asked it; the only answer is of course *Why not?*" (*A Whole New Life* [New York: Atheneum, 1994] 53). The hostility directed toward theodicies is also evident in Lewis Smedes's *My God and I: A Spiritual Memoir*, which moves beyond folk theodicies to consider (and reject) more sophisticatedly conceived theodicies. Contemplating the events of September 11, 2001, Smedes writes, "I do not want God to 'make it plain.' If he could show us that there was a good and necessary reason for such a bad thing to have happened, it must not have been a bad thing after all. And I cannot accommodate that thought. In fact, I have given up asking *why* such bad things happen" (*My God and I: A Spiritual Memoir* [Grand Rapids: Eerdmans, 2003] 125). Alvin Plantinga employs even stronger language in condemning the theodicy: "If God is omnipotent, omniscient, and wholly good, why is there any evil?... The Christian theist must concede that she doesn't know—that is, she doesn't know in any detail.... And here I must remark that many of the attempts to explain why God permits evil—theodicies, as we might call them— seem to me shallow, tepid, and ultimately frivolous" ("Epistemic Probability and Evil," in *The Evidential Argument from Evil*, ed. Daniel Howard-Snyder [Bloomington: Indiana University Press, 1996] 70). Tilley likewise denounces the theodicy: "As the predominant modern theological and philosophical discourse practice about God and evil, theodicy misportrays and effaces genuine evils, it warps the way traditional texts are read today. It consigns other discourse about God and evil to philosophical and theological irrelevance. It silences powerful voices of insight and healing. It contributes to the powers of the 'classical' Humean problem of evil, the alleged incoherence of belief in an all-powerful , all-good, all-knowing God, and that there is genuine evil in the world" (Tilley, *The Evils of Theodicy*, xiii).

and evil carry over into the conventions of public discourse. The public sphere requires of its participants the posture of hyperbolically objective, autonomous inquiry. Both the Enlightenment stage and the public sphere demand an abstracted, de-contextualized approach to the issue of evil and suffering. Such an approach creates a large phenomenological distance between evil and inquirer, operating from a de-individualized vantage point that, if successful, will render universally binding conclusions. Concrete instances of evil are held at bay while the theodicy-maker squares off against the universal problem of evil.

Many philosophers have recognized the limitations of de-localizing the problem. Before launching his own theodicy, for example, Daniel Howard-Snyder makes a distinction between the "practical problem of evil and the theoretical problem of evil."[6] He then admits that many of his readers will be disappointed by his exclusive focus on the theoretical problem: "I am in sympathy with them. After all, evil and suffering are too real to be dealt with on a merely theoretical level.... The premise here is true: for many people, there are times when 'philosophical twaddle' about God and evil cannot meet their needs."[7] Philosopher Susan J. Brison also notes how philosophical discourse often empties suffering of its lived, individualized meanings. A victim of sexual assault, Brison struggles to localize terms that are easily dislodged from their particularized context: "And I felt that I had very little control over the meaning of the word 'rape.' Using the term denied the particularity of what I had experienced and invoked in other people whatever rape scenario they had already constructed."[8] Evil assumes different hideous contours, affecting experience in alarmingly sundry ways, whenever it bridges that phenomenological distance and enters the orbit of individual lives. As Nicholas Wolterstorff writes in his moving account of the loss of his son, "Each person's suffering has its own quality. No outsider can ever fully enter it."[9] Even Lewis in *The Problem of Pain* acknowledges the limitations of a philosophical approach to suffering in the context of religious faith: "I must add, too, that the only purpose of the book is to solve the intellectual problem raised by suffering; for the far higher task of teaching fortitude and patience I was never fool enough to suppose myself

---

[6] Daniel Howard-Snyder, "God, Evil, and Suffering," in *Reason for the Hope Within*, ed. Michael J. Murray (Grand Rapids: Eerdmans, 1999) 79.

[7] Ibid., 80.

[8] Susan J. Brison, "Violence and the Remaking of a Self," *Chronicle of Higher Education* (18 January 2002): http://chronicle.com/article/Violence-the-Remaking-of-a/8258.

[9] Nicholas Wolterstorff, *Lament for a Son* (Grand Rapids: Eerdmans, 1987) 72.

qualified, nor have I anything to offer my readers except my conviction that when pain is to be borne, a little courage helps more than knowledge, a little sympathy more than much courage, and the least tincture of the love of God more than all."[10]

An alternative to the Enlightenment approach to evil and the existence of God is to eliminate the phenomenological distance between pain and the inquirer, who thus becomes the sufferer, no longer de-individualized and de-contextualized. Such an alternative occupies the personalized space of sufferers grappling with evil, eliminating that phenomenological distance and giving representation to concrete, particularized experiences of suffering; evil rushes in upon the reader as the discourse unfolds.[11] The problem of evil becomes localized.

This chapter shows how Lewis's *A Grief Observed* illustrates this process and thus provides another glimpse of Lewis beyond the public sphere. As public intellectual, Lewis mastered the de-particularized perspective, giving reasons for the hope that lay within him using Enlightenment standards of rationality. The philosophical framework of *The Problem of Pain*—its clear stance of analyzing suffering from outside the space of suffering—is a testament to that fact. As with *Till We Have Faces*, however, the movement beyond the public sphere in *A Grief Observed* occurs primarily as an exception rather than as a rule to Lewis's typical discursive position. When Joy Davidman Gresham died in 1960, he was forced to return to the problem of pain—over twenty years since the publication of his book on that subject—in a way that made him so uncomfortable that, when *A Grief Observed* was published, he resorted to the use of a pseudonym (N. W. Clerk). Lewis was forced to enter the space of suffering where the particularities of his own experience became evident. Lewis thus necessarily sheds his typical discursive identity as a dispassionate inquirer whose reasonable conclusions were irrefutable to anyone exercising good common sense and impartiality—that is, he sheds his identity as public intellectual. He abandons the neutral posture adopted in *The Problem of Pain* and begins a narrative of suffering and loss that is already embedded in a context: that of a middle-aged academic who recently lost his wife, who wants to turn to his

---

[10] C. S. Lewis, *The Problem of Pain* (San Francisco: HarperSanFrancisco, 2001) xii.

[11] Of course, narrative accounts of evil do not always bring resolution (sometimes intentionally, sometimes unintentionally) to either the characters represented or the readers themselves. A dark, pessimistic narrative might, for instance, intensify the problem. An artificial, contrived narrative might miss the mark of lived experience, actually increasing that phenomenological distance.

Christian faith but finds God's presence to be overshadowed by the tyrannizing presence of grief. Once Lewis steps inside the space of suffering, he necessarily emphasizes perspective his narrative and abandons the de-localized voice that predominates in most of his other books on faith. Unlike *The Problem of Pain*, *A Grief Observed* draws readers into a deeply contextualized scenario, and it is within this context that he narratively registers an existential account of suffering possible only outside the public sphere.[12]

---

[12] I realize my argument partially depends on the autobiographical reliability of *A Grief Observed*—that Lewis faithfully and accurately describes his own experiences. (I will add that, even if it were mostly fabricated, the text still illustrates the localization of the problem of evil.) James Como faults John Beversluis for insisting on "the literal, verbatim facticity of *A Grief Observed*..." (*Branches to Heaven: The Geniuses of C. S. Lewis* [Dallas: Spence Publishing Company, 1998] 174). Hooper recalls a conversation he had with Lewis on the subject of *A Grief Observed*: "Lewis went on to say that, while he had to make it sound like straight autobiography if the book was to help the average sufferer, he took various precautions to prevent anyone thinking it was by him or about his grief" ("C. S. Lewis and C. S. Lewises," in *G. K. Chesterton and C. S. Lewis: The Riddle of Joy*, ed. Michael H. MacDonald and Andrew A. Tadie [Grand Rapids: Eerdmans, 1989] 45–46). Como's point and Hooper's recollection about *A Grief Observed* are correct insofar as any autobiography or memoir provides a partial, interested, and subjective account of events; an autobiographer or memoirist is not a court reporter merely transcribing events. Indeed, chapter 3 showed how Lewis tended to adopt certain personas during the course of his lifetime, tendencies that well suited him to adopt the role of public intellectual. Nevertheless, evidence suggests that *A Grief Observed* is about as reliable as any autobiographical text can be. Joe Christopher offers some of that evidence: "Certainly some of the images and ideas are not fictional. The use of H. throughout for his wife refers to Joy Davidman's first name, Helen. The effect of Charles Williams's death (without his name being mentioned) is described...as Lewis describes it in letters. The anecdote of H. putting off a request from God, only to learn He wanted to give her a feeling of joy...is told in letters. The joke that, if God had wanted people to live as lilies of the field, He should have given people their constitution...is also used in letters. Most specifically, in a letter to Mary Willis Shelburne...Lewis discusses his grief over Joy's death, using the image of sorrow as a winding road, revealing new landscapes at each turn, that he also uses in *A Grief Observed* as a winding valley...." (*C. S. Lewis* [New York: Twayne, 1987] 20). George Sayer notes, "Of all his books, *A Grief Observed* is the most personal and the one that tells us most about his relationship with Joy.... It is not fiction at all. In it he is trying to understand himself and the nature of his feelings. It is analytical, cool, and clinical" (*Jack: A Life of C. S. Lewis*, 2nd ed. [Wheaton: Crossway Books, 1988] 392–93). John Lawlor states, "I think of *A Grief Observed* as truly indicative of Lewis—for its truth-telling in the depth of adversity...and, more humbly, for the authenticity of its having been written in blank pages of an exercise book containing some 'ancient arithmetic'" (*C. S. Lewis: Memories and Reflections* [Dallas: Spence Publishing, 1998] 43).

Phenomenological distance thus differentiates *The Problem of Pain* and *A Grief Observed*, shaping their approach to the same subject in radically different ways. *The Problem of Pain* abstracts itself from the particular experience of pain in order to draw universal conclusions about a philosophical problem; *A Grief Observed* remains within the space of lived suffering and likewise remains faithful to authentic experience. Lewis notes in the preface to *The Problem of Pain* that he wished to publish the book anonymously, "...since , if I were to say what I really thought about pain, I should be forced to make statements of such apparent fortitude that they would become ridiculous if anyone knew who made them."[13] The desire for anonymity implicitly acknowledges the phenomenological distance involved in suffering, the difference between encountering evil at a safe cognitive and emotional remove, and confronting evil when it invades the individualized space of personal experience and indelibly marks the human psyche. Later in *The Problem of Pain*, Lewis again deflects autobiographical considerations, distancing the problem of evil from personal experience: "All arguments in justification of suffering provoke bitter resentment against the author. You would like to know how I behave when I am experiencing pain, not writing books about it. You need not guess, for I will tell you; I am a great coward. But what is that to the purpose?"[14] Readers of *A Grief Observed* learn that Lewis's subjectivity is everything to the purpose because no one suffers abstractly. Suffering always occurs within a context, one that shapes the experience of suffering itself. The particularized context of *A Grief Observed* localizes the problem of evil and, through its focus on subjectivity, removes Lewis from the public sphere.

Before turning to the text itself and analyzing this process, I must make a qualification similar to that offered in the previous chapter. Like *Till We Have Faces*, *A Grief Observed* adopts a radically different vantage point and discursive mode than those found in his earlier works. Nevertheless, again like *Till We Have Faces*, it engages the ideas, themes, and arguments that occupied Lewis's mind since his Christian conversion; it is therefore difficult for readers to conclude that the radically different vantage point and

---

May Borhek suggests a compelling meta-critical theory to account for the motivations of those who cast *A Grief Observed* as fiction: "The only reason I can see for believing the book to be a fictionalized account are a desire to distance oneself from the extreme discomfort of confronting naked agony and an unwillingness to grant a revered spiritual leader and teacher permission to be a real, fallible, intensely real human being" ("*A Grief Observed*: Fact or Fiction?" *Mythlore* 16 issue no. 4 [Summer 1990]: 9).

[13] Lewis, *The Problem of Pain*, 105.

[14] Ibid., 103–104.

discursive mode overturn—though such readers may occasionally admit that they strain—the ideas, themes, and arguments upon which Lewis makes the case for Christian faith in earlier works.

For instance, a major theodicy offered in *The Problem of Pain* concerns God's use of human suffering: to convict people of their badness and set them on the path toward righteousness—to use Lewis's famous phrase, pain is God's " megaphone to rouse a deaf world."[15] In *A Grief Observed*, Lewis does not abandon this belief; but in the emotional tumult that characterizes a work like this, the belief comes across as desperate and unsettling. God's megaphone becomes a torture device: "But is it credible that such extremities of torture should be necessary for us? Well, take your choice. The tortures occur. If they are unnecessary, then there is no God or a bad one. If there is a good God, then these tortures are necessary. For no even moderately good Being could possibly inflict or permit them if they weren't."[16]

Passages like these enable John Beversluis not only to argue that Lewis shifted from a Platonic view of God—"that God says things are good because they are good"—to an Ockhamist view of God—"that things are good simply because God says they are" [17]: They also allow Beversluis to write the following: "Throughout the book Lewis grieves like a husband, but he thinks like an apologist. In light of this, we would be greatly oversimplifying matters if we accepted a psychological diagnosis he himself regarded as inconclusive. It is true that, psychologically speaking, he gradually comes to terms with his grief. By the end of the book he no longer feels like protesting. But it does not follow from his improved psychological and emotional condition that he has answered the logical objections he had raised earlier."[18]

Beversluis's distinction here between husband and Christian apologist, between the personal and the logical, corresponds to my categories of analysis. While Lewis in *A Grief Observed* moves beyond the public sphere— grieving as a husband—his identity as a public intellectual—the Christian apologist answering logical objections—remains with him; it remains with him in part because this identity precedes him, influencing the way all of his books are read. As public intellectual, Lewis becomes a name associated with

---

[15] Ibid., 91.

[16] Lewis, *A Grief Observed*, 60–61.

[17] John Beversluis, *C. S. Lewis and the Search for Rational Religion* (Grand Rapids: Eerdmans, 1985) 146. Beversluis confirms this position in the 2007 (revised and updated) version of his book.

[18] John Beversluis, *C. S. Lewis and the Search for Rational Religion*, rev. ed. (Grand Rapids: Eerdmans, 1985; repr. Amherst NY: Prometheus, 2007) 280.

the positions he holds. The convergence of two contrasting modes of discourse, without one silencing the other, leaves Lewis open to Beversluis's critique. Thus, contra Como, it is not that Beversluis falsely assumes the "facticity" of *A Grief Observed*; it is that he criticizes Lewis as public intellectual in a book that leaves behind public discourse. Beversluis's critique is read as merciless and unfair because it is directed toward a Lewis rarely seen in other works, a less stylized, contrived identity seeking faithfulness to personal experience rather than success in the public sphere.

## II. The Eclipse of Abstraction

*A Grief Observed* surprises and perhaps unsettles readers who came to know Lewis through his earlier faith-informed works, for in grappling with the death of his wife, Lewis reveals profound doubts, distrusting at least momentarily both God—a "cosmic Sadist"—and his faith—a "house of cards."[19] These confessional moments effect a startling jolt when contrasted with the breezy certitude typically associated with Lewis's treatment of Christian faith. As we have seen, the public intellectual normally exudes confidence in his or her beliefs; but argumentation within the public sphere is largely performance and the beliefs defended often notional. Brought within the orbit of personal experience, the abstract issues that Lewis deftly finessed and manipulated become something else entirely: an irrepressible and implacable reality resistant to all theorizing.

Various moments in *A Grief Observed* show how experience overshadows analysis and thus how the text localizes the problem of evil. Here Lewis writes about the ravages of cancer:

> Yet H. herself, dying of it, and well knowing the fact, said that she had lost a great deal of her old horror at it. When the reality came, the name and the idea were in some degree disarmed. And up to a point I very nearly understood. This is important. One never meets just Cancer, or War, or Unhappiness (or Happiness). One only meets each hour or moment that comes. All manner of ups and downs. Many bad spots in our best times, many good ones in our worst. One never gets the total impact of what we call 'the thing itself.' But we call it wrongly. The thing itself is simply all these ups and downs: the rest is a name or an idea.[20]

Theoretical analyses of experience are necessarily misleading; abstraction misrepresents the particularity of experience. Thus, while in theory "cancer"

---

[19] Lewis, *A Grief Observed*, 54, 55.
[20] Ibid., 29.

names a dreaded disease that has scourged humankind for centuries, in practice it signifies the specific pains and hardships that certain individuals endure on a daily basis. In fact, the issue localized, Lewis leans toward a nominalist position: Universals do not exist, only particulars. Forced by the throes of his own pain to abandon universalizing analyses (public discourse), Lewis finds empty meaning in abstract nouns; only experiences are real.

The eclipse of abstract analysis by particular experience constitutes the source of much cognitive dissonance in the text; this eclipse coerces Lewis to abandon his notional beliefs and reassess his religious faith. The following passage registers the cognitive dissonance, implicitly pitting the Lewis of *The Problem of Pain* against the Lewis of *A Grief Observed*:

> We were even promised sufferings. They were part of the programme. We were even told, 'Blessed are they that mourn,' and I accepted it. I've got nothing that I hadn't bargained for. Of course it is different when the thing happens to oneself, not to others, and in reality, not in imagination. Yes; but should it, for a sane man, make quite such a difference as this? No. And it wouldn't for a man whose faith had been real faith and whose concern for other people's sorrows had been real concern.[21]

The theoretical/practical dichotomy operates in this passage as well. Theoretically, Lewis understood Christ's beatitude about sufferers. He in fact incorporated it into his apologetic strategy in *The Problem of Pain*. But in doing so, the beatitude is absorbed into public discourse, becoming a polemical move to win an argument; it subsequently also becomes more notional than experiential. Thus, brought within the crucible of intense grief, the beatitude lacks traction, and Lewis concludes that his faith was flimsy. The struggle Lewis records in *A Grief Observed* occurs because the experiential eclipses the abstract.

## III. The Problem of Evil as Process

In its tendency toward abstraction, theodicy-making manages the problem of evil by suspending it in time and place, pinning it to the analytical table so that it conforms to the methods of philosophical discourse; theodicy-making fixes and stabilizes all human variables in order to make analysis and argument possible. Once the problem of evil is pressed into the service

---

[21] Ibid., 53–54.

of these discursive needs, theodicy-making yields a product: the theodicy itself, the answer to the problem of pain.

Here once again we find the Lewis of *The Problem of Pain* at odds with the Lewis of *A Grief Observed*. The latter realizes that grief is a process, an experience that cannot be rendered static:

> In so far as this record was a defence against total collapse, a safety-valve, it has done some good. The other end I had in view turns out to have been based on a misunderstanding. I thought I could describe a *state*, make a map of sorrow. Sorrow, however, turns out to be not a state but a process. It needs not a map but a history, and if I don't stop writing that history at some quite arbitrary point, there's no reason why; I should ever stop.[22]

Lewis painfully realizes his misunderstanding: Grief never sits still long enough for him to comprehend it; its shape alters, and its intensity fluctuates—thus the need for Lewis to devise a new metaphor to chart its nature. Lewis jettisons the map metaphor, for it assumes a fixed set of coordinates to plot an ever-changing experience. The history metaphor captures the protean nature of grief, its continuation as a never-ending process. Unlike a narrative, which includes the identifiable moments of climax and *denouement*, a history lacks such reference points, clear markers that chart progress. History does not reach a settled conclusion: As Lewis writes, his journal would continue indefinitely if he did not give it an arbitrary stopping point.

*A Grief Observed* is thus process. Indeed, throughout the journal, Lewis goes through stages of grief, the most intense of which is the anger stage. During one moment of temporary emotional tranquility, he reflects, "All that stuff about the Cosmic Sadist was not so much the expression of thought as of hatred. I was getting from it the only pleasure a man in anguish can get; the pleasure of hitting back."[23] Giving vent to the stages of his intensely personal grief and abandoning the map metaphor, Lewis reveals the messiness of an experience that cannot yield the sanitized product of an abstracted theodicy.

## IV. Subjectivity and Preconditionalism

As in *Till We Have Faces*, *A Grief Observed* adopts a mode of discourse that makes Christian polemics difficult. The focus is not on truth claims—

---

[22] Ibid., 76.
[23] Ibid., 57.

their expatiation and defense—but on the perspective within which truth claims are processed. The emphasis on process, rather than product, creates a writing scenario that necessarily focuses on Lewis's own subjectivity. Thus, again like *Till We Have Faces, A Grief Observed* engages the process of preconditionalism, the notion that belief-acquisition has as much or more to do with an individual's state of mind than with the rationality of potential beliefs. The beliefs that Lewis acquires fluctuate with the stages of grief that he endures.

Examples abound. Lewis's self-professed overindulgence in self-pity, for instance, clouds his faculty of recollection. He explains, "But the bath of self-pity, the wallow, the loathsome sticky-sweet pleasure of indulging it—that disgusts me. And even while I'm doing it I know it leads me to misrepresent H."[24] A pathetic absorption in grief hinders the ability to think clearly. By its very nature, the text interrogates beliefs on these terms, attending not to beliefs themselves but to the mental landscapes that situate them. Thus, Lewis's crisis of belief culminates in autobiographical considerations: "Whether there was anything but imagination in my faith, or anything but egoism in my love, God knows."[25] The text implicitly presses the point that faith depends more on the psychology of the believer than the rationality of the belief.

One of the first upward movements of the text—a positive moment during which grief abates and Lewis achieves some peace and clarity—illustrates a principle of preconditionalism: that beliefs are holistically acquired, involving not just the mind but body and soul as well. He states that, upon waking one morning, his "...heart was lighter than it had been for many weeks":

> For one thing, I suppose I am recovering physically from a good deal of mere exhaustion. And I'd had a very tiring but very healthy twelve hours the day before, and a sounder night's sleep; and after ten days of low-hung grey skies and motionless warm dampness, the sun was shining and there was a light breeze. And suddenly at the very moment when, so far, I mourned H. the least, I remembered her best.[26]

The rejuvenation of his body, along with the experience of a sunny day, seems to replenish his spirit, bringing clarity to his perspective on his wife. Lewis reiterates the embodied nature of perspective later in the text as well: "It is just at those moments when I feel least sorrow—getting into my

---

[24] Ibid., 23.
[25] Ibid., 59.
[26] Ibid., 62.

morning bath is usually one of them—that H. rushes upon my mind in her full reality, her otherness."[27] The bath in its tranquility cleanses both his body and spirit, quieting the mind so that it can apprehend reality. Adopting what amounts to an incarnational theology, Lewis affirms the role of the body as the medium for perspectives and beliefs.

Consequently, *A Grief Observed* implicitly reshapes the nature of rationality, setting forth an epistemology removed from the public sphere. After identifying "half our great theological and metaphysical problems" as unanswerable nonsense, Lewis relocates belief-acquisition to the trans-rational region of human subjectivity: "It's all about weights of feelings and motives and that sort of thing."[28] Weights of feelings and motives are influenced by embodied practices. Thus, Lewis acknowledges that his attitude toward God, alternating between belligerence and desperate neediness, limits his ability both to relate properly to God and to remember rightly his wife. His self-confessed narcissism dis-orders his loves and clouds his vision. He subsequently rediscovers a different "mode of thinking" that reorients the Christian reality that he has come to accept, bringing into focus the objects of his love:

> And I see that I have nowhere fallen into that mode of thinking about either [God or his wife] which we call praising them. Yet that would have been best for me. Praise is the mode of love which always has some element of joy in it. Praise in due order; of Him as the giver, of her as the gift. Don't we in praise somehow enjoy what we praise, however far we are from it? I must do more of this. I have lost the fruition I once had of H. And I am far, far away in the valley of my unlikeness, from the fruition which, if His mercies are infinite, I may some time have of God. But by praising I can still, in some degree, enjoy her, and already, in some degree, enjoy Him. Better than nothing.[29]

The last phrase indicates that Lewis still struggles to find peace.

Nevertheless, his willingness to engage in praise carries epistemological implications: The embodied practice of praise permits clearer knowledge of its object. Indeed, epistemology may be the wrong word to classify this phenomenon; for what Lewis's "mode of thinking" provides is, strictly speaking, not knowledge but another embodied practice: enjoyment. What Lewis begins to experience is not intellectual closure but existential fullness. Toward the end of the journal, Lewis reiterates this idea: "To see, in some

---

[27] Ibid., 73.

[28] Ibid., 87.

[29] Ibid., 79–80.

measure, like God. His love and His knowledge are not distinct from one another, nor from Him. We could almost say He sees because He loves, and therefore loves although He sees."[30] With respect to issues of faith, love precedes knowledge. Consistent with the principles of preconditionalism, Lewis becomes rightly oriented toward both God and the memory of his wife when the rational search for answers is subsumed by a holistic disposition: mind, body, spirit, and soul centered on love and praise.

### V. The "incomprehensible and unimaginable"

Detached from a strictly rational understanding, encompassing categories much larger than the mere epistemological, the experience of grief becomes difficult for Lewis to render into language and propositional terms. Lewis registers this difficulty—indeed, futility—in his startling attestation on the limitations of theology and metaphysics: "Can a mortal ask questions which God finds unanswerable? Quite easily, I should think. All nonsense questions are unanswerable. How many hours are there in a mile? Is yellow square or round? Probably half the questions we ask—half our great theological and metaphysical problems—are like that."[31] What makes this generalization so startling is the fact that Lewis, as public intellectual, repeatedly asked (and answered) those questions and engaged those problems.

Answers present themselves, however, only after philosophical and theological discourse frames the very questions, establishing terms of analysis that privilege strict standards of intelligibility. The death of Joy Davidman Gresham unmasks the narcissistic tendencies of such terms; they offer intelligibility and thus comfort by accommodating psychological needs. Thus, with the death of his wife—the reality of her presence removed— Lewis finds an "imaginary woman" materializing in his mind's eye: "Founded on fact, no doubt. I shall put in nothing fictitious (or I hope I shan't), but won't the composition inevitably become more and more my own?"[32] A disconnect develops between self-serving representational impulses and the unyielding mystery and quiddity of the object of representation: what Lewis calls something "...unmistakably other, resistant—in a word, real."[33] Made absent by death, Joy Davidman Gresham

---

[30] Ibid., 89–90.
[31] Ibid., 87.
[32] Ibid., 34.
[33] Ibid., 25.

becomes a figure increasingly subjected to representations shaped by Lewis's psychological traumas. For this reason, Lewis comes to sympathize with the man who enters the cemetery and proclaims to his friends, "'See you later, I'm just going to visit Mum.'" The man, Lewis understands, meant he was going to tend to his mother's grave. Lewis admits that such a "mode of sentiment, all this churchyard stuff, was and is simply hateful, even inconceivable to me." However, Lewis also comes to see that the actual presence of the grave imposes representational constraints upon memories of the dead, hardening the malleable images of the deceased, calibrating them to a hard and immutable reality:

> The grave and the image are equally links with the irrecoverable and symbols for the unimaginable. But the image has the added disadvantage that it will do whatever you want. It will smile or frown, be tender, gay, ribald, or argumentative just as your mood demands. It is a puppet of which you hold the string.... The flower-bed on the other hand is an obstinate, resistant, often intractable bit of reality, just as Mum in her lifetime doubtless was. As H. was.[34]

The absence of Joy Davidman Gresham simply gives Lewis too much representational space to fashion her in his desired image, which at this stage of his grieving process, assumes the form of a "mere doll to be blubbered over."[35]

In her death, Joy Davidman Gresham has become transcendently signified; her reality no longer immanent, she both defies and submits to Lewis's representations of her—which is to say she has become inscrutable and ineffable. All forms of images and discourse fail to grasp her full reality—which is to say, in turn, that she has become like God. Lewis writes, "Kind people have said to me, 'She is with God.' In one sense that is most certain. She is, like God, incomprehensible and unimaginable."[36] As transcendent objects, Joy Davidman Gresham and God unsettle all attempts at representation and understanding. What Lewis writes here about God could just as easily be applied to his wife: "Images of the Holy easily become holy images—sacrosanct. My idea of God is not a divine idea. It has to be shattered time after time. He shatters it Himself. He is the great iconoclast."[37] Lewis's reflections on images of his wife lead him to consider images of God;

---

[34] Ibid., 37–38.
[35] Ibid., 20.
[36] Ibid., 40.
[37] Ibid., 83.

in both cases, the images must be continually shattered and rebuilt. The failure of representation removes Lewis from the public sphere.

The final consolation of the journal likewise registers the inadequacy of representation. Lewis undergoes a mystical experience that

> ...can be described in similes; otherwise it won't go into language at all. Imagine a man in total darkness. He thinks he is in a cellar or dungeon. Then there comes a sound. He thinks it might be a sound from far off— waves or wind-blown trees or cattle half a mile away. And if so, it proves he's not in a cellar, but free, in the open air. Or it may be a much smaller sound close at hand—a chuckle of laughter. And if so, there is a friend just beside him in the dark. Either way, a good, good sound.[38]

Lewis thus arrives at no rationally defensible proposition that can satisfy his (or anyone else's) "incurably abstract intellect."[39] Instead, he receives an irrational experience, resistant to language, that troubles that mode of thinking: "Heaven will solve our problems, but not, I think, by showing us subtle reconciliations between all our apparently contradictory notions. The notions will all be knocked from under our feet. We shall see that there never was any problem."[40] Lewis arrives at this conclusion in part by hearing the sound of laughter in the dark and inexplicably receiving the "...sense that some shattering and disarming simplicity is the real answer."[41] Lewis acknowledges that this experience does not grant him "...an assurance of H.'s presence...." Indeed, momentarily falling back into apologetic mode, Lewis asserts, " I won't treat anything of that sort as evidence."

Nevertheless, the experience—the perception of the sound of laughter in the dark—moves Lewis beyond issues of warrant and proof, the domain of the philosopher and public intellectual: "It's the *quality* of last night's experience—not what it proves but what it was—that makes it worth putting down. It was quite incredibly unemotional. Just the impression of her *mind* momentarily facing my own."[42] The experience is not a link in the chain of any argument; it does not buttress any claim, serving as the foundation for any position. Rather, its value is self-originating, meaningful in and of itself; it makes no attempt at representing, or signifying for that matter. It is a self-referentially complete experience, compelling in its own irrepressible circularity. Perhaps most importantly, it provides a sense of presence

---

[38] Ibid., 81.
[39] Ibid.
[40] Ibid., 88.
[41] Ibid., 89.
[42] Ibid., 90–91.

without narcissistically drawn images. Lewis encounters the incomprehensible and unimaginable otherness of his deceased wife through an experience that is itself incomprehensible and unimaginable.

This experience and the thoughts that it provokes lead Lewis to a contemplation of the resurrection. He had asked Joy Davidman Gresham to come to him (from beyond the grave) when he was on his own deathbed. But Lewis brings this reflection to a quick halt: As a result of the experiences recorded in the journal, he has "...come to misunderstand a little less completely what a pure intelligence might be...."[43] Negatively framing the lessons he has learned (misunderstanding a little less), Lewis becomes more acutely aware—and, in the private space of this journal, more willing to admit—that the language of the public intellectual over-represents and over-signifies. That which is most valuable is incomprehensible and unimaginable. Such is Lewis's conclusion on the resurrection: "there is also, whatever it means, the resurrection of the body. We cannot understand. The best is perhaps what we understand least."[44]

## VI. Conclusion, in Which Not Everything Is Concluded

Such provisionality characterizes *A Grief Observed*, a work that never arrives at a settled conclusion. Pushed off-balance by grief, Lewis registers confusion throughout the journal. The opening entry, for instance, even records a confusion of emotions: "No one ever told me that grief felt so like fear. I am not afraid, but the sensation is like being afraid."[45] The tempest of grief disorders classifications of experience. Later, Lewis returns to this confusion of emotions, likening grief not only to fear but to suspense. And, in a moment of the text when the sense of unsettledness becomes particularly palpable, he suggests that grief is "...like waiting; just hanging about waiting for something to happen. It gives life a permanently provisional feeling."[46] In stark contrast to the public intellectual, Lewis here finds himself on unstable ground where he cannot avail himself of settled truths and firm conclusions; certainty in the public sphere gives way to tenuousness within the private space of grief.

In addition, the comfort Lewis does achieve often turns out to be temporary. That is, he arrives at a notion that brings peace to his troubled

---

[43] Ibid., 93.
[44] Ibid.
[45] Ibid., 19.
[46] Ibid., 50.

mind; however, he then experiences relapses of grief. For instance, he concludes that "...passionate grief does not link us with the dead but cuts us off from them,"[47] a conclusion that not only assuages his pain but yields the resolution to handle his emotions with more equanimity. The resolution is short-lived, however, for just four journal entries later, Lewis describes being overcome by another tumult of confused emotion: "Tonight all the hells of young grief have opened again; the mad words, the bitter resentment, the fluttering in the stomach, the nightmare unreality, the wallowed-in tears. For in grief nothing 'stays put.'"[48] Lewis once again registers the tentativeness of his experiences and notions; grief-induced shifting ground repeatedly destabilizes his conclusions and unsettles his experiences.

This is not to suggest that Lewis abandons the conclusion addressed above: Lewis continues to believe that intense grief clouds his memories of Joy Davidman Gresham and dulls his perception of God's presence. But unlike in the public sphere, beliefs in the private space of grief endure inexplicable fluctuations. Whereas the public sphere provides a static environment for beliefs to achieve universality, the private space of particularity records the messiness of human experience, complicating beliefs through their full immersion in the lived context of grief, hope, and emotional swings. Lewis writes, "All reality is iconoclastic."[49] Memories of the deceased, images of God, and the beliefs that develop from them both are all subject to destruction; we simply might be wrong about such matters. For Lewis, one must then begin the reassembling process, fitting the memories, images, and beliefs back together. The destruction-and-reassembling process may be interminable, a possibility Lewis acknowledges when he identifies his faith as a house of cards: "And all this time I may, once more, be building with cards. And if I am He will once more knock the building flat. He will knock it down as often as proves necessary."[50] Such destruction is necessary within the epistemological geography that *A Grief Observed* maps out, a geography characterized by provisionality and unsettled conclusions.

Consequently, some scholars wonder if Lewis ever recovered from his wife's death or if he even lost his faith. Beversluis finds the "turning point" in the text unconvincing; that is, Lewis's slow return to God leaves Beversluis suspicious: "But in Part III everything changes. The protest is

---

[47] Ibid., 73.
[48] Ibid., 75.
[49] Ibid., 83.
[50] Ibid., 85.

dropped and the charges against God are withdrawn. A turning point is reached, and the tone of the book alters so abruptly that the reader is at a loss to explain Lewis's sudden change of heart."[51] The biographical reflections of other Lewis scholars affirm a change they observed in Lewis after Davidman's death. Chad Walsh states, "Lewis never really recovered from the loss of Joy. When I next saw him in late 1961, he was subdued and at loose ends."[52] Lyle Dorsett succinctly writes, "C. S. Lewis died at the Kilns in November 1963. He was never well after Joy left him."[53] And Douglas Gresham, Lewis's stepson who lived with Lewis during much of the ordeal, explains, "Jack was half the man he had been [after the death of his wife], and in one sense he was never completely happy again. He settled back to work and to continue his life with an aching emptiness that nothing could ever fill."[54] Nevertheless, Walsh, Dorsett, and Gresham clearly do not read *A Grief Observed* as an account of Lewis's apostasy. Beversluis's suspicions return us to the discrepancy between Lewis as public intellectual and Lewis removed from the public sphere. Obviously the pseudonymously written journal allows Lewis to write more privately and personally, testifying to the change in personality that Walsh, Dorsett, and Gresham observe.

This chapter has maintained, however, that the movement beyond the public sphere in *A Grief Observed* means much more than that. Moving beyond the public sphere compels Lewis to localize the problem of evil, which re-frames the very experience of grief and undermines the distinctly philosophical approach to the subject. This, I believe, is the source of Beversluis's suspicions and objections. Localizing the problem of evil, removing it from the auspices of philosophical discourse, Lewis acknowledges doubts and uncertainties; approaches grief not as a philosophical problem but as an experiential process; experiences (and admits to experiencing) relapses of grief; and attends to the puzzling

---

[51] Beversluis, *C. S. Lewis and the Search for Rational Religion*, 147. 1985.

[52] Chad Walsh, afterword to *A Grief Observed* (New York: Bantam Books, 1976) 148.

[53] Lyle Dorsett, *Joy and C. S. Lewis: The Story of an Extraordinary Marriage* (London: Harper Collins, 1993) 149.

[54] Douglas Gresham, *Jack's Life: The Life Story of C. S. Lewis* (Nashville: Roadman & Holman, 2005) 159. Walter Hooper here once again demurs, maintaining that accounts of Lewis's grief have been greatly exaggerated: "By this time [not long after Lewis wrote *A Grief Observed*] I had heard Lewis talk a great deal about his late wife, Joy. While he, doubtless, loved her very much, he never to me seemed sad" ("C. S. Lewis and C. S. Lewises," in *G. K. Chesterton and C. S. Lewis: The Riddle of Joy*, ed. Michael H. MacDonald and Andrew A. Tadie [Grand Rapids: Eerdmans, 1989] 45).

dynamic by which his own psychology not only shapes beliefs but determines their cogency. Such a radical departure from the public sphere confuses readers who try to cohere the plaintive cries of *A Grief Observed* with the dispassionate, confident arguments found in Lewis's other works of non-fiction.[55] Consequently, while Beversluis may find the resolution of Lewis's journal unconvincing, he is wrong to do so on a strictly logical

---

[55] Even scholars who come to Lewis's defense perpetuate what I consider to be a category mistake, applying the criteria of the public sphere to the private sphere. Victor Reppert, for instance, admits that the journal is "primarily pastoral," an identification that suggests the book engages the whole person, mind, body, soul, and spirit. He continues, "Nevertheless the book does contain some argumentation to show that his grief experience does not provide any reason to adopt a worldview other than theism that includes a Platonistic conception of divine goodness." Thus framing the book as, at least in part, a philosophical argument within the public sphere, Reppert attempts to "show the continuity between Lewis's apologetic writing and *A Grief Observed*…," a continuity that I have identified as problematic at best. Reppert then comes to the flawed conclusion that "[t]he message of *A Grief Observed* is that those intellectual grounds [for maintaining trust in God] remained what they had always been" (*C. S. Lewis's Dangerous Idea: A Philosophical Defense of Lewis's Defense of Reason* [Downers Grove IL: InterVarsity Press, 1989] 23, 28). I believe this is a misreading of the text, one that is understandable for reasons previously offered: that Lewis's separation from the public sphere is never fully complete. Nevertheless, Reppert's placement of the "message" on a strictly intellectual level—the only operative level in the public sphere—suggests a misunderstanding of the text's genre and the quality of private discourse.

basis—as if Lewis has committed a *non sequitur*. Indeed, Beversluis overlooks the fundamental source of resolution in the text, as thinly developed as it may be: the mystical laughter in the dark that convinces Lewis of Joy's presence. While such an experience may be irrational, it occasions a resolution that emerges slowly, organically, though perhaps not fully and completely. But in the private space of suffering, perhaps that is the best that Lewis—or anyone—can do.

# Introduction to Part 3
## An Experiment in Meta-criticism

Part 3 constitutes an excursus into the sociology of Lewis's reputation. Lewis created a vast body of writings. Once published, however, his books—like those of any author—took on a life of their own, variously interpreted by readers with contrasting hermeneutical frameworks. Similarly, Lewis's reputation developed in varying degrees independently of Lewis himself: a public identity tugged and pulled in different directions by different readers. If, as Part 1 argued, Lewis developed a secure position within the public sphere because of his writerly persona, polemical maneuverings, and rhetorical strategies, then how have various critics, scholars, reporters, admirers, and detractors positioned Lewis's reputation within that public sphere? In other words, what might a meta-critical analysis reveal about Lewis's public reception, the third of the three phenomena explored in this book?

In chapters 10 and 11, I attempt a strictly historical, chronological survey of Lewis's formation in the public sphere. Drawing mainly from articles and reviews written between 1930 and 2010, these chapters explore the evolution of Lewis's various public identities: literary scholar, "conservative iconoclast," religious populist, and American evangelical hero, among others. Of course, these chapters cannot exhaustively survey all secondary sources on Lewis produced over the span of eighty years. The chapters do, however, try to single out representative choruses of critical voices (or particularly stentorian or influential single voices) that, through the years, produced enough volume to catch the collective ear of a larger public, thereby shaping Lewis's identity. Attending to these voices enables me to identify salient themes in the evolution of Lewis's reputation. Chapter 10 examines Lewis's meta-critical life from 1930 to 1970, chapter 11 from 1970 to 2010.

In chapter 12, I endeavor to explain distinct meta-critical curiosities that attend the study of Lewis; these curiosities mainly concern the paraphrase-heavy content and hagiographical tone found in numerous studies of Lewis. My explanations will pave the way for chapter 13, wherein I define and explore the Lewis industry.

# 10

# The Evolution of C. S. Lewis's Reputation in the Public Sphere, 1930–1970

## I. 1940s and 1930s

### a. Foundation as a Literary Scholar

In the 1930s, Lewis had not yet become a public intellectual. Published in 1933, *The Pilgrim's Regress*, Lewis's first Christian book, did not reach a broad audience, due in part to its dense allegory and arcane references. During this decade, however, Lewis did establish himself as an Oxford don and became a preeminent literary scholar, a reputation that demanded respect and earned him intellectual credibility within the scholarly world, credibility that would spill over into the public sphere. Thus, in the 1930s, Lewis built the foundation for his identity as public intellectual.

Published in 1936, *The Allegory of Love*, a scholarly work that exemplifies Lewis's mastery of a wide range of medieval and Renaissance poets in the context of the courtly-love tradition, received lavish praise, as evidenced in reviews published in 1936 and 1937. William Empson called the book "learned, witty, and sensible."[1] Oliver Elton wrote that the "general conduct of [Lewis's] story is masterly."[2] G. L. Brook offered this laudatory assessment: "This is undoubtedly one of the best books on mediaeval literature ever published in this country, and every page reveals in the author an unusual degree of scholarship and critical insight."[3] An anonymous reviewer for *Notes and Queries* asserted that the book "has a freshness and verve and directness beyond anything we have met with and enjoyed in literary study for some time."[4] And Kathleen Tillotson attributed the book with watershed significance: "It is rarely that we meet with a work of literary

---

[1] William Empson, "Love in the Middle Ages," *Critical Thought Series: C. S. Lewis*, ed. George Watson (Cambridge: Cambridge University Press, 1992) 79. Originally published in *Spectator*, 4 September 1936 241-243.

[2] Oliver Elton, review of *The Allegory of Love*, in Watson, 83. Originally published in *Medium Aevum* vol. 6 (1936): 34-39.

[3] G. L. Brook, review of *The Allegory of Love*, in Watson. Originally published in *Modern Language Review* vol. 32 (1936): 32.

[4] Anonymous, review of *The Allegory of Love*, in Watson, 105. Originally published in *Notes and Queries* vol. 3 (3 October 1936): 250-251.

criticism of such manifest and general importance as this. No one could ever read it without seeing all literature differently for ever after."[5]

Some reviewers of the book called attention to qualities in Lewis's writing that would later help brand his name in the public sphere, qualities that generate controversy and others that attune Lewis's argument to the polemical register of the public sphere. As an instance of the former, Empson observed the traditionalism of Lewis's critical orientation, the general resistance to progressivism: "Mr Lewis is rather bitter about 'the modern reader', that vulgar fool looking for excitement, and it seems fair to point out the journalism of his first pages."[6] Elton noted Lewis's tendency toward moralism, specifically his quick defense of Spenser from scholars who associate representations of the Bower of Bliss in *The Faerie Queene* with sensuality. Lewis, Elton observed, wants perhaps too desperately to show that that sensuality is corrupt and artificial, in contrast to the rectitude found in the Bower's structural parallel within Spenser's poem: the Garden of Adonis. "That may be true," wrote Elton, "but why defend Spenser at all, and why not admit that this Renaissance artist, with his passion for colour and his sense of luxury, *can* be, at times, voluptuous?"[7] As an instance of the latter—argumentative strategies that lend themselves to public discourse— L. C. Knights, in a 1939 review of Lewis's *Rehabilitations and Other Essays*, accused Lewis of some polemical strong-arming, attributing other viewpoints—namely those that Lewis himself does not hold—to straw men and adopting a polemical attitude that is quick to disagree rather than understand. Knights called Lewis out on his "trick of disparaging unnamed opponents who remain conveniently vague—'our modern impostors,' 'the new Puritanism,' 'some of Mr. Eliot's weaker disciples'; and there is at times the same irritating tone of superiority." Knights later concluded that Lewis was completely unable "to envisage any point of view other than his own except in the most ludicrous forms."[8] Knights's critique points to qualities in Lewis's writing that are endemic to public discourse: a tone of certainty read as rightness of position within the public sphere and the necessity of vigorous, no-punches-pulled argumentation within an arena created precisely for the confrontation of diverse, competing viewpoints. Once

---

[5] Kathleen Tillotson, review of *Allegory of Love*, in Watson, 96. Originally published in *Review of English Studies* vol. 13 (1936): 477.

[6] William Empson, "Love and the Middle Ages," in Watson, 79. Originally published in *Spectator* vol. 4 (September 1936): 241-243.

[7] Elton, review of *The Allegory of Love*, 88.

[8] L. C. Knights, "Mr. C. S. Lewis and the Status Quo," in Watson, 143. Originally published in *Scrutiny* vol. 8 (1939): 88-92.

again, one sees how, in the 1930s, Lewis was poised to enter the public sphere.

However, literary disputes—over, say, rival interpretations of Spenser's *Faerie Queene*—generate little publicity. Beginning in 1940 with the publication of *The Problem of Pain* and, three years later, with *The Screwtape Letters*, Lewis engaged a topic about which the entire public had an often strong opinion. Lewis's entrance into this public sphere was noticeable: iterations—in the form of book reviews—of his uniquely presented Christian position occasioned multiple reiterations, spawning a Lewis phenomenon that would become explosive.

### b. Lewis's Early Reputation in the Public Sphere: Reviews of Christian Books.

Lewis's Christian books received numerous positive reviews in the 1940s. In a 1942 review of *The Screwtape Letters* in the *Spectator*, W. J. Turner proclaimed, "From this Christian standpoint he has written the most vital restatement of religious truths produced in our time, and he has found a brilliantly original form in which to do it."[9] Turner facetiously suggested that Lewis should become the next Archbishop of Canterbury: "For who could be fitter for the task than one who could give counsel to Satan himself?"[10] Many American reviewers first encountered *The Problem of Pain* in George Shuster's 1943 review in the *New York Herald Tribune Book Review*. Shuster wrote, "I believe that Mr. Lewis has succeeded in making all these points in terms of orthodox Christianity with unusual effectiveness. He writes very well." Shuster also touched upon what would become Lewis's public-intellectual identity, noting Lewis's sensitivity to a lay audience: "The average man will find this book…decidedly able to come to grips with distressing facts."[11] A year later, Henry James Forman also spotted Lewis's aptitude as a translator of Christian doctrine in a review of *Christian Behaviour*, one of Lewis's BBC radio talks and later published in *Mere Christianity*, in the *New York Times Book Review*. James Forman underscored the book's "costly simplicity that is achieved only after much learning and thinking and pruning away of nonessentials."[12] James Forman's review is significant because it is one of the first to notice the tension inherent in the

---

[9] W. J. Turner, "The Devil at Work," *Spectator* 168 (1942): 186.

[10] Ibid.

[11] George Shuster, "Discipline," *New York Herald Tribune Book Review* 26 December 1943, 6.

[12] Henry James Forman, "Common-Sense Humanist," *New York Times Book Review*, 23 April 1944, 12.

project of the public intellectual: the yoking together of simplicity and learning, expository facility and scholarly acumen. (Indeed, as we will see, the "costly simplicity" that elicits James Forman's praise will serve precisely as the object of critique for other reviewers.)

In another 1944 review, this one of *Beyond Personality*, another BBC talk that would ultimately be published in *Mere Christianity*, the *Times Literary Supplement* asserted, "Mr. Lewis has a quite unique power of making theology an attractive, exciting and (one almost might say) an uproariously fascinating quest."[13] Touching on the tone of certainty necessary for public discourse, the review also commented, "[Lewis] can scarcely imagine any other answer than the orthodox one for any sane man who is moved to study the ultimate problems of life."[14] Reviewing *Out of the Silent Planet* for *America* in 1944, Charles A. Brady praised Lewis for "creating fantasy on an intensely imaginative plane of great beauty...."[15] Interestingly, however, Brady offered a quirky reading of Ransom's encounter with the *hrossa*, one of the inhabitants of Malacandra: an encounter "which can be interpreted, if you wish, as an allegory of racial fear and repugnance and its sublimation into deep affection through the very recognition of the fact of difference."[16] I label this interpretation "quirky" because of its contrast to the later critical preoccupation with the religious—not racial—elements of the text, a critical preoccupation made complete once Lewis's name is thoroughly branded as Christian in the public sphere. In a 1939 letter, Lewis himself observes that only two of approximately sixty reviews of *Out of the Silent Planet* showed any awareness of the Christian theology in the book or that his "...idea of the fall of the Bent One was anything but an invention of my own."[17]

Two reviews of *The Great Divorce* spotlighted characteristics that would help transform Lewis into a public intellectual. A review in the *New York Herald Tribune Weekly Book Review* praised Lewis's ability of rendering philosophical subjects interesting through the use of a winsome prose style: "Mr. Lewis is a scholar, a philosopher and a most engaging writer, a

---

[13] Anonymous, "Theology of Discovery: Mr. C. S. Lewis's Talks," *Times Literary Supplement*, 21 October 1944, 513.

[14] Ibid., 513.

[15] Charles A. Brady, "C. S. Lewis: II," *America* vol. 71 (10 June 1944): 269.

[16] Ibid.

[17] C. S. Lewis to Sister Penelope, 9 July 1939, in *The Collected Letters of C. S. Lewis*, vol. 2, *Books, Broadcasts, and the War, 1931–1949*, ed. Walter Hooper (San Francisco: HarperSanFrancisco, 2004) 262.

combination so rare that it is hard to believe."[18] Writing for the *Saturday Review of Literature*, W. H. Auden concluded, "I think it unlikely that if other books as generally entertaining as 'The Great Divorce' appear this year, they will be as generally instructive, and vice versa, so that it seems ungracious to ask for more...."[19] Delighting and instructing while marshaling arguments for Christianity enabled Lewis to leave his mark in the public sphere.

### c. Popularity

By the mid 1940s, Lewis's Christian works had garnered much publicity. However, at least one reviewer—Alistair Cooke—saw the popularity of Lewis as a mere fad, popularity owing to the emotional needs of a worried public in a time of war. Indeed, Cooke implied that Lewis exploited people's wartime fears to bring them to Christianity. Cooke admitted that *Out of the Silent Planet, The Screwtape Letters,* and *Perelandra* "have had a modest literary success" and that "multitudes of readers, and in Britain radio listeners, succumb to the charm of his more direct treatises on Christian conduct." Nevertheless, Cooke reduced Lewis's impact to an "alarming vogue" that, before radio, would have quickly evaporated.[20]

Americans seemed less inclined to ascribe evanescence to Lewis's popularity. In a 1944 piece significantly titled "Introduction to Lewis" published in *America,* Brady called *The Screwtape Letters* "the most phenomenally popular household book of applied religion of the twentieth century": The essay established Lewis as the only living Christian public intellectual: "He is the only truly popular champion of Orthodoxy...in book, pamphlet and radio address since the passing of Gilbert Keith Chesterton."[21] The American periodical *Christian Century* did not hesitate in 1946 to emphasize Lewis's popularity in grandiose terms: "...for unquestionably not a clergyman in all Britain has the influence exercised by this ordinary lay lecturer on English literature."[22]

---

[18] Thomas Sugrue, "Terrifying Realities of the Soul," *New York Herald Tribune Weekly Book Review,* 3 March 1946, 4.

[19] W. H. Auden, "Red Lizards and White Stallions," *Saturday Review of Literature* (13 April 1946): 22.

[20] Alastair Cooke, "Mr. Anthony at Oxford," *New Republic* vol. 110 (24 April 1944): 578.

[21] Charles A. Brady, "Introduction to Lewis," *America* vol. 71 (27 May 1944): 213–14.

[22] George C. Anderson, "C. S. Lewis: Foe of Humanism," *Christian Century* vol. 64 (25 December 1946): 1563.

That same year, Chad Walsh introduced Lewis to an American audience wider in scope than Brady's readers in *America*. Published in the *Atlantic Monthly*, Walsh's article, "C. S. Lewis, Apostle to the Skeptics," opened with a head-turning hook: "C. S. Lewis is now in the thirteenth year of his one-man campaign to convert the world to Christianity."[23] Indeed, Walsh, perhaps more than any other early commentator, emphasized the Christian mission of Lewis's writerly task, evident in his reading of *Out of the Silent Planet*, a reading that starkly contrasts with the one Brady offered in *America*: "Everyone worships Maleldil, who is none other than the Christian God, and one of the first acts of the Martians is to instruct Ransom in the rudiments of true religion."[24] Walsh was one of the first to observe Lewis's appeal to evangelical Christians, implicitly connecting Lewis's working class roots to the populism of evangelicalism. Walsh even provided a grassroots explanation for Lewis's rising popularity: "It is interesting that Lewis's reputation has spread largely by word of mouth. One reader 'discovers' him, and passes along the tidings to his friends."[25] Walsh concluded with mention of a Lewis-inspired Christian revival: "If Christianity revives in England and America, the odds are that it may bear strong traces of the Gospel according to C. S. Lewis."[26]

Articles in *America*, *Christian Century*, and the *Atlantic Monthly* generated the interest that culminated in a climactic publication event in 1947: Lewis's appearance on the cover of *Time* magazine, a cover story that firmly established Lewis's name in the public sphere. The article referred to Lewis as "one of the most influential spokesmen for Christianity in the English-speaking world." The article was also one of the first to make use of the phrase, "Lewis's devotees."[27] By 1947, then, Lewis had a following, admirers growing in number by word of mouth who were impassioned and motivated by his uniquely presented Christian message: Thus began the cultic following with which Lewis's name is so often associated, a following biblically charged with spreading Lewis's Christian message throughout the public sphere.

It is also important to note that by at least 1950 Lewis's Christian message had a polarizing effect on the public. In a telling 1948 letter,

---

[23] Chad Walsh, "C. S. Lewis, Apostle to the Skeptics," *Atlantic Monthly* (September 1946): 115.

[24] Ibid., 117.

[25] Ibid., 119.

[26] Ibid., 119.

[27] Anonymous, "Religion: Don V. Devil." *Time* (8 Sept. 1947): http://www.time.com/time/magazine/article/0,9171,804196,00.html accessed 6 Nov. 2009.

Dorothy Sayers asked a friend, "Do you like C. S. Lewis' work, or are you one of the people who foam at the mouth when they hear his name?"[28] Because of his message and/or method of conveying it, Lewis had become the sort of public figure who both emphatically attracts and repulses; either response generated the sort of publicity that brands the name of the public intellectual. Whether recapitulated by devotees or attacked by critics, Lewis's arguments echoed throughout the public sphere by 1950.

### d. *Metamorphosis into Transcendent Author: An Illustration from* Time

Chapter 2 showed how most public intellectuals, adopting the conventions of the public sphere, engage in a process I called *de-conversion*: the hyperbolic stripping away of assumptions and biases in an effort to pose as ideologically uncontaminated and thus preeminently reasonable. Abiding by this process earns credibility, for the public intellectual thereby becomes intellectually representative of everybody and nobody, positioned to offer universal truths by shedding the particularities that narrow viewpoints. In chapter 5, I identified a character type, found in all of Lewis's works of fiction, that I labeled the *transcendent character*: a character who possesses an Olympian perspective and trans-mortal knowledge that approximates absolute truth. Operating as Lewis's mouthpiece, ensuring that philosophical and theological truths emerge clearly from the stories, these characters become fictional simulacra of Lewis himself. That is, mediating the knowledge possessed by his transcendent characters, Lewis becomes transcendent himself. He thus adopts the role played more explicitly in his works of non-fiction in which, through the process of de-conversion, he offers eternal truths crystallized in the formulation, "Mere Christianity."

Early issues of *Time* illustrate the evolution of this identity, Lewis's metamorphosis into a transcendent author. In a 1943 review, *The Screwtape Letters* is described as narrowly conceived, confined thematically to a limited context. Screwtape and Wormwood are identified as "strictly Church of England fiends."[29] Screwtape and Wormwood are not here painted as the universal enemies of humankind, acutely aware of the psychological foibles that can render any man or woman—not just those in the Anglican fold—

---

[28] Dorothy Sayer to Mrs. Robert Darby, 31 May 1948, in *The Letters of Dorothy L. Sayers*, vol. 3., ed. Barbara Reynolds (Cambridge: The Dorothy L. Sayers Society, 1998) 135.

[29] Anonymous, "Religion: Sermons in Reverse." *Time* (19 April 1943), online http://www.time.com/time/magazine/article/0,9171,884914,00.html accessed 11 Nov. 2009.

susceptible to temptation. The review makes no gesture toward Screwtape as a transcendent character (or Lewis as a transcendent author); instead, contextualizing *The Screwtape Letters* within one specific theological tradition, the review limits the text's range.

Six months later, *Time* reviewed *Out of the Silent Planet*. The text is there limited to the generic category of "sub-Wellsian fantasy," a category that implies a subaltern, derivative status and therefore confines the scope of the book's message. The reviewer described Thulcandra as being "taken over by a Satanic eldil with Hitleresque ambitions," a phrasing that tends to reduce *Out of the Silent Planet* to a period piece, dependent for its thematic animus on a contingent, historical moment. The review concluded with this prognosis for the character of Ransom: "Back on earth, 'the silent planet,' it must be Ransom's duty to fight these men [Weston and Devine] wherever he found them."[30] This is an interpretation that underestimates the magnitude of Ransom's struggle within the narrative: a battle against mere mortals, not—as the text will later more easily be read—as spiritual warfare of cosmic importance, evident in the Thulcandrian Oyarsa's very revelation that Ransom inhabits the silent planet. The review argues that *Out of the Silent Planet* is a rather mundane text, narrow in its application, lacking the transcendent perspective with which Lewis's name would come to be associated.

The *Time* cover story solidified this association three years later, registering the evolution of Lewis's name. As previously noted, the article referred to Lewis as "one of the most influential spokesman for Christianity in the English-speaking world." Carrying the banner for the faith, Lewis is divested of all local association (Screwtape is no longer merely a Church of England fiend) and embodies mere Christianity. Indeed, as the article pointed out, "Immeasurable ministers quoted Screwtape in sermons and urged it on their congregations. Catholics enjoy it as much as Protestants." The very title of the article—"Don v. Devil"—suggests how Lewis has metamorphosed into a transcendent author. Far from the mundane assessment of *Out of the Silent Planet* in the earlier review, the cover story, with its catchy, alliterative title, likens Lewis to God, battling his cosmic foe within the public sphere. As Part I showed, Lewis appealed to forms and sources of authority that made his defense of Christianity compelling; by

---

[30] Anonymous, "Books: Little Hm." *Time* (Oct. 11, 1943) online http://www.time.com/time/magazine/article/0,9171,774702,00.html accessed 11 Nov. 2009.

1947, he became identified with that very authority within the public sphere and transformed into the transcendent author.

### e. Some Complications: Charged Public Perceptions

The story of Lewis's meteoric rise in the public sphere is not driven by mere acclaim, however. The letter of Dorothy Sayers, quoted above, reveals how Lewis's celebrity status rested on antithetical, visceral responses. Critiques of Lewis constitute complications to his identity, complications that will dog Lewis's public perception throughout his career and, as often happens within the public sphere, will serve as lightning rods that energize both devotees and detractors.

Beginning in the 1940s, Lewis's strategy of making complex ideas understandable for a diverse audience—the fundamental component of the public-intellectual identity—drew criticism that amounted to charges of anti-intellectualism. Reflecting upon the late 1940s, Chad Walsh asserts that British theologians "felt that [Lewis] was a regrettable simplifier who presented the gospel in an overly digestible form to an uncritical public."[31] Cooke served as an exponent of this sentiment; addressing Lewis's *Christian Behavior*, he wrote, "The exposition of every fundamental human problem from 'Social morality' to 'Marriage' and 'Charity,' comes out with a patness that murders the issues it pretends to clarify."[32] A 1944 article in *Ethics* maintained that Lewis's art of translation more conspicuously uncovers the weaknesses of his position than would academic discourse: "An advantage of an amateur exposition of a system of thought is that it may 'let the cat out of the bag,' that is to say, it may fail to achieve the unconsciously artful concealing of difficulties which experts are almost sure to fall into now and then."[33] Expository clarity thus renders Lewis's arguments more vulnerable to attack.

A 1946 article in the *Modern Churchman* faulted Lewis for "simply using the Church as an excuse for his dreary attacks on everything he hasn't bothered to understand. The [*Screwtape*] *Letters* are full of vague references to Liberalism, Humanitarianism, the Life-Force, Modern Art, the Historical Point of View, Psychoanalysis, Progress, etc., all asserted to have their origin in the Evil Principle and to be winning over humanity to the devil in the guise of angels of intellectual light." This article provided a snapshot of

---

[31] Chad Walsh, "Impact on America," in *Light on C. S. Lewis*, ed. Jocelyn Gibb (New York: Harcourt Brace & World, 1965) 109.

[32] Cooke, "Mr. Anthony at Oxford," 579.

[33] Charles Hartshorne, "Philosophy and Orthodoxy," *Ethics* 54/4 (July 1944): 296.

Lewis's developing stature within the public sphere, for its author—R. C. Churchill—has as his polemical animus a growing critical consensus of Lewis's works. In the following sentence, Churchill explained,

> This is what the reviewers are referring to when they say of Mr. Lewis's work in general...that it "traverses so many glibly repeated modern opinions" or "clears away a mass of shoddy assumption." They haven't stopped to think, these reviewers, whether to make a sneer do the work of a demonstration is not pretty "glib" in itself, or whether it is not a "shoddy assumption" to present the case against orthodoxy in a conveniently vague manner which leads to misrepresentation or as a mere reversal of the truth.[34]

Churchill thus attempts to apply the brakes to the C. S. Lewis phenomenon. More importantly, Churchill's polemic shows how "Mr. Lewis's work in general" has generated a debate, drawing more and more people in as it snowballs. In any case, Churchill is one of the first Lewis detractors to register a critique that will become commonplace in later decades: that Lewis misrepresented his opposition in his efforts to present a sleek, compact, winsome argument for a broad audience.

This critique, however, can strangely double as a compliment, a critique that actually commends Lewis to his popular audience. On the one hand, it is Lewis's status as lay theologian—as well as his immense popularity—that draws the ire of professional scholars. Indeed, Lewis implicitly sets himself up for critique in some of his self-effacing pronouncements of his own identity as amateur theologian: in the preface to *Mere Christianity* he refers to himself as "a very ordinary layman"; in Book II, he is "only a layman."[35] However, he goes on to dismiss the philosophy of Sigmund Freud precisely on these grounds—that is, that Freud is an amateur: "And furthermore, when Freud is talking about how to cure neurotics he is speaking as a specialist on his own subject, but when he goes on to talk general philosophy he is speaking as an amateur. It is therefore quite sensible to attend to him with respect in the one case and not in the other—and that is what I do."[36] One might logically conclude that it is likewise sensible to attend to Lewis with respect in the discipline of literary studies but not in the field of theology. Once again, a Sayers letter proves illuminating here, this one written in 1947:

---

[34] R. C. Churchill, "Mr. C. S. Lewis as an Evangelist," *Modern Churchman* vol. 35 (January–March 1946): 335–36.

[35] C. S. Lewis, *Mere Christianity*, viii, 54 (2001 version).

[36] Ibid., 89.

One trouble about C. S. Lewis, I think, is his fervent missionary zeal. I welcome his able dialectic, and he is a tremendous hammer for heretics. But he is apt to think that one should rush into every fray and strike a blow for Christendom, *whether or not one is equipped by training and temperament for that particular conflict.* If one objects that God has put nothing into one's mind on the subject, he darkly hints that one has probably mistaken one's own artistic preferences for the voice of the Holy Ghost. I am not strong on pneumatology, but I know when I am merely talking hot air without conviction, and I refuse to believe that that is the operation of the Holy Ghost. But Lewis seems to feel it wrong to refuse any challenge: if the Bishop of Bootle says that the Christian doctrine of marriage must be upheld, Lewis makes haste to uphold it, although, very obviously, he has no practical experience in the matter.[37]

On the other hand, his status as layman endears Lewis to fellow laypeople. The first sentence in a 1946 review of *That Hideous Strength* in *Time* is suggestive: "England's modern John Bunyan is a wise, witty, sad-faced Fellow of Oxford's Magdalen College named Clive Staples Lewis.[38] Bunyan was, of course, a relatively uneducated moralist; though Lewis might also be called a moralist, he was most certainly not uneducated, though the analogy here might have more resonance if one cedes to the notion (suggested, as we have seen, by detractors) that Lewis's popular writings contain strains of anti-intellectualism. More importantly—and this, I think, is the point of the analogy—Bunyan and Lewis are united in their accomplishments of creating theological bestsellers, books found in the homes of a wide range of mostly ordinary folk. Because he operated as a public intellectual, Lewis wrote books that contain strong populist appeal. Chapter 1 described Lewis's "reverence" for what he called in *Surprised by Joy* the "ordinary man"[39]; even his scholarship showed an attentiveness to the "popular imagination."[40]

The basis of E. L. Allen's 1945 critique of Lewis's theology in *Modern Churchman* obliquely addressed this populist impulse. Allen charged Lewis with equating the "central tradition" in Christianity to "a majority-

---

[37] Dorothy L. Sayers to Brother George Every, 10 July 1947, in *The Letters of Dorothy L. Sayers*, 3rd volume, ed. Barbara Reynolds (Cambridge: The Dorothy L. Sayers Society, 1998) 314. Emphasis added.

[38] Anonymous, "Religion: Theological Thriller," *Time* (10 June 1946): online. http://www.time.com/time/magazine/article/0,9171,853374,00.html accessed 15 Nov. 2009.

[39] *Surprised by Joy*, 193.

[40] C. S. Lewis, *The Allegory of Love: A Study in Medieval Tradition* (Oxford: Oxford University Press, 1936) 312.

judgment" and "mass-opinion."[41] Regardless of whether the accusation is true, Allen's argument helped shape a distinct public perception of Lewis as champion for the everyman, against the corrupting machinations of academic elites. (This perception, I will argue later, helps explain Lewis's popularity in America, where religion has historically assumed a populist shape.) Lewis's position was and is both unique and compelling: teetering on an intellectual tightrope, leaning toward anti-intellectualism by virtue of his popular appeal, ballasted against a fall by his status as preeminent scholar who, to complicate the situation even more, inveighed against the beliefs of most every other scholar as those beliefs were embodied in modernism and its various splinter movements. Lewis could never be dismissed as a charlatan. As a 1946 article in *Time* put it, Lewis was a convert to Christianity from "well-bred skepticism": Lewis earned respect in the public sphere by paying his intellectual dues.[42]

### f. Lewis as "Conservative Iconoclast"

George Watson uses the phrase "conservative iconoclast" to describe Lewis's reputation during the 1940s, a phrase that inscribes a theme of crucial importance to my narrative of Lewis's development as a public intellectual.[43] The oxymoronic title combines Lewis's theological and cultural traditionalism with his tendency to challenge popular assumptions and untested preconceptions. Watson's phrase also overlaps in meaning with a rhetorical strategy, consistently employed by Lewis, that I identified in chapter 3 as the *re-conceptualization*. Rendered an outsider by virtue of his conservative orientation within an antagonistic *milieu*, Lewis is well positioned to challenge deficient or incomplete understandings of Christianity and traditional beliefs, re-conceptualizing the ideas that have been misunderstood by a secular, modern world. Such a rhetorical strategy is powerful for a public intellectual like Lewis, for it makes his traditionalism edgy and unexpected, ripping apart the ideological box into which his opponents would like to consign him.

The 1947 *Time* cover story did much to establish Lewis as conservative iconoclast, forcing an off-balance and intrigued public to reassess its idea of a typical Christian. The article initially accomplished this rather mundanely:

---

[41] E. L. Allen, "The Theology of C. S. Lewis," *Modern Churchman* 34/1 (1945): 319.
[42] Anonymous, "Religion: Excursion from Hell," *Time* (11 March 1946), online. http://www.time.com/tme/magazine/article/0,9171,776709,00.html accessed 16 Nov. 2009.
[43] George Watson, introduction *Critical Thought Series: C.S. Lewis*, in Watson, 3.

by alluding to Lewis's predilection for consuming alcohol. The piece's opening narrative describes Lewis concluding a lecture in a packed auditorium and proceeding briskly "to the nearest pub for a pint of ale"; thus readers are surprised—some scandalized—to learn that "one of the most influential spokesmen for Christianity in the English-speaking world" is hardly a teetotaler.[44] Nor is he hesitant to tackle the subject of sex, as the article went out of its way to emphasize: "Sex in Heaven? Bachelor Lewis is no man to be afraid of that one either." Later, the article described a scene in *The Pilgrim's Regress*—complete with an explicit and titillating quotation from the book—in which the protagonist John has sex with a "Brown Girl." Singling this one scene out of the book surrounds Lewis in controversy, piquing reader interest and unsettling common conceptions about what a Christian is and what Lewis writes about.

---

[44] This scandalized reaction probably intensified as readers learned the details of Lewis's fondness for beer. Robert Havard describes Lewis's profound disappointment when, during a trip they took together, they spent a night in Wales, which outlawed the sale of beer on Sundays: "He was intrigued by the Welsh spoken in the bar on the Saturday night but was not happy about the 'dry' Welsh Sunday that followed. (At that time, though we were unaware of it, total prohibition reigned over the Welsh Sabbath.) We drove ten miles or so to plead that we were 'bona fide travelers'. This would have earned us a drink in Scotland but was no go in Wales.... In the hotel it was quickly apparent that in booking our rooms there because of its site I had overlooked the fact that it was 'dry'. The discovery was followed by one of the most eloquent silences I have ever listened to. It was long before I lived it down" (Robert Havard, "Philia: Jack at Ease," in *Remembering C. S. Lewis: Recollections of Those Who Knew Him*, ed. James Como [San Francisco: St. Ignatius Press, 2005] 366–67). Warren Lewis described a cartographic ambition he shared with his brother: "We discussed how useful it would be if there were a beer map of England, showing the areas controlled by each Beer Baron" (quoted in Humphrey Carpenter, *The Inklings: C. S. Lewis, J. R. R. Tolkien, Charles Williams and Their Friends* [Boston: Houghton Mifflin Company, 1979] 53). Carpenter also reports Lewis's response to Americans who objected to his frequent consumption of alcohol: "When some of Lewis's teetotal American readers heard of his fondness for drinking beer, and asked him how he could square the consumption of alcohol with his Christianity, they received the reply: 'I strongly object to the tyrannic and unscriptural insolence of anything that calls itself a Church and makes teetotalism a condition of membership. Apart from the more serious objection (that our Lord Himself turned water into wine and made wine the medium of the only rite He imposed on all His followers), it is so provincial (what I believe you people call 'small town')" (*The Inklings*, 185). And when Tolkien learned in 1944 that someone used the term "ascetic" to describe Lewis, he responded, "'Ascetic Mr Lewis—!!! I ask you! He put away three pints in a very short session we had this morning, and said he was 'going short for Lent'" (quoted in Hooper, *C. S. Lewis: A Companion and Guide* [San Francisco: HarperSanFrancisco, 1996] 38).

The theme of re-conceptualization becomes a bit more substantive in following paragraphs, one of which offered a phrasing that captures a key rhetorical strategy of the conservative iconoclast: "a strictly unorthodox presentation of strict orthodoxy." Later, Lewis is identified as "one of a growing band of heretics among modern intellectuals: an intellectual who believes in God."[45] Lewis is thus represented as a rarity because of his unique, unpopular position as well as the intellectual climate in which he defends it—to invoke a trope that Lewis himself would later employ to describe himself, he is a unique specimen, one that is both orthodox and unorthodox, traditional and untraditional, a believer and a heretic. These paradoxical formulations account for much of Lewis's fame in the public sphere; the conservative iconoclast proved to be a controversial, provocative, and intriguing identity.

## II. 1950s and 1960s

### a. Popularity

Lewis's growing popularity landed him a surprising place in the pages of *Vogue* in 1951. In a piece titled "Oxford Personalities," the magazine identified Lewis as "one of the most powerful forces in Oxford today as a lecturer." Invoking the conservative-iconoclast persona, the article maintained that "neither [Lewis's] Christianity nor his literary taste has destroyed the healthy, earthy gusto of his pleasure in walking, talking, eating, argument and beer."[46] In a 1954 article in the *Spectator*, John Wain maintained that, with the death of George Orwell, Lewis stood "alone as our major controversial author."[47] In 1955, the *New Statesman and Nation* drew attention to a religious revival occurring in England, a revival that has Lewis as one of its driving forces.[48]

Increasingly, articles in the 1950s and 60s acknowledged Lewis as transcendent author, exerting a lasting influence in the annals of intellectual history. A 1956 review of *Surprised by Joy* in *Time* called Lewis "a High Anglican Lorelei in the gown of a Cambridge don. The author of *The Screwtape Letters* lures not to shipwreck but salvation, and many a troubled

---

[45] Anonymous, "Religion: Don v. Devil."

[46] Anonymous, "Oxford Personalities," *Vogue* 107.11 (November 1951): 100.

[47] John Wain, "Pleasure, Controversy, Scholarship," published in *Critical Thought Series: C.S. Lewis*. Originially published in *The Spector* (1 October 1954).

[48] Tom Driberg, "Lobbies of the Soul," *New Statesman and Nation* vol. 49 (19 March 1955): 393.

20th century secularist who came to scoff at Lewis faith has fallen prey to his urbane style and good sense." The article attributed "universal meaning" to Lewis's final conversion to Christianity, suggesting that he serves as an archetypal Christian, uniting the religious experiences of diverse believers.[49] Thus we see Lewis once again embodying the concepts from the book that helped establish his name: Lewis as mere Christian. Indeed, when *Christianity Today* asked Lewis in 1962, "What imposing obstacles hinder the Christian offensive? What are the main obstructions to Christian initiative?" Lewis responded, "Next to the prevalent materialism, for which we are not to blame, I think the great obstacle lies in the dissentiences not only between Christians but between splinter groups within denominations. While the name Christianity covers a hundred mutually contradictory beliefs, who can be converted to it?"[50] Increasingly, argumentative appeals to Lewis—as *uber*-Christian—score immediate polemical points simply because his position is associated with timelessness and immutable truth.

By the 1950s, Lewis's name was strongly branded; he became more immediately associated with Christianity, thereby inflecting the way all of his texts were read. A 1957 review of *Till We Have Faces* asserted that Lewis "uses all sorts of urbane literary lures" to "scoop unbelievers out of the waters of doubt into the net of faith...." It is probably for this reason that the reviewer wrongly called *Perelandra* an "allegory."[51] The inaccurate generic classification is perhaps more understandable when one considers that allegory is a literary genre that transparently conveys beliefs; since Lewis became readily identified as an exponent of Christianity in the public sphere, a reviewer might conclude that his works of fiction are allegories. (The temptation to generic mis-labeling likewise attached to readings of the Narniad, which many interpreted—and continue to interpret—as allegory.) Name-branding is evident in some of Lewis's obituaries. *Time* wrote that, although "Oxbridge" will remember him as a literary scholar, the "rest of the Christian world" will know him as "a defender of the faith who with fashionable urbanity justified an unfashionable orthodoxy against the

---

[49] Anonymous, "The Reluctant Convert," *Time* (6 February 1956), online. http://www.time.com/time/magazine/article/0,9171,893351,00.html accessed 10 Nov. 2009.

[50] Anonymous, "Scholars Cite Obstacles to Christian Advance," *Christianity Today* 7/1 (12 October 1962): 35.

[51] Anonymous, "Books: Psyche in Paradise," *Time* (28 January 1957), online. http://www.time.com/time/magazine/article/0,9171,809015,00.html accessed 15 Nov. 2009.

heresies of his time."[52] *Christianity Today* commemorated him thusly: "The death of C. S. Lewis is a major loss to the international Christian community. His books, which in paperback alone are approaching a circulation of one million, will continue to point many to the Lord whose joy was the dominant factor in his life and work."[53]

Lewis's popularity spawned one of the first imitations of his work in 1963. *Time* printed a piece written from an infernal perspective, conceptually derived from *The Screwtape Letters,* and titled "Ecumenism: Seven Devilish Ways to Block Church Union."[54] Lewis's popularity also drew followers whose admiration for Lewis inspired critical works that, according to some readers, amounted to little more than hagiographical summary of ideas (a subject tackled fully in the next chapter). Reviewing Clyde Kilby's *The Christian World of C. S. Lewis* for *Christian Century,* A. H. Carter disdainfully observed Kilby's "enthusiasm for his hero and his unswerving presuppositions" and wrote, "Considering that Lewis' impact was due largely to his wit and style, I can but wonder what we gain from Kilby's lengthy paraphrases."[55] Admiration for Lewis eventuated in the first journal attending, at least in part, to the writings of Lewis: the first issue of *Mythlore,* a journal that publishes essays on Tolkien and Charles Williams as well, was printed on 3 January 1969. Others rapidly followed: *The Bulletin of the New York C. S. Lewis Society* in 1969; *The Chronicle of the Portland C. S. Lewis Society* in 1972; *The Lamp-Post,* published by the Southern California C. S. Lewis Society, in 1977; *The Canadian C. S. Lewis Journal* in 1979; and *VII: An Anglo-American Review,* which also prints essays on Tolkien, Williams, Sayers, Owen Barfield, George MacDonald, and G. K Chesterton, in 1980.

### b. Some Responses to the Christian Public Intellectual: Populism and Anti-intellectualism

Attempting to reach as many people as possible and thus writing to a lay audience in an accessible style, Lewis was conceived by some as a simplifier whose populist approach to Christianity amounted to anti-intellectualism. Given the rise of fundamentalism in the early twentieth

---

[52] Anonymous, "Theologians: Defender of the Faith," *Time* (6 December 1963), online. http://www.time.com/time/magazine/article/0,9171,898102,00.html accessed 12 Nov. 2009.

[53] Anonymous, "C. S. Lewis," *Christianity Today* 8/23 (20 December 1963): 23.

[54] Anonymous, "Ecumenicism: Seven Devilish Ways to Block Church Union," *Time* (10 May1963), online. http://www.time.com/time/magazine/article/0,9171,830297,00.html accessed 13 Nov. 2009.

[55] A. H. Carter, "One About, One By," *Christian Century* vol. 82 (1965): 54.

century, Lewis's identity as a distinctly Christian public intellectual becomes susceptible to such charges. Lewis aimed for a simplicity that some identified as a virtue and others read as reductionism. Lewis's obituary in *Time* registers this paradox. Although the piece affirmed that Lewis wrote about religion "with great sophistication," it also asserted that "his was, in a way, a simple faith," conveyed more "with an amateur's love than a professor's learning."[56] A 1966 article in *The Cambridge Quarterly* aligned Lewis with a populist cause, positioned antagonistically against an academic elite; the author observed Lewis's "promptness to defend the common man and common things against the facile contempt of literary intellectuals."[57]

The tension between populist and professional exploded into public controversy with W. Norman Pittenger's 1958 diatribe against Lewis in the pages of the *Christian Century*. Pittenger critiqued Lewis precisely for the qualities that make Lewis a public intellectual: translating complex ideas and arguments into accessible prose for the layperson. Pittenger charged Lewis with substituting "smart superficiality for careful thought, reasonable statement and credible theology."[58] Lewis's response appeared later that year in the magazine; Lewis appealed to his role as "translator...turning Christian doctrine...into the vernacular, into language that unscholarly people would attend to and could understand," people Lewis earlier in his response referred to as "the great mass of my unbelieving fellow-countrymen...." Invoking the divide that draws accusations of anti-intellectualism, Lewis described the strategy of his Christian books: "I was writing *ad populum*, not *ad clerum*."[59] Lewis's explanation did not satisfy Pittenger. In a subsequent letter to the editor of the *Christian Century*, Pittenger faulted Lewis's argument for its reliance on populist appeal to defend his books, "always with an eye out 'to what Jones will take.'" Pittenger concluded, "This kind of thing seems to me very *bad* 'modernism.' The apologist has two obligations laid upon him: to commend the faith, but at the same time to commend it with absolute integrity of mind—with guarding of style, with nuances, with fine shades, with ambiguity, at those places where these things are indicated as essential to a fully truthful

---

[56] Anonymous, "Theologians: Defender of the Faith," *Time* (6 December 1963), online.

[57] W.W. Robson, "C. S. Lewis," *Cambridge Quarterly* vol. 1 (Summer 1966): 261.

[58] W. Norman Pittenger, "Apologist Versus Apologist: A Critique of C. S. Lewis as 'Defender of the Faith,'" *Christian Century* vol. 75 (1 October 1958): 1107.

[59] C. S. Lewis, "Rejoinder to Dr Pittenger," in *God in the Dock: Essays on Theology and Ethics*, ed. Walter Hooper (Grand Rapids: Eerdmans, 1970) 182. Originally published in *Christian Century* vol. 75 (26 November 1958): 1359–61.

presentation of the faith."[60] During this same year, the debate spilled over onto the pages of *Christianity Today*, thanks to an article by Clyde Kilby, who defended Lewis when he wrote, "In all my reading of Lewis one of his very best qualities is his avoidance of technically theological language. It is the very thing which has made him spiritually thrilling to thousands of people around the world. This directness, this 'orthodoxy,' is the element which Dr. Pittenger appears to dislike most."[61] Kilby's claim recapitulates Lewis's own self-defense: an appeal to "thousands of people around the world" necessitates a simplified presentation and language.

Once again, then, we see that the line of argumentation regarding Lewis's theology follows a pattern: Depending upon which side of the debate one stands, Lewis's method of "translation" is either his greatest asset or his most culpable liability—a talent enabling him to bring Christianity to masses of "unscholarly people," on the one hand, or a simplistic polemic that convinces those masses through deception, masking the nuances and complexities to which scholars devote their careers. To complicate matters, even some of Lewis's closest friends belonged to the latter camp. Lyle Dorsett reports that Owen Barfield informed him that J. R. R. Tolkien "was upset that Lewis dedicated *The Screwtape Letters* to him, because Jack had no business writing such a book since he was not trained in theology."[62]

### c. Lewis among the Evangelicals and Fundamentalists

Beginning in the 1950s, Lewis was occasionally associated with fundamentalism and, later, evangelicalism. In *Reflections on the Psalms*, Lewis states that he has "been suspected of being what is called a Funda-mentalist."[63] He theorizes this might be the case because he does not dismiss an ancient document—such as one of the Gospels—as unhistorical simply because it relays the miraculous. However, fundamentalism may share a stronger conceptual kinship with Lewis's Christian position. One component of fundamentalism is adherence to orthodoxy, defined by James Davison Hunter as "a cultural system represent[ing] what could be called a 'consensus through time,'" a consensus parallel to what I described in

---

[60] Pittenger, "Pittenger-Lewis" (letter to the editor), *Christian Century* vol. 75 (24 December 1958): 1486.

[61] Clyde Kilby, "C. S. Lewis and His Critics," *Christianity Today* vol. 3 (8 December 1958): 15.

[62] Lyle W. Dorset, *Seeking the Secret Place: The Spiritual Formation of C. S. Lewis* (Grand Rapids: Brazos Press, 2004) 40 (fn #28).

[63] C. S. Lewis, *Reflections on the Psalms* (San Diego: Harcourt Brace & Company, 1958) 109.

chapter 4 as Lewis's appeal to high tradition. Fundamentalism, Davison Hunter continues, "is orthodoxy in confrontation with modernity," a confrontation assuming the shape of resistance to the "pressures that would dilute the purity of traditional religious expression,"[64] what Lewis calls in *Mere Christianity* "Christianity-and-water."[65] As a traditionalist and thus a reactionary, Lewis follows some of the positional maneuvering inherent in Davison Hunter's definition.

James Houston, who knew Lewis at Oxford, writes that Lewis "was often dubbed a fundamentalist by his friends (although fundamentalist isn't the right word in England—Evangelical is their term—but an Evangelical draws the same dirty looks there as a fundamentalist tends to do here)."[66] In 1955, Tom Driberg of *New Statesman and Nation* distanced Lewis from fundamentalism, but likened him to Billy Graham: "Professor Lewis is not a fundamentalist; but in one important respect his teaching is akin to Billy Graham's. Both of them largely ignore the 'social gospel' of William Temple and other Christians of the last generation. Both of them seem more concerned with the saving of individual souls for eternal life after death than with the creation of a just society on earth."[67]

In 1962, Lewis conducted an interview with a representative of the Billy Graham Evangelistic Association, Ltd. Moments in the interview suggest that Sherwood E. Wirt, who conducted the interview, attempted to nudge Lewis in an evangelical direction when answering questions, phrasing questions in a manner that might compel Lewis to describe his religious experiences in evangelical terms: "Mr. Wirt: Do you feel you made a decision at the time of your conversion? Lewis: I would not put it that way. What I wrote in *Surprised by Joy* was that 'before God closed in on me, I was in fact offered what now appears a moment of wholly free choice.' But I feel my decision was not so important. I was the object rather than the subject in this affair."[68] An emphasis on a defining conversion moment constitutes one fundamental component of evangelicalism. Wirt remained persistent, framing subjects in evangelical terms, though Lewis once again demurred:

---

[64] James Davison Hunter, "Fundamentalism in its Global Contours," in *The Fundamentalist Phenomenon: A View from Within; a Response from Without*, ed. Norman J. Cohen (Grand Rapids: Eerdmans, 1990) 57.

[65] Lewis, *Mere Christianity*, 40.

[66] James Houston, "Reminisces of the Oxford Lewis," in *We Remember C. S. Lewis: Essays & Memoirs*, ed. David Graham (Nashville: Broadman & Holman Publishers, 2001) 136.

[67] Driberg, "Lobbies of the Soul," 394.

[68] Lewis, "Cross Examination," in *God in the Dock*, 260–61.

"Mr. Wirt: Would you say that the aim of Christian writing, including your own writing, is to bring about an encounter with Jesus Christ? Lewis: That is not my language, yet it is the purpose I have in view."[69] By 1962, Lewis had so often been linked with evangelicalism in the public sphere that Wirt's questions did not seem unreasonably leading.

Lewis's association with fundamentalism disturbed Chad Walsh, who disconcertedly asked, "Could it be…that the very brilliance of his writing was at the service of a backward-looking way of facing the primal questions of God, man, society, and the meaning of the Christian faith?"[70] As with other aspects of Lewis's reputation in the public sphere, paradoxes characterize Lewis's affiliation with fundamentalism. Detractors like Kathleen Nott, whose 1958 work *The Emperor's Clothes* is one of the first book-length critiques of Lewis, employ the term as an aspersion.[71] Admirers like Walsh attempt to distance Lewis from fundamentalism, inoculating him from the anti-intellectual strains of the movement. Some fundamentalists are themselves made uneasy by the Lewis connection. The 1960 issue of the *Wheaton Record*, for instance, registered the dangers of Lewis's view of the Bible: that portions of it, as Lewis maintained, may not be historically accurate, though it will still act on the reader as the Word of God. The author, Kenneth Kantzer, wrote, "The question I must return to C. S. Lewis, however, is simply this: 'Does Holy Scripture really "act on me as the Word of God" when I reject its word (what it really intends to teach) as in fact not true?' I do not think so."[72] Lewis's association with fundamentalism thus carries multiple significations, putting some on the offensive and others—for contrasting reasons—on the defensive.

The historical rise of evangelicalism coincided with the prolific heart of Lewis's career. As Mary Michael explains,

Lewis's rise to fame as the "most popular theologian in the English-speaking world," as a writer in *Theology Today* called him, took place at a time when American evangelicalism was entering a new phase. Led by Billy Graham, Carl F. H. Henry, Harold Lindsell, and others after World War II, the movement sought to distance itself from the anti-intellectual aspects of fundamentalism on the one hand and from the liberalism of the

---

[69] Ibid., 261.

[70] Chad Walsh, foreword to *The Image of Man in C. S. Lewis* by William Luther White (Nashville: Abingdon Press, 1969) 7.

[71] Kathleen Nott, *The Emperor's Clothes* (Bloomington: Indiana University Press, 1958) 49.

[72] Kenneth Kantzer, "Dantzer Comments on Lewis," *Wheaton Record* alumni magazine (1960) 1.

mainline denominations on the other.... Lewis's intelligent, articulate defenses of the Christian faith made him an ideal spokesperson.[73]

Barry Hankins dates this new phase of evangelical cultural engagement later than Michael, claiming that in the mid-1960s, "most American evangelicals were still in the throes of fundamentalist separatism, in which Christian public identity manifested itself primarily in an attempt to shun the secular world."[74] However, the evangelical attitude soon changed, thanks in part—as Hankins's thesis holds—to the efforts of Francis Schaeffer. Clearly, Lewis also played a role in invigorating the evangelical mind, helping the movement turn an intellectual corner. Mark Noll writes that "Lewis's writing has constituted the single most important body of Christian thinking for American Evangelicals in the twentieth century."[75]

Lewis's spiritually rigorous, uncompromising theology helps explain his appeal to evangelicals. Roger Finke and Rodney Stark show that mainline denominations lost membership numbers during the second half of the twentieth century because of a weakened doctrinal commitment: "as denominations have modernized their doctrines and embraced temporal values, they have gone into decline." Conversely, evangelicalism thrived not only because of its unflagging commitment to doctrinal purity but because of the spiritual and moral demands it places on its members, the sort of dynamic that Finke and Starke identify as central to a proper understanding of religious sociology, rendered in the following axiom: "People tend to value religion on the basis of how costly it is to belong—the more one must sacrifice in order to be in good standing, the more valuable the religion."[76]

The cost of sacrifice operates as a leitmotif in Lewis's Christian books, aligning them in that respect with the demanding theological and moral orientation of evangelicalism. Screwtape, for instance, boils Christian sexuality down to a non-negotiable dualism: "The Enemy's [God's] demand on humans takes the form of a dilemma: *either* complete abstinence *or* unmitigated monogamy." Screwtape further makes clear that a breach of this demand carries eternal consequences: "The truth is that wherever a man lies

---

[73] Mary Michael, "Our Love Affair with C. S. Lewis," *Christianity Today* 37/12 (25 October 1993): 34.

[74] Barry Hankins, *Francis Schaeffer and the Shaping of Evangelical America* (Grand Rapids: Eerdmans, 2008) xv.

[75] Mark Noll, *The Scandal of the Evangelical Mind* (Grand Rapids: Eerdmans, 1994) 218.

[76] Roger Finke and Rodney Stark, *The Churching of America, 1776–1990: Winners and Losers in Our Religious Economy* (New Brunswick: Rutgers University Press, 2002) 238.

with a woman, there, whether they like it or not, a transcendental relation is set up between them which must be eternally enjoyed or eternally endured."[77] The enormous pressure and struggle to adhere to "complete abstinence or unmitigated monogamy," along with the guilt that attends failure, exemplify Finke and Starke's theorem for religious success: "religious organizations are stronger to the degree that they impose significant costs in terms of sacrifice and even stigma upon their members."[78] Sacrifice plays a central role in *The Great Divorce*, for the crux of nearly every scene in the foothills of heaven concerns a demand for self-sacrifice; every Ghost that wishes to continue to heaven must undergo a painful transformation that often begins with some form of self-denial. For Lewis, the process of sanctification must be laborious and demanding, perhaps explaining in part his belief in purgatory.[79] Lewis's great metaphor for transformation finds expression in the character of Eustace Scrubb, who in *The Voyage of the* Dawn Treader becomes a dragon, emblematizing his mean and selfish disposition. To become a little boy again, Eustace must submit to the razor-sharp claws of Aslan, who tears Eustace's dragonish skin to pieces, peeling off layer upon layer until Eustace is restored to normal. This process suggests how, for Lewis, salvation comes at a tremendous cost, entailing demands that appeal to the uncompromising theological and moral system of evangelicalism.

Lewis's emphasis on mere Christianity also helps explain his appeal to evangelicals. Evangelicalism has found the highest concentration of representatives in mega-churches and in an assortment of non-denominational churches, all of which, by virtue of their identities as non-denominational, tend to de-historicize Christian theology, thereby circumventing the difficulties that arise from denominational differences. Resonating with Lewis's famous phrase, evangelical theology is a transcendent theology, elevated above the contingencies of history and the messiness of denominational difference. Evangelicals emphasize the fundamentals of the faith and most of

---

[77] C. S. Lewis, *The Screwtape Letters* (San Francisco: HarperSanFrancisco, 2001) 93 and 96. It is probably also the case that Lewis's demanding stance particularly on sexuality attracts evangelicals. As Robert D. Putnam and David E. Campbell show, "...views on premarital sex (rather than abortion or homosexuality) are the most robustly associated with evangelicalism, suggesting that what sparked the growth of evangelicalism was less hot-button politics than deeply personal moral concerns" (*American Grace: How Religion Divides and Unites Us* [New York: Simon & Schuster, 2010] 119).

[78] Finke and Stark, *The Churching of America*, 238.

[79] See C. S. Lewis, *Letters to Malcolm: Chiefly on Prayer* (San Diego: Harcourt Brace, 1964) 109.

the doctrines that have stood the test of time, all of which Lewis intends to crystallize within Mere Christianity. Doing so, of course, evades the changes and developments that the church has undergone over the centuries. Alan Bede Griffiths insightfully notes that Lewis "...had very little sense of the Church as a living organism, growing by stages through the centuries."[80]

### d. C. S. Lewis in America

Lewis's popularity among evangelicals—beginning in the 1970s—cannot be divorced from his popularity in America in general. Evangelicalism is a distinctly American phenomenon, and as this section will show, certain qualities in the American religious experience harmonized well with Lewis's work as a public intellectual. According to Walsh, the two decades from 1943 to 1963 witnessed a cultural phenomenon during which Lewis "had an impact on American religious thinking and indeed on the American religious imagination which has been very rarely, if ever, equaled by any other modern writer."[81] The sensation that Lewis created in the United States contrasted with the lukewarm reception Lewis received in his home country. In Adam Gopnick's phrasing, Lewis in America is a "saint revered and revealed," while Lewis in Britain is a "slightly embarrassing polemicist, who made joke-vicar broadcasts on the BBC, but who also happened to write a few very good books about late-medieval poetry and inspire several good students."[82]

The popularity of C. S. Lewis in America constitutes a glaring irony. Lewis knew little about America and thus the readership that claimed him as its own. In a 1944 letter, Lewis declares himself to be "quite ignorant of modern American letters"[83]; and in a letter written eight years later to an American, he admits, "I seem to be as ignorant of America as you are of India."[84] Moreover, on those occasions when America is not the object of Lewis's befuddlement, it is occasionally the direction toward which he casts

---

[80] Alan Bede Griffiths, "The Adventure of Faith," in *Remembering C. S. Lewis: Recollections of Those Who Knew Him*, ed. James T. Como (San Francisco: Ignatius Press, 2005) 90.

[81] Chad Walsh, "Impact on America," 106.

[82] Adam Gopnick, "Prisoner of Narnia: How C. S. Lewis Escaped," *New Yorker*, 21 November 2005, accessed 8 November 2009, http://www.newyorker.com/archive/2005/11/21/051121crat_atlarge.

[83] C. S. Lewis to Charles Brady, 29 October 1944, *The Collected Letters of C. S. Lewis*, vol. 2, *Books, Broadcasts, and the War, 1931–1949*, ed. Walter Hooper (San Francisco: HarperSanFrancisco, 2004) 631.

[84] C. S. Lewis to Vera Matthews, 22 March 1952, *Collected Letters*, 3:172.

aspersions. Toward the end of World War I, Lewis called it a pity that a writer as inspiring as Ralph Waldo Emerson was American; years later, Lewis bemoans a pupil who, on top of her ignorance, is an American; even as late as post-World War II, Lewis's American student George Bailey affirmed that "it was widely rumored that Lewis did not like Americans."[85] Despite all of this, American devotion to Lewis remained unabated, a fact that tormented Warren Lewis after the death of his brother, as recorded in a journal entry: "CSL's home, complete with the great man's brother, is now a show piece for any American who happens to visit Oxford…. And what is the worst of it is that this situation is going to continue for the rest of my life…. I suppose that on my death-bed—or at any rate on the day before—I shall have some verbose American standing over me and lecturing on some little observed significance of Jack's work. Oh, damn, damn, DAMN!"[86]

So what accounts for Lewis's popularity in America? This section theorizes that Lewis's role as public intellectual resonated with the populist character of American religion. By attempting to win the common man and woman over to Christianity by appealing to their reason and better sense, Lewis unintentionally participated in a rhetorical maneuver that was central to the religious economy of America since its founding.

In *The Democratization of American Christianity*, Nathan Hatch characterizes the basic impulse of American Christianity as populist, a word he chooses "because it suggests leadership that is deliberate in championing the interests of common people against professional expertise and elite institutions."[87] The vitality of religion among ordinary people distinguishes the United States from other Western countries: "Deep and powerful undercurrents of democratic Christianity…insure that churches in this land do not withhold faith from the rank and file." Thus, contends Hatch, "religious populism…remains among the oldest and deepest impulses in American life."[88] The final court of arbitration in matters political, legal, or religious resides with the people: "persons who derive their authority not from their education or stature within major denominations, but from the democratic art of persuasion."[89] Finke and Stark trace this populism to religious disestablishment. Having suffered religious persecution in England

---

[85] Quoted in Schofield, *In Search of C. S. Lewis*, ed. Stephen Schofield (South Plainfield NJ: Bridge Publishing, 1983) 174.

[86] Quoted in A. N. Wilson, *C. S. Lewis: A Biography* (New York: Norton, 1990) 303.

[87] Nathan O. Hatch, *The Democratization of American Christianity* (New Haven: Yale University Press, 1989) 244–45.

[88] Ibid., 5.

[89] Ibid., 211.

and seeking religious freedom in the new land, early Americans realized "there was no other safe way to proceed but to create an unregulated, free market, religious economy."[90] Now a matter of choice, not compulsion, church affiliation becomes an issue of contestation in a highly competitive market. Whereas under the old regime church-goers attended the church in their assigned parish, the "unregulated, free market, religious economy" drives churches to compete for parishioners: and hence the rise of religious populism wherein religious claims are formulated to appeal to the widest swath of the people as possible.

This is the narrative Mark Noll relates, emphasizing the pressure placed upon denominations in this new religious economy: "[The denominations] had to convince individuals, first, that they should pay attention to God and, second, that they should do so in *their* church and not elsewhere. The primary way the churches accomplished this task was through the techniques of revival—direct, fervent address aimed at convincing, convicting, and enlisting the individual." Disestablishment and revivalism, Noll claims, gave American Christianity its dynamism, from which it gathers and maintains its current momentum: "As it was in the days of [George] Whitefield, so it has been in the two centuries since. The most visible evangelicals, with the broadest popular influence, have been public speakers whose influence rested on their ability to communicate a simple message to a broad audience."[91] Elsewhere, Noll explains that the "most popular and influential leaders among evangelicals are those who have mastered the ability to sway mass audiences. And while the evangelical community respects its scholars, it also expects them to communicate the results of research in a style that is both understandable and supports treasured beliefs."[92]

Lewis's project as a Christian public intellectual finds purchase in this environment of religious populism. Although clearly no fervid revivalist—in a preface to a work by Austin Farrer, Lewis regards with some disdain what he calls "labored *bonhomie,* emotional rhetoric, [and] conventional pietisms of phrase"[93]—Lewis does flesh out Christian truth claims (in non-fiction) and Christian suppositions (in fiction) in a register attuned to the heartbeat of American Christianity; in Hatch's phrase, Lewis was a master of the

---

[90] Finke and Stark, *The Churching of America,* 60.

[91] Noll, *The Scandal of the Evangelical Mind,* 66, 61.

[92] Mark Noll, *Between Faith and Criticism: Evangelicals, Scholarship, and the Bible in America.*
(Grand Rapids: Baker Book House, 1991) 151.

[93] C. S. Lewis, preface to *A Faith of Our Own,* by Austin Farrer (Cleveland: World Publishing Company, 1960) 8.

"democratic art of persuasion," the polemical strategy of appealing to the common man and woman. As Part 1 explained in detail, such was Lewis's strategy as a distinctly public intellectual. He embodied Noll's description of the type of evangelical who has historically exerted the strongest influence: "public speakers whose influence rested on their ability to communicate a simple message to a broad audience."

In the next chapter, I explore how Lewis's public reception evolved with the turn of the millennium, as evangelicals claimed him as their own while the public sphere continued to disintegrate, creating a charged, politicized atmosphere, pushing Lewis into an arena of ideological contestation.

# 11

# The Evolution of C. S. Lewis's Reputation
## in the Public Sphere, 1970–2010

### I. 1970s and 1980s

*a. Popularity*

Some perceptions suggest that Lewis's popularity went into decline soon after his death in 1963 but revived in the early 1970s. Significantly due to the work of Walter Hooper, who brought out numerous edited volumes on Lewis during this period, including *Poems* (1964), *Of Other Worlds* (1966), *Christian Reflections* (1967), *Narrative Poems* (1969), *Selected Literary Essays* (1969), and *God in the Dock* (1970), Lewis's name never disappeared from the public sphere. As Hooper himself wrote, "You must remember that more than anything I wanted to keep Lewis' books in print and before the public."[1] Nevertheless, reviewing Hooper's *God in the Dock* in 1970, *Christian Century* dismissively declared that it was "too late to capitalize on the C. S. Lewis fad."[2] Peter Kreeft observes that when he first proposed a longer version of his book, *C. S. Lewis: A Critical Essay*, in the late 1960s, his original publisher replied, "'We like your book, but we think Lewis' star has risen and is about to set. His day is over. No one will be reading C. S. Lewis twenty years from now.'"[3] Lewis's place in the public sphere thus seemed to be in question.

Besides Hooper's editorial work, Charles Colson's conversion to Christianity in 1973 engendered renewed interest in Lewis, for Colson asserted that *Mere Christianity* played a significant role in his coming to faith. In 1974, *Newsweek* reported, "In the last 18 months alone, Americans have bought nearly 100,000 copies of 'Mere Christianity,' the work that helped convert Colson.... Clubs of Lewis cultists have sprouted across the nation,

---

[1] Walter Hooper, "Editing C. S. Lewis," in *C. S. Lewis: Views from Wake Forest*, ed. Michael Travers (Wayne PA: Zossima Press, 2008) 18.

[2] Anonymous, "This Week," *Christian Century* 87 (1970): 1566.

[3] Peter Kreeft, *C. S. Lewis: A Critical Essay* (Front Royal VA: Christendom College Press, 1988) 5.

and at campus bookstores his works have become best-selling fare."[4] After this period, Lewis's popularity seemed to skyrocket. In 1977, *Time* reported, "Fourteen years after his death at 64, this Pascal of the Space Age is the only author in English whose Christian writings combine intellectual stature with bestseller status."[5] That same year, Hooper spearheaded a tour in support of a film he helped produced titled *Through Joy and Beyond*, a documentary intended to introduce people to the life and writings of Lewis.

By the 1980s, Lewis scholarship continued to multiply, testifying to the popularity Lewis enjoyed among many Christian scholars. The *New Oxford Review* reported in 1982: "Surely this is the moment of C. S. Lewis scholarship. In addition to the already large accumulation of studies on Lewis, hardly a month passes that does not leave a fresh view of his life and writings."[6] Lewis scholarship received more legitimation with the 1987 publication of Joe Christopher's monograph on Lewis in the Twayne English Author Series. Registering Lewis's importance among English authors, the publication of Christopher's book served notice that Lewis's popularity was no fad and that Lewis would stand the test of time. As Doris Myers writes, Christopher's book "...seemed to confirm that Lewis belonged in the canon of English authors."[7]

Often, the source of scholarly interest in Lewis mirrored the source of popular interest: Lewis's defense of Christianity, which by the 1970s branded his name as public intellectual. For both casual readers and scholars, Lewis's books operated as *the* voice of faith against secularism in a spiritually embattled world hurtling toward the apocalypse. A few sentences from Martha Sammons's 1980 book on the Ransom trilogy illustrate this attitude: "The dangers Lewis warned were approaching back in the forties are becoming realities in our world. For the myth of Deep Heaven is a true story—the story of you, your earth past and future, the choices you will make, and what side you will be on in a present and worsening battle...."[8] In 1983, when a science-fiction/fantasy convention in Chicago featured an exhibit on the Inklings, *Christianity Today* viewed the event as an evangelism

---

[4] Merrill Sheils, "Chuck Colson's Leveler," *Newsweek* vol. 84 (9 September 1974): 72.

[5] Ross Douthat, "The Apocalypse, Rated PG," *Atlantic Monthly* (May 2005): 36.

[6] Joe McClatchey, "The Praise of God in C. S. Lewis Scholarship," *New Oxford Review* (June 1982): 10.

[7] Doris T. Myers, *C. S. Lewis in Context* (Kent: Kent State University Press, 1994) x.

[8] Martha Sammons, *A Guide through C. S. Lewis' Space Trilogy* (Westchester IL: Cornerstone Books, 1980) 10–11.

opportunity for "concerned Christians…to witness to a more positive, redeeming presence."[9]

Attempts to witness this presence to the larger world (and encourage others to do the same) characterized much of the scholarly appropriation of Lewis in the 1980s, a presence that continues to characterize Lewis conferences to this day. During his address at a 2007 Lewis conference, for instance, James Como extended a metaphor that captures Lewis's appeal to Christian scholars, unifying them around their fundamental religious commitments, offering them a respite from a secularized academic world, and emboldening them to re-enter that antagonistic world with the enduring witness and presence of Lewis:

> …whenever meeting in conference on the subject of C. S. Lewis I delight in imagining my fellow conferees as medieval monks and nuns and our venue as a monastery. Consider: Are we not surrounded by a world largely bereft of manners and morality? Do we not seek to till that landscape so as to replenish it and thus grow the old faith anew? Do we not seek links to other enclaves? Moreover, is not Lewis rather like our Father Abbot Jack who, providing purpose and direction, above all cultivates that indispensable fruit which is Hope, thereby motivating us to even greater cultivation? That Lewis we know best…is the father abbot whom we commonly spirit from monastery to monastery, now and again dispatching him into the larger world (the West End, Broadway, PBS, Hollywood) for what good he may do.[10]

Over the years then, monographs on Lewis as well as Lewis societies, conferences, and journals helped establish Lewis as a public intellectual, entrenching Lewis's religious position, championing Lewis's method of appropriating and conveying authority, and elevating Lewis into transcendent author.

It is no wonder, then, that Kathryn Lindskoog caused an uproar in 1988 with the publication of *The C. S. Lewis Hoax*, a book developed from a 1978 essay titled "Some Problems in C. S. Lewis Scholarship," published in *Christianity and Literature*. In both the article and book, Lindskoog called into question the integrity of Walter Hooper, Lewis's editor, suggesting that Hooper, among other acts of malfeasance, wrote a fragment called *The Dark Tower*, subsequently published in *The Dark Tower and Other Stories* (1977),

---

[9] Steve Lawhead, "What Do C. S. Lewis and the Faith Have in Common with this Crew?" *Christianity Today* (25 November 1983): 38.

[10] James Como, "Culture and Public Philosophy: Another C. S. Lewis (Being Finally an Exhortation)," in *C. S. Lewis: Views from Wake Forest*, ed. Travers, 34–35.

and attributed it to Lewis. The crisis this book provoked within the Lewis industry will be explored in chapter 13. For now, it is sufficient to note that Lindskoog's questions and claims about forgery strike at the heart of the C. S. Lewis phenomenon, for Lewis's rise as a public intellectual was significantly propelled by his methods of harnessing and conveying authority beyond reproach (as argued in Part 1). In addition, his appeal to what I called *high tradition*, the collective wisdom of the Western world, reveals the logocentric orientation of Lewis's Christian position, the implicit and pervasive faith in language and discursive reason. Moreover, Lewis's ultimate and final authority is the Bible, and though Lewis never adhered to the doctrine of inerrancy, his belief in the Bible as a sacred text sensitizes him to the reliability of the written word—a sensitivity that becomes exaggerated in the public sphere as Lewis admirers included in increasing numbers evangelicals, who *do* adhere to biblical inerrancy and become increasingly associated with Lewis. Consequently, while any book like Lindskoog's would be provocative, her analysis proved particularly combustible because the questions she raised about authority and reliability overlap with the very formula for Lewis's success as public intellectual.

*b. Some Responses to the Public Intellectual: Populism and Anti-Intellectualism*

Critiques of Lewis in the '70s and '80s continued to fall along populist and anti-intellectual lines. A 1977 article in the *Christian Century* drew attention to "a characteristic of style [in Lewis's writing] less agreeable to the contemporary ear. I refer to a certain flippant dismissal of modern challenges to religious belief as simply lapses of good taste and reasonableness."[11] Even the scholar who helped introduce Lewis to America, Chad Walsh, found some of Lewis's arguments "flippant." Reflecting on Lewis's famous *reductio ad absurdum* argument in *Mere Christianity*, the so-called trilemma that if Jesus Christ were not God himself then the only alternatives are that he was insane or evil, Walsh wrote, "It is always possible that God can count beyond two."[12]

In 1983, the *Christian Century* once again printed an article critical of Lewis, this one considerably more scathing. Assessing Lewis's *Reflections on the Psalms*, Stanley N. Rosenbaum maintained that the "book's tone reflects

---

[11] Lawrence Cunningham, "C. S. Lewis: The Screwtape Letters," *Christian Century* (2 March 1977): 190.

[12] Chad Walsh, *Literary Legacy of C. S. Lewis* (New York: Harcourt, Brace, Jovanovich, 1979) 203.

the same smug triumphalism that is found in Lewis's better-known works." This triumphalism, Rosenbaum suggested, proceeds from thin scholarship that Lewis passes off as a virtue: the populist appeal of a layperson writing for his fellow laypeople. Faulting Lewis for not reading Hebrew—the very language of the book of Psalms—Rosenbaum wrote,

> Lewis did not read Hebrew, a fact with which he is honest enough to begin his book. He immediately goes on to propose that this very lack of scholarly training makes him better able to communicate the ideas in Psalms to others as amateur as himself. The pupil, he says, can often teach other pupils better than the master can. So Lewis's lack of Hebrew is really a virtue? (Would he apply this maxim to all fields of knowledge or only to the Old Testament? If the former, one wonders why he chose teaching instead of some more useful employment.)[13]

Rosenbaum's critique covered familiar territory, revealing, once again, how in the public sphere, amateur scholarly status can both strengthen and weaken credibility. The *Christian Century* article thus further positioned Lewis's reputation in a paradoxical position: well-credentialed Oxford don who is also an anti-intellectual populist.

These antithetical identities polarized assessments of Lewis's work, a polarization that continues to characterize Lewis's public perception. Lewis admirers, especially those without theological and philosophical training as well as those who were already committed to Lewis's Christian position, often found Lewis's authoritative defense of Christianity unanswerable, so winsomely and brazenly defended in the secularized public sphere. In 1987, Richard Harries registered concerns over this sort of populist appeal: One reason for "Lewis's continuing popularity is that he wrote with authority; and there lies a danger. For in an uncertain age people are looking for those who speak or write with confidence. Anxious, bewildered and uncertain themselves, they look to some authoritative voice. Lewis had such a voice. But the problem, dare one say it, is that there has been too much uncritical acceptance of Lewis's thought in Christian circles."[14]

Perhaps no one stemmed the tide of this uncritical acceptance as John Beversluis, who in 1985 offered a thorough and methodical critique of Lewis in *C. S. Lewis and the Search for Rational Religion*, subsequently revised and reprinted in 2007. What Beversluis called "the increasing crop of almost

---

[13] Stanley N. Rosenbaum, "Our Own Silly Faces: C. S. Lewis on the Psalms," *Christian Century* (18 May 1983): 486.

[14] Richard Harries, *C. S. Lewis: The Man and His God* (Wilton CT: Morehouse-Barlow, 1987) 14.

wholly uncritical studies of Lewis the thinker"[15] constitutes a springboard for the book, which attempts to deflate much of the Lewis fervor, unflinchingly dissecting most of Lewis arguments and finding them wanting.

Beversluis's book has as its animus Lewis's populist appeal; Beversluis noted, "Seldom, too, has an apologist come across to his readers as a person with whom they could so immediately identify."[16] Beversluis identifies Lewis as a "popularizer" in the opening pages of the book.[17] Beversluis wrote as a professional philosopher, and thus his critique unavoidably exploited the argumentative weaknesses that arise from Lewis's approach as a public intellectual. The confidence of which Harries spoke, coupled with Lewis's tendency toward the straw-man fallacy, thus became an obvious point of Beversluis's attack: "Rarely does he set forth the alternatives to his own view in philosophically recognizable form. His tendency is to rush into battle, misrepresent the opposition, and then demolish it. The demolition is often swift and the victory decisive, but the view refuted is seldom a position anyone actually holds."[18] Lewis, in short, fails to acknowledge the complexities that problematize his refutation of naturalism. To re-invoke Pittenger's 1958 phrase, Lewis's failure is one of "smart superficiality." Of course, Beversluis's critique is many-sided, faulting Lewis for much more than committing informal fallacies of logic. For my purposes, its importance lay in its very premise: a professional philosopher mercilessly critiquing the works of a public intellectual and challenging Lewis's populist appeal, a critique that foregrounds the disconnect between academic scholarship and the public sphere. The trajectory of Pittenger's 1958 critique found its end point, its logical conclusion, in Beversluis's 1985 book.

### c. Lewis among the Evangelicals

In their magisterial study of religiosity in America, Robert D. Putnam and David E. Campbell identify two aftershocks that follow the initial shock of the long 1960s, during which conventional sexual morality was upended and traditions in general were challenged. These social movements of the '60s provoked a political reaction in the form of the Religious Right. As Putman and Campbell explain, "...during the 1970s and 1980s this part of the American religious spectrum attracted attention, energy, adherents, and

---

[15] John Beversluis, *C. S. Lewis and the Search for Rational Religion* (Grand Rapids: Eerdmans, 1985) xiv.

[16] Ibid., 4.

[17] Ibid.

[18] Ibid., 41.

eventually political prominence. Thus, the rise of evangelicals and then of the Religious Right constituted the first aftershock to the tumult of the 1960s."[19] It is probably no coincidence that Lewis's re-ascent to popularity in the 1970s overlapped with this first shock; Lewis's resurgence in popularity overlapped with the mobilization of the Religious Right: Organizations of crucial importance to evangelicals—Focus on the Family, Chuck Colson's Prison Fellowship, and the Moral Majority—were all founded in the 1970s.[20] Stephen J. Nichols shows how, during this decade, "American religio-politico rhetoric took a decisive evangelical turn..."[21] C. S. Lewis studies took a decisive evangelical turn during this period as well.

Articles on Lewis in *Christianity Today* illustrate this evangelical turn. As we have seen, reviews of Lewis in the *Christian Century*, a periodical attracting a predominantly mainline Protestant, non-evangelical readership, printed articles critical—some even scathingly critical—of Lewis. Conversely, *Christianity Today*, a pro-evangelical magazine, heaped accolades upon Lewis, emblematizing the evangelical appropriation of Lewis. In a 1973 article commemorating the ten-year anniversary of Lewis's death, Calvin Linton acknowledged the monumental influence Lewis wielded on the evangelical world: "Few literary scholars, even the best, do more than add facts to our body of knowledge. Lewis has altered our sensibility, the *way* we think about things; he has given us words and phrases by which we grasp vital ideas; he has given us a pattern of feeling within which we better comprehend artistic and Christian truths. He is one of those rare writers who leave us different from what we were before we read him."[22]

Six years later, Donald T. Williams penned an article for *Christianity Today* expressly attempting to align Lewis with "conservative Christianity." In fact, Williams' article betrays a certain possessiveness, endeavoring to wrest Lewis from the classification of Chad Walsh, who in a 1969 foreword to William Luther White's *Image of Man in C. S. Lewis*, called Lewis "a more

---

[19] Robert D. Putnam and David E. Campbell, *American Grace: How Religion Divides and Unites Us* (New York: Simon & Schuster, 2010) 81. The second shock will be discussed in the conclusion to this chapter.

[20] Focus on the Family in 1977, Prison Fellowship in 1976, and the Moral Majority in 1979.

[21] Stephen J. Nichols, *Jesus Made in America: A Cultural History from the Puritans to the Passion of the Christ* (Downers Grove IL: IVP Academic, 2008) 198.

[22] Calvin Linton, "C. S. Lewis Ten Years Later," *Christianity Today* 28/3 (9 November 1973) 4.

poetic [Rudolph] Bultmann."[23] (Recall Walsh fretted over Lewis's connections with fundamentalism, perhaps offering this analogy as a corrective.) Walsh's association of Lewis with a liberal theologian raised Williams's ire, resulting in an article in which Williams attempts to situate Lewis in the evangelical camp. Although acknowledging Lewis's decidedly un-evangelical view of Scripture, Williams affirmed, "Lewis' loyalty to true Christianity and his value to the conservative cause lie in his statement and defense of positions even more basic than inerrancy. It was Lewis's belief in the *exclusivity of truth* and his brilliant defense of it, that finally make nonsense of all attempts to reinterpret him as a modern man at heart."[24] And in his rousing conclusion, Williams reassures his evangelical readers that Lewis was one of them: "Who was the real C. S. Lewis? We may say with confidence that he was the Lewis whom conservatives have long known and loved and whom liberals find embarrassing and wish to explain away."[25]

Lewis's evangelical appropriation did not go unnoticed in the secular press. The *Los Angeles Times* reported in 1979: "Evangelical Protestants particularly admire Lewis, perhaps because of his born-again style switch in adult life from atheism to fervent faith."[26] But Lewis's association with evangelicalism likewise created counter-reactions among evangelicals themselves. Like Williams, Jerry Walls in 1981 recognized the importance of Lewis to evangelicals—he wrote, "It is a safe guess that more people have read Lewis than could even identify, say, Athanasius"—but unlike Williams, Walls found it difficult to harmonize Lewis's view of Scripture with evangelicalism: "Now that it is becoming more and more public that Lewis did not believe in inerrancy, evangelicals may have to distance themselves from him if they are to be consistent."[27] Lewis's acceptance of the theory of evolution put him at odds with some evangelicals. Writing for the journal *Biblical Creation*, David Watson stated, "C. S. Lewis, like the Taj Mahal, is greater than all the photographs and eulogies. Great, but not infallible." Watson went on to explain that "how even his brilliant mind could be

---

[23] Luther White, The Image of Man in C. S. Lewis (Nashville: Abingdon Press, 1969) 8.

[24] Donald T. Williams, "A Closer Look at the 'Unorthodox' Lewis: A More Poetic Bultmann?" *Christianity Today* (21 December 1979): 24.

[25] Ibid., 27.

[26] John Dart, "Questions Raised on C. S. Lewis Lore," *Los Angeles Times*, 24 March 1979, 30.

[27] Jerry Walls, "C. S. Lewis and Evangelical Ambivalence," *Wittenburg Door* 62 (August–September 1981): 20–21.

confused when trying to reconcile two irreconcilables—the theory of Evolution and the truth of Scripture."[28]

## II. 1990s and 2000s

### a. Popularity

By the 1990s, Lewis's reputation had taken on a life of its own, wielded by both admirers and critics for various, often diametrically opposed and politically charged, purposes. In 1993, Kath Filmer offered an idea of the range of these purposes: "Acclaimed on the one hand as a twentieth-century 'apostle', despised as a thundering fundamentalist, made patron saint of some right wing think-tanks, denounced as a reactionary, Lewis has left a literary legacy which cannot be ignored."[29] Filmer's proclamation indicates the extent to which the public sphere had splintered by the '90s, fragmented by a vitriolic language that came to characterize political discourse and the so-called culture wars (see chapter 6). Indeed, this section will explore the perception that Lewis was politicized, enlisted in the culture wars by his growing evangelical readership.

Lewis's popularity energized the politicization. In 1999, Lewis's Chronicles of Narnia appeared on *Time* magazine's "Best of the Century" list as runner-up to E. B. White's *Charlotte's Web* as the best children's book.[30] In 2005, *Time* dubbed Lewis the "Christian Answer Man," reporting that HarperSanFrancisco sold 843,000 copies of his adult titles in 2005, twice as many as in 2001. The article also commented on the cultic following increasingly associated with Lewis, cataloging a list of the famous people whose lives Lewis changed: Charles Colson, Domino's Pizza billionaire Thomas Monaghan, National Human Genome Research Institute leader Francis Collins, and megapastor Rick Warren.[31] In 1993, *Christianity Today* conducted a reader's poll that included the following question: "What book (other than the Bible) has had the most significant impact on your Christian

---

[28] David Watson, "C. S. Lewis and Evolution," *Biblical Creation* 7/19 (Spring 1985): 9.

[29] Kath Filmer, *The Fiction of C. S. Lewis: Mask and Mirror* (New York: St. Martin's Press, 1993) 1.

[30] Anonymous, "The Best of the Century," *Time* (31 December 1999), online. http://www.time.com/time/magazine/article/0,9171,993039,00. Html accessed 15 Nov. 2009.

[31] David Van Biema, "Beyond the Wardrobe," *Time* (30 October 2005), online. http://www.time.com/time/magazine/article/0,9171,1124316,00. Html accessed 15 Nov. 2009.

Life?" *Mere Christianity* received more than twice as many votes as any other book, a testament to the devotion of Lewis's evangelical readership.[32]

Lewis's popularity, name branding, and evangelical appropriation was the tinderbox ignited by the publication of A. N. Wilson's controversial 1990 biography, *C. S. Lewis*. I will explore the book's place within the Lewis industry in chapter 13. For now, one need only note that not since Beversluis's *C. S. Lewis and the Search for Rational Religion* had a book on Lewis generated so much publicity, at least in part because it rankled Lewis's ardent admirers. The opening sentences of *Time*'s review of Wilson's biography pitches the compelling storyline, one that becomes increasingly popular in the secular press: "To a substantial battalion of devotees, Clive Staples Lewis—the Christian apologist, children's fabulist and Oxbridge don who died in 1963—was a contemporary saint…. But difficulties face those who would canonize the author of *Mere Christianity* and the Narnia chronicles. A. N. Wilson, a British writer who has previously taken sensitive measure of Milton, Tolstoy and Hilaire Bellow, portrays Lewis as a blustery, hard-drinking eccentric whose private life included sequential liaisons with two married women."[33] With the publication of his biography, Wilson completed the scholarly triumvirate—the other two are Lindskoog and Beversluis—who created the most dramatic meta-critical sagas within Lewis studies.

While Lindskoog's book pitted some Lewis's admirers against each other—depending upon how they felt about Walter Hooper—Wilson's text, like Beversluis's, created battle lines predictably drawn along obvious allegiances: secular critics praised the biography, applauding its unflinching honesty; Lewis admirers panned the book, charging it with interpretive overreach and overreliance on psychoanalysis. In 1990, for instance, Wilson's biography appeared on *Time*'s "Best of '90" list, further developing the storyline created in the earlier review: "Fans should be warned that Wilson's portrait of the saintly don contains some fleshy demons."[34] Meanwhile, Gilbert Meilaender, who had previously written on Lewis, disliked the book. Significantly, Meilaender's critique invokes the religious name-branding associated with Lewis's identity as public intellectual: One problem with

---

[32] Michael Maudlin, "1993 Christianity Today Books Awards," *Christianity Today* (5 April 1993): 28.

[33] John Elson, "Books: Love's Labor," *Time* (5 March 1990), online. http://www.time.com/time/magazine/article/0,9171,969533,00.html accessed 3 Nov. 2009.

[34] "Best of '90: Books," *Time* (31 December 1990), online. http://www.time.com/time/magazine/article/0,9171,972055,00.html accessed 14 Nov. 2009.

Wilson's biography is that Wilson was not a Christian when he wrote it; consequently, Wilson obviously does not write sympathetically to the religious beliefs that shaped nearly all of Lewis's books. Meilaender wrote, "More disturbing than Wilson's tone is his attitude toward religion, chiefly in asides which seem to need no argument. Wilson observes that it is not the 'rational Lewis' who has continuing appeal; rather, 'it is the Lewis who plumbed the irrational depths of childhood and religion who speaks to the present generation.' But why should religion...be irrational at its depths?"[35]

Elevated to the status of transcendent author, a timeless representative of mere Christianity, Lewis becomes a guarded subject of analysis: Believing from the outset that Christianity is false, outspoken atheists and agnostics who mount a study of Lewis immediately lose credibility with Lewis's Christian readers. Belief in Christianity operates as the subtext of many analyses of Lewis, often regardless of the ostensible focus, for consistent with the dynamic of the public intellectual, Lewis has become representative of the position he holds. Despite harsh reviews within Christian circles, Wilson's biography continued to influence Lewis scholars. In 1998, Meilaender faulted Lionel Adey's *C. S. Lewis: Writer, Dreamer, and Mentor* because "it shows at places perhaps too much influence of A. N. Wilson's rather skewed biography of Lewis."[36]

The fallout from a 2001 *New York Times* article evidenced the indelibility of Lewis's name-branding, particularly his status as an exemplar of Christianity. The article surfaced the contents of a memo from the publishing firm HarperCollins concerning its marketing plan for selling its Lewis titles. The marketing plan included the strategy of muting the connection between the Narnian chronicles and their Christian message, as an executive with the firm wrote: "'We'll need to be able to give emphatic assurances that no attempt will be made to correlate the stories to Christian imagery/theology.'"[37] Many of Lewis's Christian admirers responded to the memo leak angrily and hastily. A *Christianity Today* online article reported that Chuck Colson called for a boycott of HarperCollins; the article quoted Andrew Greeley, who began an online commentary on the memo with the

---

[35] Gilbert Meilaender, "Psychoanalyzing C. S. Lewis," *Christian Century* (16–23 May 1990): 529.

[36] Gilbert Meilaender, review of *C. S. Lewis: Writer, Dreamer, and Mentor*, by Lionel Adeys, *Christian Century* (23 September 1998): 880.

[37] Doreen Carvajal, "Marketing 'Narnia' Without a Christian Lion," *New York Times*, 3 June 2001, online. http://www.nytimes.com/2001/06/03/us/marketing-narnia-without-a-christian-lion.html/ accessed 12 October 2010.

sentence, "Plans are afoot to purge Christian content from the seven Narnia stories."[38]

Of course, HarperCollins had no such plans; again, the memo simply outlined marketing strategies. As Douglas Gresham, Lewis's stepson and adviser of the Lewis estate, exclaimed on an online Lewis e-mail list: "'This is to be my first and last post on this matter. This is an evil lie. There are no such plans and there never have been any such plans.'"[39] In the *New York Times* article, Gresham defended HarperCollins's marketing plan: "'What is wrong with trying to get people outside of Christianity to read the Narnian chronicles? The Christian audience is less in need of Narnia than the secular audience, and in today's world the surest way to prevent secularists and their children from reading it is to keep it in the Christian or Religious section of the bookstores or to firmly link Narnia with modern evangelical Christianity."[40] Gresham here implies that, in their zeal to proclaim Lewis's Christianity to the world, Lewis admirers isolate Lewis, narrowing his audience by putting off prospective readers. A *Christianity Today* editorial later that year echoed Gresham's sentiments:

> One wonders, after the vitriolic attacks by conservative Christians—Why are we so upset over how C. S. Lewis is being *marketed*? Why all the opprobrium over fear that the jacket covers on Narnia books won't say, "By C. S. Lewis, eminent Christian apologist"? Why aren't we happier that a major publishing company is spending millions upon millions of dollars to get some of the best Christian writing of all time into the hands of people who haven't read it yet? Have we really bought into the lie that "image is everything"?[41]

The issue, however, was not image. Rather, the issue was secularization, the front lines of the culture wars that were raging in the 1990s. The tense stand-off at the time between Christians and secularists helps explain the Christian overreaction to the HarperCollins memo: The very notion of disassociating Lewis from Christianity provoked the battle cry that, until cooler heads prevailed, nearly mobilized a boycott. Moreover, Christian concerns about a de-Christianized Lewis were unfounded not only for the

---

[38] Ted Olsen, "The War for Narnia Continues," *Christianity Today* (June 2001). Accessed 3 September 2009, http://www.christianitytoday.com/ct/2001/juneweb-only/6-18-32.0.html.

[39] Ibid.

[40] Carvajal, "Marketing 'Narnia' Without a Christian Lion."

[41] Anonymous, "Aslan Is Still on the Move," *Christianity Today* (6 August 2001): 32.

obvious reason (that HarperCollins had no intention of de-Christianizing him): As I have argued throughout this book, Lewis was readily associated with Christianity in the public sphere so that anyone who knew of the name C. S. Lewis was also aware of his Christian beliefs. The HarperCollins memo, in all of its misunderstood ambiguity, struck a nerve, galvanizing Christians prepared to wage cultural war in a reconstituted public sphere—a public sphere now animated by anger and distrust.

In such an environment, evangelicals turned to Lewis to combat what they considered to be the pernicious elements of the late twentieth-century *Zeitgeist*. Moral relativism was one target, especially for evangelicals influenced by the writings of Francis Schaeffer, whose emphasis on absolute truth became the linchpin for evangelical apologetics and cultural criticism. I noted earlier the basis of Donald Williams's appropriation of Lewis on behalf of the conservative-Christian cause: what Williams perceives to be Lewis's emphasis on the exclusivity of Christianity, implicitly predicated on its status as absolute truth. In 1992, David Neff wrote an article for *Christianity Today* titled "American Babel," a jeremiad against moral relativism in America. Neff enlisted the aid of Lewis: After sketching the dangers of moral relativism, Neff wrote, "This subjective approach is nothing new. C. S. Lewis had to argue against something quite similar [in *The Abolition of Man*]."[42] Later that same year, another *Christianity Today* article summoned Lewis to stem the ills of the age, this time in the form of New Age spirituality: "As C. S. Lewis wrote in *The Silver Chair*, 'And the lesson of it all is…witches always mean the same thing, but in every age they have a different plan for getting it.'… To absorb Lewis's lesson we must discern the witchery of this age."[43] In 2001, Louis A. Markos marshaled Lewis to engage evangelical Christianity's perennial antagonist: postmodernism (as well as its elder relation, modernism). Markos wrote, "We need to dig deeper to reach those unstated assumptions that gird and control our contemporary world, even as we must broaden our perspective to encompass both the multifaceted nature of the modernist and postmodernist ethos and the equally multifaceted critique that we as evangelicals must offer in response. But where shall we find the methods and the language to construct a critique?" The answer, of course, is Lewis, who not only "bequeathed us a method and language for sharing the gospel

---

[42] David Neff, "American Babel," *Christianity Today* (17 August 1992): 18.

[43] Marvin Olasky, "The Return of Spiritism," *Christianity Today* (14 December 1992): 24.

with the modern and postmodern world," but also offered a response to the "threat that postmodern theories pose to the integrity of the arts."[44]

Once again, the evangelical appropriation of Lewis illustrates the dissolution of the public sphere. Once an inclusive space of diverse, though clashing and competing, viewpoints, the public sphere fragments into walled and protected regions of defense, discrete pockets of individuals and groups united by their ideological commitments as well as their resistance to the ideological commitments of other individuals and groups: hence the distrust of ideological outsiders (i.e., Beversluis and Wilson) writing about Lewis; hence the territorialism regarding Lewis's position among rival theological orientations; hence the overreaction to the HarperCollins memo; and hence the appeal to Lewis primarily to combat those elements of the contemporary *Zeitgeist* that constitute perceived threats to evangelical Christianity.

While Lewis became what David Downing called the "Elvis of Evangelicals," a broader audience became acquainted with Lewis through the 1993 film *Shadowlands*, directed by Richard Attenborough and starring Anthony Hopkins and Debra Winger. Como credited the movie with reigniting Lewis's broad popularity: "Who in the world would have guessed that when C. S. Lewis made a Comeback—a return to the status of popcult star, 46 years after his appearance on the cover of *Time* magazine—it would be as the hero in, of all things, a movie?"[45] Indeed, Wayne Martindale enumerates the ways in which the film adrenalized interest in Lewis: sales of Lewis books, of course, increased; Como's book, *C. S. Lewis at the Breakfast Table*, went into another printing, as did Martindale's own *The Quotable Lewis*; Leanne Payne's book on Lewis, *Real Presence*, had gone out of print but was picked up by another publisher and reissued; and George Sayer's biography of Lewis, *Jack: A Life of C. S. Lewis*, was reprinted twice in 1994 and was even picked up by a book club.[46]

Expectedly, reviews of the film were often divided along religious lines. *Time*—clearly a secular periodical—praised the film as well as the liberties it took in depicting Lewis's life. Some Christians, however, were not as pleased. Bruce Edwards, for instance, disparaged the film: "A movie about

---

[44] Louis A. Markos, "Myth Matters," *Christianity Today* (23 April 2001): 34, 32, and 38.

[45] James Como, "Land of Shadows," *National Review* (7 February 1994): 72.

[46] Wayne Martindale, "Shadowland: Inadvertent Evangelism," in *C. S. Lewis, Lightbearer in the Shadowlands: The Evangelistic Vision of C. S. Lewis*, ed. Angus J. L. Menuge (Wheaton IL: Crossway Books, 1997) 37.

Jack and Joy that downplays or ignores the centrality of Christ to their lives is analogous to scripting the life of Michael Jordan with little reference to basketball."[47] Philip Yancey even anticipated the evangelical response: "Some evangelicals will complain that the movie distorts Lewis's life and waters down his Christian message. True, in some ways the producers settled for the Hollywood formula of a tearjerker love story played by named stars.... But let's not be too harsh: these stars speak substantive dialogue to each other—about spiritual matters, no less."[48] Once again, we thus see evangelical ambivalence about the methods by which Lewis is brought to the attention of a large audience.

The 2005 release of the feature film *The Lion, the Witch and the Wardrobe* generated even more publicity and controversy. Before the film's release, *Time* ran an interview with Philip Pullman, author of *His Dark Materials*, a fantasy trilogy that Pullman admits writing—at least in part—as a riposte to Lewis's Narnian stories. Asked about Lewis and Tolkien, Pullman contended that, in Tolkien's hobbit books, religious issues—specifically the "personal wrestling with God"—"is rather trivial."

> In [Lewis's] *Narnia* books these things are not trivial; the ultimate destiny of the children hangs on how they behave. But the answers Lewis came up with are abominable and appalling. The child Susan at the end of *The Last Battle* is excluded from salvation because she's become too interested in lipstick and nylons. She's growing up through the natural stages of development every teenager does and becoming aware of her body. But Lewis hated it vehemently and punished with eternal damnation the one child that succumbs to it.[49]

Pullman brought the vexed question of Susan to the attention of a large audience—not to mention an assortment of damning judgments that both generated controversy/publicity and mobilized Lewis admirers.

A couple of months before the film's release, *Time* ran a story that assessed the film's chances at the box office. David Van Biema, the author of the piece, implicitly forecasted a segmented audience, divided by faith or lack thereof: the very fate allotted to Mel Gibson's *The Passion of the Christ*

---

[47] Quoted in Martindale, "Shadowland: Inadvertent Evangelism," 45.

[48] Philip Yancey, "Surprised by Shadowlands," *Christianity Today* 38/4 (April 1994): 112.

[49] Michael Brunton, "You Don't Know How Famous You Are Until Complete Strangers Stop You in the Street to Talk," *Time* (19 January 2004), online. http://www.time.com/time/magazine/article/0,9171,579063,00.html. Accessed 6 Nov. 2009.

(2004), a film widely popular among evangelicals. If the *Lion* film is to succeed, Van Biema prognosticated, it should not downplay theological elements: "What the *Lion*'s filmmakers do with the charming storytelling that surrounds [religious ideas] is—theologically—optional. But if these key ideas are muddled, the film may be a classic, but never a Christian classic. And its revenues, large as they may be, will reflect that."[50] The *Washington Post* echoed *Time*'s assessment in an article of which the title says it all: "Hollywood U-turn? Disney Film Looks to Christian Fan Base." The piece detailed the events—special showings, evangelistic outreaches—organized by conservative Christian churches and para-church groups.[51] Indeed, I attended one of the film's pre-screenings at a mega-church in Palm Beach County, Florida, where participants received an "Official Narnia Event Kit," complete with door hangers, posters, church-bulletin inserts, and resources for using the film as an outreach opportunity; Douglas Gresham made an appearance, emphasizing how the film could occasion conversions to Christianity throughout the world.

The month after the film's release, the *Chronicle of Higher Education* printed a story documenting how one evangelical university in southern California, Biola University, went to significant and expensive lengths to seize the outreach opportunity of the film. According to the story, Biola purchased 5,000 tickets for the film and distributed them to students, alumni, and donors; Biola also placed a large advertisement for the film on the university website. Rob Westervelt, "Director of Brand Management" at Biola, described in the piece Biola's strategy of "God-branding": "'God-branding, for us, is when an organization partners its marketing efforts with what God is doing in the world. We see the Chronicles of Narnia as sharing our values.'"[52] Efforts such as these undoubtedly prompted Elizabeth Ward of the *Washington Post* to claim retrospectively in 2008 that the *Lion* film "...left the whole series more or less hijacked by Christian Fundamentalists."[53]

---

[50] David Van Biema, "How to Tell if *The Lion, the Witch and the Wardrobe* is a Christian Film," *Time* (3 October 2005), online. http://www.time/magazine/article/0,8599,1113226,00.html. Accessed 12 Nov. 2009.

[51] Julia Duin, "Hollywood U-turn? Disney film looks to Christian fan base," *Washington Post* (7–13 November 2005).

[52] Thomas Bartlett, "Short Subjects: Brought to You by God," *Chronicle of Higher Education* (20 January 2006): A6.

[53] Elizabeth Ward, "Saving C. S. Lewis: A Critic Ventures Back into the Wardrobe," *Washington Post* (14 December 2008), online. http://www.high-beam.com/doc/1P2-19623429.html. Accessed 15 Jan. 2010.

Once again, we see how the evangelical (or fundamentalist) appropriation of Lewis—and, in 2005, of the film version of *The Lion, the Witch and the Wardrobe*—reflects the polarized public reception of Lewis in a manner consistent with the reconstituted public sphere. Appreciation of Lewis is starkly divided along religious lines. Nothing illustrates this dynamic better than the challenges Disney experienced while producing and marketing the film, as reported in a 2005 *New York Times* article titled "The Narnia Skirmishes." In the piece, Charles McGrath, who described the film as a "$200 million smackdown between the religious right and godless Hollywood," outlined the evidently well-recognized dilemma confronting Disney: "Disney has backed itself into a corner. If the studio plays down the Christian aspect of the story, it risks criticism from the religious right, the argument goes; if it is too upfront about the religious references, on the other hand, that could be toxic at the box office." Consequently, Disney "is hedging its bets and has, for example, already issued two separate soundtrack albums, one featuring Christian music and musicians and another with pop and rock tunes."[54] Indeed, Disney mounted two separate advertising campaigns, one catered for Christians and the other for a more general audience. By doing so, Disney implicitly acknowledged a public sphere parceled out into warring camps with little common ground.

It is little surprise that Lewis's popularity among evangelicals would foster a public perception connecting Lewis to conservative American politics. Not only is it a truism that evangelicals tend to vote conservative and Republican, but Philip Anschutz, owner of Walden Media, which co-produced *Lion*, entered the divided public sphere already branded as a crusader of conservative causes. In a 2005 article on the film, *Atlantic Monthly* developed the formula for a plotline sure to generate publicity and controversy within a divided public sphere. Called "The Apocalypse, Rated PG," a title that evokes the perceived evangelical obsession with both the "end times" and wholesome family entertainment, the article melodramatically asked, "Can a socially conservative Christian Republican succeed in Hollywood?"[55] According to the *Atlantic Monthly*'s plotline, Anschutz wields Lewis as a weapon on behalf of socially conservative Christian Republican causes. Within a fundamentally divided public sphere, however,

---

[54] Charles McGrath, "The Narnia Skirmishes," *New York Times*, 13 November 2005, accessed 8 September 2009, http://www.nytimes.com/2005/11/13/ movies/13narnia.html?_r=1&ei=5070&en=ce321391153d8017&ex=1156996800&page wanted=print.

[55] Duin, "Hollywood U-turn? Disney film looks to Christian fan base," 1.

such a pitch yields a predictable plot, one in which Lewis operates as ideological leverage widening the gulf—and augmenting the animosity—between conservatives and liberals.

A 2006 article in the *New York Times Review of Books* fell in lockstep with the *Atlantic Monthly's* plotline, following it to its predictable outcome. In the piece, which covers the *Lion* film, Alison Lurie described Anschutze as "an evangelical Christian and supporter of George W. Bush." The political subtext (as well as a caustic tone) is sustained throughout Lurie's article:

> It is no surprise that conservative Christians admire these books. They teach us to accept authority, to love and follow our leaders instinctively, as the children in the Narnia books love and follow Aslan. By implication, they suggest that we should and will admire and fear and obey whatever impressive-looking and powerful male authority figures we come in contact with. They also suggest that without the help of Aslan (that is, of such powerful figures, or their representatives on earth) we are bound to fail. Alone, we are weak and ignorant and helpless. Individual initiative is limited—almost everything has already been planned out for us in advance, and we cannot know anything or achieve anything without the help of God. This is, of course, the kind of mindset that evangelical churches prefer and cultivate: the kind that makes people vote against their own economic and social interest, that makes successful, attractive, and apparently intelligent young men and women want to become the apprentices of Donald Trump, or of much worse rich and powerful figures.[56]

This passage is remarkable because of the way Lurie's diatribe is informed by the *Lion* film's connection with Anschutz as well as Lewis's association with evangelicals. That is, the way Lewis has been received by the public and wielded within the public sphere shapes Lurie's reading of Lewis's book. (One may forget that Lurie does not even address the film in the quoted passage.) The public sphere—a divided, acrimonious public sphere—has become a hermeneutical prism by which critics read and interpret Lewis's books. And because many critics find themselves on the other side of the ideological divide from those who have claimed Lewis as their own (*Christianity Today*, after all, calls Anschutz a "Hollywood Hellfighter"[57]), their critiques are both scathing and politicized.

---

[56] Alison Lurie, "The Passion of C. S. Lewis," *New York Review of Books*, 9 February 2006, accessed 8 September 2009, http://www.nybooks.com/articles/18672.
[57] Mark Moring, "Hollywood Hellfighters," *Christianity Today* (May 2008): 46-50.

The fears that Ralph C. Wood registered in 2005 before the film's release seemed to have been realized, at least to some extent: "A subtler form of wickedness will ensue, however, if this movie—with its obvious triumph of good over evil—is turned into the latest weapon for waging the culture wars."[58] No doubt much to Wood's chagrin, the *New York Times* declared in 2005: "Narnia, it seems, is in danger of becoming a red state." The *Times* article also illustrated how the film exposed the ideological rifts within the public sphere: "Legions of evangelicals seem poised to make the new movie an adjunct to Sunday school, while critics uncomfortable about the religious subtext of Lewis's stories have been launching preemptive strikes to alert the susceptible. Stopping short of proposing a PG-13 label ('Parental guidance strongly advised—contains religious context and fleeting Christian imagery'), they have recognized the 7 Narnia books as good escapist fantasy but please, please, don't pay any attention to the other stuff."[59] Political considerations informed Polly Toynbee's controversial 2005 invective against Lewis and Narnia in an angry piece unsubtly titled "Narnia Represents Everything that Is Most Hateful about Religion." Toynbee wrote that "in Narnia is the perfect Republican, muscular Christianity for America—that warped, distorted neo-fascist strain that thinks might is proof of right."[60]

While the film version of *The Lion, the Witch and the Wardrobe* exposed the fault lines of a fragmented public sphere, the very polarization that such fragmentation occasions accounts for much of the film's success. (The film earned $67 million on opening weekend, the second largest weekend debut ever during the month of December[61]; ultimately, the film earned $745 million at the box office and more than $1 billion in DVD sales.[62]) Contrasting the success of *Lion* with the relative failure of *Prince Caspian* at the box office, Kelly Jane Torrance observed social factors that help explain the discrepancy. The release of *Lion*, Torrance explains, capitalized on the 2004 reelection of George W. Bush and rode the strong evangelical wave

---

[58] Ralph C. Wood, "Good and Terrible: The God of Narnia," *Christian Century* (27 December 2005): 8.

[59] Peter Steinfels, "Religious Questions Emerge Ahead of Movie Based on Children's Tale," *New York Times*, 3 December 2005.

[60] Polly Toynbee, "Narnia Represents Everything that Is Most Hateful about Religion," *Guardian*, 5 December 2005, accessed 8 September 2009, http://www.guardian.co.uk/books/2005/dec/05/cslewis.booksforchildrenandteenagers/.

[61] Anonymous, "Maybe a Lewis Franchise?" *Wall Street Journal*, 12 December 2005.

[62] Bartlett, "Short Subjects: Brought to You by God," A6.

generated by *The Passion of the Christ*: "...that's when, culturally, Christian groups were stronger or coming out of the woodwork." By 2008, when *Prince Caspian* was released, evangelicals had lost much of their cultural capital: "In 2008, Narnia didn't do as well—and neither did the Republican presidential candidate." Torrance quoted in her article David J. Theroux, president of the C. S. Lewis Society of California, who said that *Prince Caspian* was weak at the box office because Disney took the Christian fan base for granted: "'[Disney] deliberately would not work with the people with a special interest in the film, whether it was people interested in Lewis' work, or churches, or schools.'"[63] Disney, in short, took for granted the one segment—the "special interest"—of a fragmented public sphere that was large enough to generate large ticket sales.

I do not want to overstate the case. Obviously people other than evangelicals and Republicans purchased tickets to watch *Lion* at the theaters. The film had much to commend it: *Time*, for instance, praised the film for improving Lewis's "soft-pedaled" climactic battle between the Narnians and the forces of the White Witch, which the film turned into the "kick-ass set piece readers have always wanted."[64] Nevertheless, in an incendiary, overly politicized public sphere, evangelicals possessed the numbers, passion, and mobilizing infrastructure to turn a film into a box office success.

*b. Some Responses to the Public Intellectual: Populism and Anti-Intellectualism.*

As mentioned earlier, A. N. Wilson's controversial biography of Lewis provoked much controversy in its unflattering depictions generated from an analytical starting point clearly unfriendly to both Lewis and Christianity. As a Lewis outsider, Wilson penned a biography that predictably elicited the contempt of Lewis insiders. One prong of Wilson's critique concerned the perceived nonchalance and triumphalism with which Lewis tackles large theological and philosophical problems, a charge that amounts to the perception of populism and anti-intellectualism revolving around Lewis at least since 1958 when Pittenger critiqued Lewis in the pages of the *Christian Century*. Wilson wrote, "His intention in the lively fifteen-minute [BBC] talks was to answer such questions as 'Can an intelligent person be a Christian?'

---

[63] Kelly Jane Torrance, "Fox saves 'Narnia' from Disney," *Washington Times*, 30 January 2009, online. http://www.washingtontimes.com/news/2009/jan/30/the-chronicle-of-narnia/?page=al/. Accessed 15 Aug. 2009
[64] Richard Corliss, "Books Vs. Movies," *Time* (27 November 2005), online. http://www.time/magazine/article/0,9171,1134742,00.html. Accessed 3 Nov. 2009.

'What should a Christian's attitude be towards war, sex or money?' 'Is there a heaven and a hell?' He answers these questions with a breeziness and self-confidence which on an academic podium would have been totally unacceptable."[65] Wilson, in fact, recapitulated Pittenger's attack, setting up academic and popular as two poles, faulting Lewis for slipping from the former to the latter. What appeared to be lost on Wilson—like Pittenger before him—was the persona Lewis adopted while delivering the broadcast talks: a public intellectual speaking about religion to the masses, a scenario that calls for a populist discourse that skirts anti-intellectualism. As Lewis himself put it in his response to Pittenger, "But I was writing *ad populum*, not *ad clerum*."[66]

What makes accusations of anti-intellectualism—and permutations of such accusations—especially resilient are the similar critiques of Lewis writing *ad clerum*. In 1992, for instance, James Como edited an influential volume that included reminiscences of Lewis's friends, colleagues, and students. One contributor was Peter Bayley, once Lewis's pupil and later his colleague. Reflecting strictly on Lewis's scholarship, Bayley wrote, "His greatness lay in extraordinary powers of clarification and illumination. His weakness lay in this very strength: he could not resist oversimplification and beautifully neat conclusions." Bayley's assessment reveals how Lewis was predisposed to become a public intellectual, consistent with my earlier analysis of Lewis's scholarly reception in the 1930s. Bayley, in fact, pointed to *The Allegory of Love* as an example of Lewis's twinned virtue/vice of clarification and oversimplification: "He oversimplified the idea of courtly love in a way that long baffled as if it were a cut-and-dried, established, codified, and neatly recorded simple phenomenon found over several centuries in many literary works in several languages."[67] Bayley's dichotomous reaction to Lewis's rhetorical strategy—both his greatness and his weakness—crystallizes, in turn, Lewis's reception as a public intellectual. To many (primarily Lewis's admirers), Lewis's ability to simplify and clarify is a component of his genius, reaching the differentiated mass of the public sphere with the truths of Christianity; to others, Lewis's ability to simplify

---

[65] Wilson, *C. S. Lewis*, 181.

[66] C. S. Lewis, "Rejoinder to Dr Pittenger," in *God in the Dock: Essays on Theology and Ethics*, ed. Walter Hooper (Grand Rapids: Eerdmans, 1970) 182. Originally published in *Christian Century* vol. 75 (26 November 1958): 1359–61.

[67] Peter Bayley, "From Master to Colleague," *Remembering C. S. Lewis: Recollections of Those Who Knew Him*, ed. James T. Como (San Francisco: Ignatius Press, 2005) 170.

and clarify is an exploitative populist discourse, betrayed by its own reductive tendencies.

In 1998, Gilbert Meilaender wrote an article sensitive to this dilemma. Published in *First Things*, a venue sympathetic to Lewis's cause, the article invoked the now-familiar polarity: Lewis emphasizes his status as an amateur theologian, "a smart rhetorical strategy that gets the reader on his side over against the presumably elitist theologians." Meilaender went on to fret over the implications of this dichotomy: "But there is a worrisome sense in which Lewis's readers might be all too ready to hear such a message, all too ready to suppose that the faith is simple and clear, that theologians are largely in the business of making complicated what ought not to be." Lewis's disarming strategy, in other words, of full disclosure—'I am an amateur, a non-specialist'—may backfire in a way that is by now familiar: Distancing himself from "elitist theologians" may land Lewis in a populist/anti-intellectual camp. Meilaender attempted to forestall such an eventuality—though, as we have seen, it had already occurred forty years earlier—by simply stating that Lewis's ideas were not unsophisticated: "Lewis' readers actually get a rather heavy dose of serious religious reflection, though generally in quite alluring literary style."[68] A simple denial of anti-intellectualism, however, is insufficient to slow the momentum accumulated within the public sphere over the span of forty years, from Pittenger to Beversluis to Wilson; a simple denial cannot resolve the complexities endemic to the public intellectual, especially a Christian public intellectual who has wielded the strongest influence in America.

Some of Meilaender's language is suggestive in this respect: Readers might be "all too ready" to align themselves with Lewis "over against" the "elitist theologians"—"all too ready to suppose that faith is simple and clear...." Lewis's American readers in particular might be "all too ready" because, as we saw earlier, they inhabit a country in which religious discourse has deep populist roots. According to Noll, religious populism constitutes one contributing factor of the scandal of the evangelical mind. Accusations of anti-intellectualism (or variations thereof) will perennially dog Lewis by virtue of the fact that he wrote as a Christian public intellectual and acquired enormous fame in a country whose religious expressions have, from its beginnings, been characterized by populist impulses.

---

[68] Gilbert Meilaender, "The Everyday C. S. Lewis," *First Things* vol. 85 (August/September 1998): 27.

### c. Lewis among the Evangelicals and Fundamentalists

*Time* ran a story in 1999 on Billy Graham, distancing him from fundamentalists. By connection, the article likewise distanced Graham from Lewis: "Graham's most important book, *Peace with God* (1953), is light-years away from C. S. Lewis' *Mere Christianity*, which is revered by Fundamentalists."[69] An article of that same year in *The Nation* described the descent of the C. S. Lewis Foundation (of Redlands, California) upon Oxford for its C. S. Lewis Summer Institute. The article observed how 750 people, "most of them Americans and most of them evangelical Christians, effectively transformed [Christopher Wren's Sheldonian Theater] into a revival tent." An American pastor led the assembled in a worship service, complete with a hymn written in Lewis's memory: "He then asked, 'How has God spoken to you this week?' and beckoned worshipers to approach microphones placed throughout the Sheldonian. 'Brothers and sisters,' he called out, 'come and give witness." The article later asserted, "Evangelicals have adopted Lewis as their ultimate answer man, an easy-to-read St. Thomas Aquinas for today's world."[70] Events such as these, as well as the press that it received, solidified Lewis's connection to evangelicals.

In 2005, David Van Biema wrote an article for *Time* that enumerated Lewis's evangelical devotees. Focusing on two names on the list, Charles Colson and Rick Warren, Van Biema noted Lewis's "posthumous migration from liberal to conservative icon." Van Biema argued that Lewis's "natural first constituency was the old Protestant denominations. But by the 1960s the mainline's interest had shifted from core orthodoxies to social action."[71] Consequently, as this chapter has repeatedly observed, evangelicals, with their commitment to orthodoxy and doctrinal purity, appropriated Lewis and wielded him as a defense against inimical forces, from secularization to New Age spiritualism.

Colson and Nancey Pearcey often identified postmodernism as one of Christianity's most formidable opponents. In a 1998 *Christianity Today* article, they enlist Lewis in their fight, identifying him as "a true prophet for our

---

[69] Harold Bloom, "Billy Graham: the Preacher," *Time* (14 June 1999), online. http://www.time.com/time/magazine/article/0,9171,991259,00.html. Accessed 20 Nov. 2009.

[70] Michael Joseph Gross, "Narnia Born Again," *Nation* (1 February 1999): 28.

[71] David Van Biema, "Beyond the Wardrobe," *Time* (30 October 2005), online. http://www.time.com/time/magazine/article/0,9171,1124316,00.html. Accessed 16 Nov. 2009.

postmodern age."[72] Later that same year, J. I. Packer called Lewis "the Aquinas, the Augustine, and the Aesop of contemporary evangelicalism." Like others, Packer assumed a nonplussed reaction to this state of affairs, noting just a few of Lewis's incompatibilities to evangelicalism: "...his noninerrantist view of biblical inspiration, plus his quiet affirmation of purgatory and of the possible final salvation of some who have left this world as nonbelievers...." Like Colson and Pearcey, however, Packer insisted that Lewis could be counted on to announce prophetically the dangerous relativism of the postmodern turn: "Thus Lewis' Narnia links up with his attempt, in *The Abolition of Man*, to recall education to its Tao-grounded roots. The attempt was ignored, and today we reap the bitter fruits of that fact."[73] Bob Smietana explored the unlikely evangelical appropriation of Lewis with focused attention in a 2005 *Christianity Today* article. Like Packer, Smietana acknowledged the incompatibilities, though Smietana also included Lewis's social behavior: "He smoked cigarettes and a pipe, and he regularly visited pubs to drink beer with friends." Smietana quoted Christopher Mitchell, director of the Marion Wade Center at Wheaton College, to explain, at least in part, Lewis's evangelical connection: "'[Lewis] had an evangelical experience, this personal encounter with the God of the universe.'"[74]

While evangelicals embraced and explored their affinities to Lewis, others bemoaned the connection. When William Griffin, for instance, asked Helen Gardner, who succeeded Lewis at Oxford, for an interview for his biography on Lewis, he was rebuffed: "Too many American Evangelicals already had sniffed around his religious writings, she felt, and one more would only drag his reputation down to the gutter."[75]

In 1995, Ralph Wood wrote a piece for the *Christian Century* that voiced concern over what Van Biema would later call Lewis's "posthumous migration from liberal to conservative icon." Writing from a non-evangelical perspective—to a predominantly non-evangelical audience—Wood argued that Lewis's non-fiction apologetics (*Mere Christianity, Miracles,* and *The*

---

[72] Charles Colson and Nancy Pearcey, "The Oxford Prophet," *Christianity Today* (15 June 1998): 72.

[73] J. I. Packer, "Still Surprised by Lewis," *Christianity Today* (7 September 1998): 54, 56, 59.

[74] Bob Smietana, "C. S. Lewis Superstar: How a Reserved British Intellectual with a Checkered Pedigree Became a Rock Star for Evangelicals," *Christianity Today* (December 2005): 31.

[75] William Griffin, *C. S. Lewis: Spirituality for Mere Christians* (New York: Crossroad Publishing Company, 1998) 15.

*Problem of Pain*) "...reveal why many Christian conservatives view Lewis as a patron saint": "Like them, Lewis sometimes regards Christian faith as a set of intellectual propositions. Because these truths can be rationally demonstrated, they should command the assent of all fair-minded people. Those who deny such argument, it follows, must be either dimwitted or stubborn." Wood wrote that these "rationalist proofs...are among his weakest writings" and conversely praised Lewis's mythopoeic works: "It is Lewis's imaginative work that presents his best and most readable confession of the gospel."[76]

Wood here offers an analysis that tellingly engages a key dynamic of my critical narrative. The objects of Wood's disapprobation are the apologetic writings that not only appeal primarily to evangelicals but also resonate most strongly in the public sphere by engaging its conventions. In short, conflating Wood's claim with my analysis, one might generalize that evangelicals gravitate toward Lewis as a distinctly public intellectual, while Christians of a less conservative stripe favor the mythopoeic Lewis and thus the Lewis who moves beyond the public sphere. After all, chapter 8 showed that the workings of Lewis's mythopoeic imagination culminated in *Till We Have Faces*, Lewis's fullest actualization of myth and a novel that abandons the conventions of the public intellectual and thus moves him beyond the public sphere. Certain qualities of evangelicalism predispose its adherents to the apologetic methods of Lewis the public intellectual—a rich area of exploration that lies beyond the purview of this chapter.

Two years later, another article in *Christian Century* re-invoked the categories of Wood's analysis. Briefly comparing Lewis and Karl Barth, Gary Dorrien contrasted Lewis's shallow theology relative to Barth's theological profundity: "Compared to Barth, Lewis's understanding of history and the problems of theology was slight, even simplistic." However, Dorrien also claimed that Barth could learn something from the mythopoeic elements of Lewis's Christian imagination: "Despite [Lewis's] lack of theological training, however, his religious writings are marked by a keen and realistic sense of the mythical character of Christianity—a sense that eluded Barth."[77] Like Wood, then, Dorrien contrasted Lewis's (thin) apologetic theology with his (rich) mythopoeic imagination, the very fault lines that ultimately create the gap separating the Lewis who flourishes as a public intellectual and the

---

[76] Ralph C. Wood, "The Baptized Imagination: C. S. Lewis's Fictional Apologetics," *Christian Century* (30 August–6 September 1995): 812 and 813.

[77] Gary Dorrien, "The 'Postmodern' Barth? The Word of God as True Myth," *Christian Century* (2 April 1997): 340.

Lewis who moves beyond the public sphere: a gap that likewise separates the theological orientations of Lewis's evangelical and non-evangelical (though Christian) readers.

### d. The Politicization of C. S. Lewis

My analysis of the public reception of the film version of *The Lion, the Witch and the Wardrobe* illustrated ways in which Lewis became associated with conservative, Republican politics. The politicization of Lewis, however, began at least as early as the 1970s. Before exploring this politicization, I must first observe that Lewis's basic philosophical and theological orientation possesses fundamental affinities to political conservatism, as it is outlined, for instance, in E. J. Dionne's three defining principles of the concept: "First, conservatives are suspicious of innovation and therefore subject all grand plans to merciless interrogation"; "Second, conservatives respect old things and old habits"; third, "...a suspicion of human nature and a belief that humans cannot be remolded into plastic.... From generation to generation, human nature doesn't really change."[78] Such principles operate throughout the Lewis corpus, embodied in principles like "chronological snobbery," exemplified in Lewis's adherence to essentialism and what I called in an earlier chapter de-conversion, and illustrated in the machinations of the N.I.C.E., an organization which, as described in *That Hideous Strength*, attempts to re-make human nature. Thus, to the delight of some and the chagrin of other Lewis readers, it would be difficult to deny that many of the ideas fundamentally associated with Lewis's Christian worldview could be used in support of a vague political conservatism. My interest in this section, however, is the way Lewis is situated in the public sphere within more specific political discourse and debates.

Although Lewis was thrust into the political arena primarily in the '90s and 2000s, I begin by backtracking, briefly examining how Lewis was earlier positioned on the political stage. One of the earliest politicized uses of Lewis occurs in a 1973 *Christianity Today* article. Joan Lloyd employs Lewis to enter the debates surrounding the sexual revolution and women's liberation. Drawing from Lewis—especially his article, "Priestesses in the Church," as well as his representations of girls in the Narniad—Lloyd concluded that "the feminine is grounded in obedience." Consistent with Lewis's own stance throughout most of his career, Lloyd's article was both reactionary

---

[78] E. J. Dionne, Jr., "Three Points for Conservatives," *Washington Post*, 23 March 2010, accessed 5 May 2010, http://www.washingtonpost.com/wp-dyn/content/article/2010/23/ar2010032302427_pf.html.

and antagonistic in tone and polemical thrust: "Today's views of sexuality and marriage are based on the belief that sex is merely a biological phenomenon and has little meaning outside its reproductive function. Therefore, divorce or the transfer of sexual characteristics is of little consequence. Lewis would take issue with this."[79]

Lloyd's article established a pattern followed by later politicized appropriations of Lewis: a pattern of mobilizing Christians inspired by the prophetic words of Lewis to stop or at least slow cultural movements perceived to have a baneful effect upon society, uprooting it from Christian moorings. Such is the pattern Colson followed in a 1988 *Breakpoint* article, informed by Lewis's *The Screwtape Letters*: "American Christians need to realize we are on the front lines in a spiritual battlefield. As good soldiers, we must stand by our buddies.... Anything less, and devil Wormwood can go ahead with his reassignment. We'll be no challenge whatsoever to his boss."[80] The secular press took notice of such maneuvers. A *Time* article during this period analyzed the sociological profile of those who voted for Pat Robertson in the 1988 presidential election, a profile that included a Lewis connection: "Religious people of various kinds may feel insulted if Robertson's belief is ridiculed. There are many products of Christian schools reading sophisticated defense of their position, books like C. S. Lewis' *Miracles: A Preliminary Study*."[81]

By the 1990s, Lewis had so often been thus positioned in the public sphere that Cal Thomas could herald the second coming of Lewis in the figure of William T. Bennett, who "...may be as close in intellectual likeness [to Lewis] as America has had at a national level." Like Bennett, Lewis "called for a return to the ideas and principles that have a proven track record and provide the inner peace that temporal pursuits and shifting standards cannot."[82]

In 1994, the Focus on the Family newsletter printed an article aptly titled "Recruiting Lewis for Today's Culture War." The article posed a number of loaded questions pertaining to culture-war politics, with answers supplied by Lewis himself, taken from a variety of Lewis books and letters, regardless

---

[79] Joan Lloyd, "Transcendent Sexuality as C. S. Lewis Saw It," *Christianity Today* (November 1973): 8 and 10.

[80] Chuck Colson, "A PS from Uncle Screwtape," *Breakpoint* (August 1988): 8.

[81] Garry Wills, "Robertson and the Reagan Gap," *Time* (22 February 1988), online. http://www.time.com/time/magazine/article/0,9171,966762,00.html. Accessed 4 Nov. 2009.

[82] Cal Thomas, "Bennett Shows the Way to Regain Our Lost Values," *Daily Herald*, 21 March 1993.

of context. For instance, the *Citizen* "asked" Lewis, "Now that President Clinton and other liberal elitists have begun talking about 'family values,' how can pro-family activists avoid being duped?" The *Citizen* then provided Lewis's "answer," taken with glaring contextual disconnect from "Learning in War-Time": "'A man who has lived in many places is not likely to be deceived by the local errors of his native village. [Likewise] the scholar who has lived in many times [through his study of history] is in some degree immune from the great cataract of nonsense that powers from the press and the microphone of his own age." The *Citizen* then queried Lewis about homosexuality: "How should pro-family activists view homosexuals?" Lewis's response is taken from one snippet of a letter he wrote to Sheldon Vanauken in 1954: "'I take it for certain that the physical satisfaction of homosexual desires is sin....'"[83] In 1994, the *New Yorker* compared Lewis's Aslan to conservative icon Oliver North, who, after being convicted of federal charges in the Iran-Contra affair, became a political commentator for the Fox News Channel: "Is Aslan North's secret identity? Is he the lionhearted Christ figure who is crucified willingly on behalf of others (the "fall guy"), yet lives again to redeem the kingdom in a holy war?"[84]

A 1998 edited volume on Lewis contained a couple of essays engaging the culture wars, thus illustrating the politicization of Lewis. Michael H. MacDonald and Mark P. Shea identified the front lines of the offensive: "Many point to a new war, a war for the soul of Western civilization, with an enemy as insidious as the enemy in World War II: the culture of death. This enemy does not do *public* violence with guns and bombs. Rather, it seeks to *privatize* (and hide) violence with abortion in clinics and euthanasia in hospital rooms." MacDonald and Shea emphasize the threat of this enemy using Lewisian categories of analysis: "And, if Christians do not fight it, this ideology will dissolve and debunk our faith in conscience, the Moral Law, and the Moral Lawgiver and replace them with faith in appetite, feeling, and, ultimately, power. After this will surely come the deluge." MacDonald and Shea went on to enlist Lewis in this war with the sort of signal phrase common in such appropriations of Lewis: "For as Lewis warned in his prophetic little book [*The Abolition of Man*]...."[85] In the same collection of

---

[83] Anonymous, "Recruiting C. S. Lewis for Today's Culture War," *Focus on the Family Citizen* (15 August 1994): 12–13.

[84] Sidney Blumenthal, "Christian Soldiers," *New Yorker* (22 August 1994): 34.

[85] Michael H. MacDonald and Mark P. Shea, "Saving Sinners and Reconciling Churches: An Ecumenical Meditation on Mere Christianity," in *The Pilgrim's Guide: C. S. Lewis and the Art of Witness*, ed. David Mills (Grand Rapids: Eerdmans, 1998) 50–51.

essays, Sheridan Gilley invoked the spirit of Lewis to combat "the common enemy of all good Christians, the evil that I can only call in the vaguest terms liberalism, which leads to what Lewis called "the abolition of man" in the name of an ultimate ethical and religious relativity."[86]

Lewis's alignment with evangelicals and political conservatives within the public sphere continued with the turn of the millennium. A 2000 *Washington Post* article explored the popularity of George W. Bush among evangelicals: "'I know what it means to be right with God,' [Bush] would say [to evangelical leaders]. Then he would follow with personal notes—'I saw your book came out.' Once, he dug up an old *Time* magazine cover of author C. S. Lewis, the evangelicals' literary favorite, to send to a Wheaton college professor he had met with."[87] Within the political arena, Lewis name-dropping curried evangelical favor. In a 2002 article in *Christianity Today*, J. I. Packer used Lewis (along with Oswald Chambers) to marshal an argument supporting Bush's decision to invade Iraq: "However burdensome, it is surely the best and only rational course." Lewis (and Chambers), according to Packer, would also be in favor of the heightened security measures implemented by the U.S. Department of Homeland Security: "In light of all this, I guess that Chambers and Lewis, were they back with us, would direct us as follows: Accept tightened security."[88]

In a 2008 book titled *Conversations with God*, Robert Velarde resurrects Lewis—"C. S. Lewis died in 1963, but I met him last week"—and puts him into dialogue with a fictional character called Thomas Clerk, who is dying of cancer. At one point, Lewis's "conversation" with Clerk engages the culture wars. Velarde summarizes Lewis's argument in *The Abolition of Man* and then, extrapolating from that position, puts the following words into Lewis's mouth:

> "For one, genetic engineering in order to 'improve' the human machine will ultimately be allowed in such a scheme. In order to mold the human race, one needs material to mold. Infants, even in the womb, will no longer be seen as valuable, but as mere biological tissue to do with what we want. If the elderly become a burden to society, then they must be allowed to do away with themselves or, perhaps, we will do away with

---

[86] Sheridan Gilley, "The Abolition of God: Relativism and the Center of Faith," in *The Pilgrim's Guide: C. S. Lewis and the Art of Witness*, ed. Mills, 162.

[87] Hanna Rosin, "Applying Personal Faith to Public Policy," *Washington Post*, 24 July 2000.

[88] J. I. Packer, "Wisdom in a Time of War: What Oswald Chambers and C. S. Lewis Teach Us about Living Through the Long Battle with Terrorism," *Christianity Today* (7 January 2002): 45 and 49.

them on our own, if a valueless system runs its course." Jack's words reminded me of contemporary debates about the status of the human fetus, euthanasia, abortion, genetic engineering and so forth.[89]

And in 2005, Florida Governor Jeb Bush encouraged children to read *The Lion, the Witch and the Wardrobe* as part of a Florida educational initiative called "Just Read, Florida!" In response, one Florida newspaper pundit made the predictable and by now unavoidable connection between Lewis and conservative politics: "Yes, of all the books the state might encourage children to read, Bush just so happened to pick the book that coincides with the Disney movie, which just so happens to be co-produced by Walden Media, which just so happens to be owned by a Colorado billionaire, who through his family and foundation has donated nearly $100,000 to the Republican Party."[90]

## III. Conclusion

The evolution of Lewis's reputation follows, to a large extent, the devolutionary trajectory of the public sphere. Early in his career as a Christian public intellectual, before the restructuring of the public sphere, Lewis was a "conservative iconoclast," that paradoxical formulation that attracted the attention of scholars and journalists who displayed thoughtful, though not always favorable, considerations of his rhetorical strategies. And because most of these strategies abided by the conventions of the public sphere itself, Lewis's publicity multiplied, branding his name not only as Christian writer but defender of Mere Christianity, a concept deified by the religious imagination and possessing enormous discursive power. Lewis, in short, became a synecdoche for the purest form of Christianity, removed from local associations and contingencies: Lewis became a transcendent author, mediating the immortal truths of his transcendent characters, from the *Oyarsu* in the Ransom trilogy to Aslan in the Narniad.

Elevated to this prominent position in the public sphere, Lewis naturally became a large target for those who opposed his project. Since Lewis became a distinctly Christian public intellectual, many of those opponents argued from a religiously agnostic or atheistic perspective. Ironically, however, it

---

[89] Robert Velarde, *Conversations with C. S. Lewis: Imaginative Discussion about Life, Christianity and God* (Downers Grove IL: IVP Books 2008) 68–69.

[90] Frank Cerabino, "A Thinly Veiled Christian Message," *Palm Beach Post*, 13 October 2005, accessed 17 September 2009, http://www.palmbeachpost.com/search/content/shared/news/nation/stories/10/1013_coxcerabino_column.html.

was a fellow believer—W. Norman Pittenger—who issued the most influential critique of Lewis—most influential, that is, if we consider that all subsequent critiques of Lewis were recapitulations of Pittenger's, following the same lines of attack either explicitly or implicitly, directly or indirectly. Those lines of attack assume the shape of a dichotomy, variously phrased depending upon one's biases: elitist versus popularizer, scholar versus amateur, apologist writing *ad clerum* versus apologist writing *ad populum*. The analytical underpinnings of nearly every critique of Lewis's apologetics were established when Pittenger, writing as a professional theologian, faulted Lewis not only for thin theology but implicitly for the facile, self-assured tone to which his status as public intellectual committed him. Consider, for instance, the critique of *Mere Christianity* offered here by Beversluis, who writes in the spirit of Pittenger: "Here is the populizer of Christianity at work: the unpretentious, no-nonsense Everyman's theologian. The tone is informal, the manner relaxed, the approach chatty. The most momentous questions are tackled in a winningly let's-see-if-we-can-make-sense-of-this fashion."[91] The Pittenger/Lewis debate thus drew particular attention to the dichotomy that operates subtextually in numerous critiques of Lewis's theology. More importantly for my purposes, the dichotomy figures centrally in conceiving Lewis as a public intellectual, testifying to the explanatory power of that identification.

The identification likewise enables us better to understand Lewis's popularity in America. The populist character of American Christianity proved to be fertile soil for Lewis's *ad-populum* apologetics, appealing winsomely within the marketplace of ideas to the rationality of any clearly thinking individual. Of course, professional theologians and philosophers, whose sensitivity to intellectual nuance and complexity renders Lewis's apologetic reductive and simplistic, were the exception. Nevertheless, Lewis's adherence to the conventions of the public sphere—his strategy, for instance, of de-conversion and his status as transcendent author—endow his writing with a tone of certainty and self-assuredness, a tone that tends to convince and win over his lay readers while, again, alienating the professional scholars.

Flourishing in the populist religious climate of America, Lewis's writings naturally gained favor among evangelicals. As we have seen, evangelicals helped to rescue Lewis from relative obscurity in the 1970s. However, Lewis's alignment with this increasingly influential body of American Christians coincided with the disintegration of the public sphere.

---

[91] Beversluis, *C. S. Lewis and the Search for Rational Religion*, 32.

Splintered into pockets of ideologically driven resistance and *ressentiment*, the reconstituted public sphere re-structured Lewis's public reception. Although always characterized by diversity and difference, the public sphere lost the standards by which rival viewpoints could be rationally adjudicated, effectively blocking off possible pathways to consensus. The result is what James Davison Hunter calls the "turn toward politics." The public sphere has transformed into the political sphere: "Politics subsumes the public so much so that they become conflated. And so instead of the political realm being seen as one part of public life, all of public life tends to be reduced to the political. Linguistically, the political becomes effectively synonymous with the public for, in fact, they come to occupy the same space. The primary if not only meaning given to a public act is its political meaning and importance."[92] Lewis assumes a politicized position in a now politicized public sphere.

A meta-critical analysis thus suggests that a species of tribalism has shaped Lewis's public reception at the beginning of the new millennium. Lewis's emergence as American evangelical hero, whether occasioned by the efforts of evangelicals themselves or by the pronouncements of secular critics and the popular press, creates an ideologically charged, often politicized critical space for engaging both Lewis and his ideas. Lewis's symbolic place within the marketplace of ideas reflects American religious patterns identified by Putnam and Campbell, who show how the rise of the Religious Right constitutes one of a series of shocks that "have gradually polarized the American religious scene, as people (especially young people) have increasingly sorted themselves out religiously according to their moral and political views, leaving both the liberal, secular pole and the conservative, evangelical pole strengthened and the moderate religious middle seriously weakened. Religious polarization has increasingly aligned Americans' religious affiliations with their political inclinations."[93] My very experiences in writing this book attest to this dynamic: After informing people—both religious and secular—that I am writing a book on Lewis, they easily make certain assumptions about not only my religious but also my political orientation. The devolution of the public sphere has re-shaped Lewis's public reception: While Lewis once occupied the universal stage of the Enlightenment, the fragmentation of the public sphere has created the ideological pressure that increasingly pushed Lewis into an evangelical

---

[92] James Davison Hunter, *To Change the World: The Irony, Tragedy and Possibility of Christianity in the Late Modern World* (Oxford: Oxford University Press, 2010) 105–106.
[93] Putnam and Campbell, *American Grace*, 132.

subculture, which, at best, is an impassioned community of faith or, at worst, an intellectual and political ghetto.

Earlier in this chapter, I described what Putnam and Campbell identify as shock that sent waves through the American religious experience: the sexual permissiveness and the challenge to authority of the long 1960s. I also noted what they call the first aftershock: the religious response to these embattled sexual mores, a response that united religion and Republican conservatism. Putnam and Campbell's second aftershock is relevant to the concluding section of this chapter:

> But beginning in the 1980s and continuing into the first decade of the new century, conservative politics became the most visible aspect of religion in America. While that development encouraged a certain kind of triumphalism among some leaders of the Religious Right, it deeply troubled many other Americans, especially those whose attachment to organized religion was weak, in part because they were just coming of age. For many Americans raised in the 1980s and 1990s, religion as they saw it around them seemed to be mostly about conservative politics and especially about traditional positions on sexual morality, like homosexuality. In effect, many of these Americans, who might have been religiously inclined, but were liberal on moral issues, said "if that's what religion is all about, then it's not for me." Thus, the second aftershock, during the 1990s and 2000s, thrust a substantial number of Americans, especially young Americans, in a decidedly nonreligious direction.[94]

The fragmented public sphere has aligned Lewis with the very group that has drawn a negative reaction from "a substantial number of Americans, especially young Americans." Consequently, public disagreements with Lewis's ideas—or their appearances on the big screen—often engage this sociological subtext; antagonism toward evangelicalism can animate critiques of Lewis. In short, Lewis inevitably experiences some of the backlash that has now been directed at those who have called him one of their own.

---

[94] Ibid., 81–82.

# 12

# Explaining Some Meta-critical Curiosities

C. S. Lewis scholarship presents distinct meta-critical curiosities. One need not delve too deeply into the various studies on Lewis published over the past fifty years before encountering similar refrains that amount to critical leitmotifs, typically registered in an introductory or prefatory chapter, or sometimes even in a book-jacket blurb. First, many studies on Lewis assume an apologetic tone, with authors sheepishly introducing their books to an audience apparently bothered and bewildered by the numerous publications on Lewis. David Mills's 1998 edited volume, *The Pilgrim's Guide: C. S. Lewis and the Art of Witness*, is a case in point. In the introductory chapter, editor Mills admits "to sharing many readers' weariness of the Lewis cult, and to feeling slightly irritated when someone prefaces a statement on almost any question with 'It's like Lewis says.'" He then clears some critical space for his volume by audaciously posing the anticipated, awkward question: "*The Pilgrim's Guide* is yet another book on C. S. Lewis, and you may well ask (I did): Why should the editor and his writers take the time to write, Eerdmans publish, and I read yet another book on C. S. Lewis?"[1] Such a question seems to dog nearly every published analysis of Lewis. In fact, the question casts such a large shadow that its presence frames the praise that G. B. Tennyson offers Lionel Adey's 1998 study of Lewis on the book's back cover: "This is not just another book on C. S. Lewis."[2]

The second critical leitmotif would seem to be a corollary of the first: the repeated asseveration that many books on Lewis are of poor quality and shoddy scholarship, consisting of routine summaries of Lewis texts and hagiographical praise of Lewis the man. In 1986, for instance, Bruce Edwards wrote, "For every scholarly treatise about Lewis's apologetics or fiction, there have been five or six superficial tributes, plot summaries, or anthologies of Lewis quotations. Judging from publishers' lists there would seem to be nothing left to be said about Lewis. Even some of Lewis's admirers refer to his canon and the range of secondary sources which

---

[1] David Mills, intro *The Pilgrim's Guide: C. S. Lewis and the Art of Witness*, ed. David Mills (Grand Rapids: Eerdmans, 1998) xi.

[2] Lionel Adey, *C. S. Lewis: Writer, Dreamer, and Mentor* (Grand Rapids: Eerdmans, 1998).

evolved around them as the 'glut of Lewisiana.' Clearly, any new book about Lewis requires some explanation."[3] In 1988, Peter Kreeft's version of the critical refrain was a bit less charitable: "Books on Lewis have multiplied like rabbits, or like flies around honey." Kreeft asserted that "most [of these books] are not worth reading because they do little more than rehash what Lewis already said much, much more effectively than any of his summarizers and commentators can."[4] And in the 2010 *Cambridge Companion to C. S. Lewis*, Robert MacSwain coined the term "Jacksploitation"; drawn from Lewis's nickname, Jack, the neologism describes "a work related to Lewis that has no scholarly substance or originality whatsoever, produced by someone whose only credential is that the work is related to Lewis. The world is awash in Jacksploitation."[5]

What explains these meta-critical curiosities? One would be hard-pressed to find similar critical refrains in scholarship devoted to some of Lewis's famous contemporaries, like J. R. R. Tolkien or T. S. Eliot. For that matter, one would be stretched to identify *any* writer from *any* period whose corpus has generated scholarship of such unique, embattled character. One could identify the plethora of books on Shakespeare, Milton, Pope, Wordsworth, Austen, Tennyson, and Pound as a "glut," but scholars do not typically apologize for writing books on them. In addition, the majority of books on these authors are not dismissed as shoddy, consisting of summary and hagiography. Moreover, although the writings of Lewis may not be as rich as those of the stellar literary lineup above, the scholars who analyze them generally would not agree—qua Edwards—that there is "nothing left to be said" about them, a claim that would seemingly be so easy to make with respect to a writer such as Shakespeare. Consistent with the critical category proposed and defended throughout this book, this chapter argues that Lewis's status as public intellectual possesses considerable explanatory power in understanding the strange contours of Lewis scholarship and what can be called the C. S. Lewis industry. My meta-critical analysis will show how the hagiographical and paraphrase-heavy quality of Lewis scholarship proceeds from Lewis's identity as a public intellectual.

---

[3] Bruce L. Edwards, *A Rhetoric of Reading: C. S. Lewis's Defense of Western Literacy* (Provo UT: Center for the Study of Values in Literature, 1986) 2.

[4] Peter Kreeft, *C. S. Lewis: A Critical Essay* (Front Royal VA: Christendom College Press, 1988) 5.

[5] Robert MacSwain, introduction to *The Cambridge Companion to C. S. Lewis*, ed. Robert MacSwain and Michael Ward (Cambridge: Cambridge University Press, 2010) 11.

## I. A Closer Examination of Lewis Studies

Before connecting the two critical curiosities mentioned above to Lewis's status as a public intellectual, I find it necessary to examine more closely the manifestations of these curiosities within Lewis studies. Doing so will underscore how deep-seated and widespread they are. My brief, closer examination will proceed chronologically, beginning with the 1960s and stretching into the 2000s.

Published in 1964, Clyde Kilby's *The Christian World of C. S. Lewis* was an early monograph in the field. While assuming a multi-faceted task, the book, as Kilby explained, adopted the primary mission of serving as "a guide" and "a help," aiding both "those who know little or nothing of Lewis" and "those who have read and yet not fully understood his books."[6] A monograph proclaiming to serve as a guide and a help must necessarily offer summaries, enabling readers to understand Lewis by paraphrasing his ideas. Nevertheless, a 1965 review faulted Kilby's book for this very reason: "Considering that Lewis's impact was due largely to his wit and style, I can but wonder what we gain from Kilby's lengthy paraphrases."[7]

Later Lewis scholars would follow in the footsteps of Kilby, publishing Lewis guides and helps that necessarily paraphrase, either introducing readers to Lewis, with the hope of expanding Lewis's readership, or explaining Lewis's ideas to those who might be confused, thereby securing the place of those who already count among that readership. Critics and reviewers subsequently fault these books for accomplishing the very task that they set out to perform. In this respect, Kilby's book and the reviewer's response above constitute a meta-critical microcosm of Lewis studies. Richard B. Cunningham's 1967 book, *C. S. Lewis: Defender of the Faith*, is likewise heavy in paraphrase as it introduces readers to Lewis's arguments for the Christian faith, thereby following the model established not only by Kilby but by Chad Walsh in his seminal 1949 study, *C. S. Lewis: Apostle to the Skeptics*. Cunningham's book thus not only summarizes Lewis's ideas, but is also derivative of earlier books that do the same. Predictably, a 1968 review of Cunningham's book laments that "...most of this territory has been covered

---

[6] Clyde Kilby, *The Christian World of C. S. Lewis* (Grand Rapids: Zondervan, 1964) 7.

[7] A. H. Carter, "One About, One By," *Christian Century* 82 (1965): 54.

by previous writers [like Walsh and Kilby]" and concludes, "The Cunningham study adds little that is new to an understanding of Lewis."[8]

The strategies of introducing readers to Lewis and explaining him to the already initiated elicit some predictable reader responses. By paraphrasing and thereby subtly—and sometimes not so subtly—commending, studies on Lewis assume hagiographical characteristics. While a writer like Walsh definitely steers clear of such characteristics—indeed, his book is often quite critical of Lewis—the model that he, along with other early Lewis scholars, establishes, consisting of much paraphrase, transforms the model into hagiography. Thus, by 1977, Edward G. Zogby could write, "It seems a fair statement of the state of Lewis criticism to date to say that most of the criticism being published falls into the category of appreciation and applause."[9] In the preface to Thomas Howard's 1980 study, *The Achievement of C. S. Lewis*, Peter Kreeft registered the sorry state of Lewis studies as the springboard for praising Howard's book:

> At last! A book about C. S. Lewis that doesn't sound like a term paper, a book that is a joy to read, a book written with Lewis's own passionate power with words, Mercurial magic. At last a book that shows us things we *didn't* see or appreciate in Lewis before, instead of trotting out a recital of the obvious things we did see (unless we were morons).... So far the plethora of Lewisiana has illustrated two maxims: that inflation cheapens value and that the more interesting the author, the duller the books about him.[10]

In 1982, James Como wrote, "The past few years have seen the publication of a rash of books on C. S. Lewis. But whether favorable to him or not—and often from publishers of religious evangelicalism—the shabby has outweighed the substantial."[11] In 1984, Humphrey Carpenter baldly stated, "C. S. Lewis was a very good man. A lot of very bad books have been written about him."[12] Bruce Edwards's 1988 assessment registered similar meta-critical disappointment: "Unfortunately, many of the earliest studies of

---

[8] Joan Kerns Ostling, "Shotgun Approach to C. S. Lewis," *Christianity Today* (19 January 1968): 29.

[9] Edward G. Zogby, "Triadic Patterns in Lewis Life and Thought," in *The Longing for Form: Essays on the Fiction of C. S. Lewis*, ed. Peter J. Schakel (Kent: Kent State University Press, 1977) 20.

[10] Peter Kreeft, preface to *The Achievement of C. S. Lewis*, by Thomas Howard (Wheaton IL: Harold Shaw Publishers, 1980) 7.

[11] James Como, "Mediating Illusions: Three Studies of Narnia," *Children's Literature* vol. 10 (1982): 163.

[12] Humphrey Carpenter, "Giddy with Awe," *Spectator* (31 March 1984): 26.

Lewis have tended to reflect more hagiography than scholarship, more paraphrase than analysis, yielding few insights into source and strength of Lewis's literary achievements." Edwards went on, however, to offer some hope: "Recently, however, scholars have begun to go beyond surface treatments of Lewis's work and consider more creditably the fuller scope of Lewis's writing career, offering students of Lewis a more critical vantage point from which to assess his work."[13] Nicolas Barker was not as optimistic in 1990, when he wrote that "...the mass of published trivia generated by Lewis's work is depressing, more so than with most 'fan club' literature. The whole business is a sad legacy, a poor memorial of a man who wished the world so much good."[14] (Edwards would probably not disagree with Barker's ascription of "fan club literature" to Lewis studies, for in 1980 Edwards wrote an article on Lewis fandom titled "On the Excesses of Appreciation."[15])

The litany of dire, meta-critical assessments continued into the 1990s and beyond. In 1993, Kath Filmer explained, "While I have felt much admiration for some of the other books about Lewis, I have had a feeling of vague dissatisfaction about all of them. There seems to be a universal tendency to hagiography pervading them; Lewis is held up for admiration by those who have enjoyed his works and a certain quality of critical reading seems to be minimized in order to extol Lewis's 'Christian' message."[16] In 2007, Edwards again commented on the deficiencies of Lewis scholarship, maintaining that Lewis biographies typically fall victim to one of two extremes. The first extreme concerns unflattering portrayals of Lewis that explore Lewis's sadomasochistic tendencies as a youth and his eyebrow-raising relationship with Janie Moore. (Edwards most likely has in mind here biographies by A. N. Wilson and Michael White.) Edwards explains the second extreme, which by this time had obviously become familiar: "(2) works so enamored of Lewis that their work borders on or exceeds hagiography and offers page after page of redundant paraphrase of his putatively unique insights."[17] And

---

[13] Bruce L. Edwards, introduction to *The Taste of the Pineapple: Essays on C. S. Lewis as Reader, Critic, and Imaginative Writer*, ed. Bruce L. Edwards (Bowling Green: Bowling Green State University Popular Press, 1988) 3.

[14] Nicholas Barker, "C. S. Lewis, Darkly," *Essays in Criticism* 40/4 (1990): 367.

[15] Bruce Edwards, "On the Excesses of Appreciation," *Christian Scholar's Review* vol. 11 (January 1980).

[16] Kath Filmer, *The Fiction of C. S. Lewis: Mask and Mirror* (New York: St. Martin's Press, 1993) 1.

[17] Bruce L. Edwards, preface to *C. S. Lewis: Life, Works, and Legacy*, vol. 1, *An Examined Life*, ed. Bruce L. Edwards (London: Praeger Perspectives, 2007) xiv.

in 2008, Adam Barkman identified what he considered to be the "most common of all mistakes in regard to Lewis scholarship—to oversimplify him and then hail him as infallible."[18]

It bears repeating how unusual and, indeed, how unprecedented is this bleak meta-critical assessment, one that attaches itself to Lewis studies from its beginnings and one that has been sustained for nearly fifty years. Before concluding this section, I might also observe how many books on Lewis, even those that condemn the others as hagiographical or unoriginal, share a key similarity: a desire to spark in their readers a return (or turn) to Lewis's books themselves, a wish to keep Lewis's books and ideas in circulation. For instance, in the preface to his 1981 book on Lewis, Robert Houston Smith asserted, "My justification for writing this book is the hope that what I say will prompt the reader to turn back to Lewis's own works, there to revel in the variegated garments with which this indefatigable imagist clothes the body of his thought."[19] In the conclusion to his 1981 study, Richard Purtill strikes a similar note: "If nothing else, I hope I have sent you to Lewis himself, or back to Lewis himself, to examine his arguments in their context and to study *in extensor* what I have been forced to summarize briefly or quote."[20] Art Lindsley went so far in 2005 as to issue his readers a rather odd enjoinder: "At this point you may ask, Why should I read a book *about* C. S. Lewis? Why not read Lewis himself? Good question! If you have not read *Mere Christianity* and you are inclined to do so, put this book down immediately and begin."[21] Even Edwards, who, as we have seen, could be critical of Lewis studies, proclaimed that "the ultimate goal" of his 1988 edited volume, *The Taste of the Pineapple: Essays on C. S. Lewis as Reader, Critic, and Imaginative Writer*, was "…to revitalize interest in Lewis as an important spokesman to a generation of writers, readers and critics who seem to have lost their moorings, conflating reading and criticism with a host of other, ancillary activities."[22]

This desire "to revitalize interest in Lewis" and to increase the circulation of his books and ideas begs explanation, for, once again, Lewis

---

[18] Adam Barkman, *C. S. Lewis & Philosophy as a Way of Life: A Comprehensive Historical Examination of His Philosophical Thoughts* (Wayne PA: Zossima Press, 2008) 7.

[19] Robert Houston Smith, *Patches of Godlight: The Pattern of Thought of C. S. Lewis* (Athens: University of Georgia Press, 1981) xi.

[20] Richard L. Purtill, *C. S. Lewis's Case for the Christian Faith* (San Francisco: Harper & Row, 1981) 134.

[21] Art Lindsley, *C. S. Lewis's Case for Christ: Insights from Reason, Imagination and Faith* (Downers Grove IL: InterVarsity Press, 2005) 24.

[22] Edwards, introduction to *Taste of the Pineapple*, 4.

studies are unusual in this respect: Most scholars study their chosen authors in a spirit of critical discovery and interpretive originality—not advocacy. On one level, the desire might reflect anxiety about Lewis's place in the canon. As we saw in the last chapter, Lewis's popularity ebbed soon after his death; the mission of Walter Hooper, Lewis's editor, from the beginning was to keep Lewis's books in circulation. A certain anxiety thus characterized the birth of Lewis studies, and many Lewis scholars consequently shared not only Hooper's unbridled love of Lewis but his mission as editor as well. This shared mission might also go some distance in explaining the hagiographical character of much Lewis scholarship; veneration is obviously a form of commendation, an implicit case that Lewis belongs in the canon. And earlier in this section, I suggested that paraphrase inflected by veneration produces hagiography—however mightily the paraphraser struggles to moderate the veneration and attain critical detachment.

All of these theories, however, have much deeper roots. In the next section, I show how the public-intellectual identity can serve as a heuristic device to explain the meta-critical curiosities of Lewis scholarship.

## II. Understanding the Meta-Critical Curiosities: The Explanatory Power of the Public-Intellectual Identity

Part 1 (and chapter 1 in particular) explained in detail the contours of Lewis's identity as public intellectual. One core quality of any public intellectual is the ability to make difficult ideas and arguments intelligible to the layperson. Lewis clearly possessed this quality, maintaining that his authorial stance as an apologist was that of a "translator": "My task was therefore simply that of a *translator*—one turning Christian doctrine, or what he believed to be such, into the vernacular, into language that unscholarly people would attend to and could understand."[23] This authorial stance sheds light on the rousing condemnations of paraphrase in Lewis scholarship. If Lewis, as public intellectual, provides in many of his works translations of Christian beliefs, then paraphrases of Lewis's works amount to translations of translations. Committed to the circulation of Lewis's books and ideas, paraphrase-heavy studies as well as Lewis "guides" purport to translate what Lewis claimed already to have translated, eventuating in unoriginal, derivative critical studies.

---

[23] C. S. Lewis, "Rejoinder to Dr Pittenger," in *God in the Dock: Essays on Theology and Ethics*, ed. Walter Hooper (Grand Rapids: Eerdmans, 1970) 183. Originally published in *Christian Century* vol. 75 (26 November 1958): 1359–61.

I wish to focus, however, on two facets of the public-intellectual identity: what Richard A. Posner calls "brand identification" and "solidarity goods." Brand identification occurs when a public intellectual's name becomes associated with his or her religious or philosophical positions; the public intellectual becomes a symbol of his or her own ideas and commitments. According to Posner, "solidarity goods" are "...symbolic goods that provide a rallying point for like-minded people."[24]

As *the* exponent of Mere Christianity, Lewis becomes not only a symbol of religious faith, but *the* symbol of a Christianity that rises above denominational difference, above contingency, historical happenstance, and localized concerns. Creating characters whose knowledge approximates absolute truth (*transcendent characters*), he is himself, as previous chapters show, a transcendent writer, perceived as purveying a faith unmediated by partial perspectives rooted in time. Distilling the timeless truths of Christianity (truths that elide the complex historical development of the faith), he thus offers solidarity goods around which Christians have rallied for two millennia, solidarity goods for which Christians would sacrifice their lives. Lewis is a transcendent writer representing the transcendent truths of the faith.

The symbolism of Lewis's identity as public intellectual provides numerous rallying points for admirers. Because of his clear brand identification, Lewis can be—and has been—readily wielded on numerous fronts: against the forces of secularization, against the forces of progress, against the forces of relativism, against the forces of postmodernism, against the forces of women's liberation, against the forces of naturalistic science, etc. The phenomena of brand identification and solidarity goods, endemic to the nature of a public intellectual, explain the paraphrases, hagiography, and the desire within much Lewis scholarship of increasing the circulation of Lewis's books and ideas. To put it simply, the paraphrases, hagiography, and desire are ways of fulfilling Jesus' great commission to spread the gospel. Thus, when Purtill expresses his hope that his book will send the reader back to Lewis, he sets up what to him is his ultimate, larger hope, as he later explains: "And, of course, Lewis himself wants you to look beyond him, to his Master, Christ...."[25] (Purtill is, by the way, correct. As I showed in chapter 1, Lewis rejects the notion of art for art's sake; as he writes, "But the Christian knows from the outset that the salvation of a single soul is more

---

[24] Richard A. Posner, *Public Intellectuals: A Study of Decline* (Cambridge MA: Harvard University Press, 2003) 72, 42.

[25] Purtill, *C. S. Lewis's Case for the Christian Faith*, 134.

important than the production or preservation of all the epics and tragedies of the world...."[26]) Moreover, admirers wish to keep Lewis's books and ideas in circulation because they combat the forces catalogued above; Lewis presciently addresses the dangers of postmodernism, debunks the tenability of relativism, provides a sound alternative to pernicious forms of literary criticism like deconstruction, prophetically warns of the dangers of progressivism and liberalism, etc. Moreover, paraphrases represent one way of continuing Lewis's mission, reiterating the values around which Lewis admirers rally.

What I have thus far described reveals, in broad strokes, the explanatory power of the public-intellectual identity in achieving a clearer understanding of the eccentricities of Lewis scholarship. In the next few subsections, I proceed more systematically, focusing on specific components of Lewis scholarship that flesh out my argument.

### a. The Religious Experience of Reading Lewis

As a transcendent symbol of Mere Christianity, relaying unmediated truths of the faith, Lewis achieves quasi-divine status. For many readers, then, the initial experience of reading a Lewis book is tantamount to a religious conversion. In prefatory or introductory material, numerous Lewis studies begin with an account of the conversion moment, proclaiming how reading Lewis transformed the author's life, analogous to a road-to-Damascus experience.

Examples are legion. In his afterword to the 1976 Bantam edition of *A Grief Observed*, Chad Walsh engages the conversion narrative:

> It all began during World War II, when a friend introduced me to Lewis's work with a copy of his philosophic science fiction novel, *Perelandra*. I could not put it down. I had always loved good science fiction, but never had I come on any as haunting; I was ready to take the next spacecraft to Venus and dwell on the sensuous, floating islands where the story takes place. I began reading everything of Lewis's I could lay hands on, and wrote him an ardent fan letter, to which he graciously replied in his own highly abbreviated handwriting.[27]

A similar narrative unfolds in Kilby's seminal Lewis study, *The Christian World of C. S. Lewis*: "It was almost a quarter century ago that I picked up at

---

[26] C. S. Lewis, "Christianity and Culture" in *Christian Reflections*, ed. Walter Hooper (Grand Rapids: Eerdmans, 1967) 10.

[27] Chad Walsh, afterword to *A Grief Observed* (New York: Bantam Books, 1976) 93–94.

my college book store a little volume by an Oxford don named C. S. Lewis. It was called *The Case for Christianity*, and when I sat down to read it I realized that a new planet had sailed into my ken."[28] James Como's conversion moment occurs during a serendipitous reading of an article, drawing from Lewis, in the *National Review*: "Before reading the article, I had never heard of C. S. Lewis; while reading it, there rose within me a mounting, incredulous excitement mingled with a sort of personal rebirth of optimism. Could it be? Could a man who so unashamedly expressed his Christian beliefs not be laughed at as a fool, scorned as a zealot, or patronized as an eccentric?"[29] Kathryn Lindskoog recalls the "time, place, and manner" of her first Lewis encounter, when a friend loaned her a Lewis book: "You could say that I was mentally 'married' to Lewis that very day." She continues that Lewis "dominated [her] intellectual life from that time on," culminating in an actual meeting with Lewis. She explains, "The fact that I was sitting on the same sofa with him made me afraid that I would fall off the sofa. I was giddy with awe…. Being with him was a bit of heaven, and I hope that heaven will include a bit of being with him."[30] Evoking imagery typical of the conversion experience, Sheldon Vanauken calls his first reading of Lewis "the encounter with Light."[31] Lyle Dorsett explains that some people gave him copies of *Mere Christianity* and *Surprised by Joy*, which "…nudged [him] closer toward faith in the Lord Jesus Christ."[32]

The religiously inflected conversion-to-Lewis narrative became so common, in fact, that in 1979 Donald T. Williams could inscribe it as an archetype, uniting Lewis readers. He states that "…the experience of discovering Lewis had formed an almost archetypal pattern in the lives of countless evangelical students of the past three decades." Williams relates that the initial phase in this archetypal pattern is a questioning and doubting of the faith. Then comes the epiphanic moment of conversion: "Into this dark night

---

[28] Kilby, *The Christian World of C. S. Lewis*, 5.

[29] James Como, preface to *Remembering C. S. Lewis: Recollections of Those Who Knew Him*, ed. James T. Como (San Francisco: Ignatius Press, 2005) 81.

[30] Kathryn Lindskoog, "Reactions from Other Women," in *In Search of C. S. Lewis*, ed. Stephen Schofield (South Plainfield NJ: Bridge Logos, 1983) 82 and 88.

[31] Sheldon Vanauken, *A Severe Mercy* (San Francisco: HarperSanFrancisco, 1987) 83.

[32] Lyle W. Dorsett, *Seeking the Secret Place: The Spiritual Formation of C. S. Lewis* (Grand Rapids: Brazos Press, 2004) 22.

of the soul swept whatever happened to be the student's first Lewis book...."[33]

Reading Lewis as a religious experience, registering the moment with conversion imagery, admirers have created the conditions for hagiography. Because Lewis's ideas have transformed their lives, these admirers want—and, indeed, are divinely called upon—to bring others into this transformative experience. Paraphrases are often the best way to accomplish this task. And in doing so, admirers are carrying on the work of Lewis himself, who, as we have seen, considered the salvation of a single soul to be vastly more important than literary artistry (for its own sake) and scholarship itself.

### b. Lewis Scholarship as Religious Work

For many Lewis scholars, Lewis is thus used as a vehicle for distinctly religious purposes: converting people to Christianity, enriching the faith of the already converted, defending Christian orthodoxy, etc. This claim may seem a truism, for much of the Lewis *corpus* consists of apologetics; again, admirers are simply carrying on Lewis's mission.

However, it is important to observe that this fundamental characteristic of Lewis scholarship as religious work has made more "secular," original approaches to writing about Lewis problematic. Doris Myers's 1994 study, *C. S. Lewis in Context*, illustrates the point. Myers endeavors a purely literary analysis of Lewis's writings, but she must first clear a critical path because of the preponderance of religiously focused studies that have preceded hers. She writes, "But for most of the earliest critics, the interest [in Lewis] was primarily in his defense of Christianity. His religious essays such as *Mere Christianity* were valued more than his fiction, and his fiction was valued more as Christian instruction than as literary art." This myopic interest constitutes a "barrier to the serious literary consideration of [Lewis's fiction]." Having cleared space for her book amid the array of religiously focused studies, Myers states her purpose: "to redirect attention to Lewis's fiction as art worthy of serious study." Testifying to the critical momentum accumulated from previous studies, however, Myers does not drop the subject; a few pages later, she emphasizes her desire "to switch the focus from whether one agrees with Lewis's Christianity...."[34] Once again we

---

[33] Donald T. Williams, "A Closer Look at the 'Unorthodox' Lewis: A More Poetic Bultmann?" *Christianity Today* (21 December 1979): 24.

[34] Doris T. Myers, *C. S. Lewis in Context* (Kent: Kent State University Press, 1994) ix, x, and xiv.

confront a meta-critical curiosity of Lewis studies: A scholar must go to significant prolegomenous lengths to announce her strictly literary analysis of Lewis's *literary* works. Due in large part to Lewis's status as a public intellectual, marketed as the exemplar of Mere Christianity, religiously focused studies have dominated the critical conversation on Lewis.

The religious focus took root in early Lewis studies, often in the form of qualifying and ultimately commending Lewis's theology to a conservative Christian audience. In introducing Lewis's theology in 1964, for instance, Kilby takes occasional measures to safeguard Lewis's orthodoxy, dulling some of Lewis's theological hard edges. Kilby approaches with care the vexed subject of Emeth, who, in *The Last Battle*, finds himself after death in Aslan's country (heaven) even though, during his mortal life, he was not a follower of Aslan. Kilby offers this explanation: "To reconcile the account of Emeth with Lewis's customary teaching that Christ is the only way to salvation it might be pointed out that the doorway in *The Last Battle* is not altogether the symbol of salvation. Indeed an unbelieving pagan and many cynical dwarfs managed to get on the other side of it, as did Tash himself. Perhaps the door is to be looked upon as similar to the purlieus of heaven in *The Great Divorce*, where a great many people caught glimpses of the glory within and yet refused to enter."[35] Emeth's entrance through the doorway, however, is not the issue; the issue is that Emeth ultimately ends up in Aslan's country. The scene is probably less analogous to the soteriology in *The Great Divorce* and more illustrative of a more latitudinarian line from *Mere Christianity*: "We do know that no man can be saved except through Christ; we do not know that only those who know Him can be saved through Him."[36]

Kilby goes on to address Lewis's view of the Bible, quoting from a letter on the subject that he received from Lewis himself, a letter in which Lewis makes the following claims: that "apparent inconsistencies" exist between the genealogies of Jesus in the Gospels of Matthew and Luke as well as between the accounts of Judas's death in Matthew and Acts; that the story of creation in Genesis is mythical; and that not all passages in the Bible are equally inspired "in the same mode and the same degree."[37] Nevertheless, Kilby once again assures his readers of Lewis's orthodoxy: "It would be a

---

[35] Kilby, *The Christian World of C. S. Lewis*, 143.

[36] C. S. Lewis, *Mere Christianity* (San Francisco, HarperSanFrancisco, 2001) 64.

[37] Quoted in Kilby, *The Christian World of C. S. Lewis*, 154.

bad mistake to infer from what has been said in the last few pages that Lewis regarded the Bible as simply another good book."[38]

During the same year his book was published, Kilby wrote an article specifically attempting to stave off evangelical fears of Lewis's more un-evangelical ideas, an article that concluded by offering "...a few rules that ought to be used in the interpretation of Lewis":

1. The Christian must always apply the rule of truth to whatever he reads, but he should avoid applying it mechanically like a grid. Truth is one, but it has many facets.

2. Try to examine all that Lewis says on a given topic, also to examine it in the spirit in which it was intended.

3. Make a distinction between his speculative ideas and his uncompromising ones.

4. Remember that Lewis is more willing than most evangelicals to "share his bewilderments". There is a rock-bottom honesty about him that should be commended, not criticized.[39]

Kilby's reassurance of Lewis's evangelical-friendly theology—verging, at times, on damage-control maneuvers—not only clears the way for a full-throttled evangelical engagement of Lewis; it also helps establish the religious focus of Lewis scholarship itself. The four interpretive guidelines enumerated above foreground theological considerations, privileging a distinctly religious—and religious-friendly—approach to Lewis.

Examples abound. Sammons's 1980 book is more than a study of Lewis's Ransom trilogy; it is also a call to arms in a spiritual battle with eternal souls at stake: "The dangers Lewis warned were approaching back in the forties are becoming realities in our world. For the myth of Deep Heaven is a true story—the story of you, your earth past and future, the choices you will make, and what side you will be on in a present and ever worsening battle...."[40] Reading and understanding the Ransom trilogy involve much more than appreciating the literary merits of the books; critically engaging Lewis means much more than applying scholarly acumen and interpretive originality to texts. Likewise, Douglas Gresham's biography of Lewis reaches for spiritual edification: "I hope that [this biography] shows how the power of the Holy Spirit of God flows through our lives and, if we allow it

---

[38] Ibid., 156.

[39] Clyde Kilby, "The Provocative Mr Lewis," *Inter-Varsity* (Autumn 1964): 31.

[40] Martha Sammons, *A Guide through C. S. Lewis' Space Trilogy* (Westchester IL: Cornerstone Books, 1980) 10–11.

to, makes us far more than we could ever be by ourselves." (Moreover, probably only a biography on Lewis could include the following sentence: "One thing that was a disadvantage about Kirk [Lewis's tutor] was that he was an atheist...."[41])

Lewis scholarship as religious work is evident also in Armand M. Nicholi Jr.'s *The Question of God: C. S. Lewis and Sigmund Freud Debate God, Love, Sex, and the Meaning of Life* (2002). Setting up Freud as a representative of the "unbeliever" worldview and Lewis as the "believer" worldview, Nicholi assesses the psychological health of both men, evaluating which of the two attitudes toward life leads to more fulfillment. Nicholi clearly sides with Lewis, ending his book with a religiously motivated call to action:

> The answer to the question of God has profound implications for our lives here on earth, both Freud and Lewis agree. So we owe it to ourselves to look at the evidence, perhaps beginning with the Old and New Testaments. Lewis also reminds us, however, that the evidence lies all around us. "We may ignore, but we can nowhere evade, the presence of God. The world is crowded with Him. He walks everywhere *incognito*. And the *incognito* is not always easy to penetrate. The real labor is to remember to attend. In fact to come awake. Still more to remain awake."[42]

Lindsley's 2005 book on Lewis begins each chapter with a running narrative involving a bookstore study group discussing the works of Lewis. Lewis's books help the fictional group leader, John, a conservative Christian, lead to Christ the group's atheist, Simon, who, after reading and discussing Lewis, confesses, "'I hate to admit it, but I am no longer as certain of my atheism as when we began this study....'" Lindsley concludes this narrative with an altar-call moment; John tells Simon, "I can give a good [Lewis] reading list, but remember faith in Christ is more than just satisfying your intellect. C. S. Lewis would not want people to focus on his personality or even his books. He wanted to point beyond that to Jesus."[43]

Even studies of Lewis's literary criticism, which may seem far removed from religious issues and defenses of the faith, conveys strong religious subtexts. Toward the end of his 1986 study of Lewis's literary theories, Edwards connects his subject to religious concerns:

---

[41] Douglas Gresham, *Jack's Life: The Life Story of C. S. Lewis* (Nashville: Broadman & Holman Publishers, 2005) 1, 27.

[42] Armand M. Nicholi, Jr., *The Question of God: C. S. Lewis and Sigmund Freud Debate God, Love, Sex, and the Meaning of Life* (New York: The Free Press, 2002) 5 and 244.

[43] Lindsley, *C. S. Lewis's Case for Christ*, 199.

For Lewis, the Christian, this means that literary inquiry is always in some sense apologetics, though, of course, rarely explicitly so. If Lewis were himself here to rescue reading and criticism from tendentiousness and solipsism, his case would be ultimately grounded on the *transcendental signified* which the Judeo-Christian tradition presents to us as the Triune God, the Great I Am, who stands apart from history and beyond time, and yet once inhabited human history to give it meaning and bring it redemption.[44]

It would seem, then, that nearly all of Lewis's books contain elements that concerned Christians can use as springboards for defending a Christian view of the world, illustrating how Lewis scholarship operates as religious work.

### c. Engaging Transcendence, Combating Postmodernism

As chapter 1 explained, public intellectuals deliver their messages to a diverse audience. One challenge for public intellectuals is thus to build arguments upon forms of authority that have wide resonance, appealing to as many people as possible despite differences in assumptions and convictions. Chapter 5 showed that Lewis develops in nearly every one of his works of fiction a character I identified as the *transcendent character*. This character possesses knowledge that approximates absolute truth, transcending localized viewpoints and partial perspectives, thereby uniting readers within the public sphere around commonalities rather than differences. And in his non-fiction, Lewis himself becomes a transcendent writer, an identity embodied in Lewis's oft-quoted apothegm: "All that is not eternal is eternally out of date."[45] Lewis thus commands transcendent authority.

Lewis's appeal to this sort of authority creates a sacrosanct image within Lewis scholarship. Linking Lewis to an epic hero, Edwards asserts that Lewis managed "to be 'in, but not of' the period in which he lived, tethering himself as a willing Odysseus to a perspective *outside that world*—that is, via divine revelation, to enable his participation in the voyage, all the while maintaining an equilibrium amid endless undulations of time and culture: hence his maxim climaxing *The Four Loves*: 'All that is not eternal is eternally out of date.'" Edwards adds that Lewis's perspective is "suprahistorical, unvested with our own petty ambitions and unreflective fallen

---

[44] Edwards, *A Rhetoric of Reading*, 110.

[45] C. S. Lewis, *The Four Loves* (New York: Harcourt Brace & Company, 1988) 137.

preferences...."[46] Unlike lesser mortals, Lewis somehow possesses an unselfish, disinterested, unmediated perspective; he is conscious (reflective) of what others are unconscious ("unreflective"). Como writes that the sources of Lewis's appeal—"brilliance and intellectual authority; reason, reasonableness, and reliability; tradition, doctrine, and the promise of glory"—"...help lift us all above our and all mere Zeitgeists—into the tides of timelessness." Como then makes the startling claim that Lewis, as a literary critic, was "theoryless," apparently engaging literature from an unmediated, transcendent perspective and thus offering a theoryless theory that cannot possibly be anything other than truth.[47] In his preface to the 1982 edition of *On Stories and Other Essays*, Hooper describes the "whirligig of fashion" that characterized literary criticism during Lewis's time; "Lewis," Hooper assures, "heard them, stayed where he was, and proved immune to the whole thing."[48] And in his preface to the 1970 edition of *God in the Dock*, Hooper states that Lewis had "...the ability to see beyond the partial perspectives which limit so many existentialists."[49]

Affirmations of Lewis's transcendent perspective proceed from other sources of authority as well (and not just Lewis's unmediated, theoryless, departicularized perspective). Chapter 4 likewise showed that Lewis summoned authority in the public sphere by operating as a cipher of what I termed *high tradition*, the collective wisdom of the Western world; Lewis distills this wisdom and then serves as its mouthpiece. Eugene McGovern asks, "'Why are [Lewis's] readers so fervent?'" His answer: "Lewis convinces his readers that he is the most reliable guide they have found on the subjects that matter most." And then, illustrating how the appeal to high tradition transforms Lewis into a transcendent author, McGovern relates that Lewis addresses questions flowing from these subjects with unassailable authority: "His answers are the ones that have been given by thousands of expositors of Christianity since Saint Paul."[50] Drawing from such unimpeachable authority, Lewis cannot help but become sacrosanct to his "fervent" readers.

---

[46] Edwards, preface to *C. S. Lewis: Life, Works and Legacy*, 13 and 14. Vol. 1. London: Praeger Perspectives, 2007.

[47] James T. Como, *Branches to Heaven: The Geniuses of C. S. Lewis* (Dallas: Spence Publishing Company, 1998) 20, 71–72.

[48] Walter Hooper, preface to *On Stories and Other Essays*, by C. S. Lewis, ed. Walter Hooper (San Diego: Harcourt Brace, 1982) ix.

[49] Walter Hooper, preface to *God in the Dock: Essays on Theology and Ethics*, by C. S. Lewis, ed. Walter Hooper (Grand Rapids: Eerdmans, 1970) 12.

[50] Eugene McGovern, "Our Need for Such a Guide," in *Remembering C. S. Lewis*, ed. Como, 232.

Lewis's transcendent status, characterized by objectivity and essentialism, likewise positions Lewis as an antidote to the perceived ills of postmodernism. In his 1998 study, Lionel Adey maintains that university literature departments influenced by postmodernism would do well to heed Lewis's warning in *The Abolition of Man*.[51] Unease with postmodernism (as it influenced literary theory likewise) informs Edwards's 1986 book, *A Rhetoric of Reading: C. S. Lewis's Defense of Western Literacy*: Edwards maintains that traditional understandings of literary meaning have been assaulted by postmodernism. Lewis leads Edwards out of the postmodern fog, emphasizing objectivity, essentialism, and the possibility of unmediated knowledge, a "platform which recommends Lewis as a perspicacious and balanced guide through a critical labyrinth."[52] Toward the end of *C. S. Lewis in Context*, Myers warns of the dangers of postmodernism, highlighting Lewis's opposition to its primary tenets. She proclaims the urgent need to find someone who can carry on the legacy of Lewis, responding to the lamentable effects of the postmodern turn. She then concludes, "that probably no one has his qualifications as intellect, mythicist, or prose stylist." "But," she adds, "one can always reread Lewis."[53] Louis Markos points to Lewis's prescience, identifying Lewis as "…a man whose vision allowed him to pierce through the modern and postmodern tree to examine the roots that sustain it."[54] Thomas L. Martin registers the now-familiar critical narrative: Postmodernism threatens the stability of meaning and the possibility of knowledge; Lewis presciently provides a counter-attack strategy. Characterizing his own words as "alarmist," Williams believes that the "…minds [of young Christians] are increasingly instructed and controlled by [postmodern] paradigms which are in deadly conflict with the Christian worldview and the Christian tradition as any of us—Protestant, Catholic, or Orthodox, Reformed, Dispensationalist, or Arminian—have ever understood it." Evoking my notion of Lewis as the mouthpiece of high tradition, Williams admonishes, "If the West [i.e., Western tradition] goes down under this assault (considered as an attack on the possibility of truth claims), [the Church] will go down with it (insofar as making a particular set of truth claims is the essence of her mission)."[55] The deficiencies of his

---

[51] Adey, *C. S. Lewis*, 102.

[52] Edwards, *A Rhetoric of Reading*, ix, 8.

[53] Myers, *C. S. Lewis in Context*, 217.

[54] Louis Markos, *Lewis Agonistes: How C. S. Lewis Can Train Us to Wrestle with the Modern and Postmodern World* (Nashville: Broadman & Holman, 2003) x.

[55] Donald T. Williams, *Mere Humanity: G.K. Chesterton, C. S. Lewis, and J. R. R. Tolkien on the Human Condition* (Nashville: Broadman & Holman, 2006) 154, 162–63.

understanding of postmodernism notwithstanding, Williams illustrates how Lewis's methods of commanding authority in the public sphere, especially the method of appealing to high tradition, elevates him to a transcendent perspective, from which he is mobilized to combat postmodernism and transformed into a sacred image.

I cannot conclude this section without first observing how postmodernism is both a blessing and a curse within Lewis studies. On the one hand, many Lewis scholars obviously perceive postmodernism as an evil entity in direct opposition to their understanding of Christianity. On the other hand, postmodernism is an animating force that keeps the Lewis industry churning. That is, postmodernism hurtles admirers back into the books of Lewis, providing the animus that unites Lewis lovers in an oppositional stance, creating solidarity at Lewis conferences, and opening numerous polemical avenues for Lewis book writers. Postmodernism may thus be deadly to the faith, but it enlivens interest in the defender of the faith.

### d. Further Solidarity Goods: The Assurances of Conservatism

The invocation of Lewis to combat the encroachment of postmodernism is one example of a larger call to critique the forces of innovation in the name of a general conservatism. As we have seen, Lewis offers solidarity goods of a clear religious nature, but they are religious goods with strong conservative inflections. Throughout his writings, Lewis remains skeptical of progress. His appeal to the Law of Human Nature in *Mere Christianity* and the *Tao* in *The Abolition of Man* reposes confidence in traditional values. Many Lewis admirers resonate with Lewis when he portrays the ills of modern society, supposedly proceeding from innovation, new philosophies, and new science. Consequently, Lewis offers to likeminded readers the assurances of conservatism: further solidarity goods around which Lewis admirers can rally.

Numerous examples can be cited. In an essay titled "Our Need for Such a Guide," Eugene McGovern maintains that a knowledge of Lewis and his writings is critical for Christians in a post-Christian day and age such as ours, when politicians attempt "...to defend the hundreds of billions we spend on the health, education, and welfare of the citizenry" without a transcendent reason—namely, that these citizens possess immortal souls and are thus infinitely worth helping. McGovern likens the dissolution of civilization to the descent down a hill: "Perhaps it is better to say that we are somewhere on a path that began at the top of a hill at a time when our civilization was called Christendom and are headed down and away from that toward something else."[56]

Como calls the middle third of the twentieth century—during which Lewis lived—"...one of the worst declines in human history." Como then corrects himself: "Did I say *one* of the worst? Let me not be cautious for caution's sake: the twentieth century offers mostly ruins and constitutes a net moral and cultural loss." This loss extends through the duration of the century, prompting Como to ask, "Is there nothing to redeem the century? So I look, and I find...the advent of movies, the maturation of baseball, and the ready availability of ibuprofen, for those of us delusional enough to think we can still play the second instead of merely watching the first." Like the advent of postmodernism, however, the destructive legacy of the twentieth century is both a blessing and a curse, leaving us with "depredations" but also "...bring[ing] us to Lewis—and Lewis to us, for he is a Providential man if ever there was one."[57]

Thomas Howard likewise paints the twentieth century as a vast wasteland, with Lewis heroically standing defiant against its onslaught of newfangled theories and technologies. Howard here recapitulates the "mythology" of twentieth-century progress:

> We now have the tools at our disposal to come at the plain truth of things: the analyst's couch, the test tube, the questionnaire, the computer. These will deliver us, where the aspergillum, the thurible, the gospel book, and the crucifix failed. It will take a long time, of course, to clear the space, but we are at last beginning, and soon can get down to building the real edifice, the temple of Man. So runs the contemporary mythology. Lewis

---

[56] McGovern, "Our Need for Such a Guide," 236, 237.

[57] James Como, "Culture and Public Philosophy: Another C. S. Lewis (Being Finally an Exhortation)," in *C. S. Lewis: Views from Wake Forest*, ed. Michael Travers (Wayne PA: Zossima, 2008) 36, 37. To be fair, Como remarks in the same essay that "the 'old Western Man' of his [Lewis's] famous inaugural lecture at Cambridge does not necessarily equal Conservative" (41). Como's phrasing here does suggest, however, that conservatism best describes Lewis's general orientation. In the second printing of *C. S. Lewis: A Critical Essay* (1988), Peter Kreeft admits trying too hard to avoid calling Lewis conservative: "I think I was...too concerned to place Lewis in the middle between the Left and the Right, bending over backwards to avoid labeling him a 'conservative.' Politically, this is essentially correct, as is clear from the passage on page 29 about what a truly Christian society would look like. But theologically and philosophically, Lewis clearly is the enemy of the Leftist, the Modernist, the revisionist. And even politically, he is a 'conservative' in the European, Burkean sense of the word, if not the American." See *C. S. Lewis: A Critical Essay* (Front Royal VA: Christendom College Press, 1988) 29–30.

struggled to find a way of speaking to an epoch with which he shared virtually no suppositions at all.[58]

For Kreeft, the twentieth century was so bad that he is "...often tempted to thank God for Hitler. For if one big Hitler and one big Holocaust had not scared the Hell out of us, we might be living in a worldwide Hitler-Holocaust-Hell right now. God rubbed our face in it—we have seen the pure logical consequences of 'the death of God' in the fires of Auschwitz." Despite the supposed palliative evil of Hitler and the Holocaust, the twentieth century nevertheless remains in a cultural abyss of decadence and decay, a narrative Kreeft relays with references to both Lewis and Christ:

> Let's take stock for a moment. How far down the slide have we slid? How much of the *Tao* is already lost? How many of the objectively Permanent Things have become subjectively impermanent? I count at least thirty-three: silence, solitude, detachment, self-control, contemplation, awe, humility, hierarchy, modesty, chastity, reverence, authority, obedience, tradition, honor, simplicity, holiness, loyalty, gentlemanliness, manliness, womanliness, propriety, ceremony, cosmic justice, pure passion, holy poverty, respect for old age, the positive spiritual use of suffering, gratitude, fidelity, real individuality, real community, courage, and absolute honesty (the passionate, or fanatical love of truth for its own sake). That's one lost value for each of the years in Christ's life.[59]

Hooper asserts that the "appalling decadence of the times, the 'enlightened' ignorance of the intelligentsia, and the shameless cowardice of the clerics..." are "...enough to make us at least *feel* we are living in a madhouse." Naturally, Lewis provides the bearings to negotiate this topsy-turvy world: "Lewis knew what was wrong with the world," in part because "...he did not believe in linear, or automatic, progress—the notion that things just somehow went on getting better and better and better. If such a thing as linear progress *is* true, then it is the liberals, not Lewis, who ought to feel stunned at the appearance of 'progress'."[60]

---

[58] Thomas Howard, *The Achievement of C. S. Lewis* (Wheaton IL: Harold Shaw Publishers, 1980) 14.

[59] Peter Kreeft, "Darkness at Noon: The Eclipse of Permanent Things," in *Permanent Things: Toward the Recovery of a More Human Scale at the End of the Twentieth Century*, ed. Andrew A. Tadie and Michael H. McDonald (Grand Rapids: Eerdmans, 1005) 208.

[60] Walter Hooper, "Oxford's Bonny Fighter," in *Remembering C. S. Lewis*, ed. Como, 291–92.

Biographical treatments of Lewis reflect the conservative strains within Lewis studies. As John Batchelor observes, biography and conservatism share a conceptual kinship: "There seems no doubt that the writing of biography is in some sense a 'conservative' activity in that it celebrates a known life of the past."[61] Like conservatism, biography preserves what is deemed valuable in history. Moreover, by generic necessity, biography resists the de-centering strategies of postmodernism, especially as they are expressed in deconstruction. Jürgen Schlaeger comments, "Biographers seem to agree that their craft is immune to, resistant to deconstruction. Biographers are 'in the business of ancestor-worship', that is to say, they believe in identity, however complex it may turn out to be under intense scrutiny."[62] Biography thus tends to assume the invalidity of postmodern theories that many Lewis scholars already reject from the outset; biography, in short, is amenable to Lewis-directed projects.

Biography is also a labor of love, enshrining the past in a figure of adoration. Biographers often revere their subjects. James Boswell, for instance, admits that, upon first being admitted into Samuel Johnson's presence, he "...felt himself elevated as if brought into another state of being."[63] Douglas Bush's biography of Milton at times offers superlative judgments: "And in no poet have religious and political, intellectual and aesthetic experience and sensibility been more completely unified."[64] And John Gardner's biography of Chaucer borders on the panegyrical: "No poet in the whole English literary tradition, not even Shakespeare, is more appealing, either as a man or as an artist, than Geoffrey Chaucer, or more worthy of biography...."[65] Given these qualities of biography, it is little wonder that biographical treatments of Lewis harmonize with the conservative and hagiographical tones of Lewis studies.

On the other hand, biography does not constitute a literal transcription of truth. All biographical accounts are, to some extent, biased, partial, and thus unreliable. As Richard Holmes observes, "Biographers base their work

---

[61] John Batchelor, introduction to *The Art of Literary Biography*, ed. John Batchelor (Oxford: Clarendon Press, 1995) 2.

[62] Jurgen Schlaeger, "Biography: Cult as Culture," in *The Art of Literary Biography*, ed. Batchelor, 65.

[63] James Boswell, *Life of Johnson*, ed. R. W. Chapman (Oxford: Oxford University Press, 1980) 681.

[64] Douglas Bush, *John Milton: A Sketch of His Life and Writings* (New York: Macmillan, 1964) 12.

[65] John Gardner, *The Life and Times of Chaucer* (New York: Alfred A. Knopf, 1977) 3.

on sources which are inherently unreliable. Memory itself is fallible; memoirs are inevitably biased; letters are always slanted towards their recipients; even private diaries and intimate journals have to be recognized as literary forms of self-invention rather than an 'ultimate' truth of private fact or being. The biographer has always had to construct or orchestrate a factual pattern out of materials that already have a fictional or reinvented element."[66] Such considerations lead Stephen Gill to exhort the Wordsworth biographer not to "succumb" to Wordsworth's own account of the first thirty years of his life.

Biographical treatments of religious figures can be particularly problematic, as Frank Schaeffer notes, "Every human being has a dark side. But when you are being hailed as a conduit-to-God, the fact that you are a mere human...has to be ignored by your followers for the same reason that the tribes of Israel really and truly had to keep on believing in Moses' abilities as they wandered lost in the desert."[67] Thus, in collecting memories of Lewis, Luke Rigby recognizes the copious factors that influence biographical accounts: "After almost thirty years, my recollections of C. S. Lewis will be hazy, to say the least. Lewis's renown has spread way beyond expectation. I must beware of fantasy, of gathering into my recollections impressions I have gained from subsequent hearsay and reading."[68]

Some Lewis biographies have implicitly denied or downplayed the subjective influences that shape biography. In an essay titled "C. S. Lewis and C. S. Lewises," for instance, Hooper wants to distinguish the real Lewis from the Lewis presented by certain other scholars. These false Lewises include "Lewis the Misogynist," "Lewis the Fundamentalist/Evangelical," and "Lewis the Doubter."[69] According to Hooper, these false Lewises flow from the pens of scholars with axes to grind, whose perceptions have been distorted by their own agendas and/or ignorance. Hooper, who presumably has no agenda, acquiring a privileged possession of truth, offers instead the one true Lewis, objectively and impartially presented. Gresham succinctly states that his biography of Lewis "...is my attempt to tell the story of his life, the way it was and the way it happened," a thesis statement that seems

---

[66] Richard Holmes, "Biography: Inventing the Truth," in *The Art of Literary Biography*, ed. Batchelor, 17.

[67] Frank Schaeffer, *Crazy for God: How I Grew Up as One of the Elect, Helped Found the Religious Right, and Live to Take All (or Almost All) of It Back* (New York: Carroll and Graf Publishers, 2007) 100.

[68] Luke Rigby, "A Solid Man," in *Remembering C. S. Lewis*, ed. Como, 111.

[69] Walter Hooper, *G. K. Chesterton and C. S. Lewis: The Riddle of Joy*, ed. Michael H. MacDonald and Andrew A. Tadie (Grand Rapids: Eerdmans, 1989) 38, 40, 43.

to discount any possibility of bias or partiality: a purely objective bio-graphical account. Of course, such a project is impossible, presupposing—vis-à-vis Lewis's transcendent perspective—an unmediated vantage point from which to relate a life. (See Appendix 1 for an extended account of the biographical contradictions in Lewis studies.)

The distinctly conservative aspects of biographical treatments of Lewis find parallels in William C. Dowling's idea of the "Boswellian hero." According to Dowling, Boswell's biography of Samuel Johnson depicts a heroic character embattled by the modern world. Significantly, this depiction is strongly colored with a sense of nostalgia and community, for the need for a hero like Johnson was for Boswell particularly acute in a world devoid of heroism. As Dowling writes, "The hero in a world where heroism is possible exists within a community of shared belief, for his personality and his actions always give expression to certain values which, taken together, sustain the society from which he has emerged." Thus, in an unheroic age, the veneration of a hero masks a desire for the virtues of a bygone era and the community that gave them shape: "When a society feels itself to be disintegrating, there is thus a nostalgia for heroes that is also a nostalgia for the community of shared belief." Boswell offers in Johnson "...a symbolic refuge from modern anxiety, being transformed into an actual myth of the heroic past."[70]

The connections here to Lewis and Lewis studies are uncanny. Like Boswell's Johnson, Lewis felt embattled by the modern age. Like Boswell's Johnson, Lewis becomes a hero living in an unheroic age. Most importantly, like Boswell's Johnson, the admirer's Lewis is a symbolic figure, representing the values of a better, once-heroic age, thus inspiring a feeling of nostalgia as well as a desire for a community of shared belief, alienated from the modern world, united by the values and virtues of its hero. Boswell's Johnson and the Lewis of much Lewis scholarship occupy the same symbolic space: "The situation of the hero in Boswellian narrative is symbolically the situation of man living in an age where reason has gone to war with faith, where abstract theories of social progress have triumphed over an older wisdom of tradition and continuity, and where society has become the enemy of the free self."[71] The conservative bent of both Lewis and, more importantly, his admirers creates a symbolical myth, in which

---

[70] William C. Dowling, *The Boswellian Hero* (Athens: University of Georgia Press, 1979) 3, 5.
[71] Ibid., 17.

Lewis becomes the hero in an unheroic age, generating a sense of nostalgia and community that animates Lewis studies.

### e. Employing Lewis's Principles

Lewis naturally provides the models for his admirers to follow. However, because Lewis was a transcendent and thus authoritative writer, dealing in such powerful solidarity goods, the influence of Lewis's models becomes a critical expectation. To mimic Lewis's interpretive strategies yields good scholarship; to defy them constitutes a critical transgression, resulting in shoddy scholarship. The interpretive parameters within Lewis studies have been defined, proceeding from the very subject of Lewis studies: C. S. Lewis himself. (We encounter here yet another meta-critical curiosity. One would be hard pressed to find, say, interpreters of Eliot's "The Waste Land" compelled to abide by the analytical guidelines of Eliot's own literary criticism.)

Lewis, for instance, downplayed the importance of originality. Como follows the principles of his master: "There are few new facts, and hardly any material new to the experienced student of Lewis, but my view of newness, not unlike Lewis's of 'originality,' is that it is much overrated."[72] Attempting to "...articulate a Lewisian model of literacy..." in his *Rhetoric of Reading*, Edwards minimizes his own critical voice: "...my rhetorical strategy is to let Lewis speak for himself as much as possible in bringing together his thinking about literacy from many sources in the canon."[73]

Perhaps no hermeneutical principle has exerted as much influence within Lewis studies as what I identified in chapter 2 as the process of *de-conversion*. According to the mechanism of this process, one must divest oneself as much as possible of all subjectivity before processing a truth claim or, as in the case of *An Experiment in Criticism*, before appreciating a work of art:

> Real appreciation demands the opposite process. We must not let loose our own subjectivity upon the pictures and make them its vehicles. We must begin by laying aside as completely as we can all our own preconceptions, interests, and associations. We must make room for Botticelli's Mars and Venus [sic], or Cimabue's Crucifixion, by emptying our own. After the negative effort, the positive. We must use our eyes. We must look, and go on looking till we have certainly seen exactly what is there. We sit down before the picture in order to have something done to

---

[72] Como, *Branches to Heaven*, xiii.
[73] Edwards, *A Rhetoric of Reading*, 11.

us, not that we may do things with it. The first demand any work of any art makes upon us is surrender. Look. Listen. Receive. Get yourself out of the way.[74]

Thus, Green and Hooper, whom Alan Jacobs refers to as Lewis's "dutiful biographers,"[75] steer clear of over-editorializing and subjective assessments in their seminal biography: "We have not attempted in this book either to criticize Lewis's works or to assess his place in literature."[76] They seemed pressed to get themselves out of the way, enabling readers to receive Lewis without the static of an intrusive critical voice. It is no wonder that Hooper uses Lewis's own critical category to dismiss "unfriendly" books on Lewis: "It should, then, come as no surprise that those determined to use C. S. Lewis instead of receive from him must make him other than he was."[77] Even a scholar like John Beversluis, who systematically rejects Lewis's arguments for Christianity, evokes Lewis's analytical principles, faulting A. N. Wilson's biography of Lewis for its infidelity to Lewis's hermeneutic. Beversluis claims that Lewis "...anticipates and (to my mind) discredits the method on which [Wilson's] biography depends."[78] Beversluis here critiques what he perceives to be Wilson's tendency to interpret Lewis's books through biographical lenses, reading the books as reflections of Lewis's personality and experiences.

To do so is, of course, a clear instance of defiance against Lewis's exhortations regarding what he calls the "personal heresy." Lewis maintains that, in order to read a writer correctly, one "...must share his consciousness and not attend to it...."[79] Such a hermeneutical injunction downplays biographical considerations as valid interpretive avenues for analysis. Such an injunction also enables David Downing to turn the page on the controversy surrounding Lewis's supposed premarital, sexual relationship with Janie Moore: "Too great an interest in such a question may bear out

---

[74] C. S. Lewis, *An Experiment in Criticism* (Cambridge: Cambridge University Press, 1961) 18–19.

[75] Alan Jacobs, *The Narnian: The Life and Imagination of C. S. Lewis* (San Francisco: HarperSanFrancisco, 2005) 275.

[76] Roger Lancelyn Green and Walter Hooper, *C. S. Lewis: A Biography*, rev. ed. (San Diego: Harcourt Brace, 1974) 10.

[77] Hooper, "C. S. Lewis and C. S. Lewises," in *G. K. Chesterton and C. S. Lewis*, ed. MacDonald and Tadie, 50.

[78] John Beversluis, "Surprised by Freud: A Critical Appraisal of A. N. Wilson's Biography of C. S. Lewis," *Christianity and Literature* 41/2 (1992): 181.

[79] C. S. Lewis and E. M. W. Tillyard, *The Personal Heresy: A Controversy* (London: Oxford University Press, 1939) 12.

Lewis's observation in *The Personal Heresy* that readers too often prefer to gossip about the frank details of writers' lives rather than to read their books."[80]

Abiding by Lewis's own interpretive principles has clear implications for Lewis studies. Broaching certain biographical issues becomes problematic; evoking the personal heresy becomes a trump card, undermining the validity by which a certain species of claims can be made. Lewis's principle of receiving, not using, provides theoretical license for extensive paraphrase. That is, following Lewis's principles, admirers want to get out of Lewis's way, letting Lewis speak for himself, and thus enabling others to receive Lewis without critical distractions. Lewis scholars might therefore feel compelled to lower their own critical voices, wary that attempts at more unconventional interpretation might be taken for "using." Finally, the fear of connecting biographical issues to interpretation, of using instead of receiving, and of committing the personal heresy tends to minimize the value of interpretive creativity and originality—as does, of course, Lewis's own dismissive attitude toward originality. The principles described above simply place hermeneutical restrictions upon the way Lewis's writings are engaged. When advocated nearly universally among a great many Lewis scholars, the principles implicitly place hermeneutical restrictions on Lewis studies itself. Similar interpretive frameworks tend to produce similar interpretations.

### f. Lewis Scholarship as Hagiography

The transformation of much Lewis scholarship into hagiography follows from the claims proffered thus far, all of which employ Lewis's designation as a public intellectual as a heuristic device. First, reading Lewis amounts to a religious experience, thus explaining the conversion-to-Lewis narratives that often begin extended studies of Lewis. These conversion accounts occur because Lewis—as public intellectual—provides the sort of "solidarity goods" for which people have the utmost passion. And since Lewis is the embodiment of Mere Christianity, discovering Lewis resembles a conversion to faith. Moreover, Lewis's solidarity goods are typically conservative, transforming Lewis into the heroic embodiment of past virtues, inspiring Lewis admirers with a strong sense of nostalgia and community. Second, again since Lewis is the embodiment of Mere Christianity, much Lewis scholarship takes on the goal of spiritual edification and even evangelization;

---

[80] David Downing, *The Most Reluctant Convert* (Downers Grove IL: InterVarsity Press, 2002) 87.

Lewis scholarship becomes religious work. These extra-scholarly *desiderata* privilege paraphrase-heavy criticism and downplay critical acumen and interpretive creativity. Third, as public intellectual, Lewis mobilizes forms of authority—loudly resonating in the public sphere—that elevate him into a transcendent figure. Lewis provides unmediated truth, immunized against the changing interpretive frameworks, conceptual lenses, and various theories that characterize normal perceptions of reality. Finally, vested with this tremendous authority, Lewis compels admirers to follow his hermeneutical principles, which implicitly sanction paraphrase and downplay interpretive originality and creativity.

Given these meta-critical phenomena, it is little wonder that Lewis has been made into a saint, a sacred figure. Aviad Kleinberg remarks that "sanctity implies separation, demarcation" and that the Latin word "*sanctus*" designates something that has been removed from the realm of the ordinary, sanctified, and is now 'untouchable.'"[81] Clearly Lewis's elevation to the status of transcendent figure removes him from the realm of the ordinary. However, Lewis has been deemed "untouchable" in other, less theoretical, more mundane ways.

The hagiographical tendencies of Walter Hooper evidence some of these ways. In 1982, Hooper claimed that Lewis was (rather literally) "untouchable," maintaining that Lewis never had sexual relations with Joy Davidman Gresham: "For religious as well as physical reasons Lewis's marriage was not consummated."[82] Lyle Dorsett reports that Hooper unsuccessfully urged him to repeat this claim in his 1983 biography of Joy Davidman Gresham, *And God Came In*: "As a historian, I refused because I saw that the evidence was mightily weighted in favor of consummation."[83] In addition to Dorsett's opinion and the evidence that Lewis himself supplies in *A Grief Observed*, Douglas Gresham (as Lewis's stepson) contradicts Hooper's claim. In an interview, Lyle Dorsett blankly asked Gresham if he believed the marriage was consummated. After informing Dorsett that "…it's nobody's goddamn business," Gresham eventually responded, "I never got a doctor to do a medical examination on my mother to find out if the marriage was consummated. But knowing my mother, as I did, and as I do, you can bet

---

[81] Aviad Kleinberg, *Flesh Made Word: Saints' Stories and the Western Imagination,* trans. Jane Marie Todd (Cambridge MA: Belknap Press, 2008) 1.

[82] Walter Hooper, *Through Joy and Beyond: A Pictorial Biography of C. S. Lewis* (New York: Macmillan Publishers Company, Inc., 1982) 151.

[83] Lyle W. Dorset, "Unscrambling the C. S. Lewis 'Hoax,'" *Christian Century* (22 February 1989): 208.

your life it was."[84] Dorsett also maintains that Hooper "marginalizes" the role Joy Davidman Gresham played in Lewis's life in the biography he co-wrote with Roger Lancelyn Green, *C. S. Lewis: A Biography* (1974). Dorsett writes, "In fact, Roger Green told me when I questioned him about this [marginalization of Davidman Gresham], that he did not write that portion of the book. Furthermore, he told Hooper that he wanted that brief part of the book expanded and clarified to present the truth. But, alas, the book went to press without Green's demands being met."[85]

Evidence suggests that Hooper not only wanted to render Lewis "untouchable" with respect to the ways of the flesh, but also from the antagonistic charges of unfriendly critics. In his 1979 study, *Past Watchful Dragons: The Narnian Chronicles of C. S. Lewis*, Hooper alludes to David Holbrook's highly critical, often condemnatory 1973 article, "The Problem with C. S. Lewis." Apparently attempting to protect Lewis—as saint—from the profane and vulgar, Hooper refused to mention Holbrook by name: "I withhold the name of the author as I cannot bear that it should appear on the same page with that of C. S. Lewis."[86] Including the name of this harsh critic alongside that of Lewis would besmirch the purity of the saint. As Lewis editor and trustee of the Lewis estate, Hooper wields considerable influence, defining the issues and setting the tone for much Lewis scholarship.

Hagiographical elements thread their way through Lewisiana from the beginning, even as early as 1948, when David Soper, then professor at Union College, reported the following words repeated by his former students: "'C. S. Lewis is Soper's Bible.'"[87] Lewis hagiography became fodder for a 1981 satirical piece in *The Wittenburg Door*. The article relates the misadventures of one Virgil Buzzy, who, wandering the desert alone, "...was captured by a group of pipe-smoking men and women who said that they were worshippers of C. S. Lewis, otherwise known as the C. S. Lewies. When asked if he had been harmed by his captors, Buzzy replied, 'I have no

---

[84] Lyle W. Dorset, interview with Douglas Gresham, Oral History Project, Wade Center at Wheaton College (4 June 1982): 33, 34–35. Manuscript stored at Wade Center.

[85] Lyle W. Dorsett, review of *Out of My Bone: The Letters of Joy Davidman*, by Don W. King, *Christian Scholar's Review* 40/1 (2010): 113.

[86] Walter Hooper, *Past Watchful Dragons: The Narnian Chronicles of C. S. Lewis* (New York: Collier Books, 1970) 26.

[87] David Soper, "An Interview with C. S. Lewis," *Zion's Herald* (14 January 1948): 28.

problem with pain.'"[88] A 1984 article in the *Los Angeles Times* reported that St. Luke's Episcopal Church in Monrovia, California, installed a representation of Lewis in one of its stained-glass windows, thereby propelling Lewis toward "another stage of canonization."[89] Reviewing Stephen Schofield's edited volume on Lewis, Humphrey Carpenter flatly states that "...several of Mr Schofield's contributors seem to be under the impression that Lewis was God."[90] A 1988 article in the *Virginia Quarterly* revealed how Lewis hagiography acquired consumerist dimensions: "Thus the Lewis devotee (and there are many, judging from the sales figures) could, upon rising, don his C. S. Lewis sweatshirt, ascertain the date from his C. S. Lewis calendar, make coffee wearing his C. S. Lewis apron and drink it from his C. S. Lewis mug, offer devotion to his maker in the words of C. S. Lewis, and meditate on what C. S. Lewis had done on that date, before setting off to work or school with his C. S. Lewis tote bag filled with C. S. Lewis books."[91] A 2001 article in the *Independent* calls Lewis a "figure of near-Messianic status to devotees of his religious apologetics...."[92]

As I have noted, the hagiographical strain within Lewis studies creates meta-critical curiosities. Before even advancing an argument in print, Lewis scholars often assume a defensive stance, compelled to justify the creation of yet another Lewis book or article. This defensive stance plays no small role in critical conversations on Lewis, often beginning and structuring monographs and articles. In Gresham's glowing biography of Lewis, for instance, Christopher Mitchell preemptively addresses in a foreword a predictable critique of the book, one that easily attaches to Lewis studies: "That said, I want to address a criticism that I anticipate is certain to be raised against the book. No doubt at points some readers will feel that the author has drawn an overly pious picture of Lewis. But one must remember that our author believes that Lewis was indeed a saint, and a saint of the most real kind: not someone without flaws, but rather one who aspired to overcome those flaws and in fact did so in many cases...."[93]

---

[88] Erik Nelson, "Survivor of New Cult Found in Desert Muttering," *Wittenburg Door* vol. 59 (February–March 1981): 24.

[89] John Dart, "C. S. Lewis Honored in Church Window," *Los Angeles Times*, 20 October 1984, 4.

[90] Carpenter, "Giddy with Awe," 26.

[91] Michael Nelson, "C. S. Lewis and His Critics," *Virginia Quarterly* 64/1 (Winter 1988): 2.

[92] D. J. Taylor, "The Lion, the Witch and the Boardroom: A Chronicle of Narnia," *Independent*, 7 June 2001, 1.

[93] Christopher Mitchell, foreword to Gresham, *Jack's Life*, v.

This scholarly tendency toward hagiography, as well as the need to defend it, creates an ironic meta-critical phenomenon. In his 1986 study, Edwards suggests that some of "Lewis's friends" betray a critical overcorrection, rendering unduly harsh judgments of Lewis's works to off-set the effusive praise that often attends Lewis studies: "Even among Lewis's friends, there is a perceptible tendency to devalue purposefully certain aspects of his work, especially his fiction, lest Lewis's admirers be written off as mere idolaters."[94] Edwards's observation is a revealing testament to the discourse-shaping power of hagiography within Lewis studies. Creating scholarly expectations and setting critical tones, hagiographical tendencies have fundamentally directed the course and structured the critical discourse of Lewis studies. In fact, six years earlier, Edwards penned an article aptly titled "On the Excesses of Appreciation." Edwards registered the now-familiar meta-critical motifs: "To be blunt, there's a glut [of Lewis scholarship], a glut to which I've contributed forgettable research papers, a lust for everything by and about Lewis that surfaces, and probably this piece." For Edwards, "the mindless proliferation of Lewisiana seems to me analogous to the 'Honk if you love Jesus' bumper stickers: something akin to 'feinting with damn praise'." This mindless proliferation, Edwards remarks, is simply counterproductive, more likely to turn people away from Lewis than turn them on to Lewis: "Is it possible to develop a kind of spiritual pedantry that drives away potential friends from our favorites, that prevents others from acknowledging their greatness precisely because of the inordinate attention these figures seem to receive?"[95]

Whether one answers it affirmatively or not, Edwards's question has unmistakably cast a large shadow over all of Lewis studies. Engaging the meta-critical baggage that accompanies Edwards's question, Lewis scholars must often carve out a critical space for their analyses before even marshaling their arguments—or, in the case of Michael Ward's *Planet Narnia*, at the conclusion of the argument. Ward considers why the astrological elements of his own argument—that each book in the Narniad corresponds to the mythical features of a planet—went undiscovered for so long. Ward's answer illuminates the meta-critical curiosities explored in this section: "[Lewis's] status as a Christian too often causes Pavlovian reactions of approval among his co-religionist readership; his interest in astrology gets

---

[94] Edwards, *A Rhetoric of Reading*, 9.
[95] Edwards, "On the Excesses of Appreciation," *CSL: Bulletin of the New York C. S. Lewis Society* vol. 123 (January 1980): 3.

overlooked in the rush to lionize him."[96] Employing the concept of public intellectual as a heuristic device, one can see that Lewis's status as a Christian has branded his name, marketing solidarity goods that generate enormous passion and that have dominated critical conversations within Lewis studies.

---

[96] Michael Ward, *Planet Narnia: The Seven Heavens in the Imagination of C. S. Lewis* (Oxford: Oxford University Press, 2008) 246.

# 13

# The C. S. Lewis Industry

## I. "Those Who Love the Same Truth": Toward a Definition of the C. S. Lewis Industry

According to the *Oxford English Dictionary*, referring to the study of a particular writer as an "industry" is a relative novelty, dating to a 1965 issue of the *New Statesman* that makes mention of a "Pindar industry." References to a "Shakespeare industry" and a "Joyce industry" soon followed. The OED's definition of the term carries a neutral connotation: "scholarly or diligent work devoted to the study of a particular author or subject."[1] At its most basic level, then, the C. S. Lewis industry may simply refer to the body of work devoted to the study of Lewis. Of course, the term's generic definition becomes more particularized when applied to the unique character of Lewis studies, adopting various connotations and triggering various reactions whenever the phrase "the Lewis industry" is invoked. The purpose of this chapter is to explore these connotations and ultimately flesh out what I consider to be the defining characteristic of the Lewis industry.

Often, the phrase "Lewis industry" seems to carry negative connotations for reasons already discussed—specifically, the apparent glut of poor-quality and/or hagiographical books. In this sense, the "Lewis industry" names the collection of unoriginal studies that paraphrase Lewis and turn him into a saint. Thus, Peter Milward contends that his "challenge" to Lewis—that is, addressing the "inadequacies of his arguments"—is necessary in part because of "...the present state of what may be called 'Lewis scholarship,' or even 'the Lewis industry.'" Lewis, Milward believes, is too often "...enshrined as a saint."[2] Other times, the phrase "Lewis industry" evokes more sinister connotations, playing on the more well-recognized definition of "industry": namely, "the practice of a profitable occupation."[3] I have already noted the 1988 *Virginia Quarterly* article that ridiculed the

---

[1] "Industry," online Oxford English Dictionary. http://www.oed.com/view/entry/94859?redirectedFrom=industry#eid. Accessed 17 Feb. 2010.

[2] Peter Milward, *A Challenge to C. S. Lewis* (London: Associated University Presses, 1995) 11.

[3] "Industry," online OED.

consumerism that has capitalized on Lewis's popularity (the hawking of Lewis calendars, mugs, tote bags, etc.). Kathryn Lindskoog remarked in 2001 that "...the C. S. Lewis industry is richer than ever."[4] And, as we have seen, Robert MacSwain coined the term "Jacksploitation," which can refer to the writing of Lewis books whose "...primary purpose is still to 'cash in' on Lewis's popularity rather than to advance significantly our understanding of his work."[5]

Once again deploying the concept of the public intellectual as a heuristic device, I wish to chart a different course in defining the Lewis industry. I begin with a consideration of Walter Hooper, whose influence on the Lewis industry, as trustee of the Lewis estate and editor of Lewis's books, is significant. Como calls him the "indefatigable and indispensable Walter Hooper."[6] A. N. Wilson comments that the "...development of the C. S. Lewis industry [was] presided over by Hooper...." Touching on the hagiographical elements of Lewis studies, Wilson writes that "Hooper is one of nature's devotees, and he had hero-worshiped C. S. Lewis for many years."[7]

Hooper's zest for Lewis sets the tone for much Lewis scholarship, especially considering that Hooper writes the prefaces for numerous Lewis texts and collections of Lewis essays. Prefaces shape the way readers understand and value a writer, providing the interpretive bearings that orient reader responses. Evoking many of the phenomena particular to Lewis as public intellectual—summoning authority in the public sphere as a transcendent writer, operating as a cipher for high tradition (of Western Civilization), etc.—Hooper reposes supreme confidence in Lewis's authority. Here Hooper describes his initial encounter with Lewis: "Lewis believed, it seemed to me, with the certainty of those who had been with Jesus."[8] In prefaces, Hooper implicitly invites Lewis readers to share in that unbreakable confidence, positioning Lewis, as we have seen in the preface to *On Stories and Other Essays on Literature*, above the "whirligig of fashion" that

---

[4] Kathryn Lindskoog, *Sleuthing C. S. Lewis: More Light in the Shadowlands* (Macon: Mercer University Press, 2001) xii.

[5] Robert MacSwain, introduction to *The Cambridge Companion to C. S. Lewis*, ed. Robert MacSwain and Michael Ward (Cambridge: Cambridge University Press, 2010) 11.

[6] Bob Smietana, "C. S. Lewis Superstar," *Christianity Today* (December 2005): 31.

[7] A. N. Wilson, *C. S. Lewis: A Biography* (New York: Norton, 1990) 302, 301.

[8] Walter Hooper, "My Original Encounter with C. S. Lewis," in *Mere Christians: Inspiring Stories of Encounters with C. S. Lewis*, ed. Mary Anne Phemister and Andrew Lazo (Grand Rapids: Baker Books, 2009) 140.

characterizes the modern age. In his preface to *God in the Dock*, Hooper laments the apostasy of the modern age and then frames the reader's reception of Lewis's essays: "It is, partly because of this, a pleasure for me to offer as an antidote this new book by C. S. Lewis."[9] Throughout his prefaces, Hooper repeatedly establishes Lewis as an antidote to the toxicity of the modern age, a God-send here to bring encouragement, solace, and answers to a godless world. Even the formation of at least part of the Lewis canon was providential. In his preface to *The Dark Tower and Other Stories*, Hooper states that Warren Lewis ordered Fred Paxford, Lewis's gardener, to burn a collection of Lewis's writings. Hooper miraculously appeared to prevent its destruction: "By what seems more than coincidence, I appeared at the Kilns that very day and learned that unless I carried the papers away with me that afternoon they would indeed be destroyed."[10]

It is with this authority and providential guidance in mind that I wish to consider a telling observation—of critical importance to my definition of the Lewis industry—that Hooper makes in his foreword to Wayne Martindale's 2005 study, *C. S. Lewis on Heaven and Hell: Beyond the Shadowlands* (2005):

> The book is important in another way as well. Shortly after Lewis died, those who knew his works were far fewer than now, and they delighted in giving and receiving new light on Lewis's books. It was a time of pleasant civility when everyone was saying to the others, "What? You like Lewis?" Those who liked Lewis liked one another. Many of us hung on the latest issue of *CSL: The Bulletin of the New York C. S. Lewis Society* and other publications, eager to know what the others were thinking and saying about this remarkable writer. We took it for granted we needed one another. But whatever attracted such an enormous number of fans to Lewis became, as well, a magnet for those who had different motives. Much of the early camaraderie seemed to have been lost for good. Before I had reached the end of this book, I knew it was a recovery of that friendship that ought to exist between those who love the same truth. It is the product of genuine appreciation and insight, a labor of love that well matches its subject, C. S. Lewis's brilliant illumination of Heaven and Hell.[11]

---

[9] Walter Hooper, preface to *God in the Dock: Essays on Theology and Ethics*, by C. S. Lewis, ed. Walter Hooper (Grand Rapids: Eerdmans, 1970) 7.

[10] Walter Hooper, preface to *The Dark Tower and Other Stories*, by C. S. Lewis, ed. Walter Hooper (San Diego: Harcourt Brace & Company, 1977) 7.

[11] Walter Hooper, foreword to *C. S. Lewis on Heaven and Hell: Beyond the Shadowlands*, by Wayne Martindale (Wheaton IL: Crossway Books, 2005) 13–14.

Hooper conceives of Lewis scholars—at least during the breezy early days—as a network of friends, united by their love of Lewis. Their love of Lewis breeds good will toward each other. In fact, they achieve solidarity by virtue of the fact that they love the same truth (a religious truth with a strong conservative bent). Their channels for expressing admiration for Lewis and good will toward each other are grassroots in structure, evident not only in *CSL: The Bulletin of the New York C. S. Lewis Society*, but the myriad other Lewis newsletters, bulletins, and journals that were formed in the 1970s and '80s (the *Chronicle of the Portland C. S. Lewis Society* in 1972; the *Lamp-Post*, published by the Southern California C. S. Lewis Society, in 1977; the *Canadian C. S. Lewis Journal* in 1979; and *VII: An Anglo-American Review* in 1980). Moreover, the books produced by this network of friends consists of "genuine appreciation and insight," an appreciation that easily becomes, as we have seen, mere paraphrase; these books are also "labor[s] of love," a love which, when directed toward the subjects of Lewis's books, becomes nearly devotional, easily slipping into the religious passion that characterizes hagiography.

I contend that Hooper's nostalgic memory of early Lewis studies is not a lost vision; rather, Hooper has described the status of the present-day Lewis industry. Although the vision has become embattled, it remains intact. The metaphor of friendship has long defined the Lewis industry. Of course, the metaphor does not suggest that Lewis scholars all know each other; rather, the metaphor conveys the idea that they are united by common beliefs and loves. To put it more strongly, Lewis scholars are often *expected* to be united by common beliefs and loves (though, as we will see, this expectation is gradually changing). Thus, in his preface to *God in the Dock*, after commending Lewis as the "antidote" for the poison of much modern theology, Hooper presumes his readers share his and Lewis's convictions, a presumption so certain that it is phrased sarcastically in the form of a false dilemma: "There are, however, I expect, others like myself who are more concerned whether a book is *true* than whether it was written last week."[12] Such an utterance has shaped the contours of the Lewis industry. What particularly unifies the Lewis industry is Lewis's own emphasis on Mere Christianity; since Lewis himself underscores what Christians have in common, Lewis scholars tend to enact what they study, solidifying the metaphorical friendships. In short, to return to the nomenclature of public-intellectual scholarship, Lewis scholars are united around Lewis's solidarity

---

[12] Hooper, preface to *The Dark Tower and Other Stories*, 7.

goods. From these goods emerge the metaphorical friendships that define the Lewis industry.

These friendships are often displayed (and literalized) at Lewis conferences. Como's characterization of these conferences bears repeating: "[W]henever meeting in conference on the subject of C. S. Lewis I delight in imagining my fellow conferees as medieval monks and nuns and our venue as a monastery."[13] This sentence crystallizes my argument. The participant in a Lewis conference is assumed to share the convictions of his or her fellow monks and nuns, cloistered for a time from the secular cataclysms of the modern world, paying homage to a transcendent figure who, as Como explains, offers "purpose and direction." The conference unites both metaphorical and literal friends who passionately rally around solidarity goods. This is probably the reason why such conferences generate the strongest rhetoric—for example, Kreeft's temptation to "thank God for Hitler," which was originally read at a 1990 conference; the presence of like-minded individuals emboldens the utterance of radical statements.

From one perspective, the formation of the Lewis industry into a metaphorical network of friends has proven to be beneficial and salutary. The network serves to spiritually edify its members, nurturing and inspiring faith. The network also serves to clarify its theological self-understanding, self-referentially examining the characteristics of Mere Christianity. The C. S. Lewis industry remains faithful to the convictions of Lewis himself, thereby forming an interpretive community that uncompromisingly builds upon shared assumptions. In this sense, the Lewis industry models the integration of faith and scholarship.

From a different perspective, however, the formation of the Lewis industry into a metaphorical network of friends is less auspicious. The quality of like-mindedness—that is, loving the same truth—might create a critical insularity and homogeneity, discouraging alternative approaches to Lewis; the result is a lack of critical diversity. Like-minded people tend to see matters in similar ways. Founding member of the New York C. S. Lewis Society Eugene McGovern engages the key concepts of my argument: "There is in the society a sense of community all too rare in most of our lives and an acknowledgment that an interest in Lewis goes far toward establishing a friendship. There is, further, an example of Lewis's Principle of Inattention: we find that, by coming together quite matter-of-factly to discuss an author

---

[13] James Como, "Culture and Public Philosophy: Another C. S. Lewis (Being Finally an Exhortation)," in *C. S. Lewis: Views from Wake Forest*, ed. Michael Travers (Wayne PA: Zossima Press, 2008) 34.

in whom we share an interest, we are led to the discovery that we are in agreement on the fundamental things." Significantly, he then wonders if anyone would benefit from reading a meta-critical analysis hypothetically titled "Literary Enthusiasm among the Nonliterary: Etiology and Symptomatology in Admirers of C. S. Lewis" (which is pretty much what I am attempting in this chapter). He answers, "Perhaps, but any such explanation would be one obtained by looking *at* the phenomenon and so could not be as revealing as one obtained by looking *along* it."[14] The idea here seems to be that in order to appreciate what I call the meta-critical C. S. Lewis phenomenon one must look along with it, sharing its loves and seeing as it sees. But to do so, the critical starting point must be "agreement on the fundamental things."

Again, such agreement promotes solidarity and community. But it also limits the range of scholars who study Lewis and narrows analytical approaches.[15] Adam Gopnick illustrates this dynamic in his critique of Alan Jacobs's *The Narnian*:

> Lewis is defended, analyzed, protected, but always in the end vindicated, while his detractors are mocked at length: a kind of admiration not so different in its effects from derision. Praise a good writer too single-mindedly for too obviously ideological reasons for too long, and pretty soon you have him all to yourself. The same thing has happened to G. K. Chesterton: the enthusiasts are so busy chortling and snickering as their man throws another right hook at the rationalist that they don't notice that the rationalist isn't actually down on the canvas; he and his friends have long since left the building.[16]

A wariness of critical homogeneity and insularity seems to inform the compilation of Robert MacSwain and Michael Ward's *The Cambridge Companion to C. S. Lewis* (2010). MacSwain explains that he and Ward made

---

[14] Eugene McGovern, "Our Need for Such a Guide," in *Remembering C. S. Lewis: Recollections of Those Who Knew Him*, ed. James T. Como (San Francisco: Ignatius Press, 2005) 230.

[15] This is not to say that no scholarly diversity exists within the Lewis industry. Different strands of interpretive approach, for instance, can be found in what Glenn Edward Sadler identifies as two different groups that revere Lewis: evangelicals and the "Anglo followers." (See Sadler, "Revering and Debunking a Saint," in *Reformed Journal* vol. 40 (November 1990): 24.) I do maintain that the scholarly diversity is significantly limited.

[16] Adam Gopnick, "Prisoner of Narnia: How C. S. Lewis Escaped," *New Yorker* (21 November 2005): accessed 8 September 2009, http:www.newyorker.com/archive/2005/11/21/051121crat_atlarge.

"...a deliberate attempt to widen the discussion of Lewis's legacy beyond 'the usual suspects' [and have therefore] invited a number of contributors who have not hitherto participated in these debates, or at least not at this public level." He further writes, "Feeling that the current situation in Lewis scholarship represented something of an impasse, we wanted to bring some fresh voices to the conversation."[17] Again, conceived as a network of metaphorical (and literal) friends, the Lewis industry both succeeds and fails in generating solidarity of belief: It creates critical discussions that inspire and edify its members while simultaneously bringing those discussions to an "impasse" that amounts to a scholarly cul-de-sac.

In addition, the solidarity cultivated among the network of friends can come at the expense of those outside the network or even those expelled from the network. To some extent, this sort of phenomenon is both natural and predictable. When the beliefs and ideals of a group of like-minded individuals are threatened, their response is vigorous; the values around which their solidarity is based are at stake. In his review of Kathryn Lindskoog's *The C. S. Lewis Hoax*, which calls into ethical question the editorial actions and character of Walter Hooper, Nicholas Barker images the Lewis industry as a "club" with a clear line of demarcation between those inside and those outside: "[The Inklings] are not unique in this; anybody from a football club to a philosopher may have fans. But they have more than most, and the rest of us (diversely as we may think of Lewis and the others with admiration or dislike) who are not visited by their enthusiasm, or rather the enthusiasm that they convey, are not members of the club. Clubs may be cosy or violent, but they thrive on common enthusiasm." Lindskoog, Barker explains, struck a nerve center when she accused Hooper of literary forgery: "In doing so she has embarrassed the Lewis 'establishment' who have retorted with surprising sharpness."[18]

The retorts to various outsiders—or, in Lindskoog's case, an insider, sharing the religious beliefs of Lewis and his admirers, who became an outsider—exemplify the protectiveness of Lewis among the Lewis industry, conceived as a network of friends with shared beliefs and commitments. To re-invoke an overarching phrase of my larger thesis, Lewis as public intellectual provides for his admirers solidarity goods of immense motivating power. Challenges to those goods—challenges that can come in various forms—mobilize the retorts that stake out the boundaries between

---

[17] MacSwain, introduction to *The Cambridge Companion to C. S. Lewis*, 9.

[18] Nicholas Barker, "C. S. Lewis Darkly," *Essays in Criticism* 40/4 (October 1990): 359, 360.

insiders and outsiders, shoring up a critical consensus around which solidarity is built, and, in effect, territorializing the study of Lewis. I therefore briefly examine in the following subsections some of those outsiders who have instigated this process.

### a. Kathryn Lindskoog

Before 1978, Lindskoog could be characterized as member of the Lewis network of friends—that is, the Lewis industry. In 1973, she published a monograph titled *The Lion of Judah in Never-Never Land: The Theology of C. S. Lewis Expressed in His Fantasies for Children.*[19] Lewis himself praised the book.[20] In 1978, however, she wrote an article published in *Christianity and Literature* titled "Some Problems in C. S. Lewis Scholarship." The piece concerned the provenance of *The Dark Tower*, published by Hooper as an unfinished Lewis manuscript. While casting doubt on the authenticity of the manuscript, questioning Hooper's account of its recovery, Lindskoog attempted to maintain a courteous tone: "The questions [of her article] are in no way meant as complaints or challenges [to or against Hooper and Owen Barfield, who helped Hooper in managing the Lewis estate]. They are only questions, and they are likely to go unanswered. But it is fitting for serious Lewis scholars to know what the questions are. Not all mysteries are interesting, and not all mysteries need solving. But a bit of curiosity is a great aid to perceptive reading."[21]

The "retort" to Lindskoog's article was quick and robust. Due to the numerous letters received in response to the piece, the editorial staff of *Christianity and Literature* published in a subsequent issue of that same year a section called "Dialogue." Owen Barfield wrote that Lindskoog's article consists of a "mass of inaccurate statements, ingenious speculations, and waspish innuendo," the latter of which may constitute "libelous insinuation."[22] McGovern called the essay "obnoxious," denouncing Lindskoog's "tasteless

---

[19] Grand Rapids, MI: Eerdman's, 1973.

[20] Lewis wrote to Kathryn Stillwell (later Lindskoog): "Your thesis [later published as *The Lion of Judah in Never-Never Land*] arrived yesterday and I read it at once. You are in the centre of the target everywhere. For one thing, you know my work better than anyone else I've met: certainly better than I do myself." (See letter to Kathryn Stillwell, 29 October 1957, *The Collected Letters of C. S. Lewis*, vol. 3, *Narnia, Cambridge, and Joy, 1950–1963*, ed. Walter Hooper [San Francisco: HarperSanFrancisco, 2007] 891.)

[21] Kathryn Lindskoog, "Some Problems in C. S. Lewis Scholarship," *Christianity and Literature* 27/4 (Summer 1978): 54.

[22] "Dialogue," *Christianity and Literature* 28/2 (Winter 1979): 10.

probing of Walter Hooper's life before he knew Lewis."[23] For her part, in her own reply to these letters, Lindskoog remained open to correction: "I do not know what the abundance of inaccurate statements in my article is. I am eager to stand corrected if Owen Barfield or anyone else will spell out my errors. My article was an inevitably fallible attempt to promote more truth and accuracy in Lewis studies." Nevertheless, Lindskoog stood behind her thesis: "The fact that my character and competence were attacked vehemently in several unpublished letters but that not one respondent has even tried to straighten out the contradictions in the [Green and Hooper] biography, which should be an elementary task if its accounts are authentic, indicates that certain questions I raised in order to put Lewis students on guard are indeed as difficult as they first seemed to me."[24]

Years later, Lindskoog stated that, after the publication of the article, she "...was shunned by many influential people in Lewis affairs, some of whom I had considered my good friends. Invitations dwindled, manuscripts were rejected, letters went unacknowledged, and my name gradually disappeared from various publications and bibliographies." Lindskoog summarized her eviction from the Lewis industry with the words from an editor at Harper & Row: "'Lindskoog doesn't know how to play this C. S. Lewis Game.'" [25]

Lindskoog's article became the basis for a book published in 1988 titled *The C. S. Lewis Hoax*, in which she notches up her rhetoric, more pointedly accusing Hooper of literary forgery and malfeasance as Lewis editor. In the book's opening pages, she registered the dangers of publishing her study: "I have been warned repeatedly that if I dare to reveal my discoveries in this book I will be hounded by libel suits and otherwise punished. I hope that is not true."[26] Lyle Dorsett's review showed how the book created a sensation: "Ever since *The C. S. Lewis Hoax* came off the press, people all over North America and the United Kingdom have been asking: Is Kathryn Lindskoog insane? Is her book accurate? Is the author right or wrong about Walter Hooper?"[27]

In 2001, Lindskoog wrote another monograph on Hooper's alleged dubious actions as Lewis editor. Titled *Sleuthing C. S. Lewis: More Light in the Shadowlands*, the book ratchets up the force, intensity, and scope of her

---

[23] Ibid., 11.

[24] Ibid., 14.

[25] Kathryn Lindskoog, *Sleuthing C. S. Lewis: More Light in the Shadowlands* (Macon: Mercer University Press, 2001) 220.

[26] Kathryn Lindskoog, *The C. S. Lewis Hoax* (Portland OR: Multnomah, 1988) 14.

[27] Lyle W. Dorsett, "Unscrambling the C. S. Lewis 'Hoax,'" *Christian Century* (22 February 1989): 208.

charges. Lindskoog proclaims, for instance, "What has happened to Lewis since his death is an amazing saga of fakery, fraud, and forgery."[28] Elsewhere, Lindskoog's charges include some rather uncharitable accusations like the following, found in one of her footnotes: "Hooper's overly colorful passages about Warren's alcoholism puzzle readers who believe that Hooper is himself an alcoholic, as some North Carolina people believed his father was."[29]

The aftermath of Lindskoog's article and two books was unsurprisingly ugly. In his introduction to *Sleuthing C. S. Lewis*, Robert S. Ellwood noted that Lindskoog "...has suffered demeaning slurs and rebukes, or worse has been given the silent treatment, from those in the multi-million dollar C. S. Lewis 'industry' who ought to take her well-documented case more seriously."[30] A. N. Wilson calls *Sleuthing* "one of the most vitriolic personal attacks on a fellow-scholar, Walter Hooper, that I have ever read in print." Wilson maintains that Lindskoog's work has divided Lewis scholars into warring camps: "Lewis idolatry, like Christianity itself, has resorted to some ugly tactics as it breaks itself into factions. Hard words are used on both sides, and there is not much evidence of Christian charity when the war is at its hottest."[31] As we have seen, Barker asserts that Lindskoog "...has embarrassed the Lewis 'establishment' 'who have retorted with surprising sharpness." J. Stanley Mattson attempted to strike a conciliatory tone in 1989, maintaining that both Lindskoog and Hooper are valuable scholars within Lewis studies. Nevertheless, as paraphrased in *Christianity Today*, Mattson admitted that "... the current conflict has produced considerable grief within the community of Lewis scholars." But he hoped that the conflict could be resolved along a "'redemptive trajectory.'"[32] In 1998, Alan Jacobs raised the possibility of a subtext animating the dispute: "The whole spectacle is immensely unedifying and becomes more so when people start to notice that Hooper is a late convert to Catholicism while Lindskoog writes for evangelical publishers."[33] In this sense, the conflict thus constitutes a betrayal of the Mere Christianity for which Lewis stood. The controversy cooled over the years, especially in 2003 when Lindskoog died and Alistair

---

[28] Lindskoog, *Sleuthing C. S. Lewis*, xii.

[29] Ibid., 90.

[30] Robert S. Ellwood, introduction to *Sleuthing C. S. Lewis*, xi.

[31] Wilson, *C. S. Lewis*, xvi.

[32] Randy Frame and Marjorie Chandler, "A 'Hoax' Observed," *Christianity Today* (16 June 1989): 65.

[33] Alan Jacobs, "Narnia Business: C. S. Lewis at 100," *Weekly Standard* (20 April 1998): 34.

Fowler wrote an article in the *Yale Review* in which he claimed that Lewis showed him the unfinished manuscript of *The Dark Tower*. A 2007 *Christianity Today* article went so far as to say that, thanks to Fowler's revelation, the mystery regarding *The Dark Tower* had been solved.[34]

Whether solved or not, the controversy exemplifies how Lindskoog threatened the solidarity of the Lewis industry. Although her initial 1978 article may have maintained a charitable tone, the questions she raised were directed at the heart of the Lewis industry. Consequently, responses to her questions were harsh and defensive. Lindskoog subsequently intensified her own rhetoric in *Hoax* and *Sleuthing*, resulting in an all-out verbal war. Criticized and shunned, Lindskoog became an outsider, displaced from the Lewis industry. What is remarkable in this expulsion is that Lindskoog, as a Christian, shared the solidarity goods of the Lewis industry, but her attack on Hooper challenged the locus of authority that has generated nearly the entire Lewis catalog of books. Lindskoog replaced the appreciation that should characterize friendship with a distrust reserved for enemies.

*b. A. N. Wilson*

A. N. Wilson's controversial 1990 biography of Lewis takes great pains to distance itself from traditional Lewis scholarship. Pointing to the hagiography that attends the study of Lewis, Wilson writes in his preface that he "...will try to be realistic, not only because reality is more interesting than fantasy, but also because we do Lewis no honour to make him into a plaster saint. And he deserves our honour."[35] Despite this warm sentiment directed toward the subject of his biography, Wilson pieces together the life of Lewis without assuming that Christianity is true. In short, Wilson does not share the solidarity goods of the Lewis industry; he is clearly an outsider. Indeed, in a 2009 article, Wilson explains how he privately "denounc[ed] Lewis' muscular defense of religious belief": "I can remember almost yelling that reading C. S. Lewis' *Mere Christianity* made me a non-believer—not just in Lewis' version of Christianity, but in Christianity itself."[36] Wilson's then

---

[34] See Harry Lee Poe, "Shedding Light on *The Dark Tower*: A C. S. Lewis Mystery Is Solved," *Christianity Today* 51/2 (2 February 2007): 44–45.

[35] Wilson, *C. S. Lewis*, xvii.

[36] A. N. Wilson, "Why I Believe Again," *New Statesman* (2 April 2009): online. http://www.newstatesman.com/religion/2009/04/conversion-experience-atheism. Accessed Aug. 6 2010. As the title of this article reveals, Wilson miraculously returned to the fold, though his newfound Christian faith hardly arose from Lewisian sorts of arguments or evidentialist paths: "When I think about atheist friends, including my father, they seem to me like people who have no ear for music, or who have never

atheistic (or at least agnostic) interpretive lens drew him to some original conclusions about Lewis's life. Moreover, some of those conclusions were informed by psychoanalytic theory, an approach never before employed by Lewis scholars in part because the theory is antithetical to the values of Lewis himself (recall that Lewis scholars tend to follow Lewis's own principles in studying Lewis): first, psychoanalysis derives from Freud, with whom Lewis largely disagreed; second, psychoanalysis constitutes an innovation in the grand sweep of Western Civilization, thus placing it at odds with Lewis's conservatism and distrust of progressivism; finally, psychoanalysis is not clearly amenable to the Christianity for which Lewis stands. Consequently, by virtue of his stance and approach, Wilson was an outsider intruding on sacred ground.

Harsh reviews from the Lewis industry predictably ensued. Admittedly, some of them may have been warranted. For instance, George Sayer convincingly casts serious doubt on Wilson's claim that Lewis had premarital sex with Joy Davidman Gresham.[37] But as we have seen, biography-making is an inexact science for the simple reason that it involves acts of interpretation, which are fallible, and the use of sources that are, to varying extents, unreliable. Nevertheless, my contention is that some of the critiques of Wilson's book, apparently directed at specific points, are in fact implicit (or occasionally explicit) critiques of Wilson's interpretive framework. Gilbert Meilaender's review illustrates this point. He calls Wilson's "attitude toward religion" "disturbing" and quotes the following passage from the biography: "'[I]t is the Lewis who plumbed the irrational depths of childhood and religion who speaks to the present generation.'" Meilaender then asks, "But why should religion (or, for that matter, childhood) be irrational at its depths?"[38] Meilaender implies that Wilson's pre-analytical beliefs about religion blemish his biographical theorizing— that in order to understand Lewis's life one must share Lewis's religious beliefs.

---

been in love. It is not that (as they believe) they have rumbled the tremendous fraud of religion—prophets do that in every generation. Rather, these unbelievers are simply missing out on something that is not difficult to grasp. Perhaps it is too obvious to understand; obvious, as lovers feel it was obvious that they should have come together, or obvious as the final resolution of a fugue."

[37] See George Sayer, *Jack: A Life of C. S. Lewis*, 2nd ed. (Wheaton IL: Crossway Books, 1994) 413–14.

[38] Gilbert Meilaender, "Psychoanalyzing C. S. Lewis," *Christian Century* (16–23 May 1990): 529.

This status as outsider helps explain some of the stronger denunciations of Wilson's book. Diana Pavlac Glyer and David Bratman, for instance, comment, "Wilson writes engagingly, but commits serious gaffes in fact, interpretation, and tone that overshadow any value in his book."[39] It remains vague how a writer can commit serious gaffes of *tone* in writing a biography; one might agree or disagree with a tone, but to call it an error or blunder obviously presupposes the existence of a correct or right tone, a presupposition that can only occur when one has very strong opinions— metamorphosing into certitude—about the subject of the biography. Like Meilaender, Pavlac Glyer and Bratman probably have in mind the tone with which Wilson describes some component of Lewis's religious beliefs, moti-vations, and actions. Nevertheless, for Pavlac Glyer and Bratman, because of its "gaffes," Wilson's book ultimately lacks value. Dorsett's denunciation of the book is likewise hyperbolic: "The biography of A. N. Wilson published in 1990 is so filled with factual errors and inaccurate interpretations that it is useless to the serious student of Lewis's life and writing."[40] As noted in the last chapter, despite such unmitigated condemnation, Wilson's biography managed to make it onto *Time* magazine's "Best of '90" list.[41] One wonders if Pavlac Glyer, Bratman, Dorsett, and the editors of *Time* are reading the same book. The source of the contradiction may be found in different interpretive frameworks; as a secular periodical, and like Wilson himself at the time when writing his biography, *Time* does not share Lewis's religious beliefs.

Since Wilson is an outsider, his claims receive intensified scrutiny. For instance, Wilson argued in his biography that Lewis not only lost the infamous 1948 debate against G. E. M. Anscombe but subsequently abandoned Christian apologetics, his confidence in defending the faith shaken, and turned to the gentler, kinder genre of children's stories. This argument has received much flak from Lewis scholars, especially Victor Reppert and Alan Jacobs. Jacobs, for instance, writes, "But the oddest [of Wilson's ideas] is his insistence that Lewis was driven to abandon

---

[39] Diana Pavlac Glyer and David Bratman, "C. S. Lewis Scholarship: A Bibliographical Overview," in *C. S. Lewis: Life, Works, and Legacy*, vol. 4, ed. Bruce Edwards (London: Prager Perspectives, 2007) 302.

[40] Lyle W. Dorset, *Seeking the Secret Places: The Spiritual Formation of C. S. Lewis* (Grand Rapids: Brazos Press, 2004) 24.

[41] "Best of '90: Books," *Time* (31 December 1990): online. http://www.time.com/time/magazine/article/0,9171,972055,00.html.

apologetics, and to turn to the making of Narnia, by being bested in a debate at the Socratic Club."[42]

While this idea is certainly open to critique, one wonders why Wilson is the brunt, for the idea is not Wilson's. Humphrey Carpenter made the same claim in 1979: "Lewis had learnt his lesson: for after this he wrote no further books of Christian apologetic for ten years, apart from a collection of sermons; and when he did publish another apologetic work, *Reflections on the Psalms*, it was notably quieter in tone and did not attempt any further intellectual proofs of theism or Christianity."[43] In 1981, Margaret Patterson Hannay offered a similar claim: "His argument having been, at least by some accounts, defeated by the Catholic philosopher Elizabeth Anscombe, he produced no more combative apologetics."[44] Sayer's 1988 biography of Lewis corroborated these assessments, complete with Sayer's recollections of his own conversations with Lewis: "'I can never write another book of that sort,' he said to me of *Miracles*. And he never did. He also never wrote another theological book. *Reflections on the Psalms* is really devotional and literary; *Letters to Malcolm*, published after his death, is also a devotional book, a series of reflections on prayer, without contentious argument."[45] Despite these numerous antecedents to Wilson's argument, Wilson, as outsider to the Lewis industry, remains most vulnerable to critique.

Wilson is, of course, aware of his status as outsider, a stance that animates his meta-critical observations, endowing them with their argumentation edge. He calls the fervent admiration for Lewis "...symptomatic of the religious temperament as a whole, the need to erect images and to worship them."[46] Wilson played the role of provocateur, and the Lewis industry took the bait, unambiguously placing Wilson on the far side of the line drawn in the sand.

### c. John Beversluis

Like Wilson, Beversluis (gleefully) played the role of provocateur, challenging the Lewis industry in a slap-in-the-face confrontation titled *C. S. Lewis and the Search for Rational Religion* (1985, second, revised edition

[42] Alan Jacobs, *The Narnian: The Life and Imagination of C. S. Lewis* (San Francisco: HarperSanFrancisco, 2005) 231.

[43] Humphrey Carpenter, *The Inklings: C. S. Lewis, J.R.R. Tolkien, Charles Williams, and Their Friends* (Boston: Houghton Mifflin, 1979) 217.

[44] Margaret Patterson Hannay, *C. S. Lewis* (New York: Frederick Ungar, 1981) 262.

[45] Sayer, *Jack: A Life of C. S. Lewis*, 308.

[46] Wilson, *C. S. Lewis*, 304.

published in 2007). And as with Wilson's biography, Beversluis's critique remained ever mindful of the Lewis industry, using it as an animus for analysis. A blurb on the back cover of Beversluis's book proclaims, "In a marketplace saturated with worshipful tributes to Lewis, this decidedly iconoclastic volume will serve as a distinctive counterpoint and should generate a good deal of discussion among Lewis's large following." The author of this commendation probably realized that most "discussion" of the book would take the form of a robust disagreement with Beversluis and a spirited defense of Lewis. Beversluis, after all, concludes that Lewis's "arguments for the existence of God fail"; "his answer to the Problem of Evil is unacceptable"; and that "his characteristic way of misrepresenting the views of the opposition stands as a permanent warning to future apologists.... Although the Lewis cult has made him out to be something he never was, and although Lewis the man must be distinguished from Lewis the myth and elemental force, his apologetic writings repay study—even if not for the reason he wrote them."[47] Clearly Beversluis did not hesitate to announce his defiance of the Lewis industry.

And it responded with equal aggression. Como called Beversluis's argument "badly overextended" and remarked that Beversluis was "generically tone-deaf."[48] Kreeft identified Beversluis's book as the "abomination of desolation."[49] Louis Markos stated that Beversluis and fellow outsider A. N. Wilson adopt a faulty approach to Lewis: "Aside from the sheer vulgarity and tastelessness of their unfounded critique, it demonstrates a misunderstanding of Lewis and his works."[50]

Assessments from reviewers not affiliated with the Lewis industry were, of course, less one-sided. In addition, many of these reviewers, like Beversluis himself, used the Lewis industry as the backdrop for their reflections, confirming the notion that the industry operates as a gateway for the discussion of Lewis. Maintaining that "Beversluis is conversant with Lewis's works to an extent probably unmatched by many ardent Lewis followers," Robert M. Price wrote, "Those who infer from the title that this is yet another hagiographic tribute to C. S. Lewis, buy it, and settle down to read it

---

[47] John Beversluis, *C. S. Lewis and the Search for Rational Religion* (Grand Rapids: Eerdmans, 1985) 167.

[48] James Como, *Branches to Heaven: The Geniuses of C. S. Lewis* (Dallas: Spence, 1998) 174.

[49] Peter Kreeft, *C. S. Lewis: A Critical Essay* (Front Royal VA: Christendom College Press, 1988) 5.

[50] Louis Markos, *Lewis Agonistes* (Nashville: Broadman & Holman Publishers, 2003) 106.

between their Lewis calendar on one wall and their Narnia map on the other, are in for a major shock."[51] A piece in the *National Review* engaged Beversluis's book by critiquing the Lewis industry: "Whether Lewis succeeds in proving this or that philosophical thesis is another matter, and Beversluis is right to be impatient with those Lewis idolaters who want to credit him with resolving problems that have baffled minds for centuries."[52] British reviewer Brian Horne seemed pleased that Britain had thus far "escaped the effects of the C. S. Lewis 'industry' of the USA" and praised Beversluis's book: "In this book we see a philosopher with a rigorous and sophisticated mind unerringly exposing Lewis's philosophical inadequacies, but never with hostility or contempt. Lewis could not have wished for a fairer critic...."[53] Singing the book's praises—"Beversluis has initiated a much more informed and profitable debate on Lewis's role as apologist than we have had to date"—William C. James likewise acknowledged the presence and influence of the Lewis industry: "Beversluis scorns the cult of Lewis followers, letting his readers know at the outset that his book is not going to be just another act of homage to the master."[54] Francis C. Rossow approved of the book and employed strong language in positioning Beversluis as outsider: "Uneasy (or even angry) as the Lewis enthusiast may be at Beversluis' attack, that attack has literary (if not theological) merit. It deserves your reading. Without question Beversluis is the great 'Anti-Lewis' of our times."[55] A testament to the meta-critical subtexts of Lewis studies, Willis D. Van Groningen's review of the book consists of two assessments, one offered inside the context of Lewis studies and one offered outside: "Considered simply as a corrective to the 'Lewis cult' phenomenon that has made Lewis into something that he was not—namely, an irreproachable apologist of the Christian faith—this book is excellent and valuable. It weakens, however, when considered more generally."[56] And in his review, John R. Willis hints that any evaluation of Beversluis's book is irrelevant, for

---

[51] Robert M. Price, review of *C. S. Lewis: A Biography*, by John Beversluis, *Religious Humanism* 20/4 (1986): 196.

[52] Joseph Sobran, "The Poor Man's Aquinas," *National Review* (31 May 1985): 42.

[53] Brian Horne, "C. S. Lewis—Christian Apologist," *Expository Times* 97/4 (1986): 124.

[54] William C. James, review of *C. S. Lewis*, by John Beversluis, *Journal of Religion* 66/2 (1986): 223.

[55] Francis C. Rossow, review of *C. S. Lewis*, by John Beversluis, *Concordia Journal* 11/5 (1985): 198.

[56] Willis D. Van Groningen, review of *C. S. Lewis*, by John Beversluis, *Journal of the Evangelical Theological Society* 29/3 (1986): 369.

the book will generate irreconcilable differences of opinion: "Beversluis' book is sure to upset the Lewis *aficionados*. Whether or not he has satisfactorily made his own case against Lewis is moot. Carefully and cogently written (although occasionally somewhat prolix), his book will evoke pros and cons in Lewis circles for some time to come. Nevertheless, it is a most significant addition to the growing corpus of Lewisiana."[57]

In the second, revised edition of his book, Beversluis himself reflects on meta-critical phenomena. He notes that the harshest critics of his book were "hard-core devotees" that include "expositors of his [Lewis's] thought, popular apologists, and even a few philosophers...." He admits to anticipating such criticism. "What I had not expected," he continues, "was the *kind* of criticism. With the market saturated with adulatory but almost completely uncritical books about Lewis, many were dismayed and, in some cases, outraged by a critical study in which his arguments were subjected to scrutiny and found wanting and his 'case for Christianity' was judged a failure." Beversluis concludes that Lewis "...has achieved such iconic status in some quarters that criticism is viewed as near-sacrilege."[58] Beversluis's claim is hard to deny when one considers that the solidarity goods of the Lewis industry *are* sacred and that Lewis is the unparalleled bearer of those goods. Consequently, Beversluis has done much more than criticize Lewis and his ideas; he has attacked the worldview that lies at the heart of the Lewis industry, positioning himself as an outsider whose views therefore must be tendentious, warped, or in some way flawed.

### d. Other Outsiders

Other Lewis scholars and commentators have self-consciously negotiated the dividing line of the Lewis industry, separating the friendly from the unfriendly, the likeminded from the un-likeminded. For instance, Christopher Derrick observes the aftermath of the publication of his 1981 monograph, *C. S. Lewis and the Church of Rome*, a book occasionally critical of Lewis's religious ideas: He received numerous hostile letters from American fans. "But," he explains, "they didn't challenge my findings, they didn't fault my arguments. In every single case, their tone was 'How *dare* you criticize our idol!' or even 'How *dare* you blaspheme our god!'" Later, Derrick positively reviewed Beversluis's book: "Once again," writes Derrick, "the

---

[57] John R. Willis, review of *C. S. Lewis*, by John Beversluis, *Theological Studies* 47/1 (1986): 188.

[58] John Beversluis, *C. S. Lewis and the Search for Rational Religion*, rev. ed. (Grand Rapids: Eerdmans, 1985; repr. Amherst NY: Prometheus, 2007) 10, 11.

angry letters came, and their dominant tone was 'Hey, Derrick—which side are you on?'"[59] Derrick's phrasing here literalizes the boundaries of the Lewis industry. Milward positions himself as outsider when he begins his 1995 study by declaring, "Considering the widespread cult of C. S. Lewis today, it may seem presumptuous of me to offer this 'challenge' to so great a man."[60] Wesley A. Kort does the same when he tries to enlarge the analytical context for studying Lewis, maintaining that most Lewis scholars define truth and goodness too narrowly: "I think the company Lewis would prefer to keep, were he working in our culture today, would not be provided mainly by those who claim and treat him now as their own."[61]

Although Michael White claims that he "write[s] as a devotee certainly," he also identifies himself as "someone less absorbed by my subject's religious or even his academic world." According to my thesis, such a distinction constitutes a contradiction in terms, for devotion to a public intellectual implies a devotion to his or her solidarity goods, an implication much stronger with Lewis than other public intellectuals, given Lewis's subject matter. White seems to reveal as much by deploying a heated tone in engaging his scholarly predecessors:

> It is clear to see why Lewis would appeal most to bigoted, hard-line, old-fashioned Christians. He was an old-fashioned Christian when he was alive and today those who consider the Church to be too interested in modernizing and who wish to keep the institution in thrall to retrograde thinking see Lewis as a hero of religious orthodoxy and conservative values.... The puritans of America...have tried desperately hard to furnish the world with another sanitized version of the real Lewis. Their influence has infiltrated some of the smaller publishers who have certain rights over Lewis's works in America and for their own misguided reasons these parties have made it their business to ensure that all references to alcohol and tobacco in his writing are eradicated.[62]

White's position as Lewis-industry outsider generates the hostile tone of this critique; rejecting Lewis's solidarity goods disqualifies White as a Lewis devotee.

---

[59] Christopher Derrick, "Some Personal Angles on Chesterton and Lewis," in *G. K. Chesterton and C. S. Lewis: The Riddle of Joy*, ed. Michael H. MacDonald and Andrew A. Tadie (Grand Rapids: Eerdmans, 1989) 10.

[60] Milward, *A Challenge to C. S. Lewis*, 12.

[61] Wesley A. Kort, *C. S. Lewis: Then and Now* (Oxford: Oxford University Press, 2001) 5.

[62] Michael White, *C. S. Lewis: A Life* (New York: Carroll & Graf, 2004) 217, 222.

Toward the end of his monograph on Lewis and war, K. J. Gilchrist identifies two reasons why he wrote his book; the first was to counter the popular image of Lewis: "First, but not foremost, I felt that the image of Lewis sustained by his adulators was like Lewis's house of cards: not solid— he is too often perceived as a plaster saint, or no, a paper prince, fun to make dance, but not rounded, not believable, not human."[63] (Gilchrist marshals a number of original and/or controversial arguments in his book: that Lewis was severely traumatized by his war experiences; that his experiences during war inform a recurrent theme in his corpus—shattering and rebuilding assumptions and beliefs; and that Lewis had a sexual relationship with Janie Moore.)

Outsiders thus share in common a critical orientation toward Lewis's ideas, the Lewis industry, or, as is most often the case, both Lewis's ideas *and* the Lewis industry. They challenge Lewis's solidarity goods, thereby placing themselves outside the pale of metaphorical friendship that unites the Lewis industry. Even Bruce Edwards, an exponent of the Lewis industry, assesses the situation along similar lines, though his take naturally proceeds from his perspective as insider. He observes that biographies on Lewis too often fall into one of two extreme categories: biographies that tend toward hagiography on the one hand or, on the other, "works furtively focused on certain presumed negative personality traits and ambiguous relationships and incidents that obscure rather than illuminate Lewis's faith and scholarship." The latter, Edwards writes, "often programmatically dismiss Lewis's readership"—or, in my account, challenge the Lewis industry. Thus, Edwards writes defensively of the Lewis industry, most likely compelling him to challenge the "underlying theme of recent works: the desire 'to rescue' Lewis from the assumed cult of his evangelical idolaters, particularly in America."[64] Edwards walks a tightrope here, for he has already granted that numerous Lewis biographies tend to be hagiographical, a concession that demands the presence of "idolaters," whether evangelical and American or not, to do the idolizing; in addition, such hagiography of Lewis, as we have already seen, is not restricted to biography, despite Edwards's specific attribution of hagiography to this genre alone.[65] Nevertheless, the boundary

---

[63] K. J. Gilchrist, *A Morning after War: C. S. Lewis and WWI* (New York: Peter Lang, 2005) 218.

[64] Edwards, preface to *C. S. Lewis: Life, Works, and Legacy*, vol. 1, ed. Bruce L. Edwards (London: Praeger Perspectives, 2007) xiv.

[65] Edwards focuses his critique on Wilson and White, quoting one of Wilson's hyperbolic, evangelical representations of Lewis: "'virginal, Bible-toting, nonsmoking, lemonade-drinking champion for Christ'" (xiv). Such a quote helps Edwards reduce

lines of the Lewis industry seem to be recognized by both those inside and outside of it, creating scholarly skirmishes that always have at their foundation disagreements about the solidarity goods that Lewis, as public intellectual, represented.

## II. The View from the Outside

In his preface to the 1992 edition of *Remembering C. S. Lewis*, Como registers his "puzzlement that the general body of professional critics, scholars, and theorists have [*sic*] not afforded [Lewis's] varied work the attention it merits."[66] Indeed, why have scholars—those outside the Lewis industry—more or less neglected Lewis's contributions to literary studies, theology, and intellectual history? Some scholars within the Lewis industry have even attempted to redress this neglect. Consider, for instance, Bruce Edwards's *The Taste of the Pineapple: Essays on C. S. Lewis as Reader, Critic, and Imaginative Writer* (1988). Edwards emphasizes that the "ultimate goal" of his volume "...is to revitalize interest in Lewis as an important spokesman to a generation of writers, readers and critics who seem to have lost their moorings, conflating reading and criticism with a host of other, ancillary activities."[67] Why has interest in Lewis not been revitalized?

In a sense, it has. The multi-million dollar film versions of the Narniad, of course, had much to do with a boost in Lewis's popularity. However, interest in Lewis had been vital long before Hollywood put Narnia on the big screen. Como himself observes, "Since his death in November 1963, sales of his books have increased sixfold (with several titles selling more than one million copies per years in some twenty languages)."[68] Como thus raises yet

---

Wilson to absurdity, although there is a basis for truth in at least one prong of Wilson's hyperbole, a basis discovered in Edwards's volume itself. An essay in the collection authored by Alice H. Cook acknowledges the perpetuation of the "virginal"-Lewis image, an image originally painted by Walter Hooper: "Walter Hooper's early treatment of Lewis as 'the perpetual virgin' bears much responsibility for turning this into a topic of interest." (See Alice H. Cook, "A Grief Observed: C. S. Lewis Meets the Great Iconoclast," in Edwards, ed., *C. S. Lewis: Life, Works, and Legacy*, 295–313).

[66] Como, preface to 1992 edition of *C. S. Lewis at the Breakfast Table*, San Diego: Harcourt Brace & Company. later published as *Remembering C. S. Lewis*, 18.

[67] Bruce L. Edwards, introduction to *The Taste of the Pineapple: Essays on C. S. Lewis as Reader, Critic, and Imaginative Writer*, ed. Bruce L. Edwards (Bowling Green: Bowling Green State University Popular Press, 1988) 4.

[68] Como, *Remembering C. S. Lewis*, 33.

another meta-critical curiosity: Why do professional scholars neglect Lewis even while Lewis's books enjoy healthy sales?

To answer this question in part, I re-invoke the concept of the public intellectual as a heuristic device. Simply put, as public intellectual, Lewis wrote for the layperson, offering translations of complex ideas and arguments. As prior chapters have shown, Lewis acquired a large grassroots following. Lewis's popularity traveled through populist channels: word of mouth and small journals. Indeed, as chapter 10 showed, the populist character of American Christianity harmonized with Lewis's discursive strategies. Lewis's following thus carried on the pattern established by Lewis himself: write for the common person; do not worry about the scholars, whose progressivism, secularism, relativism, and scientism make them inimical to Christianity anyway. Of course, the legacy of this pattern has militated against the canonization of Lewis; professional scholars and their organizations, beginning with the Modern Language Association, operate as gatekeepers on the path to inclusion in the canon.

But Lewis's followers have traveled a different path; institutional structures and procedures—especially of the secular variety—are held in suspicion. The first issue of *Mythlore*, one of those grassroots journals that helped boost Lewis's popularity, is telling in this respect. The editor of the journal, Glen Goodknight, casts the world into which the journal is launched as a hopeless system: "We can say that the present system is hopeless, and more than that, it has become abhorrent and should be overthrown." But to do that, the editor continues, one must offer another system in its place. Suspicion of the "system" thus leads the editor to another alternative: "...to temporarily withdraw a distance from the system, have a detached view, and return refreshed with a new perspective." The editor concludes, "The fantasy of Tolkien, Lewis, and Williams (among others) have this beneficial effect."[69] In obvious ways, then, the populist characteristics of the Lewis industry clash with the identity and function of professional scholars.

However, consistent with the focus of this chapter, I want to hone in on another reason to help explain the relative silence among scholars vis-à-vis the study of Lewis. Defined as an assembly of the like-minded, metaphorical friends who share the same solidarity goods, the Lewis industry either explicitly or implicitly discourages alternative approaches to Lewis. The insularity and homogeneity of the Lewis industry proves unwelcoming to the uninitiated. Just as Lewis has become associated with evangelicals, so

---

[69] Glen Goodknight, "Fantasy and Personal Involvement," *Mythlore* 1/1 (3 January 1969): 4.

has Lewis become associated with the Lewis industry. As we have seen, engaging the ideas of Lewis in critical studies often means first negotiating the Lewis industry, a negotiation that inflects and shapes interpretation, structuring the approach to Lewis. A formidable weight of meta-critical baggage has accumulated around Lewis; this baggage has influenced the way Lewis is understood and analyzed. The Lewis industry, unintentionally or not, has placed expectations on the way people read Lewis, inadvertently placing interpretive straightjackets on the study of Lewis. I believe Robert MacSwain has these sorts of limitations in mind when he notes that the "current situation in Lewis scholarship represent[s] something of an impasse...."[70]

Although I feel I have already offered a wealth of support for these claims, one other anecdote develops the picture rather dramatically. Alan Jacobs recounts an acquaintance who lost his faith because of the sort of meta-critical phenomena I have explored: "I even know a man who says that he lost his faith largely because of Lewis's *Mere Christianity*: he figured that, since all his devout friends told him that it was the last word on what Christian belief is all about, then if he loathed the book he was honor-bound to loathe Christianity as well."[71] Hagiographical treatments of Lewis cannot help but shape reader response to Lewis himself.

This is why Dabney Adams Hart's 1984 monograph, *Through the Open Door: A New Look at C. S. Lewis*, constitutes such a unique case study. She explains in the preface to her book that she wrote the first dissertation on Lewis in the 1950s. For the next twenty years, she lived in England, where Lewis was of only minor importance. Upon returning to the States, Adams Hart was made aware of Lewis's surging American popularity and turned her dissertation into a book, which is a unique case study for two reasons: the ideas that became the book germinated before the advent of the Lewis industry; and for twenty years after writing her dissertation, she was living in England, unaware of the growth of the Lewis industry and oblivious to the ways it was shaping the study of Lewis. Consequently, Adams Hart offers unique perspectives on Lewis in her book. For instance, employing the metaphor of the open door as her unifying trope, she claims that the overarching theme in the Lewis corpus is "radical reassessment": "One of his favorite images was the open door: the opportunity for new perspectives, new views, free movement of the mind and spirit." She argues that Lewis

---

[70] MacSwain, introduction to *The Cambridge Companion to C. S. Lewis*, ed. MacSwain and Ward, 9.

[71] Jacobs, *The Narnian*, x.

"...always intended to raise rather than to settle questions, to arouse rather than to satisfy curiosity."[72] Drawing from *The Discarded Image* and *Letters to Malcolm*, Adams Hart proposes that Lewis's epistemology is characterized by provisionality and limitation. Of course, other Lewis scholars have noted some of the anti-foundationalist, even postmodern qualities of Lewis's epistemology. David Downing, for instance, writes that, for Lewis, "...Reality is not self-interpreting, that a great deal of what we see depends on who we are and what we have been taught to see."[73] However, Adams Hart's study is unique in its development of Lewis's epistemological provisionality as a *systematic* explanatory model, an interpretive matrix for understanding Lewis's complete writings. The novelty of this approach suggests the analytical originality made possible from an interpretive space relatively uninfluenced by the Lewis industry. Despite being one of the pioneers in Lewis scholarship, because of the twenty years she spent in ignorance of the burgeoning Lewis industry, Adams Hart offered an analysis that in many ways is off the map.

Others have also offered original, off-the-map analyses, but they have done so in disagreement with, or even defiance of, the Lewis industry—not in oblivion to it. As we have seen, Wesley Kort believes that "...the company Lewis would prefer to keep, were he working in our culture today, would not be provided mainly by those Christians who claim and treat him now as their own."[74] Kort maintains that the evangelical language of "accepting Christ into one's life" is antithetical to the basic impulse of Lewis's thought: "The language of acceptance, appropriation, and possession is contrary to what is basic for Lewis. For him it is essential that the Christian not think of belief as a way of bringing something into his or her life, but, rather, as a way of being brought out into a larger world or sense of the world."[75] Kort's unique interpretive framework naturally yields unique interpretations of Lewis. For instance, instead of maintaining that Lewis transcends culture, Kort insists that Lewis deeply inhabits it, inevitably leading him to points of disagreement with the Lewis industry:

> I find dissonance between Lewis and some of his American devotees at this point. They seem to recruit Lewis into a sharply focused set of

---

[72] Dabney Adams Hart, *Through the Open Door: A New Look at C. S. Lewis* (Tuscaloosa: University of Alabama Press, 1984) 1, 120.

[73] David Downing, *The Most Reluctant Convert: C. S. Lewis's Journey to Faith* (Downers Grove: InterVarsity, 2002) 20.

[74] Kort, *C. S. Lewis: Then and Now*, 5.

[75] Ibid., 22.

affirmations believed to provide, in a culturally complex society, a sharply differentiated and separated identity. Lewis, in my opinion, tended to see theological and dogmatic statements not as marks of identity or battle cries in some kind of cultural conflict. They are, instead, articulations of the kind of world in which a Christian lives, statements that can be thought of as providing a framework for a constructed account of the world that clarifies relations and provides habitable space.[76]

Kort's belief in Lewis's engagement with culture in turn leads him to the radical suggestion that Lewis has a place in the academy not in departments of religious or theological studies, but in literature departments with strong emphases in cultural studies. I call this suggestion radical because of its brazen departure from the beliefs of the Lewis industry, for cultural studies as a discipline presupposes what Kort calls the "constructed account of the world." Like Adams Hart, Kort tends to minimize Lewis's essentialism and to emphasize his provisionalism, seen, again, in Lewis's later writings, especially *Letters to Malcolm*.

Laura Miller's *The Magician's Book: A Skeptic's Adventure in Narnia* (2008) constitutes another off-the-map analysis. Miller displays her unique interpretive perspective when she announces in the book's opening pages that she is not a Christian. In fact, when she first learned that Lewis *was* Christian, she was

> ...shocked, almost nauseated. I'd been tricked, cheated, betrayed. I went over the rest of the Chronicles, and in almost every one found some element that lined up with this unwelcome and, to me, ulterior meaning. I felt like a character in one of those surreal, existential 1960s TV dramas, like *The Prisoner* or *The Twilight Zone*, a captive who pulls off a daring escape from his cell only to find himself inside another, larger cell identical to the first.[77]

She naturally anticipates her reader's response: "This, to many casual observers, no doubt make my continuing enjoyment of the Chronicles perplexing."[78] Throughout her book, she attempts to account for her perplexing enjoyment of the Narniad. And, as we have seen with Adams Hart and Kort, Miller's unique interpretive framework produces unique insights. She contrasts Christianity and Narnia, asserting that they are animated by a mutually exclusive spirit:

---

[76] Ibid., 73.

[77] Laura Miller, *The Magician's Book: A Skeptic's Adventure in Narnia* (New York: Little, Brown and Company, 2008) 99.

[78] Ibid., 8.

While the Narnians' obedience to Aslan irks some adult readers, for me it was essentially different from the docility demanded by the Church. First and foremost it wasn't founded on self-denial. The Narnians did as Aslan asked because he was strong, kind, warm, and lovable, and because his requests always led to that most desirable of ends: the continuation of Narnia as it should be, the most wonderful country imaginable. Christianity instructed me to comply with a list of dreary, legalistic demands because Jesus, whom I had never met, reportedly loved me and had redeemed me from the guilt of a sin I had never committed by dying before I was even born. The proof of his love was his suffering; I owed him, and he expected to be paid in kind. Narnia and Aslan made me happy. Jesus wanted me to be miserable. ... Narnia was liberation and delight. Christianity was boredom, subjugation, and reproach. For all the similarities between *The Lion, the Witch and the Wardrobe* and the New Testament, and for all Lewis's evangelical intentions, I don't think I was that grievously mistaken. The Christianity that I knew—the only Christianity I was aware of—was the opposite of Narnia in both aesthetics and spirit. More than just opposite, really, since the Church was a major part of the lackluster world I sought refuge from in Lewis's books. For me, Narnia was Christianity's antidote.[79]

Not sharing the solidarity goods of the Lewis industry, operating on alternative assumptions, Miller opens up other avenues for analysis, avenues not possible or likely for those inside the Lewis industry.

## III. Conclusion

What is true for the study of Lewis is true for the study of any literary figure: What we bring to the analytical table shapes what and how we analyze. Obviously, scholars shape the meta-critical lives of their subjects of study; the significance of literary figures and the meanings of their texts fundamentally take shape in the hands of the scholars who study them. As Terry Eagleton observes, "The fact that we always interpret literary works to some extent in the light of our own concerns—indeed that in one sense of 'our own concerns' we are incapable of doing anything else—might be one reason why certain works of literature seem to retain their value across the centuries." Eagleton adds that, through the centuries, "...people have not actually been valuing the 'same' work [of literature] at all, even though they may think they have. 'Our' Homer is not identical with the Homer of the Middle Ages, nor 'our' Shakespeare with that of his contemporaries; it is

---

[79] Ibid., 95.

rather that different historical periods have constructed a 'different' Homer and Shakespeare for their own purposes, and found in these texts elements to value or devalue, though not necessarily the same ones."[80]

It is also true of Lewis. As I have argued throughout this book, Lewis presents a unique case when he is understood as a public intellectual. Conceived as such, Lewis adopts a writerly persona and discursive stance that encourage the very meta-critical phenomena that I have sketched in this chapter. Thus, to identify the Lewis industry as a network of metaphorical friends, sharing solidarity goods, critiquing and ostracizing outsiders, and producing scholarship characterized by hagiography, summaries, and critical homogeneity should not be understood as a critical indictment; rather, to depict the Lewis industry as such is simply to observe a natural critical response to a public intellectual—that is, a natural critical response from the large body of scholars who agree with Lewis. The unique qualities of the Lewis industry naturally result from the highly successful rhetorical and polemical strategies that Lewis deployed as a public intellectual.

Nevertheless, as we have seen, a few scholars have diverged from the typical critical approach. For the most part, these scholars have done so by explicitly or implicitly disagreeing with Lewis. And in doing so, they set off the sort of meta-critical phenomena I have observed: That is, the Lewis industry responds in kind, showing how the disagreeing scholar is wrong or tendentious, protecting the solidarity goods, and drawing the line in the sand separating metaphorical friends and enemies. Consequently, the unfriendly Lewis scholar participates in the same analytic mode as the friendly Lewis scholar; both engage, whether directly or indirectly, textually or subtextually, the fundamental question that attaches itself to the work of a public intellectual: Is Lewis right or wrong? It is this question that generates the critical skirmishes, the attacks that reveal the weaknesses in Lewis's arguments or the skeletons in his closet, thereby galvanizing the Lewis industry, which responds with spirited defenses, summaries that cast glowing admiration on Lewis's arguments, and hagiographies that admire Lewis himself. Lewis studies will remain at an impasse as long as that question remains a critical preoccupation.

---

[80] Terry Eagleton, *Literary Theory: An Introduction*, 2nd ed. (Minneapolis: University of Minnesota Press, 1996) 11.

# Conclusion

The public sphere operated as the site of meaning formation. For centuries, it shaped the structure of public discourse, supplying the guidelines by which statements could be made and the criteria by which those statements were judged to be true or false. The public sphere made room for collaborative meaning-making, a process involving intellectuals, their critics, as well as the more nebulous contributions of public opinion. All three played public roles in creating public meaning. Consequently, what I have called in this book the C.S. Lewis phenomenon is the joint accomplishment of both Lewis and the various commentators over the past seventy years who have shaped Lewis's public identity.

Part 1 attempted to show how Lewis mastered the conventions of the public sphere, securing powerful forms of authority and deftly conveying them to marshal cogent Christian arguments. These arguments had universal appeal, thus appealing to his diverse lay audience. Throughout this process, Lewis seemed to uphold the promise sustained in John Milton's *Areopagitica* (1644). Milton forestalls fears over an open marketplace of ideas and implicitly celebrates the creation of a public sphere, which at the time was just emerging, because in the end, he is sure, truth will win. For Milton, censorship is unnecessary; truth will ultimately defeat the blasphemous or harmful ideas of dubious books: "And though all the winds of doctrine were let loose to play upon the earth, so Truth be in the field, we do injuriously by licensing and prohibiting to misdoubt her strength. Let her and Falsehood grapple; who ever knew Truth put to the worse in a free and open encounter?"[1] Lewis implicitly shares Milton's optimism, not only in the eventual triumph of truth but also in the public mechanism by which the victory would be accomplished; that is, both Lewis and Milton had unspoken faith that the rules of the playing field—the conventions of the public sphere—would ensure that only the best ideas won.

What makes Lewis's accomplishment phenomenal is that he made use of the public sphere shortly before its demise or, at the least, its radical restructuring. For various reasons (explained in chapter 6), in the latter half of the twentieth century, the public sphere ceased to exist as it had for centuries. The universal stage of the Enlightenment became fragmented,

---

[1] John Milton, *Areopagitica and Of Education*, ed. George H. Sabine (Wheeling IL: Harlan Davidson, Inc., 1951) 50.

parceled into narrow pockets of specialized interest and rabid sectarianism, transforming public discourse and civil argumentation into intellectual insularity and ideological contestation. Thus, since Lewis made use of the public sphere like no other Christian, his accomplishment was unprecedented; and since the public sphere no longer exists, his accomplishment is also inimitable.

Part 2 proposed a counter-narrative to Part 1, exploring ways in which Lewis operated outside the public sphere. Beginning in the 1950s, for various reasons, Lewis created different species of texts, ones that abandoned, however momentarily, the conventions of the public sphere. These works privileged provisionality and perspective: an epistemology at odds with Enlightenment assumptions. Since intellectual history necessarily generalizes, Part 2 served as a qualification to my own generalizations, illustrating the exceptions to and thus the complexities of what I have called the C.S. Lewis phenomenon. Lewis and his commentators established the Lewis name within the public sphere before its demise, thus ensuring that his name would not fall into obscurity. Part 2 illustrated some ways in which Lewis still appeals to a new generation of readers, those who now occupy a post-public-sphere era.

Part 3 analyzed how Lewis commentators, as well as the public opinion they helped to create, contributed to the C.S. Lewis phenomenon. The fate of the public sphere modulated these contributions. That is, prior to the demise of the public sphere, Lewis was often represented as a veritable Mere Christian, an exemplary model of the faith standing boldly upon the universal stage of the Enlightenment. As the public sphere began to crumble, however, Lewis became increasingly associated with pockets of interest, primarily those who espoused American evangelical Christianity and conservative politics, both of which were energized by the sort of populist discourse that Lewis perfected as a "translator" of ideas. Lewis thus became a lightning rod for acrimonious rhetoric, the discourse of the post-public-sphere era. The polarized public of the reconstituted public sphere shaped the perception of Lewis. For many Lewis fans—the Lewis industry, what I have called the "insiders"—Lewis remains a transcendent, unimpeachable authority often specifically enlisted to combat the various particular ills of the postmodern world. Acting upon this association, outsiders often view Lewis as a symbol of the values of American evangelicalism and conservative politics; for these outsiders, Lewis is transformed from a symbol to a target, a metonymic representative of provocative, polarizing beliefs. This insider/outsider polarization has created inescapable meta-critical baggage that surrounds Lewis and shapes the study of Lewis himself. Lewis lovers and haters—those on both sides of ideological fences—have created a new Lewis, one that has intensified shouting matches and that has helped to generate poor scholarship.

My study has hopefully brought to light the powerful role played by discursive frameworks. Christians write a lot these days about the integration of faith and learning. Perhaps underexplored is the sort of discourse they adopt when carrying out that integration. Again, for centuries, the public sphere shaped discourse, providing the guidelines by which statements conveyed meaning and truth.

The arguments made throughout this book have revealed how, for the Christian, participation in the public sphere involved compromises. *The Problem of Pain*, for instance, begins with one such compromise: the assumption that God does not exist or, at the very least, the assumption that God's existence must be held in abeyance. Lewis must begin on his opponents' ground, one that privileges neutrality and objectivity, and thus establishes atheism or, at best, agnosticism as normative, the necessary starting point for any argument. Lewis must first build an argument for God's existence before he can he even release God from the dock, from the accusation—taken for granted in the public sphere—that the existence of evil constitutes a strike against the tenability of Christianity. The public sphere turns the Christian into a reactionary, answering objections that materialize from the guidelines and assumptions that attend the very creation of the public sphere.

Lewis devotees likewise adopt a reactionary pose. Critiques of Lewis double as critiques of his solidarity goods. Devotees become defensive when coming to Lewis's rescue against antagonists; at stake are both Lewis's reputation and the beliefs of which he is symbolic, however accurate or inaccurate the symbolism may be. And with the fall of the public sphere, the reactionary counterattacks and the defensiveness become politicized, transforming public discourse into the heated rhetoric of the culture wars.

The arguments made throughout this book have also revealed how participation in the public sphere required a performance. The public intellectual, after all, is a persona, a role played within the public sphere. Chapter 3 in particular explored the various formations of these roles, whether characterized by impersonality, hiddenness, mystery, secretiveness, privacy, or artificiality. Entrance into the public sphere necessitates compromises of identity.

This study has of course emphasized the fundamental bifurcation of identity necessitated by the public sphere, the division of public and private self, underscored by the narrative/counter-narrative approach of my analysis: Lewis inside the public sphere (Part 1) and Lewis outside the public sphere (Part 2). My contention was that the unique character of texts like *Till We Have Faces* and *A Grief Observed* is attributable less to any emphasis or de-emphasis on reason but more to a movement away from the public sphere. Exiting the public sphere, Lewis naturally relies less upon its conventions, creating a species of texts operating through a radically different frame of reference. The most obvious and simplistic example of this competing frame of reference is the stark contrast between *The Problem of Pain* and *A Grief Observed*, the former modeling public discourse and the latter private discourse. Given that these two texts treat the same subject, their differences highlight the intellectual and emotional schizophrenia generated by the authorial shift from public sphere to private sphere.

Indeed, from its beginnings, the public sphere divided the use put to human faculties like reason, evident in Immanuel Kant's essay "What Is Enlightenment?" (1784). Kant conceptually aligns the Enlightenment and the public sphere, defining it as an open marketplace of ideas where reason, not authority, determines truth. However, Kant makes a distinction between public reason, which should be free, and private reason, which he calls "...that which one may make of it in a particular civil post or office...."[2] Thus, working on behalf of the church and state as a civil servant, a pastor should not use reason—that is, private reason—to question the "symbol of the church"—that is, the "organization of the religious body and church." [3] To do so would be of no benefit to either the church or state. However, as a public scholar, acting independently of church and state, a pastor is welcome to use reason—that is, public reason—to question that very same symbol. After all, within the public sphere, the pastor should be free of the influence of church and state, whose biases are antithetical to the conventions of the public sphere. The public sphere thus can foster intellectual schizophrenia: A questioning spirit is permitted inside the public sphere but forbidden outside the public sphere. The intellectual schizophrenia becomes more apparent when one imagines Kant's confused congregant who, weighing his allegiance to the church, happens to witness the potentially conflicting opinions of the pastor in his capacity as public priest on the one hand and

---

[2] Immanuel Kant, *Foundations of the Metaphysics* and *What Is Enlightenment?* Trans. Lewis White Beck (Indianapolis: The Bobbs-Merrill Company, Inc., 1959), 87.
[3] Ibid., 88.

private scholar on the other, wielding his private reason as the former and civic reason as the latter. Although later definitions of private and public reason may differ from those of Kant, the public sphere nevertheless operated in the same manner insofar as it generated rival frameworks of perception and divergent guidelines for the function of reason.

This study has shown how the public sphere generated another dualism that played a prominent role in the C.S. Lewis phenomenon. As Chapter 2 explained, the public sphere ostensibly admitted all to participate. Of course, the exclusion of most women and minorities for most of the public sphere's existence severely limited its supposed inclusiveness. Nevertheless, theoretically at least, the public sphere purported to ignore status within its environs; reason served as a leveler, intended to ensure that arguments carried the day due to their own merits, not because of external influence from religious, political, or socioeconomic pressures or authorities. But as the twentieth century wore on, this supposed unifying virtue became the very source of division. Reason as defined by the scholar differed from reason as defined by the layperson, as did standards of intellectual rigor. The public intellectual, charged with the task of bringing together the intellectual and populace, specialist and non-specialist, could increasingly be accused of anti-intellectualism by the professional scholar. As we have seen, Lewis performed the art of what he called translation. In my critical narrative, this was his service as a public intellectual: translating Christian ideas to a general population. But in so doing, did he occasionally sacrifice nuance? Did he tend toward oversimplification? Were his explanations at times reductive? Did he misrepresent opponents' positions when convenient to buttress his own arguments? I have argued that nearly every unfriendly critic of Lewis, from W. Norman Pittenger to John Beversluis, has pounced on perceived argumentative weaknesses as they proceed from these sorts of questions. And these are the sorts of questions that dog a public intellectual like Lewis when he attempts to bridge the gap between scholar and non-scholar: when he writes *ad populum* rather than *ad clericum*.

Given its long-established religious populism, America tended to exaggerate the intellectual/layperson schism. Among American religious conservatives, a general distrust of professional scholars generated interest in Lewis, who, though a professional scholar himself, also tended to distrust professional scholars. Lewis achieved both credibility and popularity in America in part because he cut through supposed academic godlessness and gobbledygook to present to his lay readers a Christian intellectualism characterized by common sense, irresistible logic, and metaphysical realism, all of which bored most professional scholars while galvanizing American Bible believers whose religious roots have long found nourishment within the populist soil of American Christianity.

With the fall of the public sphere, the intellectual/populace schism became increasingly politicized. In America, the political right increasingly became associated with populism: Witness the rise of the Tea Party. In 2008, the political left, meanwhile, helped elect Barack Obama, a president known for polished speaking and intellectual rigor. These rival approaches further polarized political parties. Thus, those on the left could proclaim, "The Republicans are now the 'How great is it to be stupid?' party."[4] And those on the right could counterattack by accusing those on the left of being elitists, out of touch with the opinions of ordinary citizens: "We seem to have fallen in love with the notion that only book smarts matter when it comes to the nation's problems. At least Democrats have. Republicans, despite having a few brainiacs in their midst, have taken the opposite approach, emphasizing instead the value of being just regular folk."[5] These political orientations—"brainiacs" and "regular folk"—now polarized in the post-public-sphere era encompass the demographics that a public intellectual like Lewis was supposed to unite. Instead, the two demographic groups became further divided and helped to cement Lewis's affiliation with American conservative politics, for as Part 2 repeatedly pointed out, the rise of the Lewis industry depended on grassroots movements, most of which were politically conservative to begin with. In Lewis's own day, the task of uniting the scholar and the layperson was daunting, first evident in Pittenger's critique of Lewis in the pages of *The Christian Century*. Today, in polarized political discourse, the task seems impossible. Scholars and laypeople—now brainiacs and regular folk—cannot easily be reconciled, for reconciliation necessitates compromise, which has proven to be elusive in the reconstituted public sphere of the early twenty-first century.

The issue of compromise raises yet another instance of a dualism that proceeds from the fault line separating the public from the private sphere. As chapter 3 argued, the transformation of the private person into the public intellectual necessitated an argumentative, defensive stance that downplayed doubt and rested upon certainty, a certainty that, in the public sphere, was easily read as rightness of position, as, in fact, of argumentative

---

[4] Maureen Dowd, "Why is GOP flaunting stupidity?" *The Palm Beach Post* (19 September 2011), 15A.

[5] Kathleen Parker, "Stupid is as stupid does," *The Palm Beach Post* (19 September 2011), 15A.

facticity. This stance, which was nothing short of a public performance, made difficult not only compromise but admission of doubts. The public intellectual tended to exaggerate his or her own position for the sake of the performance. This tendency helps to explain the rigidity of some of Lewis's arguments, their resistance to compromises and concessions. Chapter 3 showed how Lewis's identity was complex and multifaceted. His *public* identity, however, was simple and transparent: Publicly, Lewis was a Christian intellectual who was certain that he was right. This sort of public stance led to intense stand-offs with the opposition, generating the publicity that branded Lewis's name.

As Part 2 illustrated, the Lewis outside the public sphere moderated his position, leaving room for uncertainty: thus the epistemology fleshed out in *Letters to Malcolm* that reins in the borderline triumphalism of earlier texts and thus the change in tone and focus in *Till We Have Faces* and *A Grief Observed*. In the latter, public certainty gives way to private provisionality.

If my assessment in Part 3 is correct, then the Lewis within the public sphere still dominates Lewis scholarship. Lewis's solidarity goods are still of prime concern for the Lewis industry. Again, this explains why a scholar like Doris T. Myers must go to such prefatory lengths in launching a distinctly *literary* analysis of Lewis's writings, first clearing a critical path because of the preponderance of religiously focused studies that have preceded hers. This likewise explains why a philosopher like Beversluis critiques the Lewis of *A Grief Observed* as a public intellectual, even though Lewis abandons the public sphere in that text. Lewis critics whose scholarship remains preoccupied with Lewis's solidarity goods mimic the performance of Lewis himself: adopting defensive, reactionary stands, exaggerating their positions, and downplaying their own doubts.

To exacerbate this scholarly dead-end, what emerged from the rubble of the public sphere's demise was not a private intellectual or persona, but a new type of public persona, a product of the reconstituted public sphere. This persona does not operate on a supposed level playing field and does not follow conventions designed to ensure fair play. Instead, this persona occupies a space already territorialized and inextricably divided. Lewis managed to make a name for himself in the public sphere; his devotees and detractors have repositioned him in ways that reflect its devolution.

Although the public-intellectual status of Lewis will most likely continue to shape Lewis scholarship,[6] this book has attempted to model

---

[6] On the other hand, a book like Michael Ward's *Planet Narnia: The Seven Heavens in the Imagination of C.S. Lewis* (2008) might encourage new critical directions for

another direction for analysis. It has explored Lewis as a public intellectual, but not to argue that, or even suggest whether, he was right or wrong; rather, it has investigated Lewis the public intellectual as a historical phenomenon. To use Lewis's spatial metaphor, it has analyzed Lewis from outside rather than inside the discursive space that he opened up as public intellectual. Perhaps with the passage of time, the creation of such critical distance is inevitable. That is, perhaps as Lewis becomes more of a distinctly historical figure, an increasing number of scholars will study him with a more sensitive historical consciousness, which will in turn suggest new literary-critical methods of approach; over time, perhaps fewer scholars will feel compelled to modulate their studies of Lewis to the dominant question, "Was he right or wrong?" I suspect, however, that such a scholarly turn is unlikely at least in the near future, for the defense of solidarity goods lies at the heart of the C.S. Lewis phenomenon.

---

analysis, leading Lewis studies out of what MacSwain calls the current "impasse." However, one might also note that Lewis's debate with Anscombe—and Ward's position that the debate did *not* occasion Lewis's retreat from apologetical conflict—serves as the springboard for his analysis of astrology in Narnia. Ward thus engages Lewis subtextually as a public intellectual.

# Appendix

## Biographical Contradictions Within Lewis Studies

### Lewis's Relationship with Janie Moore

C.S. Lewis met Janie Moore in 1916 when he became friends with her son, Edward "Paddy" Moore. She was forty-five at the time; Lewis was seventeen. After Edward was killed in battle during World War I, and after Lewis returned to civilian life at the conclusion of his own military service, he helped care for Mrs. Moore for the rest of her life. Drawing mainly from Lewis's letters, many Lewis scholars have sought to understand the exact nature of his relationship with Mrs. Moore. Were they, at some point, lovers? Or was she simply a mother-substitute for Lewis? Was their relationship strictly platonic? Opinions are divided. The following meta-critical overview surveys these divided opinions in chronological order as they were expressed in various monographs from 1974 to 2005.

In their pioneering biography, Roger Lancelyn Green and Walter Hooper feel pressured into addressing this issue because of the increasing availability of Lewis's personal letters. They at one point term the relationship a "'love affair'" (in scare quotes), attributing its genesis to "that incomprehensible passion which attractive middle-aged women seem occasionally able to inspire in susceptible youths." The phrasing here is delicate: Because she was "able," did she therefore *intend* to "inspire" erotic passion in Lewis? Is she thus the aggressor? Lewis, after all, is described as "susceptible" and thus naïve. Nevertheless, they are quick to add that the relationship "soon turned from the desire for a mistress into the creation of a mother-substitute—in many ways a father-substitute also." However, a few pages later, they equivocate: "However innocent Lewis's involvement with Mrs Moore might be, he felt that it would be quite impossible to explain it to his father."[1] What exactly do Green and Hooper mean by "innocent"? If the relationship was a "'love affair,'" how could it be innocent? Because it did not really happen? Because Lewis did not intend for it to happen (since Mrs.

---

[1] Roger Lancelyn Green and Walter Hooper, *C.S. Lewis: A Biography*. Revised Edition (San Diego: Harcourt Brace, 1974) 56 and 62.

Moore was the aggressor)? Green and Hooper's reluctance to address the issue leads to ambiguity.

In 1976, Chad Walsh's afterword was published in the Bantam Books edition of *A Grief Observed*. Here too, ambiguity surrounds the issue. Walsh calls the relationship "strange" and a "real mystery." Like Green and Hooper, he suggests that Moore operates for Lewis as some sort of "mother substitute"—but only if "one must be psychoanalytic."[2]

In his 1979 study, Humphrey Carpenter seems inclined to reject the thesis that Lewis was romantically involved with Mrs. Moore. While acknowledging those who affirm it, and admitting that Lewis's own silence on the issue gave credence to the thesis, he concludes that it is unlikely: "On the practical level, a sexual relationship with Mrs Moore would have been difficult without servants' gossip, let alone the fact another member of the household was Mrs Moore's daughter Maureen, who was eight years younger than Paddy and still a child."[3]

George Sayer flatly denies that Lewis and Mrs. Moore were lovers in his 1988 first-edition biography. (A second edition was released in 1994.) His evidence is cumulative. First, they did not share a bedroom. Second, he does not think Lewis would violate or sully his promise to Paddy Moore to look after his mother; indeed, Sayer maintains, Mrs. Moore became a second mother to Lewis (the mother-substitute thesis again). And third, during his visits to the Kilns, Sayer never saw any reason to conclude that the relationship was anything other than platonic. Like Carpenter, Sayer admits that Lewis's secretiveness seemed to be incriminating. But Sayer explains that secretiveness was necessary not to cover up a sexual relationship, but to prevent Mr. Moore from learning that his alienated wife was living with another man; if this occurred, then he would have a legitimate reason for divorcing her and would then cut off financial support. Finally, Sayer points to an incident involving one Mary Wibelin, who evidently became enamored with Lewis. According to Sayer, when Lewis related the incident to Mrs. Moore, she felt that Lewis was too harsh in rebuffing the smitten Wibelin— "which," Sayer concludes, "[Mrs. Moore] would never have said had she been Jack's mistress."[4]

---

[2] Chad Walsh, Afterword to *A Grief Observed*. (New York: Bantam Books, 1976) 112 and 122.

[3] Humphrey Carpenter, *The Inklings: C.S. Lewis, J.R.R. Tolkien, Charles Williams, and Their Friends*. (Boston: Houghton Mifflin Company, 1979) 12.

[4] George Sayer, *Jack: A Life of C.S. Lewis*. Second edition. (Wheaton: Crossway Books, 1994) 164. See pp. 154-166.

A.N. Wilson unsurprisingly delivers a rousing affirmative decision on the issue: "It would...be amazing, though no evidence is forthcoming either way, if Lewis's thirty-year relationship with Mrs Moore was entirely asexual." Wilson singles out Walter Hooper as the person most responsible for creating an image of Lewis that makes denials of this claim possible. Wilson writes that Hooper "has a natural bent for hero-worship...."[5] And thus, Wilson believes, Hooper has turned Lewis into a saint. A saint, moreover, must be celibate. Wilson is not alone in this assessment. Alice H. Cook, for instance, asserts that Hooper inadvertently sparked widespread interest in Lewis's sexuality by insisting that Lewis was a "perpetual virgin."[6] If Lewis did not consummate his own marriage—as Hooper plainly claimed in his 1982 book, *Through Joy and Beyond: A Pictorial Biography of C.S. Lewis*[7]—then Lewis certainly did not have an extramarital, sexual relationship with Moore. Nevertheless, by 1991, Hooper admitted what seemed obvious to Wilson: "The notion of sexual intimacy between the two [Lewis and Moore] must be regarded as likely."[8]

Differences of opinion continued throughout the 1990s. In 1998, Lionel Adey wrote that the idea of a sexual relationship seemed "inconceivable." Adey is skeptical "...that in the 1920s a woman with an adolescent daughter slept with a young man, yet all lived *en famille* and attended church together, without guilt."[9] That same year, James Como came to the opposite conclusion: "As the ménage progressed, the liaison of Lewis and this handsome woman in her late forties almost certainly included a brief sexual interlude...."[10]

Not surprisingly, no consensus on the nature of Lewis's relationship with Moore materialized in the last decade. Armand M. Nicholi believes that the available evidence on the matter "weighs against the notion" that the two were lovers. Nicholi takes Lewis's word for it when Lewis refers in a

---

[5] A.N. Wilson, *C.S. Lewis: A Biography* (New York: W.W. Norton & Co., 1990) xvi.

[6] Alice H. Cook, "*A Grief Observed*: C.S. Lewis Meets the Great Iconoclast," in *C.S. Lewis: Life, Works, Legacy*. Vol 1. Ed. Bruce Edwards (London: Praeger Perspectives, 2007), 306.

[7] Walter Hooper, *Through Joy and Beyond: A Pictorial Biography of C.S. Lewis* (New York: MacMillan, 1982) 151.

[8] Walter Hooper, Introduction to *All My Road Before Me: The Diary of C.S. Lewis 1922-1927*. Ed. Walter Hooper (San Diego: Harcourt Brace & Company, 1991) 9.

[9] Lionel Adey, *C.S. Lewis: Writer, Dreamer, and Mentor* (Grand Rapids, MI: Eerdmans, 1998) 15.

[10] James Como, *Branches to Heaven: The Geniuses of C.S. Lewis* (Dallas: Spence Publishing, 1998) 42.

few letters to his "mother-son relationship."[11] Colin Duriez likewise rejects the Lewis-Moore lover thesis: "Although Janie Moore was likely to have been aware of his infatuation at that time, her own feelings for him remained motherly—Jack Lewis became the replacement for her only and much beloved son Paddy."[12]

On the other hand, Alan Jacobs believes that Lewis's feelings eventually turned into "something...evidently romantic." Indeed, Jacobs offers this personal anecdote relating his experience at a Lewis conference: "I once heard a longtime friend of Lewis's give a lecture, at the end of which a member of the audience flatly asked whether Lewis and Mrs. Moore had a sexual relationship. The lecturer's face assumed a pained look, and he hesitated—but then the elegant voice of his wife piped up from the back of the room: 'Oh, *of course* they did, dear—go ahead and say it!'" Jacobs, however, remains open-minded, not willing completely to dismiss alternative accounts, including the one offered by Green and Hooper that began this overview: that Moore simply served as a mother-substitute for Lewis. Jacobs admits, "And perhaps that is indeed what happened, but Green and Hooper don't *know*, any more than you or I do, whether their statement is true." [13]

## The C.S. Lewis/G.E.M. Anscombe Debate

In 1948 during a meeting of the Oxford Socratic Club, C.S. Lewis debated the Catholic philosopher G.E.M. Anscombe on the subject of causation, as it is developed in Lewis's 1947 book, *Miracles*. By this time, Lewis's reputation as a dominating debater was well established. Debate after debate, Lewis successfully defended the faith. His exchange with Anscombe was different. Some say he was defeated; others say he was routed. In a 1950 letter, Lewis wrote, "The lady is quite right to refute what she thinks bad theistic arguments, but does this not almost oblige her as a Christian to find good ones in their place: having obliterated me as an Apologist ought she not to *succeed* me?"[14] Apparently, Lewis told Alan Bede

---

[11] Armand M. Nicholi, Jr. *The Question of God: C.S. Lewis and Sigmund Freud Debate God, Love, Sex, and the Meaning of Life* (New York: The Free Press, 2002) 34.

[12] Colin Duriez, *The C.S. Lewis Chronicles: The Indispensable Biography of the Creator of Narnia Full of Little-Known Fact, Events and Miscellany.* (New York: BlueBridge, 2005) 103-4.

[13] Alan Jacobs, *The Narnian: The Life and Imagination of C.S. Lewis* (San Francisco: HarperSanFrancisco, 2005) 81 and 92-3.

[14] C.S. Lewis, letter to Stella Aldwinckle. 6 Dec 1950, in *The Collected Letters of C.S. Lewis*, Ed. Walter Hooper, Vol. 3 (San Francisco: HarperSanFrancisco, 2007) 35.

Griffiths something similar: "I remember Lewis saying to me that she had completely demolished his argument and remarking that he thought that, as she was a Catholic, she might at least have provided an alternative argument."[15] In 1978, Lewis's student Derek Brewer contributed an essay to James Como's edited volume, *C.S. Lewis at the Breakfast Table and Other Reminisces*, in which he quoted a diary entry describing a meeting with Lewis and other friends a few days after the debate:

> None of us very cheerful—one has to work to keep up with Lewis. He was obviously deeply disturbed by his encounter last Monday with Miss Anscombe...who had disproved some of the central theory of his philosophy about Christianity. I felt quite painfully for him. Dyson said— very well—that now he had lost everything and was come to the foot of the Cross—spoken with great sympathy. Lewis described the club meeting, where Miss Anscombe had delivered, at her own request, such an onslaught against his views, with real horror. His imagery was all of the fog of war, the retreat of infantry thrown back under heavy attack....[16]

This diary entry became a central piece of evidence for assessing the Lewis/Anscombe controversy. Lewis's personal doctor, Robert Havard, also contributed an essay to Como's volume, in which he baldly stated, "She [Anscombe] out-argued Lewis, who remarked later, 'Of course, she is far more intelligent than either of us.'"[17] What cannot be denied is that, as a result of this debate, Lewis revised chapter three of *Miracles* in a subsequent edition (1960).

This debate generated over the years a flurry of vexed critical questions: Did Lewis, in fact, lose the debate with Anscombe? If so, does this loss help explain the change evident in his writings beginning in the 1950s? Like the previous section, the following meta-critical overview traces the competing perspectives on the Lewis/Anscombe debate in chronological order, this time from 1974 to 2008.

In their 1974 biography, Green and Hooper suspend judgment. They point out that the very contestants in the debate provided conflicting accounts: "Lewis told Walter Hooper he was not defeated, and Miss

---

[15] Alan Bede Griffiths, "The Adventure of Faith," in *Remembering C.S. Lewis: Recollections of Those Who Knew Him* Ed. James Como (San Francisco: Ignatius Press, 2005) 91.

[16] Derek Brewer, "A Tutor: A Portrait," in *Remembering C.S. Lewis: Recollections of Those Who Knew Him* (previously published as *C.S. Lewis at the Breakfast Table and Other Reminisces*). Ed. James Como (San Francisco: Ignatius Press, 2005) 139-140.

[17] Robert Havard, "Philia: Jack at Ease," in Como, 361.

Anscombe told Hooper that he was."[18] Green and Hooper conclude that the only certain fact is that Lewis revised *Miracles*. However, a few years later (in Como's 1978 volume), Hooper rendered a more definitive judgment: "I don't think Lewis was 'defeated.'" Hooper accounts for Lewis's own opinions to the contrary by pointing to Anscombe's manners and style: "I think it may have been Miss Anscombe's rather bullying quality that left Lewis low and dispirited afterward."[19]

Carpenter acknowledges that many of Lewis's "fervent supporters" denied that Lewis lost the debate. Carpenter himself thinks otherwise. He reported that "many who were at the meeting thought that a conclusive blow had been struck against one of his fundamental arguments," quoting Brewer's diary as evidence. Carpenter is one of the first to claim that Lewis's loss compelled him to abandon the genre of pure Christian apologetics: "Lewis had learnt his lesson: for after this he wrote no further books of Christian apologetics for ten years, apart from a collection of sermons; and when he did publish another apologetic work, *Reflections on the Psalms*, it was notably quieter in tone and did not attempt any further intellectual proofs of theism or Christianity."[20]

In 1987, Joe Christopher minced no words when he asserted that Lewis's interactions with his peers included "losing to G.E.M. Anscombe in a meeting of the Oxford Socratic Club when she challenged one of his arguments in *Miracles*."[21] One year later, Lyle Dorsett supported the account offered by Carpenter, who "...convincingly argues that Lewis was so devastated by an attack on *Miracles* by an able Christian, Elizabeth Anscombe, that he avoided writing Christian apologetics for a decade."[22] In his 1988 biography, Sayer (who, again, knew Lewis) said that Lewis himself felt that he had lost the debate: "He told me that he had been proved wrong, that his argument for the existence of God had been demolished.... He wanted to mount a counterattack, but he thought that it would be dangerous to do so unless he were quite sure of its validity." Sayer went on to offer an account that contradicted Green and Hooper's. While the latter attested that Anscombe informed them that she won the debate, Sayer painted a different picture of Anscombe: "When told years later of the effect of the discussion

---

[18] Green and Hooper, 228.

[19] Walter Hooper, "Oxford's Bonny Fighter," in Como, 275 and 277.

[20] Carpenter, 217.

[21] Joe Christopher, *C.S. Lewis* (New York: Twayne, 1987) 2.

[22] Lyle Dorset, *Joy and C.S. Lewis: The Story of an Extraordinary Marriage* (London: Harper Collins, 1993) 146. (First published in 1988 as *And God Came In*)

on Jack, Professor Anscombe was surprised and upset. 'Oh dear! I had no idea that he took it so seriously. As a matter of fact I don't think I won. All that I was doing was to argue as a modern philosopher, academically, I was not expressing my deepest beliefs.'"[23]

In 1990, Wilson wrote that "...Lewis was thoroughly trounced in argument." He also follows, and provocatively develops, Carpenter's thesis that Lewis never again wrote pure Christian apologetics. Wilson argues that with his defeat at the hands of Anscombe, along with other factors such as the deteriorating health of Janie Moore, the straining of some friendships, and Warren Lewis's binge drinking, Lewis felt a psychological need to return to childhood, to the salad days he spent with his brother in their nursery. And thus, Wilson maintained, was born Narnia:

> He has abandoned here a cerebral and superficial defence of religion of the kind attempted at the Socratic Club. He has launched back deep into the recesses of his own emotional history, his own most deeply felt psychological needs and vulnerabilities.... That is to say, we hardly need to dwell on the psychological significance of the wardrobe in the first story; we do not need, though some will be tempted to do so, to see in this tale of a world which is reached through a dark hole surrounded by fur coats any unconscious image of the passage through which Lewis first entered the world from his mother's body. We do not need to be ingenious because, by the end of *The Last Battle*, it is all spelt out for us.[24]

Adey states that Lewis's "...role as apologist came to a sudden end with his defeat by the philosopher Elizabeth Anscombe in a Socratic Society debate on *Miracles* (1947)."[25] Lindskoog writes that Anscombe "bested" Lewis in the debate. She takes issue with Hooper's report that Lewis told him he won the debate; she likewise demurs when "...Hooper attributed her apparent victory to unfair bullying." She explains, "Given Lewis's reputation as a 'butcher' even in friendly debate, and the fact that he altered the third chapter of *Miracles* because of Anscombe's input, his martyrdom at her hands is an odd proposal."[26]

Jacobs seems hesitant to pronounce a winner: "The only thing that the participants in, and the audience of, that evening seem to concur on was that the debate was vigorous, even exciting." He does critique some of the

---

[23] Sayer, 306-307.

[24] Wilson, 213 and 228.

[25] Adey, 222.

[26] Kathryn Lindskoog, *Sleuthing C.S. Lewis: More Light in the Shadowlands* (Macon, Georgia: Mercer University Press, 2001) 114.

accounts that depict Lewis as the loser. For instance, he doubts that Lewis told Sayer that "his argument for the existence of God had been demolished": this assertion, says Jacobs, "...makes no sense: the existence of God was not up for debate that session."[27] He finds merit in one of Wilson's claims: "All that had happened, humiliating as it had been at the time, was the Lewis had been shown to have no competence to debate with a professional philosopher on her own terms."[28] Even here, Jacobs qualifies his assent: "To be bested by Elizabeth Anscombe in argument, or simply to have her reveal a weakness in one's argument, would be shameful to no one."[29] Jacobs is less ambiguous in his assessment of Wilson's claim that Lewis's loss to Anscombe prompted him to abandon Christian apologetics and write children's stories, a claim that, as we have seen, predates Wilson's book.

Adam Barkman believes that the publication of the third volume of Lewis's collected letters settles the issue. Lewis's 1950 letter to Stella Aldwinckle, quoted above, was published in this volume. (Here again is the relevant sentence in that letter: "Having obliterated me as an Apologist ought she not to succeed me?") Barkman concludes, "Consequently, there is a clear lesson here for Lewis scholars: in our love for the man, we must not exercise blind devotion, but ought to follow Truth even if it appears to differ with our heroes, for such was Lewis's own approach to philosophy."[30] To be fair, Jacobs may not have had access to the third volume of Lewis's collected letters (published in 2004), since his book was published the following year.

Nevertheless, the publication of that 1950 letter has made it much more difficult for Lewis devotees not only to maintain that Lewis won the debate but to derail analyses that use Lewis's loss as their springboard for exploring the shift in Lewis's writing in the 1950s. In fact, with the publication of the 1950 letter, the testimony in 2008 of Antony Flew, who attended the debate, may be unnecessary:

> But most of my memories of that evening are more clear regarding the scene after the conclusion of the dialogue. I was heading back across the Magdalen Bridge, walking immediately behind Elizabeth Anscombe. She was absolutely exultant. A little way in front of us were a few people who had gotten out of the meeting early. But on the far side of Magdalen

---

[27] Jacobs, 232.
[28] Jacobs, 232, 214 in Wilson.
[29] Jacobs, 232.
[30] Adam Barkman, *C.S. Lewis & Philosophy as a Way of Life: A Comprehensive Historical Examination of His Philosophical Thoughts* (Wayne, Pennsylvania: Zossima Press, 2008) 67.

Bridge was C.S. Lewis, and he was obviously unhappy about the exchange that evening. He was going back hastily to his room in Magdalen College. That's about all I can say about the event, but it did indicate the mood afterward. It was very clear that Lewis was depressed and equally clear that Elizabeth was triumphant.[31]

## Lewis and Sexism

Accusations of sexism, or at least sexist tendencies, have long surrounded Lewis. Despite her lifelong fondness for Lewis, Dorothy Sayers wrote in a 1948 letter that "...he is apt to write shocking nonsense about women and marriage."[32] Sexism first surfaces as a distinctly scholarly issue in Chad Walsh's pioneering monograph, *C.S. Lewis: Apostle to the Skeptics* (1949). Walsh points out that representations of women in Lewis's book are rarely flattering: "In general Lewis does better with the men in his books than with the women, who tend to fall into types: the possessive woman, the sharp-tongued old lady, the whiner."[33] In what is most likely the first study specifically focused on gender in Lewis's writing, Doris T. Myers lamented in 1971 that Lewis perpetuates gender stereotypes. Here is her analysis of *That Hideous Strength*: "...and the one feminist in the novel is Fairy Hardcastle, a caricature complete with boots, swagger, cigar, and foul language. Apparently Lewis's brave new world is inhabited by the same old stereotypes."[34]

In 1974, Green and Hooper tried to silence the "rumor" that Lewis "looked down on female undergraduates...." Green and Hooper point out that Lewis had a number of female students and that he treated them the same as his male students. Any reports to the contrary are attributable to the fact that his female students, like his "more sensitive male pupils," might mistake his "bluff manner" and "the lightning speed at which his mind worked" as harsh, cruel, or unfair treatment. Later in the book, however, they do concur with Owen Barfield, who "...said in a meeting of the New

---

[31] Antony Flew, "From Atheism to Deism: A Conversation Between Antony Flew and Gary R. Habermas," in *C.S. Lewis as Philosopher: Truth, Goodness and Beauty*. Eds. David Baggett, Gary R. Habermas and Jerry L. Walls (Downers Grove, Illinois: IVP Academic, 2008) 37-38.

[32] Letter to Mrs. Robert Darby, 31 May 1948, in *The Letters of Dorothy Sayers, Vol. 3*, ed. Barbara Reynolds (Cambridge: The Dorothy L. Sayers Society, 1998) 375.

[33] Chad Walsh, *Apostle to the Skeptics* (New York: MacMillan, 1949) 149.

[34] Doris T. Myers, "Brave New World: The Status of Women according to Tolkien, Lewis, and Williams." *Cimarron Review*. 17 (Oct. 1971): 16-17.

York C.S. Lewis Society in 1972, that Lewis could properly be called a misogynist on at least the 'theoretical level', though decidedly not so in his personal relations with individual women." [35]

In 1975, Margaret Hannay, following the pioneering article of Doris Myers, wrote a piece entitled, "C.S. Lewis: Mere Misogyny?" She brings nuance to the issue by tracing a development in Lewis's thought, a transition from misogyny in Lewis's early writings to a more equitable treatment of women in his later work. Hannay attributes this transition to the influence of Joy Davidman. [36]

By 1976, Chad Walsh could admit, "The legends of Lewis's male chauvinism abound. And there is some documentation." According to Walsh, one piece of documentation is Lewis's self-proclaimed favorite sound: male laughter. Walsh also addressed the rumor that Lewis would hide himself in his room at Oxford whenever females appeared on campus. When Walsh shared this rumor with Lewis, Lewis replied, "...pure bosh. For one thing women are wandering through the 'college precincts' the whole blessed day. For another, having taken female pupils of all ages, shapes, sizes, and complexions for about twenty years, I am a bit tougher than the story makes out. If I ever have fled from a female visitor it was not because she was a woman but because she was a *bore*, or because she was the fifteenth visitor on a busy day." [37]

In his contribution to Como's 1979 edited volume, Brewer addressed these rumors, suggesting that they may have had a basis in fact. Drawing from his diary entry of 16 February 1946, he reveals that Lewis "...indulged in several of his more pointed antifeminist witticisms and remarks...." He also noted, "'I am told that many women are revolted by his whole personality—though this is probably an exaggeration." When Brewer broached the topic of "antifeminism" with Lewis himself, Lewis "warmly" informed Brewer of the fact that he received lots of letters from admiring female readers of his books and that some of these letters included marriage proposals. "Any antifeminism," Brewer concludes, "must have been superficial, as his idyllically happy late marriage showed."[38]

That same year, Carpenter offered this rather baffling account of Lewis's attitude toward females: "It would be wrong to say that he despised women.

---

[35] Green and Hooper, 87 and 213-214.

[36] Margaret Hannay, "C.S. Lewis: Mere Misogyny?" 1.6 *Daughters of Sarah* (Sept. 1975): 1-4.

[37] Walsh, Afterword to *A Grief Observed*, 112.

[38] Brewer, "A Tutor: A Portrait," in Como, 134.

He was no misogynist. But he did regard the female mind as inferior to the male, or at least as being incapable of the mental activities which he valued. He told Charles Williams that he thought women's minds 'not really meant for logic or great art....'" (I term this account baffling because one manifestation of misogyny is the belief that females are intellectually inferior to males.) Carpenter goes on to enumerate the qualities that Lewis valued in women: "intelligence certainly" (even though, apparently, he felt they had inherently inferior minds), "submissiveness," and "fertility." It is thus not surprising that Carpenter adds, "Moreover many women found Lewis as unbearable as he found them. If they had no 'real conversation', he had no small talk whatever, and they often felt that he was blundering, brusque, or downright rude."[39] Carpenter thus seems to point to a process producing mutual antagonism between Lewis and women "with no 'real conversation.'"

Norma Bradshaw, one of Lewis's former students, seemed to confirm the "rumor" in Stephen Schofield's 1983 book, *In Search of C.S. Lewis*, concerning Lewis's attitude toward female undergraduates: "He would not, in my time, ever act as tutor to women. He seemed almost afraid of them. It was a standing joke at Magdalen that whenever he saw a woman enter the College he would run as fast as he could and lock himself in his rooms." Bradshaw also recounted Lewis's proclivity for male-dominated society: "What for the most part he expressed preference for, when I knew him, was the heroic-age camaraderie of warriors feasting in their hall, with bards reciting the exploits of those present—and no women in sight!" Like other commentators, however, Bradshaw also noticed a change in Lewis's attitude later in life, a change engendered in no small part by Joy Davidman. Bradshaw considers whether her presence liberated Lewis from the gender stereotypes that occupied most of his books: "Did he at last, happily though so briefly, reconcile some warring our unresolved elements in his nature? Was woman no longer dangerous, because she was neither a 'brown girl' nor one 'divinely fair,' neither a temptress nor a goddess, but a human being he came to love, and who happened to be a woman?"[40]

Another of Lewis's former students attested—also in Schofield's 1983 volume—that Lewis made sexist jokes during his lectures at Oxford. As E.L. Edmonds recalls it, before Lewis began one of his lectures on medieval literature, he delivered the following *double entendre* to his female students in

---

[39] Carpenter, 165.

[40] Norma Bradshaw, "Impressions of a Pupil," in *In Search of C.S. Lewis*, ed. Stephen Schofield (South Plainfield, New Jersey: Bridge Publishing, 1983) 21 and 22.

the front row (and with tongue firmly planted in cheek): "He asked them if they had their pens at the ready...and as a young male chauvinist at the time, I joined I the laughter."[41]

Schofield's edited volume includes a number of essays written by some of Lewis's other female students. Patricia Berry writes, "Lewis was thought to be a misogynist at that time, enjoying chiefly the company of J.R.R. Tolkien, Charles Williams and other Inklings members, with whom he regularly met. He certainly did complain that the women's colleges of Oxford produced 'dull, but meritorious' candidates for the B.A.... It is impossible to imagine a girl present at his 'Beer with *Beowulf* evenings at Magdalen."[42] Muriel Jones certainly found Lewis to be sexist: "It was generally thought in the university that he didn't care much for women. My tutor tried to induce Mr. Lewis to take me and another girl as pupils and he refused. He just didn't want us. He said he was very busy with the Home Guard, and he always got flue in the Hilary term."[43] Rosamund Cowan, on the other hand, seemed to witness a completely different side of Lewis; her experience as Lewis's student was entirely positive: "At first we were a bit frightened as he had a reputation of being a 'man's man.' We rather thought he would be a bit down on women. Actually he was delightful. He told me I reminded him of a Shakespearean heroine—a compliment I've always cherished. He certainly treated me like one."[44] Later in Schofield's volume, Lindskoog explains how she, like Walsh in 1976, brought accusations of misogyny to Lewis's attention. Lewis laughed off these charges: "I told him that I was glad that he would see me, because he was said to be a woman hater who avoided women altogether. He took that as a big joke and enjoyed it."[45]

On a couple of occasions in his study, Christopher makes unfaltering references to Lewis's "male chauvinism."[46] David Barratt explains that the rise of feminist scholarship heightened awareness of this chauvinism: "Even at the time of his writing, Lewis's attitude to women was somewhat suspect. With the growth of feminist criticism, this has been highlighted, and Lewis, for most feminists, must by now be outside the pale."[47] Wilson asserts that

---

[41] E.L. Edmonds, "C.S. Lewis, The Teacher," in Schofield, 44.

[42] Patricia Berry, "Part B: With Women at College," in Schofield, 69.

[43] Muriel Jones, "Part D. With Women at College," in Schofield, 74.

[44] Rosamund Cowan, "Part A: With Women at College," in Schofield, 62.

[45] Kathryn Lindskoog, "Reactions from Other Women," in Schofield, 83.

[46] Christopher, 7 and 24.

[47] David Barratt, *C.S. Lewis and His World* (Grand Rapids, Michigan: Eerdmans, 1987) 43.

Lewis "...was frequently contemptuous in his remarks about the opposite sex."[48] Wilson theorizes that such remarks may be attributable to the fact that, for most of his younger life, Lewis lived in all-male environments. When he finally did share a house with a female when he was fifteen—Mrs. Kirkpatrick, wife of Lewis's tutor—the experience was tainted by Mr. Kirkpatrick's misogyny. As Wilson concludes, "It was an unhappy model to grow up with: the clever man matched with a woman who, though evidently no fool, had to be written down as a fool to satisfy her husband's ego and explain his dislike of her."[49]

In the first edition of his Lewis biography, Sayer describes how Lewis "...had to give up teaching a female pupil [at Oxford] because he found her so beautiful that in her presence he was rendered speechless."[50] In the afterword to the second edition (1994), Sayer directly takes on the issue of Lewis and sexism:

> I don't know how it [accusations of misogyny] came into being, and certainly I can't think of an educated and well-read woman who knew him and held this view about him. I have written "educated and well-read" because he was bored by very much ordinary social conversation about such matters as clothes, shopping, household improvements, and the schooling of children. This sort of conversation bored him just as much if it came from a man as if it came from a woman, but he was more likely to experience it from a woman. He would try to avoid or to cut short such conversation, if he politely could. He may have sometimes given women the impression that he did not like them. It is worth remembering that an important part of his work, from the writing of his great academic masterpiece *The Allegory of Love* to *Till We Have Faces*, was a celebration or glorification of femininity and romantic love. A misogynist could hardly have written these books, nor could he have appreciated, as Lewis did, the writings of Coventry Patmore, the supreme poet of married love.[51]

Douglas Gresham seems to want to ameliorate concerns that Lewis was sexist by placing the issue in Lewis's historical context: "It wasn't a men-only society or group, but in those days women with both intellect and learning were not as common as they are today. And it was rare to find one with not only the right interests but also the ability to discuss them." And if, by rare

---

[48] Wilson, xii.
[49] Ibid., 43.
[50] Sayer, 67.
[51] Ibid., 418-419.

chance, a woman in those days possessed all these requirements—intellect, learning, the right interests, and the ability to discuss them—they suffered from yet another disadvantage: the patriarchal need to protect a woman's sensitive feelings. As Gresham explains,

> Most women would have had the men wary of embarrassing them or hurting their feelings, and thus when a woman was present, they would not feel able to launch into the sort of hard and tough talk they so enjoyed. There were some exceptions to this though they were few and far between. Also the men of those times were brought up to believe that women were people whom it was their duty to protect, even or perhaps especially, from themselves (and it isn't at all a bad way to think). They would never have been able to indulge in the verbal fencing that they were so good at if each of them was always trying to protect a member of the group from all the other members of the group.[52]

Jacobs tries to bring nuance to the issue. His approach is careful, sensitive, subtle, and—perhaps as a result—dizzyingly equivocal. It is best to let Jacobs speak for himself; he begins by reflecting on Lewis's true feelings for his numerous female pen pals:

> But what did he *think* of these women whose questions he answered, whose anxieties he soothed, and whose problems he sympathized with? The answer, of course, is that he thought different things about different women, but this answer will be thought by some to be evasive, because Lewis has often been accused of being a misogynist. I think this accusation largely rests on misunderstandings, but there is no question that Lewis shared the attitudes toward women common to men, and especially Christian men, of his time (and, we should add in fairness, of many other times). He believed, for instance, that God had ordained the "headship" of man over woman, especially in marriage: he even explores and defends this teaching at some length in *Mere Christianity*. But the very fact that it is in *Mere Christianity*—the book devoted to a general summary of "the belief that has been common to nearly all Christians at all times"— tells us that he did not think it a very controversial idea. This may tell us something about the limits of his acquaintance and his experience, or it may tell us how little progress feminism had made in England to that date, or perhaps it tells us both 253 things. Nevertheless, Lewis did not

---

Douglas Gresham, *Jack's Life: The Life Story of C.S. Lewis* (Nashville: Broadman & Holman Publishers, 2005) 110-111.

believe he was weighing in on an issue of great controversy among Christians when he described the doctrine of male headship.[53]

Jacobs goes on to analyze Lewis's argument in his essay, "Priestesses in Church?" wherein Lewis defends his belief that ordination should not be extended to women. Jacobs explains that this belief was common at the time, implying that we should not fault Lewis for adhering to a doctrine that has only recently and—in many denominations—successfully been contested. What follows in Jacobs's analysis is more nuance (and ambiguity):

> Matters like this can be clarified, but beyond them, Lewis's attitude toward women becomes difficult to understand, much less to explain. The evidence points in several different directions. It was adult *male* laughter that he loved, and he rarely sought the company of women. For many years he invited groups of undergraduates to his rooms to drink beer and sing bawdy songs, and it was understood not only that no women would be invited to such sessions but also that there would be no other kinds of gatherings at which women *were* welcome. Yet, at a time when many Oxford dons openly resented the increasing presence of women in their lecture halls and among their tutorial pupils, Lewis was unfailingly kind and supportive of his female students.[54]

Jacobs later admits that Lewis "...could say some extraordinarily silly things about women." Jacobs also shows how sexism operates as a component of a Lewisian leitmotif: "One of the most powerfully recurrent themes in Lewis's work is the evil of love gone wrong—love become possessive, voracious, even consuming—and invariably it is a woman who embodies that evil."[55] Jacobs traces the condescension Lewis directs toward his character of Jane Studdock in *That Hideous Strength* and the facile development of such cookie-cutter characters as Mother Dimble and Fairy Hardcastle. Jacobs seems to reach a conclusion about the issue when he writes, "I suppose it would be easy enough to say that Lewis can represent women only as virtuous little girls, inaccessible saints, or domestic tyrants." But by now, it should be clear that it is not easy for Jacobs to say anything definitive about the issue of Lewis and sexism: "It is in the end useless to point to fictional characters and declare that they prove something about the character of their creator."[56]

---

[53] Jacobs, 252-253.
[54] Ibid., 255.
[55] Ibid., 257.
[56] Ibid., 261.

While scholarly nuance may be important in a book like Jacobs's, it had little place in the 2005 film adaptation of *The Lion, the Witch and the Wardrobe*. In Hollywood, box-office ratings preempt most other considerations, noble and important as they may be. Andrew Adamson, who directed the film, felt it necessary to make at least one change to Lewis's original: a scene that Adamson perceived to be sexist. Adamson explained, "It was a little sexist when Father Christmas gives the gifts—the weapons—to all the kids and then tells the girls not to use them because battles are ugly when girls fight. I had just come off two films that I hope are empowering for girls. I didn't want to turn that message around. I told Doug Gresham, who was somewhat concerned about changing an idea C.S. Lewis put in there, 'Yeah, but he wrote this before he met your mother.'"[57]

Indeed, the issue of Lewis and sexism seems to pivot on the influence that Joy Davidman had on Lewis. As we have seen, Hannay and Bradshaw suggested that Davidman softened Lewis's attitude toward women. In 2001, Wesley Kort joined this chorus of Lewis commentators, not denying that Lewis was sexist, but observing how that sexism was toned down later in life, primarily through the influence of Davidman.[58] Such an observation is central to Mary Stewart van Leeuwen's 2010 study of Lewis and gender, *A Sword Between the Sexes? C.S. Lewis and the Gender Debates*. Van Leeuwen "trace[s] the route"—at least in part directed by Davidman—by which Lewis moved "...from an often-polemical defense of gender essentialism and gender hierarchy to a much more gender-egalitarian view."[59]

---

[57] Erik Brady, "A Closer Look at the World of Narnia," *USA Today* (1 December 2005). http://usatoday30.usatoday.com/life/movies/news/2005-12-01-narniaside_x.htm. Accessed 10 November 2010.

[58] Wesley Kort, *C.S. Lewis: Then and Now* (Oxford: Oxford UP, 2001) 11.

[59] Mary Stewart van Leeuwen, *A Sword Between the Sexes? C.S. Lewis and the Gender Debates* (Grand Rapids, Michigan: Brazos Press, 2010) 10. A shorter version of van Leeuwen's argument first appeared in "A Sword Between the Sexes: C. S. Lewis's

Of course, as with the other two issues surveyed in the appendix, no critical argument or assessment has settled the debate. Barkman's take on van Leeuwen's argument illustrates the point: "Van Leeuwen's belief that Lewis's marriage and post-marriage books reveal a rejection of gender hierarchy is completely false."[60]

---

Long Journey to Gender Equality," in *Christian Scholar's Review*, 36.4 (Summer, 2007), 391-414.

[60] Barkman, 464.

# BIBLIOGRAPHY

Addison, Joseph. *The Spectator*. London: J. M. Dent & Sons, 1950.

Adey, Lionel. *C.S. Lewis: Writer, Dreamer, and Mentor*. Grand Rapids: Eerdmans, 1998.

Aeschliman, Michael D. *The Restitution of Man: C.S. Lewis and the Case Against Scientism*. Grand Rapids: Eerdmans, 1983.

Allen, E.L. "The Theology of C.S. Lewis." *The Modern Churchman* 34.1 (1945): 319.

Anderson, George C. "C.S Lewis: For of Humanism." *The Christian Century*, November 25, 1946.

"Anglicans: Empty Pews, Full Spirit." *Time*, August 16, 1963.

"Aslan Is Still on the Move." *Christianity Today*, August 6, 2001.

Auden, W.H. "Red Lizards and White Stallions." *Saturday Review of Literature*, April 17, 1946.

Ayer, A.J. "Introduction." In *Logical Positivism*. New York: The Free Press, 8.

Baker, Leo. "Near the Beginning." In *Remembering C.S. Lewis: Recollections of Those Who Knew Him*. Ed. James T. Como. San Francisco: Ignatius Press, 2005. 67.

Barfield, Owen. "Introduction." In *Light on C.S. Lewis*. Ed. Jocelyn Gibb. New York: Harcourt Brace & World, 1965. xiv.

---. *Poetic Diction: A Study in Meaning*. New York: McGraw-HillCompany, 1964.

---. *Saving the Appearances: A Study in Idolatry*. London: Faber and Faber, 1959.

Barker, Nicholas. "C.S. Lewis, Darkly." *Essays in Criticism* 40.4 (1990): 367.

Barkman, Adam. *C.S. Lewis & Philosophy as a Way of Life: A Comprehensive Historical Examination of His Philosophical Thoughts*. Wayne, PN: Zossima Press, 2008.

Barron, Neil. *Anatomy of Wonder: A Critical Guide to Science Fiction*. 5th ed. London: Libraries Unlimited, 2004.

Bartlett, Thomas. "Short Subjects: Brought to You by God." *Chronicle of Higher Education* January (2006): A6.

Batchelor, John. *The Art of Literary Biography*. Oxford: Clarendon Press, 1995.

Bayley, Peter. *Remembering C.S. Lewis: Recollections of Those Who Knew Him*. Ed. James Como. San Francisco: Ignatius Press, 2005.

Bender, John. *Imagining the Penitentiary*. Cambridge: Cambridge University Press, 1977.

"Best of 90's: Books." *Time*, December 31, 1990.

Bevan, Edwyn. *Symbolism and Belief*. Port Washington NY: Kennikat Press, Inc, 1938.

Beversluis, John. "Surprised by Freud: A Critical Appraisal of A.N. Wilson's Biography of C.S. Lewis." *Christianity and Literature* 41.2 (1992): 181.

---. *C.S. Lewis and the Search for Rational Religion*. Grand Rapids: Eerdmans, 1985.

---. *C.S. Lewis and the Search for Rational Religion, Revised and Updated*. Amherst NY: Prometheus Books, 2007.

Blair, Hugh. *Lectures of Rhetoric and Belles Lettres*. Carbondale IL: Southern Illinois University Press, 1965.

Blamires, Harry. "Teaching the Universal Truth: C.S. Lewis among the Intellectuals." In *The Pilgrim's Guide: C.S. Lewis and the Art of Witness*. ed. David Mills. Grand Rapids: Eerdmans, 1998: 16.

Bloom, Harold. "Billy Graham: the Preacher." *Time*, June 14, 1999.

Blumenthal, Sidney. "Christian Soldiers." *The New Yorker* August (1994): 34.

Boa, Kenneth D., and Robert M. Bowman. *Faith Has Its Reasons: Integrative Approaches to Defending the Christian Faith.* 2nd ed. Waynesboro GA: Paternoster, 2005.

Borhek, May. "A Grief Observed: Fact or Fiction?" *Mythlore* 16 (1990): 9.

Boswell, James. *Life of Johnson.* Ed. R.W. Chapman. Oxford: Oxford University Press, 1980.

Brady, Charles A. "C.S. Lewis: II." *America,* June 10, 1944. Ed. George Watson. Cambridge: Cambridge University Press, 1992: 94.

Briggs, Asa and Peter Burke. *A Social History of the Media: From Gutenberg to the Internet* . Cambridge: Polity Press, 2002.

Brison, Susan J. "Violence and the Remaking of a Self." *The Chronicle of Higher Education,* January 18, 2002.

Brunton, Michael. "You Don't Know How Famous You Are Until Complete Strangers Stop You in the Street to Talk." *Time,* January 19, 2004.

Burke, Edmund. *An Enquiry.* Oxford: Oxford University Press, 1998.

Bush, Douglas. *John Milton: A Sketch of His Life and Writings.* New York: Macmillan, 1964.

"C.S Lewis." *Christianity Today,* December 20, 1963.

Carnell, Corbin Scott. *Bright Shadow of Reality: C.S. Lewis and the Feeling Intellect.* Grand Rapids: Eerdmans, 1974.

Carpenter, Humphrey. "Giddy with Awe." *The Spectator* March (1984): 26.

---. *The Inklings: C.S. Lewis, J.R.R. Tolkien, Charles Williams, and Their Friends.* Boston: Houghton Mifflin Company, 1979.

Carter, A.H. "One About, One By." *The Christian Century,* January 1965.

Carvajal, Doreen. "Marketing 'Narnia' Without a Christian Lion." *The New York Times,* June 3, 2001.

Cerabino, Frank. "A Thinly Veiled Christian Message." *The Palm Beach Post (West Palm Beach, FL),* October 13, 2005. (accessed September 17, 2009). url: http://www.palmbeachpost.com/search/content/shared/news/nation/stories/10/1013_coxcerabino_column.html.

Chesterton, G.K. *The Everlasting Man.* Radford VA: Wilder Publications, 2008.

Churchill, R.C. "Mr. C.S. Lewis as an Evangelist." *The Modern Churchman,* Spring 1946.

Clapp, Rodney. "Our Stalker Culture." *Christian Century,* November 17, 2009.

Coghill, Nevill. "The Approach to English." In *Light on C.S. Lewis.* Ed. Jocelyn Gibb. New York: Harcourt Brace & World, 1965: 65.

Colson, Charles and Nancy Pearcey. "The Oxford Prophet." *Christianity Today,* June 15, 1998.

Colson, Chuck. "A PS from Uncle Screwtape." *Breakpoint* August (1988): 8.

Como, James. "Culture and Public Philosophy: Another C.S. Lewis (Being Finally an Exhortation)." In *C.S. Lewis: views from Wake Forest.* Ed. Michael Travers. Wayne PA: Zossima, 2008: 36, 37.

---. "Land of Shadows." *National Review* February (1994): 72.

---. "Mediating Illusions: Three Studies of Narnia." *Children's Literature* 10 (1982): 163.

---. "Preface." In *Remembering C.S. Lewis: Recollections of Those Who Knew Him.* San Francisco: Ignatius Press, 2005: 81.

---. *Branches to Heaven: The Geniuses of C.S. Lewis.* Dallas: Spence Publishing Company, 1998.

Cook, Alice H. "A Grief Observed: C.S. Lewis Meets the Great Iconoclast." In *C.S Lewis: Life Works and Legacy, Vol. I*. Ed. Bruce L. Edwards. London: Praeger Perspectives: 2007: 295-313.

Cooke, Alastair. "Mr. Anthony at Oxford." *The New Republic* 24 April (1944): 578.

Corliss, Richard. "Books Vs. Movies." *Time*, November 27, 2003.

Coser, Lewis A. *Men of Ideas: A Sociologist's View*. New York: The Free Press, 1965.

Cunningham, Lawrence. "C.S. Lewis: The Screwtape Letters." *The Christian Century*, March 2, 1977.

Damrosch, Leo. *Fictions of Reality in the Age of Hume and Johnson*. Madison: University of Wisconsin Press, 1989.

Dart, John. "Questions Raised on C.S. Lewis Lore." *The Los Angeles Times*, March 24, 1979.

Dawkins, Richard. *The God Delusion*. Boston: Houghton Mifflin Company, 2006.

Delacampagne, Christian. *A History of Philosophy in the Twentieth Century*. trans. M.B. DeBevoise Baltimore: The Johns Hopkins University Press, 1999.

Derrick, Christopher. "Some Personal Angles on Chesterton and Lewis." In *G.K. Chesterton and C.S. Lewis: The Riddle of Joy*. Eds. Michael H. MacDonald and Andrew A. Tadie. Grand Rapids: Eerdmans, 1989: 10.

Descartes, Rene. *Discourse on Method and the Meditations*. Trans. F. E. Sutcliffe. New York: Penguin Books, 1968.

Detienne, Marcel. *Dionysos at Large*. Trans. Arthur Goldhammer. Cambridge: Harvard University Press, 1989.

Diggins, John Patrick. "The Changing Role of the Public Intellectual in American History." In *The Public Intellectual: Between Philosophy and Politics*. New York: Rowman & Littlefield Publishers, 2003: 114.

Dionne, Jr., E. J . "Three Points for Conservatives." *The Washington Post*, March 23, 2010. http://www.washingtonpost.com/wp-dyn/content/article/2010/23/ar2010032302427_pf.html. (accessed May 5, 2010).

Dobree, Bonamy. *English Literature in the Early Eighteenth Century*. Oxford: Oxford University Press, 1959.

Dorrien, Gary. "The 'Postmodern' Barth? The Word of God as True Myth." *Christian Century*, April 2, 1997.

Dorsett, Lyle W. "Review of Don W. King's Out of My Bone: The Letters of Joy Davidman." *Christian Scholar's Review* 40.1 (2010): 113.

---. "Unscrambling the C.S. Lewis 'Hoax'." *Christian Century* February (1989): 208.

---. *Seeking the Secret Place: The Spiritual Formation of C.S Lewis*. Grand Rapids, MI: BrazosPress, 2004.

---. *Joy and C.S. Lewis: The Story of an Extraordinary Marriage*. London: Harper Collins, 1993.

Douthat, Ross. "The Apocalypse, Rated PG." *The Atlantic Monthly* May (2005): 36.

Dowd, Maureen. "Why is GOP flaunting stupidity?" *The Palm Beach Post (West Palm Beach)*, September 19, 2011.

Dowling, William C. *The Boswellian Hero*. Athens GA: University of Georgia Press, 1979.

Downing, David. *Planets in Peril: A Critical Study of C.S. Lewis's Ransom Trilogy*. Amherst: University of Massachusetts Press, 1992.

---. *The Most Reluctant Convert*. Downers Grove IL: InterVarsity Press, 2002.

Driberg, Tom. "Lobbies of the Soul." *New Statesman Nation* 48 (1955): 393.

Dryden, John. *Religio Laici, in Eighteenth-Century English Literature*. New York: Harcourt Brace Jovanovich, 1969.

Duin, Julia. "Hollywood U-turn? Disney film looks to Christian fan base." *The Washington Post*, November 7, 2005.

Dulles, Avery. *A History of Apologetics*. London: Hutchinson, 1971.

"Dream of the After-World." *Times Literary Supplement*, February 2, 1946.

Eagleton, Terry. *Literary Theory: An Introduction*. 2nd ed. Minneapolis: University of Minnesota Press, 1996.

"Ecumenism: Seven Devilish Ways to Block Church Union." *Time*, May 10, 1963.

Edwards, Bruce L. "On the Excesses of Appreciation." *CSL: The Bulletin of the New York C.S. Lewis Society*, January 1980.

---. "Introduction." In *The Taste of the Pineapple: Essays on C.S. Lewis as Reader, Critic, and Imaginative Writer*. Bowling Green, OH: Bowling Green State University Popular Press, 1988: 3.

---. "Preface." In *C.S. Lewis: Life, Works, and Legacy, Vol. 1: An Examined Life*. London: Praeger Perspectives, 2007: xiv.

---. *A Rhetoric of Reading: C.S. Lewis's Defense of Western Literacy*. Provo, UT: Center for the Study of Values in Literature, 1986.

---. "On the Excesses of Appreciation." *Christian Scholar's Review* 11, (1980).

---. *C.S. Lewis: Life, Works, and Legacy, Vol. 1*. Ed. Bruce L. Edwards. London: Praeger Perspectives, 2007.

Eiesland, Nancy. "Barriers and Bridges: Relating the Disability Rights Movement and Religious Organizations." In *Human Disability and the Service of God: Reassessing Religious Practice*. Eds.Nancy Eiesland and Don Saliers. Nashville: Abingdon, 1998: 218.

Eliot, T.S. "Tradition and the Individual Talent." In *Selected Essays*. New York: Harcourt, Brace & World, 1932: 4.

Ellwood, Robert S. "Introduction." In *Sleuthing C.S. Lewis: More Light in the Shadowlands* . Macon GA: Mercer University Press, 2001: xi.

Elson, John. "Books: Love's Labor." *Time*, March 5, 1990.

Empson, William. "Love in the Middle Ages." In *Critical Thought Series: C.S. Lewis*. Ed. George Watson. Cambridge: Cambridge University Press, 1992: 79.

---. *Critical Thought Series: C.S. Lewis*. Cambridge: Cambridge University Press, 1992.

Euripedes. *The Bacchae*. Trans. C.K. Williams. New York: Farrar Straus Giroux, 1990.

Fielding, Henry. *Joseph Andrews*. Oxford: Oxford University Press, 1991.

---. *Tom Jones*. Oxford: Oxford University Press, 1991.

Filmer, Kath. *The Fiction of C.S. Lewis: Mask and Mirror*. New York: St. Martin's Press, 1993.

Finke, Roger , and Rodney Starke. *The Churching of America, 1776-1990: Winners and Losers in Our Religious Economy*. New Brunswick: Rutgers University Press, 2002.

Fish, Stanley. "Milton, Thou Shouldst Be Living in this Hour." In *There's No Such Thing as Free Speech and It's a Good Thing, Too*. Oxford: Oxford University Press, 1994: 269.

---. "Why We Can't All Just Get Along." In *First Things* 1996: 21.

---. *Self-Consuming Artifacts: The Experience of Seventeenth-Century Literature*. Berkeley: University of California Press, 1972.

Forman, Henry James. "Common-Sense Humanist." *The New York Times Book Review*, April 23, 1944.

Frame, Randy, and Marjorie Chandler. "A 'Hoax' Observed." *Christianity Today*, June 16, 1989.

Fremantle, Anne. "Beyond Personality." *Commonweal* September (1945): 528.

Fuller, Edmund. "The World of His Mind Was Freely Available." *The Wall Street Journal (Washington DC)*, July 16, 1979.

Gardner, John. *The Life and Times of Chaucer*. New York: Alfred A. Knopf, 1977.

Gay, Peter. *The Enlightenment: An Interpretation*. New York: Knopf, 1966.

Gilchrist, K.J. *A Morning After War: C.S. Lewis and WWI*. New York: Peter Lang, 2005.

Gilley, Sheridan. "The Abolition of God: Relativism and the Center of Faith." In *The Pilgrim's Guide: C.S. Lewis and the Art of Witness*. Ed. David Mills. Grand Rapids: Eerdmans, 1998: 162.

Girard, Rene. *I See Satan Fall like Lightning*. Trans. James G. Williams. Maryknoll NY: Orbis Books, 2001.

Glyer, Diana Pavlac, and David Bratman. "C.S. Lewis Scholarship: A Bibliographical Overview." In *C.S. Lewis: Life, Works, and Legacy, Vol. 4*. London: Prager Perspectives, 2007: 302.

Goodknight, Glen. "Fantasy and Personal Involvement." *Mythlore* 1.1 (1969): 4.

Gopnick, Adam. "Prisoner of Narnia: How C.S Lewis Escaped." *The New Yorker* (2005). (accessed November 8, 2009). url: http://www.newyorker.com/archive/2005/11/21/051121crat_atlarge.

Green, Roger Lancelyn, and Walter Hooper. *C.S. Lewis: A Biography*. San Diego: Harcourt Brace, 1974.

Green, V.H.H. *Religion at Oxford and Cambridge* . London: SCM Press, 1964.

Gresham, Douglas. Interview by Lyle W Dorset. Personal interview. Wade Center at Wheaton College, June 4, 1982.

---. *Jack's Life: The Life Story of C.S. Lewis* . Nashville: Broadman & Holman Publishers, 2005.

Gresham, Joy Davidman. *Out of My Bone: The Letters of Joy Davidman*. Ed. Don W. King. Grand Rapids: Eerdmans, 2009.

Griffin, William. *C.S. Lewis: Spirituality for Mere Christians*. New York: Crossroad Publishing Company, 1998.

Griffiths, Alan Bede. "The Adventure of Faith." In *Remembering C.S. Lewis: Recollections of Those Who Knew Him*. Ed. James T. Como. San Francisco: Ignatius Press, 2005: 77.

Gross, Michael Joseph. "Narnia Born Again." *The Nation*, February 1, 1999.

Habermas, Jurgen. *The Structural Transformation of the Public Sphere: An Inquiry into a Category of Bourgeois Society*. Trans. Thomas Burger. Cambridge: The MIT Press, 1989.

Hampshire, S.N. "David Hume: A Symposium." In *Hume's Place in Philosophy*. New York: St. Martin's Press, 1966: 6-7.

Hankins, Barry. *Francis Schaeffer and the Shaping of Evangelical America*. Grand Rapids: Eerdmans, 2008.

Hannay, Margaret Patterson. *C.S. Lewis*. New York: Frederick Ungar Publishing Company, 1981.

Harries, Richard. *C.S. Lewis: The Man and His God*. Wilton CN: Morehouse-Barlow, 1987.

Harris, Sam. *Letter to a Christian Nation*. New York: Knopf, 2006.

Hart, Dabney Adams. "A Sword Between the Sexes: C. S. Lewis's Long Journey to Gender Equality." *Christian Scholar's Review* 36.4 (2007): 391-414.

---. *Through the Open Door: A New Look at C.S. Lewis*. Alabama: University of Alabama Press, 1984.

Hartshorne, Charles. "Philosophy and Orthodoxy." *Ethics* 54.4 (1944): 296.

Hastings, Adrian. *A History of English Christianity*. London: SCM Press, 1991.

Hatch, Nathan O. *The Democratization of American Christianity*. New Haven: Yale University Press, 1989.

Hauerwas, Stanley. *Naming the Silences*. Grand Rapids: Eerdmans, 1990.

Havard, Robert. "Philia: Jack at Ease." In *Remember C.S. Lewis: Recollections of Those Who Knew Him*. Ed. James Como. San Francisco: St. Ignatius Press, 200: 366-367.

Heie, Harold. "The Postmodern Opportunity: Christians in the Academy." *Christian Scholars Review* 26.2 (1996): 138.

Himmelfarb, Gertrude. *The Roads to Modernity: The British, French, and American Enlightenments*. New York: Vintage, 2005.

Holmes, Richard. "Biography: Inventing the Truth." In *The Art of Literary Biography*. Oxford: Clarendon Press: 1995: 17.

Home: Oxford English Dictionary. http://www.oed.com/view/Entry/94859?redirectedFrom=industry#eid (accessed October 16, 2011).

Hooker, Richard. *Of the Laws of Ecclesiastical Polity*. Ed. A.S. McGrade. New York: St. Martin's Press, 1975.

Hooper, Walter. "My Original Encounter with C.S. Lewis." In *Mere Christians: Inspiring Stories of Encounters with C.S. Lewis*. Eds. Mary Anne Phemister and Andrew Lazo. Grand Rapids: BakerBooks, 2009: 140.

---. "Preface." In *On Stories and Other Essays*. Ed. Walter Hooper San Diego: Harcourt Brace, 1982: ix.

---. *The Collected Letters of C.S. Lewis*. Ed. Walter Hooper. San Francisco: HarperSanFrancisco, 2007.

---. *C.S. Lewis on Heaven and Hell: Beyond the Shadowlands*. Wheaton IL: Crossway Books, 2005.

---. *C.S. Lewis: A Companion and Guide*. San Francisco: HarperSanFrancisco, 1996.

---. *C.S. Lewis: Views from Wake Forest*. Ed. Michael Travers. Wayne, PN: Zossima Press, 2008.

---. *G.K. Chesterton and C.S. Lewis: The Riddle of Joy*. Eds. Michael H. McDonald and Andrew A. Tadie. Grand Rapids: Eerdmans, 1989.

---. *God in the Dock: Essays on Theology and Ethics*. Ed. Walter Hooper. Grand Rapids: Eerdmans, 1970.

---. *Past Watchful Dragons: The Narnian Chronicles of C.S. Lewis* . New York: Collier Books, 1979.

---. *The Dark Tower and Other Stories*. San Diego: Harcourt Brace & Company, 1977.

---. *Through Joy and Beyond: A Pictorial Biography of C.S. Lewis*. New York: Macmillan Publishers, 1982.

Hoover, Stewart M. *Religion in the Media Age*. London: Routledge, 2006.

Horne, Brian. "C.S. Lewis' Christian Apologist." *Expository Times* 97.4 (1986): 124.

Hough, Graham. "Old Western Man." In *Critical Thought Series: C.S. Lewis*. Ed. George Watson. Cambridge: Cambridge UP, 1992: 241-243.

---. "The Screwtape Letters." *The London Times*, December 10, 1966.

Houston, James. "Reminisces of the Oxford Lewis." In *We Remember C.S Lewis: Essays & Memoirs*. Nashville: Broadman & Holman Publishers, 2001: 136.

Howard-Snyder, Daniel. "God, Evil, and Suffering." In *Reason for the Hope Within*. Grand Rapids: Eerdmans, 1999: 79.

Howard, Thomas. *The Achievement of C.S. Lewis*. Wheaton IL: Harold Shaw Publishers, 1980.

Hume, David. *An Enquiry Concerning Human Understanding, in Modern Philosophy*. Eds. Baird, Forrest E., and Walter Kaufmann. Upper Saddle River NJ: Prentice Hall, 1996.

Humphreys, A.R. *The Augustan World*. New York: Harper & Row, 1963.

Hunter, James Davidson. "Fundamentalism it its Global Contours." In *The Fundamentalist Phenomenon: A View from Within; a Response from Without*. Grand Rapids: Eerdmans, 1990. 57.

---. *Culture Wars: The Struggle to Define America*. New York: Basic Books, 1990.

---. *To Change the World: The Irony, Tragedy and Possibility of Christianity in the Late Modern World*. Oxford: Oxford University Press, 2010.

Jacobs, Alan. "Narnia Business: C.S. Lewis at 100." *The Weekly Standard* April (1998): 34.

---. *The Narnian: The Life and Imagination of C.S. Lewis*. San Francisco: HarperSanFrancisco, 2005.

Jacoby, Russell. *The Last Intellectuals: American Culture in the Age of Academe*. New York: Basic Books, 1987.

James, William C. "Review of Beversluis' C.S. Lewis." *The Journal of Religion* 66.2 (1986): 223.

---. *Pragmatism*. Indianapolis: Hackett, 1981.

Johnson, Samuel. "enthusiasm." In *Samuel Johnson's Dictionary: Selections from the 1755 Work that Defined the English Language*. Ed. Jack Lynch. New York: Walker Publishing Company, Inc., 2003: 166.

Johnson, Samuel. *The Yale Edition of the Complete Works of Samuel Johnson*. Eds. Jean H. Hagstrum and James Gray. New Haven: Yale University Press, 1978.

Kant, Immanuel. *Foundations of the Metaphysics and What Is Enlightenment?* Indianapolis: The Bobbs-Merrill Company, Inc, 1959.

Kanter, Kenneth. "Dantzer Comments on Lewis." *Wheaton Record*, January 1960.

Kilby, Clyde. "C.S Lewis and His Critics." *Christianity Today*, December 8, 1958.

---. "The Provocative Mr. Lewis." *Inter-Varsity* Autumn (1964): 31.

---. *The Christian World of C.S. Lewis*. Grand Rapids: Zondervan, 1964.

Kleinberg, Aviad. *Flesh Made Word: Saints' Stories and the Western Imagination*. Trans. Jane Marie Todd. Cambridge MA: Belknap Press, 2008.

Knights, L.C. *Critical Thought Series: C.S. Lewis*. Ed. George Watson. Cambridge: Cambridge University Press, 1992.

Kort, Wesley A. *C.S. Lewis: Then and Now*. Oxford: Oxford University Press, 2001.

Kreeft, Peter. "Darkness at Noon: The Eclipse of Permanent Things." In *Permanent Things: Toward the Recovery of a More Human Scale at the End of the Twentieth Century*. Grand Rapids: Eerdmans, 2005: 208.

---. "Preface." In *The Achievement of C.S. Lewis*. Wheaton, IL: Harold Shaw Publishers, 1980: 7.

---. *C.S Lewis: A Critical Essay*. Front Royal, VA: Christendom College Press, 1988.

Ladborough, Richard W. "In Cambridge." In *Remembering C.S. Lewis: Recollections of Those Who Knew Him*. Ed. Como. San Francisco: Ignatius Press, 2005. 192.

Lawhead, Steve. "What Do C.S. Lewis and the Faith Have in Common with this Crew." *Christianity Today*, November 25, 1983.

Lawlor, John. *C.S. Lewis: Memories and Reflections*. Dallas: Spence Publishing, 1998.

Leavis, F.R. *For Continuity*. Freeport, NY: Books for Libraries Press, 1933.

Lewis, C.S. "'Bulverism' or, the Foundation of 20th Century Thought." In *God in the Dock*. Grand Rapids: Eerdmans, 1970: 272.

---. "Afterword." In *The Pilgrim's Progress, The Pilgrim's Regress*. 3rd (illustrated) ed. Grand Rapids: Eerdmans, 1981: 205.

---. "Christian Apologetics." In *God in the Dock*. Ed. Walter Hooper. Grand Rapids: Eerdmans, 1970: 94.

---. "Christianity and Culture." In *Christian Reflection*. Ed. Walter Hooper. Grand Rapids: Eerdmans, 1967: 18.

---. "Christianity and Literature." In *Christian Reflections*. Ed. Walter Hooper. Grand Rapids: Eerdmans, 1967: 10.

---. "Dogma and the Universe." In *God in the Dock*. Grand Rapids: Eerdmans, 1970: 44-45.

---. "Historicism." In *Christian Reflections*. Grand Rapids: Eerdmans, 1967: 104.

---. "Introduction." In *George MacDonald: 365 Readings*. New York: Collier Books, 1974: xxviii.

---. "Is Theology Poetry?" In *The Weight of Glory and Other Addresses*. New York: Simon & Schuster, 1980: 98.

---. "Learning in War-Time." In *The Weight of Glory*. Ed. Walter Hooper. New York: Simon & Schuster, 1980: 41-52.

---. "Myth Became Fact." In *God in the Dock*. Grand Rapids: Eerdmans, 1970: 66.

---. "On Criticism." In *On Stories and Other Essays on Literature*. San Diego: Harcourt Brace & Company, 1982: 139.

---. "On Stories." In *On Stories and Other Essays on Literature*. San Diego: Harcourt Brace & Company, 1982: 12.

---. "On the Reading of Old Books." In *God in the Dock*. Grand Rapids: Eerdmans, 1970: 202.

---. "Preface." In *A Faith of Our Own*. Cleveland: The World Publishing Company, 1960: 8.

---. "Rejoinder to Dr. Pittenger." In *God in the Dock*. Ed. Walter Hooper. Grand Rapids: Eerdmans, 1970: 182.

---. "Religion: Reality or Substitute?" In *Christian Reflections*. Grand Rapids: Eerdmans, 1967: 42.

---. "Revival or Decay?" In *God in the Dock*. Grand Rapids: Eerdmans, 1970: 251.

---. "Sometimes Fairy Stories May Say Best What's to Be Said." In *On Stories and Other Essays on Literature*. San Diego: Harcourt Brace & Company, 1982: 46.

---. "The Poison of Subjectivism." In *Christian Reflections*. ed. Walter Hooper. Grand Rapids: Eerdmans, 1967: 73.

---. "The Seeing Eye." In *Christian Reflections*. Grand Rapids: Eerdmans. 175.

---. "Tolkien's The Lord of the Rings." In *On Stories and Other Essays*. San Diego: Harcourt Brace & Company, 1982: 90.

---. "Why I Am Not a Pacifist." In *The Weight of Glory and Other Addresses*. New York: Simon & Schuster, 1980: 65.

---. *A Grief Observed*. San Francisco: HarperSanFrancisco, 1994.

---. *A Preface to Paradise Lost*. Oxford: Oxford University Press, 1961.

---. *An Experiment in Criticism*. Cambridge: Cambridge University Press, 1961.

---. and E.M.W. Tillyard. *The Personal Heresy: A Controversy*. London: Oxford University Press, 1939.

---. *Letters to Malcolm: Chiefly on Prayer*. San Diego: Harcourt Brace, 1964.

---. *Miracles: A Preliminary Study*. New York: Collier Books, 1947.

---. *On Stories and Other Essays on Literature*. San Diego: Harcourt Brace & Company, 1982.

---. *Out of the Silent Planet*. New York: Collier Books, 1944.

---. *Prince Caspian*. New York: HarperTrophy, 1979.

---. *Reflections on the Psalms*. San Diego: Harcourt Brace & Company, 1958.

---. *Screwtape Proposes a Toast*. New York: Macmillan, 1982.

---. *Studies in Medieval and Renaissance Literature*. Cambridge: Cambridge University Press, 1998.

---. *Studies in Words*. Cambridge: Cambridge University Press, 1967.

---. *Surprised by Joy: The Shape of My Early Life*. San Diego: Harcourt Brace & Company, 1984.

---. *That Hideous Strength*. New York: Simon & Schuster, 1996.

---. *The Abolition of Man*. New York: Collier Books, 1955.

---. *The Allegory of Love: A Study in Medieval Tradition*. Oxford: Oxford University Press, 1936.

---. *The Collected Letters of C.S. Lewis*. San Francisco: HarperSanFrancisco, 2004.

---. *The Collected Letters of C.S. Lewis. Vol. III. Narnia, Cambridge, and Joy*. Ed. Walter Hooper. San Francisco: HarperSanFrancisco, 2007.

---. *The Discarded Image: An Introduction to Medieval and Renaissance Literature*. Cambridge: Cambridge University Press, 1946.

---. *The Four Loves*. New York: Harcourt Brace & Company, 1988.

---. *The Great Divorce*. San Francisco: HarperSanFrancisco, 2001.

---. *The Last Battle*. New York: Harper Trophy, 1994.

---. *The Lion, the Witch and the Wardrobe*. New York: Harper Trophy, 1994.

---. *The Magician's Nephew*. New York: HarperTrophy, 1980.

---. *The Personal Heresy: A Controversy*. London: Oxford University Press, 1939.

---. *The Pilgrims Regress*. Grand Rapids: Eerdmans, 1992.

---. *The Screwtape Letters*. San Francisco: HarperSanFrancisco, 2001.

---. *The Voyage of the Dawn Treader*. New York: HarperTrophy, 1980.

---. *Till We Have Faces: A Myth Retold*. San Diego: Harcourt Brace & Company, 1984.

Lindbeck, George. *The Nature of Doctrine: Religion and Theology in a Postliberal Age*. Philadelphia: Westminster, 1984.

Lindskoog, Kathryn. "Reactions from Other Women." In *In Search of C.S. Lewis*. South Plainfield NJ: Bridge Logos, 1983: 82, 88.

---. "Some Problems in C.S. Lewis Scholarship." *Christianity and Literature* 27.4 (1978): 54.

---. *Sleuthing C.S. Lewis: More Light in the Shadowlands* . Macon GA: Mercer University Press, 2001.

---. *The C.S. Lewis Hoax*. Portland OR: Multnomah, 1988.

Lindsley, Art. *C.S. Lewis's Case for Christ: Insights from Reason, Imagination and Faith*. Downers Grove, IL: InterVarsity Press, 2005.

Linton, Calvin. "C.S. Lewis Ten Years Later." *Christianity Today*, November 9, 1973.

Lloyd, Joan. "Transcendent Sexuality as C.S. Lewis Saw It." *Christianity Today*, November 1973.

Lobdell, Jared C. "C.S. Lewis's Ransom Stories and Their Eighteenth-Century Ancestry." In *Word and Story in C.S. Lewis*. Eds. Peter J. Schakel and Charles A. Huttar. Columbia: University of Missouri Press, 1991: 214-216.

Louthan, Stephen. "On Religion: A Discussion with Richard Rorty, Alvin Plantinga and Nicholas Wolterstorff." *Christian Scholar's Review* 26.2 (1996): 177-183.

Luce, Henry R. "Robertson and the Reagan Gap." *Time*, February 22, 1988.

Lurie, Alison. "The Passion of C.S. Lewis." *The New York Review of Books*, September 8, 2009. http://www.nybooks.com/articles/18672. (accessed September 8, 2009).

MacDonald, George. *Unspoken Sermons*. Whitethorn CA: Johannesen, 1997.

MacDonald, Michael H, and Mark P Shea. "Saving Sinners and Reconciling Churches: An Ecumenical Meditation on Mere Christianity." In *The Pilgrim's Guide: C.S. Lewis and the Art of Witness*. Grand Rapids: Eerdmans, 1995: 50-51.

MacIntyre, Alasdair. *Whose Justice? Which Rationality?* Notre Dame: University of Notre Dame Press, 1988.

MacSwain, Robert. "Introduction." In *The Cambridge Companion to C.S. Lewis*. Cambridge: Cambridge University Press, 2010: 11.

Manlove, Colin. *Christian Fantasy: From 1200 to the Present*. Notre Dame: University of Notre Dame Press, 1992.

---. *The Chronicles of Narnia: The Patterning of a Fantastic World*. New York: Twayne Publishers, 1993.

Markos, Louis A. "Myth Matters." *Christianity Today*, April 23, 2001.

---. *Lewis Agonistes: How C.S. Lewis Can Train Us to Wrestle with the Modern and Postmodern World*. Nashvilee: Broadman & Holman, 2003.

Marsden, George. *The Outrageous Idea of Christian Scholarship*. Oxford: Oxford University Press, 1997.

---. *The Soul of the American University: From Protestant Establishment to Established Nonbelief*. Oxford: Oxford University Press, 1994.

Martin, Thomas L. *Reading the Classics with C.S. Lewis*. Ed. Thomas L. Martin. Grand Rapids: Baker Academic, 2000.

Martindale, Wayne. "C.S. Lewis, Lightbearer in the Shadowlands: The Evangelistic Vision of C.S. Lewis." In *Shadowland: Inadvertent Evangelism*. Wheaton IL: Crossway Books, 1997: 37.

Maudlin, Michael. "1993 Christianity Today Books Awards." *Christianity Today*, April 5, 1993.

"Maybe a Lewis Franchise?" *The Wall Street Journal (New York)*, December 12, 2005.

McClatchey, Joe. "The Praise of God in C.S. Lewis Scholarship." *New Oxford Review* June (1982): 10.

McCormack, Elissa. "Inclusivism in the Fiction of C.S. Lewis: The Case of Emeth." *Logos* 11:4 (2004).

McGovern, Eugene. *Remembering C.S. Lewis.* Ed. Como. San Francisco: Ignatius Press, 2005.

Medcalf, Stephen. "Language and Self-Consciousness: The Making and Breaking of C.S. Lewis's Personae." In *Word and Story in C.S. Lewis.* Eds. Peter J. Schakel and Charles A. Huttar. Columbia: University of Missouri Press, 1991: 129, 135.

Meilaender, Gilbert. "Psychoanalyzing C.S. Lewis." *Christian Century*, May 1990.

---. "Review of Lionel Adey's C.S. Lewis: Writer, Dreamer, and Mentor." *The Christian Century*, September 23, 1998.

---. "The Everyday C.S. Lewis." *First Things* 85 (1998): 27.

Melzer, Arthur M. "What is an Intellectual?" In *The Public Intellectual: Between Philosophy and Politics.* New York: Rowman & Littlefield Publishers, Inc.

---. "What Is an Intellectual?" In *The Public Intellectual: Between Philosophy and Politics.* Ed. Arthur M. Melzer. New York: Rowman & Littlefield Publishers, Inc, 2003: 11.

Meyer, Birgit and Moors, Annelies. "Introduction." In *Religion, Media, and the Public Sphere.* Bloomington IN: Indiana University Press, 2006.

Michael, Mary. "Our Love Affair with C.S Lewis." *Christianity Today*, October 25, 1993.

Miller, Laura. *The Magician's Book: A Skeptic's Adventure in Narnia.* New York: Little, Brown and Company, 2008.

Mills, David. *The Pilgrim's Guide: C.S. Lewis and the Art of Witness.* Ed. David Mills. Grand Rapids: Eerdmans, 1998.

Milton, John. *Areopagitica and Of Education.* Ed. George H. Sabine. Wheeling IL: Harlan Davidson, Inc, 1951.

Milward, Peter. *A Challenge to C.S. Lewis.* London: Associated University Presses, 1995.

Molner, Thomas. *The Decline of the Intellectual.* New York: Meridian Books, 1961.

Moring, Mark. "Hollywood Hellfighters." *Christianity Today*, May 2008.

Morris, Jan. *Oxford.* Oxford: Oxford University Press, 1965.

Muggeridge, Malcolm. "The Mystery." In *In Search of C.S. Lewis.* Ed. Stephen Schofield. South Plainfield NJ. 1983: 127.

Munz, Peter. *The Place of Hooker in the History of Thought.* London: Routledge & Kegan, 1952.

Murpey, Nancey. "Philosophical Resources for Postmodern Evangelical Theology." *Christian Scholar's Review* 26.2 (1996): 205.

--- and James Wm. McClendon. "Distinguishing Modern and Postmodern Theologies." *Modern Theology* 5.3 (1898): 192.

---. *Theology in the Age of Scientific Reasoning.* Ithaca NY: Cornell University Press, 1990.

Myers, Doris T. *Bareface: A Guide to C.S. Lewis's Last Novel* . Columbia MO: University of Missouri Press, 2004.

---. *C.S. Lewis in Context.* Kent OH: Kent State University Press, 1994.

Neff, David. "American Babel." *Christianity Today*, August 17, 1992.

Nehamas, Alexander. *Nietzsche: Life as Literature.* Cambridge: Harvard University Press, 1985.

Neil, Strauss. *Radiotext(e)*. New York: Semiotext(e), 1993.

Nelson, Erik. "Survivor of New Cult Found in Desert Muttering." *The Wittenburg Door* 59 (1981): 24.

Nelson, Michael. "C.S. Lewis and His Critics." *The Virginia Quarterly* 64.1, no. Winter (1988): 2.

Neumann, Erich. *Amor and Psyche: The Psychic Development of the Feminine: A Commentary on the Tale by Apuleius*. Trans. Ralph Manheim. New York: Pantheon Books, 1956.

Nicholi, Jr. Armand M. *The Question of God: C.S. Lewis and Sigmund Reud Debate God, Love, Sex, and the Meaning of Life*. New York: The Free Press, 2002.

Nichols, Aidan. *The Panther and the Hind: A Theological History of Anglicanism*. Edinburgh: T & T Clark, 1993.

Nichols, Stephen J. *Jesus Made in America: A Cultural History from the Puritans to the Passion of the Christ*. Downers Grove IL: IVP Academic, 2008.

Noll, Mark. *Between Faith and Criticism: Evangelicals, Scholarship, and the Bible in America*. Grand Rapids: Baker Book House, 1991.

---. *The Scandal of the Evangelical Mind*. Grand Rapids: Eerdmans, 2008.

Nott, Kathleen. *The Emperor's Clothes*. Bloomington: Indiana University Press, 1958.

Olasky, Marvin. "The Return of Spiritism." *Christianity Today*, December 14, 1992.

Olsen, Ted. "The War for Narnia Continues." *Christianity Today*, June 2001. http://www.christianitytoday.com/ct/article_print.html.?id=7716. (accessed September 3, 2009).

Ostling, Joan Kerns. "Shotgun Approach to C.S. Lewis." *Christianity Today*, January 19, 1986.

Otto, Rudolf. *The Idea of the Holy*. Oxford: Oxford University Press, 1969.

Otto, Walter. *Dionysus: Myth and Cult*. Trans. Brian B. Palmer. Bloomington: University of Indiana Press, 1965.

"Oxford Personalities." *Vogue*, November 1951.

Packer, J.I. "Still Surprised by Lewis." *Christianity Today*, September 7, 1998.

---. "Wisdom in a Time of War: What Oswald Chambers and C.S. Lewis Teach Us about Living Through the Long Battle with Terrorism." *Christianity Today*, January 7, 2002.

Pangle, Thomas L. "A Platonic Perspective on the Idea of the Public Intellectual." In *The Public Intellectual: Between Philosophy and Politics*. Ed. Arthur M. Melzer. New York: Rowman & Littlefield Publishers, Inc., 2003: 15.

Parker, Kathleen. "Stupid is as stupid does." *The Palm Beach Post (West Palm Beach)*, September 19, 2011.

Patrick, James. *The Magdalen Metaphysicals: Idealism and Orthodoxy at Oxford 1901-1945*. Macon: Mercer University Press, 1985.

Peter, Bayley. "From Master to Colleague." In *Remembering C.S. Lewis: Recollections of Those Who Knew Him*. Ed. James T. Como. San Francisco: Ignatius Press, 2005.

Pittenger, W. Norman. "Apologist Versus Apologist: A Critique of C.S. Lewis as 'Defender of the Faith.'" *The Christian Century* 1 October (1958): 1107.

---. "Pittenger-Lewis (letter to the editor)." *The Christian Century*, November 26, 1958.

Placher, William. *Unapologetic Theology: A Christian Voice in a Pluralistic Conversation*. Louisville KY: Westminster/John Knox Press, 1989.

Plantinga, Alvin. "Advice to Christian Philosophers." *Faith and Philosophy* 1.3 (1984): 268.

---. "Augustinian Christian Philosophy." *The Monist* 75.3 (1992): 294.

---. "Reason and Belief in God." In *Faith and Rationality: Reason and Belief in God*. Indiana: Notre Dame University Press, 1983: 52.

---. "The Reformed Objection to Natural Theology." *Christian Scholar's Review* 11.3 (1982): 193.

---. *The Evidential Argument from Evil*. Ed. Daniel Howard-Snyder. Bloomington: Indiana University Press, 1996.

Poe, Harry Lee. "Shedding Light on The Dark Tower: A C.S. Lewis Mystery is Solved." *Christianity Today*, February 2, 2007.

Pope, Alexander. "The Rape of the Lock." In *Eighteenth-Century English Literature*. Eds. Geoffrey Tillotson et al. New York: Harcourt Brace Jovanovich, 1969: 39-46.

Posner, Richard A.. *Public Intellectuals: A Study of Decline*. Cambridge, MA: Harvard UP, 2002.

Postman, Neil. *Amusing Ourselves to Death: Public Discourse in the Age of Show Business*. New York: Penguin Books, 1985.

Potkay, Adam. *The Passion for Happiness: Samuel Johnson and David Hume*. ed. Walter Hooper. Ithaca NY: Cornell University Press, 2000.

Price, Reynolds. *A Whole New Life*. New York: Atheneum, 1994.

Price, Robert M. "Review of Beversluis' C.S. Lewis." *Religious Humanism* 20.4 (1986): 196.

Pullman, Phillip. "Don't Let Your Children Go to Narnia." *The Independent* (1998).

Purtill, Richard L. *C.S. Lewis's Case for the Christian Faith*. San Francisco: Harper & Row, 1981.

---. *Lord of the Elves and Eldils: Fantasy and Philosophy in C.S. Lewis and J.R.R. Tolkien*. Grand Rapids: Eerdmans, 1974.

Putnam, Robert D. and David E. Campbell. *American Grace: How Religion Divides and Unites Us*. New York: Simon & Schuster, 2010.

Quine, Willard V. O. *Problems in the Philosophy of Language*. Ed. T. Olshewsky. New York: Holt, 1969.

"Recruiting C.S. Lewis for Today's Culture War." *Focus on the Family Citizen*, August 15, 1994.

"Religion: Excursion from Hell." *Time*, March 11, 1946.

"Religion: Sermons in Reverse." *Time*, April 19, 1943.

"Religion: Theological Thriller." *Time*, June 1946.

Reppert, Victor. *C.S. Lewis's Dangerous Idea: A Philosophical Defense of Lewis's Defense of Reason* . Downers Grove IL: InterVarsity Press, 1989.

Reynolds, Joshua. *Discourses*. New York: E.P. Dutton & Company, 1906.

Richards, I.A. *Practical Criticism*. London: Transaction Publishers, 2004.

---. *Principles of Literary Criticism*. Ed. Walter Hooper. New York: Harcourt Brace & World, 1925.

---. *Principles of Literary Criticism*. New York: Harcourt Brace & World, 1925.

Rigby, Luke. *Remembering C.S. Lewis*. Ed. James T. Como. San Francisco: Ignatius Press, 2005.

Roberts, Adam. *Science Fiction*. London: Routledge, 2000.

Robson, W.W. "C.S Lewis." *The Cambridge Quarterly*, Summer 1966.

Rogers, Melissa. "Navigating the new Media News Filter." *Christian Century* 20
  September (2009): 24.
Rorty, Richard. "Solidarity or Objectivity." In *Post-Analytic Philosophy*. New York:
  Columbia University Press, 1985: 4.
---. *Consequences of Pragmatism*. Minneapolis: University of Minnesota Press, 1982.
---. *Contingency, Irony and Solidarity*. Cambridge: Cambridge University Press, 1989.
Rosenbaum, Stanley N. "Our Own Silly Faces: C.S. Lewis on the Psalms." *The
  Christian Century*, May 18, 1983.
Rosin, Hannah. "Applying Personal Faith to Public Policy." *The Washington Post*, July
  24, 2000.
Rossow, Francis C. "Review of Beversluis' C.S. Lewis." *Concordia Journal* 11.5 (1985):
  198.
Sacks, Sheldon. *Fiction and the Shape of Belief*. Berkeley: University of California Press,
  1967.
Sadler, Glenn Edward. "Revering and Debunking a Saint." *The Reformed Journal* 40
  (1990): 24.
Sammons, Martha. *A Guide through C.S. Lewis Space Trilogy*. Westchester IL:
  Cornerstone Books, 1980.
Sayer, George. *Jack: A Life of C.S. Lewis*. 2nd ed. Wheaton IL: Crossway Books, 1994.
Sayers, Dorothy. *The Letters of Dorothy Sayers, Volume Three, 1944-1950*. ed. Barbara
  Reynolds. Cambridge: The Dorothy L. Sayers Collection, 1998.
Schaeffer, Frank. *Crazy for God: How I Grew Up as One of the Elect, Helped Found the
  Religious Right, and Live to Take All (or Almost All) of It Back*. New York: Carrol and
  Graf Publishers, 2007.
Schakel, Peter J. *Reason and the Imagination in C.S. Lewis: A Study of Till We Have Faces*.
  Grand Rapids: Eerdmans, 1984.
---. *Reason and the Imagination in C.S. Lewis: A Study of Till We Have Faces*. Grand
  Rapids: Eerdmans, 1984.
Schlaeger, Jurgen. "Biography: Cult as Culture." In *Art of Literary Biography*. Ed. John
  Bachelor. Oxford: Clarendon Press, 1995: 65.
"Scholars Cite Obstacles to Christian Advance." *Christianity Today*, October 12, 1962.
Shaftesbury, Anthony Earl of. *Characteristics of Men, Manners, Opinions, Times, etc.* Ed.
  John M. Robertson. Gloucester MA: Peter Smith, 1963.
Sheils, Merrill. "Chuck Colson's Leveler." *Newsweek*, September 9, 1974.
Sherburn, George. "The Restoration and Eighteenth Century." In *A Literary History of
  England*. Ed. Albert C. Baugh. New York: Appleton-Century Crofts, 1948: 705.
Shuster, George. "Discipline." *New York Herald Tribune Book Reviews*, December 26,
  1943.
Sidney, Philip. *A Defence of Poetry*. Ed. Jan Van Dorsten. Oxford: Oxford University
  Press, 1996.
Smedes, Lewis. *My God and I: A Spiritual Memoir*. Grand Rapids: Eerdmans, 2003.
Smietana, Bob. "C.S. Lewis Superstar: How a Reserved British Intellectual with a
  Checkered Pedigree Became a Rock Star for Evangelicals." *Christianity Today*,
  December 2005.
Smith, Adam. *The Theory of Moral Sentiments*. Amherst: Prometheus Books, 2000.
Smith, James K.A. . *Desiring the Kingdom: Worship, Worldview, and Cultural Formation*.
  Grand Rapids: Baker Academic, 2009.

Smith, Robert Houston. *Patches of Godlight: The Pattern of Thought of C.S. Lewis.* Athens GA: University of Georgia Press, 1981.

Smollett, Tobias. *The Expedition of Humphrey Clinker.* Oxford: Oxford University Press, 1984.

Sobran, Joseph. "The Poor Man's Aquinas." *National Review* May (1985): 42.

Soper, David. "An Interview with C.S. Lewis." *Zion's Herald,* January 14, 1948.

Spacks, Patricia. *Imagining a Self: Autobiography and the Self in Eighteen-Century England.* Cambridge: Harvard University Press, 1976.

Speaight, Robert. "To Mixed Congregations." *The Tablet* June (1943): 308.

Steele, Joseph. *The Tatler.* New York: Clarendon, 1977.

Steinfels, Peter. "Of Lions and Donkeys." *The New York Times,* December 3, 2005.

Sugrue, Thomas. "Terrifying Realities of the Soul." *New York Herald Tribune Weekly Book Review,* March 3, 1946.

Surin, Kenneth. *Theology and the Problem of Evil.* Oxford: Basil Blackwell, 1986.

Suvin, Darko. *Metamorphoses of Science Fiction: On the Poetics and History of a Literary Genre.* New Haven: Yale University Press, 1979.

Taylor, Charles. *A Secular Age.* Cambridge MA: The Belknap Press of Harvard University, 2007.

Taylor, D.J. "The Lion, the Witch and the Boardroom: A Chronicle of Narnia." *The Independent,* June 7, 2001.

"The Best of the Century." *Time,* December 31, 1999.

*The New York Times,* "The Narnia Skirmishes," November 13, 2005. http://www.nytimes.com/2005/11/13/movies/13narnia.html?_r=1&ei=5070&en=ce321391153d8017&ex=1156996800&pagewanted=print (accessed September 9, 2008).

"The Reluctant Convert." *Time,* February 6, 1955.

"Theologians: Defender of the Faith." *Time,* December 6, 1963.

"Theology of Discovery: Mr. C.S. Lewis's Talks." *Times Literary Supplement (New York),* October 21, 1944.

"This Week." *The Christian Century,* January 1, 1970.

Thomas, Cal. "Bill Bennett Seeks the Moral 'Correction' that Must Be Made in America." *The Salt Lake Tribune (Salt Lake City),* March 21, 1993.

Tickle, Phyllis. *The Great Emergence: How Christianity Is Changing and Why.* Grand Rapids: Baker Books, 2008.

Tilley, Terrence W. *The Evils of Theodicy.* Washington, D.C: Georgetown University Press, 1991.

Tillotson, Kathleen. "Review of Allegory of Love." In *Critical Thought Series: C.S. Lewis.* Ed. George Watson. Cambridge: Cambridge University Press, 1992: 96.

Torrance, Kelly Jane. "Fox saves 'Narnia' from Disney." *The Washington Times,* January 30, 2007.

Toynbee, Polly. "Narnia Represents Everything that Is Most Hateful about Religion." *The Guardian* (London), December 5, 2005. http://www.guardian.co.uk/books/2005/dec/05/cslewis.booksforchildrenandteenagers/. (accessed September 8, 2009).

Turner, W.J. "The Devil at Work." *Spectator* 168 (1942): 186.

Van Biema, David. "Beyond the Wardrobe." *Time,* October 30, 2005.

---. "How to Tell if The Lion, the Witch and the Wardrobe is a Christian Film." *Time*, October 3, 2005.

Van Groningen, Willis D. "Review of Beversluis' C.S. Lewis." *Journal of the Evangelical Theological Society* 29.3 (1986): 369.

Van Til, Cornelius. *The Defense of the Faith*. 3rd. Reprint, Phillipsburg, NJ: Presbyterian and Reformed Publishing Company, 1967.

Vanauken, Sheldon. *A Severe Mercy*. San Francisco: HarperSanFrancisco, 1987.

Velarde, Robert. *Conversations with C.S. Lewis: Imaginative Discussion about Life, Christianity and God*. Downers Grove IL: IVP Books, 2008.

von Drehle, David. "Mad Man: Is Glenn Beck for America." *Time*, September 29, 2009.

Wain, John. "Pleasure, Controversy, Scholarship." In *Critical Thought Series: C.S Lewis*. Ed. George Wastosn. Cambridge: Cambridge University Press, 1992. 201.

Walls, Jerry. "C.S. Lewis and Evangelical Ambivalence." *The Wittenburg Door* 62 (1981): 20-21.

Walsh, Chad . "Impact on America." In *Light on C.S Lewis*. Ed. Jocelyn Gibb New York: Harcourt Brace & World, 1965: 109.

---. "Afterword." In *A Grief Observed*. New York: Bantam Books, 1976: 93-94.

---. "C.S Lewis Apostle to the Skeptics." *Atlantic Monthly*, September 1946.

---. "Foreword." In *The Image of Man in C.S Lewis*. Nashville: Abingdon Press, 1969: 7.

---. *C.S. Lewis: Apostle to the Skeptics*. New York: Macmillan, 1949.

---. *Literary Legacy of C.S. Lewis*. New York: Harcourt, Brace, Jovanovich, 1979.

Ward, Elizabeth. "Saving C.S. Lewis: A Critic Ventures back into the Wardrobe." *The Washington Post*, December 14, 2008.

---. *Planet Narnia: The Seven Heavens in the Imagination of C.S. Lewis*. Oxford: Oxford University Press, 2008.

Warner, Michael. "The Mass Public and the Mass Subject." In *Habermas and the Public Sphere*. Ed. Craig Calhoun. Cambridge: The MIT Press, 1992: 376.

Watson, David. "C.S. Lewis and Evolution." *Biblical Creation* 7.19, no. Spring (1985): 9.

Watson, George. "Introduction." In *Critical Thought Series: C.S. Lewis*. ed. George Watson. Cambridge: Cambridge University Press, 1992: 1.

Watt, Ian. *The Rise of the Novel: Studies in Defoe, Richardson and Fielding*. Berekely: University of California Press, 2001.

Weinsheimer, Joel C. *Eighteenth-Century Hermeneutics: Philosophy of Interpretation in England from Locke to Burke*. New Haven: Yale University Press, 1993.

White, Michael. *C.S. Lewis: A Life*. New York: Carroll & Graf, 2004.

Willey, Basil. *The Eighteenth Century Background*. London: Chatto & Windus, 1946.

Williams, Charles. "The Way of Exchange." In *The Image of the City and Other Essays*. Oxford: Oxford University Press, 1958: 147-54.

Williams, Donald T. "A Closer Look at the 'Unorthodox' Lewis: A More Poetic Bultmann?" *Christianity Today*, December 21, 1979.

---. *Mere Humanity: G.K. Chesterton, C.S. Lewis, and J.R.R. Tolkien on the Human Condition* . Nashville: Broadman & Holman, 2006.

Willis, John R. "Review of Beversluis' C.S. Lewis." *Theological Studies* 47.1 (1986): 188.

Wilson, A.N. "Why I Believe Again." *New Statesman* April (2009).

---. *C.S. Lewis: A Biography*. New York: Norton, 1990.

Wolterstorff, Nicholas. *Lament for a Son*. Grand Rapids: Eerdmans, 1987.

---. *Reason within the Bounds of Religion*. Grand Rapids: Eerdmans, 1976.

Wood, Ralph C. "Good and Terrible: The God of Narnia." *The Christian Century*, December 27, 2005.

---. "The Baptized Imagination: C.S. Lewis's Fictional Apologetics." *The Christian Century*, Aug. - Sep. 1995.

Wordsworth, William. "Preface." In *Lyrical Ballads*. Eds. R.L. Brett and A.R. Jones. 2nd (1800 ed.) Ed. London: Routledge, 1991: 250.

Yancey, Philip. "Surprised by Shadowlands." *Christianity Today*, April 4, 1994.

Zogby, Edward G. *The Longing for Form: Essays on the Fiction of C.S. Lewis*. Ed. Peter J. Schakel. Kent, OH: Kent State University Press, 1977.

# Index